1992
GUIDE TO
LITERARY AGENTS
&
ART/ PHOTO REPS

Edited by Robin Gee

Writer's
Digest
Books

Cincinnati, Ohio

Distributed in Canada by McGraw-Hill,
300 Water Street,
Whitby Ontario L1N 9B6.
Also distributed in Australia by Kirby Books, Private Bag No. 19, P.O. Alexandria NSW2015.

Managing Editor, Market Books Department: Constance J. Achabal; Assistant Managing Editor: Glenda Tennant Neff

1992 Guide to Literary Agents & Art/Photo Reps. *Copyright © 1991 by Writer's Digest Books. Published by F&W Publications, 1507 Dana Ave., Cincinnati, Ohio 45207. Printed and bound in the United States of America.*
International Standard Serial Number
ISSN 1055-6087
International Standard Book Number
0-89879-485-4

Contents

Art/Photo Reps

Resources

Indexes

From the Editor

Welcome to the first edition of *Guide to Literary Agents and Art/Photo Reps*. Chances are you've purchased this book because you are seriously considering obtaining or changing representation. You want to know if you really need an agent or rep and what to expect from one. Well, you're not alone.

As the publisher of books for writers, artists and photographers, our readers ask us questions all the time on a variety of topics of concern to creative people—how to find markets, how to approach those markets, how best to present work to interested buyers—and, especially in recent years, about representation—why get it, how to get it and what to expect from it. In fact, all the editors at Writer's Digest Books agree a major topic of concern—the one that seems to generate the most questions currently—is representation.

This book gives you the opportunity to have your questions about this topic answered. The ins and outs of finding and working with literary and art/photo reps are explained fully in articles by experts—many of whom are agents or reps themselves.

Literary agents

Literary agents are fast becoming the stable factor in many writers' careers. With the shrinking of the number of commercial publishers there are fewer editors on the front lines and those that are left have less time to devote to helping promising new talent. Increasingly, agents have assumed the role previously filled by editors—helping writers make their work more marketable and helping them plan career moves, as well as acting as the writer's inside advocate. The first article in the *Guide*, The New Breed of Agents, explores this role shift.

The better informed you are about what agents do and how they operate, the easier it will be to choose an agent. To help you understand just what an agent can and cannot do for you, there are articles on what you need to know before approaching an agent, what skills good agents bring to their profession and how they sell work on a day to day basis.

You also will find articles on how to choose the right agent and what to do if you feel it's time to change agents. To round off this section, Finding and Working With Literary Agents tackles the nitty gritty aspects of submitting to and dealing with agents.

Art/photo reps

Unlike new writers looking for literary agents, those who seek representation in the fine or commercial art or photography fields are usually already established. They want representation to help them expand their client list and to handle the paper work. For more information on working with reps, we asked New York rep Barbara Gordon to write Finding and Working with Art and Photo Reps. I'd also like to take this opportunity to thank rep Maria Piscopo, author of *The Photographer's Guide to Marketing & Self-Promotion*, for her help with the development of the questionnaires we used to solicit information for the rep listings.

We took special care to include as much information as possible on what promotional materials you will need even before approaching a rep. And we've given the specifics on the type of advertising and other promotional material favored by the each of the reps listed.

Plus . . .

We offer two additional sections in the *Guide*. Screenwriter and editor of *Hollywood Scriptwriter*, Kerry Cox wrote Finding and Working with a Script Agent to lead off the section of agents who are primarily interested in handling scripts. And our commercial art/ photo rep section is followed by a smaller, but no less important Fine Art Reps section. While the number of fine art reps is small, it is growing as more and more artists seek help finding galleries and other outlets for their work.

Much of the other material in this book comes as a result of our experience with publishing other annual directories. For example, we've found category indexes to be most helpful in identifying appropriate listings for our readers with specific needs. The Literary Agents and Script Agents sections are indexed by nonfiction and fiction subjects while the Art/ Photo Reps and Fine Art Reps sections are indexed by state. Many of the agents and reps listed are interested in handling work in other categories and these are cross-referenced in the Additional list at the end of each section. Listings are ranked by levels of openness to submissions and there is a Glossary and a list of resources helpful to writers, illustrators and photographers.

We're very proud of the number of listings and quality of information provided in this first edition, but our aim is to continue to improve this information with each subsequent edition. Your questions about representation led us to develop this edition of *Guide to Literary Agents & Art/Photo Reps*. Your comments, suggestions and concerns will help us improve it and refine the information. I invite you to let me know what information you need and what questions you'd like to see answered. I look forward to hearing from you and best of luck finding representation for your work.

Robin L. Gee

Literary Agents

The New Breed of Literary Agents

by Richard Curtis

Who is the most influential member of the editorial board of your publishing company?

The answer is—your literary agent.

Wait a moment. Since when have literary agents been attending publishers' meetings? Well, they don't actually attend in the physical sense. But so great is their power over publishers that it could well be said they are an unseen presence at every publishing committee meeting. In fact, I would go so far as to say that some agents cast the decisive votes at such meetings. Who will paint the cover of your book? Who will be assigned to edit it? Where will it be advertised, and how many cities will you tour with it? Such is the influence of some agents that a publisher would not dare make such decisions without consulting their wishes.

How did agents come to have so much clout? How is it exerted? And what other roles do agents serve beyond the stereotyped image so many writers have of them?

Coming into their own

I entered the publishing business in 1959, on the cusp of a revolution in the relationships among writers, agents and publishers. Until late in the nineteenth century, authors relied on their own business acumen to deal with their publishers—which may explain why so many were horribly exploited, robbed of their copyrights, cheated out of their money, and even hoodwinked out of their bylines. The introduction of authors' representatives afforded some measure of protection to authors who engaged them. But such was publishers' hostility to agents that many authors were afraid to hire them for fear their publishers would drop agented authors in favor of authors negotiating for themselves. And they were right.

Agents gained ground in the first half of this century, but even well into the 1960s publishers regarded them as necessary nuisances. Although the hostility, you will not be surprised to know, focused on the agents' demands for better pay and other contractual terms, there was more to it than just money. Editors felt intensely paternalistic or maternalistic towards their authors, and resented the formation of strong emotional bonds between those authors and literary agents.

All that was to change as the post-World War II paperback revolution took firm hold in the 1960s. Popular priced mass market paperbacks boomed and demand for "product" reached a point where we had an almost unprecedented situation—a seller's market. Whereas in the past, writers would usually have to complete a book in order to merit a

Richard Curtis established his agency, Richard Curtis Associates, in 1978. The New York agency handles fiction and nonfiction, but specializes in genre fiction including mystery, romance, western, science fiction and fantasy. Curtis writes a regular column for Locus, the magazine for the science fiction field, and is the author of Beyond the Bestseller: A Literary Agent Takes You Inside Publishing.

contract, during the buying spree of the 1960s, smart agents realized they could make deals with publishers merely on the basis of a portion and outline, an outline only, or even a one-page sketch.

The emerging breed of powerful dealmaker agents attracted many fine writers who felt that their publishers' professed appreciation of them did not extend to their contracts. Like it or not, publishers began to depend more and more heavily on agents to furnish them with desirable, profitable writers. A major byproduct of this dependency was the elimination of the slush pile as a source of new writing talent, thus intensifying the updraft of reliance on agents by both writers and publishers.

The intense competition for writing talent drove many undercapitalized publishers into the arms of better heeled companies, shrinking the number of important trade houses by, in my own estimation, 80%. Many editors were squeezed out of their jobs, while those that demonstrated skill at acquiring profitable authors were lured away from one house by another. Authors discovered that the stable, nurturing, affectionate relationships they had cultivated with their editors in the course of many books were shattered. My files are rife with horror stories of authors whose books were orphaned by the departure of their editor at a critical moment in the publishing process.

Agents abhor a vacuum, and few resisted the opportunity these conditions created to tighten their control over both authors and publishers. Disillusioned authors, feeling abandoned by their editors who had been stalwart friends over the course of many books, transferred their feelings of affection and loyalty to their agents. The bonding was not without its price, however, for in order to satisfy their affection- and support-starved clients, agents had to learn or improve skills they had been used to leaving to editors. In particular they had to become more active in the editorial process, criticizing their clients' work and even helping them develop ideas and projects from scratch.

Answering the call

The most important role an editor can play in an author's career is that of advocate at a publishing company. The editor sponsors your book through each phase of the publishing process, defending it from the countless dangers lurking to kill it before birth, ranging from bad luck to human error. But with the musical-chairs mentality that swept the editorial world in the 1970s and 1980s, authors lost these powerful allies. And when they realized there was nobody at their publishing company standing up for their books, they turned to their agents and a cry was heard throughout the land: "Do something!"

What the agents did was step into the breach and start telling publishers what to do. Today there is almost no area of the publication process that agents do not get involved with. I have reviewed page design and typography, criticized cover paintings, buttonholed sales representatives, managed publicity campaigns, and of course brainstormed book ideas and edited manuscripts. I don't consider myself unique; I know few of my fellow agents who have not played a similar role on behalf of their clients. Although we sometimes encounter resistance and resentment, more often agent input is thoughtfully considered and adopted, for it represents a viewpoint that publishers don't always have the opportunity to consider. But, if a publisher doesn't want to hear our two cents—well, that's too bad: They're going to hear it anyway. For many of us pack heavy armament in the form of important authors whose wishes and whims can make even the most powerful publishing executive tremble with fear.

Luckily, most agents are not bullies. We realize that the publishing process is a three-way partnership. As such, the agent's most important task is to lubricate the sometimes abrasive interface between publisher and author through patient diplomacy and gentle influence. I genuinely believe that if literary agents were to vanish overnight, publishers would miss them as keenly as authors.

But believe me, we're not going to vanish overnight.

For the Love of Books: Becoming an Agent

by Michael Larsen

Dream Job Opportunity
Literary Agents Needed Immediately

Start a new high-income, low-risk career today. Enter the glamorous, high-stakes world of big-time publishing. No experience, training, testing or degree necessary. Salary potential unlimited. If you have a room with a desk, a telephone, a typewriter, business cards and stationery, you can be a literary agent right now.

Be in constant demand by America's millions of writers. Get paid to read potentially bestselling manuscripts. Meet new people anxious to know you. Be wined and dined at top-rated restaurants by New York editors eager to work with you. Get invited to chic publishing parties. Feast on juicy gossip.

Become indispensable to eternally grateful authors. Have books dedicated to you. Make a fortune with your stable of bestselling authors. Become a power broker in the industry. Be quoted in columns. Have stories written about you. Sell your books to the movies and meet the stars.

Set your own hours. Sleep late. Wear whatever you like. Take long vacations. Write your memoirs. Don't delay. Realists need not apply.

According to publishing industry figures there are more than 1,000 agents in the U.S. and Canada. Most of them answered this imaginary ad even though they never saw it. How else can you account for a 20% rise in the number of literary agents in the last three years?

If you like books, have an entrepreneurial spirit, and perhaps a working spouse, being a literary agent is tempting. Discovering wonderful new writers and helping them get their books published is a noble ambition.

Of course, there are some days when, if agents were asked how they became agents, they would answer: "Just unlucky, I guess." But most agents, like most editors, do the job for love, not money. They do it because they like books and they like people, and because they're eternal optimists.

The better prepared new agents are for the job when they start or the faster they can pick up the skills they need, the more agents relish the perpetual challenges they face. Every book is a unique combination of author, subject, timing, editor, publisher and agent.

This article was adapted from the revised edition of **Michael Larsen's** *book* Literary Agents: How to Get and Work with the Right One for You, *to be published fall 1992 by Paragon House. Michael is a partner in Michael Larsen/Elizabeth Pomada, the San Francisco Bay Area's oldest literary agency. He's the author of* How to Write a Book Proposal *and co-author with Hal Bennett of* How to Write with a Collaborator, *both published by Writer's Digest Books.*

Harmonizing all those elements so that a book is as successful as it can be is always a new, creative challenge for everyone involved. Agents who help writers to do it well earn their keep.

Like editors, agents spend their lives slogging through ream after ream of proposals and manuscripts looking for something publishable. They reject more than 99% of what they see. And even when they find a project they like, there's no certainty that they're right and that they will be able to make the project work.

Why editors do it between the lines

There are as many ways to become agents as there are agents. The traditional and still the best path to agenting goes around an editor's desk. After years of being overworked and underpaid slaving for a conglomerate, editors find moving to the other side of the desk to help writers get their just desserts an easy and satisfying transition.

What do editors bring to their new calling?

● A knowledge and love of writing and books.

It's been said that a writer is a reader moved to emulation. Most editors we know are readers moved to edit. Editors love good books and, one of the things that new writers aren't aware of is how much editors love to discover promising new writers.

● Creativity in judging books and in guiding writers to make their books better.

Submissions are almost never ready for publication. Two most important gifts that editors bring to the challenge to make their books successful are: 1) having a vision of not just what a proposal or manuscript is when they first read it, but what it can be when it is 100%, as well conceived and crafted as the writer can make it; and 2) being able to convince, encourage, cajole, criticize, praise, wait, and whatever else it takes to help writers to come as close as they can to achieving that vision.

● An understanding of the business.

Editors know the business from the inside. They understand how it works or fails and why. They know the problems of getting a book sold, and as the in-house agent for the books they buy, they know what has to be done to build and maintain momentum for a book inside the house, in the publishing world at large, and with media and subsidiary rights people.

They also know how to work within the daily, weekly, monthly, seasonal, and yearly cycles in which publishers operate.

● A professional network.

The trade journal *Publishers Weekly* once reported that editors switched jobs every 2.6 years. Because the sales, publicity, and subsidiary rights people who editors work with also ride the publishing merry-go-round, an experienced editor has developed useful contacts at many houses. Editors also get to know the agents who try to sell books to them, creating a network of agents to call on for help.

● Negotiating skill.

Every time they buy a book, editors negotiate at least the major points of the deal. They learn where the give is in the contracts of the publishers they work for. And although no two publishers' contracts are exactly alike, they all cover the same territory. As agents, editors just go from keeping as much money as possible from writers to squeezing as much as they can get out of publishers for their clients.

As agents, they have an obvious interest in wrangling as much money as possible out of publishers: The more money their clients make, the bigger their commissions.

● Perseverance.

Another important gift editors have is being the relentless in-house agents for the books they buy. Editors have to be persistent and creative in guiding a book through all the phases of the publication process: reading it, convincing the house to buy it, the writing and rewriting of the book, editing, copyediting, design of the text and cover, sales, trade and consumer advertising, publicity, reviews, subsidiary rights sales (if it's a hardcover), publication in paperback and more. Following through on the publication of a book can take years.

Other ways to learn the business

Working for major publishers in other positions will also provide on-the-job training in how publishing works, and the opportunity to learn skills that agents need. Successful agents have learned about the business as sales representatives, subsidiary rights salespeople, publicists, promotion directors, house counsels and from other positions.

My partner Elizabeth Pomada and I did promotion work for a total of six major New York houses before moving to San Francisco in 1970, giving us a ready-made network when we set up our agency two years later.

After being an editor, the second best way to learn how to be an agent is to work for one. At the William Morris agency, one of the two largest agencies in the business, would-be agents start out in the mailroom and work their way up.

Booksellers learn on the front lines what sells and what dies. This is excellent experience for developing a sense of what kinds of books sales reps can convince booksellers to stock, and what motivates people to spend their hard-earned money on books.

Lawyers who become agents may not have publishing background, but they bring a knowledge of contracts and negotiation that make them effective at the bargaining table.

These are only the most obvious ways to learn about agenting, but there are many others such as being an author, working in the movie business or in other media as a magazine editor or a journalist, or being a writing teacher.

The write stuff

Agents have become successful without any of this experience. What's important to you is not so much what an agent did before becoming an agent but what happens after the business cards arrive.

Writers may get upset or depressed when their work is rejected, but agents get rejected all the time. Being thick skinned about accepting rejection (admittedly easier for someone's else work than your own) comes with the territory. So does negotiating the best possible contract, hitting up slow-paying publishers, and mediating between writer and publisher when problems arise about the acceptability of a manuscript, cover design, promotion, a royalty statement, or the editor abandoning the book for a better job. Besides knowing the art of the possible, agents have to be able to stick up for their writers' rights.

Agents must have the ability to ride the rapids. In *Life on the Mississippi*, Mark Twain's wonderful classic, he writes about how a riverboat captain knows every changing bend in the 2,000-mile river. He knows where he is all the time, even when he's asleep.

Agents have to be able to stay afloat while awash in an endless, daily changing melange of meetings, phone calls, correspondence, submissions from writers, submissions to editors, deals, projects in different stages, and dealing with other publishing professionals such as, foreign and subsidiary rights agents. This is like trying to keep track of 2,000 miles worth of people and the mix changes every day. Agents have to go with the flow, staying afloat on the swift current and dangerous eddies of uncertainty that are in the nature of publishing.

How can you determine if an agent can do the job? Here are three suggestions:
1. Ask your professional network of writers, booksellers, reviewers, sales reps, librarians, and anyone else you know in the world of books about an agent you are considering.
2. Research the agent in directories to find out the agent's policies and specific interests.
3. After you have submitted your book to an agent, and the agent wants to represent you, meet with the agent if possible. Your relationship with your agent is a working marriage, but as one comedian once quipped: "Marriage is grounds for divorce." So before you accept an agent's proposal, decide if the chemistry between you is right for a mutually

satisfying relationship. See what the agent's office looks like. Look at the books the agent has sold.

Feel free to ask any questions that come to your mind or arise in the course of the conversation. Agents who work with new writers are used to answering questions about their business. A bad agent is worse than no agent at all, so convince yourself that you are hiring the agent you need on both a personal and professional level.

Even with the best of precautions, your working marriage with your agent may wind up on the rocks. It may turn out that, despite the best of intentions, you and your agent were not meant to work together.

If this turns out to be the case, look at it as a learning experience that will help you to choose more wisely the next time.

Go for it!

The hardest part of our job is finding books to sell. Elizabeth spent ten years selling a literary first novel, but our biggest deals always happen fast because it is easy to sell a well-conceived, well-written, well-presented book that meets the needs of the marketplace. Indeed, if you're writing to meet the needs of the marketplace and you're tireless in promoting your work, this is far and away the best time ever to be a writer.

I have always thought that the idea that it is hard to get an agent is a myth. I believe that all of the agents listed in this directory will work with any book if they love it enough or if they think they can sell it for enough money.

There are more than 1,000 agents out there. The vast majority of them must keep finding new writers or they will go out of business. You won't know whether the agent you find is the perfect agent for you until the honeymoon is over. But finding an agent for a salable book with a significant national audience is easy. The challenge is writing one.

One editor used to give this advice to aspiring writers: "If anything can stop you from becoming a writer, let it. If nothing can stop you, do it and you'll make it." Good luck and keep on writing!

Taking Stock: Are You Ready for an Agent?

by Rod Pennington

The most frequently asked question whenever writers gather is, "Do you have an agent?" The better question might be, are you ready for an agent and do you really need one? Many aspiring writers make the mistake of looking for an agent before they have anything to sell. Agents are brokers and their commodity is the written word. Unless you are an established writer with a track record of producing marketable books or scripts, you will need to have a completed project in hand before you will get the attention of an agent.

Agents are not super humans who will solve all of a writer's problems with one phone call to the right editor. In fact, an agent cannot sell anything you couldn't sell yourself if you were willing to do the leg work. Agents will look after your interests and usually squeeze enough extra out of a publisher so that they more than earn their fee. However, the best agent in the world cannot sell a badly flawed manuscript.

What agents will handle

Few agents handle poetry or short stories so if those are your markets then you probably don't need, nor could you find, representation. Category fiction such as romance novels, westerns, science fiction and so on, is fairly open to newcomers. The rates of compensation do not vary much in category fiction for beginning writers and an agent, while able to open a few doors and move your manuscript to the top of the stack, probably isn't going to get you a better deal than you could get for yourself. Nonfiction is usually written by an expert in a field who is known to agents and publishers before he even begins writing. This type of writer is often approached directly by publishers and has little trouble finding representation if the project is large enough. Celebrities and their "close personal friends" have little trouble finding someone to represent them. If you are the disgruntled ex-mistress of a New York crime boss who wants to tell all, the agents will find you.

So, what is left? Novels and screenplays. Most book publishers are located in New York and most screenplays are sold in Hollywood. It would logically follow that if you have a literary work you will want a New York agent and if you are trying to sell a screenplay you will want a California agent. New York agents can sell screenplays and California agents can sell books and many bigger agencies have offices on both coasts. In the age of fax machines and overnight mail, however, an agent does not have to live near either of the major markets. But, since this agent is out of the "loop" of day-to-day activity, they will have to be well-connected or deal with a specialized market to be effective.

It is not the job of an agent to fix plot problems, correct the spelling or tie up your dangling participles.

Before approaching an agent

Your work must be professional and polished and you must have the right attitude toward a career in writing before you embark on the task of securing an agent. Answering

Author of five novels and more than 300 articles and short stories, **Rod Pennington** *has three screenplays in development, one with an independent producer and two with major studios. He is a Writer's Digest School instructor and teaches writing in adult education classes. He originally developed his Agent Acquisition Checklist for use in the classroom.*

the questions on page 11 will help you determine where you stand on these matters.

First, your work must be in the proper format; *The Writer's Digest Guide to Manuscript Formats*, by Dian Dincin Buchman and Seli Groves, is a good place to look and there are many other excellent books on the subject. A manuscript or script which is not in the proper format will wave a red flag to an editor that he is not dealing with a "pro." The copy which you present for review must be clean with dark type. Don't cost yourself a contract because you were too lazy to change a typewriter ribbon. If you use a computer, avoid dot matrix printers, use a letter quality printer. Do not use justified margins, the added spacing can lead to typesetting errors and can be annoying to read.

Before you approach an agent, you must be confident that you are writing at a professional, marketable level. Do your homework. Read what's being published or produced in your field. Be honest with yourself: Is your work as good or better than what's currently on the market?

Writing can be a brutal career path. Editors make decisions based on what they feel their readers will want to read and occasionally reject otherwise excellent projects simply because they are not what they currently need. Are you mentally prepared to accept the inevitable rejections and understand that a rejection is a professional decision and not a personal rebuff?

Do you have the self-confidence to compete with other experienced writers? Do you know in your heart that this is the best possible writing which you are capable of producing at this time?

Selecting an agent

Perhaps the most important thing you will ever write is the query letter you use to solicit an agent. The only thing an agent will have to judge you by is your query. In about five hundred words you must sell your project and, more importantly, yourself. Your query must be professional and compelling if you want to tickle the fancy of a top agent. Don't exaggerate or make false claims such as, "a sure best seller" or "I'm the next Tom Clancy." False bravado will make the eyes of most agents glaze over. In crisp, concise language explain your project, give a brief description of your skills and experiences, and ALWAYS enclose a self-addressed, stamped envelope.

The selection of the right agent can be tricky. The more you know about a potential agent the greater the likelihood there will be a fruitful relationship. If you are writing a novel, is the agent you plan to query a member of the Independent Literary Agents Association (ILAA) or the Society of Authors' Representatives (SAR)? If you plan to sell more than one screenplay, your agent must have signed the Writers Guild of America Artists Managers' Basic Agreement. All of these organizations provide lists of agents who have agreed to abide by the groups' codes of ethics and standards. See Resources for contact information for ILAA, SAR and the Writers Guild.

Agents are frequent speakers at writers' conferences and this offers an excellent opportunity to meet them face-to-face and see if there is a possible match. If you "network" with other writers you often can get an introduction to an agent. An excellent source of agent referrals is from editors whom you respect; they will refer you to someone they are comfortable working with.

Know what you want

What type of relationship are you looking for from your agent? Are you an able business person who is good at sales and likes to have control over every phase of your work? Do you only need an agent to be sure that you are getting the best possible deal? Do you want to turn the entire business side of your career over to your agent so that you can get back to your writing? Do you want your agent to just be the middle-man and not comment on your work or do you want a nurturing sounding board? Or, are you somewhere in between?

Agent Acquisition Checklist

My Manuscript or Screenplay

Answer the following questions: Yes (Y), No (N), Uncertain (U)

☐ I have a completed manuscript or screenplay.

☐ I am writing at a professional level.

☐ I have the self-confidence in my work to compete with other experienced writers.

☐ I realize that rejection letters are inevitable but I am prepared to accept them and continue writing.

If you answered all of these questions "YES," then proceed to the next section. If you answered any of these questions "No" or "Uncertain" then go back to working on your manuscript or screenplay. You are not ready for an agent.

Manuscript or Screenplay Checklist

☐ My manuscript or screenplay is in the proper format.

☐ ALL spelling, typographical and grammatical errors have been corrected.

☐ This is the best possible writing I am capable of producing at this time.

My Plan of Action

☐ I have prepared a professional quality query letter to send to prospective agents.

☐ I have prepared a list of potential agents who are experienced in my area of interest.

☐ I know if my prospective agent charges a reading fee.

☐ I am aware of my prospective agent's commission structure.

Choosing the Right Agent

☐ After an agent has expressed a willingness to represent me, we will discuss my career goals before any contracts are signed.

© 1991 Rod Pennington

Before you sign on with an agent you should discuss your career goals and needs. It is not necessary to jump into a relationship with the first agent who bats his eyes in your direction. Ask a few questions first!

Has the agent successfully represented a project in your field of interest? What is the agent's commission structure? Does the agent charge a reading fee? What items will be charged to you — photocopies, long distance phone calls, courier serivces, etc. — and what will be paid by the agent?

Is the agent sensitive to your needs? Is the agent interested in your writing goals for the next year, five years, 20 years? Will the agent help you in planning your "next move?"

Working with an agent is like a marriage; some last a lifetime, some end in an ugly divorce. If you approach the relationship with a professional attitude you will increase your chances for success.

How Agents Find Their Clients

by Eileen Fallon

When Writer's Digest Books asked me to write this piece on how agents find their clients, I was struck by their approach. I'd heard the lament "How do I find an agent?" innumerable times during my publishing career, yet I'd never really sat down and thought about exactly how I found my clients.

Of course, I always knew that clients came to me in one of four or five ways—being referred by an editor or by another agent, through a writers' conference, through a query letter, referred by another client (sometimes, I even get excellent clients through friends or relatives of clients) or due to the fact that many writers either knew me or knew of me from my days as an editor. But I never really knew which one of these approaches had given me the greatest number of clients.

So, with pencil and paper in hand, I actually went through my entire client list to find out just how the writers had made their initial contact and I'll share with you the results.

Initial contact through:
A query letter 22%
A writers' conference 22%
Referral from a current client 24%
Referral from an editor 13%
Referral from another agent 3%
Having known me as an editor 13%
Referral from a bookseller 3%

What a lucky break for me in terms of this assignment! Almost 50% of my clients came to me through those old (and evidently very productive) standbys, the query letter and writers' conferences. For the reader of *The Guide to Literary Agents and Art/Photo Reps*, the task of finding an agent is not that onerous. You don't have to have connections, but you do have to have some knowledge of what agents are looking for and you have to use common sense.

So, before you write to the first agent listed in the *Guide*, or sign up for the first writers' conference you hear about, keep in mind another statistic. I have a current list of about 45 clients. So when I note that 22% of my list came to me through a query letter, I'm talking about a total of 10 writers. That same (and yes, very small) number came to me through conferences.

I can receive from five to 25 query letters a day. From that number, I will request material about twice a week (that's right, not twice a day, twice a week). And in the eight years I've been an agent, I've spoken at a wide variety of conferences across the country. Still, both approaches combined have yielded a total of 20 writers.

How do you put the odds in your favor?

Well, definitely *not* by dashing off a letter to the first agent whose name your eye lights upon in the *Guide*, and definitely *not* by signing up for just any conference.

Eileen Fallon *was an agent for Lowenstein Associates for eight years before establishing her own agency, The Fallon Literary Agency, in 1990. The agency handles a range of fiction and nonfiction and is building a reputation in the field for handling mainstream fiction, mystery and romance fiction.*

You're going to have to use those same skills that are called upon in your writing—organization, choice, discrimination—to find out how to write a successful query letter or how to select the conference that's best for you.

The main thing to keep in mind when choosing a conference is this: Will at least one of the speakers be someone to whom you could submit material, meaning an agent or editor in your field? Think about what you write. If you're a mystery writer, you don't want to be at a conference focusing on another genre, or at a general interest writers' conference that does not feature an agent who handles mysteries or an editor who acquires them. Take some time to research and target conferences just as you do when you market your work.

But since the query letter is certainly a less expensive option than attending a writers' conference, and one that many more readers will want to pursue, I'll concentrate on that avenue.

Ask any agent to name the most frequent mistake writers of the query letter make, and I believe you'll get the same response—all too often, *the query is sent to an agent who does not represent the kind of project discussed in the letter.*

I'll never forget a phone call that came in very late one afternoon to the agency in which I first worked. Since the receptionist had already left for the day, I picked up the phone. The caller wanted to pitch a science fiction novel. I told him that no one at our agency handled that genre, but I did give him the names and addresses of two other agents known for working in that field. "Well," the caller asked me, "if neither of them wants it, would you take a look at it?"

Recall that I'd just told him that no one in the firm knew the first thing about science fiction. While we could certainly judge if the manuscript were well written, we would have no idea if it were the greatest SF novel to come along in a number of years, or if the idea had been seen a thousand times and it would be impossible to interest an editor in the novel (not to mention the fact that our contact with science fiction editors would not be as strong as those of an agent who dealt in the field).

How do you find the right agent to query?

First it's important for you to know what you've written. The caller I mentioned knew that his project was a science fiction novel (what he didn't know was how important it is to contact an agent who handled work in that area). If you've written a novel in a known genre, such as science fiction, mystery, romance, technothriller, etc., the path is pretty much laid out for you.

A source such as the one you're currently reading will list agents and their areas of expertise. But keep in mind that even such non-genre books as the literary novel, or the big mainstream novel, are a discernable part of the market. Just because they are non-genre does not mean that an agent therefore sends them to any old editor for consideration. Certain editors acquire genre books and certain editors acquire literary novels or mainstream fiction. An agent may list one or a number of genres among the kind of project he/she represents and those who handle mainstream or literary fiction will mention that fact in their listings.

Or perhaps you haven't written a novel at all. You may have credentials in an area of expertise—psychology, law, medicine, etc.—and have written a book on a topic in your field. Similar to a novelist, you would consult the list of agents in this volume to see which of them handles nonfiction. This area is also further broken down into types of nonfiction—self-help, popular culture, biography, history, etc.

Obviously, those agents who note in a listing that they handle the kind of project you've written are most likely to be receptive to your letter.

Another good way to find an appropriate agent to query is to check the dedication or acknowledgments page in a recent book that appeals to the same market that yours does. The agent is often mentioned.

Now you've found the right person to whom to direct your query. Since most of the queries an agent receives are not appropriate (meaning that the agent does not handle the kind of project discussed), you've already favorably impressed a carefully chosen agent. How do you further that good impression?

Query letters

Here are two composite query letters. The first would likely get a favorable reaction. The second would not.

Query #1
Dear Agent X:

I have recently completed a mystery novel, *Miss Johnson Finds a Body*. Though set in a small town on the east coast of the U.S., the novel is very much in the tradition of Agatha Christie's Miss Marple stories in that it features an elderly woman sleuth in a small town setting. Of course, she is much more savvy than others initially realize. Another series my novel brings to mind is the one featuring Miss Seeton. I have noticed that Berkley is still publishing new titles in this series.

I have long been a reader of the softer kind of mystery novel mentioned above (hardboiled mysteries have never appealed to me). When I saw your name on the dedication page of several softer mysteries, I thought you would be a good agent to query about my novel.

I have enclosed a one-page synopsis of *Miss Johnson Finds a Body*. The completed novel is 80,000 words in length. Could I send you the novel, or a longer synopsis and sample chapters? A SASE is enclosed for your reply.

I look forward to hearing from you at your convenience.

Sincerely,

Aspiring Author #1

Aspiring Author #1

Query #2
Dear Agent X:

I have written a romance and would like to know if you would consider representing it.

I am a happily married woman with two young children. I have always loved to read, and now that my younger child is finally in school, I hope to fulfill a desire I've had since childhood—to write a novel and have it published.

I've enclosed a SASE for your reply, and look forward to hearing from you at your convenience.

Sincerely,

Aspiring Writer #2

Aspiring Author #2

Let's see what the first query shows us about the person who wrote it. She or he has directed the letter to Agent X since she knows from seeing the agent's name on the dedication pages of novels similar to hers, that the agent not only handles mysteries, but specifi-cally the kind of mystery she's written—what she described as a "softer" mystery (usually referred to as a "cozy" in the publishing business).

We also see that this author has done her homework in that we know she has obviously read a number of books in the area she hopes to publish in. And not only has she read the novels of a superstar in her genre, she is also aware that a publishing house is still putting out new titles in a certain series. This is an aspiring writer who goes to bookstores and keeps up with what is being published. Her mentioning the length of her project in words is a further indication of professionalism (so often when agents ask a writer how long a proposed submission is, we're told that the writer doesn't know!). As an agent who values my own time, but who also hopes to take on new, qualified clients, I would request material from this writer.

Now on to the second letter. First of all, I hope that our Agent X handles romance novels. There's no indication in the letter why the writer chose to query this agent about her novel. Further, she does not give enough information about her project. Just as there are many sub-genres of mystery, there are many in romance. Has this woman written a 120,000 contemporary love story, similar perhaps to the novels of Danielle Steele? Or maybe she's really pitching a smaller contemporary romance, one suitable for Silhouette, Harlequin or Bantam's Loveswept series. Further, the facts she mentions in her second paragraph have no bearing on the novel. The agent really doesn't care about personal facts that have nothing to do with a writer's project. Of course, at times such facts are important. Say that you lived in Alaska for ten years, and though you now live elsewhere, you've set your novel there—that fact has something to do with your novel.

While I represent romance fiction, I would hesitate to request material based on this letter, since it only gives me the strong impression that I would be wasting my time in so doing. I have no indication that the writer is up on the current market and the general impression that the letter gives is one of lack of professionalism.

Remember agents are always looking for that next bestseller. The competition is stiff, but you can tip the scale in your favor if you spend time researching the appropriate agents for your work.

How to Find an Agent: One Agent's View

by Frank Weimann

Whenever I speak to a group of writers, my main suggestion for how to find an agent is to look in one of your favorite books. If in the acknowledgment section there's an agent's name listed, it must mean that the writer and agent had a good relationship. Taking that a step further, you should probably look in the acknowledgment section of a number of books within your genre. Then just get the agent's number either from this book or *Literary Market Place* or even the publishing house's public relations department. Tell them you're working on a book within the same genre and would like an agency that can help promote your work in a mutually beneficial relationship.

Making contact

If you call a publishing house and they give you the names of several agents (in all likelihood they will), call them and see how responsive they are to you. Ask them if you can submit a query letter or a sample chapter or proposal.

When you contact an agent, keep in mind that writers are as important to agents as agents are to writers. Don't let them feel as if they have the upper hand, but neither should you come across as being difficult.

Another way to find an agent is to attend writers' conferences. If *I* were a writer attending a conference, I would bring whatever I wanted to sell with me. Immediately prior to the agent's session, I would just walk directly up to him and tell him I have a proposal that is unique and well-written.

What to ask

What kinds of questions should you ask a potential agent? You simply ask him the types of books he sells, what kinds of authors has he worked with, and if the agent has any interest in whatever you're writing about. If the answer to that last question is "yes," you go into the pitch about why your work should be published, and how both parties would greatly benefit from working together. Then, if you're at a conference, you suggest that the agent read the proposal on his or her flight home.

You must be very aggressive, but you also must be prepared to capsulize what your book's about in 25 words or less.

If you're dealing with a potential agent on the phone, get right to the point. You tell him where you got his name, then you tell him about, for example, this wonderful mystery you've been working on. Then you say, "Let me capsulize it for you. The story's about . . . . Why this book would sell is . . . . I can help by doing public appearances, book signings, whatever." Most important, be respectful of the agent's time. If he's interested, ask for a client list. Also, offer to give the proposal or manuscript to the agency on a two-week or 30-day exclusivity basis.

Frank Weimann *founded The Literary Group in 1985 and represents approximately 50 clients, including Aissa Wayne* (My Father, John Wayne), *ex-mobster Sam Giancana* (Double-Cross) *and David Jacobsen* (My Nightmare in Beirut). *He is also the author of two books, the most recent being* Everything You Wanted to Know About Woody Allen.

The reason you want to make an exclusivity offer is that if the agency's not competing against another agency just to read it, the likelihood is that they'll take it more seriously. Given a choice between two books that the agency's looking at, one on an exclusivity basis and the other on multiple submission, the multiple submission will sit around because the agency feels that it's making a commitment to the writer by reading his or her work. They want the writer to make that same commitment to the agency.

What to look for

Without hesitating, I would say the first quality you should look for in an agent is aggressiveness, then for someone who is looking for a long-term arrangement with a writer; also someone who can maximize the writer's profit on a book by means of ancillary rights (foreign sales, movie deals, etc.). I would look at current successes, not those of 10 or 15 years ago. What is he doing now? Also, I would ask the agency if I could contact anyone on its client list, not necessarily to do so but more to find out what the reaction is.

Personality is important, too. Do you like the personality of the person you'd be dealing with? Or do you think there's something about him or her that gets on your nerves? The best line I've heard about something like that is from a forthcoming book by one of the authors I represent, and it goes like this: "Have you ever met a jerk that got better?" They don't. Once a jerk, always a jerk. So it's important to realize that you'll be dealing with this person, you have to get along with them.

After an agent's interested in your work, find out what his or her plans are for the book. Does he think he can close the deal for you in 30 days, or six months or a year and a half? What type of commitment is he making to you?

What to avoid

What shouldn't you do when seeking an agent? Never handwrite a letter or envelope; never address a letter "Dear Sir or Madam"; never send poor quality copies (which indicate that everybody and their brother have seen the proposal); never forget to enclose a self-addressed, stamped envelope; and never send inferior work (such as a first draft or rough outline). The presentation you make has to be very professional. If you commit any of the above-mentioned pet peeves of agents, it shows that you aren't thorough enough to work on proposed projects.

At a writers' conference, you shouldn't insult the agent by saying, "I've got this great idea, but I can't tell you about it because I don't want anyone to steal it." That blows any possibility of trust between you and the agent.

Also, don't bad-mouth any other agent or publishing house (or anyone else, for that matter) in front of the agent.

Finally, don't monopolize the agent's time. Make your point right away, offer the possibilities, and try to be positive and upbeat.

Finding the Right Agent: One Writer's Experience

by Katina Z. Jones

I've often heard it said that, at least in love, the right relationship will come along as soon as you stop needing it.

That's almost how I got my agent—I wasn't convinced I needed one.

Meeting Frank Weimann, my agent, was a happy accident. I was at a writers' conference in Detroit, and I ran into Writer's Digest School's Kirk Polking, whom I had met one year earlier. Kirk remembered me and introduced me to Frank, who had a crowd of writers around him. We started talking about some of my ideas; he expressed some interest; and I went to his session the next day, ironically titled, "How to Find the Right Agent for You."

How I really found my agent

I'd like to stop here for a minute to point out two of the most used techniques for finding an agent (I had used them unwittingly but you should try a little more consciously); they are: 1) networking and 2) using writers' conferences to meet agents (and editors and lots of other people, which really leads you back to the first technique). I've talked to a lot of writers over the last year or so, curious about how they went about finding agents, and the majority of them said they'd met their agents at writers' conferences. Some had sent letters to the agents listed in the *Literary Market Place (LMP)* and other directories with varying degrees of success.

Don't get me wrong. Directories are terrific sources, a wealth of information that every writer should keep at his or her disposal. But there's a lot to be said about meeting someone face to face; in fact, it's been shown that, at least in job interviews, the interviewer makes up his or her mind within the first 30 seconds. Every good business person (you should be one of them, your agent should be another) knows the fundamental rule of sales: People buy people, then they buy ideas.

There are, as usual, exceptions. One friend of mine was lucky enough to have an agent notice his short stories in a literary magazine. He was in the rather enviable position of having that agent call him to set up a meeting. He subsequently "hired" her, and she is now "shopping around" his first collection of short stories.

Stories like this are what we all dream of from the moment we decide to become writers. But unfortunately, for most of us, it's not what actually happens. What actually does happen is often quite surprising.

As I said earlier, even having been introduced to an agent who was receptive to some of my ideas, I wasn't convinced I was ready for an agent.

I became convinced

I'd started a proposal for a nonfiction book on writing for trade journals and was most of the way through it. I had begun mapping out a plan for selling it myself. I was so convinced that I could sell it to one particular publishing house that I balked at Frank's

Katina Z. Jones *is the former editor of* EveryBody's News *(a Cincinnati art & entertainment biweekly), and has written for* McCall's, Midwest Living, Writer's Digest, The Cincinnati Post *and several business and trade journals. She lives in Akron, Ohio.*

suggestion to let him have a look at it. I wasn't being arrogant, just a little ignorant, I guess.

But then external events (twists of fate?) led me to think about seeking an agent. Two months after I'd met Frank and told him, "I can sell this one on my own, thanks," my regular job as creative director for an engineering consultant was eliminated. When your job is phased out, you seriously begin to reconsider a lot of things.

I did. I finished the final draft of my proposal, called Frank and told him it would be on his desk the following day. I really did need help and I knew it. I was finally ready for an agent.

One week later, I got a letter from him saying he'd like to represent me on the project.

Like any relationship, it's give and take

One year and lots of rejections later, we mutually decided to abandon the idea because it just wasn't selling. The lesson there: Just because you have an agent doesn't guarantee a sale. The marketplace is a strange beast, and no one can predict what will or won't sell.

But I will tell you this, too: One of the rejections was the most glowing rejection I've ever received, and it was from Henry Holt & Sons, a publishing company I really respect. It basically said that, although they couldn't buy the book, the proposal was one of the nicest they'd seen. That helped build Frank's trust in me as a writer, and it's probably what later led him to try me out on another project.

That brings me to another important point: As in any type of close relationship, you've got to have a lot of trust in whomever you choose to be your agent. Not only that, you've got to stick by them for awhile even if they can't, for some reason, sell your work. And because, as in love, the relationship's a two-way street, your agent must have more than a little trust in your abilities, too.

Frank and I have worked together now for more than a year, and we've had a few ups and downs along the way. But that's the way any good relationship is, whether it's a working or personal one. We have all the qualities of a decent relationship: We communicate easily, work as a team and have lots of faith in each other.

Sticking with Frank wound up bringing me a book collaboration with the president of a national organization (which we recently sold to Longmeadow Press) and the promise of future collaborations.

Eventually, I hope to come up with another proposal of my own, something else for Frank to pound the pavement with. So far, I've been too busy, which I think is a good sign.

EDITOR'S NOTE: We did not assign or plan the following two articles as a unit, but they go so well together we are making it a point to present them to you in that way. Jeff Herman's article, The Literary Agent: A User's Guide, is an excellent description of the way an agent sells work and Evan Marshall's An Agent's Day illustrates this description by giving you a play-by-play of how works are actually sold on any typical day.

The Literary Agent: A User's Guide

by Jeff Herman

You've read enough and heard enough to know that as a writer, it is difficult to get very far without an agent. Of course, there is always that almost mythic story about the writer from Usk, Washington whose brilliant novel was discovered in the slush pile by a diligent editorial assistant who passed it on to a top editor. But you've wisely decided to get yourself an agent, and this article is about what you should expect once you have one.

There are almost as many kinds of literary agents as there are people, and the relationships between agents and clients are equally varied, ranging from best buddies who vacation together to snarling combatants. Your best bet is to aim for something in between. This article will outline what you should expect from an agent, as well as give you a few tips on what your agent can expect from you, for this is, after all, a reciprocal arrangement.

Agent as critic

You've just received a letter or a phone call from an agent who is not only agreeing to represent you, but is also waxing enthusiastic about your project. Then comes the big blow: You're hearing suggestions about how you could—in fact, should—improve your manuscript or proposal. This is a good sign—it means the agent is doing the job.

Your agent reads thousands of pages of writing a year, and has a sense of what works and what doesn't. He or she also knows the markets for and the commercial potential of a manuscript. Don't let the egotism of the sensitive artist in you blind you to good criticism and advice; on the other hand, don't be pushed into changes that you feel will compromise rather than enhance your project.

There is room for discussion and negotiation at this stage, but you must be willing to listen. Sometimes it's tough to know what to do. However, if your gut response is to like and trust your agent, and if you want to continue with him or her, make the leap of faith. Of course, you might be among the lucky ones whose writing requires no revision.

Agent as advocate

The next step is for your agent to find you a publisher. It is here that his or her expertise and contacts are invaluable—this is why you sought out an agent in the first place. The agent is your advocate, trying to find the best possible home for your book, as well as the

Jeff Herman *founded The Jeff Herman Literary Agency in 1985 and has since sold more than 100 titles. His agency has become known for general adult nonfiction. He has taught courses for writers at New York's West Side YMCA Writer's Voice program and frequently addresses writers' groups across the country. He is author of the book,* The Insider's Guide to Book Editors & Publishers: Who They Are! What They Want! And How to Win Them Over!.

biggest advance. This is not motivated by philanthropy as much as it is by self-interest — although you may be lucky enough to have an agent whose love for books is a part of the incentive for showing up at the office — because your agent gets a cut of whatever money you make. (Similarly, if you make no money, neither does your agent.)

Agents have different methods at this stage. The general idea is that your manuscript will be sent to editors who are interested in your kind of work, and with whom your agent has developed a relationship over time. Some agents believe that manuscripts should be sent to one editor at a time — this is genteel old-style publishing — while others will submit simultaneously to editors at different houses, informing all of them that this is happening, in the hopes of speeding up the process and possibly generating an auction.

Granting one publisher an "exclusive" has some advantages; the publisher will be given a reasonable deadline within which to respond or lose the exclusive option, and if your agent has in mind a particular editor whose sensibility almost entirely coincides with that of your project, this may be the best route to take. It is also a way to test the waters — if you are rejected altogether, the editor may offer some insights into ways to further improve your work.

It's your right to ask your agent at the outset what the marketing methods will be and which publishers and editors will be targeted. You should also ask what kind of advance you can reasonably expect, as well as discuss what would be acceptable to you and the agent.

Agent as caretaker

Now you've entered the awful limbo of waiting for word. You have to remember that some editors take six to eight weeks to respond, which means calling in to your agent for daily updates will not help your cause any, and may lead your agent to think you're being a pain in the neck.

Your agent should, however, let you know when your material was submitted and to whom, and then keep you informed about the good news or bad news as it develops. This should include sending you copies of all publishers' rejection letters, since some of their comments may be helpful. If this kind of information isn't forthcoming within ten weeks of the submission date, you should call your agent to find out what's going on. What you want to be sure about is that your agent hasn't forgotten you, or given up on your project.

If it seems to you that your agent isn't putting in a reasonable effort towards getting your work published, you might want to terminate the relationship. But if your manuscript has received 20 rejection letters within six months, you should feel secure that the agent has been getting your materials out, and that you may have to rethink or shelve your project.

Agent as negotiator

Back to our more positive scenario: The editor has called your agent and said, "I love it! Let's make a deal." Although some editors have nasty things to say about agents, whom they often consider sharks, this is one of the main reasons you need an agent — to procure the best deal possible. The agent will negotiate the advance and all other contract terms, including the publisher's commitment to publicity — which can make or break your book — and then will explain it all to you in plain English so you know what you've agreed to when you sign on the dotted line.

Your agent is your advocate when dealing with the publishing company, and even if you cultivate a lovely relationship with your editor, the agent will help keep track of royalties, book club sales, serial rights and foreign sales, and other possible financial and legal complications.

If all goes well, the agent will also take an interst in your development as a writer, nurturing your future projects as they evolve and making suggestions about options that will foster the growth of your career. If you're willing to be a "hired pen," your agent might be able to help you obtain lucrative freelance and "ghosting" jobs in addition to representing the projects you do in your own name.

Agent as business partner

When you as a writer embark on this most important of relationships, here are some smart questions to ask your agent:

• How are you going to market my material to publishers?
• What kind of time frame will this involve?
• Is it okay for me to call you with questions or suggestions? How often?
• Will you help me develop ideas for new projects?
• Will you be honest with me if you lose faith in any of my projects?
• What kind of money can we reasonably expect for the project(s) in question?

A good agent will be a legal advisor, a sounding board, a development editor and a financial manager, but not a therapist or whipping post. Treat your agent with respect and honesty—expecting the same in return—and you will be able to cultivate a durable and profitable relationship.

An Agent's Day

by Evan Marshall

Monday, 9 a.m. As I unlock the door to my office, I'm smiling because in my briefcase is one of the most exciting manuscripts I've seen in a long time. I read it over the weekend. It's a courtroom thriller called *Hit*, reminiscent of *Presumed Innocent* yet completely fresh. Better yet, it's by one of my clients who thus far has published only category mysteries. This book, I am certain, will be her break-out book, a turning point in her career.

I am dialing the author's number even as I sit down. When I reach her, she is, of course, delighted. I promise to keep her posted as to the results of my marketing efforts.

I've already decided to submit *Hit* to a number of editors simultaneously, since it is definitely a hot book that more than one major publisher will want. This competition will, I hope, lead to an auction, which will drive up the price of the book as well as the excitement surrounding it. I begin to draw up my submission list, remembering that my lunch date today is with the editor-in-chief of a top publisher. I'll make my first pitch then.

9:14 a.m. I call an editor at a large publisher of romances who told me Friday that she wants to buy a first novel by a new client of mine. We begin the negotiation, the editor offering an advance that is several thousand dollars less than what I had in mind. When I tell her so, she surprises me by offering a two-book contract (for the first book and an untitled book to be determined later), but with the same advance on the second as what she has just offered on the first, and with joint accounting—*both* books must earn back their advances before the author receives any royalties. I tell her the advance that was unacceptable for the first book is even more so for the second, and that in any case I would advise my client not to accept a multibook contract at all if the books were joint-accounted. The editor says she'll talk to her editor-in-chief and get back to me.

Evan Marshall is president of the Evan Marshall Agency which specializes in adult fiction and nonfiction as well as original screenplays. He is a contributor to Writer's Digest *magazine. Before starting his own agency, he worked for Sterling Lord Literistic, Inc. and has held editorial positions in Dodd, Mead; Everest House and New American Library.*

9:31 a.m. I begin reading a horror novel that a client has just completed. It reads well, but a few inconsistencies occur to me and I jot down a few notes.

9:59 a.m. I take a call from a long-time client who has attained considerable success writing psychological thrillers. He has just delivered his latest book, has sketchy ideas for three more but cannot decide which one to develop. I listen to the three story ideas, then tell him my choice, based on what the editors are buying. He agrees to send me a preliminary outline of the book for us to discuss before he proceeds.

10:40 a.m. I call three editors to whom I have sent a proposal for a psychological self-help book by an author with a solid track record. The first editor drops out immediately, saying he has discovered that the book is too close to a book his house has recently signed up. The second editor says she intends to make an offer and will call back. The third editor is unsure and will also call.

10:55 a.m. Back to the horror novel. Getting scary.

11:10 a.m. The mail arrives. In it are five checks representing signing payments on recently sold books, three queries from would-be clients, a new contract (I'll study this tonight in order to negotiate the fine points tomorrow), two bills, and a carton of author's copies of a book just published. I ask my secretary to remove a dozen copies before forwarding the rest to the author; we'll use these copies to send, along with reviews, to our sub-agents in England, Europe and Japan.

11:18 a.m. The editor who said she intended to make an offer on the pop-psych book calls to offer $40,000 for hard/soft (hardcover and paperback) rights. I thank her, remind her that this project is on multiple submission and say I'll get back to her. I call the remaining editor, who says she's waiting to speak to her editor-in-chief and will call back within the hour. I ask her to call after lunch.

11:28 a.m. Before leaving for lunch, I read the queries that have arrived in today's mail. The first is from an author referred to me by an editor with whom I have worked on a number of books. The query describes a historical romance that seems rather trite in its plot line; however, the author has been referred by an editor and also has been published, so I make a note on the letter asking my secretary to ask to see the manuscript.

The second and third queries are poorly written; one contains numerous grammatical and spelling errors. I make a note on each asking my secretary to decline.

12:37 p.m. My lunch date is already at the table when I arrive at the restaurant. It's good to see her. Though we talk often on the telephone, I enjoy sitting down with her from time to time, learning more about her as a person and, inevitably, about her taste in books. We have no sooner placed our order than she asks me what books I've got that are really hot. I'm still feeling chills from reading that last page of *Hit*, so it's easy to convey my excitement over this book.

The editor's eyes widen as I relate the plot in a nutshell. "When can I have it?," she asks, and I tell her I'll be sending it out next week. Making a note in her datebook, she assures me she'll read the manuscript as soon as it arrives and, if the book is as good as it sounds, be in touch about making a floor bid—an offer that, if accepted, would allow her to sit out while other publishers bid, then take the book by topping the highest bid by an agreed-upon percentage (usually 10%). I tell her I'll be happy to entertain a floor offer.

As lunch progresses, she tells me about her company's list, and I take some notes about projects my clients are working on that may be right. Then she tells me about a new series of male-adventure novels she is developing for paperback, and asks if any of my clients might be suitable as authors. I recommend a young man I represent who has published six male-adventure novels with a competing house and promise to send her copies of the books. As we part, she reminds me to get *Hit* to her as soon as I can.

3:15 p.m. I take a call from my film and television agent. Terrific news! After a lively auction among four major producers, an option on a recently published women's novel has gone to a respected independent with a number of high-quality feature and television projects under his belt. His plan is to produce this book as a four-hour TV miniseries. I thank my film agent for the good work and say I'll call my author and get back.

I call the author, who is ecstatic, this being her first option. She instructs me to accept the offer; I then call my film agent and say to go ahead with the contracts.

3:23 p.m. The third editor who has the pop-psych proposal calls to up the offer to $50,000, also for hard/soft rights. I thank her and say I'll call back. I call the other editor and inform her of the better offer. She immediately goes to $60,000, obviously already having been authorized to do so.

I call the first editor, who says she cannot better her offer. She is disappointed not to get this book, but thanks me for including her in the submission and asks me to continue to keep her in mind. I call my client, who is pleased with the offer and agrees that we should accept it (when I submitted the material, I stated in my covering letter that my client and I reserved the right not to accept the highest offer, or to accept no offer at all). I call the winning editor and accept, saying that I look forward to receiving contracts.

3:33 p.m. I read more of the horror novel and jot some more notes.

3:38 p.m. The romance editor calls to say that she has been authorized to offer a thousand dollars more on the first novel, but that she must still insist on the joint accounting. I thank the editor for the improved offer, call my client to discuss it, then call back the editor and tell her that I'll take the extra thousand on the first book, but will agree to a one-book contract only. At first the editor balks, saying that the advances were based on a two-book deal, but at last she agrees, saying I can expect the contracts soon.

3:48 p.m. I call a client who has sent me a proposal for his next book, a mainstream novel à la Sidney Sheldon. This is a departure for him, as his six previous books have been rather quiet, almost literary novels. I have read his material twice and tell him that in all honesty I do not feel it is yet strong enough to submit, that the story itself must be more original, the writing tighter, the characters more fleshed out. I say that perhaps subconsciously he felt that commercial fiction of this type need not be as fresh or substantial as the fiction he has written, and he says this may be so. At any rate, I tell him he must produce more than the 200 pages he has shown me—at least half of the 800 pages he proposes. The author is disappointed but grateful for the candid feedback, and says he will rework the material with my comments in mind.

4:15 p.m. The food editor of a major women's magazine calls offering to buy first serial rights to a cookbook that will be published later in the year. I call the book's two authors, clear the deal with them and phone back the editor to accept. The editor says she wants to run several color photos from the book, and I suggest that she call the editor directly to arrange this.

4:33 p.m. I call my male-adventure author and tell him about the new series my lunch friend is developing. Though his goal is to graduate to bigger books and leave category behind, he feels these books would be a good source of money in the interim and encourages me to propose him for the series.

4:46 p.m. Back to the horror novel. So far, I feel that it's good but not as good as it could be, that the author has missed opportunities to make the story more complex and less linear. More notes.

5:23 p.m. I close my office door behind me. In my briefcase is the still-unfinished manuscript and the contract to be studied.

I'm tired but smiling. All in all, it's been a good day.

When It's Time for a Change

by James Lee Young

The writer was distraught. Her novel languished somewhere between two or three publishers and the office of a literary agent who hadn't contacted her in six months. Nor would he return her calls or letters.

What should she do?

That's nothing compared to the writer who didn't hear from his agent in three years and wondered if it was time for a change. Get real!

For those who surmount the hurdle of "getting an agent," as we phrase it among writers, it's an initial high—akin to winning a sporting event. We experience the next best thing to actually seeing our book or script sold and published. Yet, the relationship between writers and agents is one of ongoing tensions, of necessity.

Every writer wants to believe in his or her agent. And every agent wants to sell every book he or she represents. Everyone enters the relationship with high hopes and usually a congenial attitude. Both parties want it to work. But sometimes it doesn't. What then?

Some points to consider first

First, let's clear up some misconceptions about working with agents. For one, agents are not superhuman, although it is amazing how much work some of them can do on speculation and still survive. Agents have to sell or they can't live. Payment comes only through selling and the overhead between sales can be horrendous. No wonder some—not nearly all—appear to be habitually short with writers, unwilling to spend their time cultivating aspiring authors or communicating regularly.

Agents have families and pets, apartments and houses to pay for, illness and crises, and 24-hours per day, like the rest of us. If someone is representing you, the relationship should be professional and courteous, one of trust. But it must also allow for the things in life that beset all of us—which sometimes prevent us from doing exactly what we promised with good intentions.

Second, if an agent is representing you, he or she does owe you a periodic update on how things are coming in marketing your work. You have a right as a client to that information. However, if the agency has several clients, too frequent reporting to you can eat up a lot of time, letterhead and postage or telephone calls.

Two or three weeks usually is not enough time for a busy agent to respond to your query, whether you're a client or not. Calling or writing to the agent at that point won't win you points, or likely representation, nor is failure to get back to you in that time frame a reason to change.

If the time between reports is excessive or not at all, then you should begin to look at making a change. But remember, the agent's job is to sell your work, not run to you every time something new is done on your behalf.

Sometimes the agent's workload is so tremendous that he or she, like writers and editors,

James Lee Young is Executive Director of the National Writers Club. He is co-editor of The Professional Writer's Guide, Revised Expanded Edition, *National Writers Press. National Writers Club runs the National Writers Literary Agency for selected works from its members.*

loses track of time, misses deadlines and may appear not to care. Realizing this, as a writer you may be able to maintain or even salvage a good relationship that will benefit both of you.

Third, agents are not writers' baby-sitters. Good ones will not hold your hand, rewrite or edit your work. That's your job, or you can find other services to help you prepare the manuscript. So if the agent fails to cater to you in these areas, that's not a reason to change.

Having noted what agents will or will not do for you—the writer—how do you know when to leave or change agents?

The warning signs

Sometimes an agent loses enthusiasm or simply runs out of ideas for marketing a particular manuscript, script, or even an author's work in general. In that case, he or she should let the writer know, or the writer may take the initiative. Either way, it may be time to part company. A new agent might have more success selling the work, and the writer can get on with marketing his or her wares. Everyone gets a fresh start.

Then there are those cases where the writer and agent have a personality clash, or some misunderstanding or event occurs and one or both parties are unwilling to bend on an opinion, issue or method of operation.

If that happens to you, try to work it out. If you can't work it out, don't fight it. Part company as amicably as possible. Conflict happens in the best of families. Move away as gracefully and courteously as you can. It's time.

Reporting time varies among the agencies, but it's advisable to find out what your agent's method and time frame are, and expect that you will be contacted regularly, at least every quarter.

If you have queried the agent or inquired and have had no response, say, within four to six weeks, it's time for a courteous letter by mail or fax. At two months, another professional and courteous letter is in order. If you feel comfortable doing so, and/or you know the agent well enough, give him a telephone call.

Periodic telephone calls, fax messages, and/or letters between the agent and writer usually are anticipated and welcomed, within reason. Most agents will be courteous and responsive to inquiries, might apologize for not contacting you sooner and will update you. A few are habitually hostile. The response may be, for example, "I don't have time to run to every client with each little thing. When I've got something for you, I'll let you know."

Unless you have been an absolute pest (a relative term, I realize), reconsider the relationship and whether to change agents. If, however, you have been overzealous by writing or calling too often, and the rebuke is justified, resolve to stay busy on your next book or other project, freeing the agent to market your work.

Selling books is difficult, even for an experienced agent. It takes time to sell manuscripts, and publishers usually have a 12- to 18-month production schedule. Yet, if you haven't heard from your representative in six months to let you know the status of your work, it's high time you reestablished contact. A polite letter inquiring about the status of your work is certainly in order.

With no response beyond that and depending on your contractual obligation, I'd consider withdrawing the material, ask that it be returned and move on. If your material is more timely, you may have to adjust the time frame considerably to ensure your material isn't dated. Just be sure the project is realistic in terms of salability and production.

In fact, from a writer's view and possibly from an agent's as well, it might be advantageous to set a time limit on your contract, either written or verbal. Six months to a year, depending on the manuscript or script, are general time limit agreements set by some agents and their clients. That way, if the work doesn't sell the writer and agent can move on to new projects.

Raise your antennae

Suppose an agent agrees to represent you as a writer and praises your work but notes that the manuscript needs work. Raise your antennae and be wary.

Although more and more agencies are providing evaluation and editing services, you must be careful about which ones you choose for these tasks. Some so-called agencies run editorial mills, making their money by providing critiques and editing, rather than selling manuscripts.

Reputable agents who offer evaluation and/or editorial and rewrite services will say up front that such work does not guarantee they will represent you. Be aware that unless representation is guaranteed you can spend considerable dollars and still have no agent to represent your work. Some writers feel an agent who agrees to edit your work should have enough confidence and belief in the work to represent it once you have made the changes or corrections to the manuscript.

Of course, if you agree to an evaluation of your work and you fail to come up to the standards or revise the manuscript in the way the agent considers salable, that's another story. That's the ruse used by disreputable agent/editorial mills. The manuscript almost never measures up and, of course, that way he or she has your money and doesn't even have to try to sell your work. These people prey on beginners and are not legitimate agents. And if it looks like you're about to enter a deal where the agent wants even more money but isn't giving you any guarantee, look elsewhere for representation.

Your representative should be up front with you as to his or her agency's policies. Often writers will enter such relationships, amid great encouragement from the agent, only to be dropped after paying for a reading fee, evaluation and/or editing fee, creating hostility and the feeling on the writer's part that he or she has been fleeced, whether that's the case of not.

Another point when it comes to money

Consider changing agents if yours fails to pay you promptly. You are in business with expenses and overhead, perhaps a family to support, and the next manuscript or script to write. You have done your job. The book or script has sold. You earned the money; the agent has the right to his or her percentage. His or her obligation is to pay you quickly.

Why should the agency draw interest on your money when you can put it to good use on your own behalf? If the agency does hang on to your money for more than a reasonable period—certainly not more than 30 days—find another agent. Reputable agents will forward your money immediately, and give you an accurate accounting.

Keep communication lines open

These are some examples of reasons and times when you might want to consider changing agents, or at least leaving one. There are exceptions and usually extenuating circumstances to consider. Not every situation will be the same.

If you belong to a good writers' organization, its staff or members may strategize with you over how to choose an agent, whether your agent is treating you properly or vice versa, and provide general guidelines on agent/writer relationships.

A good agent/writer relationship, one that lasts, is where the two parties work as a team. Give your agent the same courtesies and flexibility you expect for yourself.

Where it's possible, the best communication is between you and your agent—without either overstepping acceptable bounds. Generally, the best advice I can give is to work with your agent, keep the lines of acceptable communication open, and change only when you and/or your agent realize it has to be done.

I wish you and your agent a long, happy, and profitable relationship.

Finding and Working with Literary Agents

by Robin Gee

The articles included in this book cover a number of very important aspects of the author/agent relationship, including how agents work, what to look for in an agent, when to know you are ready for an agent and how to know if you and your agent are working well together. We're pleased also to offer almost 400 detailed listings of literary agents and script agents. Yet, with all this information, it's still possible to overlook some of the more basic requirements of working with an agent.

We've included this section to make sure these fundamentals are covered. Written especially for those of you looking for an agent for the first time, the information provided here will help you with querying an agent, preparing and presenting your work to an agent, and knowing what you can and cannot expect from your agent. Authors who may be considering changing agents will also find this material helpful.

Thinking about getting an agent

If you've just completed a manuscript or have been sending out your work directly to publishers for awhile without success, you may be thinking of getting an agent. Before you start to query agents, however, you must first have a clear idea of what you want and of what you expect your agent to accomplish.

Many agents complain of writers who expect too much; it's important to note what agents do not do. Agents are not teachers. They may give advice or recommend changes based on their experience and what they know about the market, but no agent is able or willing to try to sell an unsalable manuscript. Before contacting any agent, you must be certain your work is of publishable quality.

For the most part, agents do not handle short pieces such as magazine articles, poetry or short stories. A few agents will handle short work if they also handle a writer's book-length material, more as a friendly gesture than for profit. The reason is agents' commissions on short work are just too small to make handling such material profitable.

In general you don't need an agent to sell very specialized or experimental work or to sell work to a small or specialized publisher. Most agents work with the big, commercial publishers and look for books with wide appeal, although there are exceptions.

Simply put, an agent's job is to sell your work, help you maximize your earnings from your work, help keep track of your earnings and, thus, advance your career. It is often said agents are one part salesperson, one part business partner.

If you have a book-length manuscript you feel is publishable, and would like someone to manage the marketing of your work, an agent can help. Agents can open doors to publishers who do not take unagented manuscripts. They can put an unsolicited manuscript on an editor's desk that on its own might lie buried under the "slush" pile in the outer office.

Robin Gee *is editor of two Writer's Digest Books' titles:* Guide to Literary Agents and Art/Photo Reps *and* Novel and Short Story Writer's Market *and a regular contributor to* The Artist's Magazine.

Looking for an agent

Yet finding the right agent can be almost as hard as finding the right publisher. It's important to put just as much effort into your search. Start by reading all you can about the agent/author process. The articles and introductions in this book were chosen to help answer some of the most frequently asked questions writers have about agents. We've also included within the Resources section a list of books on agents.

Most agents find clients in one of two ways—direct contact or through referrals. One way to make direct contact is to send a query or a proposal package to the agent. Agents list in directories such as this book to let writers know how to get in touch with them. Examine the listings included in this book and check the Subject Indexes (located before the Listings Index at the back of the book) to find an agent who handles the type of work you write.

Another way to make direct contact with an agent is to meet one at a writers' conference. Often conferences will invite agents to participate in a panel, give a speech and be the "resident agent" for the conference. Although most agents would not appreciate your just "stopping by" their office for a chat, agents set aside time at conferences to do just that. Writers can sign up to talk with an agent. Some agents will look at material writers send in before the conference, but many just want to meet writers and talk generally about their work. If interested, the agent will ask the writer to send a query and samples after the conference is over.

Many agents find referrals very helpful. A recommendation from an editor, another agent or one of the agent's other clients tells the agent someone else thinks your work is worth considering. Even if you do not know any big-name authors or editors, you can make helpful contacts with them at conferences, readings and any place writers gather. Ask around. Some experienced writers are more than happy to share information and contacts.

Approaching an agent

Most agents will accept unsolicited queries. Many will also look at outlines and sample chapters. Few are interested in seeing unsolicited manuscripts, but those who handle fiction may be more willing to do so. Agents, for the most part, are slow in responding to queries, so they understand the writer's need to contact several at one time. When sending a manuscript, however, it is best to send it to one agent at a time.

This should go without saying, but submitting to an agent requires the same professional approach you would use when approaching a publisher. Work must be clean, typed, double-spaced and relatively free of cross-outs and typos. If you are sending a computer printout copy, make sure it is printed on at least a near-letter quality printer and the type is dark and easy-to-read. Always include a self-addressed, stamped envelope large enough to return your material. To save money, many writers do not want their outlines or manuscripts returned—they just send a self-addressed, stamped envelope or postcard for a reply.

Queries to agents should be brief (one-page) and to-the-point. The first paragraph should quickly state your purpose—you are looking for representation. In the second paragraph you might mention why you are querying this agent and whether you were referred to them by someone. If you chose that agent because of their interest in books like yours, be sure to mention this—in other words, show you have done a little research and are informed about this agent's business.

In the next paragraph or two describe the project. Include the type of book or script it is and the proposed audience. If your book fits into a genre or specific category, be sure to mention this. For example, if you have written a private eye detective novel, a cookbook or a movie-of-the-week, be sure to say so. This saves the agent (and yourself) time. You may also want to mention approximate length and any special features.

Follow this with a very short paragraph of personal information. Include some publica-

WILL I. DREW
122 22nd Drive
Louisville, Colorado 80077
Telephone: (303)555-5432

Ms. Mary Miller
The Wilbert Will Agency
1776 No. Houston Street
New York, NY 10077

Dear Ms. Miller:

I have a manuscript I propose to submit for publication some time
soon. I do not have an agent at this time, and would like to discuss
the possibility of your representing me.

I was referred to you by Dudley Jenkins, one of your clients, who told
me of your interest in how-to books.

I have prepared an outline and two chapters for a book I call, Time-
and Trouble-Savers at Home. This book contains 50 time- and energy-
saving tips and techniques that would be of interest to homemakers,
nursing home managers, hoteliers, health spa managers and others.

I teach home economics at Johnson High School in Louisville. I also
teach courses in time and motion studies for corporate clients.

I have had two articles on home care published in Homelife Magazine.
I can provide you with copies.

Please let me know if you would like me to send you the outline and
chapters for my book. I look forward to hearing from you.

Sincerely,

Will I. Drew

Will I. Drew

*This agent query is concise and direct. The writer mentions a referral from one of the
agent's clients, while in the same sentence he demonstrates a knowledge of the type
of work the agent handles. He follows with a one-paragraph description of the project, his credentials and background and publishing credits. This sample is from* The
Writer's Digest Guide to Manuscript Formats, *copyright ©1987, Dian Dincin Buchman
& Seli Groves. Used with permission of Writer's Digest Books.*

tion credits, if you have any, especially other published books or scripts. For nonfiction,
list your professional credentials or experience related to the project. For fiction, you may
want to relate something personal that lends credibility to your story. For example, if your
novel is about a dentist and you are a dentist, by all means mention this. If it takes place
in Mexico City and you once lived there, you want to mention this too. The rule of thumb
is to include only that information directly related to your project or what lends credibility.

Close your query with an offer to send either an outline, sample chapters or the complete manuscript. Some agents ask for an outline and/or sample chapters with the query, while some want queries only and will ask for more, if interested. Within this section we've included a sample agent query from *Guide to Manuscript Formats*. This book is also a good source for standard formats for just about any type of material, including scripts, novels, outlines, proposals and cover letters. Script and screen writers will also want to see the article by Kerry Cox on working with script agents featured at the beginning of the Script Agents section.

Making an informed decision

Unfortunately, in most states, agents are not required to have a license or formal training. Basically anyone who can afford a phone can call themselves an agent, but there are ways to determine if an agent is legitimate, recognized in the publishing industry and has enough professional experience and potential to sell your work.

Remember you are entering a business agreement. You have the right to ask for references or other information that will help you determine if the agent is the right one for you. Some agents freely give out client names, recent sales or editorial references. Others feel it is an invasion of their client's privacy, but you should ask.

Do some checking by talking to other writers about their experiences with agents. Several writers' clubs have information on agents on file and share this by written request or through their club newsletters.

While some very reputable agents are not affiliated with any agent group, those who do belong to a professional organization are required to maintain certain standards. Agents who are members of the Society of Authors' Representatives (SAR), the Independent Literary Agents Association (ILAA) or signatories of the Writers Guild of America East or West have met certain qualifications and have agreed to a code of ethics. We have listed these affiliations within the listings.

Here's a list of questions you may wish to ask a potential agent. Much of this material is contained in the listings in this book, but it's always good to check if there have been any policy changes.

- How soon do you report on queries? On manuscripts?
- Do you charge a reading fee or a critique fee? If so, how much? If a critique is involved, who will do it? What kind of feedback will I receive? Is the fee nonrefundable? Or will it be credited toward my expenses or refunded, if I become a client?
- Do you offer a written contract? If so, how long is it binding? What projects will it cover? Will (or must) it cover all of my writing?
- What is your commission on domestic, foreign, dramatic and other rights? Will I be responsible for certain expenses? If so, which ones and will they be deducted from earnings, billed directly or paid by an initial deposit?
- How can our agreement be terminated? After termination, what will happen to work already sold, current submissions, etc.?
- Will I receive regular status reports? How often can I expect to receive this information? Will I receive all information or good news only? Copies of editors' letters?
- Which subsidiary rights do you market directly? Which are marketed through subagents? Which are handled by the publisher?
- Do you offer editorial support? How much?
- Do you offer other services such as tax/legal consultation, manuscript typing, book promotion? Which cost extra and which would be covered by the commission?

How agencies make money

The primary way agents make money is by taking a commission on work sold. This is usually a 10 to 20 percent commission taken from a writer's advance and royalties. Most agents charge a slightly higher commission on the sale of foreign rights or other special rights, because they may have to split some of the money with a foreign or specialized agent.

The agents listed in our Nonfee-charging Agents section and many of those listed in the Script Agents section make almost all of their money from commissions earned on sales. Most, however, do deduct some expenses from an author's earnings in addition to the commission. These expenses may include postage costs, long-distance calls, extensive photocopying or express mail fees. Be sure you know exactly what expenses you might be charged before signing an agreement with an agency. Ask your agent to give you prior notification of any large or unusual expenses.

Many agents also charge reading or critique fees. In our book we've put these literary agents into the Fee-charging Agents section. Some script agents also charge for reading and/or critiquing and they are marked with an open box symbol (□) in the Script Agent section.

Reading fees are intended to be used as payment for an outside person to read and report on a manuscript. This saves the agent time and effort. Reading fees can range from $25-$50 on up to $300-$400. Quite often the fee is nonrefundable. Reading fees almost never obligate the agent to agree to represent you, but some agents will refund the fee, if they decide to take you as a client. Others will refund the fee after they sell your work or will credit your account. Some agents also include a report or even a critique with the fee. Before you pay any fees, make sure you have a clear understanding of what the fee will cover.

Many agents also offer critique or editorial services. The fees for these services vary widely as do the quality and extent of the critiques. It's important to ask for a fee schedule and to check the credentials of agents offering these services. Remember, too, while many agents have some editing and writing background, most are unable or unwilling to rewrite entire manuscripts.

Agents may also offer a variety of other services including consultation, publicity and ghostwriting. A few agents are also lawyers and may be available for legal consultation or representation. Keep in mind, however, that if an agent's income is mostly generated by additional services, there is less incentive to sell your book for a commission.

What agencies do

In order to sell your work, an agent must keep up with the market. Agents must maintain constant contact with editors and publishers. They must study the market and know what publishers want. This sounds easier than it really is. Publishing companies are being bought out at a dizzying rate these days and editors change jobs frequently. Until recently, agents near New York (for publishing) and the West Coast (for film) had an advantage of being close to the market. Today, proximity, while still helpful, is less important thanks to modern office technology—faxes, computers, special phone services, etc.

An agent's job is to get the most money or the best deal for your work. Agents try to help you hold onto your rights so that you can maximize your profits from one piece of work. Depending on your work and the market, an agent may submit your work to various publishers and wait for the best offer. Agents also conduct "auctions" in which publishers are invited to bid for the work at a set time. Work is then sold to the highest bidder.

The agent will represent you in contract negotiations. The final decision is ultimately yours, but the agent will advise you on how to get the best deal, what rights to sell and what rights to try to keep. Once you've sold the work, the agent may continue to try to sell additional rights or options to other publishers, movie or television producers, book clubs, audio or video producers, etc.

Agents also keep track of your business. Some agents will give you periodic reports about the status of your work. This may include a list of publishers contacted and copies of publishers' letters. Some only report on good news, while others will send you copies of reject letters as well. After the sale, the agent will keep records of your income. Publishers will send the money to the agent for you. Once the agent has deducted the commission and expenses (if any), a check will be forwarded to you.

You can also call on your agent to handle disputes or problems that come up while you are working with an editor or publisher. The agent will check your royalty statements and will ask for an audit, if needed.

Some additional information

For more information on working with agents, see the articles written by agents or other writing professionals in the Literary Agents section. Check also the introductions to each section. These cover material directly related to the entries contained within a section and will help you understand more about each type of agent listed.

At the end of the Literary Agents: Nonfee-charging and the Literary Agents: Fee-charging section introductions you will find sample listings. These samples describe each item included in the listing in detail. We explain why each piece of information is important and how it can help you make an informed decision.

We've also included a number of indexes. The Subject Index for each section contains a list of subjects in both nonfiction and fiction. Agencies who have specified interest in handling particular types of material are listed within each subject section. The Agents and Reps Index lists the names of agents and their agency affiliation. This index will be most helpful to writers who have heard or read about a good agent, but do not know the agency for which the agent works.

Important Listing Information

Listing Policy and Complaint Procedure

Listings appearing in Guide to Literary Agents & Art/Photo Reps *are compiled from detailed questionnaires, phone interviews and information provided by agents and representatives. The industry is volatile and agencies change addresses, needs and policies frequently. We rely on our readers for information on their dealings with agents and policies or fees that are different from what has been reported to the editor. Write to us if you have new information, questions about agents or if you have any problems dealing with the agencies listed or suggestions on how to improve our listings.*

Remember, while we work hard to present the most accurate information available, we do not endorse or recommend any agency listed in the book. If you feel you have not been treated fairly by an agent or representative listed in Guide to Literary Agents & Art/Photo Reps, *we advise you to take the following steps:*

• *First try to contact the listing. Sometimes one phone call or a letter can quickly clear up the matter. Be sure to document all your correspondence with the listing.*

• *If you do not hear back within a reasonable amount of time, we will then write on your behalf. When you write to us with your complaint, give us the name of your manuscript or type of artwork, the date of your first contact with the agency (query or submission) and the nature of your subsequent correspondence.*

• *We will ask the agency to contact you and resolve the problem and then enter your letter into our files.*

• *The number, frequency and severity of unresolved complaints will be considered in our decision whether or not to delete the listing from our next edition.*

Key to Symbols and Abbreviations

* *Agents who charge fees to previously unpublished writers only*

□ *Script agents who charge reading or other fees*

■ *Art/photo representatives who charge a one-time or monthly fee for handling, marketing or other services in addition to commission and advertising costs*

ms/mss — manuscript/manuscripts

SASE — self-addressed, stamped envelope

SAE — self-addressed envelope

FAX — a communications system used to transmit documents over telephone lines.

ILAA — Independent Literary Agents Association

SAR — Society of Authors Representatives

SPAR — Society of Photographers and Artists Representatives

WGA (East or West) — Writers Guild of America (East or West divisions)

See the Glossary for definitions of words and expressions used through out the book.

Literary Agents: Nonfee-charging

In this section you will find literary agents who do not charge reading fees or other fees for services such as critiquing, editing or marketing. These agents derive from 98 to 100 percent of their business from commissions made on the sale of their clients' work.

One advantage to working with this type of literary agent is, of course, you do not have to pay a fee before you sell your work. Another important advantage is the agent has a built-in incentive to selling your work—if these agents do not sell, they do not make money. They are not involved in making money in other ways such as editing manuscripts or promoting published books. They devote all their time to selling. Their job is to know the market and establish valuable contacts in the field.

A disadvantage may be that these agents are very selective. Many prefer to work with established authors, celebrities or those who have professional expertise in a particular field. Almost all will look at queries from new writers, but they are looking for outstanding talent and the competition is keen.

To save time and money, check the listing or query first to find out if the agent you are interested in is open to new clients. A few ask to see outlines or sample chapters with queries, but send them only if they are requested within the listing. Always include a self-addressed, stamped envelope or postcard for reply. Agents tend to take a long time looking at queries, so you may want to send queries to more than one agent. When sending a requested manuscript, however, it is best to let one agent at a time consider the piece.

Commissions range from 10 to 20 percent for domestic sales and usually slightly higher for foreign or dramatic sales. The additional commission is used to pay a foreign agent or a subagent.

Many of the agents in this section charge for expenses in addition to taking a commission. Expenses can include foreign postage, fax charges, long-distance phone calls, messenger services, express mail and photocopying. Most of the agents listed only charge for what they consider extraordinary expenses. Make sure you have a clear understanding of what these "extraordinary" expenses might be before signing an agency agreement. Most agents will agree to discuss these expenses as they come up and negotiate with their clients on payment.

While most agents take expenses from the money made on sales, a few agents included in this section charge a low (no more than $40) one-time-only expense fee. Sometimes these are called "marketing" fees. These are fees charged every client to cover general expenses. Agents charging more than $40 were included in the Literary Agents: Fee-charging section.

To help you with your search for an agent, we've included a number of special indexes in the back of this book. The Subject Index is divided into sections for nonfee-charging and fee-charging literary agents and script agents. Each of these sections in the index is then divided by nonfiction and fiction subject categories. If you have written a romance novel and you are interested in nonfee-charging agents, turn to the fiction subjects listed in that section of the Subject Index. You will find a subject heading for romance and then the names of agencies interested in this type of work. Some agencies did not want to restrict themselves to specific subjects. We've grouped them in the subject heading "open" in both nonfiction and fiction.

We've included the Agents and Reps Index as well. Often you will read about an agent, but since that agent is an employee of a large agency, you may not be able to find that person's business phone or address. We've asked agencies to give us the names of agents on their staffs. Then we've listed the names in alphabetical order along with the name of their agency. Find the name of the person you would like to contact and then check the agency listing. You will find the page number for the agency's listing in the Listings Index.

Some art representatives, especially those interested in humor (cartoons and comics) and children's books, are also looking for writers. If the agency is primarily an art representative, but is also interested in writers, we've included them in a list (Additional Nonfee-charging Agents) in this section. For example, if ABC Art Reps, Inc. primarily handles the work of artists, but is also interested in writers who can draw, it is in the Additional Nonfee-charging Agents list. The company's complete listing, however, appears in the Commercial Art/Photo Reps section.

Many of the literary agents in this section are also interested in scripts and vice versa. If the agency's primary function is selling scripts, but it is interested in seeing some book manuscripts, we've also included them in Additional Nonfee-charging Agents. Their complete listings, however, appear in the Script Agent section.

For more information on approaching agents and the specifics of our listings, please see Finding and Working with Literary Agents and the following sample agent listing for this section. See also the various articles at the beginning of this book for the answers to a wide variety of questions concerning the author/agent relationship.

We've ranked the agencies listed in this section according to their openness to submissions. Below is our ranking system:

I   New agency (less than one year in business) actively seeking clients.

II Agency seeking both new and established writers.

III Agency prefers to work with established writers, mostly obtains new clients through referrals.

IV Agency handling only certain types of work or work by writers under certain circumstances.

V   Agency not currently seeking new clients. (If an agency chose this designation, only the address is given). We have included mention of agencies rated V only to let you know they are not open to new clients at this time. In addition to those ranked V, we have included a few well-known agencies' names who have declined listings. *Unless you have a strong recommendation from someone respected in the field, our advice is to approach only those agents ranked I-IV.*

Sample listing

The following is a sample listing for nonfee-charging literary agents. Each element of the listing is numbered and numbers correspond to explanations following the listing. For more information on specific terms see the glossary and introductions to the listings.

(1) RAY E. NUGENT LITERARY AGENCY (II), 170 10th St. N., Naples FL 33940. (813)262-3683. FAX: (813)262-3683. **(2)** Contact: Ray E. Nugent. **(3)** Estab. 1976. **(4)(5)** Represents 17 clients. **(6)** 50% of clients are new/previously unpublished authors. **(7)** Specializes in nonfiction: true crime, celebrity biographies, true war, fiction (limited). **(8)** Currently handles: 100% nonfiction books. **(9)**
(10) Will Handle: Nonfiction books, novels. **(11)** Will consider these nonfiction areas: biography/autobiography (celebrity); military/war; music/dance/theater/film; photography; true crime/investigative. **(12)** Will consider these fiction areas: detective/police/crime; erotica; mystery/suspense. **(13)** Query with outline plus 3 sample chapters. **(14)** Will report in 1 month on queries; 2 months on mss.
(15) Recent Sales: *A POW's Story*, by L. Guarino (Ballantine); *The Day I Died*, by J. Barbree (New Horizon); *How to Retire on the House*, by A. McLean (Contemporary Books); *50 Plus*

Wellness, by D. Bruce et al (John Wiley & Sons).
(16) Terms: Agent receives 15% commission on domestic sales; 20% on foreign sales. **(17)** Offers written contract, binding for 1 year. **(18)** Charges for photocopying, fax, telephone calls, postage.
(19) Writers' Conferences: Attends South Florida Romance Writers and South Florida Mystery Writers conferences.
(20) Tips: Obtains new clients from recommendations from others, solicitation, at conferences, etc. "Carefully prepare submissions; adhere to the agent's policy on submission format; enclose SASE."

(1) Names, addresses, phone number, ranking. Take special note of the ranking codes **(I-V)** which appear after the name of the agency. Those ranked **I** or **II** and some ranked **IV** are most open to new writers. Agencies ranked **III** prefer established writers or those with strong referrals. Those with rankings of **V** are not looking for new clients and are included only to inform our readers. A few well-known agencies which prefer not to be listed are also included (name and address only). For the most part these agencies do not wish to list because they are not looking for new clients and will only accept queries from writers with very strong references. For a complete explanation of the different rankings, please see the section introduction.
(2) Contact name/s. Send your query or manuscript to the name or one of the names listed. If you are not sure of the gender, it is best to use the full name, such as "Dear Robin Jones." Occasionally no contact name is given. In such a case, "Dear Agency Director" usually is acceptable. If the agency has listed other member agents (see #9) and has indicated a specialty with the name, address your query to the agent who handles the work you do.
(3) Establishment date. While an agency that has been in business a number of years is a good sign the agent is stable and has built up a network of helpful contacts in the industry, new agencies are often most open to new clients and eager to work with new or previously unpublished writers.
(4) Memberships. While no memberships appear in this sample listing, many agents in this section are members of agent organizations. We use the blanket term "member of" in the listings, but agents listed as members of writers' organizations are actually signatories or associate members. This is especially true of the Writers Guild of America. While there are respectable agencies who are not members of any group, membership in a recognized agent or writer organization suggests the agency has met certain requirements and has agreed to adhere to a code of ethics. For more information on some of the groups listed see Finding and Working with Literary Agents. For addresses for these groups see Resources following the Glossary.
(5) Number of clients. The number of clients will give you an indication of the size of the agency. This must be weighed by the number of agents working in the agency. To determine the client to agent ratio, see the agents listed in #2 (contact names) and #9 (member agents) or ask the agent how many agents they have.
(6) Percentage of new/previously unpublished writers. If you are a new writer, an agency with a high percentage of new writers may be a good bet for you.
(7) Specialties. If an agency specializes in any type of book or script, it is mentioned here.
(8) Currently handles. This gives you a rough breakdown of the types of material the agency is currently handling. Usually this is an indication of what the agency will consider representing, but sometimes the agency may be looking for something different or may feel they already have too many of one thing and not enough of another.
(9) Member agents. Many smaller agencies are one- or two-person operations. In other cases, however, there may be several agents on staff. We've asked agents to list staff members and, if given, would appear in this spot in the listing. This information is also included in the Agents and Reps Index. You may read about a particular agent, but not know where the agent works. You can find out where an agent works by locating their name in the Agents and Reps Index. We've also asked the agencies to list specialties, if any, next to the member agents listed. This will help you determine which agent on staff will be most interested in your work.
(10) Will handle. This is the type of material the agent is interested in handling. If the agency handles some scripts in addition to books, this will be indicated here. The names of other agents who primarily handle scripts, but who also handle books appear in Additional Nonfee-charging Agents (full listings in Script Agents section).
(11) Nonfiction areas. If the agent has indicated specific nonfiction subject areas, they are listed here. Check the Nonfiction Subject Index to find agencies listed by subject matter.
(12) Fiction areas. If an agent has indicated specific fiction subject areas, they are listed here. Check the Fiction Subject Index to find agencies listed by subject matter.
(13) How to contact. Most agencies request either a query or a query with an outline or sample chapters first. Follow the contact directions carefully. Whether or not the agency specifically requests a SASE (self-addressed, stamped envelope), *always* include one with any of your agent correspondence.
(14) Reporting time. Wait at least 3 weeks beyond the time the agent has indicated before writing

to check on the status of your query or submission.

(15) Recent sales. Check this section to see what type of work the agent has sold and some examples of the writers and publishers with whom the agent works. Some agencies did not give this information as a matter of privacy, but when making your decision whether to become a client of any agency, you should be able to obtain from the agency the names of its industry references.

(16) Commission terms. Agents make money by taking a percentage (usually 10-15%) commission from sales of a manuscript. This includes commission on advance and royalties. While some agencies also earn income from a variety of services and fees, agents listed in this section earn 98-100% of their income from sales only. Commissions on foreign and some dramatic sales may be slightly higher because the agent will pay a foreign agent or subagent a percentage from their own income on the sale.

(17) Other terms. Additional information on terms will appear here. In the past agencies usually worked on verbal agreements, but today many offer a written contract. Before making any decisions, ask to see this contract and find out how long it is binding and how it may be terminated. The distribution of commission from sales made after termination is an important clause in most contracts. Often the agent will be entitled to money from any sales made up to six months after termination or from additional sales made on work they handled under contract.

(18) Expenses. Although agents who charge reading, evaluation or other fees are listed in the Fee-charging Agents section, almost all agents ask clients to cover unusual expenses. These expenses may include postage, faxes, long-distance calls, photocopying, messenger, express mail charges. Ask your agent about expense fees. Will you receive an accounting of these fees? Will you be required to pay a lump sum for expenses upfront, or will you be billed as the expenses occur? Some agencies take expenses off the top of your sales. Many agencies will agree to discuss major expenses with you before they are incurred.

(19) Writers' conferences. Although we have used the word "attends" in this section, the agents who list conferences may not attend each one every year. It is best to check with the agents to find out their upcoming conference schedule or check with the conference directors. You can find names and addresses for most conferences in *The Guide to Writers Conferences*, by Shaw Associates, Suite 1406, 625 Biltmore Way, Coral Gables FL 33134. For fiction writers, *Novel & Short Story Writer's Market* will have a conference section in its 1992 edition. Also check writers' magazines for information on upcoming conferences. Each year the May issue of *Writer's Digest* includes an extensive list of writers' conferences and information on attending.

(20) Tips. Listed here is information on how agents usually obtain new clients. Any other helpful advice from the agent is included here.

DOMINICK ABEL LITERARY AGENCY, INC. (II), Suite 1B, 146 W. 82nd St., New York NY 10024. (212)877-0710. President: Dominick Abel. Estab. 1975. Member of ILAA.
Will Handle: Nonfiction, novels. Query with outline. Reports in 2 weeks on queries. "Enclose SASE."
Recent Sales: *The Last Camel Died at Noon*, by Elizabeth Peters (Warner); *Second Chance*, by Jonathan Valin (Delacorte); *The Daisy Chain*, by James O'Shea (Pocket Books).
Terms: Agent receives 10% commission on domestic sales; 15% on dramatic sales; 20% on foreign sales. Charges for overseas postage, phone and cable expenses.

ACTON AND DYSTEL, INC. (II), 928 Broadway, New York NY 10128. (212)473-1700. FAX: (212)475-0890. Contact: Jay Acton or Jane Dystel. Estab. 1976. Member of ILAA. Represents 100 clients. 50% of clients are new/previously unpublished writers. Specializes in commercial nonfiction and fiction; some category fiction; some literary fiction. Currently handles: 90% nonfiction books; 10% novels.
Will Handle: Nonfiction books, novels. Will consider these nonfiction areas: animals; biography/autobiography; business; child guidance/parenting; cooking/food/nutrition; current affairs; ethnic/cultural interests; gay/lesbian issues; government/politics/law; health/medicine; history; military/war; money/finance/economics; music/dance/theater/film; nature/environment; psychology; true crime/investigative; science/technology; self-help/personal improvement; sports; women's issues/women's studies. Will consider these fiction areas: action/adventure; contemporary issues; detective/police/crime; ethnic; family saga; glitz; historical; literary; mainstream; mystery/suspense; romance; sports; thriller/espionage. Query. Will report in 1 week on queries; 1 month on fiction mss and 3 weeks on nonfiction mss.
Terms: Agent receives 15% on domestic sales; 19% on foreign sales. Offers a written contract. Charges for photocopying and Federal Express.
Tips: Obtains new clients through recommendations from others.

AGENCY CHICAGO (I), P.O. Box 11200, Chicago IL 60611. Contact: Ernest Santucci. Estab. 1990. Represents 4 clients. 50% of clients are new/previously unpublished writers. Specializes in ghost writing. Currently handles: 40% nonfiction books; 20% scholarly books; 10% novels; 10% movie scripts; 20% TV scripts.
Will Handle: Nonfiction books, movie and TV scripts, sports books. Will consider these nonfiction areas: animals; art/architecture/design; ethnic/cultural interests; music/dance/theater/film; sports. Will consider these fiction areas: detective/police/crime; erotica; experimental; humor/satire; regional. Send outline/proposal and SASE. Will report in 1 month on queries and mss.
Terms: Agent receives 10% commission on domestic sales; 15% on foreign sales. Offers a written contract, binding for 1 year.
Writers' Conferences: Attends Midwest Writers Conference; International Writers and Translators Conference.
Tips: Obtains new clients through recommendations. "Do not send dot matrix printed manuscripts. Manuscripts should have a clean professional look, with correct grammar and punctuation."

AGENTS INC. FOR MEDICAL AND MENTAL HEALTH PROFESSIONALS (II), P.O. Box 4956, Fresno CA 93744-4956. (209)226-0761. FAX: (209)226-0761 (press asterisk). Director: Sydney H. Harriet, Ph.D. Estab. 1987. Member of APA. Represents 20 clients. 45% of clients are new/previously unpublished writers. Specializes in "writers who have education and experience in the medical and mental health professions. It is helpful if the writer is licensed, but not necessary. Prior book publication not necessary." Currently handles: 85% nonfiction books; 5% scholarly books; 5% textbooks; 3% novels; 2% syndicated material.
Will Handle: Nonfiction books, textbooks, scholarly books, novels, syndicated material. Will consider these nonfiction areas: child guidance/parenting; nutrition; health/medicine; psychology; science/technology; self-help/personal improvement; sociology; sports; sports medicine/psychology; mind-body healing; how-to; reference. Will consider these fiction areas: contemporary issues; literary; "fiction focused toward health professions." Query with vita. Will report in 2 weeks on queries; 1 month on mss.
Recent Sales: *Not Getting Any Better*, by Joseph Wolpe, M.D. and Tom Giles, Psy.D. (Avery).
Terms: Agent receives 15% commission on domestic sales; 20% on foreign sales. Offers a written contract, binding for 3-9 months. "After contract with a publisher is signed, office expenses are negotiated."
Writers' Conferences: Attends writers' conferences in California. "Plans are being made to present marketing workshops at nationwide medical and mental health conferences."
Tips: "45% of our clients are referred. The rest are obtained from writers using this guide. Our specialty has been to help writers with their manuscripts. If the idea is unique, but the writing needs work, that's where we have done our best work. We rarely receive a manuscript that's immediately contracted by a publisher. Unfortunately, we cannot respond to queries or proposals without receiving a return envelope and sufficient postage."

THE JOSEPH S. AJLOUNY AGENCY (II), 8400 Kenwood Ave., Oak Park MI 48237. (313)546-9123. FAX: (313)546-3010. Contact: Joe Ajlouny. Estab. 1987. Member of WGA. "Represents humor and comedy writers, humorous illustrators, cartoonists." Member agents: Joe Ajlouny (original humor, how-to); Renee Cooper (music, popular culture); Lisa McDonald (general nonfiction).
Will Handle: "In addition to humor and titles concerning American popular culture, we will consider general nonfiction in the areas of 'how-to' books, history, health, cookbooks, self-help, social commentary, criticism, biography and memoirs." Query first with SASE. Reports in 2-4 weeks.
Recent Sales: *Soviet Humor: The Best of Krokodil* (anthology) (Andrews & McMeel); *DeficitBusters*, by Joe West (Price, Stern, Sloan); *Russian Cuisine*, by Vladimir Mogilev (Progress Publishers); *Guessing Games*, by Tamara Weston (Doubleday).
Terms: Agent receives 15% commission on domestic sales. Charges for postage, photocopying, office expenses only if specifically negotiated.
Tips: Obtains new clients "typically from referrals and by some advertising and public relations projects. We also frequently speak at seminars for writers on the process of being published. Just make sure your project is marketable and professionally prepared. We see too much material that is limited in scope and appeal. It helps immeasurably to have credentials in the field or topic being written about."

LEE ALLAN AGENCY (II), P.O. Box 18617, Milwaukee WI 53218. (414)357-7708. Contact: Lee Matthias. Estab. 1983. Member of WGA. Represents 15 clients. 50% of clients are new/previously unpublished writers. Specializes in suspense fiction. Currently handles: 3% nonfiction books; 75% novels; 20% movie scripts; 2% TV scripts. Member agents: Lee A. Matthias (all types of genre fiction and screenplays, nonfiction); Andrea Knickerbocker (fantasy and science fiction, juvenile fiction, nonfiction).

Will Handle: Nonfiction books, juvenile books, novels, movie scripts. Will consider these nonfiction areas: biography/autobiography; business; child guidance/parenting; computers/electronics; cooking/food/nutrition; current affairs; government/politics/law; health/medicine; history; juvenile nonfiction; military/war; money/finance/economics; music/dance/theater/film; nature/environment; psychology; true crime/investigative; science/technology; self-help/personal improvement; sports. Will consider these fiction areas: action/adventure; detective/police/crime; fantasy; historical; humor/satire; juvenile; literary; mainstream; mystery/suspense; psychic/supernatural; romance (contemporary, historical); science fiction; thriller/espionage; westerns/frontier; young adult. Query. Will report in 2-3 weeks on queries; 6 weeks-3 months on mss.
Recent Sales: *Valley of the Shadow*, by Franklin Allen Leib (NAL); "Hollow Pursuits/Star Trek: The Next Generation," by Sally Caves (Paramount TV); *Under the Thousand Stars*, by John Deakins (ROC Fantasy).
Terms: Agent receives 10% commission on domestic sales; 20% on foreign sales. Offers a written contract. Charges for "occasional shipping/mailing costs; photocopying; international telephone calls and/or excessive long-distance telephone calls."
Writers' Conferences: Attends World Fantasy Conference.
Tips: Obtains new clients through "recommendations and solicitations, mainly." If interested in agency representation, "read agency listings carefully and query the most compatible. Always query by letter with SASE or IRC with envelope. A very brief, straightforward letter (1-2 pages, maximum) introducing yourself, describing or summarizing your material will suffice. Avoid patronizing or "cute" approaches. We *do not reply* to queries *without* SASE. Do not expect an agent to sell a manuscript which you know is not a likely sale if nonagented. Agents are not magicians; they serve best to find better and more of the likeliest publishers or producers. And they really do their work after an offer by way of negotiating contracts, selling subsidiary rights, administrating the account(s), advising the writer with objectivity, and acting as the buffer between writer and editor."

JAMES ALLEN, LITERARY AGENCY (III), P.O. Box 278, Milford PA 18337. Estab. 1974. Member of WGA. Represents 40 clients. 10% of clients are new/previously unpublished writers. "I handle all kinds of genre fiction (except westerns) and specialize in science fiction and fantasy." Currently handles: 2% nonfiction books; 6% juvenile books; 90% novels; 1% novellas; 1% short story collections.
Will Handle: Novels. Will consider these fiction areas: detective/police/crime; fantasy; historical; mainstream; mystery/suspense; romance (historical, regency); science fiction. Query. Will respond in 1 week on queries; 2 months on mss. "I prefer first contact to be a query letter with 2-3 page plot synopsis and SASE with a response time of 1 week. If my interest is piqued, I then ask for the first 4 chapters, response time again 1 week. If I'm impressed by the writing, I then ask for the balance of the ms, response time about 2 months."
Recent Sales: *The Circle*, by David C. Poyer (St. Martin's Press); fantasy trilogy, by James Pierce (Berkley); *The Veiled Vixen*, by Virginia Bown (Walker).
Terms: Agent receives 10% on domestic print sales; 20% on film sales; 20% on foreign sales. Offers a written contract, binding for 3 years "automatically renewed. I reserve the right to charge for extraordinary expenses: international airmail (to get copies of books to foreign publishers), really long phone calls to the author, photocopying of novel-length manuscripts. I do not bill the author, but deduct the charges from incoming earnings."
Tips: *First time at book length need not apply—only works with established writers.* "A cogent, to-the-point query letter is necessary, laying out the author's track record (if any) and giving a brief blurb for the book. The response to a mere 'I have written a novel, will you look at it?' is universally 'NO!' "

LINDA ALLEN LITERARY AGENCY (II), Suite 5, 1949 Green St., San Francisco CA 94123. (415)921-6437. Contact: Linda Allen. Estab. 1982. Represents 35-40 clients. Specializes in "good books and nice people. We don't rep picture books."
Will Handle: Nonfiction, novels (adult and juvenile). Will consider all nonfiction and fiction areas. Query. Will report in 2-3 weeks on queries.
Terms: No information provided. Charges for photocopying.
Tips: Obtains new clients "by referral mostly."

MARCIA AMSTERDAM AGENCY (II), 41 W. 82 St., New York NY 10024. (212)873-4945. FAX: (212)873-4945. Contact: Marcia Amsterdam. Estab. 1969. Member of WGA.
Will Handle: Novels, movie and TV scripts. Will consider these fiction areas: action/adventure; glitz; historical; humor; mainstream; mystery/suspense; romance (contemporary, historical); science fiction; thriller/espionage; westerns/frontier; young adult; horror. Send outline plus first 3 sample chapters and SASE. Will report in 1 month on queries.

Recent Sales: *SeaGhost*, by William Lovejoy (Avon); *Killing Suki Flood*, by Robert Leininger (St. Martin's); *Piano Man*, by Joyce Sweeney (Delacorte).
Terms: Agent receives 15% commission on domestic sales; 20% on foreign sales. Offers a written contract, binding for 1 year, "renewable." Charges for "cable, legal fees (chargeable only when agreed to), foreign postage."
Tips: "We are always looking for interesting literary voices."

BART ANDREWS & ASSOCIATES INC. (III), 1321 N. Stanley Ave., Los Angeles CA 90046. (213)851-8158. FAX: (213)851-9738. Contact: Bart Andrews. Estab. 1982. Member of ILAA. Represents 25 clients. 25% of clients are new/previously unpublished authors. Specializes in nonfiction only, and in the general category of entertainment (movies, TV, biographies, autobiographies). Currently handles: 100% nonfiction books.
Will Handle: Nonfiction books. Will consider these nonfiction areas: biography/autobiography; music/dance/theater/film; TV. Query. Will report in 1 week on queries; 1 month on mss.
Recent Sales: *Film Flubs*, by Bill Givens (Citadel Press); *Michael Jackson: Magic & Madness*, by J. Randy Taraborrelli (Birch Lane Press).
Terms: Agent receives 15% on domestic sales; 15% on foreign sales (after sub-agent takes his 10%). Offers a written contract, "binding on a project-by-project basis." Author/client is charged for all photocopying, mailing, phone calls, postage, etc.
Writers' Conferences: Frequently lectures at UCLA in Los Angeles.
Tips: "Recommendations from existing clients or professionals are best, although I find a lot of new clients by seeking them out myself. I rarely find a new client through the mails. Spend time writing a query letter. Sell yourself like a product. The bottom line is writing ability, and then the idea itself. It takes a lot to convince me. I've seen it all! I hear from too many first-time authors who don't do their homework. They're trying to get a book published and they haven't the faintest idea what is required of them. There are plenty of good books on the subject and, in my opinion, it's their responsibility — not mine — to educate themselves before they try to find an agent to represent their work. When I ask an author to see a manuscript or even a partial manuscript, I really must be convinced I want to read it — based on a strong query letter — because I have no intention of wasting my time reading just for the fun of it."

APPLESEEDS MANAGEMENT (II), Suite #302, 300 E. 30th St., San Bernardino CA 92404; for screenplays and teleplays only, send to Suite #560, 1870 N. Vermont, Hollywood CA 90027. (714)882-1667. Executive Manager: S. James Foiles. Estab. 1988. Member of WGA, licensed by state of California. Represents 25 clients. 40% of clients are new/previously unpublished writers. Specializes in action/adventure, fantasy, horror/occult, mystery and science fiction novels; also in nonfiction, true crime, biography, health/medicine and self-help; also in materials that could be adapted from book to screen; and in screenplays and teleplays. "We're not accepting unsolicited screenplays and teleplays at this time." Currently handles: 25% nonfiction books; 40% novels; 20% movie scripts; 15% teleplays (movie of the week).
Will Handle: Nonfiction books, novels, movie and TV scripts (no episodic), teleplays (MOW). Will consider these nonfiction areas: biography/autobiography; business; health/medicine; money/finance/economics; music/dance/theater/film; psychology; true crime/investigative; self-help/personal improvement; general nonfiction. Will consider these fiction areas: action/adventure; detective/police/crime; fantasy; historical; humor/satire; mainstream; mystery/suspense; psychic/supernatural; science fiction; thriller/espionage; occult, horror novels. Query. Will report in 2 weeks on queries; 2 months on mss.
Terms: Agent receives 10-15% commission on domestic sales; 20% on foreign sales. Offers a written contract, binding for 1-7 years.
Tips: "In your query, please describe your intended target audience and distinguish your book/script from similar works."

AUTHORS AND ARTISTS GROUP, INC. (III), Suite 703, 14 E. 60th St., New York NY 10022. (212)754-9393. FAX: (212)755-8237. Estab. 1983. Represents 70 clients. 10% of clients are new/previously unpublished writers. Specializes in adult fiction and nonfiction. Currently handles: 60% nonfiction books; 40% novels, "a smattering of the rest." Member agents: Alfred P. Lowman; B.G. Dilworth.
Will Handle: Nonfiction books, novels, short story collections. Will consider these nonfiction areas: biography/autobiography; business; child guidance/parenting; cooking/food/nutrition; history; language/literature/criticism; new age/metaphysics; psychology; self-help/personal improvement; sociology; women's issues/women's studies. Will consider these fiction areas: erotica; family saga; glitz; historical; literary; mainstream; thriller/espionage. Send an outline plus 2 sample chapters, plus a "short bio/publishing history of author." Will report in 2 months on queries; 1 month on mss.

Recent Sales: *Parent and Child* (4 book series), by Lawrence Kutner, Ph.D. (William Morrow); *Family Matters*, by Lee Salk (Simon & Schuster); *Shakkai*, by Lynn Andrews (HarperCollins).
Terms: Agent receives 15 % commission on domestic sales; 25% on foreign sales. Offers a written contract, "cancelable with 60 days' notice." Charges for messenger service, express/overnight mail, photocopying.
Writers' Conferences: Attends Breadloaf Conference and Rope Walk Conference.
Tips: Obtains new clients through referrals; "active pursuit of high-profile magazine writers." If interested in agency representation, "don't hype without product. Pitch your book clearly in 60 seconds or less."

THE AXELROD AGENCY (III), Rm. 5805, Empire State Bldg., New York NY 10118. (212)629-5620. FAX: (212)629-5624. Estab. 1983. Member of ILAA. Represents 30 clients. Specializes in commercial fiction and nonfiction. Currently handles: 50% nonfiction books; 50% fiction.
Will Handle: Will consider these nonfiction areas: art; business; computers; government/politics/law; health/medicine; history; money/finance/economics; music/dance/theater/film; nature/environment; science/technology. Will consider these fiction areas: cartoon/comic; detective/police/crime; family saga; historical; literary; mainstream; mystery/suspense; picture book; romance; thriller/espionage. Query. Will report in 10 days on queries; 2-3 weeks on mss.
Terms: Agent receives 10% commission on domestic sales; 20% on foreign sales. Charges for photocopying.
Writers' Conferences: Attends Romance Writers of America conferences.
Tips: Obtains new clients through referrals.

JULIAN BACH LITERARY AGENCY (II), 747 3rd Ave., New York NY 10017. (212)753-2605. FAX: (212)688-8297. Contact: Julian Bach or Emma Sweeney. Estab. 1956. Member of SAR. Represents 300 clients. 65% of clients are new/previously unpublished writers. Currently handles: 50% nonfiction books, 50% novels. Member agents: Julian Bach; Emma Sweeney; Susan Merritt; Ann Rittenberg (Chicago).
Will Handle: Nonfiction books, novels. Will consider these nonfiction areas: anthropology/archaeology; biography/autobiography; business; cooking/food/nutrition; current affairs; government/politics/law; history; language/literature/criticism; military/war; music/dance/theater/film; nature/environment; new age/metaphysics; photography; psychology; religious/inspirational; true crime/investigative; self-help/personal improvement; sports; women's issues/women's studies. Will consider these fiction areas: detective/police/crime; feminist; gay; humor/satire; literary; mainstream; picture book; psychic/supernatural; religious/inspirational. Query.
Terms: No information provided. Offers a written contract.

MALAGA BALDI LITERARY AGENCY (II), P.O. Box 591, Radio City Station, New York NY 10101. (212)222-1221. Contact: Malaga Baldi. Estab. 1985. Represents 40-50 clients. 80% of clients are new/previously unpublished writers. Specializes in quality fiction and nonfiction. Currently handles: 60% nonfiction books; 30% novels; 5% novellas; 5% short story collections.
Will Handle: Nonfiction books, novels, novellas, short story collections. Will consider any well-written nonfiction, but do *not* send child guidance, crafts, juvenile nonfiction, new age/metaphysics, religious/inspirational or sports material. Will consider any well-written fiction, but do *not* send confessional, family saga, fantasy, glitz, juvenile, picture book, psychic/supernatural, religious/inspirational, romance, science fiction, western or young adult. Query, but "prefers entire manuscript for fiction." Will report within 10 weeks. "Please enclose self-addressed jiffy bag with submission and self-addressed postcard for acknowledgement of receipt of manuscript."
Recent Sales: *Small Beer: A Handbook to the 19th Century English Novel*, by Daniel Pool (Prentice Hall Press); *Take These Chains From My Heart*, by Steven Nielsen and Eugenia Debranskaya (Aaron Asher Books/HarperCollins); *Henfield Prize Stories*, by the Henfield Foundation (Warner Books).
Terms: Agent receives 15% commission on domestic sales; 20% on foreign sales. Offers a written contract. Charges "initial $50 fee to cover photocopying expenses. If the manuscript is lengthy, I prefer the author to cover expense of photocopying."
Tips: "From the day I agree to represent the author, my role is to serve as his or her advocate in contract negotiations and publicity efforts. Along the way, I wear many different hats. To one author I may serve as a nudge, to another a confidante, and to many simply as a supportive friend. I am also a critic, researcher, legal expert, messenger, diplomat, listener, counselor and source of publishing information and gossip. I work with writers on developing a presentable submission and make myself available during all aspects of a book's publication."

BALKIN AGENCY, INC. (III), 317 S. Pleasant St., Amherst MA 01002. (212)781-4198 (call to get updated number). President: R. Balkin. Estab. 1972. Member of ILAA, Author's Guild. Represents 48 clients. 10% of clients are new/previously unpublished writers. Specializes in adult nonfiction.

Currently handles: 85% nonfiction books; 5% scholarly books; 10% textbooks. **Will Handle:** Nonfiction books, textbooks, scholarly books. Will consider these nonfiction areas: animals; anthropology/archaeology; biography; child guidance/parenting; current affairs; health/medicine; history; language/literature/criticism; music/dance/theater/film; nature/environment; true crime/investigative; science/technology; sociology; translations, travel. Query with outline/proposal. Will report in 2 weeks on queries; 3 weeks on mss.
Recent Sales: *There Was No Big Bang,* by Lerner (Random House); *George Sanders: An Exhausted Life* (Madison Books); *A Natural History of the Grand Canyon* (Houghton Mifflin).
Terms: Agent receives 15% on domestic sales; 20% on foreign sales. Offers a written contract, binding for 1 year. Charges for photocopying, trans-Atlantic long-distance calls or faxes, and express mail.
Tips: Obtains new clients through referrals. "I do not take on books described as bestsellers or potential bestsellers."

VIRGINIA BARBER LITERARY AGENCY, INC., 353 W. 21st St., New York NY 10011. Prefers not to be listed.

LORETTA BARRETT BOOKS INC. (II), Suite 601, 121 W. 27th St., New York NY 10001. (212)242-3420. FAX: (212)727-0280. President: Loretta A. Barrett. Associate: Morgan Barnes. Estab. 1990. Represents 40 clients. Specializes in general interest books. Currently handles: 40% fiction; 60% nonfiction.
Will Handle: Will consider all areas of nonfiction and fiction. Query first, then send partial ms and a synopsis. Will report in 4-6 weeks on queries and mss.
Terms: Agent receives 15% commission on domestic sales; 20% on foreign sales. Offers a written contract. Charges for "all professional expenses."

HELEN BARRETT LITERARY AGENCY (II), 175 W. 13th St., New York NY 10011. (212)645-7430. Contact: Helen Barrett. Estab. 1988. ("After 14 years as a literary agent at William Morris, where I handled many bestsellers, I went on my own.") Currently handles: 30% nonfiction books; 70% novels.
Will Handle: Nonfiction books, novels. Will consider these nonfiction areas: anthropology/archaeology; biography/autobiography; current affairs; government/politics/law; history; interior design/decorating; true crime/investigative; self-help/personal improvement; women's issues/women's studies. Will consider these fiction areas: action/adventure; confessional; contemporary issues; detective/police/crime; family saga; historical; mainstream; mystery/suspense; romance; thriller/espionage. Query first with SASE. Will report in 2 weeks on queries; 3-4 weeks on mss.
Terms: Agent receives 15% commission on domestic sales; 20% on foreign sales.
Tips: Obtains new clients through recommendations from others, "mainly, or they seek me out. Be straightforward. Do not hype. If you have never been published, tell enough in a bio to give a good picture of your background that would relate to material to be submitted and education, etc."

DAVID BLACK LITERARY AGENCY, INC. (II), 220 5th Ave., New York NY 10001. (212)689-5154. FAX: (212)684-2606. Associate: Janice Gordon. Estab. 1990. Member of ILAA. Represents 150 clients. Specializes in sports, politics, novels. Currently handles: 80% nonfiction; 20% novels.
Will Handle: Nonfiction books, novels. Will consider these nonfiction areas: politics, sports. Query with outline. Reports in 1 month on queries.
Recent Sales: *Bo,* by Glenn "Bo" Schembechler and Mitch Albom (Warner); *If I Had a Hammer,* by Henry Aaron and Lonnie Wheeler (HarperCollins); *Birdsong Ascending,* by Sam Harrison (HBJ); *There Are No Children Here,* by Alex Kotlowitz.
Terms: Agent receives 15% commission. Charges for photocopying manuscripts and for books purchased for sale of foreign rights.

BLASSINGAME, MCCAULEY & WOOD (II), Suite 1503, 111 8th Ave., New York NY 10011. (212)691-7556. Contact: Eleanor Wood. Represents 50 clients. Currently handles: 95% fiction, 5% nonfiction books.
Will Handle: Will consider these nonfiction areas: biography/autobiography; business; child guidance/parenting; health/medicine; history. Will consider these fiction areas: contemporary issues; historical; literary; mainstream; mystery/suspense; romance; science fiction. Query with SASE. Will report in 1 month on queries.
Terms: Agent receives 10% commission on domestic sales.
Tips: Obtains new clients through recommendations from authors and others.

HARRY BLOOM (II,III), 16272 Via Embeleso, San Diego CA 92128-3219. Estab. 1967. Member WGA. 5% of clients new/unpublished writers. Prefers to work with published/established authors; works with small number of new/unpublished authors. Specializes in mainstream fiction, love, mystery, action/adventure and nonfiction. "No science fiction."

Will Handle: Nonfiction books, novels, movie scripts, syndicated material. Will consider these fiction areas: action/adventure, romance, mainstream, mystery. Query with outline. Does not read unsolicited mss. Reports in 2 weeks on queries. "If our agency does not respond within 2 weeks to your request to become a client, you may submit requests elsewhere."
Terms: No information provided.

REID BOATES LITERARY AGENCY (II), P.O. Box 328, 274 Cooks Crossroad, Pittstown NJ 08867. (908)730-8523. FAX: (908)730-8931. Contact: Reid Boates. Estab. 1985. Represents 45 clients. 15% of clients are new/previously unpublished writers. Specializes in general fiction and nonfiction, investigative journalism/current affairs; bios and autobiographies; serious self-help; literary humor; issue-oriented business; popular science; "no category fiction." Currently handles: 85% nonfiction books; 15% novels; "very rarely accept short story collections."
Will Handle: Nonfiction books, novels. Will consider these nonfiction areas: animals; anthropology/archaeology; art/architecture/design; biography/autobiography; business; child guidance/parenting; current affairs; ethnic/cultural interests; government/politics/law; health/medicine; history; language/literature/criticism; nature/environment; psychology; true crime/investigative; science/technology; self-help/personal improvement; sports; women's issues/women's studies. Will consider these fiction areas: contemporary issues; crime; family saga; mainstream; mystery/suspense; thriller/espionage. Query. Will report in 2 weeks on queries; 6 weeks on mss.
Recent Sales: *Dave's Way: Autobiography*, by David Thomas (Putnam); *A Killing in the Family*, by Stephen Singular (Avon/Morrow); *Love, Honor and Obey*, by Larry Taylor (Morrow).
Terms: Agent receives 15% commission on domestic sales; 20% on foreign sales. Offers a written contract, binding "until terminated by either party." Charges for photocopying costs above $50.
Tips: Obtain new clients through recommendations from others.

ALISON M. BOND LTD., 171 W. 79th St., New York NY 10024. Prefers not to be listed.

GEORGE BORCHARDT INC. (III), 136 E. 57th St., New York NY 10022. (212)753-5785. FAX: (212)838-6518. Estab. 1967. Member of SAR. Represents 200+ clients. 10% of clients are new/previously unpublished writers. Specializes in literary fiction and outstanding nonfiction. Currently handles: 60% nonfiction books; 1% juvenile books; 37% novels; 1% novellas; 1% poetry books.
Will Handle: Nonfiction books, novels. Will consider these nonfiction areas: anthropology/archaeology; biography/autobiography; current affairs; history; women's issues/women's studies. Will consider these fiction areas: literary. "Must be recommended by someone we know." Will report in 1 week on queries; 3-4 weeks on mss.
Recent Sales: Has sold fiction book by Charles Johnson (Atheneum); nonfiction book by Tracy Kidder (Houghton Mifflin); and *Flow Chart* (poetry), by John Ashbery (Knopf).
Terms: Agent receives 10% on domestic sales; 15% British sales; 20% on foreign sales (translation). Offers a written contract. "We charge cost of (outside) photocopying and shipping mss or books overseas."
Tips: Obtains new clients through recommendations from others.

THE BARBARA BOVA LITERARY AGENCY (II), 207 Sedgwick Rd., West Hartford CT 06107. (203)521-5915. Estab. 1974. Represents 20 clients. Specializes in nonfiction science. Currently handles: 50% nonfiction books; 50% novels.
Will Handle: Will consider these nonfiction areas: science/technology; social sciences. Will consider these fiction areas: contemporary issues; mainstream; mystery/suspense. Query with SASE. Will report in 1 month on queries.
Terms: Agent receives 10% commission on domestic sales.
Tips: Obtains new clients through recommendations from others.

BRANDENBURGH & ASSOCIATES LITERARY AGENCY (III), 24555 Corte Jaramillo, Murrieta CA 92362. (714)698-5200. Owner: Don Brandenburgh. Estab. 1986. Represents 30 clients. "We prefer previously published authors, but will evaluate submissions on their own merits." Works with a small number of new/unpublished authors. Specializes in adult nonfiction for the religious bookstore market; limited fiction for religious market. Currently handles: 70% nonfiction books; 20% novels; 10% textbooks.
Will Handle: Nonfiction books, novels and textbooks. Query with outline or send entire ms. Reports in 2 weeks on queries; 3 months on mss.
Recent Sales: *Eve*, by Evelyn Minshull (HarperCollins); *Audeh Rantisi: A Christian Arab in the Occupied West Bank*, by Audeh Rantisi and Ralph Beebe (Zondervan); *The Throne of Tara*, by John Dejarlais (Crossway).
Terms: Agent receives 10% commission on domestic sales; 20% on dramatic sales; 20% on foreign sales. Charges a $35 mailing/materials fee with signed agency agreement.

THE JOAN BRANDT AGENCY (II), 697 West End Ave., New York NY 10025. (212)749-4771. FAX: (212)678-4588. Contact: Joan Brandt. Estab. 1990. Reprsents 100 clients. Also handles movie rights for other agents.
Will Handle: Novels, nonfiction books, scripts. Will consider these fiction areas: fiction: contemporary issues; detective/police/crime; literary; mainstream; mystery/suspense; thriller/espionage; "also will consider "popular, topical" nonfiction." Query with SAE, outline plus 100 pages. Will report in 2 weeks on queries.
Terms: Agent receives 15% commission on domestic sales, 20% on foreign sales (co-agents in all major marketplaces). Charges for photocopying and long-distance postage.
Tips: Obtains new clients through recommendations from others and over-the-transom submissions.

BRANDT & BRANDT LITERARY AGENTS INC. (III), 1501 Broadway, New York NY 10036. Contact: Carl Brandt, Gail Hochman, Charles Schlessiger. Estab. 1913. Member of SAR. Represents 200 clients.
Will Handle: Nonfiction books, scholarly books, juvenile books, novels, novellas, short story collections. Will consider these nonfiction areas: agriculture/horticulture; animals; anthropology/archaeology; art/architecture/design; biography/autobiography; business; child guidance/parenting; cooking/food/nutrition; crafts/hobbies; current affairs; ethnic/cultural interests; gay/lesbian issues; government/politics/law; health/medicine; history; interior design/decorating; juvenile nonfiction; language/literature/criticism; military/war; money/finance/economics; music/dance/theater/film; nature/environment; psychology; true crime/investigative; science/technology; self-help/personal improvement; sociology; sports; women's issues/women's studies. Will consider these fiction areas: action/adventure; contemporary issues; detective/police/crime; erotica; ethnic; experimental; family saga; feminist; gay; historical; humor/satire; lesbian; literary; mainstream; mystery/suspense; psychic/supernatural; regional; romance; science fiction; sports; thriller/espionage; westerns/frontier; young adult. Query. Will report in 2-4 weeks on queries.
Terms: Agent receives 10% commission on domestic sales; 20% on foreign sales. Charges for "manuscript duplication or other special expenses agreed to in advance."
Tips: Obtains new clients through recommendations from others or "upon occasion, a really good letter. Write a letter which will give the agent a sense of you as a professional writer, your long-term interests as well as a short description of the work at hand."

MARIE BROWN ASSOCIATES INC. (II,III), Rm. 902, 625 Broadway, New York NY 10012. (212)533-5534. FAX: (212)533-0849. Contact: Marie Brown. Estab. 1984. Represents 100 clients. Specializes in multicultural African-American writers. Currently handles: 50% nonfiction books; 25% juvenile books; 25% other.
Will Handle: Will consider these nonfiction areas: art; biography; business; child guidance/parenting; cooking/food/nutrition; ethnic/cultural interests; gay/lesbian issues; history; juvenile nonfiction; money/finance/economics; music/dance/theater/film; new age; photography; psychology; religious/inspirational; self-help/personal improvement; sociology; women's issues/women's studies. Will consider these fiction areas: contemporary issues; ethnic; family saga; feminist; gay; historical; humor/satire; juvenile; literary; mainstream; mystery/suspense; picture book; regional; science fiction. Query with SASE. Will report in 8-10 weeks on queries.
Terms: Agent receives 15% commission on domestic sales; 25% on foreign sales. Offers a written contract.
Tips: Obtains new clients through recommendations from others.

ANDREA BROWN LITERARY AGENCY, INC. (III,IV), Suite 71, 1081 Alameda, Belmont CA 94002. (415)508-8410. FAX: (415)592-8846. Contact: Andrea Brown. Estab. 1981. Member of ILAA, WNBA. 25% of clients are new/previously unpublished writers. Specializes in "all kinds of juveniles—illustrators and authors." Currently handles: 99% juvenile books, 1% novels.
Will Handle: Juvenile books. Will consider these nonfiction areas: animals; juvenile nonfiction; science/technology. Will consider these fiction areas: juvenile; picture book; young adult. Query. Will report in 2 weeks on queries; 2 months on mss.
Recent Sales: *7 Little Hippos*, by Mike Thaler and Jerry Smath (Simon & Schuster); *Ethics*, by Susan Terkel (Lodestar/Dutton); *Panda*, by Caroline Arnold (Morrow).
Terms: Agent receives 15% commission on domestic sales; 20% on foreign sales.
Writers' Conferences: Attends Jack London Writers Conference; UCLA Writer's Workshop Conference and various SCBW conferences.

CURTIS BROWN LTD. (II), 10 Astor Pl., New York NY 10003. (212)473-5400. Queries: Laura J. Blake. Chairman & CEO: Perry Knowlton. President: Peter L. Ginsberg. Member agents: Emilie Jacobson, Irene Skolnick, Henry Dunow, Clyde Taylor, Maureen Walters, Timothy Knowlton (film screenplays

and plays), Laura J. Blake, Virginia Knowlton, Marilyn Marlowe, Jess Taylor (audio rights), Jeanine Edmunds (film screenplays and plays), Jeff Melnick (television).
Will Handle: Nonfiction books, juvenile books, novels, novellas, short story collections, poetry books, movie and TV scripts, stage plays. All categories of nonfiction and fiction considered. Query. Will report in 2 weeks on queries; 3-4 weeks on mss "only if requested."
Terms: Agent receives 15% on domestic sales; 20% on foreign sales. Offers a written contract. Charges for photocopying, some postage, "but only with prior approval of author."
Tips: Obtains new clients through recommendations from others, solicitation, at conferences and query letters.

JANE BUCHANAN LITERARY AGENCY (II), P.O. Box 569, Radio City Station, New York NY 10101. (212)757-7493. President: Jane Buchanan. Estab. 1985. 40% of clients are new/previously unpublished writers. Currently handles: 35% nonfiction books; 65% novels.
Will Handle: Nonfiction books, novels. Will consider these nonfiction areas: anthropology/archaeology; biography/autobiography; business; child guidance/parenting; health/medicine; history; money/finance/economics; nature/environment; self-help/personal improvement; women's issues/women's studies. Will consider these fiction areas: family saga; historical; literary; mainstream. Query with outline/proposal, plus 3 sample chapters and SASE. "We do not read unsolicited manuscripts." Will report in 2 weeks on queries; 4-6 weeks on mss.
Terms: Agent receives 15% on domestic sales; 20% on foreign sales. Offers a written contract. Charges for photocopying mss, messenger services, special mailing and telephone expenses.
Tips: Obtains new clients through "recommendations from clients, colleagues, speaking at conferences and seminars. I am looking for strong mainstream literary fiction, historical tales and family sagas. I am particularly interested in novels with a wide sociological scope. I want to see serious but accessible and lively nonfiction including history, biography, business, health, child care and family concerns by writers with proven credentials and expertise in their fields. I am eager to work with new writers who have work that is professionally presented and in final draft form."

HOWARD BUCK AGENCY, Suite 1107, 80 8th Ave., New York NY 10011. (212)807-7855. Contact: Howard Buck and Mark Frisk. Estab. 1981. Represents 75 clients. "All-around agency." Currently handles: 75% nonfiction books; 25% novels.
Will Handle: Nonfiction, novels. Will consider all nonfiction and fiction areas. Query with SASE. Will report in 6 weeks on queries.
Terms: Agent receives 15% commission on domestic sales. Offers a written contract. Charges for office expenses, postage and photocopying.
Tips: Obtains new clients through recommendations from others.

KNOX BURGER ASSOCIATES LTD., 39 ½ Washington Square South, New York NY 10012. Prefers not to be listed.

JANE BUTLER, ART AND LITERARY AGENT (II, III), 212 3rd St., Milford PA 18337. (717)296-2629. Estab. 1981. "Prefers published credits, but all queries are welcome; no SASE, no reply." Specializes in fiction. Currently handles: 15% nonfiction books; 80% novels; 5% juvenile books.
Will Handle: Nonfiction books and novels. Will consider these fiction areas: fantasy, historical, horror, historical fantasy. Reports in 1 month on queries.
Recent Sales: *Alexander*, by Judith Tarr (Bantam Books); *Fleeting Fancy*, by Rosemary Edgehill (St. Martin's Press); *Borderland*, by S.K. Epperson (Donald Fine, Inc.).
Terms: Agent receives 10% commission on domestic sales; 15% on dramatic sales; 20% on foreign sales.

SHEREE BYKOFSKY ASSOCIATES (IV), Suite 11-D, Box WM, 211 E. 51st St., New York NY 10022. Estab. 1984. Represents "a limited number of" clients. Specializes in popular reference nonfiction. Currently handles: 100% nonfiction.
Will Handle: Nonfiction books. Will consider all nonfiction areas. Query with SASE. "No unsolicited manuscripts. No phone calls." Will report in 1 month on queries.
Terms: Agent receives 15% commission on domestic sales; 15% on foreign sales. Offers a written contract, binding for 1 year "usually." Charges for postage, photocopying and fax.
Tips: Obtains new clients through recommendations from others. "Read the agent listing carefully and comply with guidelines."

CANTRELL-COLAS INC., LITERARY AGENCY (II), 229 E. 79th St., New York NY 10021. (212)737-8503. Contact: Maryanne C. Colas. Estab. 1980. Represents 80 clients. Currently handles: 50% nonfiction books; 25% juvenile books; 25% mainstream.

Will Handle: Will consider these nonfiction areas: anthropology; art; biography; child guidance/parenting; cooking/food/nutrition; current affairs; ethnic/cultural interests; government/politics/law; health/medicine; history; juvenile nonfiction; language/literature/criticism; military/war; money/finance/economics; nature/environment; new age/metaphysics; psychology; true crime/investigative; science/technology; self-help/personal improvement; sociology; women's issues/women's studies. Will consider these fiction areas: contemporary issues; detective/police/crime; ethnic; experimental; family saga; feminist; historical; humor/satire; juvenile; literary; mainstream; mystery/suspense; psychic/supernatural; science fiction; thriller/espionage; young adult. Query with SASE and outline plus 2 sample chapters, and "something about author also." Will report in 2 months on queries.
Recent Sales: *Well and Truly,* by Evelyn Wilde-Mayerson (NAL); *Roosevelt and DeGaulle,* by Raoul Aglion (McMillan/The Free Press); *White Hare's Horses,* by Penina Spinka (Atheneum).
Terms: Agent receives 15% commission on domestic sales; commission varies on foreign sales. Offers a written contract. Charges for foreign postage and photocopying.
Tips: Obtains new clients through recommendations from others. "Make sure your manuscript is in excellent condition both grammatically and cosmetically. In other words, check for spelling, typing errors and legibility."

MARIA CARVAINIS AGENCY, INC. (II), Apt. 15F, 235 West End Ave., New York NY 10023. (212)580-1559. FAX: (212)877-3486. Contact: Maria Carvainis. Estab. 1977. Member of ILAA, WGA, Authors Guild. Represents 60 clients. 10% of clients are new/previously unpublished writers. Currently handles: 25% nonfiction books; 15% juvenile books; 55% novels; 5% poetry books.
Will Handle: Nonfiction books, scholarly books, juvenile books, novels, poetry books. Will consider these nonfiction areas: biography/autobiography; business; current affairs; government/politics/law; health/medicine; history; military/war; money/finance/economics; psychology; true crime/investigative; women's issues/women's studies; popular science. Will consider these fiction areas: action/adventure; contemporary issues; detective/police/crime; family saga; fantasy; glitz; historical; humor/satire; juvenile; literary; mainstream; mystery/suspense; romance; thriller/espionage; westerns/frontier; young adult. Query. Will report in 2-3 weeks on queries; 4-12 weeks on mss.
Recent Sales: *Workplace 2000,* by Joseph H. Boyett & Henry P. Conn (Dutton/Penguin); *Breath of Scandal,* by Sandra Brown (Warner); *Dun & Bradstreet's Guide to Your Investments,* by Nancy Dunnan (HarperCollins).
Terms: Agent receives 15% commission on domestic sales; 20% on foreign sales. Offers a written contract, binding for 2 years "on a book-by-book basis." Charges for foreign postage and bulk copying.
Tips: "75% of new clients derived from recommendations or conferences. 25% of new clients derived from letters of query."

MARTHA CASSELMAN LITERARY AGENT (III), P.O. Box 342, Calistoga CA 94515. (707)942-4341. Estab. 1978. Member of ILAA. Represents 30 clients. Specializes in "all types of nonfiction, but mainly food books, some fiction and children's books. No poetry." Currently handles: scholarly books; textbooks; movie scripts; stage plays.
Will Handle: Nonfiction books, juvenile books, novels. Will consider these nonfiction areas: anthropology/archaeology; biography/autobiography; child guidance/parenting; cooking/food/nutrition; current affairs; ethnic/cultural interests; government/politics/law; health/medicine; juvenile nonfiction; language/literature/criticism; money/finance/economics; music/dance/theater/film; nature/environment; true crime/investigative; self-help/personal improvement; sociology. Will consider these fiction areas: contemporary issues; detective/police/crime; juvenile; literary; mainstream; young adult. Send outline/proposal. Will report in 2-3 weeks on queries; 6 weeks on mss.
Terms: Would not disclose. Charges for photocopying, overnight and overseas mailings.
Tips: Obtains new clients through referrals, conferences. "Know material in your field. Read and analyze other books, if writing nonfiction, and know similarities and differences."

FAITH CHILDS LITERARY AGENCY (III), 275 W. 96th St., New York NY 10025. (212)662-1232. Contact: Faith Childs. Estab. 1986. Represents approximately 70 clients. Specializes in literary fiction and nonfiction (politics).
Will Handle: Will consider literary fiction. Query. Will report in 3 weeks on queries.
Terms: Agent receives 15% commission on domestic sales; 20% on foreign sales. Charges for postage, photocopying, foreign postage, fax.
Tips: Obtains new clients through referrals.

CONNIE CLAUSEN ASSOCIATES (II), #16H, 250 E. 87th St., New York NY 10128. (212)427-6135. FAX: (212)996-7111. Contact: Connie Clausen. Estab. 1976. 10% of clients are new/previously unpublished writers. Specializes in true crime, autobiography, biography, health, women's issues, psychology, celebrity, beauty-fashion, how-to, financial. Currently handles: 100% nonfiction books (in New York).

Member Agents: Lisa S. Bach (in New York).
Will Handle: Nonfiction books. Will consider these nonfiction areas: biography/autobiography; business; cooking/food/nutrition; current affairs; ethnic/cultural interests; gay/lesbian issues; health/medicine; money/finance/economics; music/dance/theater/film; nature/environment; psychology; true crime/investigative; self-help/personal improvement; women's issues/women's studies. Send outline/proposal. Will report in 3 weeks on queries; 4-6 weeks on mss.
Recent Sales: *Forever Fit*, by Cher and Robert Haas (Bantam); *The David Letterman Book of Top Ten Lists*, by David Letterman (Pocket); *On a Clear Day You Can See Yourself*, by Dr. Sonya Friedman and Guy Kettelhack (Little, Brown).
Terms: Agent receives 15% commission on domestic sales; 20% on foreign sales. Offers a written contract, terms vary. Charges for photocopying and office expenses.
Tips: Obtain new clients through referrals by other clients, publishers, magazine editors and *Writer's Digest.* "Always include SASE. Go to the library and read a book or two on publishing and proposal writing."

RUTH COHEN INC. LITERARY AGENCY (II), P.O. Box 7626, Menlo Park CA 94025. (415)854-2054. Contact: Ruth Cohen or associates. Estab. 1982. Member of ILAA, Authors Guild, SCBW. Represents 75 clients. 20% of cients are new/previously unpublished writers. Specializes in "quality writing in adult women's fiction; juvenile fiction; mysteries; historical romances." Currently handles: 15% nonfiction books; 40% juvenile books; 45% novels.
Will Handle: Nonfiction books, juvenile books, novels. Will consider these nonfiction areas: ethnic/cultural interests; juvenile nonfiction; true crime/investigative; women's issues/women's studies. Will consider these fiction areas: action/adventure; detective/police/crime; ethnic; family saga; historical; juvenile; literary; mainstream; mystery/suspense; romance; young adult. Send outline plus 2 sample chapters. Will report in 2 weeks on queries. No unsolicited mss.
Terms: Agent receives 15% commission on domestic sales; 20% on foreign sales, "if a foreign agent is involved." Offers a written contract, binding for 1 year "continuing to next." Charges for foreign postage and photocopying for submissions.
Tips: Obtains new clients through recommendations from others. "A good writer cares about the words he/she uses—so do I. Also, if no SASE is included, material will not be read."

HY COHEN LITERARY AGENCY LTD. (II), #1400, 111 W. 57th St., New York NY 10019. (212)757-5237. Contact: Hy Cohen. Estab. 1975. Represents 25 clients. 50% of clients are new/previously unpublished writers. Currently handles: 20% nonfiction books; 5% juvenile books; 75% novels.
Will Handle: Nonfiction books, novels. All categories of nonfiction and fiction considered. Send 100 pages with SASE. Will report in about 2 weeks (on 100-page submission).
Terms: Agent receives 10% commission.
Tips: Obtains new clients through recommendations from others and unsolicited submissions. "Send double-spaced, legible scripts and SASE. Good writing helps."

COLLIER ASSOCIATES (III), 2000 Flat Run Rd., Seaman OH 45679. (513)764-1234. Contact: Oscar Collier. Estab. 1976. Member of SAR, ILAA. Represents 75+ clients. 10% of clients are new/previously unpublished writers. Specializes in "adult fiction and nonfiction books only." Currently handles: 50% nonfiction books; 50% novels. Member agents: Oscar Collier (category fiction, nonfiction); Carol Cartaino (how-to and self-help nonfiction). "This is a small agency that rarely takes on new clients because of the many authors it represents already."
Will Handle: Nonfiction, novels. Query with SASE. Will report in 6-8 weeks on queries; 3-4 months "or longer" on mss.
Recent Sales: *Honorable Treachery*, by G.J.A. O'Toole, Morgan Entrekin Books (Atlantic Monthly Press); *Hearst: Father and Son*, by W.R. Hearst, Jr. with Jack Casserly (Roberts Rinehart, Inc.); *Blood on the Bayou*, by D.J. Donaldson (St. Martin's Press).
Terms: Agent receives 10-15% commission on domestic sales; 20% on foreign sales. Offers a written contract "sometimes." Charges for photocopying and express mail, "if requested, with author's consent, and for copies of author's published books used for rights sales."
Tips: Obtains new clients through recommendations from others. "Send biographical information with query; must have SASE. Don't telephone. Read my books *How to Write and Sell Your First Novel* and *How to Write and Sell Your First Nonfiction Book.*"

Check the literary and script agents subject indexes to find the agents who indicate an interest in your nonfiction or fiction subject area.

COLUMBIA LITERARY ASSOCIATES, INC. (II,IV), 7902 Nottingham Way, Ellicott City MD 21043. (301)465-1595. Contact: Linda Hayes. Estab. 1980. Member of ILAA. Represents 30-40 clients. 10% of clients are new/previously unpublished writers. Specializes in women's contemporary fiction (mainstream/genre), commercial nonfiction, especially cookbooks. Currently handles: 40% nonfiction books; 60% novels.
Will Handle: Nonfiction books, novels. Will consider these nonfiction areas: business; parenting; cooking/food/nutrition; health/medicine; self-help/personal improvement. Will consider these fiction areas: mainstream; mystery/suspense; romance (contemporary); thriller/espionage. Will report in 2-4 weeks on queries; 4-8 weeks on mss, "rejections faster."
Recent Sales: *Sing To Me, Saigon*, by Kathryn Jenson (Pocket); *Forty-Three Light Street* series, by Rebecca York (Harlequin Intrigue); *International Chocolate Cookbook*, by Nancy Baggett (Stewart, Tabori and Chang).
Terms: Agent receives 15% commission on domestic sales; 20% on foreign sales. Offers single-book written contract, binding for 6-12 months. "Standard expenses are billed against book income (e.g., books for subrights exploitation, tolls, UPS)."
Writers' Conferences: Attends Romance Writers of America conferences.
Tips: Obtains new clients through referrals and mail. "For fiction, send a query letter with author credits, narrative synopsis, first few chapters, manuscript submission history (publishers/agents); self-addressed, stamped mailer mandatory for response/ms return. Same for nonfiction, plus note audience, how project is different and better than competition. Please note that we do *not* handle: juvenile/ young adult, sf/fantasy, historical/Regencies, military books, poetry or short stories."

DON CONGDON ASSOCIATES INC. (III), Suite 625, 156 5th Ave., New York NY 10010. (212)645-1229. FAX: (212)727-2688. Contact: Don Congdon, Michael Congdon. Estab. 1983. Member of SAR. Represents 100+ clients. Currently handles: 50% fiction; 50% nonfiction books.
Will Handle: Nonfiction books, novels. Will consider all nonfiction and fiction areas, especially literary fiction. Query. "If interested, we ask for sample chapters." Will report in 3-4 weeks on queries.
Terms: No information given.
Tips: Obtains new clients through referrals from other authors. "Writing a query letter is a must."

JULIA COOPERSMITH LITERARY AGENCY (III), P.O. Box 1106, Cooper Station, New York NY 10276. (212)477-4418. Estab. 1976. Represents 20 clients. Currently handles: 75% nonfiction books; 25% novels.
Will Handle: Will consider these nonfiction areas: self-help/personal improvement; sociology; education; self-help. Will consider contemporary issues in fiction. Query only. "Not accepting unsolicited material at this time."
Terms: Agent receives 15% commission on domestic sales.
Tips: Obtains new clients through recommendations from clients.

THE DOE COOVER AGENCY (II), 58 Sagamore Ave., Medford MA 02155. (617)488-3937. FAX: (617)488-3153. President: Doe Coover. Estab. 1985. Represents 45 clients. Specializes in serious nonfiction. Currently handles: 100% nonfiction.
Will Handle: Nonfiction books. Will consider these nonfiction areas: anthropology; biography/autobiography; business; child guidance/parenting; cooking/food; ethnic/cultural interests; health/medicine; history; language/literature/criticism; finance/economics; nature/environment; psychology; religious/ inspirational; true crime; science/technology; sociology; women's issues/women's studies. Query with outline. Reporting time varies on queries.
Terms: Agent receives 15% commission on domestic sales; 15% on foreign sales.
Tips: Obtains new clients through recommendations from others and solicitation.

BONNIE R. CROWN INTERNATIONAL LITERATURE AND ARTS AGENCY (IV), 50 E. 10th St., New York NY 10003. (212)475-1999. Contact: Bonnie Crown. Estab. 1976. Represents 8-11 clients. 100% of clients are previously published writers. Specializes in cross-cultural and translations of literary works, American writers influenced by one or more Asian culture. Currently handles: 10% nonfiction books; 40% novels; 50% poetry books (translations only).
Will Handle: Nonfiction books, novels. Will consider these nonfiction areas: animals; ethnic/cultural interests; nature/environment; translations; women's issues/women's studies. Will consider these fiction areas: ethnic; family saga; historical; literary; religious/inspiration. Query with SASE. Will report in 1 week on queries.
Terms: Agent receives 15% commission on domestic sales; 20% on foreign sales. Charges for processing, usually $25, on submission of ms.
Tips: Obtains new clients through "referrals through other authors and listings in reference works." If interested in agency representation, "follow the policy for submission first."

THE CURTIS BRUCE AGENCY (II), Suite A, 3015 Evergeen Dr., Plover WI 54467. FAX: (715)345-2630. Contact: Curtis H.C. Lundgren. Estab. 1990. Represents approximately 20 clients. 25% of clients are new/previously unpublished writers. Specializes in "adult fiction of all types—sci-fi, fantasy, mystery, western. Children's picture books. We also represent illustrators, especially for children's books." Currently handles: 15% nonfiction books; 5% scholarly books; 15% juvenile books; 65% fiction (novels).
Will Handle: Nonfiction, juvenile books, novels. Will consider these nonfiction areas: biography/autobiography; child guidance/parenting; juvenile nonfiction; psychology; religious/inspirational; self-help/personal improvement; sports. Will consider these fiction areas: action/adventure; family saga; fantasy; humor/satire; juvenile; mystery/suspense; religious/inspiration; science fiction; sports; thriller/espionage; westerns/frontier; young adult. Query with outline/proposal plus 1-3 sample chapters. Will report in 2-3 weeks on queries; 6-8 weeks on mss.
Recent Sales: *The Borning Chamber*, by Carolyn Nystrom (InterVarsity Press); *The Song of Albion Trilogy*, by Stephen R. Lawhead (Lion Publishing, U.K.).
Terms: Agent receives 10% commission on domestic sales; 20% on foreign sales. Offers a written contract, binding for either 1 or 2 years. "Unpublished authors are charged for postage, phone calls, photocopies and various expenses incurred—*always in prior consultation with the client.*"
Tips: Obtains new clients by referral.

RICHARD CURTIS ASSOCIATES, INC. (III), 171 E. 74th St., New York NY 10021. (212)772-7363. FAX: (212)772-7393. Contact: Richard Curtis. Estab. 1969. Member of ILAA. Represents 150 clients. 5% of clients are new/previously unpublished writers. Specializes in genre paperback fiction such as science fiction, women's romance, horror, fantasy, action-adventure. Currently handles: 9% nonfiction books; 1% juvenile books; 90% novels. Member agents: Roberta Cohen, Richard Henshaw.
Will Handle: Nonfiction books, novels. Will consider these nonfiction areas: biography/autobiography; business; child guidance/parenting; history; military/war; money/finance/economics; music/dance/theater/film; true crime/investigative; science/technology; self-help/personal improvement; sports. Will consider these fiction areas: action/adventure; detective/police/crime; family saga; fantasy; feminist; historical; mainstream; mystery/suspense; romance; science fiction; thriller/espionage; westerns/frontier. Query. Will report in 1 week on queries.
Recent Sales: *Summer of Night*, by Dan Simmons (Putnam); *Masquerade*, by Janet Dailey (Little, Brown); *TV Movies*, by Leonard Maltin (Viking Penguin).
Terms: Agent receives 15% commission on domestic sales; 20% on foreign sales. Charges for photocopying, express, fax, international postage, book orders.
Tips: Obtains new clients through recommendations from others.

DARHANSOFF & VERRILL LITERARY AGENTS (II), 1220 Park Ave., New York NY 10128. (212)534-2479. FAX: (212)996-1601. Estab. 1975. Member of ILAA. Represents 100 clients. 10% of clients are new/previously unpublished writers. Specializes in literary fiction. Currently handles: 25% nonfiction books; 60% novels; 15% short story collections. Member agents: Liz Darhansoff; Charles Verrill; Abigail Thomas.
Will Handle: Nonfiction books, novels, short story collections. Will consider these nonfiction areas: anthropology/archaeology; biography/autobiography; current affairs; health/medicine; history; language/literature/criticism; nature/environment; science/technology. Will consider literary and thriller fiction. Query. Will report in 2 weeks on queries.
Recent Sales: *A Case of Curiosities*, by Allen Kuzzweil (HBJ); *Gayle Avenue*, by Kaye Gibbons (Putnam); *Heart Earth*, by Ivan Doig (Atheneum).
Terms: Agent receives 10% commission on domestic sales; 20% on foreign sales. Offers a written contract, "on a per-book basis." Charges for photocopying, foreign postage.
Tips: Obtains new clients through recommendations from others.

ELAINE DAVIE LITERARY AGENCY (II), Village Gate Square, 274 N. Goodman St., Rochester NY 14607. (716)442-0830. President: Elaine Davie. Estab. 1986. Represents 70 clients. 30% of clients are new/unpublished writers. Works with a small number of new/unpublished authors. Specializes in adult fiction and nonfiction, particularly books by and for women and genre/fiction. Currently handles: 30% nonfiction; 60% novels; 10% juvenile books.
Will Handle: Nonfiction books, novels (no short stories, children's books or poetry). Will consider these nonfiction areas: self-help, true crime, women's issues. Will consider these fiction areas: genre fiction, history, horror, mystery, romance, western. Query with outline or synopsis and brief description. Reports in 2 weeks on queries.

Recent Sales: *The Black Rose,* by Christina Skye (Dell); *Guardian Spirit,* by Marcia Evanick (Bantam); *Across a Wine Dark Sea,* by Jessica Bryan.
Terms: Agent receives 15% commission on domestic sales; 20% on dramatic sales; 20% on foreign sales.
Tips: "Our agency specializes in books by and for women. We pride ourselves on our prompt responses to queries and that we never charge a fee of any kind."

THE LOIS DE LA HABA AGENCY (II), 142 Bank St., New York NY 10014. (212)929-4838. FAX: (212)924-3885. Contact: Lois de la Haba. Estab. 1978. Represents 100 clients. Currently handles: 65% nonfiction books; 25% juvenile books; 15% novels.
Will Handle: Nonfiction books, juvenile books, novels. Will consider these nonfiction areas: agriculture/horticulture; animals; anthropology/archaeology; art/architecture/design; biography/autobiography; health/medicine; history; juvenile nonfiction; science/technology. Will consider these fiction areas: contemporary issues; experimental; historical; juvenile; literary; mainstream; mystery/suspense; picture book; psychic/supernatural; science fiction; sports; thriller/espionage; westerns/frontier; young adult. Send outline/proposal plus 2 sample chapters. Will report in 3-4 weeks on queries.
Recent Sales: *Financial Self Defense,* by Charles J. Givens (Simon & Schuster).
Terms: Agent receives 15% commission on domestic sales; 20% on foreign sales. Offers a written contract. Charges for "out-of-pocket expenses."
Tips: Obtains new clients through recommendations from others.

ANITA DIAMANT, THE WRITER'S WORKSHOP, INC. (II), 310 Madison Ave., New York NY 10017. (212)687-1122. Contact: Anita Diamant. Estab. 1917. Member of SAR. Represents 120 clients. 25% of clients are new/previously unpublished writers. Currently handles: 20% nonfiction books; 80% novels. Member agents: Robin Rue (fiction and nonfiction).
Will Handle: Nonfiction books, juvenile books, novels. Will consider these nonfiction areas: animals; art/architecture/design; biography/autobiography; business; child guidance/parenting; cooking/food/ nutrition; crafts/hobbies; current affairs; government/politics/law; health/medicine; history; juvenile nonfiction; money/finance/economics; nature/environment; new age/metaphysics; psychology; religious/inspirational; true crime/investigative; science/technology; self-help/personal improvement; sports; women's issues/women's studies. Will consider these fiction areas: action/adventure; contemporary issues; detective/police/crime; experimental; family saga; fantasy; feminist; gay; historical; juvenile; literary; mainstream; mystery/suspense; psychic/supernatural; religious/inspiration; romance; science fiction; thriller/espionage; westerns/frontier; young adult. Query. Will report "at once" on queries; 3 weeks on mss.
Recent Sales: *Dawn,* by V.C. Andrews (Pocket Books); *Month of the Freezing Moon,* by Duane Schultz (St. Martin's); *Death of a Joyce Scholar,* by Bartholomew Gill (Morrow); *The Play of Words,* by Richard Lederer (Pocket).
Terms: Agent receives 15% on domestic sales; 20% on foreign sales. Offers a written contract.
Writers' Conferences: Attends the Romance Writers of American Annual Conference.
Tips: Obtains new clients through "recommendations from publishers and clients, appearances at writers' conferences, and through readers of my written articles."

DIAMOND LITERARY AGENCY, INC. (III), 3063 S. Kearney St., Denver CO 80222. (303)759-0291. Contact: Carol Atwell. President: Pat Dalton. Estab. 1982. Represents 20 clients. 10% of clients are new/previously unpublished writers. Specializes in romance, romantic suspense, women's fiction, thrillers, mysteries. Currently handles: 25% nonfiction books; 70% novels; 3% movie scripts; 2% TV scripts.
Will Handle: Nonfiction books, novels, scripts. Will consider these nonfiction areas: animals; biography/autobiography; business; child guidance/parenting; computers/electronics; cooking/food/nutrition; crafts/hobbies; current affairs; ethnic/cultural interests; health/medicine; history; military/war; money/ finance/economics; music/dance/theater/film; nature/environment; photography; psychology; religious/inspirational; true crime/investigative; science/technology; self-help/personal improvement; sociology; women's issues/women's studies. Will consider these fiction areas: action/adventure; contemporary issues; detective/police/crime; erotica; ethnic; family saga; feminist; glitz; historical; humor/satire; mainstream; mystery/suspense; religious/inspiration; romance; thriller/espionage. Will report in 1 month on mss (partials).
Recent Sales: *Home Fires,* by Sharon Brondos (Harlequin); *Moriah's Mutiny,* by Elizabeth Beverly (Silhouette); *Full Steam,* by Cassia Miles (Meteor).
Terms: Agent receives 10-15% commission on domestic sales; 20% on foreign sales. Offers a written contract, binding for two years "unless author is well established." Charges a "$15 submission fee for writers who have not previously published/sold the same type of project." Charges for express and foreign postage. "Writers provide the necessary photostat copies."

Tips: Obtains new clients through "referrals from writers, or someone's submitting salable material. We represent only clients who are professionals in writing quality, presentation, conduct and attitudes—whether published or unpublished. Send an SASE for agency information and submission procedures. People who are not yet clients should not telephone. We consider query letters a waste of time—most of all the writer's, secondly the agent's. Submit approximately first 50 pages and complete synopsis for books, or full scripts, along with SASE and standard-sized audiocassette tape for possible agent comments. Nonclients who haven't sold the SAME TYPE of book or script within five years must include a $15 submission fee by money order or cashier's check. Material not accompanied by SASE is not returned. We are not encouraging submissions from unpublished writers at this time."

JANET DIGHT LITERARY AGENCY (II), 3075 Inspiration Dr., Colorado Springs CO 80917. (719)597-7675. Contact: Janet Dight. Estab. 1988. Member of Authors' Guild. Represents 20 clients. 25% of clients are new/previously unpublished writers. Currently handles: 30% nonfiction books; 30% juvenile books; 40% novels.
Will Handle: Nonfiction books, juvenile books, novels, novellas, short story collections. Will consider these nonfiction areas: animals; anthropology/archaeology; biography/autobiography; business; child guidance/parenting; cooking/food/nutrition; crafts/hobbies; current affairs; ethnic/cultural interests; government/politics/law; health/medicine; history; interior design/decorating; juvenile nonfiction; language/literature/criticism; money/finance/economics; music/dance/theater/film; nature/environment; new age/metaphysics; psychology; religious/inspirational; true crime/investigative; science/technology; self-help/personal improvement; sociology; sports; women's issues/women's studies. Will consider these fiction areas: action/adventure; confessional; contemporary issues; detective/police/crime; ethnic; family saga; fantasy; feminist; glitz; historical; humor/satire; juvenile; literary; mainstream; mystery/suspense; picture book; psychic/supernatural; regional; religious/inspiration; romance; science fiction; sports; thriller/espionage; westerns/frontier; young adult. Send outline plus 1 sample chapter for nonfiction, first 3 chapters for fiction. Send SASE (29¢ postage) for submission guidelines and agency information. Will report in 4-6 weeks on proposal, 8-10 weeks on full mss.
Terms: Agent receives 15% commission on domestic sales; 20% on foreign sales. Offers a written contract, binding for 1 year. Charges for postage, photocopying.
Tips: Obtains new clients through recommendations from others and direct submissions from authors. "We encourage authors to send for our guidelines (enclose an SASE with 29¢ postage) before making a submission."

DONADIO & ASHWORTH INC. LITERARY REPRESENTATIVES, 231 W. 22nd St., New York NY 10011. Prefers not to be listed.

SANDRA DIJKSTRA LITERARY AGENCY (II), #515, 1155 Camino del Mar, Del Mar CA 92014. (619)755-3115. Contact: Katherine Goodwin. Estab. 1981. Member of Authors Guild, PENN West, Poets and Editors, Mystery Writers of America, ILAA. Represents 80-100 clients. 60% of clients are new/previously unpublished writers. "We specialize in a number of fields." Currently handles: 50% nonfiction books; 5% juvenile books; 35% novels. Member agents: Sandra Dijkstra, president (adult nonfiction, literary and mainstream fiction, selected children's projects, mysteries and thrillers); Katherine Goodwin, associate agent (adult nonfiction, mystery and thrillers, literary and mainstream fiction, science fiction/fantasy, adventure, horror and historical/sagas).
Will Handle: Nonfiction books, novels, some juvenile books. Will consider these nonfiction areas: horticulture; anthropology; art/architecture/design; biography/autobiography; business; child guidance/parenting; cooking/food/nutrition; current affairs; ethnic/cultural interests; government/politics; health/medicine; history; lit studies (trade only); military/war (trade only); money/finance/economics; music/dance/theater/film; nature/environment; new age/metaphysics; psychology; true crime/investigative; science/technology; self-help/personal improvement; sociology; sports; translations; women's issues/women's studies. Will consider these fiction areas: action/adventure; contemporary issues; detective/police/crime; ethnic; family saga; fantasy; feminist; glitz; historical; humor/satire; juvenile; literary; mainstream; mystery/suspense; picture book; psychic/supernatural; romance (historical); science fiction; sports; thriller/espionage; young adult; horror. Send "outline/proposal with sample chapters for nonfiction, synopsis and first 50 pages for fiction and SASE." Will report in 2 weeks on queries; 1-6 weeks on mss.
Recent Sales: *The Kitchen God's Wife*, by Amy Tan (G.P. Putnam).
Terms: Agent receives 15% commission on domestic sales; 20% on foreign sales. Offers a written contract, 2-year term. Charges "an expense fee to cover domestic costs so that we can spend time selling books instead of accounting expenses. We also charge for the photocopying of the full manuscript or nonfiction proposal and for foreign postage."
Writers' Conferences: "Attends Squaw Valley, Santa Barbara, Asilomar, Southern California Writers Conference, Rocky Mt. Fiction Writers, "to name a few. We also speak regularly for writers groups such as PENN West and the Independent Writers Association."

Tips: Obtains new clients "primarily through referrals/recommendations, but also through queries and conferences and often by solicitation. Be professional and learn the standard procedures for submitting your work. Give full biographical information on yourself, especially for a nonfiction project. Always include SAE with correct return postage for your own protection of your work. Call if you don't hear within a reasonable period of time. Be a regular patron of bookstores and learn what kind of books are being published. Check out your local library and bookstores—you'll find lots of books on writing and the publishing industry that will help you! At conferences, ask published writers about their agents. Don't believe the myth that an agent has to be in New York to be successful—we've already disproved it!"

THE JONATHAN DOLGER AGENCY (II), Suite 9B, 49 E. 96th St., New York NY 10128. (212)427-1853. President: Jonathan Dolger. Estab. 1980. Represents 70 clients. 25% of clients are new/unpublished writers. Writer must have been previously published if submitting fiction. Prefers to work with published/established authors; works with a small number of new/unpublished writers. Specializes in adult trade fiction and nonfiction, and illustrated books.
Will Handle: Nonfiction books, novels and illustrated books. Query with outline and SASE.
Terms: Agent receives 15% commission on domestic sales; 10% on dramatic sales; 25-30% on foreign sales. Charges for "standard expenses."

THOMAS C. DONLAN (II, IV), 143 E. 43rd St., New York NY 10017. (212)697-1629. Agent: Thomas C. Donlan. Estab. 1983. Represents 12 clients. "Our agency limits itself to philosophy and theology, mainly, but not exclusively Roman Catholic. No special requirements of earlier publication." Prefers to work with published/established authors. Specializes in philosophical and theological writings, including translations. Currently handles: 2% magazine articles; 90% nonfiction books; 8% textbooks.
Will Handle: Nonfiction books, textbooks. Will consider these nonfiction areas: philosophy, theology, translations. Query with outline. Reports in 2 weeks on queries.
Recent Sales: *Did Jesus Know He Was God*, by F. Dreyfus (Franciscan Herald); *Duty or Pleasure?— A New Approach to Christian Ethics*, by A. Ple (Paragon House).
Terms: Agent receives 10% commission on domestic sales; 6% on foreign sales.

ROBERT DUCAS (II), 350 Hudson St., New York NY 10014. (212)924-8120. FAX: (212)924-8079. Contact: R. Ducas. Estab. 1981. Represents 55 clients. 15% of clients are new/previously unpublished writers. Specializes in nonfiction, journalistic exposé, biography, history. Currently handles: 70% nonfiction books; 1% scholarly books; 28% novels; 1% novellas.
Will Handle: Nonfiction books, novels, novellas. Will consider these nonfiction areas: animals; biography/autobiography; business; current affairs; gay/lesbian issues; government/politics/law; health/medicine; history; military/war; money/finance/economics; nature/environment; true crime/investigative; science/technology; sports. Will consider these fiction areas: action/adventure; contemporary issues; detective/police/crime; family saga; feminist; gay; historical; humor/satire; lesbian; literary; mainstream; mystery/suspense; sports; thriller/espionage; westerns/frontier. Send outline/proposal. Will report in 2 weeks on queries; 1 month on mss.
Terms: Agent receives 12½% commission on domestic sales; 20% on foreign sales. Charges for photocopying and postage. "I also charge for messengers and overseas couriers to subagents."
Tips: Obtains new clients through recommendations.

DUPREE/MILLER AND ASSOCIATES INC. LITERARY (II), Suite 3, 5518 Dyer St., Dallas TX 75206. (214)692-1388. FAX: (214)987-9654. Contact: Jan Miller. Estab. 1984. Represents 120+ clients. 20% of clients are new/previously unpublished writers. Specializes in commercial fiction and nonfiction. Currently handles: 50% nonfiction books; 35% novels. Member agents: Jan Miller; Katherine Hazelwood.
Will Handle: Nonfiction books, scholarly books, novels, movie scripts, syndicated material. Will consider all nonfiction areas. Will consider these fiction areas: action/adventure; cartoon/comic; contemporary issues; detective/police/crime; family saga; feminist; gay; glitz; historical; humor/satire; literary; mainstream; mystery/suspense; psychic/supernatural; romance (contemporary, historical); science fiction; sports; thriller/espionage; westerns/frontier. Send outline plus 3 sample chapters. Will report in 1 week on queries; 8-12 weeks on mss.
Recent Sales: *The Seven Habits of Highly Effective People*, by Dr. Stephen Covey and *Unlimited Power*, by Anthony Robbins (Simon & Schuster); *Storming Intrepid*, by Payne Harrison (Crown).
Terms: Agent receives 15% commission on domestic sales. Offers a written contract, binding for "no set amount of time. The contract can be cancelled by either agent or client, effective 30 days after cancellation." Charges $10 processing fee and Federal Express charges.

Writers' Conferences: "Will be attending many national conventions. Also have lectures at colleges across nation."
Tips: Obtains new client through conferences, lectures, clients and "very frequently through publisher's referrals." If interested in agency representation "it is vital to have the material in the proper working format. As agents' policies differ it is important to follow their guidelines. The best advice I can give is to work on establishing a strong proposal that provides sample chapters, an overall synopsis (fairly detailed) and some bio information on yourself. Do not send your proposal in pieces; it should be complete upon submission. Remember you are trying to sell your work and it should be in its best condition."

ROBERT EISENBACH INC. (III), Suite 203, 6072 Franklin Ave., Los Angeles CA 90028. (213)962-5809. Contact: Robert Eisenbach. Estab. 1972. Member of WGA. Currently handles: 80% fiction; 20% nonfiction books.
Will Handle: Will consider all nonfiction and fiction areas. Query. Will report in 1 month on queries.
Terms: Agent receives 15% commission on domestic sales.
Tips: Obtains new clients through recommendations from others. "We're accepting only writers who are previously published."

VICKI EISENBERG LITERARY AGENCY (II), Suite 217, 4514 Travis St., Dallas TX 75205. (214)521-8430. FAX: (214)521-8454. Contact: Evan Fogelman. Estab. 1985. Represents 30 clients. Currently handles: 60% nonfiction books; 40% novels.
Will Handle: Will consider all nonfiction areas. Will consider mainstream and mystery/suspense fiction. Query with SASE. Will report in 6 weeks on queries.
Terms: Agent receives 15% commission on domestic sales. Offers a written contract.
Tips: Obtains new clients through referrals from other agencies and authors.

JOSEPH ELDER AGENCY (II), 150 W. 87th St., Apt. 6D, New York NY 10024. (212)787-5722. Contact: Joseph Elder. Estab. 1975. Member of ILAA. Represents approximately 30 clients. Specializes in commercial fiction. Currently handles: 10% nonfiction books; 10% young adult books; 80% adult novels.
Will Handle: Will consider all nonfiction areas. Will consider these fiction areas: contemporary issues; detective/police/crime; family saga; fantasy; historical; literary; mainstream; mystery/suspense; science fiction; sports; thriller/espionage; westerns/frontier; young adult. Query with SASE. No unsolicited mss. Will report in 1-2 weeks on queries.
Recent Sales: *Ruler of the Sky*, by Pamela Sargent (Crown Publishers); *Stranger Suns*, by George Zebrowski (Bantam Books).
Terms: Agent receives 10% commission on domestic sales; 20% on foreign sales. Charges for photocopying, express mail, unusual costs.
Tips: Obtains most new clients through referrals from other clients or editors. "Write a very persuasive query letter."

PETER ELEK ASSOCIATES (II, IV), Box 223, Canal Street Station, New York NY 10013. (212)431-9368. FAX: (212)966-5768. Contact: Michelle Roberts. Estab. 1979. Represents 20 clients. 5% of clients are new/previously unpublished writers. Specializes in children's books—picture books, adult nonfiction and juvenile art. Currently handles: 30% juvenile books.
Will Handle: Juvenile books (fiction, nonfiction, picture books). Will consider juvenile nonfiction. Will consider these fiction areas: juvenile, picture books. Query with outline/proposal. Reports in 2 weeks on queries; 3 weeks on mss.
Recent Sales: *My First Computer Book*, by Tedd Arnold (beginner, Workman); *Secrets of Vesuvius*, by Sara Bisel (middle reader, Scholastic); *The Simple People*, by Tedd Arnold, illustrated by Andrew Schachat (picture book; Dial Books for Young Readers); *Titantic: An Illustrated History*, by Donald Lynch (adult illus, Hyperion/Disney).
Terms: Agent receives 15% commission on domestic sales; 20% commission on foreign sales. If required, charges for photocopying, typing, courier charges.
Tips: Obtains new clients through recommendations and studying consumer and trade magazines.

ETHAN ELLENBERG LITERARY AGENCY (II), #5-E, 548 Broadway, New York NY 10012. (212)431-4554. FAX: (212)941-4652. Contact: Ethan Ellenberg. Estab. 1983. Represents 65 clients. 35% of clients are new/previously unpublished writers. Specializes in first novels, military fiction and nonfiction, thrillers, mystery, science fiction and fantasy, horror. Currently handles: 25% nonfiction books; 75% novels.
Will Handle: Nonfiction books, novels. Will consider these nonfiction areas: biography/autobiography; business; child guidance/parenting; cooking/food/nutrition; crafts/hobbies; current affairs; government/politics/law; health/medicine; history; juvenile nonfiction; military/war; money/finance/econom-

ics; nature/environment; new age/metaphysics; psychology; religious/inspirational; true crime/investigative; science/technology; self-help/personal improvement; sports. Will consider these fiction areas: action; cartoon/comic; detective/police/crime; family saga; fantasy; glitz; historical; humor/satire; juvenile; literary; mainstream; mystery/suspense; picture book; romance; science fiction; sports; thriller/ espionage; westerns/frontier; young adult. Send outline plus 3 sample chapters. Will report in 10 days on queries; 3-4 weeks on mss.
Recent Sales: *Eyes of the Hammer,* by Bob Mayer (Presidio); *Termite Hill,* by Tom Wilson (Bantam); *Central Park Jogger,* by Tim Sullivan (Simon & Schuster).
Terms: Agent receives 15% on domestic sales; 10% on foreign sales. Offers a written contract, "flexible." Charges for "direct expenses only: photocopying, postage."
Writers' Conferences: Attends University of Oklahoma Conference, Vassar Conference on Children's Publishing.
Tips: "I obtain clients by client and editor recommendation, active recruitment from magazines, newspapers, etc. and my unsoliciteds. I very seriously consider all new material and have done very well through unsolicited manuscripts including clients Tom Wilson, Tom Willard, Bill Keith, Bob Broomall, David Westwood and Catherine Hepworth. Write a good, clear letter, with a succinct description of your book. Show that you understand the basics and don't make outrageous claims for your book. Make sure you only submit your best material and that it's prepared professionally—perfectly typed with good margins. Find out what any prospective agent will do for you, make sure you have some rapport. Don't be fooled by big names or phony pitches—what will the agent do for you. Good agents are busy, don't waste their time, but don't be afraid to find out what's going on. Besides my professionalism, my greatest skills are editorial—helping novelists develop. We give ample editorial advice for no charge to clients the agency takes."

NICHOLAS ELLISON, INC. (II), 55 5th Ave., 15th Floor, New York NY 10003. (212)206-6050. Affiliated with Sanford J. Greenburger Associates. Contact: Jennifer Reavis. Estab. 1983. Represents 70 clients. Currently handles: 25% nonfiction books; 75% novels.
Will Handle: Nonfiction, novels. Will consider most nonfiction areas. No biography, gay/lesbian issues or self-help. Will consider these fiction areas: literary; mainstream. Query with SASE. Reporting time varies on queries.
Recent Sales: *The Gold Coast,* by Nelson De Mille (Warner Books); *Tygers of Wrath,* by Philip Rosenberg (St. Martin's Press); *Typhoon,* by Mark Joseph (Simon & Schuster).
Terms: Agent receives 15% commission on domestic sales; 20% commission on foreign sales.
Tips: Usually obtains new clients from word-of-mouth referrals.

ANN ELMO AGENCY INC. (III), 60 E. 42nd St., New York NY 10165. (212)661-2880, 2881, 2883. Contact: Ann Elmo or Lettie Lee. Estab. 1961. Member of SAR, MWA, Authors Guild.
Will Handle: Nonfiction, novels. Will consider these nonfiction areas: cooking/food/nutrition; juvenile nonfiction; women's issues. Will consider these fiction areas: historical; romance. Query with outline/ proposal. Will report in 4-6 weeks "average" on queries.
Terms: Agent receives 15% commission on domestic sales; 20% on foreign sales. Offers a written contract (standard SAR contract).
Tips: Obtains new clients through referrals. "Send properly prepared manuscript. A readable manuscript is the best recommendation. Double space."

FELICIA ETH LITERARY REPRESENTATION (II), Suite 350, 555 Bryant St., Palo Alto CA 94301. (415)375-1276. Contact: Felicia Eth. Estab. 1988. Member of ILAA. Represents 25-30 clients. Eager to work with new/unpublished writers; "for nonfiction, established expertise is certainly a plus, as is magazine publication—though not a prerequisite." Specializes in "provocative, intelligent, thoughtful nonfiction on a wide array of subjects which are commercial and high-quality fiction; preferably mainstream and contemporary. I am highly selective, but also highly dedicated to those projects I represent." Currently handles: 75% nonfiction, 25% novels.
Will Handle: Nonfiction books, novels. Query with outline. Reports in 3 weeks on queries; 1 month on proposals and sample pages.
Recent Sales: *The Female Hero,* by Kate Noble, Ph.D. (Ballantine); *Forms of Gold: Essays from the Southwest,* by Sherman Russell (Addison-Wesley); *A Breed Apart: A Journey to the Backside of Racetrack Life,* by Mike Helm (Henry Holt).
Terms: Agent receives 15% commission on domestic sales; 20% on dramatic sales; 20% on foreign sales. Charges for photocopying, fax, Federal Express service—extraordinary expenses.

EVANS AND ASSOCIATES (II), 14330 Caves Rd., Novelty OH 44072. (216)338-3264. Agent/Owner: Clyde Evans. Estab. 1987. "This agency will represent any author whose work, based on agency review, is of such quality that it is deemed salable." Eager to work with new/unpublished writers.

Will Handle: Various types of material. Query with outline or send entire manuscript. Reports in 3 weeks on queries; 2 months on mss.
Terms: Agent receives 15% commission on domestic sales; 10% on dramatic sales; 20% total on foreign sales—10% to foreign agent. Charges for photocopying over 75 pages, legal advice beyond normal agency services, messenger.

THE FALLON LITERARY AGENCY (III), Suite 13B, 301 W. 53rd St., New York NY 10019. (212)399-1369. FAX: (212)315-3823. Contact: Eileen Fallon. Estab. 1990. Member of ILAA. Represents 40 clients. 20% of clients are new/previously unpublished writers. Specializes in mainstream and literary fiction, romance, mystery and nonfiction. Currently handles: 20% nonfiction books; 80% novels.
Will Handle: Nonfiction, novels. Will consider these nonfiction areas: biography/autobiography; health/medicine; history; language/literature/criticism; natural history; psychology; self help/personal improvement; women's issues/women's studies. Will consider these fiction areas: literary; mainstream, mystery/suspense; romance. Query first. "I *must* see a query letter and agree to have the material sent before I will consider the material—no over-the-transom partials or manuscripts." Will report in 2 weeks on queries; usually 2 months on ms.
Terms: Agent receives 15% commission on domestic sales; 20% on foreign sales. Does not usually offer a written contract, unless requested. Charges for photocopying.
Tips: Usually obtains new clients through referrals from editors or and sometimes other agents. "Target your material—send it only to an agent who handles the kind of project you've written."

JOHN FARQUHARSON LTD., 250 W. 57th St., New York NY 10107. Prefers not to be listed.

FLORENCE FEILER LITERARY AGENCY (III), 1524 Sunset Plaza Dr., Los Angeles CA 90069. (213)652-6920/652-0945. Associate: Joyce Boorn. Estab. 1976. Represents 40 clients. No unpublished writers. "Quality is the criterion." Specializes in fiction, nonfiction, screen and TV. No short stories.
Will Handle: Textbooks (for special clients), juvenile books, movie scripts. Query with outline only. Reports in 2 weeks on queries. "We will not accept simultaneous queries to other agents."
Recent Sales: *Babette's Feast* (best foreign film); *Logic of the Heart*, by Patricia Veryan (St. Martin's); *Nightwares*, by Collin McDonald (Dutton); *Midnight Extacy* (Zebra); *Psychward*, by Dr. Stephen Seager (Putnam).
Terms: Agent receives 10% commission on domestic sales; 10% on dramatic sales; 20% on foreign sales.

MARJE FIELDS-RITA SCOTT INC. (II), #1205, 165 W. 46th, New York NY 10036. Member of ILAA. Represents 40 clients. 20% of clients are new/previously unpublished writers. Specializes in fiction and nonfiction. Currently handles: 5% nonfiction books; 10% juvenile books; 75% novels; 10% stage plays.
Will Handle: Nonfiction books, novels. Will consider these nonfiction areas: biography/autobiography; cooking/food/nutrition; gay/lesbian issues; health/medicine; true crime/investigative; self-help/personal improvement; sports. Will consider these fiction areas: action/adventure; confessional; detective/police/crime; family saga; gay; historical; literary; mainstream; mystery/suspense; historical romance; sports; thriller/espionage; westerns/frontier; young adult. Query. Will report in 1 week on queries; 2 weeks on mss.
Recent Sales: *Sweet Deal*, by John Westermann (Soho Press); *Live Free or Die*, by Ernest Hebert (Viking); *Summer Girl*, by Deborah Moulton (Dial); *Hearts of Glass*, by Nicole Jeffords (Crown).
Terms: *At presstime we were notified this agency charges reading fees to new writers.* Agent receives 15% on domestic sales; 20% on foreign sales. Offers a written contract, binding for 1 year.
Tips: Obtains new cilents through referrals and queries.

FLAMING STAR LITERARY ENTERPRISES (II), 320 Riverside Dr., New York NY 10025. Contact: Joseph B. Vallely. Estab. 1985. Represents 50 clients. 25% of clients are new/previously unpublished writers. Currently handles: 50% nonfiction books; 50% novels.
Will Handle: Nonfiction books, novels. Will consider these nonfiction areas: animals; biography/autobiography; business; child guidance/parenting; current affairs; government/politics/law; health/medicine; history; military/war; nature/environment; psychology; true crime/investigative; science technology; self-help/personal improvement; sports; women's issues/women's studies. Will consider these fiction areas: action/adventure; confessional; contemporary issues; detective/police/crime; experimental; family saga; glitz; historical; literary; mainstream; mystery/suspense; psychic/supernatural; science fiction; sports; thriller/espionage; westerns/frontier. Query. Will report in 1 week on queries; 2 weeks on mss.
Terms: Agent receives 10% commission on published authors; 15% on unpublished authors. Offers a written contract. Charges "actual expenses only; no fees."
Tips: Obtains new clients through over the transom and referrals.

FOGELMAN PUBLISHING INTERESTS INC. (I), Suite 241, 5050 Quorum, Dallas TX 75240. (214)980-6975. FAX: (214)980-6978. Contact: Evan Fogelman. Estab. 1990. Represents 20-25 clients. Specializes in "contemporary women's fiction and nonfiction, contemporary women's issues." Currently handles: 40% nonfiction books; 60% novels.
Will Handle: Will consider these nonfiction areas: biography; business; parenting; nutrition; current affairs; government/politics/law; money/finance/economics; true crime; self-help/personal improvement; women's issues/women's studies; gardening. Will consider these fiction areas: contemporary issues; detective/police/crime; family saga; historical; regional; romance. Query with SASE, outline and 3 sample chapters "for any work of fiction that involves women characters or work of nonfiction involving contemporary women's issues." Will report in 6 weeks on queries.
Terms: Agent receives 15% commission on domestic sales; varying on foreign sales.
Writers' Conferences: "I speak at many writers conferences, such as The New Orleans Writers Conference, The UTD Craft of Writing Conference, and various Romance Writers of America conferences."
Tips: Obtains new clients through referrals, through writers conferences and through mailed submissions. "If you have any questions, call. All books can't be treated alike. Call when in doubt."

THE FOX CHASE AGENCY INC. (II), Rm. 930, Public Ledger Bldg., Independence Square, Philadelphia PA 19106. (215)625-2450. FAX: (212)683-4520. Contact: Al Hart or J. Hart. Estab. 1972. Member of SAR. Represents 50 clients. Currently handles: 35% nonfiction books; 65% novels.
Will Handle: Will consider these nonfiction areas: current affairs; health/medicine; money/finance/economics; nature/environment; self-help/personal improvement; sociology; sports; women's issues/women's studies. Will consider these fiction areas: mystery/suspense; religious/inspiration; science fiction; sports. Query with SASE. Will report in 2-3 weeks on queries.
Terms: Agent receives 15% commission on domestic sales; varies on foreign sales. Charges for photocopying.
Tips: Obtains new clients through recommendations from others.

CANDICE FUHRMAN LITERARY AGENCY, (II), Box F, Forest Knolls, Forest Knolls CA 94933. (415)488-0161. Contact: Candice Fuhrman. Estab. 1987. Represents 45 clients. 80% of clients are new/previously unpublished writers. 95% nonfiction books; 5% novels.
Will Handle: Nonfiction books, novels. Will consider these nonfiction areas: animals; anthropology/archaeology; art/architecture/design; biography/autobiography; business; child guidance/parenting; cooking/food/nutrition; crafts/hobbies; current affairs; ethnic/cultural interests; health/medicine; history; interior design/decorating; language/literature/criticism; money/finance/economics; music/dance/theater/film; nature/environment; new age/metaphysics; psychology; religious/inspirational; true crime/investigative; science/technology; self-help/personal improvement; sociology; sports; women's issues/women's studies; recovery. Will consider these fiction areas: literary, mainstream. Send outline plus 1 sample chapter. Will report in 1 month on queries.
Terms: Agent receives 15% commission on domestic sales; 20% on foreign sales. Offers a written contract, binding for 6 months to 1 year. Charges postage and photocopying.
Tips: Obtains new clients through recommendations and solicitation. "Please do not call. Send succinct query and well-thought-out proposal. Check out your idea with *Subject Books in Print* and look at the competition to see how your book is different. (This is for nonfiction, of course)."

JAY GARON-BROOKE ASSOC. INC. (II), 17th Floor, 415 Central Park West, New York NY 10025. (212)866-3654. Contact: Jean Free or Jay Garon. Estab. 1952. Member of ILAA, WGA. Represents 80 clients. 10% of clients are new/previously unpublished writers. Specializes in mainstream fiction and nonfiction. Currently handles: 15% nonfiction books; 75% novels; 5% movie scripts; 2% stage plays; 3% TV scripts.
Will Handle: Nonfiction books, novels, movie and TV scripts, stage plays. Will consider these nonfiction areas: biography/autobiography; child guidance/parenting; gay/lesbian issues; health/medicine; history; military/war; music/dance/theater/film; psychology; true crime/investigative; self-help/personal improvement. Will consider these fiction areas: action/adventure; contemporary issues; detective/police/crime; family saga; fantasy; gay; glitz; historical; literary; mainstream; mystery/suspense; romance; science fiction. Query. Will report in 3 weeks on queries; 5-8 weeks on mss.

Agents ranked I and II are most open to both established and new writers. Agents ranked III are open to established writers with publishing-industry references.

Recent Sales: *The Master Stroke*, by Elizabeth Gage (Pocket Books); *The Firm*, by John Grisham (Doubleday-Dell); *Aces*, by Robert Denny (Donald I. Fine Inc.); *Cold Wind*, by T. Chris Martindale (Pocket Books).
Terms: Agent receives 15% on domestic sales; 30% on foreign sales. Offers a written contract, binding for 3-5 years. Charges for "photocopying if author does not provide copies."
Tips: Obtains new clients through referrals and from queries. "Send query letter first giving the essence of the manuscript and a personal or career bio."

MAX GARTENBERG, LITERARY AGENT (II,III), Suite 1700, 521 5th Ave., New York NY 10175. (212)860-8451. FAX: (201)535-5033. Contact: Max Gartenberg. Estab. 1954. Represents 30 clients. 5% of clients are new/previously unpublished writers. Currently handles: 90% nonfiction books; 10% novels.
Will Handle: Nonfiction books, novels. Will consider these nonfiction areas: agriculture/horticulture; animals; art/architecture/design; biography/autobiography; child guidance/parenting; current affairs; health/medicine; history; military/war; money/finance/economics; music/dance/theater/film; nature/environment; psychology; true crime/investigative; science/technology; self-help/personal improvement; sports; women's issues/women's studies. Will consider mainstream and mystery/suspense fiction. Query. Will report in 2 weeks on queries; 6 weeks on mss.
Recent Sales: *The Dying of the Trees*, by Charles E. Little (Viking Penguin); *Encyclopedia of Climbing*, by Greg Child (Facts on File); *Bears*, by Art Wolfe and William Ashworth (Crown Publishers).
Terms: Agent receives 10% on domestic sales; 15% on foreign sales. Offers a written contract.
Tips: Obtains new clients "primarily, by recommendations from others, but often enough by following up on good query letters. Take pains in drafting your query letter. It makes the important first impression an agent has of you. If it is sloppy, badly written, ungrammatical—as, unfortunately, so many are—the agent will probably be too busy to follow up with you. Without going on at great length, be specific about what you have to offer and include a few relevant facts about yourself. The most exasperating letter an agent receives is the one which reads, 'I have just completed a novel. If you would like to read the manuscript, please let me know. An SASE is enclosed for your convenience.' "

GOLDFARB, KAUFMAN, & O'TOOLE (II), 918-16 St., NW, Washington DC 20006. (202)466-3030. FAX: (202)293-3187. Contact: Ronald Goldfarb. Estab. 1966. Represents "hundreds" of clients. "Minority" of clients are new/previously unpublished writers. Specializes in nonfiction, "books with TV tie-ins." Currently handles: 80% nonfiction books; 1% scholarly books; 1% textbooks; 1% juvenile books; 10% novels; 1% novellas; 1% poetry books; 1% short story collections; 1% movie scripts; 1% stage plays; 1% TV scripts; 1% syndicated material. Member agents: Joshua Kaufman; Carol Randolph; Nina Graybill; Ronald Goldfarb.
Will Handle: Nonfiction books, textbooks, scholarly books, juvenile books, novels, novellas, short story collections, poetry books, movie and TV scripts, stage plays, syndicated material. Will consider all nonfiction and fiction areas. Send outline plus 1 or 2 sample chapters. Will report in 1 week on queries; within a month on mss.
Writers' Conferences: Attends Washington Independent Writers Conference; Medical Writers Conference.
Tips: Obtains new clients mostly through recommendations from others. "We are a law firm which can help writers with related problems, Freedom of Information Act requests, libel, copyright, contracts, etc. We are published writers."

GOODMAN ASSOCIATES (III), 500 West End Ave., New York NY 10024. Contact: Elise Simon Goodman. Estab. 1976. Member of ILAA (Arnold Goodman is president of ILAA). Represents 100 clients. "Presently accepting new clients on a very selective basis."
Will Handle: Nonfiction, novels. Will consider most adult nonfiction and fiction areas. No "poetry, articles, individual stories, children's or YA material." Query with SASE. Will report in 10 days on queries; 1 month on mss.
Terms: Agent receives 15% commission on domestic sales; 20% on foreign sales. Charges for certain expenses: faxes, toll calls, overseas postage, photocopying, book purchases.

IRENE GOODMAN LITERARY AGENCY (II), 17th Floor, 521 5th Ave., New York NY 10017. (212)682-1978. Contact: Irene Goodman, president. Estab. 1978. Member of ILAA. Represents 75 clients. 20% of clients are new/unpublished writers. Works with a small number of new/unpublished authors. Specializes in women's fiction, popular nonfiction, reference and genre fiction. Currently handles: 20% nonfiction books; 80% novels.
Will Handle: Novels and nonfiction books. Will consider these nonfiction areas: popular and reference. Will consider these fiction areas: historical romance, romance, mainstream, mystery, genre fiction. Query only (no unsolicited mss). Reports in 6 weeks. "No reply without SASE."
Terms: Agent receives 15% commission on domestic sales; 20% on foreign sales.

CHARLOTTE GORDON AGENCY (II), 235 E. 22nd St., New York NY 10010. (212)679-5363. Contact: Charlotte Gordon. Estab. 1986. Represents 20 clients. 20% of clients are new/unpublished writers. "I'll work with writers whose work is interesting to me." Specializes in "books (not magazine material, except for my writers, and then only in special situations). My taste is eclectic." Currently handles: 30% nonfiction books; 40% novels; 30% juvenile.
Will Handle: Nonfiction books, novels and juvenile books (all ages). Query. Does not read unsolicited manuscripts. Reports in 2 weeks on queries.
Terms: Agent receives 15% commission on domestic sales; 10% on dramatic sales; 10% on foreign sales. Charges writers for photocopying manuscripts.

GOTHAM ART & LITERARY AGENCY INC. (II), Suite 10H, 1133 Broadway, New York NY 10010. (212)989-2737. FAX: (212)633-1004. Contact: Anne Elisabeth Suter. Estab. 1983. Currently handles: 10% nonfiction books; 45% juvenile books; 45% novels.
Will Handle: Will consider all nonfiction areas. Will consider juvenile, literary and mainstream fiction. Query with SASE. Reports in 2 weeks on queries.
Recent Sales: *Ripley Under Water*, by Patricia Highsmith (Knopf); *Follow the Dream: Story of Christopher Columbus*, by Peter Sis (Knopf); *Heidi*, by Tomi Ungerer (Delacorte).
Terms: Agent receives 15% commission on domestic sales; 20% on foreign sales. Offers written contract "on demand." If postage expenses get excessive, will discuss with author.
Writers' Conferences: Attends book fairs in Frankfort and Bologna (International Children Book Fair).

JOEL GOTLER INC., (III), 8955 Norma Place, Los Angeles CA 90069. (213)275-6330. FAX: (213)550-7719. Contact: Joel Gotler. Estab. 1986. Represents 50 clients. Specializes in selling movies and TV rights from books.
Will Handle: Nonfiction and novels. Will consider these nonfiction areas: biography/autobiography; history; film; true crime/investigative. Will consider these fiction areas: action/adventure; contemporary issue; detective/police/crime; ethnic; family saga; fantasy; historical; humor/satire; literary; mainstream; mystery/suspense; science fiction; thriller/espionage. Query with SASE and outline plus 2 sample chapters. Will report in 1 month on queries.
Terms: Agent receives 15% commission on domestic book; 10% on film.
Tips: Obtains news clients through recommendations from others.

STANFORD J. GREENBURGER ASSOCIATES (II), 55 Fifth Ave., New York NY 10003. (212)206-5600. FAX: (212)463-8718. Contact: Heide Lange. Estab. 1945. Represents 500 clients. Member agents: Francis Greenburger, Heide Lange, Faith Hamlin, Beth Vesel, Diane Cleaver.
Will Handle: Nonfiction books, textbooks, novels. Will consider all nonfiction areas. Will consider these fiction areas: action/adventure; contemporary issues, detective/police/crime; ethnic; family sage; fantasy; feminist; gay; glitz; historical; humor/satire; juvenile; lesbian; literary; mainstream; mystery/suspense; picture books; psychic/supernatural; regional; science fiction; sports; thriller/espionage; westerns/frontier. Query first. Will report in 1-2 weeks on queries; 1-2 months on mss.
Terms: Agent receives 15% commission on domestic sales; 19% on foreign sales. Charges for photocopying, books for foreign and subsidiary rights submissions.

MAIA GREGORY ASSOCIATES (II), 311 E. 72nd St., New York NY 10021. (212)288-0310. Contact: Maia Gregory. Estab. 1978. Represents 10-12 clients. Currently handles: 80% nonfiction books; 20% novels.
Will Handle: Will consider these nonfiction areas: art; history; language; music/dance/theater/film; religious/inspirational. Will consider literary fiction. Query with SASE and outline plus 1 sample chapter. Will report in 2 weeks on queries.
Terms: Agent receives 10% commission on domestic sales; varies on foreign sales.
Tips: Obtains new clients "through recommendations and queries."

MAXINE GROFFSKY LITERARY AGENCY, 2 Fifth Ave., New York NY 10011. Prefers not to be listed.

THE CHARLOTTE GUSAY LITERARY AGENCY (II, IV), 10532 Blythe, Los Angeles CA 90064. (213)559-0831. FAX: (213)559-2639. Contact: Charlotte Gusay. Estab. 1988. Represents 20 clients. 50% of clients are new/previously unpublished writers. Specializes in fiction, nonfiction, children's with illus-

Agents who specialize in a specific subject area such as children's books or in handling the work of certain writers such as Southwestern writers are ranked IV.

trations. "Percentage breakdown of the manuscripts different at different times."
Will Handle: Nonfiction books, scholarly books, juvenile books, novels, movie scripts. Will consider all nonfiction and fiction areas. No science fiction or horror. Query. Reports in 2-4 weeks on queries; 6-8 weeks on mss.
Recent Sales: *A Visit to the Art Galaxy,* by Annie Reiner (Green Tiger Press); *The Potty Chronicles,* by Annie Reiner (Magination Press); *Love, Groucho: Letters from a Father to His Daughter,* by Groucho Marx and Miriam Marx Allen (Faber & Faber).
Terms: Agent receives 15% commission on domestic sales; 10% on dramatic sales. Charges for "some basic costs for printing, photocopying and mailing may be later assessed, usually agreed upon between author and agent."
Tips: Usually obtains new clients through recommendations.

THE MITCHELL J. HAMILBURG AGENCY (II), Suite 312, 292 S. La Cienega Blvd., Beverly Hills CA 90211. (213)657-1501. Contact: Michael Hamilburg. Estab. 1960. Member of WGA. Represents 40 clients. Currently handles: 75% nonfiction books; 25% novels.
Will Handle: Nonfiction, novels. Will consider all nonfiction areas and most fiction areas. No romance. Send outline plus 2 sample chapters. Reports in 3-4 weeks on mss.
Recent Sales: *A Biography of the Leakey Family,* by Virginia Marrell (Simon & Schuster); *A Biography of Agnes De Mille,* by Carol Easton (Viking).
Terms: Agent receives 10-15% on domestic sales.
Tips: Usually obtains new clients through recommendations from others, at conferences or personal search. "Good luck! Keep writing!"

JOHN HAWKINS & ASSOCIATES, INC. (II), 71 W. 23rd St., New York NY 10010. (212)807-7040. FAX: (212)807-9555. Contact: John Hawkins, William Reiss, Sharon Friedman. Estab. 1893. Member of SAR. Represents 100+ clients. 5-10% of clients are new/previously unpublished writers. Currently handles: 40% nonfiction books; 20% juvenile books; 40% novels.
Will Handle: Nonfiction books, juvenile books, novels. Will consider all nonfiction areas except computers/electronics; religion/inspirational; translations. Will consider all fiction areas except confessional; erotica; fantasy; romance. Query with outline/proposal. Will report in 1 month on queries.
Terms: Agent receives 15% on domestic sales; 20% on foreign sales. Charges for photocopying.
Tips: Obtains new clients through recommendations from others.

GARY L. HEGLER LITERARY AGENCY (III), P.O. Box 890751, Houston TX 77289-0751. (713)486-8478. Contact: Gary L. Hegler or Nikki Cane. Estab. 1985. Member of WGA. 10% of clients are new/ previously unpublished writers. Specializes in young adult, nonfiction. Currently handles: 50% nonfiction books; 30% juvenile books; 5% novels; 5% movie scripts; 10% TV scripts.
Will Handle: Nonfiction books, textbooks, juvenile books, poetry books, movie and TV scripts. Will consider these nonfiction areas: animals; biography/autobiography; health/medicine; juvenile nonfiction; military/war; money/finance/economics; nature/environment; psychology; religious/inspirational; true crime/investigative; science/technology; self-help/personal improvement. Will consider these fiction areas: action/adventure; detective/police/crime; juvenile; mainstream; mystery/suspense; regional (Texas only); romance (contemporary); westerns; young adult. Query with outline plus 3 sample chapters. "First query; then we'll ask for the outline." Will report in 1 week on queries; 2 months on mss.
Recent Sales: *The Ruination of Dan Becker,* by Robin Gibson (Avalon Books); *Blue Hills Robbery,* by Leola Kahrimanis (Eakin Press).
Terms: Agent receives 10% commission on domestic sales; 10% on foreign sales. Offers a written contract, binding for 1 year.
Writers' Conferences: Attends Bay Area Writers Conference; Golden Triangle Writers Guild Conference.
Tips: Obtains new clients through recommendations from authors, from WGA referral listing and conferences. "Be sure the submission is the best you can do, this includes its neatness, accuracy and suspense (if fictional). We will not represent writers who won't actively promote their books."

Agents ranked I-IV are actively seeking new clients. Those ranked V or those who prefer not to be listed have been included to inform you they are not currently looking for new clients.

THE JEFF HERMAN AGENCY INC. (II), #501C, 500 Greenwich St., New York NY 10013. (212)941-0540. Contact: Jeffrey H. Herman. Estab. 1985. Member of ILAA. Represents 50 clients. 20% of clients are new/previously unpublished writers. Specializes in adult nonfiction. Currently handles: 85% nonfiction books; 5% scholarly books; 5% textbooks; 5% novels.
Will Handle: Nonfiction books, textbooks, scholarly books. Will consider all nonfiction areas. Query. Will report in 2 weeks on queries; 1 month on mss.
Recent Sales: *The Insider's Guide to Book Editors, Publishers, and Literary Agents* (St. Martin's Press); *Living With Food In a Fat World* (Simon & Schuster); *The Silva Method for Sales Professionals* (Putnam).
Terms: Agent receives 15% commission on domestic sales. Offers a written contract. Charges for manuscript/proposal photocopying.
Tips: Obtains new clients through referrals and over the transom. "Sell yourself."

SUSAN HERNER RIGHTS AGENCY (II), Suite 1403, 110 W. 40th St., New York NY 10018. (212)221-7515. Contact: Susan Herner or Sue Yuen. Estab. 1987. Represents 50 clients. 25% of clients are new/unpublished writers. Eager to work with new/unpublished writers. Currently handles: 60% nonfiction books; 40% novels.
Will Handle: Nonfiction books and novels. Will consider these fiction areas: literary, romance, science fiction, mystery, thriller, horror, mainstream (genre). Query with outline or send entire manuscript SASE. Reports in 1 month on queries; 2 months on mss.
Recent Sales: *Style Is Not a Size*, by Hara Marano (Bantam); *Dead Ringers*, by Tim Underwood (NAL); *Dream Lovers*, by Mary and Don Kelly (Simon & Schuster).
Terms: Agent receives 15% commission on domestic sales; 20% on dramatic sales; 20% on foreign sales. Charges for extraordinary postage, handling and photocopying. "Agency has two divisions: one represents writers on a comission-only basis; the other represents the rights for small publishers and packagers who do not have in-house subsidiary rights representation. Percentage of income derived from each division is currently 70-30."

FREDERICK HILL ASSOCIATES, 1325 B, N. Olive Dr., West Hollywood CA 90069. (415)921-2910. FAX: (415)921-2802. Contact: Bonnie Nadell. Estab. 1979. Represents 100 clients. 50% of clients are new/unpublished writers. Specializes in general nonfiction, fiction, young adult fiction.
Will Handle: Nonfiction books and novels.
Terms: Agent receives 15% commission on domestic sales; 15% on dramatic sales; 20% on foreign sales. Charges for overseas airmail (books, proofs only), overseas Telex, cable, domestic Telex.

JOHN L. HOCHMANN BOOKS (III), 320 E. 58th St., New York NY 10022. (212)319-0505. President: John L. Hochmann. Estab. 1976. Represents 23 clients. Member of ILAA. Writers must have demonstrable eminence in field or previous publications for nonfiction, and critically and/or commercially successful books for fiction. Prefers to work with published/established authors. Currently handles: 60% nonfiction; 25% textbooks; 15% fiction.
Will Handle: Nonfiction books, textbooks, novels. Query with outline first. Include SASE. Reports in 1 week on queries; 1 month on mss (solicited).
Recent Sales: *500 Years of American Clothing*, by Lee Hall (Little, Brown); *Nutrition Challenge for Women*, by Louise Lambert-Lagacé (General Publishing); *Strategic Communications: How to Make Your Ideas Their Ideas*, by Burton Kaplan (HarperCollins).
Terms: Agent receives 15% commission on domestic sales; additional commission on foreign sales.

BERENICE HOFFMAN LITERARY AGENCY (III), 215 W. 75th St., New York NY 10023. (212)580-9051. FAX: (212)721-8916. Contact: Berenice Hoffman. Estab. 1978. Member of ILAA. Represents 55 clients.
Will Handle: Nonfiction, novels. Will consider all nonfiction areas and most fiction areas. No romance. Query with SASE. Reports in 3-4 weeks on queries.
Terms: Agent receives 15% on domestic sales. Sometimes offers a written contract. Charges of out of the ordinary postage, photocopying.
Tips: Usually obtains new clients through referrals from people she knows.

HOLUB & ASSOCIATES (II), 24 Old Colony Rd., North Stanington CT 06359. (203)535-0689. Contact: William Holub. Estab. 1967. Specializes in Roman Catholic publications. Currently handles: 100% nonfiction books.
Will Handle: Nonfiction books. Will consider these nonfiction areas: biography; religious/inspirational; theology. Query with SASE and outline plus 2 sample chapters.
Terms: Agent receives 15% commission on domestic sales. Charges for postage and photocopying.
Tips: Obtains new clients through recommendations from others.

HULL HOUSE LITERARY AGENCY (II), 240 E. 82nd St., New York NY 10028. (212)988-0725. FAX: (212)794-8758. President: David Stewart Hull. Associate: Lydia Mortimer. Estab. 1987. Represents 38 clients. 15% of clients are new/previously unpublished writers. Specializes in military and general history, true crime, mystery fiction, general commercial fiction. Currently handles: 60% nonfiction books; 40% novels. Member agents: David Stewart Hull (history, biography, military books, true crime, mystery fiction, commercial fiction by published authors); Lydia Mortimer (new fiction by unpublished writers, nonfiction of general nature including women's studies).
Will Handle: Nonfiction books, novels. Will consider these nonfiction areas: anthropology/archaeology; art/architecture/design; biography/autobiography; business; current affairs; ethnic/cultural interests; government/politics/law; history; military/war; money/finance/economics; music/dance/theater/film; true crime/investigative; sociology. Will consider these fiction areas: action/adventure; detective/police/crime; historical; literary; mainstream; mystery/suspense; thriller/espionage. Query with SASE. Will report in 1 week on queries; 1 month on mss.
Terms: Agent receives 15% commission on domestic sales; 20% on foreign sales, "split with foreign agent." Written contract is optional, "at mutual agreement between author and agency." Charges for photocopying, express mail, extensive overseas telephone expenses.
Tips: Obtains new clients through "referrals from clients, listings in various standard publications such as *LMP*, *Writer's Market*, etc." If interested in agency representation, send "a single-page letter outlining your project, always accompanied by an SASE. If nonfiction, sample chapter(s) are often valuable. A record of past publications is a big plus."

INTERNATIONAL CREATIVE MANAGEMENT, 40 W. 57th St., New York NY 10019. Prefers not to be listed.

INTERNATIONAL PUBLISHER ASSOCIATES INC. (II), 746 W. Shore, Sparta NJ 07871. (201)729-9321. Contact: Joseph De Rogatis. Estab. 1983. Represents 15 clients. Currently handles: 90% nonfiction books; 10% novels.
Will Handle: Will consider all nonfiction areas. Will consider mainstream fiction "mostly." Query with SASE. Will report in 3 weeks on queries.
Recent Sales: *A Venom in the Blood*, by Eric Van Hoffmann (Don Fine, hardcover; Zebra, paperback).
Terms: Agent receives 15% commission on domestic sales; 20% on foreign sales. Offers a written contract, binding for life of book. Charges for postage and photocopying.
Tips: Obtains new clients through word of mouth and *Writer's Market*.

SHARON JARVIS & CO., INC. (III), 260 Willard Ave., Staten Island NY 10314. (718)720-2120. Contact: Sharon Jarvis, Joan Winston. Estab. 1984. Member of ILAA. Represents 85 clients. 20% of clients are new/previously unpublished writers. Specializes in genre fiction, popular nonfiction. Currently handles: 25% nonfiction books; 75% novels.
Will Handle: Nonfiction books, "genre fiction." Will consider these nonfiction areas: agriculture/horticulture; biography/autobiography; business; crafts/hobbies; health/medicine; military/war; money/finance/economics; nature/environment; new age/metaphysics; psychology; true crime/investigative; science/technology; self-help/personal improvement. Will consider these fiction areas: action/adventure; detective/police/crime; fantasy; glitz; historical; mainstream; mystery/suspense; psychic/supernatural; romance; science fiction; thriller/espionage. Query only with SASE. Will report in 2 weeks on queries.
Recent Sales: *Encyclopedia Fantastica*, by Kurland & Marano (Prentice Hall); *Moonfire*, by Elizabeth Lane (Silhouette); *Blood Brothers*, by T. Lucien Wright (Zebra).
Terms: Agent receives 15% commission on domestic sales; 10% on foreign sales. Offers a written contract, binding for 1 year. Charges for special services such as overnight mail.
Tips: Obtains new clients through recommendations from publishing professionals and at conferences.

J DE S ASSOCIATES INC. (II), 9 Shagbark Rd., Wilson Point, South Norwalk CT 06854. (203)838-7571. Contact: Jacques de Spoelberch. Estab. 1975. Represents 50 clients. Currently handles: 50% nonfiction books; 50% novels.
Will Handle: Nonfiction books, novels. Will consider these nonfiction areas: biography/autobiography; business; current affairs; ethnic/cultural interests; government/politics/law; health/medicine; history; military/war; new age; self-help/personal improvement; sociology; sports; translations. Will consider these fiction areas: detective/police/crime; historical; juvenile; literary; mainstream; mystery/suspense; westerns/frontier; young adult; new age. Query with SASE. Will report in 2 months on queries.
Terms: Agent receives 15% commission on domestic sales; 20% on foreign sales. Charges for foreign postage and photocopying.
Tips: Obtains new clients through recommendations from others, authors and other clients.

MELANIE JACKSON AGENCY, Suite 1119, 250 W. 57th St., New York NY 10107. Prefers not to be listed.

JANKLOW & NESBIT ASSOCIATES, 598 Madison Ave., New York NY 10022. Prefers not to be listed.

JET LITERARY ASSOCIATES, INC. (III), 124 E. 84th St., New York NY 10028. (212)879-2578. President: James Trupin. Estab. 1976. Represents 85 clients. 5% of clients are new/unpublished writers. Writers must have published articles or books. Prefers to work with published/established authors. Specializes in nonfiction. Currently handles: 50% nonfiction books; 50% novels.
Will Handle: Nonfiction books and novels. Does not read unsolicited mss. Reports in 2 weeks on queries; 1 month on mss.
Recent Sales: *How to Win at Nintendo,* by Jeff Rovin (St. Martin's); *Hoopstats! The Basketball Abstract,* by Josh Trupin (Bantam); *Do Penguins Have Knees?,* by David Feldman; *Boneyards,* by Robert Campbell (Pocket Books).
Terms: Agent receives 15% commission on domestic sales; 15% on dramatic sales; 25% on foreign sales. Charges for international phone and postage expenses.

LEON JONES AGENCY (II), 670 Pine Grove Rd., Roswell GA 30075. (404)640-0714. Contact: Leon Jones. Estab. 1989. Member of SPAR. Represents approximately 20 clients. 50% of clients are new/ previously unpublished writers. Specializes in books on war, movie and tv scripts. Currently handles: 35% nonfiction books; 10% juvenile books; 30% novels; 5% poetry books; 10% movie scripts; 10% tv scripts.
Will Handle: Nonfiction books, juvenile books, novels, novellas, poetry books, movie scripts, tv scripts. Will consider these nonfiction areas: biography/autobiography; child guidance/parenting; history; juvenile nonfiction; military/war; music/dance/theater/film; religious/inspirational; true crime/investigative; self-help/personal improvement; sports; women's issues/women's studies. Will consider these fiction areas: action/adventure; contemporary issues; detective/police/crime; family saga; historical; humor/satire; juvenile; mainstream, mystery/suspense; picture books; regional; religious/inspirational; romance; science fiction; sports, thriller/espionage;young adult. Send entire manuscript or query with outline plus 3 sample chapters. Will report in 1-2 weeks on queries; 2-3 weeks on mss.
Terms: Agent receives 10% commission on domestic sales; 15% on foreign sales. Offers written contract, binding for 1 year. "Sometimes we charge a nominal fee for postage, phone calls, etc."
Writers' Conferences: Attends Dixie Council of Authors Conference; Randell House Conference, Creative Writing Workshop, Biola University Writers Institute.
Tips: "Writers write. Make a commitment to write daily and *never give up!*"

LLOYD JONES LITERARY AGENCY (II), 4301 Hidden Creek, Arlington TX 76016. (817)483-5103. FAX: (817)483-8791. Contact: Lloyd Jones. Estab. 1988. Represents 32 clients. 40% of clients are new/previously unpublished writers. Currently handles: 60% nonfiction books; 10% juvenile books; 30% novels. Member agent: Sheree Sutton (new writers).
Will Handle: Nonfiction books, juvenile books, novels. Will consider these nonfiction areas: business; current affairs; ethnic/cultural interests; health/medicine; juvenile nonfiction; money/finance/economics; psychology; true crime/investigative; self-help/personal improvement; sports; women's issues/ women's studies. Will consider these fiction areas: action/adventure; confessional; contemporary issues; detective/police/crime; erotica; ethnic; juvenile; mainstream; mystery/suspense; picture book; romance; thriller/espionage. Send outline/proposal. Will report in 2 weeks on queries; 6-8 weeks on mss.
Recent Sales: *On My Honor, I Will,* by Marc Bockmon and Randy Pennington (Warner Books); *Tammy Wynette, A Southern Cookbook,* by Tammy Wynette (Pelican Books); *300 New Ways to Get a Job,* by Eleanor Baldwin (Bob Adams Publishing).
Terms: Agent receives 15% commission on domestic sales; 15% on foreign sales. Offers a written contract "for project only."
Tips: Obtains new clients through recommendations from publishers and writers. "Include a bio on writing projects, and define the target market for the proposed book."

LAWRENCE JORDAN LITERARY AGENCY (II), A Division of Morning Star Rising, Inc., Suite 1527, 250 W. 57th St., New York NY 10107. (212)690-2748. President: Lawrence Jordan. Estab. 1978. Represents 30 clients. 25% of clients are new/unpublished writers. Works with a small number of new/ unpublished authors. Specializes in general adult fiction and nonfiction. Currently handles: 1% magazine articles; 1% magazine fiction; 60% nonfiction; 25% novels; 3% textbooks; 2% juvenile books; 3% movie scripts; 5% stage plays.
Will Handle: Magazine articles, magazine fiction, nonfiction books, novels, textbooks, juvenile books, movie scripts, stage plays. Will handle these nonfiction areas: autobiography; business; computer manuals; health; religion; science; self-help; sports. Query with outline. Reports in 3 weeks on queries; 6 weeks on mss.

Recent Sales: *Great Black Russian*, by John Oliver Killens (Wayne State University Press); *Muhammed Ali's Greatest Fights*, by Dr. Ferdie Pacheco (Birch Lane Press); *Sippi*, by John Oliver Killens (Thunder's Mouth Press).
Terms: Agent receives 15% commission on domestic sales; 20% on dramatic sales; 20% on foreign sales. Charges long-distance calls, photocopying, foreign submission costs, postage, cables and messengers. Makes 1% of income from fees.

THE KARPFINGER AGENCY (II), Suite 2800, 500 5th Ave., New York NY 10110. Prefers not to be listed.

LOUISE B. KETZ AGENCY (II), Suite 4B, 1485 1st Ave., New York NY 10021. (212)535-9259. Contact: Louise B. Ketz. Estab. 1983. Represents 16 clients. 15% of clients are new/previously unpublished writers. Specializes in science, business, sports, history and reference. Currently handles: 100% nonfiction books.
Will Handle: Nonfiction books. Will consider these nonfiction areas: anthropology/archaeology; biography/autobiography; business; current affairs; history; military/war; money/finance/economics; true crime/investigative; science/technology; sports. Send outline plus 2 sample chapters. Will report in 4-6 weeks on queries; 4-6 weeks on mss.
Terms: Agent receives 10-15% commission on domestic sales; 10% on foreign sales. Offers a written contract.
Tips: Obtains new clients through "recommendations, idea development."

VIRGINIA KIDD, LITERARY AGENT (V), Box 278, Milford PA 18337. Agency not currently seeking new clients.

KIDDE, HOYT & PICARD (III), 335 E. 51st St., New York NY 10022. (212)755-9401. Contact: Katherine Kidde. Estab. 1980. Member of SAR. Represents 50 clients. Specializes in mainstream fiction. Currently handles: 12% nonfiction books; 5% juvenile books; 80% novels; 2% novellas; 1% poetry books. Member agent: Mary Nichols.
Will Handle: Nonfiction books, novels. Will consider these nonfiction areas: animals; biography; gay/lesbian issues; photography; psychology; religious/inspirational; self-help; women's issues. Will consider these fiction areas: detective/police/crime; feminist; gay; humor/satire; lesbian; literary; mainstream; mystery/suspense; romance; thrillers. Query. Will report in a few weeks on queries; 3-4 weeks on mss.
Recent Sales: *Murder Uptown*, by Donna Hill (Carroll & Graf); *Calling Home*, by Michael Cadnum (Viking); *A Murder in the Family*, by Lydia Long (St. Martin's); *Best Friends*, by Martha Humphreys (Houghton Mifflin).
Terms: Agent receives 10% on domestic sales; 10% on foreign sales. Charges for photocopying.
Tips: Obtains new clients through recommendations from others, "former authors from when I was an editor at NAL, Harcourt, etc.; listings in *LMP*, writers guides."

KIRCHOFF/WOHLBERG, INC., AUTHORS' REPRESENTATION DIVISION (II), 866 United Nations Plaza, #525, New York NY 10017. (212)644-2020. FAX: (212)223-4387. Director of Operations: John R. Whitman. Estab. 1930's. Member of Association of American Publishers, Society of Illustrators, SPAR, Bookbuilders of Boston, New York Bookbinders' Guild, AIGA. Represent 30 authors. 33% of clients are new/previously unpublished writers. Specializes in juvenile and young adult trade books and textbooks. Currently handles: 5% nonfiction books; 80% juvenile books; 5% novels; 5% novellas; 5% young adult. Member agent: Elizabeth Pulitzer (juvenile and young adult authors).
Will Handle: "We are interested in any original projects of quality that are appropriate to the juvenile and young adult trade book markets." Send "either a query or a query that includes an outline and a sample; SASE required." Will report in 1 month on queries; 6 weeks on mss.
Recent Sales: *Color Farm*, by Lois Ehlert (Lippincott); *Fish Eyes*, by Lois Ehlert (HBJ); *Last Summer With Maizon*, by Jacqueline Woodson (Delacorte Press).
Terms: Agent receives standard commission "depends upon whether it is an author only, illustrator only, or an author/illustrator book." Offers a written contract, binding for not less than six months.
Tips: "Usually obtains new clients through recommendations from authors, illustrators and editors. Kirchoff/Wohlberg has been in business for over 50 years."

HARVEY KLINGER, INC. (III), 301 W. 53 St., New York NY 10019. (212)581-7068. FAX: (212)315-3823. Contact: Harvey Klinger. Estab. 1977. Represents 100 clients. 25% of clients are new/previously unpublished writers. Specializes in "big, mainstream contemporary fiction and nonfiction." Currently handles: 50% nonfiction books; 50% novels.

Will Handle: Nonfiction books, novels. Will consider these nonfiction areas: biography/autobiography; cooking/food/nutrition; health/medicine; psychology; true crime/investigative; science/technology; self-help/personal improvement; sports; women's issues/women's studies. Will consider these fiction areas: action/adventure; detective/police/crime; family saga; glitz; literary; mainstream; mystery/suspense; romance (contemporary); thriller/espionage. Query. Will report in 2 weeks on queries; 6-8 weeks on mss.

Recent Sales: *Secrets About Men Every Woman Should Know*, by Barbara DeAngelis (Delacorte); *The Dreaming*, by Barbara Wood (Random House); *Stars*, by Kathryn Harvey (Villard).

Terms: Agent receives 15% commission on domestic sales; 25% on foreign sales. Offers a written contract. Charges for photocopying manuscripts, overseas postage for manuscripts.

Tips: Obtains new clients through recommendations from others. "Perservere!"

BARBARA S. KOUTS, LITERARY AGENT (II), P.O. Box 558, Bellport NY 11713. (516)286-1278. Contact: Barbara Kouts. Estab. 1980. Member of ILAA. Represent 50 clients. 50% of clients are new/previously unpublished writers. Specializes in adult fiction and nonfiction and children's books. Currently handles: 20% nonfiction books; 40% juvenile books; 40% novels.

Will Handle: Nonfiction books, juvenile books, novels. Will consider these nonfiction areas: biography/autobiography; business; child guidance/parenting; current affairs; ethnic/cultural interests; health/medicine; history; juvenile nonfiction; music/dance/theater/film; nature/environment; psychology; self-help/personal improvement; women's issues/women's studies. Will consider these fiction areas: contemporary issues; family saga; feminist; historical; juvenile; literary; mainstream; mystery/suspense; picture book; romance (gothic, historical); young adult. Query. Will report in 2-3 days on queries; 4-6 weeks on mss.

Recent Sales: *Carnal Acts*, by Nancy Mairs (HarperCollins); *The Talking Eggs*, by Robert San Souci (Dial); *Bed and Breakfast Across North America*, by Hal Gieseking (Simon & Schuster).

Terms: Agent receives 10% commission on domestic sales; 20% on foreign sales. Charges for photocopying.

Writers' Conferences: Attends Trenton State College Conference and Society of Children's Book Writers Conference.

Tips: Obtains new clients through recommendations from others, solicitation, at conferences, etc. "Write, do not call. Be professional in your writing."

LUCY KROLL AGENCY (II,III), 390 W. End Ave., New York NY 10024. (212)877-0627. FAX: (212)769-2832. Agent: Barbara Hogenson. Member of SAR and WGA East and West. Represents 60 clients. 5% of clients are new/unpublished writers. Specializes in nonfiction, screenplays, plays. Currently handles: 45% nonfiction books; 15% novels; 15% movie scripts; 25% stage plays.

Will Handle: Nonfiction, movie and TV scripts, stage plays. Query with outline and SASE. Does not read unsolicited manuscripts. Reports in 1 month.

Terms: Agent receives 10% commission on domestic sales; 10% on dramatic sales; 20% on foreign sales.

EDITE KROLL LITERARY AGENCY (II), 12 Grayhurst Park, Portland ME 04102. (207)773-4922. FAX: (207)773-3936. Contact: Edite Kroll. Estab. 1981. Represents 40 clients. Currently handles: 60% adult books; 40% juvenile books.

Will Handle: Nonfiction, juvenile books, novels. Will consider these nonfiction areas: social issues (especially feminist); child guidance/parenting; current affairs; health/medicine; juvenile nonfiction. Will consider these fiction areas: contemporary issues; feminist; humor/satire; juvenile; literary; mainstream; mystery/suspense; picture book. Query with SASE. For nonfiction, send outline/proposal. For fiction, send outline plus 1 sample chapter. Reports in 2 weeks on queries; 6 weeks on mss.

Terms: Agent receives 15% on domestic sales; 20% on foreign sales. Offers a written contract if requested. Charges for photocopying, legal fees.

Tips: Obtains new clients through referrals from writers, agents and publishers.

PETER LAMPACK AGENCY, INC. (II), Suite 2015, 551 5th Ave., New York NY 10017. (212)687-9106. FAX: (212)687-9109. Contact: Peter Lampack. Estab. 1977. Represents 40 clients. 10% of clients are new/previously unpublished writers. Specializes in commercial fiction, male-oriented action/adventure, contemporary relationships, distinguished literary fiction, nonfiction by a recognized expert in a given field. Currently handles: 15% nonfiction books; 80% novels; 5% movie scripts. Member agents: Peter Lampack (commercial fiction, action/adventure, literary fiction, nonfiction, contemporary relationships); Anthony Gardner (international thrillers, important nonfiction, humor); Sandra Blanton (contemporary relationships, psychological thrillers, mysteries).

Will Handle: Nonfiction books, novels, movie scripts. Will consider these nonfiction areas: biography/autobiography; business; current affairs; government/politics/law; health/medicine; history; money/finance/economics; true crime/investigative. Will consider these fiction areas: action/adventure; car-

toon/comic; contemporary relationships; detective/police/crime; family saga; glitz; historical; literary; mystery/suspense; thriller/espionage. Query. Will report in 2 weeks on queries; 1 month on mss.
Recent Sales: *The Wild Rose*, by Doris Montman (Bantam Books); *Age of Iron*, by V.M. Goetzee (Random House); *Pomp and Circumstance*, by Fred Mustard Stewart (NAL); *Private Lies*, by Warren Adler (William Morrow); *Playing With the Pros*, by John Coyne (NAL); *Someone's Watching*, by Judith Kelman.
Terms: Agent receives 15% commission on domestic sales; 20% on foreign sales. Offers a written contract, binding for 1-3 years. "Writer is required to furnish copies of his/her work for submission purposes."
Tips: Obtains new clients from referrals made by clients. "Submit only your best work for consideration. Have a very specific agenda of goals you wish your prospective agent to accomplish for you. Provide the agent with a comprehensive statement of your credentials — educational and professional."

THE ROBERT LANTZ-JOY HARRIS LITERARY AGENCY (II), (Division of the Lantz Office), 888 7th Ave., New York NY 10106. (212)586-0200. FAX: (212)262-6659. Contact: Joy Harris. Member of SAR. Represents 150 clients. Currently handles: 30% nonfiction books; 70% novels.
Will Handle: Will consider "adult-type books, not juvenile." Will consider all fiction areas except fantasy; juvenile; science fiction; westerns/frontier. Query with SASE and outline/proposal. Will report in 1-2 months on queries.
Terms: Agent receives 10% commission on domestic sales; 20% on foreign sales. Offers a written contract. Charges for extra expenses.
Tips: Obtains new clients through recommendations from clients and editors. "No unsolicited manuscripts, just query letters."

MICHAEL LARSEN/ELIZABETH POMADA LITERARY AGENTS (II), 1029 Jones St., San Francisco CA 94109. (415)673-0939. Contact: Mike Larsen or Elizabeth Pomada. Estab. 1972. Member of ILAA. Represents 100 clients. 50-55% of clients are new/unpublished writers. Eager to work with new/unpublished writers. "We have very catholic tastes and do not specialize. We handle literary, commercial, and genre fiction, and the full range of nonfiction books." Currently handles: 60% nonfiction books; 40% novels.
Will Handle: Adult nonfiction books and novels. Query with the first 30 pages and synopsis of completed novel, or nonfiction book proposal. Reports in 2 months on queries. For nonfiction, call first. "Always include SASE. Send SASE for brochure."
Recent Sales: *The Last Innocent Hour*, by Margot Abbott (St. Martin's); *Guerrilla Selling*, by Jay Levinson (Houghton); *The Victorian Wedding*, by Georgene M. Lockwood (Prentice Hall).
Terms: Agent receives 15% commission on domestic sales; 15% on dramatic sales; 20% on foreign sales. May charge writer for printing, postage for multiple submissions, foreign mail, foreign phone calls, galleys, books, and legal fees.

M. SUE LASBURY LITERARY AGENCY (I), 4861 Ocean Blvd., San Diego CA 92109. (619)483-7170. FAX: (619)483-1853. Contact: Sue Lasbury or John Cochran, Associate. Estab. 1990. Represents 12 clients. 40% of clients are new/previously unpublished writers. "We focus primarily, but not exclusively, on West Coast academics who want to write for the general trade book market." Currently handles: 80% nonfiction books; 20% novels. Member agents: M. Sue Lasbury; John C. Cochran.
Will Handle: Will consider these nonfiction areas: animals; biography/autobiography; business; current affairs; government/politics/law; health/medicine; history; money/finance/economics; nature/environment; psychology; true crime/investigative; science/technology; self-help/personal improvement; sociology; sports; women's issues/women's studies. Will consider these fiction areas: contemporary issues; detective/police/crime; historical; literary; mainstream; mystery/suspense. Query. Will report in 3 weeks on queries; 6 weeks on mss.
Terms: Agent receives 15% commission on domestic sales; 20% on foreign sales. Offers a written contract, which varies book by book and can be cancelled by author at any time. Charges for long-distance phone calls, photocopying, shipping, fax, etc.
Writers' Conferences: Attends Pacific Northwest Writers Conference, California Writers Club Conference at Asilomar and UCSD Extension Conference.
Tips: Obtains new clients through recommendations from others. "I travel to meet with potential clients all over the West. Sometimes I seek out authors, they are recommended to me, or they contact me directly. Nonfiction authors should have a strong, well-developed book idea. They should carefully research the market and be prepared to do a thoughtful proposal and at least one or two sample chapters. For first time authors, a novel should be completed before seeking an agent."

THE LAZEAR AGENCY INCORPORATED (II), Suite 416, 430 1st Ave., Minneapolis MN 55401. (612)332-8640. FAX: (612)332-4648. Contact: Kate Garfield. Estab. 1984. Represents 350 clients. 20% of clients are new/previously unpublished writers. Currently handles: 40% nonfiction books; 20%

juvenile books; 29% novels; 1% short story collections; 5% movie scripts; 2.5% TV scripts; 2.5% syndicated material. Member agents: Mary Meehan (vp, director of books, non-book related licensing and marketing); Bonnie Blodgett (director of book packaging and literary development); Peggy Kelly (director of audio and video rights); Jack Caravela (director of science fiction, fantasy, horror, new fiction) and 4 other generalist agents.
Will Handle: Nonfiction books, juvenile books, novels, novellas, short story collections, movie and TV scripts, syndicated material. Will consider all nonfiction areas, plus "recovery, humor, heavily illustrated books." Will consider all fiction areas. Query with outline/proposal. No unsolicited mss. Will report in 3 weeks on queries.
Terms: Agent receives 15% commission on domestic sales; 20% on foreign sales. Offers a written contract, binding "for term of copyright." Charges for "photocopying, international Federal Express."
Tips: Obtains new clients through recommendations from others, "through the bestseller lists, word of mouth. The writer should first view himself as a salesperson in order to attain an agent. Sell yourself, your idea, your concept. Do your homework. Notice what is in the marketplace that is or is not like what you're doing. Be sophisticated about the arena in which you are aiming your work."

THE NED LEAVITT AGENCY (I,II), #4F, 70 Wooster St., New York NY 10012. (212)334-0999. Contact: Ned Leavitt. Estab. 1990. Represents 40 clients. 20% of clients are new/previously unpublished writers. Specializes in literary and commercial fiction, strong narrative nonfiction, psychology and spirituality. Currently handles: 55% nonfiction books; 45% novels.
Will Handle: Novels, novellas, short story collections. Will consider these nonfiction areas: biography/ autobiography; business; child guidance/parenting; health/medicine; history; nature/environment; new age/metaphysics; psychology; religious/inspirational; true crime/investigative; science/technology; self-help/personal improvement; sports; translations; women's issues/women's studies; men's issues/men's studies. Will consider these fiction areas: action/adventure; contemporary issues; detective/police/ crime; erotica; family saga; fantasy; glitz; historical; humor/satire; literary; mainstream; mystery/suspense; psychic/supernatural; religious/inspirational; science fiction; sports; thriller/espionage; westerns/frontier. Query with outline/proposal. Will report in 1 week on queries; 3 weeks on mss. "SASE is *required* or material will not be returned. Postage alone is not acceptable."
Terms: Agent receives 15% commission on domestic sales; 20-25% on foreign sales. Offers written contract. Charges for postage, phone, photocopying directly related to work.
Tips: Obtains new clients through recommendations, solicitation, conferences. "Although I began my own agency in 1990, I spent 15 years with the William Morris Agency."

THE ADELE LEONE AGENCY, INC. (II), 26 Nantucket Pl., Scarsdale NY 10583. (914)901-2965. FAX: (914)337-0361. Contact: Ralph Leone. Estab. 1978. Represents 50 clients. 20% of clients are new/ previously unpublished writers. Specializes in women's fiction, romance (historical, contemporary), horror, science fiction, nonfiction, hard science, self-help, parenting, nutrition. Currently handles: 40% nonfiction books; 60% novels. Member agents: Adele Leone, Ralph Leone, Richard Monaco.
Will Handle: Nonfiction books, novels. Will consider these nonfiction areas: biography/autobiography; business; child guidance/parenting; cooking/food/nutrition; crafts/hobbies; current affairs; ethnic/cultural interests; gay/lesbian issues; government/politics/law; health/medicine; history; interior design/ decorating; language/literature/criticism; military/war; money/finance/economics; music/dance/theater/film; nature/environment; new age/metaphysics; psychology; true crime/investigative; science/ technology; self-help/personal improvement; sports; women's issues/women's studies. Will consider these fiction areas: action/adventure; detective/police/crime; family saga; fantasy; glitz; historical; literary; mainstream; mystery/suspense; psychic/supernatural; romance; science fiction; thriller/espionage; westerns/frontier. Query. Will report in 2 weeks on queries; 6 weeks on mss.
Recent Sales: *Cold Fusion,* by F. David Peat (Contemporary Books); *Fire in the Crucible,* by John Briggs (St. Martin's Press, Jeremy Tarcher); *Wings of a Dove,* by Elaine Barbieri (Berkley).
Terms: Agent receives 15% commission on domestic sales; 15% on foreign sales, "unless foreign agent is used, then 10%." Offers a written contract, binding "no less than 1 year." Charges "only for special services performed at author's request."
Writers' Conferences: Attends RWA Conference; PENN Writers Conference; Harper's Ferry Conference.
Tips: Obtains new clients through recommendations from others, at conferences. "Send simple clear queries and return postage."

LESCHER & LESCHER LTD. (II), 67 Irving Pl., New York NY 10003. (212)529-1790. FAX: (212)529-2719. Contact: Robert or Susan Lescher. Estab. 1967. Member of SAR. Represents 150 clients. Currently handles: 75% nonfiction books; 13% juvenile books; 12% novels.
Will Handle: Nonfiction, juvenile books, novels. Will consider these nonfiction areas: biography/ autobiography; parenting; cooking/food; current affairs; government/politics/law; health/medicine; history; juvenile nonfiction; film; psychology; women's issues/women's studies. Will consider these

fiction areas: contemporary issues; historical; humor/satire; juvenile; literary; mystery/suspense; thriller/espionage. Query with SASE. Reports in 2 weeks on queries.
Terms: Agent receives 15% commission on domestic sales; 20-25% on foreign sales. Charges for photocopying mss and copywriting fees.
Tips: Usually obtains new clients through recommendations from others.

LEVANT & WALES, LITERARY AGENCY, INC. (IV), 108 Hayes St., Seattle WA 98109. (206)284-7114. FAX: (206)286-1025. Agents: Elizabeth Wales and Dan Levant. Estab. 1988. Member of Pacific Northwest Writers' Conference, Book Publishers' Northwest. Represents 40 clients. We are interested in published and not yet published writers. Prefers writers from the Pacific Northwest. Specializes in nonfiction and mainstream fiction. Currently handles: 75% nonfiction books; 25% novels.
Recent Sales: *Riding in a Convertible With the Top Down,* by Killien and Bender (Warner); *Aftermath: A Survivor's Story of Rape,* by Scherer (Prentice Hall).
Will Handle: Nonfiction books and novels. Will consider these nonfiction areas: biography, business, cookbooks, gardening, health, lifestyle, nature, popular culture, psychology, science. Will consider these fiction areas: mainstream (no genre fiction). Query first. Reports in 3 weeks on queries; 1 month on mss.
Terms: Agent receives 15% commission on domestic sales. We make all our income from commissions. We offer editorial help for some of our clients and help some clients with the development of a proposal, but we do not charge for these services. We do charge, after a sale, for express mail, ms photocopying costs, foreign postage and outside USA telephone costs.

JAMES LEVINE COMMUNICATIONS (II), 330 7th Ave., New York NY 10001. (212)268-4846. FAX: (212)465-8637. Contact: James A. Levine. Estab. 1989. Specializes in early childhood education, family issues. Currently handles: 80% nonfiction books; 5% scholarly books; 10% juvenile books; 5% novels.
Will Handle: Nonfiction books, juvenile books, novels. Will consider these nonfiction areas: business; child guidance/parenting; computers/electronics; current affairs; government/politics/law; health/medicine; money/finance/economics; psychology; true crime/investigative. Will consider these fiction areas: contemporary issues; juvenile; young adult. Query with outline plus 1 or 2 sample chapters. Will report in 2 weeks on queries; 1 month on mss.
Recent Sales: *Bionomics,* by Michael Rothschild (Henry Holt); *Parenting by Heart,* by Ron Taffel (Addison-Wesley).
Terms: Agent receives 15% commission on domestic sales; 15% on foreign sales. Offers a written contract. Charges miscellaneous office expenses, postage, telephone, etc.
Tips: Obtains new clients through recommendations from others, solicitations.

ELLEN LEVINE LITERARY AGENCY, INC. (II, III), Suite 1801, 15 E. 26th St., New York NY 10010. (212)889-0620. FAX: (212)725-4501. Contact: Ellen Levine, Diana Finch, Anne Dubuisson. "My two younger colleagues at the agency (Anne Dubuisson and Diana Finch) are seeking both new and established writers. I prefer to work with established writers, mostly through referrals." Estab. 1980. Member of SAR, ILAA. Represents over 100 clients. 20% of clients are new/previously unpublished writers. Specializes in literary fiction, women's fiction, women's issues, books by journalists, biographies. Currently handles: 45% nonfiction books; 8% juvenile books; 45% novels; 2% short story collections.
Will Handle: Nonfiction books, textbooks, juvenile books, novels, short story collections. Query. Will report in 2-3 weeks on queries, if SASE provided; 4-6 weeks on mss, if submission requested.
Terms: Agent receives 15% commission on domestic sales; 20% on foreign sales. Charges for overseas postage, photocopying, messenger fees, overseas telephone and fax, books ordered for use in rights submissions.
Tips: Obtains new clients through recommendations from others.

ROBERT LEWIS, 65 E. 96th St., New York NY 10128. Agency not currently seeking new clients. Published writers may query.

RAY LINCOLN LITERARY AGENCY (II), Suite 107-B, Elkins Park House, 7900 Old York Rd., Elkins Park PA 19117. (215)635-0827. Contact: Mrs. Ray Lincoln. Estab. 1974. Represents 34 clients. 35% of clients are new/previously unpublished writers. Specializes in "biography, nature, the sciences, fiction in both adult and children's categories." Currently handles: 30% nonfiction books, 20% juvenile books, 50% novels.
Will Handle: Nonfiction books, scholarly books, juvenile books, novels. Will consider these nonfiction areas: horticulture; animals; anthropology/archaeology; art/architecture/design; biography/autobiography; business; child guidance/parenting; cooking/food/nutrition; crafts/hobbies; current affairs; ethnic/cultural interests; gay/lesbian issues; government/politics/law; health/medicine; history; interior design/decorating; juvenile nonfiction; language/literature/criticism; money/finance/economics; music/

dance/theater/film; nature/environment; psychology; science/technology; self-help/personal improvement; sociology; sports; women's issues/women's studies. Will consider these fiction areas: action/adventure; contemporary issues; detective/police/crime; ethnic; family saga; fantasy; feminist; gay; historical; humor/satire; juvenile; lesbian; literary; mainstream; mystery/suspense; psychic/supernatural; regional; romance (contemporary, gothic, historical); science fiction; sports; thriller/espionage; young adult. Query "first, then send outline plus 2 sample chapters with SASE. I send for balance of ms if it is a likely project." Will report in 2 weeks on queries; 1 month on mss.
Recent Sales: A biography by Willard S. Randall (Henry Holt); a young adult novella by Jerry Spinelli (Simon & Schuster); a young adult novella by Joel Schwartz (Dell).
Terms: Agent receives commission 15% on domestic sales; 20% on foreign sales. Offers a written contract, binding "but with notice, may be cancelled." Charges "only for overseas telephone calls. I request authors to do manuscript photocopying themselves. No other expenses."
Tips: Obtains new clients usually from recommendations. "I always look for polished writing style, fresh points of view and professional attitudes."

WENDY LIPKIND AGENCY (II), 165 E 66th St., New York NY 10021. (212)628-9653. FAX: (212)628-2693. Contact: Wendy Lipkind. Estab. 1977. Member of ILAA. Represents 60 clients. Specializes in adult nonfiction. Currently handles: 80% nonfiction books; 20% novels.
Will Handle: Nonfiction, novels. Will consider these nonfiction areas: biography; current affairs; health/medicine; history; science/technology; social history. Will consider mainstream and mystery/suspense fiction. No mass market originals. For nonfiction query with outline/proposal. For fiction query with SASE only. Reports in 1 month on queries.
Terms: Agent receives 15% commission on domestic sales; 20% on foreign sales. Sometimes offers a written contract. Charges for foreign postage and messenger service.
Tips: Usually obtains new clients through recommendations from others. "Send intelligent query letter first. Let me know if you sent to other agents."

LITERARY AND CREATIVE ARTISTS AGENCY (III), 3539 Albemarle St. NW, Washington DC 20008. (202)362-4688. President: Muriel Nellis. Associate: Jane Roberts. Estab. 1982. Member of Authors Guild and associate member of American Bar Association. Represents 42 clients. "While we prefer published writers, it is not required if the proposed work has great merit." Requires exclusive review of material; no simultaneous submissions. Currently handles: 65% nonfiction books; 20% novels; 5% juvenile books; 5% movie scripts; 5% cookbooks and other one-shots.
Will Handle: Nonfiction books, novels, theatrical and TV scripts. Will consider these nonfiction areas: business, cooking, health, how-to, human drama, lifestyle, memoir, philosophy, politics. Query with outline and bio. Does not read unsolicited mss. Reports in 2 weeks on queries.
Recent Sales: *Quantum Healing*, by Dr. D. Chopra (Bantam); *100 Over 100*, by Heynen/Boyer (Fulcrum); *Asian Grills*, by A. Greeley (Doubleday); *Snake In, Snake Out*, by L. Banchek; *Quantum Golf*, by K. Enhager (Warner).
Terms: Agent receives 15% commission on domestic sales; 20% on dramatic sales; 25% on foreign sales. Charges for long-distance phone and fax, photocopying and shipping.

THE LITERARY GROUP (II), #7A, 153 E. 32nd St., New York NY 10016. (212)873-0972. FAX: (212)873-6169. Contact: Frank Weimann. Estab. 1985. Represents 45 clients. 75% of clients are new/previously unpublished writers. Specializes in nonfiction (true crime; biography; sports; how-to). Currently handles: 80% nonfiction books; 20% novels.
Will Handle: Nonfiction books, novels. Will consider these nonfiction areas: animals; biography/autobiography; business; child guidance/parenting; current affairs; gay/lesbian issues; health/medicine; history; music/dance/theater/film; nature/environment; psychology; true crime/investigative; self-help/personal improvement; sociology; sports; women's issues/women's studies. Will consider these fiction areas: action/adventure; detective/police/crime; humor/satire; mystery/suspense; sports; thriller/espionage. Query with outline plus 3 sample chapters. Will report in 1 week on queries; 1 month on mss.
Recent Sales: *Doublecross*, by Sam Giancana (Warner); *My Father, John Wayne*, by Aissa Wayne/Steve Delsohn (Random House); *Purple Haze*, by Joel Selvin (E.P. Dutton).
Terms: Agent receives 15% commission on domestic sales; 20% on foreign sales. Offers a written contract, which "can be cancelled after 30 days."
Writers' Conferences: Attends Florida Suncoast Writers Conference; Southwest Writers Conference; Palm Springs Writers Group.
Tips: Obtains new clients through referrals, writers conferences, query letters.

LIVING FAITH LITERARY AGENCY (II), P.O. Box 566397, Atlanta GA 30356. (404)640-0714. Agent: M.L. Jones. Estab. 1988. Represents 16 clients. 20% of clients are new/unpublished writers. Specializes in inspirational/religious books.

Will Handle: Nonfiction and fiction books, poetry, textbooks, children's books. Send first 3 chapters and chapter synopsis of remaining chapters.
Terms: Charges 15% commission on domestic sales; 20% on foreign sales. Charges for photocopying, postal and delivery expenses, ms retyping "if required" and phone calls.

STERLING LORD LITERISTIC, INC. (III), One Madison Ave., New York NY 10010. (212)696-2800. FAX: (212)686-6976. Contact: Peter Matson. Estab. 1952. Member of SAR, WGA. Represents 500 + clients. Specializes in "mainstream nonfiction and fiction." Currently handles: 50% nonfiction books, 50% novels. Member agents: Peter Matson, Sterling Lord; Jody Hotchkiss (film scripts); Elizabeth Kaplan; Phillipa Brophy; Stuart Krichevsky; Elizabeth Grossman.
Will Handle: Nonfiction books, novels. Will consider "mainstream nonfiction and fiction." Query. Will report in 1 month on mss.
Terms: Agent receives 10% commission on domestic sales; 20% on foreign sales. Offers a written contract. Charges for photocopying.
Tips: Obtains new clients through recommendations from others.

LOS ANGELES LITERARY ASSOCIATES (II), 6324 Tahoe Dr., Los Angeles CA 90068. (213)464-6444. Contact: Andrew Ellinger. Estab. 1984. Specializes in nonfiction books. Currently handles: 70% non-fiction books; 30% novels.
Will Handle: Nonfiction and novels. Will consider these nonfiction areas: biography; business; history; money/finance/economics; self-help/personal improvement; inspirational. Will consider these fiction areas: contemporary issues; mainstream; thriller/espionage. Query with SASE and outline/proposal. Reports in 1 month on queries.
Terms: Agent receives 10-15% commission on domestic sales; varies on foreign sales.
Writers' Conferences: Attends Santa Barbara Writers Conference.
Tips: Usually obtains new clients by word of mouth and referrals. "Do your grass roots market research, in bookstores and the library. It's important not to forget about your libraries because they'll give you a depth of knowledge that can't be found in cruising a typical bookstore."

NANCY LOVE LITERARY AGENCY (III), 250 E. 65th St., New York NY 10021. (212)980-3499. FAX: (212)308-6405. Contact: Nancy Love. Estab. 1984. Member of ILAA. Represents 60 clients. Specializes in adult nonfiction. Currently handles: 90% nonfiction books; 10% novels.
Will Handle: Nonfiction books, novels. Will consider these nonfiction areas: biography/autobiography; business; child guidance/parenting; cooking/food/nutrition; current affairs; ethnic/cultural interests; government/politics/law; health/medicine; history; money/finance/economics; nature/environment; psychology; true crime/investigative; science/technology; self-help/personal improvement; sociology; women's issues/women's studies. Will consider these fiction areas: action/adventure; contemporary issues; detective/police/crime; ethnic; literary; mainstream; mystery/suspense; thriller/espionage. "For nonfiction, send a proposal, chapter summary and sample chapter. For fiction, send the first 40-50 pages plus summary of the rest (will consider only *completed* novels)." Will report in 2 weeks on queries; 3 weeks on mss.
Recent Sales: *Cracking the Nutrition Code*, by Victor Herbert, M.D. (Macmillan); *Reclaiming Pleasure*, by Susan Bakos (St. Martin's Press); *Cruelty-Free Products*, by Lori Cook (Bantam Books).
Terms: Agent receives 15% commission on domestic sales; 20% on foreign sales. Offers a written contract. Charge for photocopying, "if it runs over $20."
Tips: Obtains new clients through recommendations and solicitation. "Many also come through the Writer's Union, where I have a number of clients and a very high rating. I prefer a call to a query letter. That cuts out a step and allows me to express my preference for an exclusive and to discuss the author's credentials. I can also tell a writer that I won't return material without an SASE."

LOWENSTEIN ASSOCIATES, INC. (II), #601, 121 W. 27th St., New York NY 10001. (212)206-1630. President: Barbara Lowenstein. Agents: Norman Kurz and Nancy Yost. Estab. 1976. Member of ILAA. Represents 120 clients. 15% of clients are new/unpublished writers. Specializes in nonfiction — especially science and medical-topic books for the general public — general fiction. Currently handles: 2% magazine articles; 55% nonfiction books; 43% novels.
Will Handle: Nonfiction books and novels. Will consider these nonfiction areas: medicine, science. Will consider these fiction areas: romance (historical, contemporary) and "bigger women's fiction," mainstream. Query. Will not accept unsolicited mss.
Terms: Agent receives 15% commission on domestic sales; 15% on dramatic sales; 20% on foreign sales. Charges for photocopying, foreign postage and messenger expenses.

MARGRET MCBRIDE LITERARY AGENCY (II), Suite 225, 4350 Executive Dr., San Diego CA 92121. (619)457-0550. FAX: (619)457-2315. Contact: Winifred Golden. Estab. 1980. Member of ILAA. Represents 25 clients. 10% of clients are new/unpublished writers. Specializes in historical biographies, literary fiction, mainstream fiction and nonfiction.

Will Handle: Nonfiction books, novels, syndicated material. Query with outline. Does not read unsolicited mss. Reports in 6 weeks on queries. "We are looking for two more novelists to complete our client list."
Recent Sales: *Consequences*, by John G. Tower (Little, Brown); *Why Men Don't Get Enough Sex and Women Don't Get Enough Love*, by Jonathon Kraner and Diane Dunaway (Pocket); *Discovering the Future*, by Joel Arthur Barker (William Morrow).
Terms: Agent receives 15% commission on domestic sales; 10% on dramatic sales; 25% on foreign sales.

DONALD MACCAMPBELL INC. (III), 12 E. 41st St., New York NY 10017. (212)683-5580. Editor: Maureen Moran. Estab. 1940. Represents 50 clients. "The agency does not handle unpublished writers." Specializes in women's book-length fiction in all categories. Currently handles: 100% novels.
Will Handle: Novels. Query; does not read unsolicited mss. Reports in 1 week on queries.
Recent Sales: *Love & Smoke*, by Jennifer Blake (Ballantine); *Special Assistant*, by Emilie McGee (Silhouette); *Tycoon's Daughter*, by Lynn Drennan (Doubleday).
Terms: Agent receives 10% commission on domestic sales; 20% on foreign sales.

GERARD MCCAULEY (III), P.O. Box AE, Katonah NY 10536. (914)232-5700. FAX: (914)232-1506. Estab. 1970. Member of SAR. Represents 60 clients. 10% of clients are new/previously unpublished writers. Specializes in history, biography and general nonfiction. Currently handles: 65% nonfiction books; 15% scholarly books; 20% textbooks. "Developing commercial fiction list through Henry O. Houghton. Write 53 Garland Rd., Concord MA 01742."
Will Handle: Nonfiction books, textbooks, novels ("novels go to Henry Houghton"). Will consider these nonfiction areas: biography/autobiography; current affairs; history; military/war; sports. Query. Will report in 1 month on queries; 2 months on mss.
Recent Sales: *Baseball*, by Ken Burns and Geoffrey Ward (Knopf); *Freedom Land*, by Robert J. Norell (Oxford); Alsop biography, by Robert Merrie (Viking).
Terms: Agent receives 15% commission on domestic sales; 20% on foreign sales. Charges for "postage for all submissions and photocopying."
Tips: Obtains new clients through recommendations. "Always send a personal letter – not a form letter with recommendations from published writers."

ANITA D. MCCLELLAN ASSOCIATES (III), 50 Stearns St., Cambridge MA 02138. (617)864-3448. Estab. 1988. Member of ILAA. 25% of clients are new/previously unpublished writers. Specializes in general book-length trade fiction and nonfiction.
Will Handle: Query with SASE only. "No certified mail, no unsolicited manuscripts." Will report in 3 weeks on queries.
Terms: Agent receives 15% commission on domestic sales; 20% on foreign sales. Charges for photocopying, postage, copies of galleys and books, fax and telephone.
Writers' Conferences: Attends International Women's Writing Guild Conference; International Feminist Book Fair; National Writers Union Conference.

GINA MACCOBY LITERARY AGENCY (II), Suite 1010, 1123 Broadway, New York NY 10010. (212)627-9210. Contact: Gina Maccoby. Estab. 1986. Represents 30 clients. Currently handles: 50% nonfiction books; 25% juvenile books; 25% novels.
Will Handle: Nonfiction, juvenile books, novels. Will consider these nonfiction areas: biography; current affairs; ethnic/cultural interests; juvenile nonfiction; dance/theater/film; women's issues/women's studies. Will consider these fiction areas: literary; juvenile; mainstream; mystery/suspense; thriller/espionage; young adult. Query with SASE. Reports in 4-6 weeks.
Terms: Agent receives 10% commission on domestic sales; 20% on foreign sales. May charge for expenses to recover certain costs such as airmail postage to Europe or Japan or legal fees.
Tips: Usually obtains new clients through recommendations from own clients.

The publishing field is constantly changing! If you're still using this book and it is 1993 or later, buy the newest edition of Guide to Literary Agents & Art/Photo Reps *at your favorite bookstore or order directly from Writer's Digest Books.*

RICHARD P. MCDONOUGH, LITERARY AGENT (II), P.O. Box 1950, Boston MA 02130. (617)522-6388. Contact: Richard P. McDonough. Estab. 1986. Represents 30 clients. 50% of clients are new/unpublished writers. Works with unpublished and published writers "whose work I think has merit and requires a committed advocate." Specializes in nonfiction for general contract and fiction. Currently handles: 80% nonfiction books; 10% novels; 10% juvenile.
Will Handle: Nonfiction books, novels. Query with outline and SASE or send 3 chapters and SASE. Reports in 2 weeks on queries; 5 weeks on mss.
Recent Sales: *The Way That Water Enters Stone*, by Dufresne (Norton); *The Way of the Trout*, by Montgomery (Knopf); *The Living Will*, by Smith-Brallier (Crown).
Terms: Agent receives 15% commission on domestic sales; 15% on dramatic sales; 15% on foreign sales. Charges for photocopying, phone beyond 300 miles; postage for sold work only.

HELEN MCGRATH (III), 1406 Idaho Ct., Concord CA 94521. (415)672-6211. Contact: Helen McGrath. Estab. 1977. Currently handles: 50% nonfiction books; 50% novels.
Will Handle: Nonfiction and novels. Will consider these nonfiction areas: biography; business; current affairs; health/medicine; history; military/war; psychology; self-help/personal improvement; sports; women's issues/women's studies; how-to. Will consider these fiction areas: contemporary issues; detective/police/crime; family saga; literary; mainstream; mystery/suspense; psychic/supernatural; science fiction; sports; thriller/espionage; westerns/frontier. Query with SASE and proposal. No unsolicited mss. Reports in 6-8 weeks on queries.
Recent Sales: *Mass Dreams of the Future*, by Chet Snow (McGraw-Hill); *Point Blank*, by Jayson Livingston (St. Martin's Dunn Imprint); *Paper Bridges*, by Jann Janson (NAL).
Terms: Agent receives 15% commission on domestic sales. Sometimes offers a written contract. Charges for photocopying.
Writers' Conferences: Attends California Writers Club Conference, Romance Writers of America Conference and Pacific Northwest Writers Conference.
Tips: Usually obtains new clients through recommendations from others and directory listings.

CAROL MANN AGENCY (II,III), 55 5th Ave., New York NY 10003. (212)206-5635. FAX: (212)463-8718. Contact: Carol Mann. Estab. 1977. Member of ILAA. Represents 100+ clients. 25% of clients are new/previously unpublished writers. Specializes in current affairs; self-help; psychology; parenting; history. Currently handles: 80% nonfiction books; 15% scholarly books; 5% novels. Member agent: Christine Lazor (contemporary and historical fiction).
Will Handle: Nonfiction books. Will consider these nonfiction areas: anthropology/archaeology; art/architecture/design; biography/autobiography; business; child guidance/parenting; current affairs; ethnic/cultural interests; government/politics/law; health/medicine; history; interior design/decorating; money/finance/economics; psychology; true crime/investigative; self-help/personal improvement; sociology; women's issues/women's studies. Will consider literary fiction. Query with outline/proposal. Will report in 2 weeks on queries.
Recent Sales: *Every Spy a Prince*, by Raviv and Melman (Houghton); *The Content of Our Character*, by Shelby Steele (St. Martin's); *Route 66: The Mother Road*, by Michael Wallis (St. Martin's); *Second Chance*, by Judith Wallerstein (Ticknor & Fields).
Terms: Agent receives 15% commission on domestic sales; 20% on foreign sales. Offers a written contract, binding for 1 year.

JANET WILKENS MANUS LITERARY AGENCY (II, III), Suite 5-D, 417 E. 57th St., New York NY 10022. (212)644-8020. President: Janet Wilkens Manus. Estab. 1981. Member of ILAA. Represents 40 clients. 20% of our clients are new/unpublished writers. Prefers to work with published/established authors; works with a small number of new/unpublished authors. Specializes in general adult trade fiction and nonfiction. Currently handles: 40% nonfiction books; 45% novels; 15% juvenile books.
Will Handle: Nonfiction books (trade oriented); novels (adult and young adult); juvenile books. Query with outline. Reports in 2 weeks on queries; 5 weeks on mss.
Recent Sales: *A Cold Killing*, by Deforest Day (Caroll & Graf); *The London Connection*, by Rubin Hunter (William Morrow & Co.); *Secrets*, by Carlton Stouers (Pocket Books).
Terms: Agent receives 15% commission on domestic sales; 15% on dramatic sales; and 20% on foreign sales. Charges for photocopying, messenger, overseas phone, and postage expenses.

MARCH TENTH, INC. (III), 4 Myrtle St., Haworth NJ 07641. (201)387-6551. FAX: (201)387-6552. President: Sandra Choron. Estab. 1982. Represents 40 clients. 5% of clients are new/unpublished writers. "Writers must have professional expertise in the field in which they are writing." Prefers to work with published/established writers. Currently handles: 100% nonfiction books.
Will Handle: Nonfiction books. Query. Does not read unsolicited mss. Reports in 1 month.
Recent Sales: *Sue Finn's Real Life Nutrition Book*, by Sue Finn and Linda Kass Stern (Viking); *The Heart of Rock and Soul*, by Dave Marsh (NAL); *Bitch, Bitch, Bitch*, by David Wheeler and Mike Wrenn (Dell).

Terms: Agent receives 15% commission on domestic sales; 20% on dramatic sales; 20% on foreign sales. Charges writers for postage, photocopying and overseas phone expenses.

BARBARA MARKOWITZ LITERARY AGENCY (II), 117 N. Mansfield Ave., Los Angeles CA 90036. (213)939-5927. Literary Agent/President: Barbara Markowitz. Estab. 1980. Represents 12 clients. Works with a small number of new/unpublished authors. Specializes in mid-level and young adult only; adult trade fiction and nonfiction. Currently handles: 25% nonfiction books; 25% novels; 25% juvenile books; 15% syndicated material.
Will Handle: Nonfiction books, novels and juvenile books. Query with outline. SASE required for return of any material. Reports in 3 weeks.
Recent Sales: *The Legend of Jimmy Spoon*, by K. Gregory (HBJ); *Nature's Tricksters*, by Mary Batten (Sierra Club/Little, Brown).
Terms: Agent receives 15% commission on domestic sales; 10% on dramatic sales; 15% on foreign sales. Charges writers for mailing, postage.

ELAINE MARKSON LITERARY AGENCY (II), 44 Greenwich Ave., New York NY 10011. (212)243-8480. Estab. 1972. Member of ILAA. Represents 200 clients. 10% of clients are new/unpublished writers. Specializes in literary fiction, commercial fiction and trade nonfiction. Currently handles: 30% nonfiction books; 40% novels; 20% juvenile books; 5% movie scripts. Member Agents: Geri Thomas; Sally Wofford; Karin Beisch; Lisa Callamaro (screenplays only); Joanna Cole (children's and young adults only).
Will Handle: Novels and nonfiction books. Query with outline (must include SASE). SASE is required for the return of any material.
Terms: Agent receives 15% commission on domestic sales; 10% on dramatic sales; 20% on foreign sales. Charges for postage, photocopying, foreign mailing, faxing, long-distance telephone and other special expenses.

MILDRED MARMUR ASSOCIATES LTD., Suite 607, 310 Madison Ave., New York NY 10017. Prefers not to be listed.

THE MARTELL AGENCY (III), 555 5th Ave., New York NY 10017. (212)692-9770. Contact: Paul Raushenbush or Alice Fried Martell. Estab. 1984. Represents 75 clients. Currently handles: 65% nonfiction books; 35% novels.
Will Handle: Nonfiction and novels. Will consider all nonfiction areas. Will consider most fiction areas. No science fiction or poetry. Query with SASE and outline plus 2 sample chapters. If interested, will report in 3 weeks on queries.
Terms: Agent receives 15% on domestic sales; 20% on foreign sales. Offers a written contract, binding for 1 year. Charges for foreign postage, photocopying.
Tips: Usually obtains new clients by recommendations from agents and editors.

HAROLD MATSON CO. INC., 276 Fifth Ave., New York NY 10001. Prefers not to be listed.

TONI MENDEZ INC. (II), 141 E. 56th St., New York NY 10022. (212)838-6740. FAX: (212)755-5170. President: Toni Mendez. Estab. 1966.
Will Handle: Nonfiction, novels (adult and juvenile). Also handles features, columns, comic strips for syndication; licensing of literary properties, film and TV rights. Query first with SASE and outline, plus 3 sample chapters.
Terms: Information not given.

GREG MERHIGE-MERDON MARKETING/PROMO CO. INC. (II), Suite #17, 810 Saturn St., Jupiter FL 33477. (407)747-9951. FAX: (407)747-6516. Contact: Greg Merhige. Estab. 1989. Member of WGA and Actors Guild. Represents 20 clients. 90% of clients are new/previously unpublished writers. Currently handles: 5% nonfiction books; 40% juvenile books; 5% novels; 5% novellas; 15% movie scripts; 5% stage plays; 20% TV scripts.
Will Handle: Nonfiction books, juvenile books, novels, novellas, short story collections, poetry books, movie and TV scripts, stage plays. Will consider these nonfiction areas: animals; art/architecture/design; biography/autobiography; child guidance/parenting; cooking/food/nutrition; ethnic/cultural interests; juvenile nonfiction; military/war; music/dance/theater/film; photography; true crime/investigative; self-help/personal improvement; sociology; sports; women's issues/women's studies. Will consider these fiction areas: action/adventure; cartoon/comic; confessional; detective/police/crime; ethnic; family saga; fantasy; feminist; humor/satire; juvenile; literary; mainstream; mystery/suspense; picture book; psychic/supernatural; regional; religious/inspiration; romance; science fiction; sports; thriller/espionage; westerns/frontier; young adult. Send entire ms plus outline. Will report in 2 days on queries; 30 days on mss.

Recent Sales: *Hector Hatches*, by Lauron Kingston (Golden Books).
Terms: Agent receives 10% commission on domestic sales; 15% on foreign sales. Offers a written contract, binding for 1 or 1½ years. Charges expenses on special situations.
Tips: Obtains new clients through recommendations from others. "Listen to your agent. Do not try to make your own deal."

MGA AGENCY INC. (II), Suite 510, 10 St. Mary St., Toronto, ON M4Y 1P9 Canada. (416)964-3302. FAX: (416)975-9209. Contact: Carol Bonnett, Lesley Harrison or Linda McKnight. Estab. 1989. Represents approximately 200 clients. Currently handles: 50% nonfiction books; 50% picture books, juvenile books.
Will Handle: Nonfiction, novels. Will consider all nonfiction areas. Will consider these fiction areas: family saga; juvenile; mystery/suspense; picture book; romance; science fiction; young adult. Query with résumé and SASE. Reports in 4-6 weeks on queries.
Recent Sales: *The Elizabeth Stories*, by Isabel Huggan (Viking); *Redwork*, by Michael Bedard (Atheneum).
Terms: Agent receives 15% commission on domestic sales; 20% on foreign sales. Offers a written contract. Charges for postage, photocopying, fax.
Tips: Usually obtains new clients through recommendations from others, and at conferences.

MARTHA MILLARD LITERARY AGENCY (II), 204 Park Ave., Madison NJ 07940. (201)593-9233. FAX: (201)593-9235. Contact: Martha Millard. Estab. 1980. Member of ILAA. Represents 40 clients. 3% of clients are new/previously unpublished writers. Currently handles: 45% nonfiction books; 50% novels; 5% short story collections.
Will Handle: Nonfiction books, novels. Will consider these nonfiction areas: art/architecture/design; biography/autobiography; business; child guidance/parenting; cooking/food/nutrition; current affairs; ethnic/cultural interests; health/medicine; history; money/finance/economics; music/dance/theater/ film; nature/environment; photography; psychology; true crime/investigative; science/technology; self-help/personal improvement; sports; women's issues/women's studies. Will consider these fiction areas: action/adventure; contemporary issues; detective/police/crime; experimental; family saga; fantasy; feminist; historical; literary; mainstream; mystery/suspense; science fiction; thriller/espionage. Query with SASE. Will report in 2 weeks on queries.
Terms: Agent receives 15% commission on domestic sales; 20% on foreign sales.
Tips: Obtains new clients through "referrals from publishing professionals and writers."

MOORE LITERARY AGENCY, 4 Dove St., Newburyport MA 01950. (508)465-9015. FAX: (508)465-8817. Contact: Claudette Moore. Estab. 1989. 50% of clients are new/previously unpublished writers. Specializes in trade computer books. Currently handles: 10% nonfiction books; 90% computer-related books.
Will Handle: Nonfiction books, computer books. Will consider these nonfiction areas: computers/ electronics; science/technology. Send outline/proposal. Will report in 1 week on queries; 3 weeks on mss.
Recent Sales: *Undocumented DOS*, by Andrew Schulman (Addison-Wesley); *PC Magazine's DOS 5 Power Tools*, by Jeff Prosise (Ziff-Davis Press); *Running Lantastic*, by Adrian King (Bantam).
Terms: Agent receives 15% commission on all sales. Offers a written contract, varies book by book.
Tips: Obtains new clients through recommendations/referrals and conferences.

WILLIAM MORRIS AGENCY (III), 1350 Avenue of the Americas, New York NY 10019. (212)586-5100. Estab. 1898. Member of SAR. Works with a small number of new/unpublished authors. Specializes in novels and nonfiction.
Will Handle: Nonfiction books and novels. Query only. Reports in 6 weeks.
Terms: Agent receives 10% commission on domestic sales; 10% on dramatic sales; 20% on foreign sales.

HENRY MORRISON, INC. (II), P.O. Box 235, Bedford Hills NY 10507. (914)666-3500. FAX: (914)241-7846. President: Henry Morrison. Estab. 1965. Represents 51 clients. Writer may be totally unpublished, but we prefer to work on book-length material only. Works with a small number of new/ unpublished authors. Specializes in novels, some nonfiction, science fiction novels. Currently handles: 3% nonfiction books; 95% novels; 2% movie scripts.
Will Handle: Nonfiction books, novels, juvenile books, movie scripts. Query with outline. Reports in 2 weeks on queries.
Recent Sales: *The Moscow Club*, by Joseph Finder (Viking); *The Covenant of the Flame*, by David Morrell (Warner Books); *Angel Eyes*, by Eric Van Lustbader (Random House); *DreamWeavers*, by Philip Shelby (Bantam).

Terms: Agent receives 15% commission on domestic sales; 20% on foreign sales. Charges writers for making ms copies, ordering galleys and bound books.

MULTIMEDIA PRODUCT DEVELOPMENT, INC. (III), Suite 724, 410 S. Michigan Ave., Chicago IL 60605. (312)922-3063. FAX: (312)922-1905. President: Jane Jordan Browne. Estab. 1971. Member of ILAA, ASJA-MWA; SCBW. Represents 100 clients. 5% of clients are new/previously unpublished writers. "Generalists." Currently handles: 60% nonfiction books; 5% juvenile books; 35% novels. Member agent: Matthew Rettenmund.
Will Handle: Nonfiction books, novels. Will consider these nonfiction areas: biography/autobiography; business; cooking/food/nutrition; current affairs; health/medicine; money/finance; nature; true crime/ investigative; science. Will consider these fiction areas: detective/police/crime; family saga; glitz; historical; mainstream; mystery/suspense; romance (contemporary, historical, regency); thriller/espionage; westerns/frontier. Query "by mail with SASE required. We answer queries with SASE's same or next day, 4-6 weeks on mss."
Recent Sales: *Time Off From Good Behavior,* by Susan Sussman (Pocket Books, hardcover); *Purgatory,* by Monty Mickelson (St. Martin's); *This Job Should Be Fun,* by Bob Basso and Judi Klosek (Bob Adams, Inc.).
Terms: Agent receives 15% commission on domestic sales; 20% on foreign sales. Offers a written contract, binding for 2 years. Charges for photocopying, overseas postage, faxes, phone calls.
Tips: Obtains new clients through "referrals, queries by professional, marketable authors." If interested in agency representation, "be well informed."

JEAN V. NAGGAR LITERARY AGENCY (III), 1E, 216 E. 75th St., New York NY 10021. (212)794-1082. Contact: Jean Naggar. Estab. 1978. Member of SAR, ILAA. Represents 100 clients. 20% of clients are new/previously unpublished writers. Currently handles: 30% nonfiction books; 5% scholarly books; 15% juvenile books; 40% novels; 5% short story collections. Member agent: Teresa Cavanaugh. Agentat-large: Anne Engel (nonfiction).
Will Handle: Nonfiction books, juvenile books, novels. Will consider these nonfiction areas: biography/ autobiography; business; child guidance/parenting; cooking/food/nutrition; current affairs; gay/lesbian issues; government/politics/law; health/medicine; history; interior design/decorating; juvenile nonfiction; money/finance/economics; music/dance/theater/film; new age/metaphysics; psychology; religious/ inspirational; true crime/investigative; self-help/personal improvement; sociology; women's issues/ women's studies. "We would, of course, consider a query regarding an exceptional mainstream manuscript touching on any area." Will consider these fiction areas: action/adventure; contemporary issues; detective/police/crime; ethnic; family saga; fantasy; feminist; gay; glitz; historical; juvenile; lesbian; literary; mainstream; mystery/suspense; picture book; psychic/supernatural; regional; science fiction; thriller/espionage; young adult. Query. Will report in 24 hours on queries; 2 months on mss.
Recent Sales: *Liberty Hall,* by Nancy Willard (Knopf); *How Adulthood Works: The Art of Growing Up,* by Charles Spezzano (Morrow); *Strangers at the Vigil,* by Richard Dooling (Morrow).
Terms: Agent receives 15% commission on domestic sales; 20% on foreign sales. Offers a written contract. Charges for overseas mailing; messenger services; book purchases; long-distance telephone; photocopying. "These are deductible from royalties received."
Writers' Conferences: Has attended Willamette Writers Conference; Wildacre, Bread Loaf, Pacific Northwest, Southwest and many others.
Tips: Obtains new clients through "recommendations from publishers, editors, clients and others, and from writers' conferences, as well as from query letters. Use a professional presentation."

RUTH NATHAN (II), Suite 402B, 648 Broadway, New York NY 10012. (212)529-1133. FAX: (212)529-6068. Estab. 1980. Member of ILAA. Represents 12 clients. 10% of clients are new/previously unpublished writers. Specializes in art, decorative arts, fine art; theater; film; show business. Currently handles: 90% nonfiction books; 10% novels.
Will Handle: Nonfiction books and novels. Will consider these nonfiction areas: art/architecture/ design; biography/autobiography; theater/film. Query. Will report in 2 weeks on queries; 1 month on mss.
Recent Sales: *The Art of Mickey Mouse,* by Craig Yoe (Disney Books); *Oh What a Beautiful Morning,* by Max Wilk (Grove); *My Dog Ate It,* by Lou Anne Johnson (St. Martin's).
Terms: Agent receives 15% commission on domestic sales; 20% on foreign sales. Charges for office expenses, postage, photocopying, etc.
Tips: "Read carefully what my requirements are before wasting your time and mine."

CHARLES NEIGHBORS, INC. (II), Suite 300D, 13333 Blanco Rd., San Antonio TX 78216. (512)492-6243. FAX: (512)492-6220. Contact: Charles or Margaret Neighbors. Estab. 1966. Represents 45 clients. Currently handles: 50% nonfiction books; 50% novels.

Will Handle: Nonfiction, novels. Will consider these nonfiction areas: cooking/food/nutrition; crafts/ hobbies; military/war; money/finance/economics; science/technology; legal. Will consider these fiction areas: contemporary issues; detective/police/crime; literary; mainstream; romance; science fiction; westerns/frontier. Query with SASE and outline plus 2 sample chapters. Reports in 3 weeks on queries.
Terms: Agent receives 15% on domestic sales; 20% on foreign sales.
Writers' Conferences: Attends Romance Writers of America Conference, Western Writers of America Conference.
Tips: Obtains 90% of new clients through referrals. "Write your query as carefully as you do your work."

NEW ENGLAND PUBLISHING ASSOCIATES, INC. (II), P.O. Box 5, Chester CT 06412. (203)345-4976. FAX: (203)345-3660. Contact: Elizabeth Frost Knappman or Edward W. Knappman. Estab. 1983. Member of ILAA. Represents 70 clients. 25% of clients are new/previously unpublished writers. Specializes in "adult nonfiction books of serious purpose." Currently handles: 100% nonfiction books.
Will Handle: Nonfiction books. Will consider these nonfiction areas: biography/autobiography; business; child guidance/parenting; government/politics/law; health/medicine; history; language/literature/ criticism; military/war; money/finance/economics; nature/environment; psychology; true crime/investigative; science/technology; self-help/personal improvement; sociology; women's issues/women's studies. Send outline/proposal or "phone us to describe your book." Will report in 2 weeks on queries; 3-4 weeks on mss.
Recent Sales: *The Art of Poetry Writing*, by Bill Packard (St. Martin's Press); *The Direction of Cities*, by Edmund Bacon and John Guinther (Viking-Penguin); *Cook's Dictionary*, by John Bartlett (NAL).
Terms: Agent receives 15% commission on domestic sales; 20% foreign sales (split with overseas agent). Offers a written contract, binding for 6 months.
Tips: Obtains new clients through recommendations from other clients or editors; calls from writers who see our listing in *LMP*, etc., personal contacts. "Never give up. There is usually a publisher who will see the value in your work if you are persistent."

REGULA NOETZLI LITERARY AGENCY (II), 444 E. 85th St., New York NY 10028. (212)628-1537. FAX: (212)744-3145. Contact: Regula Noetzli. Estab. 1989. Represents 35 clients. 85% of clients are new/previously unpublished writers. Specializes in psychology, popular science, history, biographies, literary fiction, mysteries. Currently handles: 80% nonfiction books, 20% novels.
Will Handle: Nonfiction books, novels. Will consider these nonfiction areas: animals; anthropology/ archaeology; biography/autobiography; child guidance/parenting; current affairs; ethnic/cultural interests; health/medicine; history; money/finance/economics; nature/environment; new age/metaphysics; psychology; true crime/investigative; science/technology; self-help/personal improvement; sociology; sports; women's issues/women's studies. Will consider these fiction areas: contemporary issues; detective/police/crime; ethnic; family saga; feminist; historical; humor/satire; literary; mainstream; mystery/ suspense; psychic/supernatural; sports; thriller/espionage. Send outline/proposal for nonfiction and outline plus sample chapters for fiction. Will report in 2 weeks on queries; 1 month on mss.
Terms: Agent receives 15% commission on domestic sales; 20% on foreign sales. "If I submit multiple copies, I ask authors to provide copies."

THE BETSY NOLAN LITERARY AGENCY (II), Suite 9 West, 50 W. 29th St., New York NY 10001. (212)779-0700. FAX: (212)689-0376. President: Betsy Nolan. Agents: Donald Lehr and Carla Glasser. Estab. 1980. Represents 100 clients. 30% of clients are new/unpublished writers. Works with a small number of new/unpublished authors. Currently handles: 70% nonfiction books; 30% novels.
Will Handle: Nonfiction books and novels. Query with outline. Reports in 2 weeks on queries; 2 months on mss.
Recent Sales: *Gardens of the World* (Macmillan); *Blackbird* (Dutton); *How to Manage Your Mother* (Simon & Schuster); *Surviving Siblings* (Ballantine).
Terms: Agent receives 15% commission on domestic sales; 20% on foreign sales.

THE NORMA-LEWIS AGENCY (II), 521 5th Ave., New York NY 10175. (212)751-4955. Contact: Norma Liebert. Estab. 1980. 50% of clients are new/previously unpublished writers. Specializes in juvenile books (pre-school-high school). Currently handles: 60% juvenile books; 40% adult books.
Will Handle: Juvenile and adult nonfiction and fiction, movie and tv scripts, radio scripts, stage plays. Query first.
Terms: Agent receives 15% commission on domestic sales; 20% on foreign sales.

RAY E. NUGENT LITERARY AGENCY (II), 170 10th St. N., Naples FL 33940. (813)262-3683. FAX: (813)262-3683. Contact: Ray E. Nugent. Estab. 1976. Represents 17 clients. 50% of clients are new/ previously unpublished authors. Specializes in nonfiction: true crime, celebrity biographies, true war; fiction (limited). Currently handles: 100% nonfiction books.

Will Handle: Nonfiction books. Will consider these nonfiction areas: biography/autobiography (celebrity); military/war; music/dance/theater/film; photography; true crime/investigative. Will consider these fiction areas: detective/police/crime; erotica; mystery/suspense. Query with outline plus 3 sample chapters. Will report in 1 month on queries; 2 months on mss.
Recent Sales: *A POW's Story*, by L. Guarino (Ballantine); *The Day I Died*, by J. Barbree (New Horizon); *How to Retire on the House*, by A. McLean (Contemporary); *50 Plus Wellness*, by D. Bruce et al (John Wiley & Sons).
Terms: Agent receives 15% on domestic sales; 20% on foreign sales. Offers written contract, binding for 1 year. Charges for photocopying, fax, telephone calls, postage.
Writers' Conferences: Attends South Florida Romance Writers and South Florida Mystery Writers conferences.
Tips: Obtains new clients from recommendations from others, solicitation, at conferences, etc. "Carefully prepare submissions; adhere to the agent's policy on submission format; enclose SASE."

HAROLD OBER ASSOCIATES (III), 425 Madison Ave., New York NY 10017. (212)759-8600. FAX: (212)759-9428. Estab. 1929. Member of SAR. Represents 250 clients. 15% of clients are new/previously unpublished writers. Currently handles: 35% nonfiction books, 15% juvenile books, 50% novels. Member agents: Claire Smith, Phyllis Westberg; Peter Shepherd; Craig Tenney; Wendy Schmalz (film rights).
Will Handle: Nonfiction books, juvenile books, novels. Will consider all nonfiction and fiction subjects. Query with outline plus 3 sample chapters. Will report in 1 week on queries; 2-3 weeks on mss.
Terms: Agent receives 10% commission on domestic sales; 15-20% on foreign sales. Charges for photocopying for multiple submissions.
Tips: Obtains new clients through recommendations from others.

THE ODENWALD CONNECTION (II), Suite 1296, 3010 LBJ Freeway, Dallas TX 75234. (214)221-5793. FAX: (224)221-1081. Contact: Sylvia Odenwald. Estab. 1984. Represents 25 clients. Specializes in business and how-to books. Currently handles: 100% nonfiction books.
Will Handle: Nonfiction. Will consider these nonfiction areas: business; current affairs; self-help/personal improvement. Query with SASE and outline/proposal. Reports in 1 month on queries.
Terms: Agent receives 15% on domestic sales; 20% on foreign sales.
Writers' Conferences: Attends the American Society for Training and Development Conference.
Tips: Usually obtains new clients through referrals from other clients and publishers.

FIFI OSCARD ASSOCIATES (II), 19 W. 44th St., New York NY 10036. (212)764-1100. Contact: Ivy Fischer Stone, Literary Department. Estab. 1956. Member of SAR and WGA. Represents 108 clients. 5% of clients are new/unpublished writers. "Writer must have published articles or books in major markets or have screen credits if movie scripts, etc." Specializes in literary novels, commercial novels, mysteries and nonfiction, especially celebrity biographies and autobiographies. Currently handles: 40% nonfiction books; 40% novels; 5% movie scripts; 5% stage plays; 10% TV scripts.
Will Handle: Nonfiction books, novels, movie scripts, stage plays. Query with outline. Reports in 1 week on queries if SASE enclosed.
Recent Sales: *TekLords*, by William Shatner (Putnam's); *Dick Tracy, The Official Biography*, by Jay Maeder (NAL).
Terms: Agent receives 15% commission on domestic sales; 10% on dramatic sales; 20% on foreign sales. Charges for photocopying expenses.

THE OTTE COMPANY (II), 9 Goden St., Belmont MA 02178. (617)484-8505. Contact: Jane H. Otte or L. David Otte. Estab. 1973. Represents 35 clients. 33% of clients are new/unpublished writers. Works with a small number of new/unpublished authors. Specializes in quality adult trade books. Currently handles: 40% nonfiction books; 60% novels.
Will Handle: Nonfiction books and novels. "Does not handle poetry, juvenile or 'by-the-number' romance." Query. Reports in 1 week on queries; 1 month on mss.
Terms: Agent receives 15% commission on domestic sales; 7½% on dramatic sales; 10% on foreign sales plus 10% to foreign agent. Charges for photocopying, overseas phone and postage expenses.

THE RICHARD PARKS AGENCY (III), 5th Floor, 138 E. 16th St., New York NY 10003. (212)254-9067. FAX: (212)777-4694. Contact: Richard Parks. Estab. 1988. Member of ILAA. Currently handles: 50% nonfiction books; 5% juvenile books; 40% novels; 5% short story collections.
Will Handle: Nonfiction books, novels. Will consider these nonfiction areas: horticulture; animals; anthopology/archaeology; art/architecture/design; biography/autobiography; business; child guidance/parenting; cooking/food/nutrition; crafts/hobbies; current affairs; ethnic/cultural interests; gay/lesbian issues; government/politics; health/medicine; history; language/literature/criticism; military/war; money/finance/economics; music/dance/theater/film; nature/environment; psychology; true crime/in-

vestigative; science/technology; self-help/personal improvement; sociology; women's issues/women's studies. Will consider these fiction areas: action/adventure; contemporary issues; detective/police/ crime; family saga; gay; glitz; historical; lesbian; literary; mainstream; mystery/suspense; psychic/super-natural; science fiction; thriller/espionage; westerns/frontier; young adult. Query with SASE. "We will not accept any unsolicited material." Will report in 2 weeks on queries.

Recent Sales: *Dangerous Waters*, by Bill Eidson (Henry Holt & Co.); *The Road to Bobby Joe*, by Louis Berney (HBJ).

Terms: Agent receives 15% commission on domestic sales; 20% on foreign sales. Charges for "photo-copying or any unusual expense incurred at the writer's request."

Tips: Obtains new clients through recommendations and referrals.

KATHI J. PATON LITERARY AGENCY (II), 19 W. 55th St., New York NY 10019-4907. (212)265-6586. FAX: available (call first). Contact: Kathi Paton. Estab. 1987. Specializes in adult nonfiction. Currently handles: 65% nonfiction books; 35% fiction.

Will Handle: Nonfiction, novels, short story collections. Will consider these nonfiction areas: business; sociology; psychology; women's issues/women's studies; how-to. Will consider these fiction areas: liter-ary; mainstream; short stories. For nonfiction, send proposal, sample chapter and SASE. For fiction, send first 40 pages and plot summary or 3 short stories.

Recent Sales: *Total Customer Service*, by Bro Uttal (HarperCollins); *The Myth of the Bad Mother*, by Jane Swigart (Doubleday); *The Rat Becomes Light*, by Donald Secreast (HarperCollins).

Terms: Agent receives 15% commission on domestic sales; 20% on foreign sales. Offers written contract. Length of time binding is on a per-book basis. Charges for photocopying.

Writers' Conferences: Attends International Womens Writing Guild panels and the Pacific North-west Writers Conference.

Tips: Usually obtains new clients through recommendations from other clients. "Write well."

JOHN K. PAYNE LITERARY AGENCY, INC. (III), P.O. Box 1003, New York NY 10276. (212)475-6447. President: John K. Payne. Estab. 1923 (as Lenniger Literary Agency). Represents 30 clients. 20% of clients are new/unpublished writers. Prefers writers who have 1-2 books published. No unsolicited material accepted. Specializes in popular women's fiction, historical romance, biographies, sagas. Currently handles: 20% nonfiction books; 80% novels.

Will Handle: Nonfiction books, novels, juvenile books (young adult fiction, nonfiction). Query with SASE required.

Recent Sales: *Cloud Dancer*, by Peggy Bechko (Harlequin).

Terms: Agent receives 15% commission on first novel; 10% on domestic sales; 10% on dramatic sales; 20% on foreign sales. Small handling fee.

RODNEY PELTER (II), 129 E. 61st St., New York NY 10021. (212)838-3432. Contact: Rodney Pelter. Estab. 1978. Represents 10-12 clients. Currently handles: 25% nonfiction books; 75% novels.

Will Handle: Nonfiction books and novels. Will consider all nonfiction areas. Will consider most fiction areas. No juvenile, romance or science fiction. For nonfiction, query with SASE. For fiction, send outline and 50-75 pages with SASE. Reports in 1-3 months.

Terms: Agent receives 15% on domestic sales; 20% on foreign sales. Offers a written contract. Charges for foreign postage, photocopying.

Tips: Usually obtains new clients through recommendations from others.

L. PERKINS ASSOCIATES (IV), 301 W. 53rd St., New York NY 10019. (212)581-7679. Contact: Lori Perkins. Estab. 1990. Member of ILAA, HWA. Represents 50 clients. 10% of clients are new/pre-viously unpublished writers. Specializes in horror, dark thrillers, literary fiction, pop culture. Currently handles: 35% nonfiction books; 65% novels.

Will Handle: Nonfiction books, novels. Will consider these nonfiction areas: art/architecture/design; current affairs; ethnic/cultural interests; music/dance/theater/film; "subjects that fall under pop cul-ture – TV, music, art, books and authors, film, etc." Will consider these fiction areas: adventure; cartoon; detective/police/crime; ethnic; literary; mainstream; mystery/suspense; psychic/supernatural; thriller. Query with SASE. Will report immediately on queries "with SASE"; 6-10 weeks on mss.

If you're looking for a particular agent, check the Agents and Reps Index to find at which agency the agent works. Then look up the listing for that agency in the appropriate section.

Recent Sales: *Rap*, by B. Adler and Janette Beckman (St. Martin's Press); *Dark Channel*, by Ray Garton (Bantam); *How to Shop Like a Coupon Queen*, by Michelle Easter (Berkley).
Terms: Agent receives 15% commission on domestic sales; 20% on foreign sales. Offers a written contract "if requested." Charges for photocopying.
Writers' Conferences: Attends Horror Writers of America Conference; World Fantasy Conference; Necon and Lunacon.
Tips: Obtains new clients through recommendations from others, solicitation, at conferences, etc. "Sometimes I come up with book ideas and find authors (*Coupon Queen*, for example). Be professional. Read *Publishers Weekly* and genre-related magazines. Join writers' organizations. Go to conferences. Know your market."

PERKINS' LITERARY AGENCY (V), P.O. Box 48, Childs MD 21916. Agent not currently seeking new clients.

JAMES PETER ASSOCIATES, INC. (III,IV), P.O. Box 772, Tenafly NJ 07670. (201)568-0760. FAX: (201)568-2959. Contact: Bert Holtje. Estab. 1971. Member of ILAA. Represents 47 clients. 5% of clients are new/previously unpublished writers. Specializes in nonfiction (history, politics, psychology, health, popular culture, business, biography, reference). Currently handles: 100% nonfiction books.
Will Handle: Nonfiction books. Will consider these nonfiction areas: anthropology/archaeology; art/architecture/design; biography/autobiography; business; crafts/hobbies; current affairs; ethnic/cultural interests; government/politics/law; health/medicine; history; interior design/decorating; military/war; money/finance/economics; psychology; self-help/personal improvement. Send outline/proposal. Will report in 3-4 weeks on queries.
Recent Sales: *The War Between the Spies*, by Alan Axelrod (Atlantic Monthly Press/Morgan Entrekin Books); *100 Drugs That Work*, by Michael Oppenheim, M.D. (Dell); *More Than Friends, Less Than Lovers*, by David Eyler and Andrea Baridon (Jeremy Tarcher).
Terms: Agent receives 15% commission on domestic sales; 20% on foreign sales. Offers a written contract; "separate contracts written for each project." Charges for photocopying.
Tips: Obtains new clients through "recommendations from other clients and publishing house editors. I read widely in areas which interest me and contact people who write articles on subjects which could be books. Be an expert in an interesting field, and be able to write well on the subject. Be flexible."

ALISON J. PICARD LITERARY AGENT (II), P.O. Box 2000, Cotuit MA 02635. (508)420-6163. FAX: (508)420-0762. Contact: Alison Picard. Estab. 1985. Represents 60 clients. 25% of clients are new/previously unpublished writers. "Most interested in nonfiction at this time, especially self-help/recovery, pop psychology, how-to, business and current affairs." Currently handles: 40% nonfiction books; 30% juvenile books; 30% novels.
Will Handle: Nonfiction books, juvenile books, novels. Will consider these nonfiction areas: art/architecture/design; biography/autobiography; business; child guidance/parenting; cooking/food/nutrition; current affairs; ethnic/cultural interests; gay/lesbian issues; government/politics/law; health/medicine; history; interior design/decorating; juvenile nonfiction; military/war; money/finance/economics; music/dance/theater/film; nature/environment; new age/metaphysics; psychology; true crime/investigative; science/technology; self-help/personal improvement; sports; women's issues/women's studies. Will consider these fiction areas: action/adventure; contemporary issues; detective/police/crime; ethnic; family saga; feminist; gay; glitz; historical; humor/satire; juvenile; lesbian; literary; mainstream; mystery/suspense; psychic/supernatural; romance; sports; thriller/espionage; westerns/frontier; young adult. Query with SASE. Will report in 1 week on queries; 1 month on mss.
Recent Sales: *How to Sell Your Home*, by Pete Davidson (Perigee/Putnam); *Over on the Lonesome Side*, by James Ritchie (Walker & Co.); *Rainbow Wishes*, by Jacqueline Case (Meteor); *Married to Kings: The Queen Consorts of England*, by Margot Arnold (Prentice-Hall).
Terms: Agent receives 15% commission on domestic sales; 15% on foreign sales.
Writers' Conferences: Attends Cap Cod Writer's Conference.
Tips: Obtains new clients through recommendations.

AARON M. PRIEST LITERARY AGENCY (II), Suite 3902, 122 E. 42nd St., New York NY 10168. (212)818-0344. Contact: Aaron Priest, Molly Friedrich or Laurie Liss. Currently handles: 50% nonfiction books; 50% fiction.
Will Handle: Fiction and nonfiction books. Query only (must be accompanied by SASE). Unsolicited mss will be returned unread.
Recent Sales: *Disappearing Acts*, by Terry McMillan; *Ordinary Love and Good Will*, by Jane Smiley; *Longing for Darkness*, by China Galland.
Terms: Agent receives 15% commission on domestic sales. Charges for photocopying and foreign postage expenses.

PRINTED TREE, INC. (II), 2357 Trail Dr., Evansville IN 47711. (812)476-9015. Contact: Jo Frohbieter-Mueller. Estab. 1983. Represents 29 clients. 80% of clients are new/previously unpublished writers. Specializes in selling serious nonfiction and textbooks. Currently handles: 50% nonfiction books; 50% textbooks.
Will Handle: Nonfiction books, textbooks. Send outline/proposal and SASE. Will report within 3 weeks on proposal/outline.
Recent Sales: *Your Home Business Can Make Dollars and Sense* (Chilton).
Terms: Agent receives 15% commission on domestic sales; 20% on foreign sales. Offers a written contract. Charges for mailing, phone calls, photocopying and other out-of-pocket expenses.
Tips: Obtains new clients through recommendations, listings. "Along with an outline/proposal, include a list of similar books on the market and identify your targeted readers."

SUSAN ANN PROTTER LITERARY AGENT (II), Suite 1408, 110 W. 40th St., New York NY 10018. (212)840-0480. Contact: Susan Protter. Estab. 1971. Member of ILAA. Represents 50 clients. 10% of clients are new/unpublished writers. Writer must have book-length project or manuscript that is ready to be sold. Works with a small number of new/unpublished authors. Currently handles: 5% magazine articles; 45% nonfiction books; 45% novels; 5% photography books.
Will Handle: Nonfiction books and novels. Will consider these nonfiction areas: general nonfiction, health, medicine, psychology, science. Will consider these fiction areas: mystery; science fiction, thrillers. Query with outline. "Must include SASE." Reports in 2 weeks on queries; 6 weeks on solicited mss. "Please do not call; mail queries only."
Recent Sales: *Voyage to the Red Planet*, by Terry Bisson (Morrow/Avon); *Parenting Our Schools*, by Jill Bloom (Little, Brown); *Roosevelt and Hitler*, by Robert E. Herzstein (Paragon House).
Terms: Agent receives 15% commission on domestic sales; 15% on TV, film and dramatic sales; 25% on foreign sales. Charges for long distance, photocopying, messenger, express mail and airmail expenses.
Tips: "Be professional in your presentation. Do not call to see if I've received your query. I am small-staffed and get 50-100 queries per week and it takes time to look at them. A SASE is a must for a reply. Please don't telephone—you will be answered if you enclose a SASE."

ROBERTA PRYOR, INC. (II), 24 W. 55th St., New York NY 10019. (212)245-0420. President: Roberta Pryor. Estab. 1985. Member of ILAA. Represents 50 clients. Prefers to work with published/established authors; works with a small number of new/unpublished writers. Specializes in serious nonfiction and (tends toward) literary fiction. Special interest in natural history and good cookbooks. Currently handles: 10% magazine fiction; 40% nonfiction books; 40% novels; 10% textbooks; 10% juvenile books.
Will Handle: Nonfiction books, novels, textbooks, juvenile books. Query. SASE required for any correspondence. Reports in 10 weeks on queries.
Recent Sales: *The Bear Flag*, by Cecilia Holland (Houghton Mifflin); *Devices and Desires*, by P.D. James (Knopf); *Seeing Through Movies*, by Mark C. Miller (Pantheon).
Terms: Charges 10% commission on domestic sales; 10% on dramatic sales; 20% on foreign sales. Charges for photocopying, Federal Express service sometimes.
Writer's Conferences: Attends Antioch Writers Conference.

QUICKSILVER BOOKS-LITERARY AGENTS (II), 50 Wilson St., Hartsdale NY 10530. (914)946-8748. Contact: Bob Silverstein. Estab. 1973 as packager; 1987 as literary agency. Represents 50+ clients. 50% of clients are new/previously unpublished writers. Specializes in literary and commercial mainstream fiction and nonfiction (especially psychology, new age, holistic healing, consciousness, ecology, environment, spirituality). Currently handles: 75% nonfiction books; 25% novels.
Will Handle: Nonfiction books, novels. Will consider these nonfiction areas: anthropology/archaeology; business; child guidance/parenting; cooking/food/nutrition; health/medicine; literature; nature/environment; new age/metaphysics; psychology; inspirational; true crime/investigative; self-help/personal improvement. Will consider these fiction areas: contemporary issues; literary; mainstream. Query, "always include SASE." Will report in "2 weeks or sooner" on queries; "1 month or sooner" on mss.
Recent Sales: *Morning Has Been All Night Coming*, by John Harricharan (Berkley Books); *Being Home: A Book of Meditations*, by Gunilla Norris (Bell Tower/Harmony); *The 7 Secrets of Influence*, by Elaina Zuker (McGraw-Hill).
Terms: Agent receives 15% commission on domestic sales; 20% on foreign sales. Offers a written contract, "only if requested. It is open ended, unless author requests time frame." Charges for postage. "Authors are expected to supply SASE for return of manuscripts and for query letter responses."
Writers' Conferences: Attends National Writers Union Conference.
Tips: Obtains new clients through recommendations, listings in sourcebooks, solicitations, workshop participation.

HELEN REES LITERARY AGENCY (II, III), 308 Commonwealth Ave., Boston MA 02116. (617)262-2401. FAX: (617)262-2401. Contact: Joan Mazmamian. Estab. 1981. Member of ILAA. Represents 75 clients. 70% of clients are new/previously unpublished writers. Specializes in general nonfiction, health, business, world politics, autobiographies, psychology, women's issues. Currently handles: 60% nonfiction books; 30% novels; 10% syndicated material.
Will Handle: Nonfiction books, novels. Will consider these nonfiction areas: biography/autobiography; business; crafts/hobbies; current affairs; ethnic/cultural interests; government/politics/law; health/medicine; history; new age/metaphysics; psychology; religious/inspirational; true crime/investigative; science/technology; self-help/personal improvement; sociology; sports; women's issues/women's studies. Will consider these nonfiction areas: cartoon/comic; confessional; contemporary issues; detective/police/crime; family saga; feminist; glitz; historical; humor/satire; mainstream; mystery/suspense; regional; science fiction; sports; thriller/espionage. Query with outline plus 2 sample chapters. Will report in 1 week on queries; 3 weeks on mss.
Recent Sales: *Women's Bodies, Women's Wisdom*, by Dr. Chris Northrup (Bantam); *Machine That Changed the World*, by Jones, Womack, Morton (Rawson); *Masterspy*, by Carpenter/Rapoport (Warner).
Terms: Agent receives 15% commission on domestic sales; 20% on foreign sales. Offers a written contract, binding for 30 days.
Tips: Obtains new clients through recommendations from others, solicitation, at conferences, etc.

RHODES LITERARY AGENCY (II), 140 West End Ave., New York NY 10023. (212)580-1300. Estab. 1971. Member of ILAA.
Will Handle: Nonfiction books, novels (a limited number), juvenile books. Query with outline. Include SASE. Reports in 2 weeks on queries.
Terms: Agent receives 15% commission on domestic sales; 20% on foreign sales.

JOHN R. RIINA LITERARY AGENCY (II), 5905 Meadowood Rd., Baltimore MD 21212. (301)433-2305. Contact: John R. Riina. Estab. 1977. Works with "authors with credentials to write on their subject." Specializes in college textbooks, professional books and serious nonfiction. Currently handles: 50% nonfiction books. 50% textbooks.
Will Handle: Textbooks. Query only. Does not read unsolicited mss. Reports in 3 weeks.
Terms: Agent receives 10% commission on domestic sales; 10% on dramatic sales; 15% on foreign sales. Charges for "exceptional long-distance telephone and express of mss."

RIVERSIDE LITERARY AGENCY (I, II), #132, 2673 Broadway, New York NY 10025. (212)666-0622. FAX: (212)749-0858. Contact: Susan Lee Cohen. Estab. 1991. Represents 30 clients. 20% of clients are new/previously unpublished writers. Currently handles: 65% nonfiction books; 30% novels; 5% short story collections.
Will Handle: Nonfiction books, novels, short story collections. Will consider these nonfiction areas: animals; biography/autobiography; business; child guidance/parenting; cooking/food/nutrition; gay/lesbian issues; health/medicine; history; language/literature/criticism; military/war; money/finance/economics; music/dance/theater/film; nature/environment; new age/metaphysics; psychology; true crime/investigative; science/technology; self-help/personal improvement; women's issues/women's studies. Will consider these fiction areas: contemporary issues; detective/police/crime; ethnic; fantasy; feminist; gay; glitz; historical; lesbian; literary; mainstream; mystery/suspense; psychic/supernatural; science fiction; thriller/espionage. Query. Reports in 1 week on queries; 3 weeks on mss.
Recent Sales: *Presumption of Guilt*, by Herb Brown (Donald I. Fine); *Making a Miracle Marriage*, by Paul Pearsall (Prentice Hall); *Larry Rivers—Autobiography*, by Larry Rivers (HarperCollins); *After Great Pain*, by Diane Cole (Summit Books).
Terms: Agent receives 15% commission on domestic sales; 20% on foreign sales. Offers written contract, binding until terminated by either party. Will charge extraordinary expenses (photocopying, foreign postage) to the author's account.
Tips: Usually obtains new clients through recommendations.

THE ROBBINS OFFICE, INC. (II), 866 2nd Ave., New York NY 10017. (212)223-0720. FAX: (212)223-2535. Contact: Kathy P. Robbins, Elizabeth Mackey, Julia Null. Specializes in selling mainstream nonfiction, commercial and literary fiction.
Will Handle: Nonfiction books, novels and magazine articles for book writers under contract. Does not read unsolicited mss.
Terms: Agent receives 15% commission on all domestic, dramatic and foreign sales. Bills back specific expenses incurred in doing business for a client.

ROCK LITERARY AGENCY (II), P.O. Box 625, Newport RI 02840. (401)849-4442. FAX: (401)849-3440. Contact: Andrew T. Rock. Estab. 1984. Represents 26 clients. Specializes in recreation, health, politics and business. Currently handles: 90% nonfiction books; 10% fiction (package and projects).

Will Handle: Nonfiction books. Will consider these nonfiction areas: business; health; money/finance/ economics; recreation. Will consider "only general, adult" fiction areas. Query with SASE. Reports in 10 days on queries.
Terms: Agent receives 15% commission on domestic sales; 20% on foreign sales. Offers written contract.
Tips: Usually obtains new clients through recommendations from others, and "I go out and get people I want to represent."

IRENE ROGERS, LITERARY REPRESENTATIVE (III), Suite 600, 9454 Wilshire Blvd., Beverly Hills CA 90212. (213)837-3511. Estab. 1977. Currently represents 10 clients. 10% of clients are new/previously unpublished authors. "Not presently accepting new clients, but this changes from month to month." Currently handles: 50% nonfiction, 50% novels.
Will Handle: Nonfiction and novels. Query. Responds to queries in 6-8 weeks.
Recent Sales: *Cross of Stone*, by V. Gregory (Random House); *King James*, by S. Stewart (Crown); *A Gathering*, by J. Kelley (Macmillan).
Terms: Agent receives 10% commission on domestic sales; 5% on foreign sales.

JEAN ROSENTHAL LITERARY AGENCY (III), 28 E. 11th St., New York NY 10003. (212)677-4248. Contact: Jean Rosenthal. Estab. 1980. Specializes in "co-productions and series of titles." Currently handles: 60% nonfiction books; 20% textbooks; 20% juvenile books.
Will Handle: Nonfiction books, textbooks, scholarly books, juvenile books. Will consider these nonfiction areas: animals; anthropology/archaeology; art/architecture/design; biography/autobiography; business; child guidance/parenting; health/medicine; history; interior design/decorating; juvenile nonfiction; language/literature/criticism; self-help/personal improvement; sports. Will consider these fiction areas: historical; literary; mystery/suspense. Query with outline/proposal. Will report in 1 month on queries.
Recent Sales: A nine volume series of paperback travel books entitled *Off The Beaten Track Italy, France, Switzerland, Spain, Austria, Germany* (HarperCollins); a five-volume *Encyclopedia of Mammals*, by Bernhard Grzimek (McGraw Hill); *CD Rom Program* (McGraw Hill London); *The Ponds of Kalambayi (An African Sojourn)*, by Mike Tidwell.
Terms: Agent receives 15% commission on domestic sales; 25% on foreign sales. Offers a written contract, binding for "6 months as agent, in perpetuity for sales. I charge postage, fax, telephone and ask that an advance of $50 is sent to me as a draw against expenses if I take on a client."
Tips: Obtains new clients "any way they come. Write a tight proposal, enclose an SASE and indicate if query is being simultaneously sent to lots of agents. Put telephone number on query letter."

JANE ROTROSEN AGENCY (II), 318 E. 51st St., New York NY 10022. (212)593-4330. Estab. 1974. Member of ILAA. Represents 100 clients. Works with published and unpublished writers. Specializes in trade fiction and nonfiction. Currently handles: 40% nonfiction books; 60% novels.
Will Handle: Nonfiction books, novels and juvenile books. Query with "short" outline. Reports in 2 weeks.
Terms: Receives 15% commission on domestic sales; 15% on dramatic sales; 20% on foreign sales. Charges writers for photocopying, long-distance/transoceanic telephone, telegraph, Telex, messenger service and foreign postage.

PESHA RUBINSTEIN, LITERARY AGENT (II), #1D, 37 Overlook Terrace, New York NY 10033. (212)781-7845. Contact: Pesha Rubinstein. Estab. 1990. Represents 25 clients. 90% of clients are new/ previously unpublished writers. Specializes in romance and children's (juvenile and young adult) books. Currently handles: 20% juvenile books; 80% novels.
Will Handle: Nonfiction books, juvenile books, novels. Will consider these nonfiction areas: child guidance/parenting; crafts/hobbies; health/medicine; juvenile nonfiction; nature/environment; true crime/investigative; self-help/personal improvement; translations. Will consider these fiction areas: cartoon/comic; detective/police/crime; glitz; historical; juvenile; mystery/suspense; picture book; romance; young adult. "No science fiction." Send outline plus 3 sample chapters "with SASE." Will report in 1 month on queries; 2 months on mss.
Recent Sales: 3 untitled historical romances, by Penelope Neri (Zebra Books); 2 untitled historical romances, by Danelle Harmon (Avon); 1 romantic suspense, by Sheryl Lynn (Harlequin); 1 young adult ethnic novel by Sara Gogol (Lerner).
Terms: Agent receives 15% commission on domestic sales; 15% on foreign sales. Offers a written contract. Charges for photocopying. "No collect calls."
Tips: "I advertise with writers' groups, with *Romantic Times*, the RWA. For children's book illustrators, I go to galleries, keep an eye on magazine ads. Keep the query letter and synopsis short. The work speaks for itself better than any description can. A phone call after 1 month is acceptable. Always include an SASE with the material."

SANDUM & ASSOCIATES (II), 144 E. 84th St., New York NY 10028. (212)737-2011. Fax number by request. President: Howard E. Sandum. Estab. 1987. Represents 35 clients. 20% of clients are new/unpublished writers. Specializes in general nonfiction—all categories of adult books; commercial and literary fiction. Currently handles: 60% nonfiction books; 40% novels.
Will Handle: Nonfiction books and novels. Query with outline. "Do not send full ms unless requested. Include SASE." Reports in 2 weeks on queries.
Terms: Agent receives 15% commission. Agent fee adjustable on dramatic and foreign sales. Charges writers for photocopying, air express, long-distance telephone.

SBC ENTERPRISES, INC. (II), 11 Mabro Dr., Denville NJ 07834-9607. (201)366-3622. Contact: Alec Bernard and Eugenia Cohen. Estab. 1979. Represents 25 clients. 80% of clients are new/previously unpublished writers. Currently handles: 10% nonfiction books; 70% novels; 20% movie scripts.
Will Handle: Nonfiction books, novels, movie scripts. "Query first with SASE." Will report immediately on queries; 1 month on mss "that are requested by us."
Terms: Agent receives 10-15% sliding scale (decreasing) on domestic sales; 20% on foreign sales. Offers a written contract, binding for 1 year "with renewals."
Tips: Obtains new clients through referrals and listings.

SCHAFFNER AGENCY, INC. (II), 6625 N. Casas Adobes Rd., Tucson AZ 85704. (602)797-8000. FAX: (602)797-8271. Contact: Timothy Schaffner. Estab. 1948. Represents approximately 40 clients. Specializes in literary fiction and nonfiction, nature and ecology issues, Southwestern and Latin American writers.
Will Handle: Nonfiction books, novels. Will consider these nonfiction areas: biography/autobiography; nature/environment; conservation issues. Will consider these fiction areas: feminist, literary. Query with SASE. Will report within 1 month on queries.
Recent Sales: *Talking to High Monks in the Snow*, by Lydia Minatoya (HarperCollins).
Terms: Agent receives 15% commission on domestic sales; 20% on foreign sales. Offers written contract, if requested. Charges $15 to cover postage costs.

SCHLESSINGER-VAN DYCK AGENCY (III), 2814 PSFS Bldg., 12 S. 12th St., Philadelphia PA 19107. (215)627-4665. FAX: (215)627-0488. Contact: Barrie Van Dyck. Estab. 1987. Represents 50 clients. 25% of clients are new/previously unpublished writers. Specializes in children's books, cookbooks, true crime, mysteries, medical (trade), biographies. Currently handles: 60% nonfiction books; 35% juvenile books; 5% novels. Member agents: Blanche Schlessinger (true crime, celebrity bios, cookbooks, mysteries); Barrie Van Dyck (children's books, literary fiction and nonfiction, bios, medical/trade, mysteries).
Will Handle: Nonfiction books, juvenile books, novels. Will consider all nonfiction areas except computers/electronics; gay/lesbian issues; new age/metaphysics; religious/inspirational. Will consider these fiction areas: contemporary issues; detective/police/crime; family saga; historical; juvenile; literary; mainstream; mystery/suspense; picture book. Query. Will report in 1 week on queries; 5-6 weeks on mss.
Recent Sales: *Score! My 25 Years with the Broad St. Bullies*, by Gene Hart with Buzz Ringe (Bonus Books); *New Traditions*, by Susan Lieberman (Noonday [Farrar, Straus & Giroux]); *Good Eating, Good Health Cookbook*, by Phyllis Kaufman (Consumer Reports Books).
Terms: Agent receives 15% on domestic sales; 20-30% on foreign sales. Offers a written contract, "30 days cancellation." Charges for long-distance phone, photocopying, UPS mailing. "Separate fee structure if author uses our publicity services."
Writers' Conferences: Attends ASJA Conference, Philadelphia Writers Organization Conference.
Tips: Obtains new clients through recommendations from others, solicitation, at conferences, etc.

HAROLD SCHMIDT LITERARY AGENCY (II), Suite 1005, 668 Greenwich St., New York NY 10014. (212)727-7473. FAX: (212)807-6025. Contact: Harold Schmidt. Estab. 1983. Member ILAA. Represents 30 clients. 20% of clients are new/previously unpublished writers. Currently handles: 45% nonfiction books; 5% scholarly books; 50% novels.
Will Handle: Nonfiction books, scholarly books, novels, short story collections. Will consider these nonfiction areas: anthropology/archaeology; art/architecture/design; biography/autobiography; business; current affairs; ethnic/cultural interests; gay/lesbian issues; government/politics/law; health/medicine; history; language/literature/criticism; military/war; money/finance/economics; music/dance/theater/film; nature/environment; new age/metaphysics; psychology; true crime/investigative; science/technology; self-help/personal improvement; sociology; translations; women's issues/women's studies. Will consider these fiction areas: action/adventure; contemporary issues; detective/police/crime; ethnic; family saga; feminist; gay; glitz; historical; lesbian; literary; mainstream; mystery/suspense; psychic/supernatural; science fiction; thriller/espionage; westerns/frontier; horror. Query. Will report within 2 weeks on queries; 4-6 weeks on mss.

Terms: Agent receives 15% commission on domestic sales; 20% commission on foreign sales. Offers a written contract "on occasion — time frame always subject to consultation with author." Charges for "larger than incidental photocopying, long distance telephone calls and faxes, manuscript submission postage costs."
Tips: Obtains new clients through recommendations from others and solicitation. "I cannot stress enough how important it is for the new writer to present a clear, concise and professionally presented query letter."

LAURENS R. SCHWARTZ, ESQUIRE (II), Suite 15D, 5 E. 22nd St., New York NY 10010-5315. (212)228-2614. Contact: Laurens R. Schwartz. Estab. 1984. Primarily nonfiction, some adult and juvenile fiction. Within nonfiction, half of authors have doctoral and post-doctoral degress and write for both the academic and crossover (education and trade) markets; other half are general trade (astrology through Zen) and professional/business (real estate, finances, teleconferencing, graphics, etc). Also works with celebrities. Adult fiction: contemporary; fantasy; literary/mainstream. Juvenile: illustrated; series. Currently handles: 60% nonfiction books; 40% fiction (adult and juvenile).
Will Handle: Everything described above, plus ancillaries (from screenplays to calendars). Does movie tie-in novelizations. "Do not like receiving mass mailings sent to all agents. Be selective—do your homework. Do not send *everything* you have ever written. Choose *one* work and promote that. *Always* include an SASE. *Never* send your only copy. *Always* include a background sheet on yourself and a *one*-page synopsis of the work (too many summaries end up being as long as the work)." No longer handle screenplays except as tied in to a book, or unless we solicit the screenwriter directly. Does not read unsolicited mss. Reports in 1 month.
Terms: Agent receives 10% commission on domestic sales; up to 20% on foreign sales. "No fees except for photocopying, and that fee is avoided by an author providing necessary copies or, in certain instances, transferring files on diskette—must be IBM compatible." Where necessary to bring a project into publishable form, editorial work and some rewriting provided as part of service. Works with authors on long-term career goals and promotion.

LYNN SELIGMAN, LITERARY AGENT (II), 400 Highland Ave., Upper Montclair NJ 07043. (201)783-3631. Contact: Lynn Seligman. Estab. 1985. Represents 32 clients. 15% of clients are new/previously unpublished writers. Currently handles: 75% nonfiction books; 15% novels; 10% photography books.
Will Handle: Nonfiction books; novels; short story collections; photography books. Will consider these nonfiction areas: anthropology/archaeology; art/architecture/design; biography/autobiography; business; child guidance/parenting; cooking/food/nutrition; current affairs; ethnic/cultural interests; government/politics/law; health/medicine; history; interior design/decorating; language/literature/criticism; money/finance/economics; music/dance/theater/film; nature/environment; psychology; true crime/investigative; science/technology; self-help/personal improvement; sociology; translations; women's issues/women's studies. Will consider these fiction areas: contemporary; detective/police/crime; ethnic; fantasy; feminist; historical; humor/satire; literary; mainstream; mystery/suspense; romance (contemporary, historical). Query with outline/proposal plus 1 sample chapter. Will report in 2 weeks on queries; 1-2 months on mss.
Recent Sales: *Professional Presence,* by Susan Bixler (Putnam's); *Raising Happy Kids in a Troubling World,* by Lynne Dumas (Ballantine); *A is for Abigail, Z is for Zachary,* by Carol McD Wallace (Avon).
Terms: Agent receives 15% commission on domestic sales; 25% on foreign sales. Charges for "photocopying, unusual postage or telephone expenses (checking first with the author), Express Mail."
Writers' Conferences: Attends Dorothy Canfield Fisher Conference.
Tips: Obtains new clients "usually from other writers or from editors."

CHARLOTTE SHEEDY LITERARY AGENCY, INC. (II), 41 King St., New York NY 10014. (212)633-2288. FAX: (212)633-6261. President: Charlotte Sheedy. Member of ILAA. Represents 250 clients. Specializes in fiction and nonfiction. Currently handles: 70% nonfiction books, 25% novels, 3% juvenile books, 2% poetry.
Will Handle: Query with outline or entire ms. Reports in 1 week on queries; 3 weeks on mss.
Recent Sales: *Current Affairs,* by Barbara Raskin (Random House); *Fear of Falling,* by Barbara Ehrenreich (Pantheon); *sex, lies and videotape,* by Stephen Soderberg (HarperCollins).
Terms: Agent receives 15% commission on domestic sales; 15% on dramatic sales; 20% on foreign sales. Charges writers for messenger service, Federal Express and overnight courier services, foreign mail, foreign faxes and foreign telephone calls.

THE SHEPARD AGENCY (II), 73 Kingswood Dr., Bethel CT 06801. (203)790-4230; 790-1780. FAX: (203)743-1879. Contact: Jean or Lance Shepard. Specializes in "some fiction; nonfiction: business, biography, homemaking; inspirational; self-help." Currently handles: 75% nonfiction books; 5% juvenile books; 20% novels.

Will Handle: Nonfiction books, scholarly books, novels. Will consider these nonfiction areas: agriculture; horticulture; animals; biography/autobiography; business; child guidance/parenting; computers/ electronics; cooking/food/nutrition; crafts/hobbies; current affairs; government/politics/law; health/ medicine; history; interior design/decorating; juvenile nonfiction; language/literature/criticism; money/ finance/economics; music/dance/theater/film; nature/environment; psychology; religious/inspirational; self-help/personal improvement; sociology; sports; women's issues/women's studies. Will consider these fiction areas: contemporary issues; family saga; historical; humor/satire; literary; regional; sports; thriller/espionage. Query with outline, sample chapters plus SASE. Will report in 1 month on queries; 2 months on mss.
Terms: Agent receives 10% on domestic sales. Offers written contract. Charges for extraordinary postage, photocopying and long-distance phone calls.
Tips: Obtains new clients through referrals and listings in various directories for writers and publishers. "Provide info on those publishers who have already been contacted, seen work, accepted or rejected same. Provide complete bio and marketing info."

BOBBE SIEGEL LITERARY AGENCY (II), 41 W. 83rd St., New York NY 10024. (212)877-4985. FAX: (212)877-4985. Contact: Bobbe Siegel. Estab. 1975. Represents 60 clients. 30% of clients are new/ previously unpublished writers. Currently handles: 65% nonfiction books; 35% novels.
Will Handle: Nonfiction books, novels. Will consider these nonfiction areas: archaeology; biography/ autobiography; child guidance/parenting; nutrition; ethnic; health/medicine; history; literature; music/ dance/theater/film; nature/environment; psychology; inspirational; true crime/investigative; self-help/ personal improvement; sports; women's issues. Will consider these fiction areas: action/adventure; contemporary issues; detective/police/crime; family saga; fantasy; feminist; glitz; historical; literary; mainstream; mystery/suspense; psychic/supernatural; romance (historical); science fiction; thriller/ espionage. Query. Will report in 2 weeks on queries; 2 months on mss.
Recent Sales: *North of the Sun,* by Fred Hatfield (Birch Lane); *Voices of Silence,* by Frank Bianco (Paragon); *The Color of His Skin,* by John DeSantis (Pharos Books).
Terms: Agent receives 15% on domestic sales; 20% on foreign sales. Offers a written contract. Charges for photocopying; long-distance or overseas telephone calls or fax messages; airmail postage, both foreign and domestic.
Writers' Conferences: Attends Santa Barbara Writers Conference.
Tips: Obtains new clients through "word of mouth; editors' and authors' recommendations; through conferences and from people who see my name in publications. Write clear and neat letters of inquiry; always remember to include SASE. Never use dot matrix. In your letter never tell the agent why your book is great. Letters should be spaced and paragraphed so they are easy to read and should not be more than 2 pages."

SIERRA LITERARY AGENCY (II), P.O. Box 1090, Janesville CA 96114. (916)253-3250. Contact: Mary Barr. Estab. 1988. Eager to work with new/unpublished writers. Specializes in contemporary women's novels, mainstream fiction and nonfiction, self-help, self-esteem books.
Will Handle: Fiction, nonfiction books and novels. Query with outline or entire ms. Reports in 2 weeks on queries; 6 weeks on mss.
Recent Sales: *Breaking the Circle,* by Daniel Ryder (CompCare); *Perfect Just the Way I Am,* by Judith Wagner (St. John's).
Terms: Agent receives 10% commission on domestic sales; 15% on dramatic sales; 20% on foreign sales. Charges writers for photocopying, phone and overseas postage.

EVELYN SINGER LITERARY AGENCY (III), P.O. Box 594, White Plains NY 10602. (914)631-5160/ 1147. Contact: Evelyn Singer. Estab. 1951. Represents 45 clients. 25% of clients are new/previously unpublished writers. Specializes in nonfiction (adult/juvenile, adult suspense).
Will Handle: Nonfiction books, juvenile books, novels. Will consider these nonfiction areas: anthropology/archaeology; biography; business; child guidance; computers/electronics; current affairs; government/politics/law; health/medicine; juvenile nonfiction; money/finance/economics; science/technology; self-help/personal improvement. Will consider these fiction areas: contemporary issues; detective/police/crime; historical; mystery/suspense; thriller/espionage. Query. Will report in 2 weeks on queries; 6-8 weeks on mss. "SASE must be enclosed for reply or return of manuscript."
Terms: Agent receives 15% on domestic sales; 20% on foreign sales. Offers a written contract, binding for 3 years. Charges for long-distance phone calls, overseas postage ("authorized expenses only").
Tips: Obtains new clients through recommendations. "I am accepting writers who have earned at least $20,000 from freelance writing. SASE must accompany all queries and material for reply and or return of ms."

VALERIE SMITH, LITERARY AGENT (III), RD Box 160, Modena NY 12548. (914)883-5848. Contact: Valerie Smith. Estab. 1978. Represents 30 clients. 1% of clients are new/previously unpublished writers. Specializes in science fiction and fantasy. Currently handles: 2% nonfiction books; 96% novels; 1% novellas; 1% short story collections.
Will Handle: Novels. Will consider these fiction areas: fantasy; literary; mainstream; science fiction; young adult. Query. Will report in 2 weeks on queries; 2 months on mss.
Recent Sales: *A Deeper Sea*, by Alexander Jablokov (William Morrow); *Talking to Dragons*, by Patricia C. Wrede (HBJ/Yolen); *Phoenix Guards*, by Steven Boust (Tor Books).
Terms: Agent receives 15% on domestic sales; 20% on foreign sales. Offers a written contract. Charges for "extraordinary expenses by mutual consent."
Tips: Obtains new clients through "recommendations from other clients, various respected contacts."

MICHAEL SNELL LITERARY AGENCY (II), Box 655, Truro MA 02666. (508)349-3718. Contact: Michael Snell. Estab. 1980. Represents 200 clients. 25% of clients are new/previously unpublished authors. Specializes in "all types of business and computer books, from low-level how-to to professional and reference." Currently handles: 90% nonfiction books, 10% novels. Member agents: Michael Snell (nonfiction); Patricia Smith (fiction and children's books).
Will Handle: Nonfiction books, textbooks, scholarly books, juvenile books. Open to all nonfiction categories. Will consider these fiction areas: literary; mystery/suspense; thriller/espionage. Query with SASE. Will report in 1 week on queries; 2 weeks on mss.
Recent Sales: *Life's Parachutes*, by Paul Coleman (Dell/Delacorte); *Recession-Proof Your Business*, by Larry Tuller (Bob Adams, Inc.); *The Seamless Enterprise*, by Don Dimancescu (HarperCollins); *Vax Cobol*, by James Janossy (John Wiley & Sons).
Terms: Agent receives 15% on domestic sales; 15% on foreign sales.
Tips: Obtains new clients through unsolicited manuscripts, word-of-mouth, *LMP* and *Writer's Market*. "Send a half- to a full-page query. We offer a booklet, 'How to Write a Book Proposal,' available on request with SASE."

ELYSE SOMMER, INC. (II), P.O. Box E, 110-34 73rd Rd., Forest Hills NY 11375. (718)263-2668. President: Elyse Sommer. Estab. 1952. Member of ILAA. Represents 20 clients. Works with a small number of new/unpublished authors. Specializes in nonfiction: reference books, dictionaries, popular culture. Currently handles: 90% nonfiction books; 5% novels; 5% juvenile.
Will Handle: Novels (some mystery but no sci-fi), juvenile books (no pre-school). Query with outline. Reports in 2 weeks on queries.
Recent Sales: The Panel Digest (annuals), Kids' World Almanac Books, several reference books, *Falser Than a Weeping Crocodile*.
Terms: Agent receives 15% commission on domestic sales (when advance is under 20,000, 10% over); 20% on dramatic sales; 20% on foreign sales. Charges for photocopying, long distance, express mail, extraordinary expenses.

DAVID M. SPATT, ESQ. (II), P.O. Box 19, Saunderstown RI 02874. (401)789-5686. Contact: David M. Spatt. Estab. 1989. 33% of clients are new/previously unpublished writers. Specializes in "mostly novel-length fiction in science fiction, fantasy and horror genres." Currently handles: 5% nonfiction books; 95% novels.
Will Handle: Juvenile books, novels, illustrated fiction. Will consider these fiction areas: erotica; fantasy; juvenile; psychic/supernatural; science fiction; young adult; illustrated fiction; horror. Send outline plus 2 sample chapters. Will report in 1 month on queries; 2 months on mss.
Terms: Agent receives 15% on domestic sales; 15% on foreign sales. Offers a written contract, binding for at least 1 year. "Certain office expenses related directly to the marketing of a writer's ms may be charged, but such would be spelled out in any written contract."
Tips: Obtains new clients through recommendations from others. "This is an arts/entertainment law practice which also acts as a literary agent on behalf of a small number of writers who are past clients, as well as promising new writers. Advice? Always deal with agents and others in written contracts, which you read and understand before signing. Get it right the first time, and you probably won't get burnt later."

F. JOSEPH SPIELER (V), 13th Fl., Room 135, 154 W. 57th St., New York NY 10019. Agency not currently seeking new clients.

PHILIP E. SPITZER LITERARY AGENCY (III), 788 9th Ave., New York NY 10019. (212)265-6003. FAX: (212)765-0953. Contact: Philip Spitzer. Estab. 1969. Member of SAR. Represents 60 clients. 10% of clients are new/previously unpublished writers. Specializes in mystery/suspense, literary fiction, sports, general nonfiction (not how-to). Currently handles: 50% nonfiction books; 45% novels; 5% short story collections.

Will Handle: Nonfiction books, novels. Will consider these nonfiction areas: biography/autobiography; business; current affairs; ethnic/cultural interests; government/politics/law; health/medicine; history; military/war; music/dance/theater/film; nature/environment; psychology; true crime/investigative; sociology; sports. Will consider these fiction areas: contemporary issues; detective/police/crime; literary; mainstream; mystery/suspense; sports. Send outline plus 1 sample chapter and SASE. Reports in 1 week on queries; 6 weeks on mss.

Terms: Agent receives 15% commission on domestic sales; 20% on foreign sales. Charge for photocopying.

Tips: Usually obtains new clients on referral.

NANCY STAUFFER ASSOCIATES (II,III), 137 5th Ave., New York NY 10010. (212)995-9716. FAX: (212)979-1696. Contact: Nancy Stauffer. Estab. 1989. Member of PEN Center USA West. Represents 50 clients. 10% of clients are new/previously unpublished writers. Currently handles: 65% nonfiction books; 35% novels.

Will Handle: Nonfiction books, novels, novellas, short story collections. Will consider these nonfiction areas: biography/autobiography; current affairs; ethnic/cultural interests; language/literature/criticism; music/dance/theater/film; nature/environment; self-help/personal improvement; sociology; sports; translations; women's issues/women's studies; popular culture. Will consider these fiction areas: contemporary issues; literary; mainstream; regional. Query with outline or sample chapter and SASE. Will report in 2 weeks on queries; 1 month on mss.

Recent Sales: Untitled novel by Leon Uris (HarperCollins); *I Married a Communist*, by Michael Barson (Hyperion Books); *Shoeless Joe Jackson*, by Harvey Frommer (Taylor Publishing); *Lucy Companion*, by Bart Andrews (Putnam).

Terms: Agent receives 15% commission on domestic sales; 20% on foreign sales. Offers a written contract. Charges for "long-distance telephone and fax; messenger and express delivery; photocopying."

Writers' Conferences: "I teach a regular seminar at the UCLA Extension Writers' Program titled 'Getting Published: A One Day Tour Through the World of New York Publishing,' which is given every other semester at the UCLA campus."

Tips: Obtains new clients through word of mouth; the UCLA seminar; active solicitation.

LYLE STEELE & CO., LTD. (II), Suite 7, 511 E. 73rd St., New York NY 10021. (212)288-2981. Contact: Lyle Steele. Estab. 1985. Member of WGA. Represents 125 clients. 20% of clients are new/previously unpublished writers. "In nonfiction we are particularly interested in current events, unique personal stories, biography and autobiography, popular business, true crime, health, parenting, personal growth and psychological self-help. In fiction we are interested in good mysteries not of the hard-boiled type, horror and occult of all types, thrillers and historical novels. We are also open to quality fiction." Currently handles: 70% nonfiction books; 30% novels. Member agents: Joe Vitale (Houston, nonfiction); Jim Kepler (Chicago, nonfiction).

Will Handle: Nonfiction books, novels. Will consider these nonfiction areas: anthropology/archaeology; biography/autobiography; business; child guidance/parenting; cooking/food/nutrition; current affairs; ethnic/cultural interests; gay/lesbian issues; government/politics/law; health/medicine; history; money/finance/economics; nature/environment; new age/metaphysics; psychology; true crime/investigative; science/technology; self-help/personal improvement; sociology; sports. Will consider these fiction areas: detective/police/crime; family saga; gay; historical; lesbian; literary; mystery/suspense; psychic/supernatural; thriller/espionage; horror. Send outline plus 2 sample chapters. Will report in 10 days on queries; 2 weeks on mss.

Terms: Agent receives 10% commission on domestic sales. Offers a written contract, binding for 1 year.

Tips: Obtains new clients through recommendations and solicitations. "Our goal is to represent books that provide readers with solid information they can use to improve and change their personal and professional lives. In addition, we take the long view of an author's career. A successful writing career is built step by step, and our goal is to provide the long-term professional management required to achieve it. Be prepared to send your material quickly once an agent has responded. Frequently, we'll have room to take on only a few new clients and a slow response may mean the openings will be filled by the time your material arrives."

GLORIA STERN LITERARY AGENCY (II,III,IV), 15E, 1230 Park Ave., New York NY 10128. (212)289-7698. Contact: Gloria Stern. Estab. 1976. Member of ILAA. Represents 35 clients. 20% of clients are new/previously unpublished writers. Specializes in history, biography, women's studies, child guidance, parenting, business, cookbooks, health, cooking, finance, true crime, sociology. Currently handles: 75% nonfiction books; 5% scholarly books; 5% juvenile books; 15% novels.

Will Handle: Nonfiction books, scholarly books, juvenile books, novels. Will consider these nonfiction areas: anthropology/archaeology; art/architecture/design; biography/autobiography; business; child guidance/parenting; cooking/food/nutrition; current affairs; ethnic/cultural interests; government/politics/law; health/medicine; history; young adult nonfiction; language/literature/criticism; money/finance/economics; psychology; true crime/investigative; science/technology; self-help/personal improvement; sociology; sports; women's issues/women's studies. Will consider these fiction areas: contemporary issues; detective/police/crime; ethnic; experimental; family saga; fantasy; feminist; literary; mainstream; mystery/suspense; romance (contemporary); science fiction; thriller/espionage; young adult. Query with outline plus 2 sample chapters. Will report in 1 week on queries; 1 month on mss.
Recent Sales: *Majoring in the Rest of Your Life*, by Carol Carter (Farrar, Straus & Giroux); *Stephan in Love*, by Joseph Machlis (W.W. Norton).
Terms: Agent receives 15% on domestic sales; 20% on foreign sales (shared). Offers a written contract, binding for 60 days.
Tips: Obtain new clients through editors, previous clients, listings. "I prefer fiction authors that have some published work such as short stories in either commercial or literary magazines or come recommended by an editor or writer. I need a short outline of less than a page, 1 or 2 chapters and SASE. For nonfiction, I need credentials, an outline, competitive books and 1 or 2 chapters and SASE. No unsolicited mss."

PATRICIA TEAL LITERARY AGENCY (III), 2036 Vista Del Rosa, Fullerton CA 92631. (714)738-8333. Contact: Patricia Teal. Estab. 1978. Member of ILAA, RWA. Represents 50 clients. 10% of clients are new/previously unpublished writers. Specializes in category fiction and commercial, how-to and self-help nonfiction. Currently handles: 10% nonfiction books, 90% novels.
Will Handle: Nonfiction books, novels. Will consider these nonfiction areas: biography/autobiography; child guidance/parenting; health/medicine; psychology; true crime/investigative; self-help/personal improvement; women's issues. Will consider these fiction areas: glitz; mainstream (published authors only); mystery/suspense; romance. Query. Will report in 10 days on queries; 6 weeks on mss.
Terms: Agent receives 10-15% on domestic sales; 20% on foreign sales. Offers written contract, binding for 1 year. Charges for postage, photocopying.
Writers' Conferences: Attends several Romance Writers of America conferences, Asilomar (California Writers Club) and Bouchercon.
Tips: Usually obtains new clients through recommendations from others or at conferences. "Attend writing classes and writers' conferences to learn your craft before submitting to agents. Include SASE with all correspondence."

2M COMMUNICATIONS LTD. (II), #601, 121 W. 27th St., New York NY 10003. (212)741-1509. FAX: (212)691-4460. Contact: Madeleine Morel. Estab. 1982. Represents approximately 40 clients. 50% of clients are new/previously unpublished writers. Specializes in pop psychology, medical; cookbooks; biography; pop culture; parenting; women's issues; alternative medical. Currently handles: 100% nonfiction books.
Will Handle: Nonfiction books. Will consider these nonfiction areas: anthropology/archaeology; biography/autobiography; child guidance/parenting; cooking/food/nutrition; current affairs; health/medicine; history; music/dance/theater/film; nature/environment; psychology; self-help/personal improvement; women's issues/women's studies. Send outline/proposal. Will report in 2 weeks on queries; 1 month on mss.
Recent Sales: *Extraordinary Uses for Everyday Things*, by Cy Tymony (Bantam Books); *Sarah Vaughan: A Biography*, by Leslie Gourse (Scribners); *What to Do When He Has a Headache*, by Janet Wolfe (Hyperion Books).
Terms: Agent receives 15% on domestic sales; 25% on foreign sales. Offers a written contract, binding for 2 years. Charges for overseas faxes, postage, photocopying, messengers.
Tips: Obtains new clients through recommendations from others and solicitation.

VAN DER LEUN & ASSOCIATES (II), 464 Mill Hill Dr., Southport CT 06490. (203)259-4897. Contact: Patricia Van der Leun. Estab. 1984. Represents 20 clients. 50% of clients are new/previously unpublished authors. Specializes in fiction, science, biography. Currently handles: 50% nonfiction books; 40% novels; 10% short story collections.
Will Handle: Nonfiction books, novels, short story collections. "Any nonfiction subject OK." Will consider these fiction areas: cartoon/comic; contemporary issues; ethnic; historical; literary; mainstream. Query. Will report in 2 weeks on queries; 1 month on mss.
Recent Sales: *Goatwalking*, by Jim Corbett (Viking-Penguin); *History of Light*, by Arthur Zajonc (Bantam); *Uh-Oh*, by Robert Fulghum (Villard).
Terms: Agent receives 15% on domestic sales; 25% on foreign sales. Offers written contract.
Tips: "We are interested in high-quality, serious writers only."

MARY JACK WALD ASSOCIATES, INC. (III), 111 E. 14th St., New York NY 10003. (212)254-7842. Contact: Danis Sher. Estab. 1985. Member of Authors' Guild, SCBW. Represents 40 clients. 10% of clients are new/previously unpublished writers. Specializes in literary works, juvenile, TV/film scripts. Currently handles: 10% nonfiction books; 50% juvenile books; 20% novels; 5% novellas; 5% short story collections; 5% movie scripts; 5% TV scripts. Member agents: Danis Sher; Lem Lloyd.

Will Handle: Nonfiction books, juvenile books, novels, novellas, short story collections, movie and TV scripts. Will consider these nonfiction areas: biography/autobiography; current affairs; ethnic/cultural interests; health/medicine; history; juvenile nonfiction; language/literature/criticism; military/war; money/finance/economics; music/dance/theater/film; nature/environment; photography; true crime/investigative; science/technology; self-help/personal improvement; sociology; sports; translations. Will consider these fiction areas: action/adventure; contemporary issues; detective/police/crime; ethnic; experimental; family saga; fantasy; feminist; gay; glitz; historical; humor/satire; juvenile; literary; mainstream; mystery/suspense; picture book; psychic/supernatural; romance (gothic, historical, regency); science fiction; sports; thriller; westerns/frontier; young adult. Query. Will report in 2 weeks on queries; 1 month on mss.

Recent Sales: *The Time of Trimming*, by Haim Be'er (Random House); *The Rabbi in the Attic*, by Eileen Pollack (Delphenium Books); *Little Eight John*, by Jan Wahl, author; Wil Clay, artist (Penguin USA).

Terms: Agent receives 15% commission on domestic sales; 15-30% on foreign sales. Offers a written contract, binding for 1 year.

Tips: Obtains new clients through recommendations from others. "Send a query letter with brief description and credits, if any. If we are interested, we'll request 50 pages. If that interests us, we'll request entire ms, which should be double-spaced. SASE should be enclosed."

JOHN A. WARE LITERARY AGENCY (II), 392 Central Park West, New York NY 10025. (212)866-4733. Contact: John Ware. Estab. 1978. Represents 60 clients. 40% of clients are new/previously unpublished writers. Currently handles: 75% nonfiction books; 25% novels.

Will Handle: Nonfiction books, novels. Will consider these nonfiction areas: anthropology; biography/autobiography (memoirs); current affairs; investigative journalism, health, history (including oral history, Americana and folklore), psychology (academic credentials required); science; sports. Will consider these fiction areas: accessible noncategory fiction; mystery/suspense; thriller/espionage. Query with outline first. Will report in 2 weeks on queries.

Recent Sales: *Black Holes, White Holes, Wormholes: Gateways to the Cosmos*, by Paul Halpern, Ph.D. (Dutton); *Lowney and Jim: A Dual Biography of James Jones and Lowney Handy*, by Alice Cornett (Prentice Hall); *The Enduring Sex: The World of Women Triathletes*, by Jeff Scott Cook (St. Martin's).

Terms: Agent receives 10% commission on domestic sales; 10% on dramatic sales; 20% on foreign sales. Charges for messenger service, photocopying, extraordinary expenses.

Tips: "Writers must have appropriate credentials for authorship of proposal (nonfiction) or manuscript (fiction); no publishing track record required. Open to good writing and interesting ideas by new or veteran writers."

HARRIET WASSERMAN LITERARY AGENCY (III), 137 E. 36th St., New York NY 10016. (212)689-3257. Contact: Harriet Wasserman. Specializes in foreign, Great Britain fiction.

Will Handle: Nonfiction books, novels. Will consider "mostly fiction (novels)." Query only. No unsolicited material.

Terms: Information not provided.

WATKINS LOOMIS AGENCY, INC. (II), Suite 530, 150 E. 35th St., New York NY 10016. (212)532-0080. Contact: Kendra Taylor. Estab. 1908. Represents 85 clients. Specializes in literary fiction, London/UK translations.

Will Handle: Nonfiction books, novels. Will consider these nonfiction areas: art/architecture/design; history; science/technology; translations; journalism. Will consider these fiction areas: contemporary issues; literary; mainstream; mystery/suspense; science fiction. Query with SASE. Will report within 3 weeks on queries.

Terms: Agent receives 10% commission on domestic sales; 20% on foreign sales.

WECKSLER-INCOMCO (III), 170 W. End Ave., New York NY 10023. (212)787-2239. FAX: (212)496-7035. Contact: Sally Wecksler. Estab. 1970. Represents 15 clients. 10% of clients are new/previously unpublished writers. Specializes in nonfiction with illustrations (photos and art). Currently handles: 70% nonfiction books, 30% novels. Member agent: Joann Amparan.

Will Handle: Nonfiction books, novels. Will consider these nonfiction areas: anthropology/archaeology; art/architecture design; biography/autobiography; business; current affairs; history; music/dance/theater/film; nature/environment; photography. Will consider these fiction areas: historical; literary;

thriller/espionage. Query with outline plus 3 sample chapters. Will report in 6 weeks-2 months on queries; 3 months on mss.
Terms: Agent receives 12-15% commission on domestic sales; 20% on foreign sales. Offers a written contract, binding for 3 years.
Tips: Obtains new clients through recommendations from others.

THE WENDY WEIL AGENCY, INC. (V), 747 Third Ave., New York NY 10017. Agency not currently seeking new clients.

CHERRY WEINER LITERARY AGENCY (III), 28 Kipling Way, Manalapan NJ 07726. (908)446-2096. Contact: Cherry Weiner. Estab. 1977. Represents 40+ clients. 10% of clients are new/previously unpublished writers. Specializes in science fiction, fantasy, all the genre romances. Currently handles: 2-3% nonfiction books; 97% novels.
Will Handle: Nonfiction books, juvenile books, novels. Will consider self-help/improvement and sociology nonfiction. Will consider these fiction areas: action/adventure; contemporary issues; detective/police/crime; family saga; fantasy; glitz; historical; mainstream; mystery/suspense; psychic/supernatural; romance; science fiction; thriller/espionage; westerns/frontier; young adult. Query. Will report in 1 week on queries; 6-8 weeks on mss.
Terms: Agent receives 15% on domestic sales; 15% on foreign sales. Offers a written contract. Charges for extra copies of manuscripts "but would prefer author do it"; 1st class postage for author's copies of books; Express Mail for important document/manuscripts.
Writers' Conferences: Attends Western Writers Convention; Golden Triangle; Fantasy Convention.
Tips: Obtains new clients through recommendations from others and at conferences.

THE WEINGEL-FIDEL AGENCY (III), #21E, 310 E. 46th St., New York NY 10017. (212)599-2959. Contact: Loretta Fidel. Estab. 1989. Represents 30 clients. 50% of clients are new/previously unpublished writers. Specializes in commercial and literary fiction and nonfiction. Currently handles: 50% nonfiction books; 50% novels.
Will Handle: Nonfiction books, novels. Will consider these nonfiction areas: anthropology/archaeology; art/architecture/design; biography/autobiography; health/medicine; music/dance/theater/film; psychology; true crime/investigative; science; sociology; women's issues/women's studies. Will consider these fiction areas: contemporary issues; detective/police/crime; literary; mainstream; mystery/suspense; thriller/espionage. Query with cover letter, résumé and SASE. Will report in 2 weeks on queries; "do not send manuscript."
Recent Sales: *A Deadline for Murder,* by Valerie Frankel (Pocket Books); untitled memoir/true crime by Lorenzo Carcaterra (Villard); Ross Macdonald biography by Tom Nolan (Atheneum).
Terms: Agent receives 15% on domestic sales; 20% on foreign sales. Offers a written contract, binding for "1 year automatic renewal." Bill back to clients all reasonable expenses such as UPS, Federal Express, photocopying, etc.
Tips: Obtains new clients through referrals. "Be forthcoming about prior representation and previous submissions to publishers."

RHODA WEYR AGENCY (II, III), 151 Bergen St., Brooklyn NY 11217. (718)522-0480. President: Rhoda A. Weyr. Estab. 1983. Member of ILAA, SAR. Prefers to work with published/established authors; works with a small number of new/unpublished authors. Specializes in general nonfiction and fiction.
Will Handle: Nonfiction books and novels. Query with outline and sample chapters with SASE.
Terms: Agent receives 15% commission on domestic sales; 20% on foreign sales.

WINGRA WOODS PRESS/Agenting Division (II), Suite 3, 33 Witherspoon St., Princeton NJ 08542. (609)683-1218. Agent: Anne Matthews. Estab. 1985. Member of American Booksellers Association and American Book Producers Association. Represents 12 clients. 70% of clients are new/unpublished writers. Works with small number of new/unpublished authors. Currently handles: 70% nonfiction books; 30% juvenile books.
Will Handle: Nonfiction and juvenile books. "Books must be completed and designed for a distinct market niche."
Recent Sales: *A Rose for Abby,* by Donna Guthrie (Abingdon); *The Gone With the Wind Handbook,* by Pauline Bartel (Taylor); *Encore,* by Graciela de Armas (Humbert Books).
Terms: Receives 15% commission on domestic sales; 15% on dramatic sales; 15% on foreign sales.

RUTH WRESCHNER, AUTHORS' REPRESENTATIVE (II, III), 10 W. 74th St., New York NY 10023. (212)877-2605. FAX: (212)595-5843. Agent. Ruth Wreschner. Estab. 1981. Represents 60 clients. 70% of clients are new/unpublished writers. "In fiction, if a client is not published yet, I prefer writers who have written for magazines; in nonfiction, a person well qualified in his field is acceptable." Prefers to work with published/established authors; works with new/unpublished authors. "I will always pay

attention to a writer referred by another client." Specializes in popular medicine, health, how-to books and fiction (no pornography, screenplays or dramatic plays). Currently handles: 5% magazine articles; 80% nonfiction books; 10% novels; 5% textbooks; 5% juvenile books.
Will Handle: Adult and young adult fiction, nonfiction, textbooks, magazine articles (only if appropriate for commercial magazines). Particularly interested in mainstream and mystery fiction. Query with outline. Reports in 2 weeks on queries.
Recent Sales: *When Good Kids Do Bad Things*, by Katherin Gordy Levine (W.W. Norton); *Pay for Play*, by Reed E. Bunzel (Avon); *The Alzheimer Trust: Quest for the Familial Gene in Alzheimer's Disease*, by Daniel A. Pollen, M.D. (Oxford University Press).
Terms: Agent receives 15% commission on domestic sales; 20% on foreign sales. Charges for photocopying expenses. "Once a book is placed, I will retain some money from the second advance to cover airmail postage of books, long-distance calls, etc. on foreign sales. I may consider charging for reviewing contracts in future. In that case I will charge $50/hour plus long-distance calls, if any."

WRITERS HOUSE (III), 21 W. 26th St., New York NY 10010. (212)685-2400. FAX: (212)685-1781. Contact: Albert Zuckerman. Estab. 1974. Member of ILAA. Represents 280 clients. 50% of clients are new/unpublished writers. Specializes in all types of popular fiction and nonfiction. "No scholarly, professional, poetry and no screenplays." Currently handles: 25% nonfiction books; 35% juvenile books; 40% novels. Member agents: Albert Zuckerman (major novels, thrillers, women's fiction, important nonfiction); Amy Berkower (major juvenile authors, women's fiction, art and decorating, cookbooks, psychology); Merrillee Heifetz (science fiction and fantasy, popular culture, literary fiction); Susan Cohen (juvenile and young adult fiction and nonfiction, Judaism, women's issues); Susan Ginsberg (serious and popular fiction, true crime, narrative nonfiction, personality books, cookbooks).
Will Handle: Nonfiction books, juvenile books, novels. Will consider these nonfiction areas: animals; art/architecture/design; biography/autobiography; business; child guidance/parenting; cooking/food/nutrition; health/medicine; history; interior design/decorating; juvenile nonfiction; military/war; money/finance/economics; music/dance/theater/film; nature/environment; psychology; true crime/investigative; science/technology; self-help/personal improvement; women's issues/women's studies. Will consider any fiction area. "Quality is everything." Query. Will report in 1 month on queries.
Terms: Agent receives 15% on domestic sales; 20% on foreign sales. Offers a written contract, binding for 1 year.
Tips: Obtain new clients through recommendations from others. "Write a wonderful book."

WRITERS' PRODUCTIONS (II), P.O. Box 630, Westport CT 06881. (203)227-8199. Contact: David L. Meth. Estab. 1982. Represents 25 clients. Specializes in "literary-quality fiction and nonfiction, with a special interest in Asia." Currently handles: 40% nonfiction books, 60% novels.
Will Handle: Nonfiction books, novels. "Literary quality fiction." Send outline plus 2 or 3 sample chapters (30-50 pages). Will report in 1 week on queries; 1 month on mss.
Recent Sales: *Night of the Milky Way Railway*, by Miyazawa Kenji (M.E. Sharpe); *Children of the Paper Crane*, by Masamoto Nasu (M.E. Sharpe); *Jinsei Annai: Letters to the Advice Column*, by John and Asako McKinsing (M.E. Sharpe); *Trial by Fire*, by Kathleen Barnes (Thunder's Mouth).
Terms: Agent receives 15% on domestic sales; 20-25% on foreign sales. Offers a written contract. Charges for electronic transmissions, long-distance calls, express or overnight mail, courier service, etc.
Tips: Obtain new clients through word of mouth. "Send only your best, most professionally prepared work. Do not send it before it is ready. We must have SASE for all correspondence and return of manuscripts. No telephone calls, please."

WRITERS' REPRESENTATIVES, INC. (II), 25 W. 19th St., New York NY 10011-4202. (212)620-9009. Contact: Glen Hartley or Lynn Chu. Estab. 1985. Represents 40 clients. 25% of clients are new/previously unpublished writers. Currently handles: 90% nonfiction books; 10% novels.
Will Handle: Nonfiction books, novels. Will consider literary fiction. "Nonfiction submissions should include book proposal, detailed table of contents and sample chapter(s). For fiction submissions send sample chapters – not synopses. All submissions should include author biography, publication list and, if available, reviews. SASE required." Will report in 2-3 weeks on queries; 4-6 weeks on mss.
Recent Sales: *Signs of the Times*, by David Lehman (Poseidon Press); *The Making of a Cop*, by Harvey Rachlin (Pocket Books); *Black Hills/White Justice*, by Edward Lazarus (HarperCollins).
Terms: Agent receives 15% commission on domestic sales; 20% on foreign sales. "We charge for out-of-house photocopying as well as messengers, courier services (e.g., Federal Express), etc."
Tips: Obtains new clients "mostly on the basis of recommendations from others. Always include an SASE that will ensure a response from the agent and the return of material submitted."

SUSAN ZECKENDORF ASSOC. INC. (II), 171 W. 57th St., New York NY 10019. (212)245-2928. Contact: Susan Zeckendorf. Estab. 1979. Member of ILAA. Represents 35 clients. 25% of clients are new/previously unpublished writers. Currently handles: 50% nonfiction books; 50% fiction.

Will Handle: Nonfiction books, novels, short story collections. Will consider these nonfiction areas: art/architecture/design; biography/autobiography; business; child guidance/parenting; health/medicine; history; music/dance/theater/film; psychology; true crime/investigative; science/technology; sociology; women's issues/women's studies. Will consider these fiction areas: action/adventure; contemporary issues; detective/police/crime; ethnic; family saga; glitz; historical; literary; mainstream; mystery/suspense; romance (contemporary, gothic, historical); thriller/espionage. Query. Will report in 10 days on queries; 2-3 weeks mss.

Recent Sales: *Winter of the Wolves,* by James N. Frey (Henry Holt); *People That We Trust,* by Paul Patti (St. Martin's Press); *The Vanderbilts,* by Jerry E. Patterson (Harry Abrams).

Terms: Agent receives 15% commission on domestic sales; 20% on foreign sales. Charges for photocopying, messenger services.

Writers' Conferences: Attends Central Valley Writers Conference and the Tucson Publishers Association Conference.

Tips: Obtains new clients through recommendations, listings in writer's manuals.

Additional Nonfee-charging Agents

The following nonfee-charging agencies have full listings in other sections of this book. These agencies have indicated they are *primarily* interested in handling the work of scriptwriters, artists or photographers, but are also interested in book manuscripts. After reading the listing (you can find the page number in the Listings Index), send them a query to obtain more information on their needs and manuscript submission policies.

Beal Agency, The Mary
Cinema Talent International
Circle of Confusion Ltd.
Coconut Grove Talent Agency
Diskant & Associates
Farber & Freeman
International Artists

Kohner, Inc., Paul
Lake & Douroux Inc.
Merrill Ltd., Helen
Montgomery-West Literary
    Agency
Raintree Agency
Scagnetti Talent & Literary

Agency, Jack
Scribe Agency
Steele & Associates, Ellen
    Lively
Stewart, Charles
Swanson Inc., H.N.

Literary Agents:
Fee-charging

Over the years the cost of marketing manuscripts to publishers has soared. Postage, long-distance telephone charges, travel expenses, legal fees, salaries and freelance wages continue to rise. At the same time more publishers are looking to agents to screen incoming manuscripts and more writers are turning to agents for editorial advice as well as marketing help. To remain competitive, some agents have hired outside readers and editors and are charging fees to help cover the costs. Others are supplementing their income from commissions with fees from other services such as editing, consulting and publicizing books.

All the literary agents included in this section charge a fee to writers in addition to a commission on sales. The commissions from sales of work are the same as those taken by agents who do not charge fees. For domestic sales, the average commission is 10 to 15 percent and for foreign or dramatic sales, it's slightly higher—10 to 20 percent. The additional commission is usually charged to help pay a foreign agent or subagent.

If an agent charges a one-time fee to cover expenses such as postage or long-distance calls and that fee is more than $40, we've included that agency in this section. Agents who charge less than $40 for expenses and do not charge for other services have been included in the Literary Agents: Nonfee-charging section.

Several agencies only charge fees to previously unpublished writers. We've indicated these agencies by placing an asterisk (*) at the beginning of the listing. If you have local or small press publication credits only, some of these agencies will consider you "unpublished" and may charge the fee. If you are not sure if your publishing credits will be acceptable, you may want to check with the agency before sending material.

One problem with grouping fee-charging agents together is the wide variety of fees and the differences in terminology used to describe these fees from agency to agency. Some charge for reading a manuscript, some for reading and evaluation. Others will read manuscripts for free but charge for critiquing or editing. A few offer consultation for a fee and still others offer typing services.

Be sure to ask for a fee schedule and to ask questions about fees. It's important for writers to have a clear understanding of what the fees cover, how they will be charged and what they can expect for their money. Here's a list of some of the terms used and how each is generally defined:

- Reading fees—This is a fee charged for reading a manuscript. Most agents do not charge to look at queries alone. For many agents, the fee is used to pay an outside reader to sift through the unsolicited manuscripts. It is generally a one-time, nonrefundable fee, but some agents will return the money if they agree to take you on as a client.

- Evaluation fees—Sometimes a reading fee will include a written evaluation, but many agents charge for evaluations separately. The evaluation may be a one-paragraph report on the marketability of the manuscript or a full, several page evaluation covering marketability, flaws and strengths.

- Critiquing service—Although some agents use the terms critique and evaluation interchangeably, a critiquing service is usually a more extensive report with suggestions on ways to improve the manuscript. Many agents offer critiques as a separate service and have a standard fee scale. Fees may be based on the extent of the service—from a one-page overview to complete line-by-line commentary. Some agents charge fees based on a per-page or word-length basis.

● Editing service—While we do not list businesses whose primary source of income is providing editing services, we do list agencies who also offer some editing. Many do not make the distinction between critiques and edits, but we define editing services as critiques that also include detailed suggestions on how to improve the work and reduce weaknesses in the piece. As with critiques, editing services may be charged on an extent basis, a per-page basis or on a word-length basis.

● Marketing fees—These fees are usually one-time fees. They are used to offset the costs of handling your work. They usually cover a variety of expenses and may include initial reading or evaluation. Sometimes these fees are refunded after the manuscript is sold.

● Consultation service—Some agents will charge an hourly rate to act as a marketing consultant. This service is usually offered to writers who are not clients and who just want advice on marketing or on a publisher's contract. A few agents are also lawyers and may offer legal advice for an hourly rate.

● Other services—Depending on an agent's background or abilities, the agent may offer a variety of other services to writers including typing, copyediting, proofreading and even book publicity.

Payment of a reading or other fee hardly ever ensures that an agent will agree to take you on as a client. Ask for references or sample critiques, so you have a good idea what you will receive for your money.

Because they are charging for the additional service, fee-charging agents tend to be more open to reading and handling the work of new writers. If you feel you need more than sales help and would not mind paying for an evaluation or critique from a professional, then the agents listed in this section may interest you. We cannot stress enough, however, the importance of researching these agencies. Do not hesitate to ask any questions you feel will help you to make your decision. (A list of possible questions and other important information on agents appears in Finding and Working with Literary Agents starting on page 28.)

To help you with your search for an agent, we've included a number of special indexes in the back of this book. The Subject Index is divided into sections for fee-charging and nonfee-charging literary agents and script agents. Each of these sections in the index is then divided by nonfiction and fiction subject categories. If you have written a book on psychology finance and you would consider a fee-charging agent, turn to the nonfiction subjects listed in that section of the Subject Index. You will find a subject heading for psychology followed by the names of agencies interested in this type of work. Some agencies did not want to restrict themselves to specific subjects. We've grouped them in the heading "open" in the nonfiction and fiction categories.

We've included an Agents and Reps Index as well. Often you will read about an agent, but since that agent is an employee of a large agency, you may not be able to find that person's business address or phone number. We've asked agencies to give us the names of agents on their staffs. Then we've listed the names in alphabetical order along with the name of their agency. Find the name of the person you would like to contact and then check the listing for that agency. You will find the page number for the agency's listing in the Listings Index at the end of the book.

Some art representatives, especially those interested in humor (cartoons and comics) and children's books, are also looking for writers. If the agency is primarily an art representative, but also interested in writers and that agency charges a reading or submission fee, we've included it in Additional Fee-charging Agents at the end of the listings in this section. For example if ABC Art Reps, Inc. handles the work of artists, but may be interested in writers who can draw, they would be mentioned in the list, but their complete listing will appear in the Commercial Art/Photo Reps section.

Many of the literary agents listed in this section are also interested in scripts and vice versa. If the agency's primary function is selling scripts, but is interested in seeing some book manuscripts and charges a reading fee, we've also included them in Additional Fee-charging Agents. Their complete listings, however, appear in the Script Agent section.

For more information on approaching agents and the specifics of our listings, please see Finding and Working with Literary Agents and the following sample agent listing. See also the various articles included at the beginning of this book for the answers to a wide variety of questions concerning the author/agent relationship.

We've ranked the agencies listed in this section according to their openness to submissions. Below is our ranking system:

I New agency (less than one year in business) actively seeking clients.

II Agency seeking both new and established writers.

III Agency prefers to work with established writers, mostly obtains new clients through referrals.

IV Agency handling only certain types of work or work by writers under certain circumstances.

V Agency not currently seeking new clients. (If an agency chose this designation, only the address is given). We have included mention of agencies rated V only to let you know they are not open to new clients at this time. In addition to those ranked V, we have included a few well-known agencies' names who have declined listings. *Unless you have a strong recommendation from someone well respected in the field, our advice is to approach only those agents ranked I-IV.*

Sample listing

The following is a sample listing for fee-charging literary agents. Each element of the listing is numbered and numbers correspond to explanations following the listing. For more information on specific terms see the Glossary and introductions to the listings.

(1) *SOUTHERN WRITERS (II), Suite 1020, 635 Gravier St., New Orleans LA 70130. (504)525-6390. FAX: (504)524-7349. (2) Contact: Pamela G. Ahearn. (3) Estab. 1979. (4) Member of Romance Writers of America. (5) Represents 30 clients. (6) 40% of clients are new/previously unpublished writers. (7) Specializes in fiction/nonfiction based in the Deep South; romance (both historical and contemporary). (8) Currently handles: 30% nonfiction books; 10% juvenile books; 60% novels. (9)
(10) Will Handle: Nonfiction books, juvenile books, ("young adult and young readers, not children's picture books"), novels. (11) Will consider these nonfiction areas: biography; business; child guidance/parenting; current affairs; gay/lesbian issues; health/medicine; history; juvenile nonfiction; money/finance/economics; music/dance/theater/film; psychology; religious/inspirational; true crime/investigative; self-help/personal improvement; women's issues/women's studies. (12) Will consider these fiction areas: action/adventure; contemporary issues; detective/police/crime; family saga; fantasy; feminist; gay; glitz; historical; humor/satire; juvenile; lesbian; literary; mainstream; mystery/suspense; psychic/supernatural; regional; religious/inspiration; romance; science fiction; thriller/espionage; westerns/frontier; young adult. (13) Query. (14) Will report in 2-3 weeks on queries; 6-8 weeks on mss.
(15) Recent Sales: *Lions and Lace*, by Meagan McKinney (Dell); *Deadly Currents* and *Fatal Ingredients*, by Caroline Burnes (Harlequin Intrigue); *Second Son*, by Kate Moore (Avon).
(16) Terms: Agent receives 15% commission on domestic sales; 20% on foreign sales. (17) Offers a written contract, binding for 1 year.
(18) Fees: Charges a reading fee of up to $450 for 200,000-word ms. "Reading fees are charged to unpublished authors, and to authors writing in areas other than those of previous publication (i.e., nonfiction authors writing fiction). Fee is nonrefundable. We offer criticism at a fee slightly higher than our reading fees. Authors who pay a reading fee or criticism fee receive a 3-5 page, single-spaced letter, explaining what we feel the problems of their books are from both a qualitative and marketing standpoint. Letters are written by Pamela G. Ahearn. (19) We charge for postage on an author's first book only if it is sold. On subsequent books there's no charge." (20) 75% of business is derived from commissions on ms sales. 25% is derived

from reading fees or criticism services. **(21)** Payment of a criticism fee does not ensure representation.

(22) Writers' Conferences: Attends Romance Writers of America Conference; Gulf Coast Writers Association; New Orleans Writer's Conference.

(23) Tips: Obtains new clients through solicitation at conferences and most frequently through recommendations from others. "You should query an agent first, and only send what he/she asks to see. If asked to send 3 chapters, make sure they're the first 3, not the ones you consider to be the strongest. Your manuscript should be in complete form and polished before you contact an agent. It should be double-spaced on 8½ × 11 white bond paper, unbound. Make your query letter brief and to the point, listing publishing credentials, writer's groups and organizations you may belong to, awards, etc. Do *not* make it cute, outlandish or hostile!"

(1) Symbols, names, addresses, phone number, ranking. Agencies which only charge fees to previously unpublished writers or only under very specific circumstances receive an asterisk. If you are self-published or published by a very small press, some of these agencies will consider you unpublished and subject to the fee. If you are unsure, ask for a clarification of their requirements. Take special note of the ranking codes (I-V) which appear after the name of the agency. Those ranked I or II and some ranked IV are most open to new writers. Agencies ranked III prefer established writers or those with strong referrals. Those with rankings of V are not looking for new clients and are included only to inform our readers. A few well-known agencies which prefer not to be listed are also included (name and address only). For the most part these agencies do not wish to list because they are not looking for new clients and will only accept queries from writers with very strong references. For a complete explanation of the different rankings, please see the section introduction.

(2) Contact name/s. Send your query or manuscript to the name or one of the names listed. If you are not sure of the gender, it is best to use the full name, such as "Dear Robin Jones." Occasionally no contact name is given. In such a case, "Dear Agency Director" usually is acceptable. If the agency has listed other member agents (see #9) and has indicated a specialty with the name, address your query to the agent who handles the work you do.

(3) Establishment date. While an agency that has been in business a number of years is a good sign the agent is stable and has built up a network of helpful contacts in the industry, new agencies are often most open to new clients and eager to work with new or previously unpublished writers.

(4) Memberships. Many agents in this section are members of agent organizations. We use the blanket term "member of" in the listings, but agents listed as members of writers' organizations are actually signatories or associate members. This is especially true of the Writers Guild of America. While there are respectable agencies who are not members of any group, membership in a recognized agent or writer organization suggests the agency has met certain requirements and has agreed to adhere to a code of ethics. For more information on some of the groups listed see Finding and Working with Literary Agents. For addresses of these groups see Resources following the Glossary.

(5) Number of clients. The number of clients will give you an indication of the size of the agency. This must be weighed by the number of agents working in the agency. To determine the client to agent ratio, see the number of agents listed in #2 (contact names) and #9 (member agents) or ask the agent how many agents they have.

(6) Percentage of new/previously unpublished writers. If you are a new writer, an agency with a high percentage of new writers may be a good bet for you.

(7) Specialties. If an agency specializes in any type of book or script, it is mentioned here.

(8) Currently handles. This tells you the rough breakdown of the types of material the agency is currently handling. Usually this is an indication of what the agency will consider representing, but sometimes the agency may be looking for something different or may feel they already have too many of one thing and not enough of another.

(9) Member agents. Many smaller agencies are one- or two-person operations. In other cases, however, there may be several agents on staff. We've asked agents to list staff members and, if given, they would appear in this portion of the listing. This information is also included in the Agents and Reps Index. You may read about a particular agent, but not know where the agent works. You can find out where an agent works by locating their name in the Agents and Reps Index. We've also asked the agencies to list specialties, if any, next to the member agents listed. This will help you determine which agent on staff will be most interested in your work.

(10) Will handle. This is the type of material the agent is interested in handling. If the agency handles some scripts in addition to books, this will be indicated here. The names of other agents who primarily handle scripts, but who also handle books appear in Additional Fee-charging Agents (full listings in Script Agents section).

(11) Nonfiction areas. If the agent has indicated specific nonfiction subject areas, they are listed here. Check the Nonfiction Subject Index to find agencies listed by subject matter.

(12) Fiction areas. If an agent has indicated specific fiction subject areas, they are listed here. Check the Fiction Subject Index to find agencies listed by subject matter.

(13) How to contact. Most agencies request either a query or a query with an outline or sample chapters first. Follow the contact directions carefully. Whether or not the agency specifically requests a SASE (self-addressed, stamped envelope), *always* include one with any of your agent correspondence.

(14) Reporting time. Wait at least 3 weeks beyond the time the agent has indicated before writing to check on the status of your query or submission.

(15) Recent sales. Check this section to see what type of work the agent has sold and some examples of the writers and publishers with whom the agent works. Some agencies did not give this information as a matter of privacy, but when making your decision whether to become a client of any agency, you should be able to obtain from the agency the names of its industry references.

(16) Commission terms. Agents make money by taking a percentage (usually 10-15%) commission from sales of a manuscript. This includes commission on advance and royalties. Commissions on foreign and some dramatic sales may be slightly higher, because the agent will pay a foreign agent or subagent a percentage from their own income on the sale.

(17) Other terms. Additional information on terms will appear here. In the past agencies usually worked on verbal agreements, but today many offer a written contract. Before making any decisions, ask to see this contract and find out how long it is binding and how it may be terminated. The distribution of commission from sales made after termination is an important clause in most contracts. Often the agent will be entitled to money from any sales made up to six months after termination or from additional sales made on work they handled under contract.

(18) Fees. Agents in this section charge a variety of fees in addition to commissions from the sales of the manuscript. Many charge reading or handling fees. (Some charge these fees only to new writers— see #1.) Reading fees are used to cover the agent's time spent reading manuscripts or the cost of hiring an outside reader. Some agents offer criticism or evaluation services. We've asked the agents to provide specifics on who does the evaluation and what type of evaluation you will receive in addition to rates charged. Read this section carefully to be sure you understand what you will be charged. For more information on fees, see the introduction to the Fee-charging Agents section.

(19) Expenses. Some agents who charge fees use these to cover marketing expenses, but many others charge for expenses separately. These expenses may include postage, faxes, long-distance calls, photocopying, messenger, express mail charges. Ask your agent about expense fees. Will you receive an accounting of these fees? Will you be required to pay a lump sum for expenses upfront, or will you be billed as the expenses occur? Some agencies take expenses off the top of your sales. Many agencies will agree to discuss major expenses with you before they are incurred.

(20) Income distribution. This indicates how much of an agent's income is derived from sales and how much comes from reading and other fees. The information can give you a better picture of the nature of the agent's business. If more than 50% of the agent's income comes from an editing or criticism service, then you may be dealing with an agent who pays as much attention to editing as selling your work. This can be valuable to a beginning writer, but more established writers may be more interested in agencies whose emphasis is on sales.

(21) Payment of fees. Payment of fees rarely ensures agency representation, but some agencies say they won't bother with critiquing a work unless they are very interested in representing the writer. If you are paying for a critique, however, and do not make the changes suggested by such an agency, they may decide not to represent you.

(22) Writers' conferences. Although we have used the word "attends" in this section, the agents who list conferences may not attend each one every year. It is best to check with the agents to find out their upcoming conference schedule or check with the conference directors. You can find names and addresses for most conferences in *The Guide to Writers Conferences*, by Shaw Associates, Suite 1406, 625 Biltmore Way, Coral Gables FL 33134. For fiction writers, *Novel & Short Story Writer's Market* will have a conference section in its 1992 edition. Also check writers' magazines for information on upcoming conferences. Each year the May issue of *Writer's Digest* includes an extensive list of writers' conferences and information on attending.

(23) Tips. Listed here is information on how agents usually obtain new clients. Any other helpful advice from the agent is also included here.

ABOUT BOOKS INC. (II, IV), Box 1500, 425 Cedar St., Dept. WM, Buena Vista CO 81211. (719)395-2459. FAX: (719)395-8374. Contact: Ann Markham. Estab. 1979. Represents 16 clients. Specializes in books on business, marketing, how-to, writing and publishing. Currently handles: 100% nonfiction books.

Will Handle: Nonfiction books. Will consider these nonfiction areas: business; money/finance/economics; marketing; advertising; writing/publishing. Query with SASE and 1 sample chapter. Will report within 3 weeks on queries.

Recent Sales: *Big Marketing Ideas for Small Service Businesses,* by Marilyn and Tom Ross (Dow Jones Irwin); *The Analogy Book of Related Words,* by Selma Glasser (Communication Creativity).
Terms: Works on a per-project fee (check with agency for details). Offers letter of agreement.
Fees: Charges a reading fee, includes written evaluation. Charges $1.50 per double-space typed page, $250 minimum. Expenses included in project fee.
Tips: Obtains new clients through "word-of-mouth, listings, repeat business and referrals. Do your homework! Learn how to be a good wordcrafter before you try to sell. We specialize in working with professionals, speakers, entreprenuers and executives who want to share their unique know-how."

ACACIA HOUSE PUBLISHING SERVICES LTD. (II, III), 51 Acacia Rd., Toronto Ontario M4S 2K6 Canada. (416)484-8356. Contact: Frances Hanna. Estab. 1985. Represents 30 clients. "I prefer that writers be previously published, with at least a few articles to their credit. Strongest consideration will be given to those with, say, three or more published books. However, I *would* take on an unpublished writer of outstanding talent." Works with a small number of new/unpublished authors. Specializes in contemporary fiction: literary or commercial (no horror, occult or science fiction); nonfiction: all categories but business/economics—in the trade, not textbook area; children's: a few picture books; young adult, mainly fiction. Currently handles: 35% nonfiction books; 35% novels; 30% juvenile books.
Will Handle: Nonfiction books, novels and juvenile books. Query with outline. Does not read unsolicited manuscripts. Reports in 3 weeks on queries.
Recent Sales: *Dear M. . . . ,* by Jack Pollock (McClelland & Stewart & Bloomsbury—UK); *The Daycare Handbook,* by Judy Rasminsky and Barbara Kaiser (Little, Brown—Canada); *The Greek Letter Murders,* by Maurice Gagnon (Stoddart-Canada); *Working Without a Laugh Track and Other Stories,* by Fred Stenson (Coteau-Canada).
Terms: Agent receives 15% commission on domestic sales; 15% on dramatic sales; and 30% on foreign sales.
Fees: Charges a reading fee on manuscripts over 300 pages (typed, double-spaced) in length; waives reading fee when representing the writer. 4% of income derived from reading fees. Charges $200/300 pages. "If a critique is wanted on a ms under 300 pages in length, then the charge is the same as the reading fee for a longer ms (which incorporates a critique)." 5% of income derived from criticism fees. Critique includes "two- to three-page overall evaluation which will contain any specific points that are thought important enough to detail. Marketing advice is not usually included, since most mss evaluated in this way are not considered to be publishable." Charges writers for photocopying, courier, postage, telephone/fax "if these are excessive."

FAREL T. ALDEN–LITERARY SERVICE (I), P.O. Box 1813, Fallbrook CA 92028. (619)728-7288. Contact: Farel T. Alden. Estab. 1990. Represents 18 clients. 50% of clients are new/previously unpublished writers. Currently handles: 60% novels; 10% nonfiction books; 10% juvenile books; 10% movie scripts; 10% TV scripts. Member agents include Farel T. Alden (action/adventure, mystery/suspense, historical, scripts, nonfiction); Joan Reynolds (consultant, fiction and nonfiction); Doris Cerea (consultant, scripts).
Will Handle: Nonfiction books, juvenile books, novels, movie scripts, TV-movie scripts. Will consider these nonfiction areas: animals; biography/autobiography; history; juvenile nonfiction; music/dance/theater/film; new age/metaphysics; true crime/investigative; self-help/personal improvement. Will consider these fiction areas: action/adventure; detective/police/crime; experimental; family saga; fantasy; historical; humor/satire; juvenile; mainstream; mystery/suspense; picture book; psychic/supernatural; romance; science fiction; thriller/espionage; westerns/frontier. Query with outline plus 3 sample chapters. Will report in 3 weeks on queries; 2 months on mss.
Terms: Agent receives 15% commission on domestic sales; 20% on foreign sales. Offers a written contract, "which can be cancelled with 60 days notice. We use a standard contract compiled by an attorney specializing in the literary field."
Fees: Does not charge a reading fee. Offers criticism service: "If the writer wishes a critique, he/she may request one. The charge is $1 per double-spaced, manuscript page. We also prefer to make notations on manuscripts in addition to the formal critique. We do them ourselves. They are detailed. We find one of the major problems is an inadequate knowledge of grammar and punctuation! We show the corrections directly on manuscript." Charges for postage, photocopying, telephone. Also offers a manuscript typing service if the writer has a need. Cost is $1.10/page (double-spaced). 75% of business is derived from commissions on ms sales; 25% derived from reading fees or criticism service. "We expect to derive most of our income from sales commissions. The critiquing is a service offered our clients." Payment of a criticism fee does not ensure representation.
Tips: Obtains new clients through recommendations from others. "All our clients to date have come through recommendations. Eventually, we plan to attend conferences and obtain further clients through this avenue. Our agency does not send a publisher a manuscript that is not properly formatted, correctly spelled and properly punctuated. If the writer is not a good typist and lacks in the foregoing areas, we suggest hiring someone to do it; either us or someone locally. Naturally, our emphasis is on

content, but why prejudice a publisher with a sloppy manuscript? At this time, we are very open to anything a writer would like to send us."

*MAXWELL ALEY ASSOCIATES OF ASPEN (II, III), P.O. Box 5098, Aspen CO 81612. (303)925-6500. Directors/Partners: Maxwell Aley and Elizabeth Aley. Estab. 1936. Represents 15 clients. Prefers to work with published/established authors; works with a small number of new/unpublished authors. Specializes in nonfiction. Currently handles: 100% nonfiction.
Will Handle: Nonfiction books.
Terms: Agent receives 15% commission on domestic sales; 20% on dramatic sales; 25% on foreign sales.
Fees: Does not charge a reading fee. May charge a criticism fee to unpublished authors or service charge for work performed after the initial reading. Charges writers for long-distance telephone; other charges by mutual agreement.

JOSEPH ANTHONY AGENCY (II), 8 Locust Ct. Rd., Mays Landing NJ 08330. (609)625-7608. Contact: Joseph Anthony. Estab. 1964. Member of WGA. Represents 30 clients. 80% of clients are new/previously unpublished writers. "Specializes in general fiction and nonfiction. Always interested in screenplays." Currently handles: 5% juvenile books; 80% novellas; 5% short story collections; 2% stage plays; 10% TV scripts. Member agent: Lena Fortunato.
Will Handle: Nonfiction and juvenile books, novels, movie and TV scripts. Will consider these nonfiction areas: health/medicine; military/war; psychology; true crime/investigative; science/technology; self-help/personal improvement. Will consider these fiction areas: action/adventure; confessional; detective/police/crime; erotica; fantasy; mystery/suspense; psychic/supernatural; romance (gothic, historical, regency); science fiction; thriller/espionage; young adult. Query, "SASE required." Will report in 2 weeks on queries; 1 month on mss.
Terms: Agent receives 15% commission on domestic sales; 20% on foreign sales.
Fees: Charges $85 reading fee for novels up to 100,000 words "fees are returned after a sale of $30,000 or more." Charges for postage and photocopying up to 3 copies. 10% of business is derived from commissions on ms sales; 90% is derived from reading fees or criticism service (because I work with new writers). Payment of criticism fee does not ensure representation.
Tips: Obtains new clients through recommendations from others, solicitation. "If your script is salable, I will try to sell it to the best possible markets. I will cover sales of additional rights through the world. If your material is unsalable but can be rewritten and repaired, I will tell you why it has been turned down. After you have rewritten your script, you may return it for a second reading without *any additional fee*. But . . . if it is completely unsalable in our evaluation for the markets, I will tell you why it has been turned down again and give you specific advice on how to avoid these errors in your future material. I do not write, edit or blue pencil your script. I am an *agent* and an agent is out to sell a script."

*AUTHOR AID ASSOCIATES (II), 340 E. 52nd St., New York NY 10022. (212)758-4213; 980-1979. Editorial Director: Arthur Orrmont. Estab. 1967. Represents 150 clients. Specializes in "aviation, war, biography, autobiography." Currently handles: 5% magazine fiction; 35% nonfiction books; 38% novels; 5% juvenile books; 5% movie scripts; 2% stage plays; 5% poetry and 5% other. Member agent: Leonie Rosenstiel, vice president "is a musicologist and authority on New Age subjects and healthy nutrition."
Will Handle: Magazine fiction, nonfiction books, novels, juvenile books, movie scripts, stage plays, TV scripts and poetry collections. Query with outline. "Short queries answered by return mail." Reports within 6 weeks on mss.
Terms: Agent receives 15% commission on domestic sales; 15% on dramatic sales; 20% on foreign sales.
Fees: Charges a reading fee "to new authors, refundable from commission on sale." Charges for cable, photocopying and messenger express. Offers a consultation service through which writers not represented can get advice on a contract. 85% of income from sales of writers' work; 15% of income derived from reading fees.
Tips: Publishers of *Literary Agents of North America*.

 An asterisk indicates those agents who only charge fees to new or previously unpublished writers or to writers only under certain conditions.

THE AUTHORS AND ARTISTS RESOURCE CENTER/TARC LITERARY AGENCY (II), P.O. Box 64785, Tucson AZ 85740-1785. (602)325-4733. Contact: Martha R. Gores. Estab. 1984. Represents 30 clients. Interested in working with new/unpublished writers. Specializes in mainstream adult fiction and nonfiction books. Currently handles: 80% nonfiction books; 20% novels.
Will Handle: Nonfiction books, novels. Will consider all nonfiction areas except essays, autobiography (unless celebrity) and journals. "Especially interested in how-to or self-help books by professionals; parenting books by psychologists or M.D.s." Query with outline. Does not read unsolicited manuscripts. Reports in 2 months if SASE.
Recent Sales: *Wings of Desire*, by Williamson [Lambert] (Avon); *Grey Pilgrim*, by Hays (Walker); and *Breakthrough*, by McConnell (Harbinger House).
Terms: Agent receives 15% commission on domestic sales; 20% on dramatic sales; 20% on foreign sales.
Fees: Does not charge a reading fee. Charges a criticism fee "only if it is requested by the author." No set fee. "Each critique tailored to the individual needs of the writer. We hire working editors who are employed by book publishers to do critiquing, editing, etc." Charges writers for mailing, photocopying, faxing, telephone calls.
Tips: "We do ghosting for professional people. In order to do ghosting, you must be published by a professional, reputable publisher. To be considered, send a business card with your résumé to our AZ address."

*AUTHORS' MARKETING SERVICES LTD. (II), 217 Degrassi St., Toronto, Ontario M4M 2K8 Canada. (416)463-7200. FAX: (416)469-4494. Contact: Larry Hoffman. Estab. 1978. Represents 17 clients. 25% of clients are new/previously unpublished writers. Specializes in thrillers, romance, parenting and self-help. Currently handles: 65% nonfiction books; 10% juvenile books; 20% novels; 5% other.
Will Handle: Nonfiction books and novels. Will consider these nonfiction areas: biography/autobiography; business; child guidance/parenting; current affairs; military/war; true crime/investigative. Will consider these fiction areas: action/adventure; detective/police/crime; mystery/suspense; romance; thriller/espionage. Query. Will report in 1 week on queries; 1-2 months on mss.
Recent Sales: *The Minstrel Boy*, by Dennis Jones (Random House); *Child's Play*, by Elaine Martin (Random House); *Nobody's Child*, by Martyn Kendrick (Macmillan); *Concerto*, by D. Jones (Europa Picture Investment).
Terms: Agent receives 15% commission on domestic sales; 20% on foreign sales. Offers a written contract, binding for 6-9 months to complete first sale.
Fees: Charges $250 reading fee. "A reading/evaluation fee of $250 applies only to unpublished authors, and the fee must accompany the completed manuscript." Criticism service is included in the reading fee. "The critique averages 3-4 pages in length, and discusses strengths and weaknesses of the execution, as well as advice aimed at eliminating weaknesses." 95% of business is derived from commissions on ms sales; 5% is derived from reading fees or criticism service. Payment of a criticism fee does not ensure representation.
Tips: Obtains new clients through recommendations from other writers and publishers, occasional solicitation. "Never submit first drafts. Prepare the manuscript as cleanly and as perfect, in the writer's opinion, as possible."

ELIZABETH H. BACKMAN (II), Box 536, Johnnycake Hollow Rd., Pine Plains NY 12567. (518)398-6408. FAX: (518)398-6449. Contact: Elizabeth H. Backman. Estab. 1981. Represents 50 clients. Specializes in nonfiction, women's interest and positive motivation. Currently handles: 33-66% nonfiction books; 33% scholarly books; 33-50% novels.
Will Handle: Will consider these nonfiction areas: biography/autobiography; business; child guidance/parenting; cooking/food/nutrition; crafts/hobbies; current affairs; ethnic/cultural interests; government/politics/law; health/medicine; history; interior design/decorating; dance; photography; psychology; religious/inspirational; pop science; self-help/personal improvement; sports; women's issues/women's studies. Will consider these fiction areas: ethnic; fantasy; historical; mystery/suspense; regional; science fiction; sports; thriller/espionage; men's adventure and suspense; women's contemporary fiction. Query with sample ms. Will report in 3 weeks on queries; 3-6 weeks on mss.
Recent Sales: *And Soon I'll Come to Kill You* and *Until Proven Innocent*, by Susan Kelly; *Cathy Cooks . . . Low Cholesterol and Vegetarian*, by Cathy Hoshijo.
Terms: Agent receives 15% commission on domestic sales; commission varies on foreign sales. Offers a written contract on request, binding for 1-3 years.
Fees: Charges $25 reading fee for proposal/3 sample chapters, $50 for complete ms. Offers a criticism service. Charges for photocopying, postage, telephone, fax, typing, editing, special services.
Writers' Conferences: Attends International Women's Writing Guild Conferences.
Tips: Obtains new clients through referrals from other editors. "I help writers prepare their proposals in best possible shape so they can get best possible deal with publisher. May not be the highest advance, but best overall deal."

MAXIMILIAN BECKER (II), 115 E. 82nd St., New York NY 10028. (212)988-3887. President: Maximilian Becker. Associate: Aleta Daley. Estab. 1950. Works with a small number of new/unpublished authors.
Will Handle: Nonfiction books, novels and stage plays. Query. Does not accept unsolicited mss. Reports in 2 weeks on queries; 3 weeks on mss.
Recent Sales: *Goering*, by David Irving (William Morrow); *Enigma*, by David Kahn (Houghton Mifflin); and *Cecile*, by Jamine Boissard (Little Brown).
Terms: Agent receives 15% commission on domestic sales; 20% on foreign sales.
Fees: Does not charge a reading fee. Charges a criticism fee "if detailed criticism is requested. Writers receive a detailed criticism with suggestions—five to ten pages. No criticism is given if manuscript is hopeless."

*MEREDITH BERNSTEIN LITERARY AGENCY (II), Suite 503 A, 2112 Broadway, New York NY 10023. (212)799-1007. FAX: (212)799-1145. Contact: Meredith Bernstein. Estab. 1981. Member of ILAA. Represents approximately 75 clients. 20% of clients are new/previously unpublished writers. Does not specialize; "very eclectic." Currently handles: 50% nonfiction books; 50% novels.
Will Handle: Nonfiction books. Will consider all nonfiction and fiction areas. Query first; if requested, then send outline and 3 chapters. Will report immediately on queries; 3-4 weeks on mss.
Recent Sales: *I.O.U.*, by Nancy Pickard (Pocket Books); *The Year of the Turtle*, by David Carroll (Camden House); *Tale of the Wind*, by Kay Nolte Smith (Villard).
Terms: Agent receives 15% commission on domestic sales; 20% on foreign sales.
Fees: Charges reading fee of up to $85 for new writers only. Charges "a $75 disbursement fee per year." 98% of business is derived from commissions on ms sales; 2% is derived from reading or criticism services. Payment of criticism fees does not ensure agency representation.
Tips: Obtains new clients through recommendations from others, solicitation, at conferences.

THE BLAKE GROUP LITERARY AGENCY (II, III), Suite 600, One Turtle Creek Village, Dallas TX 75219. (214)520-8562. Director/Agent: Ms. Lee B. Halff. Estab. 1979. Member of Texas Publishers Association (TPA) and Texas Booksellers Association (TBA). Represents 45 clients. Prefers to work with published/established authors; works with a small number of new/unpublished authors. Currently handles: 11% fiction; 30% nonfiction books; 43% novels; 2% textbooks; 9% juvenile books; 2% poetry; 3% science fiction.
Will Handle: Nonfiction books, novels, textbooks and juvenile books. Query; send synopsis 2 sample chapters. Reports within 3 months. Pre-stamped return mailer must accompany submissions or they will not be read.
Recent Sales: *Captured Corregidor: Diary of an American P.O.W. in WWII*, by John M. Wright, Jr. (McFarland & Co); *Modern Languages for Musicians*, by Julie Yarbrough (Pendragon Press); and *Weight Loss for Super Wellness*, by Ted L. Edwards Jr., M.S.
Terms: Agent receives 10% commission on domestic sales; 15% on dramatic sales; 20% on foreign sales.
Fees: Does not charge a reading fee. Charges criticism fee; $100 for 3-page critique. Sometimes offers a consultation service through which writers not represented can get advice on a contract; charges $50/hour. Income derived from commission on ms sales and critique fees.

BRADY LITERARY MANAGEMENT (III), 267 Dudley Rd., Bedford MA 01730. (617)275-1892. Contact: Sally Ryder Brady; Upton Birnie Brady. Estab. 1989. Represents 50 clients. 20% of clients are new/unpublished writers. Currently handles: 35% nonfiction books; 5% scholarly books; 15% juvenile books; 35% novels; 10% short story collections.
Will Handle: Nonfiction books, juvenile books, novels. Will consider these nonfiction areas: animals; biography/autobiography; child guidance/parenting; current affairs; government/politics/law; history; juvenile nonfiction; military/war; music/dance/theater/film; nature/environment; psychology; true crime/investigative; self-help/personal improvement; women's issues/women's studies. Will consider these fiction areas: action/adventure; contemporary issues; detective/police/crime; family saga; glitz; historical; juvenile; literary; mainstream; mystery/suspense; picture book; psychic/supernatural; thriller/espionage; westerns/frontier; young adult. Query with outline/proposals or outline plus 2 sample chapters. Will report in 6 weeks on queries; 2 months on mss, "but we try to acknowledge receipt of mss or queries promptly."
Terms: Agent receives 15% commission on domestic sales; 20% on foreign sales.
Fees: Does not charge a reading fee. Offers criticism service. Charges $350 and up, depending on length, for criticism. "Critiques are normally 2-3 single-spaced typewritten pages; often flagged notes on manuscript itself as well. Criticism is specific with suggestions how to make changes, if possible. We often charge for photocopying, and sometimes postage, if exorbitant." 85% of business derived from commissions on ms sales; 15% derived from reading fees or criticism services. Payment of criticism fee does not ensure representation.

Tips: Obtains new clients through recommendations.

RUTH HAGY BROD LITERARY AGENCY (III), 15 Park Ave., New York NY 10016. (212)683-3232. FAX: (212)269-0313. President: A.T. Brod. Estab. 1975. Represents 10 clients. 10-15% of clients are new/unpublished authors. Prefers to work with published/established authors. Specializes in trade books. Currently handles: 95% nonfiction books; 5% novels.
Will Handle: Nonfiction books. Query or send entire manuscript. Reports in 5 weeks on queries; 2 months on mss.
Terms: Agent receives 15% commission on domestic sales; 20% on foreign sales.
Fees: Charges a reading fee; waives reading fee when representing writer. 5% of income derived from reading fees. Charges a criticism fee. 5% of income derived from criticism fees.

PEMA BROWNE LTD. (II), Pine Rd., HCR Box 104B, Neversink NY 12765. (914)985-2936. FAX: (914)985-7635. Contact: Perry Browne or Pema Browne. Estab. 1966. Member of WGA and Society of Children's Book Writers. Represents 34 clients. Handles "any commercial fiction or nonfiction and juvenile." Currently handles: 25% nonfiction books; 25% juvenile books; 45% novels; 5% movie scripts.
Will Handle: Nonfiction books, textbooks, scholarly books, juvenile books, novels. Will consider these nonfiction areas: anthropology/archaeology; art/architecture/design; biography/autobiography; business; child guidance/parenting; cooking/food/nutrition; government/politics/law; health/medicine; juvenile nonfiction; military/war; nature/environment; new age/metaphysics; psychology; religious/inspirational; true crime/investigative; science/technology; self-help/personal improvement; sports; women's issues/women's studies. Will consider these fiction areas: action/adventure, contemporary issues; detective/police/crime; feminist; glitz; historical; humor/satire; juvenile; literary; mainstream; mystery/suspense; picture book; psychic/supernatural; religious/inspiration; romance; science fiction; thriller/espionage; young adult. Query with SASE. Will report in 1 week on queries; 2 weeks on mss.
Recent Sales: *The Deer Killers*, by Gunnard Landers (Walker & Company); *Red Hair 3*, by Charlotte St. John (Fawcett); *Pillow Talk*, by Valerie Mangrum (Silhouette).
Terms: Agent receives 15% commission on domestic sales; 15% on foreign sales.
Fees: Charges reading fee. "Reading fee is nonrefundable inasmuch as we hire an outside editor/reader for a review of manuscript. A copy is sent to the author." Criticism service: $160 for ms up to 80,00 words; $215 for up to 100,000 words; $260 for up to 125,000 words. "Outside editor/reader reports as to plot, character development, writing style, etc." 98% of business is derived from commissions on ms sales; 2% is derived from reading fees or criticism services. Payment of a criticism fee does not ensure representation.
Tips: Obtains new clients through "editors, authors, *LMP*, *Writer's Digest* and as a result of longevity! If writing romance, be sure to receive guidelines from various romance publishers. In nonfiction, one must have credentials to lend credence to a proposal. Make sure of margins, double-space and use heavy-weight type."

THE CATALOG™ LITERARY AGENCY (II), P.O. Box 2964, Vancouver WA 98668. (206)694-8531. Contact: Douglas Storey. Estab. 1986. Represents 31 clients. 50% of clients are new/previously unpublished writers. Specializes in business, health, psychology, money, science, how-to, self-help, technology, women's interest. Currently handles: 60% nonfiction books; 10% juvenile books; 30% novels.
Will Handle: Nonfiction books, textbooks, juvenile books, novels. Will consider these nonfiction areas: agriculture/horticulture; business; child guidance/parenting; computers/electronics; crafts/hobbies; health/medicine; juvenile nonfiction; money/finance/economics; nature/environment; psychology; science/technology; self-help/personal improvement; women's issues/women's studies. Will consider these fiction areas: juvenile and mainstream. Query. Will report in 2 weeks on queries; 3 weeks on mss.
Recent Sales: *Your Child's Dental Care* (Insight Publishers); *Patrick's Corner* (Pelican Publishers); *Doctors Who Rape* (Longwood); and *The Gun's Secret* (Winston-Derek).
Terms: Agent receives 15% on domestic sales; 20% on foreign sales. Offers a written contract, binding for about 9 months.
Fees: Does not charge a reading fee. Charges an up-front handling fee from $85-250 that covers photocopying, telephone and postage expense.

Check the literary and script agents subject indexes to find the agents who indicate an interest in your nonfiction or fiction subject area.

CHADD-STEVENS LITERARY AGENCY (I), 926 Spur Trail, Granbury TX 76049. (817)579-1405. Contact: L.F.Jordan. Estab. 1991. Represents 3 clients. Specializes in working with previously unpublished authors.
Will Handle: Novels, novellas, short story collections. Will consider these fiction areas: action/adventure; experimental; fantasy; mystery/suspense; psychic/supernatural; horror. Send entire ms or 3 sample chapters with SASE. Will report within 6 weeks on mss.
Terms: Agent receives 10% commission on domestic sales; 15% on foreign sales. Offers written contract, binding for 6 months.
Fees: Does not charge a reading fee. Charges a $35 handling fee for entire ms only. Charges for expenses. Payment of handling fee does not ensure agency representation.
Writers' Conferences: Attends several regional (Texas and Southwest) writers' conferences.
Tips: "I'm interested in working with people who have been turned down by other agents and publishers. I'm interested in first-time novelists—there's a market for your work if it's good. Don't give up. I think there is a world of good unpublished fiction out there and I'd like to see it."

LINDA CHESTER LITERARY AGENCY (II), 265 Coast, LaJolla CA 92037. (619)454-3966. FAX: (619)454-7338. Contact: Linda Chester. Estab. 1978. Represents 60 clients. 25% of clients are new/ previously unpublished writers. Specializes in "quality fiction and nonfiction." Currently handles: 70% nonfiction books; 25% novels; 5% short story collections. Member agents: Laurie Fox (associate agent).
Will Handle: Nonfiction books, novels, short story collections. Will consider these nonfiction areas: art/architecture/design; biography/autobiography; business; child guidance/parenting; current affairs; health/medicine; history; language/literature/criticism; money/finance/economics; performing arts; environment; psychology; true crime/investigative; women's issues. Will consider these fiction areas: contemporary issues; ethnic; feminist; literary; mainstream; mystery/suspense. Query first, then send outline/proposal. Will report in 2 weeks on queries; 3 weeks on mss.
Recent Sales: *Two Halves of New Haven*, by Martin Schecter (Crown Publishers Inc.); *What Makes Wolfgang Run? Doing Business with the Germans*, by Philip Glouchevitch (Simon & Schuster); *Investing From the Heart: A Guide to Socially Responsible Investment*, by Jack Brill and Alan Reder (Crown).
Terms: Agent receives 15% commission on domestic sales; 30% on foreign sales. Offers a written contract, binding for 1 year.
Fees: Does not charge a reading fee. Criticism service: $350 for manuscripts up to 400 pages. Consists of a "3-5 page critique/evaluation of manuscripts in terms of presentation, marketability, writing quality, voice, plot, characterization, style, etc. In-house professional editors write the critiques." Charges for photocopying of manuscript and other office expenses. 95% of business is derived from commissions on ms sales; 5% is derived from reading fees or criticism services. Payment of a criticism fee does not ensure representation.
Writers' Conferences: Attends Santa Barbara Writers' Conference.
Tips: Obtains new clients through recommendations from others and solicitation.

COLBY: LITERARY AGENCY (I), 2864-20 Jefferson Ave., Yuba City CA 95993. (916)674-3378. Contact: Pat Colby. Estab. 1990. Represents 2 clients. 100% of clients are new/previously unpublished writers. Specializes in fiction—mystery and comedy. Currently handles: 100% novels. Member agent: Richard Colby.
Will Handle: Novels, novellas, short story collections. Will consider these fiction areas: cartoon/comic; detective/police/crime; humor/satire; mystery/suspense; sports; thriller/espionage; westerns/frontier. Query or send entire ms. Will report within 1 week on queries; 1 month on mss.
Terms: Agent receives 12% commission on domestic sales; 15% commission on foreign sales. Offers a written contract, binding for 1 year.
Fees: Charges a reading fee. Charges $95 for up to 100,000 words, prorated if more than 100,000. Fee is nonrefundable. Offers criticism service, but this is covered by reading fee. Criticisms are done by Pat Colby. Charges for photocopying and postage. Payment of reading or criticism fees does not ensure agency representation.

CONNOR LITERARY AGENCY (III, IV), 640 W. 153rd St., New York NY 10031. (212)491-5233. FAX: (212)491-5233. Contact: Marlene K. Connor. Estab. 1985. Represents 25 clients. 30% of clients are new/previously unpublished writers. Specializes in popular fiction and nonfiction. Currently handles: 50% nonfiction books; 50% novels.
Will Handle: Nonfiction books, novels, children's books (especially with a minority slant). Will consider these nonfiction areas: child guidance/parenting; cooking/food/nutrition; crafts/hobbies; current affairs; ethnic/cultural interests; health/medicine; money/finance/economics; photography; true crime/ investigative; self-help/personal improvement; sports. Will consider these fiction areas: contemporary issues; ethnic; glitz; humor/satire; literary; mystery/suspense; picture book; sports. Query with outline/ proposal. Will report in 4 weeks on queries; 4-6 weeks on mss.

Recent Sales: *Miss America*, by Ann-Marie Bivans (Master-Media); *Simplicity's Home Decorating Book*, by Simplicity Pattern Company (Prentice-Hall); *Doll Eyes*, by Randy Russell (Bantam Books). **Terms:** Agent receives 15% commission on domestic sales; 25% on foreign sales. Offers a written contract, binding for 1 year.

Fees: Charges a reading fee. "Fee depends on length: $75-125. Deductible from commissions; reader's reports provided for all manuscripts read with fees charged." Charges for general expenses—messenger, photocopying, postage. "Less than $100 in most cases. Deducted from commissions and explained." 99% of business derived from commissions on ms sales; 1% is derived from reading fees or criticism services.

Writers' Conferences: Attends Heart of America Writer's Conference and Howard University Publishing Conference.

Tips: Obtains new clients through queries, recommendations, conferences, grapevine, etc. "Seeking previously published writers with good sales records."

WARREN COOK LITERARY AGENCY (II), 109 Riverside Dr., New York NY 10024. (212)769-1705. Owner: Warren Cook. Estab. 1983. Represents 23 clients. Works with a small number of new/unpublished authors. Currently handles: 35% nonfiction books; 35% novels; 15% juvenile books; 15% movie scripts.

Will Handle: Nonfiction books, novels, juvenile books and movie scripts. Will consider these nonfiction areas: biography, history, ecology, medicine, politics, social issues, science, true crime. Will consider these fiction areas: adventure, humor, literary, mystery, thriller, coming-of-age. Query with outline. Reports in 3 weeks on queries.

Recent Sales: *Client*, by Parnell Hall (Donald I. Fine, Inc.); *The Chase*, by Alejo Carpentier (Farrar Straus & Giroux); and *Harem: The World Behind the Veil*, by Alev Croutier (Abbeville Press).

Terms: Agent receives 15% commission on domestic sales; 15% on dramatic sales; 20% on foreign sales.

Fees: Charges a reading fee. "A reading fee is charged to consider for representation the work of writers who have not previously been published by a mainstream book publisher or national magazine or who have not previously sold a script to a major producer." 2% of income derived from reading fees. $350/300 pages. Charges writers for photocopying manuscripts, messengers and overseas airmail.

*BILL COOPER ASSOC., INC. (II), Suite 411, 224 W. 49th St., New York NY 10019. (212)307-1100. Contact: William Cooper. Estab. 1964. Represents 10 clients. 10% of clients are new/unpublished writers. Prefers to work with published/established authors; works with a small number of new/unpublished authors. Specializes in contemporary fiction. Currently handles: 90% novels; 10% movie scripts.

Will Handle: Novels and movie scripts. Reports in 2 weeks on queries and mss. No unsolicited submissions.

Terms: Agent receives 15% commission on domestic sales; 15% on dramatic sales; 20% on foreign sales.

Fees: May charge a reading fee for unpublished authors. Payment of a reading or criticism fee does not ensure represention.

*CREATIVE CONCEPTS LITERARY AGENCY (II), P.O. Box 10261, Harrisburg PA 17105-0261. (717)432-5054. Contact: Michele Glance Sewach. Estab. 1987. Represents 12 clients. 50% of clients are new/previously unpublished writers. Specializes in self-help books, how-to books, travel guides and career books. Currently handles: 60% nonfiction books; 2% scholarly books; 2% textbooks; 5% juvenile books; 20% novels; 2% short story collections; 5% movie scripts; 2% TV scripts; 2% syndicated material.

Will Handle: Nonfiction books, textbooks, scholarly books, juvenile books, novels, novellas, short story collections, movie scripts, TV scripts. Will consider these nonfiction areas: animals; biography/autobiography; business; child guidance/parenting; computers/electronics; cooking/food/nutrition; crafts/hobbies; current affairs; ethnic/cultural interests; government/politics/law; health/medicine; interior design/decorating; juvenile nonfiction; language/literature/criticism; military/war; money/finance/economics; nature/environment; psychology; science/technology; self-help/personal improvement; sociology; women's issues/women's studies; gardening; journalism/writing; career books; travel guides. Will consider these fiction areas: action/adventure; contemporary issues; detective/police/crime; family saga; glitz; historical; literary; mainstream; mystery/suspense; religious/inspirational; romance; science fiction; thriller/espionage; young adult. Query. Will report "promptly" on queries and mss.

Recent Sales: *A Visitors Guide to the Amish Country*, by Bill Simpson (Pelican); *Staccato* (movie), by Deb Ledford (IOF Productions); *Poetry*, by Amy Cox Collins (Dally Meditation).

Terms: Agent receives 10% commission on domestic sales; 10% on foreign sales. Offers a written contract.

Fees: Does not charge a reading fee. "We charge a *critiquing* fee of $95, refundable upon author's first book sale. There is no fee for authors who have already had a book published in the same area. Critiques are 2-5 typed pages addressing marketability, writing style, etc. Critiques are done by the agency director or agency editors." Other expenses are "individually negotiated when the contract is written between the agency and author." 90% of business is derived from commissions on ms sales; 10% is derived from reading fees or criticism services. Payment of criticism fee does not ensure representation.

Tips: Obtains new clients through "over-the-transom queries and recommendations from publishers and writers. Writers should include information on their writing credits and background that will convince agents they are well qualified to write their book."

DOROTHY DEERING LITERARY AGENCY (II), Suite A, 1507 Oakmont Dr., Acworth GA 30101. (404)591-2051. FAX: (404)591-0369. Contact: Dorothy Deering or V.L. Richardson. Estab. 1988. Represents 97 clients. 65% of clients are new/previously unpublished writers. Specializes in historical fiction, science fiction, romance, historical and gothic romances and mainstream fiction. Currently handles: 8% nonfiction books; 5% scholarly books; 1% textbooks; 10% juvenile books; 55% novels; 1% poetry books; 3% short story collections; 8% movie scripts; 4% stage plays; 5% TV scripts. Member agents: Dorothy Deering, director/agent; V.L. Richardson, co-director/agent.

Will Handle: Nonfiction books, scholarly books, juvenile books, novels, novellas, short story collections, poetry books, movie scripts, stage plays, TV scripts, syndicated material. Will consider all nonfiction and fiction areas. Query or send entire ms. Will report in 2 weeks on queries; 6-8 weeks on mss.

Recent Sales: *The Falcon Rises*, by Michael Staudinger (TSR, Inc.); *Prayer of Jesus — Prayer of the Heart*, by Ted Nottingham (Paulist Press); and *Olive The Other Reindeer*, by Michael Christie (Pacific Post Productions).

Terms: Agent receives 12% on domestic sales; 15% on foreign sales; 18% on dramatic or television sales. Offers a written contract, binding for 1 year.

Fees: Charges $100 reading fee for under 100,000 words; $125 reading fee for over 100,000 words. "We return this fee if we succeed in marketing the manuscript." Criticism service is free with the reading. "A 1-2-page critique is done by myself, Dorothy Deering, or one of the editors on my staff." Charges for postage, office expenses, packaging, photocopying. "Because I send to 20 or so publishers or producers, expenses can average $500 per year. I provide quarterly, detailed expense reports to clients." 70% of business is derived from commissions on ms sales; 30% is derived from reading fees or criticism services. Payment of a reading fee does not ensure representation.

Writers' Conferences: Attends Moonlight & Magnolias Conference, Southeastern Writer's Association Conference, Summer Writer's Institute & Festival, and Caribbean Seminar at Sea.

Tips: Obtains new clients through listings, recommendations and at conferences. "It always helps to expedite the process if the manuscript is presented in good form, as suggested in the *Writer's Market*. We are dealing with highly sophisticated publishers, and it is no longer feasible to present them with a manuscript that needs editing, either copy or content. I specialize in new authors."

DORESE AGENCY LTD. (III), 37965 Palo Verde Dr., Cathedral City CA 92234. (619)321-1115. FAX: (619)321-1049. Contact: Alyss Barlow Dorese. Estab. 1977. Represents 30 clients. Currently handles: 65% nonfiction books; 35% novels.

Will Handle: Will consider these nonfiction areas: art; biography/autobiography; business; child guidance/parenting; cooking/food/nutrition; crafts/hobbies; current affairs; gay/lesbian issues; government/politics/law; health/medicine; history; interior design/decorating; language/literature/criticism; military/war; money/finance/economics; music/dance/theater/film; new age/metaphysics; photography; psychology; true crime/investigative; self-help/personal improvement; sociology; sports; women's issues/women's studies. Will consider these fiction areas: action/adventure; contemporary issues; detective/police/crime; ethnic; family saga; feminist; gay; glitz; historical; lesbian; literary; mainstream; mystery/suspense; psychic/supernatural; regional; inspirational; sports; young adult. Send outline/proposal and SASE. Will report in 6 weeks on queries.

Recent Sales: *The Rape of Kuwait*, by Jean T. Sasson (Knightsbridge).

Terms: Agent receives 15% commission on domestic sales; 20% on foreign sales. Offers a written contract, binding for 2 years.

Fees: Does not charge a reading fee. Offers criticism service. Criticism service "depends on length of book."

Tips: Obtains new clients through referrals from past clients. "Don't say, 'I've written The Great American Novel.' It's an immediate turnoff."

*DOYEN LITERARY SERVICES, INC. (II), R.R. 1, Box 103, Newell IA 50568. (712)272-3300. President: B.J. Doyen. Estab. 1988. Member of NWC, RWA, HWA, SCBA, SFWA. Represents 50 clients. 20% of clients are new/previously unpublished writers. Specializes in all genre and mainstream fiction and nonfiction mainly for adults (some children's). Currently handles: 40% nonfiction books; 5% juvenile books; 50% novels; 1% poetry books; 2% movie scripts; 2% TV scripts.
Will Handle: Nonfiction books, juvenile books, novels. Will consider most nonfiction areas. No gay/lesbian issues, religious/inspirational, sports or translations. Will consider these fiction areas: action/adventure; contemporary issues; detective/police/crime; ethnic; experimental; family saga; fantasy; glitz; historical; humor/satire; juvenile; mainstream; mystery/suspense; picture book; psychic/supernatural; romance; science fiction; thriller/espionage; westerns/frontier; young adult. Query first with SASE. Will report in 1-2 weeks on queries; 6-8 weeks on mss.
Terms: Agent receives 15% commission on domestic sales; 20% commission on foreign sales. Offers a written contract, binding for 1 year.
Fees: Charges a reading fee to beginning writers only. "Our fees are very nominal—$50—so we do not refund them if we represent the author. Any criticism we give is free." May charge for international calls and postage, if excessive. "Author is expected to provide a set number of manuscript copies. We have no hidden fees." 99% of business is derived from manuscript sales; 1% is derived from reading or criticism fees.
Tips: "Many writers come to us from word-of-mouth, but we also get quite a few who initially approach us with query letters. Do *not* use phone queries unless you are successfully published, a celebrity or have an extremely hot, timely idea that can't wait. Send us a sparkling query letter with SASE. It is best if you do not collect editorial rejections prior to seeking an agent, but if you do, be up-front and honest about it. Do not submit your manuscript to more than one agent at a time—querying first can save you (and us) much time. We're open to established or beginning writers—just send us a terrific manuscript!"

THE ERIKSON LITERARY AGENCY (II), 223 Via Sevilla, Santa Barbara CA 93109. (805)564-8782. Contact: George or Lois Erikson. Estab. 1988. Represents 24 clients. Currently handles: 25% nonfiction books; 50% novels; 25% movie scripts.
Will Handle: Will consider these nonfiction areas: anthropology, sociology, general. Will consider all fiction areas. Query with SASE.
Recent Sales: *Elvis My Brother*, by Billy Stanley (St. Martins Press).
Terms: Agent receives 15% commissions on domestic sales; 20% on foreign sales. Offers a written contract, binding for 1 year.
Fees: Charges a reading fee of $125 for novel manuscript; $100 for screenplays. Criticism service: money deducted from agency expenses or commissions. Charges for office expenses, postage, photocopying.
Writers' Conferences: Attends Santa Barbara Writers Conference.
Tips: Obtains new clients through recommendations from others, queries, mail.

EXECUTIVE EXCELLENCE, 8 West Center, Provo UT 84601. (801)375-4014. FAX: (801)377-5960. President/Agent: Ken Shelton. Estab. 1984. Represents 40 clients. Specializes in nonfiction trade books/management and personal development—books with a special focus such as ethics in business, managerial effectiveness, organizational productivity. Currently handles: 95% nonfiction; 5% novels.
Will Handle: Nonfiction books, novels, magazine articles. 90% of business is derived from commissions on ms sales; 10% is derived from reading fees or criticism services.
Recent Sales: *Inventing for Profit*, by John Ilich (John Wiley & Sons); *Straight Talk for Monday Morning*, by Allan Cox (John Wiley & Sons).
Terms: Agent receives 15% commission on domestic sales.
Fees: "We charge a $1 per page ($150 minimum) critical reading and review fee." Waives reading fee "if we represent the writer." Charges $300/300 pages. "A $500 deposit is made by the author at the time of signing a contract to cover expenses (calls, mail, etc.) If expenses exceed $500, the author must approve expenditures."

*FRIEDA FISHBEIN LTD. (II), 2556 Hubbard St., Brooklyn NY 11235. (212)247-4398. Contact: Janice Fishbein. Estab. 1928. Represents 30 clients. 50% of clients are new/previously unpublished writers. Currently handles: 10% nonfiction books; 5% young adult; 60% novels; 10% movie scripts; 10% stage plays; 5% TV scripts. Member agents: Wendell Edgar; Heidi Carlson; Douglas Michael.

Agents ranked I and II are most open to both established and new writers. Agents ranked III are open to established writers with publishing-industry references.

Will Handle: Nonfiction books, young adult books, novels, movie scripts, stage plays, TV scripts ("not geared to a series"). Will consider these nonfiction areas: animals; biography/autobiography; cooking/food/nutrition; current affairs; juvenile nonfiction; military/war; nature/environment; true crime/investigative; self-help/personal improvement; women's issues/women's studies. Will consider these fiction areas: action/adventure; contemporary issues; detective/police/crime; family saga; fantasy; feminist; historical; humor/satire; mainstream; mystery/suspense; romance (contemporary, historical, regency); science fiction; thriller/espionage; young adult. "Query letter a must before sending ms or fees." Will report in 2-3 weeks on queries; 4-6 weeks on mss accepted for evaluation.
Recent Sales: *Doctor Death*, by Herbert L. Fisher (Berkley); *The Queen's War*, by Jeanne Mackin (St. Martins); *Double Cross* (play), by Gary L. Bohlke (Producer—Roger Stevens).
Terms: Agent receives 10% commission on domestic sales; 15% on foreign sales. Offers a written contract, binding for 30 days, "cancelable by either party, except for properties being marketed or already sold."
Fees: Charges $75 reading fee first 50,000 words, $1 per 1,000 words thereafter for new authors; $75 for plays, TV, screenplays. Criticism service offered together with reading fee. Offers "an overall critique. Sometimes specific staff readers may refer to associates for no charge for additional readings if warranted." 60% of business is derived from commissions on ms sales; 40% is derived from reading fees or criticism services. Payment of a criticism fee does not ensure representation.
Tips: Obtains new clients through recommendations from others. "*Always* submit a query letter first with an SASE. Manuscripts should be done in large type, double-spaced and one and one-half-inch margins, clean copy and edited for typos, etc."

*JOYCE A. FLAHERTY, LITERARY AGENT (II, III), 816 Lynda Ct., St. Louis MO 63122. (314)966-3057. Contact: Joyce or John Flaherty. Estab. 1980. Member of ILAA, RWA, MWA, WWA. Represents 75 clients. 15% of clients are new/previously unpublished writers. Currently handles: 30% nonfiction books; 70% novels.
Will Handle: Nonfiction books, novels. Will consider these nonfiction areas: animals; biography/autobiography; business; child guidance/parenting; cooking/food/nutrition; crafts/hobbies; health/medicine; history; military/war; money; nature/environment; psychology; true crime/investigative; self-help/personal improvement; sports; women's issues/women's studies; Americana. Will consider these fiction areas: action/adventure; contemporary issues; crime; family saga; feminist; historical; literary; mainstream; mystery/suspense; psychic/supernatural; romance; sports; thriller/espionage; frontier; military/aviation/war. Send outline plus 1 sample chapter and SASE. "No unsolicited manuscripts." Will report in 6 weeks on queries; 2-3 months on mss "unless otherwise agreed on."
Recent Sales: *Rules of Engagement*, by Joe Weber (Presidio Press); *Southern Secrets*, by Marcia Martin (Berkley Publishing Group); *Missing Pieces*, by Audrey Becker (Pocket Books); *Talking Back to Sexual Pressure*, by Elizabeth Powell (CompCare).
Terms: Agent receives 15% commission on domestic sales; 25-30% on foreign sales.
Fees: Charges $50 marketing fee for new clients unless currently published book authors.
Writers' Conferences: Attends Romance Writers of America; Missouri Romance Writers Conference; Love Designers Writers' Club; Western Writers of America Conference; Moonlight and Magnolias; Heartland Writers Guild Conference.
Tips: Obtains new clients through recommendations from editors and clients, writers conferences and from queries. "Be concise in a letter or by phone and well focused. Always include an SASE as well as your phone number. If you want an agent to return your call, leave word to call you collect if you're not currently the agent's client. If a query is a multiple submission, be sure to say so and mail them all at the same time so that everyone has the same chance. Know something about the agent beforehand so that you're not wasting each other's time. Be specific about word length of project and when it will be completed if not completed at the time of contact. Be brief!"

FLANNERY, WHITE AND STONE (II), Suite 404, 180 Cook St., Denver CO 80206. (303)399-2264. FAX: (303)399-3006. Contact: Barbara Schoichet. Estab. 1987. Member of Society of Children's Literature. Represents 40 clients. 75% of clients are new/previously unpublished writers. Specializes in screenplays, mainstream and literary fiction, true crime, unique nonfiction, business and medical books. Currently handles: 25% nonfiction books; 15% juvenile books; 25% novels; 25% movie scripts; 10% TV scripts. Member agents: Barbara Schoichet (screenplays, literary fiction, true crime, juvenile); Constance Solowiej (mainstream and literary fiction, nonfiction, business books); Robert FitzGerald (business, medical).

Agents who specialize in a specific subject area such as children's books or in handling the work of certain writers such as Southwestern writers are ranked IV.

Will Handle: Nonfiction and juvenile books; novels; short story collections; movie scripts; stage plays; TV scripts. Will consider these nonfiction areas: business; child guidance/parenting; current affairs; ethnic/cultural interests; gay/lesbian issues; government/politics/law; health/medicine; juvenile nonfiction; money/finance/economics; music/dance/theater/film; nature/environment; psychology; true crime/investigative; science/technology; self-help/personal improvement; sociology; sports; women's issues/women's studies. Will consider these fiction areas: action/adventure; cartoon/comic; contemporary issues; detective/police/crime; ethnic; experimental; family saga; fantasy; feminist; gay; historical; humor/satire; juvenile; lesbian; literary; mainstream; mystery/suspense; picture book; psychic/supernatural; regional; romance (contemporary, historical); science fiction; sports; thriller/espionage; young adult. Send outline/proposal with outline plus 2 sample chapters. Will report in 2 weeks on queries; 6 weeks on mss.
Recent Sales: *The Kind of Light That Shines on Texas*, by Reginald McKnight (Little, Brown & Co.); *Day of Delight*, by Maxine Schur (Doubleday); *Marketing Without Mystery*, by Dirks & Daniels (Amacom).
Terms: Agent receives 10% commission for screenplays; 15% on domestic sales; 20% on foreign sales. Offers written contract.
Fees: "FW&S will read submissions at no charge, but may charge a criticism fee or service charge for work performed after the initial reading." Criticism service: "$1 per page of manuscript for reading/ evaluation. Critiques are 3-5 pages of both line-by-line and overall evaluation. Marketing advice is included and the critiques are done by professional editors and/or published authors." Charges for photocopying "unless author provides copies." 75% of business is derived from commissions on ms sales; 25% is derived from reading fees or criticism service. Payment of a criticism fee does not ensure representation.
Writers' Conferences: Attends Aspen Writers Conference; Bruebaker's Writers Conference.
Tips: Obtains new clients through recommendations, listings in *Writer's Market, Novel & Short Story Writers Market*. "Make your nonfiction proposals professional, your screenplays by the book, and your fiction stretched to the limit. Do a little background work before contacting an agent with questions like, 'What do agents do?' "

JOAN FOLLENDORE LITERARY AGENCY (II), 1286 Miraleste, San Luis Obispo CA 93401. (805)545-9297. FAX: (805)545-9297. Contact: Joan Follendore. Estab. 1988. Member of Book Publicists of Southern California. Represents 35 clients. 85% of clients are new/previously unpublished writers. Specializes in adult nonfiction; children's and young adult fiction and nonfiction. "Adult fiction handled only after we have sold one of the author's books in the areas we specialize." Currently handles: 45% nonfiction books; 20% scholarly books; 25% juvenile books; 5% novels; 2% poetry books; 3% short story collections.
Will Handle: Nonfiction books, textbooks, scholarly books, juvenile books, short story collections. Will consider all nonfiction areas. Will consider young adult fiction. Query first. Will report in 1 month on queries.
Recent Sales: *Breastfeeding Your Baby*, by Carl Jones (Macmillan); *How to Hypnotize Yourself & Others*, by Dr. Rachel Copelan (HarperCollins); *Endangered Animals of the Rainforest*, by Sandra Uchitel (Price/Stern/Sloan).
Terms: Agent receives 15% on domestic sales; 15% on foreign sales. Offers a written contract.
Fees: Charges a reading fee. Offers an editing service. "Authors who've been published in the prior few years by a major house are not required to have their work edited by me, but most of them desire it. I was an editor for 15 years, so I completely edit the proposal/outline and sample chapter. My editing includes questions, comments, suggestions for expansion, cutting and pasting, etc." Also offers other services: proofreading, rewriting, proposal development, public relations, etc. 55% of business is derived from commissions on ms sales; 45% is derived from reading or editing fees. Payment of fees does not ensure representation unless "revisions meet our standards"
Tips: Obtains new clients through recommendations from others. "Study and make your query as perfect and professional as you possibly can."

GELLES-COLE LITERARY ENTERPRISES (II), Woodstock Towers, Suite 411, 320 E. 42nd St., New York NY 10017. (212)573-9857. President: Sandi Gelles-Cole. Estab. 1983. Represents 50 clients. 25% of clients are new/unpublished writers. "We concentrate on published and unpublished, but we try to

Agents ranked I-IV are actively seeking new clients. Those ranked V or those who prefer not to be listed have been included to inform you they are not currently looking for new clients.

avoid writers who seem stuck in mid-list." Specializes in commercial fiction and nonfiction. Currently handles: 50% nonfiction books; 50% novels.
Will Handle: Nonfiction books and novels. "We're looking for more nonfiction—fiction has to be complete to submit—publishers buying fewer unfinished novels." Does not read unsolicited mss. Reports in 3 weeks.
Recent Sales: *Legacy*, by Robin Helmsley-Grimes (Berkley); and *The Beyond*, by Barry Harrington (Berkley).
Terms: Agent receives 15% commission on domestic sales; 15% on dramatic sales; 20% on foreign sales.
Fees: Charges reading fee of $75 for proposal; $100/ms under 250 pages; $150/ms over 250 pages. "Our reading fee is for evaluation. Writer receives total evaluation, what is right, what is wrong, is book 'playing' to market, general advice on how to fix." Charges writers for overseas calls, overnight mail, messenger. 5% of income derived from fees charged to writers. 50% of income derived from sales of writer's work; 45% of income derived from editorial service.

GLADDEN UNLIMITED (II), Box 7912, San Diego CA 92107. (619)224-5051. Agent Contact: Carolan Gladden. Estab. 1987. Member of WGA. Represents 10 clients. 95% of clients are new/previously unpublished writers. Currently handles: 20% nonfiction; 70% novels; 10% movie scripts.
Will Handle: Novels and nonfiction. Will consider these nonfiction areas: celebrity biography; how-to; self-help; business. Will consider these fiction areas: action/adventure, fantasy, horror, mainstream, science fiction, thriller. "No romance or children's." Query. Responds in 2 weeks on queries; 2 months on mss.
Recent Sales: *Crime Prevention: America & Japan*, by Robert Y. Thornton (ME Sharpe).
Terms: Agent's commission: 15% on domestic sales; 10% on film sales; 20% on foreign sales.
Fees: Does not charge a reading fee. Charges evaluation fee: $100 (refundable on placement of project) is charged for diagnostic marketability evaluation. Offers 6-8 pages of specific recommendations to turn the project into a salable commodity. "We also include a copy of our handy guide 'The Writer's Simple, Straightforward, Comon Sense Rules of Marketability.' Also offers range of editorial services and is dedicated to helping new authors achieve publication."

GLENMARK LITERARY AGENCY (I), 5041 Byrne Rd., Oregon WI 53575. (608)255-1812. Contact: Glenn Schaeffer. Estab. 1990. Represents 6 clients. Currently handles: 50% nonfiction books; 50% novels.
Will Handle: Nonfiction books, novels. Will consider all mainstream nonfiction and fiction areas. Query first. Will report in 1 week on queries; 2 weeks on mss.
Terms: Agent receives 15% commission on domestic sales; 15% commission on foreign sales. Offers a written contract, binding for 1 year.
Fees: Charges a $50 reading fee. "The charge is for first-time offerings only. When we receive a query, we tell the client we will thoroughly review the manuscript for $50. If we like the manuscript and decide to represent the writer, the money is refunded." Offers criticism, but it is covered by the reading fee. "We try to cover all aspects of the writing—presentation, use of language, characterization, plot, dialogue, subject matter and more. My wife, who has a Ph.D. in English literature and I both review. Outside of the one-time charge, there are no other charges or fees." 100% of business is derived from reading or criticism fees. "Note, this is because we are new; we have not sold any manuscripts yet. However, we have at least one manuscript from each client in front of at least one publisher. Eventually we want 100% to come from sales."
Tips: "Generally, writers hear about us through the grapevine . . . discover that there is indeed a literary agency that has time for them, will respond to queries . . . Writing skill usually comes only after a great deal of practice. A writer can't expect the world to be willing to accept, with open arms, whatever they decide to write. They must do a great deal of research, take painstaking effort to perfect their manuscript, always make sure they write what the public is interested in. In short, if they slap something out without giving it thought, without making a great deal of effort, chances are remote that we, or anyone else will be interested."

LUCIANNE S. GOLDBERG LITERARY AGENTS, INC. (II), Suite 6-A, 225 W. 84th St., New York NY 10024. (212)799-1260. Editorial Director: Sandrine Olm. Estab. 1974. Represents 65 clients. 10% of clients are new/unpublished writers. "Any author we decide to represent must have a good idea, a good presentation of that idea and writing skill to compete with the market. Representation depends solely on the execution of the work whether writer is published or unpublished." Specializes in nonfiction works, "but will review a limited number of novels." Currently handles: 75% nonfiction books; 25% novels.
Will Handle: Nonfiction books and novels. Query with outline. Reports in 2 weeks on queries; 3 weeks on mss. "If our agency does not respond within 1 month to your request to become a client, you may submit requests elsewhere."

Recent Sales: *Senatorial Privilege*, by Leo Damore (Delacorte-Dell); *Who's Who in Hollywood*, by David Ragan (Facts on File); and *Nina's Journey*, by Nina Markovna (Regnery-Gateway).
Terms: Agent receives 15% commission on domestic sales; 25% on dramatic sales; 25% on foreign sales.
Fees: Charges reading fee on unsolicited mss: $150/full-length ms. Criticism is included in reading fee. 1% of income derived from reading fees. "Our critiques run 3-4 pages, single-spaced. They deal with the overall evaluation of the work. Three agents within the organization read and then confer. Marketing advice is included." Payment of fee does not ensure the agency will represent a writer. Charges for phone expenses, cable fees, photocopying and messenger service after the work is sold. 80% of income derived from commission on ms sales.

LARNEY GOODKIND (II), (Div. of Representing the Arts) (IV), 180 E. 79th St., New York NY 10021. (212)249-3185. Contact: Larney Goodkind. Estab. 1949. Have sponsored concert artists. Represents artists. Currently handles: 60% nonfiction books; 40% novels.
Will Handle: Will consider all nonfiction and fiction areas. Query with SASE. Will report in 2-4 weeks on queries.
Terms: Agent receives 10% commission on domestic sales.
Fees: Charges $100 reading fee for novels. "A set amount is returnable to writer in royalties." Offers a criticism service.
Tips: Obtains new clients through "people who know about me."

THE HAMERSFIELD AGENCY (I,II), Rt. 2, Box 48, Marianna FL 32446. (904)526-7631. Senior Partner: J.P.R. Ducat. Estab. 1990. Represents 72 clients. 80% of clients are new/previously unpublished writers. Specializes in English and French nonfiction, children's/juvenile literature, photo-travel books and quality photo-journal "table top" books. Currently handles: 70% nonfiction books; 10% photo/travel books; 2% photo-journal books; 18% juvenile books.
Will Handle: Nonfiction books, novels, juvenile books, photo/travel/journal books. No poetry, lyrics, "absolutely no" TV, movie scripts or pornography. Query with outline or send entire ms (if prior arrangement is made). SASE required. Will report within 4-6 weeks on queries.
Terms: Agent receives 15% commission on domestic sales; 20% on foreign sales.
Fees: No reading fee for first reading. Charges a reading fee for a second reading/criticism for new writers. "Reading fee may be waved at our discretion." Charges $150 for 200 pages, $250 for 350 pages, typed, double-spaced mss. Offers critique service and ghostwriting. Charges $75 per hour for contract reviewing. Charges for expenses. 70% of business is derived from commissions on ms sales; 30% from reading fees or criticism service. Payment of fees does not ensure agency representation.
Tips: "Our interest is in a good writer whether he is a new writer or one who has a book previously published—our purpose is to market and promote our client onto the 'bestsellers' list.' "

HEACOCK LITERARY AGENCY, INC., Suite #14, 1523 6th St., Santa Monica CA 90401. (213)393-6227. Contact: Jim or Rosalie Heacock. Estab. 1978. Member of ILAA, Association of Talent Agents, Writers Guild of America. Represents 60 clients. 30% of clients are new/previously unpublished writers. Specializes in "nonfiction on a wide variety of subjects: health, nutrition, exercise, sports, psychology, crafts, women's studies, business expertise, pregnancy and parenting, alternative health concepts, contemporary celebrity biographies, a very limited selection of the top children's book authors." Currently handles: 85% nonfiction books; 5% juvenile books; 5% novels; 5% movie scripts. Member agents: Jim Heacock (business expertise, parenting, psychology, sports, health, nutrition); Rosalie Heacock (psychology, philosophy, women's studies, alternative health).
Will Handle: Nonfiction books, movie scripts. Query with sample chapters. Will report in 2 weeks on queries; 2 months on mss.
Recent Sales: *Piggies*, by Don and Audrey Wood (HBJ); *Once Upon a Noontime*, by Allan Chinen, M.D. (Jeremy P. Tarcher, Inc.); *Winning With Your Voice*, by Dr. Morton Cooper (Berkley Publishing Co.).
Terms: Agent receives 15% commission on domestic sales; 25% on foreign sales, "if foreign agent used; if sold directly, it is 15%." Offers a written contract, which is binding for 1 year.
Fees: Does not charge a reading fee. "We provide consultant services to authors who need assistance. Charge is $125/hour and no commission charges (10% of our business). Charges for "actual expense for telephone, postage, packing, photocopying. We provide copies of each publisher submission letter and the publisher's response." 90% of business is derived from commission on ms sales.
Writers' Conferences: Attends Santa Barbara City College Annual Writer's Workshop; Pasadena City College Writer's Forum; Palm Springs Writer's Guild Conference.
Tips: Obtains new clients through "referrals from present clients and industry sources as well as mail queries. Take time to write an informative query letter expressing your book idea, the market for it, your qualifications to write the book, the 'hook' that would make a potential reader buy the book. Always enclose SASE, compare your book to others on similar subjects and show how it is original."

INDEPENDENT PUBLISHING AGENCY (I), Box 176, Southport CT 06490. (203)268-4878. Contact: Henry Berry. Estab. 1990. Represents 25 clients. 30% of clients are new/previously unpublished writers. Especially interested in topical nonfiction (historical, political, social topics) and literary fiction. Currently handles: 50% nonfiction books; 10% juvenile books; 20% novels; 20% short story collections. **Will Handle:** Nonfiction books, juvenile books, novels, short story collections. Will consider these nonfiction areas: anthropology/archaeology; art/architecture/design; biography/autobiography; business; child guidance/parenting; cooking/food/nutrition; crafts/hobbies; current affairs; ethnic/cultural interests; government/politics/law; history; juvenile nonfiction; language/literature/criticism; military/war; money/finance/economics; music/dance/theater/film; nature/environment; photography; psychology; religious; true crime/investigative; science/technology; self-help/personal improvement; sociology; sports; women's issues/women's studies. Will consider these fiction areas: action/adventure; cartoon/comic; confessional; contemporary issues; crime; erotica; ethnic; experimental; fantasy; feminist; historical; humor/satire; juvenile; literary; mainstream; mystery/suspense; picture book; psychic/supernatural; thriller/espionage; young adult. Will consider outline/proposal but prefers synopsis outline plus 2 sample chapters. Reports in 2 weeks on queries; 4-6 weeks on mss.
Terms: Agent receives 15% commission on domestic sales; 20% on foreign sales. Offers "agreement that spells out author-agent relationship."
Fees: Does not charge a reading fee. Offers a criticism service if requested. Charges average $1/page, with $50 minimum for poetry and stories; $100 minimum for novels and nonfiction. Written critique averages 3 pages—includes critique of the material, suggestions on how to make it marketable and advice on marketing it. Charges for postage, photocopying and U.P.S. mailing, legal fees (if necessary). All expenses over $25 cleared with client. 90% of business is derived from commissions on ms sales; 10% derived from reading fees or criticism services.
Tips: Usually obtains new clients through referrals from clients, notices in writer's publications. Looks for "proposal or chapters professionally presented, with clarification of the distinctiveness of the project and grasp of intended readership."

*GARY F. IORIO, ESQ. (I,II), 3530-47 Long Beach Rd., Oceanside NY 11572. (516)536-5152. Contact: Gary Iorio. Estab. 1990. Represents less than 10 clients. Currently handles 10% nonfiction books; 40% novels; 10% short story collections; 40% movie scripts.
Will Handle: Nonfiction books, novels, novellas, short story collections, movie scripts, stage plays, TV scripts (includes scripts and treatments for TV documentaries). Will consider these nonfiction areas: biography/autobiography; business; government/politics/law; history; military/war; money/finance/economics; true crime/investigative; sociology; sports. Will consider these fiction areas: action/adventure; contemporary issues; detective/police/crime; erotica; experimental; fantasy; historical; literary; mainstream; mystery/suspense; science fiction; sports; thriller/espionage; westerns/frontier. Query with outline plus 3 sample chapters. Will report in 3 weeks on queries; 3 months on mss.
Terms: Agent receives 15% commission on domestic sales; 20% on foreign sales. Offers a written contract.
Fees: Charges a reading fee only for short story collections. Fee schedule will be negotiated in writing in response to a query. "I will critique short stories and/or collections myself for the reading fee. There are no other reading fees charged for other materials." Charges for postage, photocopying and charges directly related to the marketing of the writer's work. 95% of business is derived from commissions on ms sales; 5% from reading or critique fees. Payment of the reading fee ensures agency representation, "because reading/criticism fee is part of the contract of representation."
Tips: "I am an attorney who also graduated from the Iowa Writers' Workshop in 1976. I have obtained all my clients to date from either my law practice or from Iowa associates."

CAROLYN JENKS AGENCY (II), 205 Walden St., Cambridge MA 02140. (617)876-6927. Contact: Carolyn Jenks. Estab. 1966. Represents 45 clients. Currently handles: 25% nonfiction books; 75% fiction.
Will Handle: Nonfiction books and novels. Will consider all nonfiction and fiction areas. Query with SASE.
Terms: Agent receives 15% commission on domestic sales. Offers written contract, binding for 3 years.
Fees: Charges $60 reading fee but no critique of novel. "May offer suggestions or resources for editorial help."
Tips: Usually obtains new clients through referrals. "I prefer projects that have a potential film or TV sale. I was the agent who first introduced Avery Corman ("Kramer vs Kramer"); Joan Micklin Silver (who later directed Hester Street); and Spike Lee's father."

*JLM LITERARY AGENTS (III), Suite L, 17221 E. 17th St., Santa Ana CA 92701. (714)547-4870. FAX: (714)840-5660. Contact: Judy Semler. Estab. 1985. Represents 35 clients. 30% of clients are new/previously unpublished writers. Agency is "generalist with an affinity for high-quality, self-help psychology and mystery/suspense." Currently handles: 90% nonfiction books; 10% novels.

Will Handle: Nonfiction books, novels. Will consider these nonfiction areas: biography/autobiography; business; current affairs; military/war; money/finance/economics; nature/environment; psychology; religious/inspirational; true crime/investigative; science/technology; self-help/personal improvement; sociology; women's issues/women's studies. Will consider these fiction areas: glitz; mystery/suspense; psychic/supernatural; contemporary romance; thriller/espionage. Send an outline with 2 sample chapters for nonfiction, query with 3 chapters for fiction—except for mystery/suspense, send entire ms. Will report in 1 month on queries; 8-10 weeks on mss.

Recent Sales: *Save L.A.*, by Tricia Hoffman and Nan Fuchs Ph.D. (Chronicle); *The Secret Laboratory Journals of Dr. Victor Frankenstein*, by Jeremy Kay (Overlook).

Terms: Agent receives 15% commission on domestic sales; 10% on foreign sales plus 15% to subagent. Offers a written contract, binding for 1 year.

Fees: Does not charge a reading fee. Does not do critiques, but will refer to freelancers. Charges $150 marketing fee for unpublished authors or to authors changing genres. Charges for routine office expenses associated with the marketing. 100% of business is derived from commissions on manuscript sales.

Tips: "Most of my clients are referred to me by other clients or editors. If you want to be successful, learn all you can about proper submission and invest in the equipment or service to make your project *look* dazzling. Computers are available to everyone and the competition looks good. You must at least match that to even get noticed."

LARRY KALTMAN LITERARY AGENCY (II), 1301 S. Scott St., Arlington VA 22204. (703)920-3771. Contact: Larry Kaltman. Estab. 1984. Represents 15 clients. 75% of clients are new/previously unpublished writers. Currently handles: 10% nonfiction books; 75% novels; 10% novellas; 5% short story collections.

Will Handle: Nonfiction books, novels, novellas, short story collections. Will consider these nonfiction areas: health/medicine; science/technology; self-help/personal improvement; sports. Will consider these fiction areas: action/adventure; confessional; contemporary issues; detective/police/crime; erotica; ethnic; humor/satire; literary; mainstream; mystery/suspense; romance (contemporary); sports; thriller/espionage; young adult. Query. Will report in 1 week on queries; 2 weeks on mss.

Recent Sales: *Rastus on Capitol Hill*, by Samuel Edison (Hunter House); *Anything That's All*, by Shirley Cochrane (Signal Books); *Throwing for a Loop*, by Larry Kaltman (The Washington Post).

Terms: Agent receives 15% commission on domestic sales; 25% on foreign sales. Offers a written contract, binding for 1 year.

Fees: Charges a reading fee "for all unsolicited manuscripts; for up to 300 pages, the fee is $150. For each additional page the charge is 50¢/page. The criticism and reading services are indistinguishable. Author receives an approximately 1,200-word report commenting on writing quality, structure and organization and estimate of marketability. I write all critiques." Charges for postage, mailing envelopes and long-distance phone calls.

Writers' Conferences: Attends Washington Independent Writers Spring Conference.

Tips: Obtains new clients through query letters, solicitation. "Plots, synopses and outlines have very little effect. A sample of the writing is the most significant factor. I also sponsor the Washington Prize for Fiction, an annual competition for unpublished works."

ALEX KAMAROFF ASSOCIATES (II), Suite 303 E., 200 Park Ave., New York NY 10166. (212)557-5557. Contact: Alex Kamaroff, Logan Kamaroff. Estab. 1985. Represents 75 clients. 30% of clients are new/previously unpublished writers. Currently handles: 5% nonfiction books; 95% novels.

Will Handle: Novels, nonfiction books. Will consider all nonfiction and fiction areas. Query. Will report in 2 weeks on queries; 1 month on mss.

Recent Sales: *Chapel Hill*, by Diana Morgan (Warner); *Louis Rukeyser Business Almanac*, (updated) by Louis Rukeyser (Simon & Schuster).

Terms: Agent receives 10% commission on domestic sales; 20% on foreign sales. Offers a written contract.

Fees: Charges a "returnable $85 reading fee." 100% of business is derived from commissions on ms sales.

Tips: Obtains new clients through editorial lunches, solicited manuscripts, conferences and authors' recommendation. "Tell a good story. Keep us turning those pages." Specializes in developing new authors.

*J. KELLOCK & ASSOCIATES LTD. (II), 11017 80th Ave., Edmonton, Alberta T6G 0R2 Canada. (403)433-0274. Contact: Joanne Kellock. Estab. 1981. Member of Writer's Guild of Alberta. Represents 50 clients. 10% of clients are new/previously unpublished writers. "I do very well with all works for children; adult fiction (all genre and literary); serious nonfiction. Currently handles: 20% nonfiction books; 5% scholarly books; 50% juvenile books; 25% novels.

Will Handle: Nonfiction, scholarly and juvenile books and novels. Will consider these nonfiction areas: animals; anthropology/archaeology; art/architecture/design; biography/autobiography; business; child guidance/parenting; cooking/food/nutrition; current affairs; government/politics/law; health/medicine; history; juvenile nonfiction; language/literature/criticism; money/finance/economics; music/dance/theater/film; nature/environment; new age/metaphysics; true crime/investigative; self-help/personal improvement; sports; women's issues/women's studies. Will consider these fiction areas: action/adventure; contemporary issues; detective/police/crime; ethnic; experimental; family saga; fantasy; feminist; glitz; historical; humor/satire; juvenile; literary; mainstream; mystery/suspense; picture book; psychic/supernatural; romance; science fiction; sports; thriller/espionage; westerns/frontier; young adult; horror. Query with outline plus 3 sample chapters. Will report in 6 weeks on queries; 3 months on mss.
Recent Sales: *The Delaney Bride*, by Jo Beverley (Zebra Books); *Please Remove Your Elbow From My Ear*, by Martyn Godfrey (Avon Books); *A Parent's Guide To Children's Medication*, by Jackie Webber (Prentice-Hall/Canada).
Terms: Agent receives 15% commission on domestic sales (English language); 20% on foreign sales. Offers a written contract, binding for 3 years.
Fees: Charges $75 reading fee. "Fee under no circumstances is refundable. *New writers only are charged.* $75 (U.S.) to read three chapters plus brief synopsis of any work; $50 for children's picture book material. If style is working with subject, the balance is read free of charge. Criticism is also provided for the fee. If style is not working with the subject, I explain why not; if talent is obvious, I explain how to make the manuscript work. I either do critiques myself or my reader does them. Critiques concern themselves with use of language, theme, plotting—all the usual. Return postage is always required. I cannot mail to the U.S. with U.S. postage so always enclose a self-addressed envelope, plus either international postage or cash. Canadian postage is more expensive, so double the amount for either international or cash. I do not return on-spec long-distance calls, if the writer chooses to telephone, please request that I return the call collect. However, a query letter is much more appropriate." 75% of business is derived from commissions on ms sales; 25% is derived from reading fees or criticism service. Payment of criticism fee does not ensure representation.
Tips: Obtains new clients through recommendations from others. "Do not send first drafts. Always double space. Very brief outlines and synopsis are more likely to be read first. For the picture book writer, the toughest sale to make in the business, please study the market before putting pen to paper. All works written for children must fit into the proper age groups regarding length of story, vocabulary level. For writers of the genre novel, read hundreds of books in the genre you've chosen to write, first. In other words, know your competition. Follow the rules of the genre exactly. For writers of science fiction/fantasy and the mystery, it is important a new writer has many more than one such book in him/her. Publishers are not willing today to buy single books in most areas of genre. Publishers who buy Sci/Fi/Fantasy usually want a two/three book deal at the beginning."

*NATASHA KERN LITERARY AGENCY (II), P.O. Box 2908, Portland OR 97208-2908. (503)297-6190. Contact: Natasha Kern. Estab. 1986. Member of ILAA. Specializes in commercial and literary fiction.
Will Handle: Nonfiction books, novels. Will consider these nonfiction areas: biography/autobiography; business; child guidance/parenting; cooking/food/nutrition; current affairs; health/medicine; psychology; science/technology; self-help/personal improvement; women's issues/women's studies. Will consider these fiction areas: action/adventure; historical; mainstream; mystery/suspense; romance; thriller/espionage; westerns/frontier; young adult. "Send a detailed, one-page query with an SASE, including the submission history, writing credits and information about how complete the project is. For fiction, send a two- or three-page synopsis, a one-paragraph precis in addition to the first three chapters. Also send a blurb about the author and information about the length of the manuscript. For category fiction, a 5-10-page synopsis should be sent with the chapters. For children's books, send the entire manuscript if it is a picture book. "Do not send illustrations." Will report in 5-6 weeks on queries.
Recent Sales: *Creating Eden*, by Marilyn Barrett (HarperCollins); *Freedom Angel*, by Robin Wiete (Penguin USA); *How to Raise a Hyperactive Child*, by Pat Kennedy (St. Martins).
Terms: Agent receives 15% commission on domestic sales; 20% on foreign sales.
Fees: Charges $35 ($20 for picture books) reading fee for new authors. "When your work is sold, your fee will be credited to your account."
Writers' Conference: Attends RWA National Conference; Santa Barbara Writer's Conference; Pacific Northwest Writer's Conference.

DORIS FRANCIS KULLER ASSOCIATES (II), Suite 7C, 2211 Broadway, New York NY 10024. (212)877-3604. Contact: Doris Francis Kuller. Estab. 1984. Represents 16 clients. Currently handles: 30% nonfiction books, 70% fiction, movie and TV scripts.
Will Handle: Nonfiction, novels, movie scripts, TV scripts. Will consider these nonfiction areas: true crime/investigative. Will consider all fiction areas. Query with SASE, outline/proposal. Reports in 1 month on queries.

Terms: Agent receives 15% commission on domestic sales; percent varies on foreign sales.
Fees: Charges $100 reading fee. Offers criticism service at no charge. Charges for unusual expenses.
Tips: Usually obtains new clients by word of mouth referrals.

LAW OFFICES OF ROBERT L. FENTON PC, #390, 31800 Northwestern Hwy., Farmington Hills MI 48334. (313)855-8780. FAX: (313)855-3302. Contact: Robert L. Fenton. Estab. 1960. Represents 25 clients. 25% of clients are new/previously unpublished writers. Currently handles: 20% nonfiction books; 50% novels; 15% movie scripts; 15% TV scripts.
Will Handle: Nonfiction books, novels, movie and TV scripts. Will consider these nonfiction areas: biography/autobiography; business; child guidance/parenting; current affairs; government/politics/law; military/war; money/finance/economics; music/dance/theater/film; religious/inspirational; true crime/investigative; self-help/personal improvement; sports; women's issues/women's studies. Will consider these fiction areas: action/adventure; contemporary issues; detective/police/crime; glitz; humor/satire; mystery/suspense; romance; science fiction; sports; thriller/espionage; westerns/frontier. Send 3 or 4 sample chapters (approximately 75 pages). Will report in 2 weeks on queries.
Recent Sales: *Black Tie Only*, by Julia Fenton (Contemporary Books); *Clash of Eagles*, by Leo Rutman (Fawcett); *Blue Orchids*, by Julia Fenton (Berkley).
Terms: Agent receives 15% on domestic sales. Offers a written contract, binding for 1 year.
Fees: Charges a reading fee. "To waive reading fee, author must have been published at least three times by a mainline New York publishing house." Criticism service: $350. Charges for office expenses, postage, photocopying, etc. 75% of business is derived from commissions on ms sales; 25% derived from reading fees or criticism service. Payment of a criticism fee does not ensure representation.
Tips: Obtains new clients through recommendations from others, individual inquiry.

LEE SHORE AGENCY (II), 440 Friday Rd., The Sterling Building, Pittsburgh PA 15209. (412)821-0440. FAX: (412)821-6099. Owner: Cynthia Sterling. Estab. 1988. Represents 46 clients. 50% of clients are new/unpublished writers "who have a strong desire to publish and a serious and professional approach to their work." We prefer to handle self-help, how-to, textbooks, quality mainstream fiction, military and genre. Please do not send children's or poetry. Currently handles: 20% self-help, 20% New Age, 50% novels, 10% young adult.
Recent Sales: *The Phoenix Cards*, by Susan Sheppard (Inner Traditions); *Horyo*, by Jesse Richardson (Hero Books); screenplay by Jeff Coe (Mixed Nuts Productions); "Birthday Toast," by Jack Ewing (Pittsburgh Press Magazine).
Will Handle: Young adult, nonfiction and mass market fiction. Query with outline. Reports on query in 1 week; 6 weeks on mss.
Terms: Agent receives 15% commission on domestic sales; 15% on dramatic sales; 20% on foreign sales.
Fees: Charges a reading fee for proposal and first 100-150 pages; 10% of income derived from reading fees. No additional reading fee once the balance of manuscript is requested. Charges for "standard expenses."

LIGHTHOUSE LITERARY AGENCY (II), P.O. Box 1000, Edgewater FL 32132-1000. (904)345-1515. Contact: Sandra Kangas. Estab. 1988. Member of WIF, Authors Guild, ABA. Represents 37 clients. 54% of clients are new/previously unpublished writers. Specializes in fiction and nonfiction adult books. Currently handles: 27% nonfiction books; 21% juvenile books; 37% novels; 3% novellas; 3% poetry books; 4% short story collections; 4% movie scripts; 1% humor.
Will Handle: Nonfiction, juvenile books, novels, novellas, short story collections, poetry books, movie scripts. Will consider these nonfiction areas: agriculture/horticulture; animals; anthropology/archaeology; art/architecture/design; biography/autobiography; business; child guidance/parenting; computers/electronics; cooking/food/nutrition; crafts/hobbies; current affairs; ethnic/cultural interest; health/medicine; history; interior design/decorating; juvenile nonfiction; military/war; money/finance/economics; music/dance/theater/film; nature/environment; photography; psychology; true crime/investigative; self-help/personal improvement; sports; women's issues/women's studies. Will consider these fiction areas: action/adventure; cartoon/comic; contemporary issues; detective/police/crime; ethnic; experimental; family saga; feminist; historical; humor/satire; juvenile; literary; mainstream; mystery/suspense; picture book; regional; science fiction; sports; thriller/espionage; westerns/frontier; young adult. Query with outline plus 3 or more sample chapters for nonfiction or entire ms for fiction. Will report in 2 weeks on queries; 2 months on mss.
Recent Sales: *Help Save Florida*, by Nicole Duplaix, Ph.D. (Pineapple Press).
Terms: Agent receives 15% commission on domestic sales; 20% on foreign sales. Offers a written contract, "author or agent may cancel at any time with 30-days' notice."
Fees: Charges $45 reading fee. "Waived for recent/trade published authors. Waived for clients and industry referrals. Fee is applied toward marketing expenses if author is accepted as client." Criticism service: $1 per manuscript page, minimum $150. Longer works may be discounted. "Critiques are

done by writers who have been published in the field they are asked to judge. A typed critique is provided pointing out the work's strengths, weak points and how it can be improved." Charges "marketing fee, payable each six months, covers all normal marketing expenses such as phone, postage, domestic fax. We charge $150 for the first six months, then $60 for subsequent six-month periods. No charge for currently, trade-published authors." 82% of business is derived from commissions on ms sales; 18% derived from reading fees or criticism services. Payment of fee does not ensure representation. "If author rewrites the work, we agree to read it again at no charge, no guarantee."

Tips: Obtains new clients through professional organizations, recommendations from clients and editors. "Send a short query or cover letter with brief description of the project—a clear description free of hype. Mention qualifications and experience. If this is a first book, say what made you decide to write it, why there's a need for it, what your book will have that others don't. Always enclose a stamped return mailer. Even if the work is accepted for marketing, we might have to return it for changes."

*LITERARY MARKETING CONSULTANTS (II), Suite 701, One Hallidie Plaza, San Francisco CA 94102. (415)979-8170. Associate: K. Allman. Estab. 1984. Represents 20 clients. 15% of clients are new/unpublished writers. Eager to work with new/unpublished writers. Specializes in nonfiction: religious and scholarly works and magazine articles and fiction. Religious fiction is a growing area of interest for us." Currently handles 10% magazine articles; 20% magazine fiction; 10% nonfiction books; 45% novels; 15% juvenile books.

Will Handle: Nonfiction books, scholarly books and novels. Will consider these nonfiction areas: religious, scholarly. Will consider these fiction areas: mystery, religious, romance, science fiction. Query with outline/synopsis only. Reports in 1 month.

Terms: Agent receives 15% commission on domestic sales; 20% on dramatic sales; and 20% on foreign sales.

Fees: Does not charge a reading fee. Charges per-ms marketing fee for photocopying, postage and phone for new/unpublished clients. 90% of income derived from commission on ms sales; 10% from fees charged to writers. "We will only take the time to provide a critique if we also have the opportunity to market the work."

LITERARY/BUSINESS ASSOCIATES (II), P.O. Box 2415, Hollywood CA 90078. (213)465-2630. Contact: Shelley Gross. Estab. 1980. Represents 5 clients. 90% of clients are new/previously unpublished writers. Specializes in pop psychology, philosophy, mysticism, Eastern religion, self-help, business, health, philosophy, contemporary novels. ("No fantasy or SF.") Currently handles: 40% nonfiction; 60% fiction (novels).

Recent Sales: A rock music reference book (Simon & Schuster); a novel (Avon); an anthology (Bantam).

Terms: Agent receives 15% commission on domestic sales; 20% on foreign sales. Offers a written contract, binding for 6 months.

Fees: Does not charge a reading fee. Charges $85 critique fee for manuscripts up to 300 pages, $10 each additional 50 pages. "Critique fees are 100% refundable if a sale is made." Critique consists of "detailed analysis of manuscript in terms of structure, style, characterizations, etc. and marketing potential, plus free guidesheets for fiction or nonfiction." Charges $60 marketing fee. 50% of business is derived from commission on ms sales; 50% is derived from criticism services. Payment of a criticism fee does not ensure agency representation.

Tips: Obtains new clients through recommendations from others, solicitation.

MARCH MEDIA INC., Suite 256, 7003 Chadwick Dr., Brentwood TN 37027. (615)370-3148. FAX: (615)370-3148. Contact: Etta Wilson. Estab. 1989. Represents 20 clients. Specializes in juvenile authors and illustrators. Currently handles: 30% nonfiction books; 70% juvenile books.

 An asterisk indicates those agents who only charge fees to new or previously unpublished writers or to writers only under certain conditions.

Will Handle: Will consider juvenile nonfiction and fiction. Send entire ms with SASE. Will report in 1 month on ms.

Terms: Agent receives 12% commission on domestic sales, "depends on whether they are author or author/illustrator." Offers a written contract, binding for 5 years.

Fees: Does not charge a reading fee. Offers criticism service: $25 per chapter; picture book hourly rated.

Tips: Obtains new clients through contacts from having been editor. "The agent is helpful in 2 ways: 1) specific knowledge about publisher's current needs; 2) reviews and negotiates contract."

THE DENISE MARCIL LITERARY AGENCY (II), 685 West End Ave., New York NY 10025. Contact: Denise Marcil. Estab. 1977. Member of ILAA. Represents 100 clients. 40% of clients are new/previously unpublished authors. Specializes in women's commercial fiction, how-to, self-help and business books. Currently handles: 30% nonfiction books; 70% novels.

Will Handle: Nonfiction books and novels. Will consider these nonfiction areas: design; business; child guidance/parenting; nutrition; health/medicine; interior design/decorating; money/finance/economics; music/dance/theater/film; nature/environment; psychology; true crime/investigative; self-help/personal improvement; women's issues/women's studies. Will consider these fiction areas: family saga; historical; romance (contemporary, historical, regency). Query with SASE *only*! Will report in 2-3 weeks on queries; "we do not read unsolicited mss."

Recent Sales: *Pulling Ahead of the Pack: The Fine Art of Motivating Everyone*; by Saul Gellerman (Dutton); *The Baby Book*, by William Sears, M.D. and Martha Sears, R.N. (Little Brown); *Song of the Wolf*, by Rosanne Bittner (Bantam).

Terms: Agent receives 15% commission on domestic sales; 20% on foreign sales. Offers a written contract, binding for 2 years.

Fees: Charges $45 reading fee for 3 chapters and outline "that we request only." Charges $100 per year for postage, photocopying, long-distance calls, etc. 99.9% of business is derived from commissions on ms sales; .1% is derived from reading fees and criticism.

Writers' Conferences: Attends University of Texas Conference at Dallas.

Tips: Obtains new clients through recommendations from other authors and "35% of my list is from query letters! Only send a one-page query letter. I read them all and ask for plenty of material. I find many of my clients this way and *always* send an SASE."

*THE EVAN MARSHALL AGENCY (III), 228 Watchung Ave., Upper Montclair NJ 07043. (201)744-1661. FAX: (201)744-6312. Contact: Evan Marshall. Estab. 1987. Member of ILAA and Romance Writers of America. Currently handles: 48% nonfiction books; 48% novels; 2% movie scripts; 2% TV scripts.

Will Handle: Nonfiction books; novels; movie scripts. Will consider these nonfiction areas: biography/autobiography; business; child guidance/parenting; cooking/food/nutrition; current affairs; government/politics/law; health/medicine; history; interior design/decorating; money/finance/economics; music/dance/theater/film; new age/metaphysics; psychology; true crime/investigative; self-help/personal improvement. Will consider these fiction areas: action/adventure; contemporary issues; detective/police/crime; family saga; glitz; historical; mainstream; mystery/suspense; psychic/supernatural; romance; thriller/espionage. Query. Will report in 1 week on queries; 2 months on mss.

Terms: Agent receives 15% on domestic sales; 20% on foreign sales. Offers written contract.

Fees: Charges a fee to consider for representation material by *writers who have not sold a book or script*: "Send SASE for fee schedule. There is no fee if referred by a client or an editor or if you are already published in the genre of your submission."

Tips: Obtains many new clients through referrals from clients and editors.

*SCOTT MEREDITH, INC. (II), 845 3rd Ave., New York NY 10022. (212)245-5500. FAX: (212)755-2972. Vice President and Editorial Director: Jack Scovil. Estab. 1946. Represents 2,000 clients. 10% of clients are new/unpublished writers. "We'll represent on a straight commission basis writers who've sold one or more recent books to major publishers, or several (three or four) magazine pieces to major magazines, or a screenplay or teleplay to a major producer. We're a very large agency (staff of 51) and handle all types of material except individual cartoons or drawings, though we will handle collections of these as well." Currently handles 5% magazine articles; 5% magazine fiction; 23% nonfiction books; 23% novels; 5% textbooks; 10% juvenile books; 5% movie scripts; 2% radio scripts; 2% stage plays; 5% TV scripts; 5% syndicated material; 5% poetry.

Will Handle: Magazine articles, magazine fiction, nonfiction books, novels, textbooks, juvenile books, movie scripts, radio scripts, stage plays, TV scripts, syndicated material and poetry. Query with outline or entire manuscript. Reports in 2 weeks.

Recent Sales: *Murder at the Kennedy Center*, by Margaret Truman (Random House); *Rendezvous with Rama II*, by Arthur C. Clarke (Bantam Books); *Stand Up!*, by Roseanne Barr (Harper & Row).
Terms: Agent receives 10% commission on domestic sales; 10% on dramatic sales; 20% on foreign sales.
Fees: Charges "a single fee which covers multiple readers, revision assistance or critique as needed. When a script is returned as irreparably unsalable, the accompanying letter of explanation will usually run 2 single-spaced pages minimum on short stories or articles, or from 4-10 single-spaced pages on book-length manuscripts, teleplays or screenplays. All reports are done by agents on full-time staff. No marketing advice is included, since, if it's salable, we'll market and sell it ourselves." 90% of business is derived from commission on ms sales; 10% is derived from fees.

*MEWS BOOKS LTD., 20 Bluewater Hill, Westport CT 06880. (203)227-1836. FAX: (203)227-1144. Contact: Sidney B. Kramer. Estab. 1972. Represents 35 clients. Prefers to work with published/established authors; works with small number of new/unpublished authors "producing professional work." Specializes in juvenile (pre-school through young adult), cookery, self-help, adult nonfiction and fiction, technical and medical. Currently handles 20% nonfiction; 20% novels; 50% juvenile books; 10% miscellaneous. Member agents: Fran Pollak (assistant).
Will Handle: Nonfiction books, novels, juvenile books, character merchandising and video use of illustrated published books. Will read unsolicited queries which include a precis, outline, character description and a few pages of writing sample and author's bio.
Terms: Agent receives 10% commission for published, 15% for unpublished authors; 20% foreign sales.
Fees: Does not charge a reading fee. "If material is accepted, agency asks for $350 circulation fee (4-5 publishers), which will be applied against commissions (waived for published authors)." Charges for photocopying, postage expenses, telephone calls and other direct costs.
Tips: "Principle agent is an attorney and former publisher. Offers consultation service through which writers can get advice on a contract or on publishing problems."

THE PETER MILLER AGENCY, INC. (II), Suite 501, 220 W., 19th St., New York NY 10011. (212)929-1222. FAX: (212)206-0238. President: Peter Miller. Associate Agent: Anthony Schneider. Estab. 1975. Represents 50 clients. 50% of clients are new/unpublished writers. Eager to work with new/unpublished writers, as well as with published/established authors (especially journalists). Specializes in true crime, celebrity books (biographies and self-help), mysteries, thrillers, historical fiction/family sagas and "fiction with *real* motion picture and television potential." Writer's guidelines for 5×8½ SASE and 2 first-class stamps. Currently handles 45% nonfiction books; 35% novels; 20% movie scripts.
Recent Sales: *Ted Sennett's On-Screen, Offscreen Movie Guides*, by Ted Sennett (Prentice-Hall Press); *Laughing in the Dark: From Groucho to Woody*, by Ted Sennett (St. Martins Press); *Get Published! Get Produced! A Literary Agent's Tips on How to Sell Your Writing*, by Peter Miller (Shapolsky Books); *Fatal Freeway*, by Steven Salerno (Knightsbridge).
Will Handle: Nonfiction books, novels and movie scripts. Query with outline. Reports in 1 week on queries; 2-4 weeks on mss.
Terms: Agent receives 15% commission on domestic sales; 20-25% on foreign sales.
Fees: Does not charge a reading fee. Charges a criticism fee for unpublished writers. Fee is refunded if book sells. 5% of income derived from criticism fees. "The agency offers a reading evaluation, usually 2-4 pages in length, which gives a detailed analysis of literary craft, commercial potential and recommendations for improving the work, if necessary." Charges for photocopying expenses.

*MORGAN LITERARY AGENCY, INC. (II), P.O. Box 14810, Richmond VA 23221. (804)359-4225. Contact: David Morgan or Katherine Morgan. Estab. 1987. Represents 25-30 clients. Currently handles: 70% nonfiction; 30% novels.
Will Handle: Nonfiction, novels. Will consider all nonfiction and fiction areas. Query with SASE. Will report in 1 week on queries.
Recent Sales: *The Love Your Heart Guide for the 1990s*, by Lee Belshin (Contemporary); *Prophecies & Predictions: Everyone's Guide to the Coming Changes*, by Moira Timms Valentine.
Terms: Agent receives 15% commission on domestic sales; 20% on foreign sales. Offers a written contract.
Fees: Charges a reading fee to unpublished authors. Offers critique service. Charges $55 for reading—includes a one-page response; charges $185 for 5-6-page critique. "Please query for details." Charges for postage, photocopying. 95% of business is derived from commissions on ms sales; 5% is derived from reading or criticism fees.
Writers' Conferences: Attends Austin Writers Conference, Writers in the Rockies; Willamette Writers Conference.
Tips: Obtains new clients through recommendations from others.

*BK NELSON LITERARY AGENCY & LECTURE BUREAU (II, III), 84 Woodland Rd., Pleasantville NY 10570. (914)741-1322. FAX: (914)741-1324. Contact: Bonita Nelson, John Benson or Charles Romine. Estab. 1980. Represents 52 clients. 45% of clients are new/previously unpublished writers. Specializes in business/self-help/how-to/computer books. Currently handles: 50% nonfiction books; 5% scholarly books; 5% textbooks; 20% novels; 5% movie scripts; 10% TV scripts; 5% stage plays. Member agents: Bonita Nelson (business books); John Benson (Director of Lecture Bureau); Charles Romine (novels and television scripts); Dave Donnelly (videos); Bill Appel (editorial assistant).
Will Handle: Nonfiction books, textbooks, scholarly books; novels; movie scripts; stage plays; TV scripts. Will consider these nonfiction areas: animals; anthropology/archaeology; biography/autobiography; business; child guidance/parenting; computers/electronics; cooking/food/nutrition; crafts/hobbies; current affairs; health/medicine; military/war; money/finance/economics; music/dance/theater/film; nature/environment; psychology; religious/inspirational; true cime/investigative; science/technology; self-help/personal improvement; sociology; sports; women's issues/women's studies. Will consider these fiction areas: action/adventure; contemporary issues; family saga; feminist; literary; mainstream; mystery/suspense; romance; sports; thriller/espionage. Query. Will report in 1 week on queries; 2-3 weeks on ms.
Recent Sales: *Notebooks of Gertrude Stein*, by Dr. Leon Katz (Ticknor Fields); *Memos Right & Left*, by Helen Gorenstein (Houghton Mifflin); *Databases & Marketing*, by Herman Holtz (John Wiley & Sons); *Complete Book of Laptops*, by David Rothman (St. Martins Press); *Employee Benefits*, by Jane White (Simon & Schuster).
Terms: Agent receives 15% on domestic sales; 10% on foreign sales. Offers a written contract, exclusive for 6 months.
Fees: Charges $325 reading fee for *new writers' material only.* "It is not refundable. We usually charge for the first reading only. The reason for charging in addition to time/expense is to determine if the writer is salable and thus a potential client."
Tips: Obtains new clients through referrals and reputation with editors. "We handle the business aspect of the literary and lecture fields. We handle careers as well as individual book projects. If the author has the ability to write and we are harmonious, success is certain to follow with us handling the selling/business."

NEW AGE WORLD SERVICES (II, IV), 62091 Valley View Circle, Joshua Tree CA 92252. (619)366-2833. Owner: Victoria Vandertuin. Estab. 1957. Member of New Age Publishing and Retailing Alliance and the Institute of Mentalphysics. Represents 35 clients. 100% of clients are new/unpublished writers. Eager to work with new/unpublished writers. Specializes in all New Age fields: occult, astrology, metaphysical, yoga, U.F.O., ancient continents, para sciences, mystical, magical, beauty, political and all New Age categories in fiction and nonfiction. Writer's guidelines for #10 SASE with four first-class stamps. Currently handles 40% nonfiction books; 30% novels; 10% poetry.
Will Handle: Nonfiction books, novels and poetry. Query with outline or entire manuscript. Reports in 6-8 weeks.
Terms: Receives 15% commission on domestic sales; 20% on foreign sales.
Fees: Charges reading fee of $150 for 300-page, typed, double-spaced ms; reading fee waived if representing writer. Charges criticism fee of $135 for new writers (300-page ms.); 10% of income derived from criticism fees. "I personally read all manuscripts for critique or evaluation, which is typed, double-spaced with about 4 or more pages, depending on the manuscript and the service for the manuscript the author requests. If requested, marketing advice is included. We charge a representation fee if we represent the author's manuscript." Charges writer for editorial readings, compiling of query letter and synopsis, printing of same, compiling lists and mailings.

*NORTHEAST LITERARY AGENCY (II), 69 Broadway, Concord NH 03301. (603)225-9162. Contact: Victor A. Levine. Estab. 1973. Represents 11 clients. 50% of clients are new/previously unpublished writers. Specializes in category fiction, children's picture books. Currently handles 10% nonfiction books; 5% scholarly books; 20% juvenile books; 40% novels; 10% poetry books; 5% short story collections; 5% movie scripts; 5% TV scripts.
Will Handle: Nonfiction books, juvenile books, novels, novellas, short story collections, poetry books, movie scripts. Will consider all nonfiction areas. Will consider all fiction areas except erotica, gay, lesbian. Query. Will report in 5 days on queries; 10 days on mss.
Recent Sales: *Christmas Babies*, by Keane & Black (Pocket Books).
Terms: Agent receives 15% commission on domestic sales; 20% on foreign sales. Offers a written contract "cancellable on 3-months' notice."
Fees: Charges a reading fee to unpublished writers, "refundable following a sale." Criticism service: costs depend on type of criticism and whether conducted by mail or in a classroom, workshop or seminar." Charges for "extraordinary expenses, such as express mail, long-distance phone calls, extensive photocopying but not for marketing or ordinary office expenses."

Writers' Conferences: Underwrites Wells Writer's Workshop.
Tips: Obtains new clients through classes, workshops, conferences, advertising in *Writer's Digest*, referrals. "Please be very specific about writing background and current project(s)."

NORTHWEST LITERARY SERVICES (II), P.O. Box 165, Shawnigan Lake, British Columbia V0R 2W0 Canada. (604)743-9169. Contact: Brent Laughren. Estab. 1986. Represents 20 clients. 25% of clients are new/previously unpublished writers. Specializes in working with new writers. Currently handles: 40% nonfiction books; 1% scholarly books; 1% textbooks; 10% juvenile books; 35% novels; 1% novellas; 1% short story collections; 5% movie scripts; 1% stage plays; 4% TV scripts; 1% illustrations.
Will Handle: Nonfiction books; textbooks; scholarly books; juvenile books; novels; movie scripts; stage plays; TV scripts and illustrations. Will consider these nonfiction areas: agriculture/horticulture; animals; anthropology/archaeology; art/architecture/design; biography/autobiography; business; child guidance/parenting; cooking/food/nutrition; crafts/hobbies; ethnic/cultural interests; health/medicine; history; juvenile nonfiction; language/literature/criticism; music/dance/theater/film; nature/environment; new age/metaphysics; photography; psychology; true crime/investigative; self-help/personal improvement; sports; translations; women's issues/women's studies. Will consider these fiction areas: action/adventure; confessional; contemporary issues; detective/police/crime; erotica; ethnic; experimental; family saga; fantasy; feminist; historical; humor/satire; juvenile; literary; mainstream; mystery/suspense; picture book; psychic/supernatural; regional; romance; science fiction; sports; thriller/espionage; westerns/frontier; young adult. Query with outline/proposal. Will report in 2 weeks on queries; 6 weeks on mss.
Terms: Agent receives 15% on domestic sales; 20% on foreign sales. Offers a written contract.
Fees: Does not charge a reading fee. Charges criticism fee: $100 for book outline and sample chapters up to 20,000 words. Charges 75¢-$1/page for copyediting and content editing; $1/page for proofreading; $10-20/page for research. "Other related editorial services available at negotiated rates." Critiques are "2-3 page overall evaluations, with suggestions." All fees, if charged "are authorized by the writer in advance." 95% of business is derived from commissions on ms sales; 5% is derived from reading fees or criticism service. Payment of criticism fee doesn't ensure representation.
Writers' Conferences: Attends Festival of the Written Arts, Vancouver International Writers Conference, Port Townsend Writers Conference.
Tips: Obtains new clients through recommendations. "Northwest Literary Services is particularly interested in the development and marketing of new and unpublished writers, though not exclusively, since this can be a long-term project without monetary reward. We are also interested in literary fiction, though again not exclusively."

*OCEANIC PRESS (II), P.O. Box 6538, Buena Park CA 90622-6538. (714)527-5650; 527-5651. FAX: (714)527-0268. Contact: Peter Carbone. Estab. 1956. Represents 25 clients. 15% of clients are new/previously unpublished writers. Specializes in celebrity interviews. Currently handles: 20% nonfiction books; 20% novels; 60% syndicated material. Member agent: Katherine Singer (child development, family relations).
Will Handle: Nonfiction books, novels, syndicated material, biographies. Will consider these nonfiction areas: biography/autobiography; business; child guidance/parenting; computers/electronics; health/medicine; money/finance/economics; music/dance/theater/film; new age/metaphysics; psychology; true crime/investigative; science/technology; self-help/personal improvement; sports; women's issues/women's studies; movies. Will consider these fiction areas: detective/police/crime; erotica; experimental; family saga; mainstream; mystery/suspense; psychic/supernatural; romance (contemporary, gothic, regency); science fiction; sports; thriller/espionage; westerns/frontier; young adult. Send outline/proposal and list of published work. Will report in 1 month on queries; 6 weeks on mss.
Recent Sales: *Capricorn Woman*, by Marian Jones (Hutchinson/Bantam); syndication package for Pan African Services; horror book series by Kurt Singer (Quelle Books/S. Fischer).
Terms: Agent receives 15% commission on domestic sales; 20% on foreign sales; "50% syndication only if wanted." Offers a written contract, binding for 1 year.
Fees: Charges a $250 reading fee to new writers only. Criticism service is included in reading fee. Criticism done by professional readers. 98% of business is derived from commissions on ms sales; 2% is derived from reading fees or criticism service. Payment of a criticism fee ensures representation.
Tips: Obtains new clients through recommendations. Do "good writing and good research. Study the market."

OCEANIC PRESS SERVICE, 3164 W. Tyler Ave., Anaheim CA 92801. (714)527-5650. FAX: (714)527-0268. Associate Editor: John J. Kearns. Estab. 1940. Represents 100 clients. Prefers to work with published/established authors; will work with a small number of new/unpublished authors. Specializes in selling features of worldwide interest; romance books, mysteries, biographies, westerns, nonfiction of timeless subjects, reprints of out-of-print titles. Currently handles: 20% nonfiction books; 30% novels; 10% juvenile books; 40% syndicated material.

Will Handle: Magazine articles, nonfiction books, novels, juvenile books, syndicated material. Will read—at no charge—unsolicited queries and outlilnes. Reports in 2 weeks on queries.
Recent Sales: *Sex and Love*, by Dr. Frank Caprio; and *Dictionary of Home Repair*, by K. Singer (Ottenheimer).
Terms: Agent receives 15% commission on domestic sales; 20% on foreign sales.
Fees: Charges reading fee: $250/300 pages. Reading fee includes detailed critique. "We have authors who published many books of their own to do the reading and give a very thorough critique." 1% of income derived from reading fees.

THE PANETTIERI AGENCY (II), 142 Marcella Rd., Hampton VA 23666. (804)825-1708. Contact: Eugenia Panettieri. Estab. 1988. Member of Romance Writers of America and Horror Writers. Represents 40 clients. 20% of clients are new/previously unpublished writers. Specializes in fiction of substantial commercial value; larger women's fiction, suspense. "However, we do handle almost all types of projects." Currently handles: 10% nonfiction books; 10% juvenile books; 80% novels. Member agents: Eugenia Panettieri (women's fiction, romances, thrillers, horror); Cynthia Richey (historical and contemporary romances); Kay Reynolds (horror, sci-fi, fantasy, mystery).
Will Handle: Juvenile books, novels and nonfiction books. Will consider these nonfiction areas: child guidance/parenting; health/medicine; psychology; true crime/investigative; self-help/personal improvement; women's issues/women's studies. Will consider these fiction areas: action/adventure; detective/police/crime; erotica; family saga; fantasy; glitz; historical; juvenile; mainstream; mystery/suspense; psychology; true crime/investigative; self-help/personal improvement; women's issues/women's studies. Will consider these fiction areas: action/adventure; detective/police/crime; erotica; family saga; fantasy; glitz; historical; juvenile; mainstream; mystery/suspense; psychic/supernatural; romance; science fiction; thriller/espionage; young adult. Query with outline plus 3 sample chapters. Will report in 2 weeks on queries; 1 month on mss.
Recent Sales: *The Forsaken*, by Steven Ray Fulgham (Berkley/Charter Diamond); *The Defiant Heart*, by Anita Gordon (Berkley/Jove); *Wild Card Bride*, by Joy Tucker (Avon).
Terms: Agent receives 10% commission on domestic sales; 10% on foreign sales. Offers a written contract, binding for 1 year.
Fees: Does not charge a reading fee. Offers criticism service: $25 for partial ms and outline, no more than 75 pages; $50 for complete mss of no more than 65,000 words; $75 for complete mss of no more than 85,00 words; $100 for mss between 85-150,000 words. "Writers receive a written analysis of their work, 3-5 single-spaced pages in length, commenting on the major elements of the book and the project's salability. It is done by office agents only." 90% of business is derived from commissions on ms sales; 10% is derived from reading fees and criticism service. "This is because we charge only a 10% commission on sales, 50% less than most agencies. Payment of criticism fee does not ensure representation. "We offer representation based on the project's salability only. A critique does insure an unbiased, well-detailed evaluation of the project, with suggestions for revisions."
Writers Conferences: Romance Writers of America, Romantic Times Convention.
Tips: "Most of our clients come from normal submissions, either solicited or over-the-transom. Some are through recommendations from existing clients, but a recommendation isn't necessary to merit a thorough consideration. We have been very pleased with the submissions that have come through our listing in *Writer's Market*! Because most agencies, including this one, get an enormous number of queries, we place a lot of emphasis on a quick, to-the-point cover letter or query. Show us that you've studied your market, where you think your project fits in, and whether it is complete or still 'in the works.' If your cover letter or query seems unfocused or rambles, we tend to believe the project may be the same way. First impressions can be very important! Also, don't try to overwhelm the agent with too much material. Send in a partial, at first, if you're coming in unsolicited. Often we read those first (they're less intimidating than a huge box!). Don't sweat the synopsis too much. If your chapters are great, that's what really counts. Just be sure the synopsis accurately describes the plot without loose ends or breaks. Be professional. Please don't try to 'bully' an agent to show her how much you know about the industry. An agent loves a considerate, well-mannered client, and will return your respect with her enthusiasm for you as well as your work!"

PEGASUS INTERNATIONAL, INC., LITERARY & FILM AGENTS (II), P.O. Box 5470, Winter Park FL 32793-5470. (407)831-1008. Contact: Carole Morling. Estab. 1987. Represents 350 clients. 85% of clients are new/previously unpublished writers. Specializes in "literary assistance to unpublished au-

If you're looking for a particular agent, check the Agents and Reps Index to find at which agency the agent works. Then look up the listing for that agency in the appropriate section.

thors." Currently handles: 15% nonfiction books; 5% scholarly books; 5% textbooks; 5% juvenile books; 25% novels; 30% movie scripts; 10% TV scripts; 5% cookbooks. Member agents: Carole Morling (novels, creative writing, line-editing, styling and trade presentation); Gene Lovitz (biography, crime, law, health, business, film/TV, photography, firearms).

Will Handle: Nonfiction books, textbooks, scholarly books, juvenile books, novels, short story collections, movie scripts, TV scripts, video. Will consider these nonfiction areas: animals; anthropology/ archaeology; art/architecture/design; biography/autobiography; business; child guidance/parenting; computers/electronics; cooking/food/nutrition; crafts/hobbies; current affairs; ethnic/cultural interests; government/politics/law; health/medicine; history; juvenile nonfiction; military/war; money/finance/ economics; nature/environment; new age/metaphysics; photography; psychology; religious/inspirational; true crime/investigative; science/technology; self-help/personal improvement; sociology; sports; translations. Will consider these fiction areas: action/adventure; confessional; contemporary issues; detective/police/crime; erotica; ethnic; experimental; family saga; fantasy; historical; humor/satire; juvenile; literary; mainstream; mystery/suspense; picture book; psychic/supernatural; religious/inspiration; romance; science fiction; sports; thriller/espionage; westerns/frontier; young adult; horror; new age fiction. Query with outline/proposal plus 2 sample chapters. "Also call." Will report immediately on queries; 6 weeks on mss ("depending on length; it could take a little longer").

Recent Sales: *Art Theatre Makeup on Stage and Screen*, by Michael Westmore (Macmillan/McGraw-Hill); *Short Stories*, by Anton Chekhov (Kensington Pub. Corp./Zebra); *Star Trek* episode, by Lee Shackleford (Paramount Pictures). "Production companies have quite a few options taken on screenplays we represent."

Terms: Agent receives 10% commission on domestic sales; 15% on foreign sales. Offers a written contract "at client's request," binding for 6 months to 1 year.

Fees: Charges a $200 reading fee for up to 400 double-spaced pages. "Lower fees for pamphlets, chapbooks, etc. Fees refundable upon publication. Installments acceptable. Fees apply to all clients. We have one fee only, which is all-inclusive of reading, critique, marketing and line-by-line editing. There are no hidden costs. We pay postage, phone calls, etc. to publishers. Critiques are done by our senior editor and staff. Outside content reports are often used with technical and/or nonfiction manuscripts. Critiques are delivered on an individual basis by phone or mail." 85% of business is derived from commissions on ms sales; 15% is derived from reading fees or criticism services. Payment of a criticism fee ensures representation.

Tips: Obtains new clients through queries, client referrals and publisher(s) recommendations. "Phone calls and/or written queries are equally welcomed. (Prompt global RSVP by phone.) We will read—at no charge—unsolicited queries and outlines accompanied by SASE. We do not read unsolicited manuscripts. Unpublished authors needing editorial help are welcomed. Manuscripts with high film potential need not be submitted in screenplay form, whereby we will endeavor to place with filmmakers and publishers alike at no additional fee. Once an author becomes a client, we will work as long as necessary to edit and market the material. We consider our clients as family, and work with them on a friendly one-to-one basis (usually by phone). Beginning authors should remember: 'There is no such thing as a dumb question, only unasked questions.' "

PENMARIN BOOKS (II), Suite 8L, 2171 E. Francisco Blvd., San Rafael CA 94901. (415)457-7746. FAX: (415)454-0426. President: Hal Lockwood. Editorial Director: John Painter. Estab. 1987. Represents 20 clients. 80% of clients are new/unpublished writers. "No previous publication is necessary. We do expect authoritative credentials in terms of history, politics, science and the like." Handles general trade nonfiction and illustrated books exclusively.

Will Handle: Nonfiction books. Query with outline. Will read submissions at no charge, but may charge a criticism fee or service charge for work performed after the initial reading. Reports in 2 weeks on queries; 1 month on mss.

Recent Sales: *Little Girl Lost*, by Joan Merriam (Zebra); *Fast and Fabulous Hord'oeuvres*, by Michele Braden (Macmillan); *The Life and Wines of Robert Mondavi*, by Steve Strauss (Rizzoli).

Terms: Agent receives 10% commission on domestic sales; 10% on dramatic sales; 10% on foreign sales.

Fees: "We normally do not provide extensive criticism as part of our reading but, for a fee, will prepare guidance for editorial development." Charges $200/300 pages. "Our editorial director writes critiques. These may be 2-10 pages long. They usually include an overall evaluation and then analysis and recommendations about specific sections, organization or style."

PETERSON ASSOCIATES LITERARY AGENCY (I,II), 803 N. Euclid Ave., Upland CA 91786. (714)949-0260. Contact: Lawerence Peterson, Ph.D. Estab. 1990. Represents 10 clients. 75% of clients are new/ previously unpublished writers. Currently handles: 50% nonfiction books; 10% textbooks; 30% novels; 10% poetry books.

Will Handle: Nonfiction books, novels, poetry books. Will consider these nonfiction areas: anthropology/archaeology; business; new age/metaphysics; psychology; science/technology; self-help/personal improvement. Will consider these fiction areas: action/adventure; erotica; fantasy; humor/satire; mainstream; psychic/supernatural; science fiction; thriller/espionage. Query or send entire manuscript. Will report in 1 week on queries; 1 month on mss.
Terms: Agent receives 15% commission on domestic sales; 20% on foreign sales. Offers a written contract.
Fees: Charges a reading fee, refundable upon sale of work. Offers a criticism service. "Fees contingent upon amount of work and complexity of material—i.e., if research is required . . . Comprehensive writing critiques done by Lawerence Peterson." Charges for postage, photocopying, phone calls. Payment of reading or criticism fees does not ensure agency representation.
Tips: Obtains new clients through referrals and advertising.

ARTHUR PINE ASSOCIATES, INC. (III), 250 W. 57th St., New York NY 10019. (212)265-7330. Estab. 1966. Represents 100 clients. 25% of clients are new/previously unpublished writers. Specializes in fiction and nonfiction. Currently handles: 75% nonfiction; 25% novels.
Will Handle: Nonfiction books, novels. Will consider these nonfiction areas: business; current affairs; money/finance/economics; psychology. Will consider these fiction areas: action/adventure; detective/police/crime; family saga; literary; thriller/espionage. Send outline proposal. Will report in 3 weeks on queries. "All correspondence must be accompanied by a SASE. Will not read manuscripts before receiving a letter of inquiry."
Recent Sales: *Sunday Nights at Seven,* by Joan Benny (Warner); *The Power in You,* by Wally Amos (Donald I. Fine); *Geek Love,* by Katherine Dunne (Knopf/Warner).
Terms: Agency receives 15% commission on domestic sales; 25% on foreign sales. Offers a written contract, which varies from book to book.
Fees: Charges a reading fee based on number of words in the manuscript. Offers a criticism service. 98% of business is derived from commissions on ms sales; 2% is derived from reading fees or criticism service. Payment of a criticism fee does not ensure representation.
Tips: Obtain new clients through recommendations from others.

JULIE POPKIN/NANCY COOKE (II), #204, 15340 Albright St., Pacific Palisades CA 90272 (Popkin). (213)459-2834. FAX: (213)459-4128. 236 E. Davie St., Raleigh NC 27601 (Cooke). (919)834-1456. Estab. 1989. Represents 16 clients. 33% of clients are new/unpublished writers. Specializes in selling book-length mss including fiction—all genres—and nonfiction. Especially interested in social issues. Currently handles 50% nonfiction books, 50% novels and some scripts.
Recent Sales: *Moments of Light,* by Fred Chappell (New South); *Speak out for Age,* by Grace Goldin (Third Age Press) (poetry); *Chapter and Verse,* by Joel Barr (Peregrine Smith).
Will Handle: Nonfiction books and novels. Will consider these nonfiction areas: how-to; self-help; history; art. Will consider these fiction areas: mainstream; literary; romance; science fiction; mystery; juvenile. Reports in 1 month on queries; 2 months on mss.
Terms: Agent receives 15% commission on domestic sales; 10% on dramatic sales; 20% on foreign sales.
Fees: Does not charge a reading fee, but may charge a criticism fee or service charge for work performed after the initial reading. Charges writers for photocopying, extraordinary mailing fees.

*SIDNEY E. PORCELAIN (II,III), 414 Leisure Loop, Milford PA 18337-1229. (717)296-6420. Manager: Sidney Porcelain. Estab. 1952. Represents 20 clients. 50% of clients are new/unpublished writers. Prefers to work with published/established authors; works with a small number of new/unpublished authors. Specializes in fiction (novels, mysteries and suspense) and nonfiction (celebrity and exposé). Currently handles: 2% magazine articles; 5% magazine fiction; 5% nonfiction books; 50% novels; 5% juvenile books; 2% movie scripts; 1% TV scripts; 30% "comments for new writers."
Will Handle: Magazine articles, magazine fiction, nonfiction books, novels, juvenile books. Query with outline or entire ms. Reports in 2 weeks on queries; 3 weeks on mss.
Terms: Agent receives 10% commission on domestic sales; 10% on dramatic sales; 10% on foreign sales.
Fees: Does not charge a reading fee. Offers a criticism service to new writers. 50% of income derived from commission on ms sales.

D. RADLEY-REGAN & ASSOCIATES (II), P.O. Box 243, Jamestown NC 27282. (919)454-5040. President and Editor: D. Radley-Regan. Estab. 1987. Eager to work with new/unpublished writers. Specializes in fiction, nonfiction, mystery, thriller. Currently handles 10% nonfiction books; 40% novels; 25% movie scripts; 25% TV scripts.

Will Handle: Nonfiction books, novels, movie and TV scripts. Query. Reports in 2 weeks on queries; 10 weeks on mss.

Recent Sales: *Wentworth Place*, and *Return to Wentworth Place*, by D. Radley-Regan.

Terms: Agent receives 25% commission on domestic sales; 25% on dramatic sales; 25% on foreign sales.

Fees: Charges reading fee for full mss. Writer receives overall evaluation, marketing advice and agency service. 10% of income derived from commission on mss sales. Payment of criticism fee does not ensure that writer will be represented.

RIGHTS UNLIMITED (II), 156 5th Ave., New York NY 10010. (212)741-0404. FAX: (212)691-0546. Agent: B. Kurman. Estab. 1984. Represents 57 clients. Works with a small number of new/unpublished authors. Specializes in fiction and nonfiction. Currently handles 35% novels; 50% textbooks; 15% movie scripts.

Will Handle: Nonfiction books, novels and juvenile books. Query or send entire manuscript. Reports in 2 weeks on queries; 1 month on manuscripts.

Recent Sales: *The Dragon Triangle*, by Charles Berlitz (Wynwood Press); *The Adventures of Taxi Dog*, by D.S. Barracca (The Dial Press); *The Last Ramadan*, by Norman Lang (Harper Paperback).

Terms: Agent receives 15% commission on domestic sales; 15% on dramatic sales; 20% on foreign sales.

Fees: Does not charge a reading fee, but may charge a criticism fee or service charge for work performed after the initial reading.

THE RISING SUN LITERARY GROUP (I, II), Suite C, 1507 Oakmont Dr., Acworth GA 30101. (404)591-3397. FAX: (404)591-0369. Contact: Lee Morrow or Lynn Watson. Estab. 1990. Represents 17 clients. 88% of clients are new/previously unpublished writers. Specializes in "book-length fiction manuscripts." Currently handles: 5% nonfiction books; 5% scholarly books; 5% juvenile books; 70% novels; 5% short story collections; 5% movie scripts; 5% TV scripts.

Will Handle: Nonfiction books, scholarly books, juvenile books, novels, short story collections, poetry books, movie scripts, stage plays, TV scripts. Will consider these nonfiction areas: animals; art/architecture/design; business; child guidance/parenting; computers/electronics; cooking/food/nutrition; crafts/hobbies; current affairs; history; juvenile nonfiction; money/finance/economics; music/dance/ theater/film; nature/environment; photography; psychology; religious/inspirational; true crime/investigative; self-help/personal improvement; sports; translations; women's issues/women's studies. Will consider these fiction areas: action/adventure; contemporary issues; detective/police/crime; erotica; ethnic; experimental; family saga; fantasy; feminist; gay; historical; humor/satire; juvenile; lesbian; literary; mainstream; mystery/suspense; picture book; psychic/supernatural; regional; religious/inspiration; romance; science fiction; sports; thriller/espionage; westerns/frontier; young adult. Query with entire manuscript. Reports in 2 weeks on queries; 6 weeks on mss.

Terms: Agent receives 13% commission on domestic sales; 14% on foreign sales; 18% on dramatic sales. Offers written contract, binding for 1 year.

Fees: Charges reading fee. Charges $125/ms, all authors. Refundable upon sale of manuscript. "Authors receive a 1-2-page critique. They are prepared by editors on the staff." Charges for postage, phone calls, fax transmissions, photocopying, packaging and office expense. 65% of business is derived from commissions on ms sales; 35% derived from reading fees or criticism services. Paying fee does not ensure representation.

Tips: Obtains new clients through recommendations from others, solicitation and at conferences. "It is very important for an author to know what experience an agent has and how they handle submissions of their manuscripts to publishers and producers, also how many publishers/producers the agent will submit their work to. We specialize in working with new authors."

SHERRY ROBB LITERARY PROPERTIES (III), #102, 17250 Beverly Blvd., Los Angeles CA 90036. (213)965-8780. FAX: (213)965-8784. Contact: Sherry Robb and Sasha Goodman or Vik Malo. Estab. 1982. Member of ILAA. Represents 60 clients. 20% of clients are new/previously unpublished writers. Currently handles: 30% nonfiction books; 40% novels; 10% movie scripts; 20% TV scripts. Member agents: Sasha Goodman (fiction); Vik Malo (film and television); Jim Pinkston (nonfiction); Sherry Robb (TV scripts/sit com).

Will Handle: Novels, movie and TV scripts. Will consider these nonfiction areas: biography/autobiography; true crime/investigative. Will consider these nonfiction areas: glitz; literary; mainstream; mystery/suspense. Send outline plus 3 sample chapters. Will report in 2 weeks on queries; 2 months on mss.

Recent Sales: *Star Trek: The Technical Manual* (Pocket Books); *The James Bond Encyclopedia* (Contemporary Books); *The Godmother* (Simon & Schuster).
Terms: Agent receives 15% on domestic sales; 15% on foreign sales. Offers a written contract, binding for one year.
Fees: Does not charge a reading fee. Offers criticism service: $2 per page. "We use two editors who line edit manuscripts and give a 10-page critique at least." Charges for postage and photocopying. Payment of a criticism fee does not ensure representation.
Tips: Obtains new clients through recommendations.

RICHARD H. ROFFMAN ASSOCIATES (III), Suite 6A, 697 West End Ave., New York NY 10025. (212)749-3647/3648. President: Richard H. Roffman. Estab. 1967. 70% of clients are new/unpublished writers. Prefers to work with published/established writers. Specializes in "nonfiction primarily, but other types, too." Currently handles: 10% magazine articles; 5% magazine fiction; 5% textbooks; 5% juvenile books; 5% radio scripts; 5% movie scripts; 5% TV scripts; 5% syndicated material; 5% poetry; 50% other.
Will Handle: Nonfiction books. Query only. Does not read unsolicited mss. Reports in 2 weeks. "SASE if written answer requested, please."
Terms: Agent receives 10% commission on domestic sales; 10% on dramatic sales; 10% on foreign sales.
Fees: "We do not read material (for a fee) actually, only on special occasions. We prefer to refer to other people specializing in that." 10% of income derived from reading fees. "We suggest a moderate monthly retainer." Charges for mailings, phone calls, photocopying and messenger service. Offers consultation service through which writers can get advice on a contract. "I am also an attorney at law."

*THE SUSAN SCHULMAN LITERARY AGENCY, INC., 454 W. 44th St., New York NY 10036. (212)713-1633/4/5. FAX: (212)586-8830. President: Susan Schulman. Estab. 1978. Member of ILAA. 10-15% of clients are new/unpublished writers. Prefers to work with published/established authors; works with a small number of new/unpublished authors. Currently handles: 50% nonfiction books; 40% novels; 10% stage plays.
Will Handle: Nonfiction, fiction and plays, especially genre fiction such as mysteries. Query with outline. Reports in 2 weeks on queries; 6 weeks on mss as long as SASE enclosed.
Recent Sales: *Runes*, by Christopher Fowler (Ballantine); *Sweet Narcissus*, by Margaret Kerlstrap (Bantam); and *The Wife-in-Law Trap*, by Ann Cryster (Simon & Schuster).
Terms: Agent receives 15% commission on domestic sales; 10-20% on dramatic sales; and 7½-10% on foreign sales (plus 7½-10% to co-agent).
Fees: Charges a $50 reading fee if detailed analysis requested; fee will be waived if representing the writer. Less than 1% of income derived from reading fees. Charges for foreign mail, special messenger or delivery services.

STACY ANN SCOTT, SYNERGY CREATIVE AGENCY (III), #110, 3232 San Mateo Blvd. NE, Albuquerque NM 87110. Contact: Stacy Ann Scott. Specializes in novels and nonfiction books, "but we will consider screenplays." Estab. 1990. Member of WGA. Represents 8 clients. 90% of clients are new/previously unpublished writers. Currently handles: 10% textbooks; 10% juvenile books; 20% novels; 20% poetry books; 20% movie scripts; 10% stage plays; 10% TV scripts. Member agents: Stacy Ann Scott (novels and nonfiction manuscripts; how-to, self-help, educational books and materials); Chris Sturgess (screenplays, TV scripts, stage plays).
Will Handle: Nonfiction books, textbooks, juvenile books, novels, movie scripts, stage plays, TV scripts. Will consider these nonfiction areas: biography/autobiography; business; child guidance/parenting; cooking/food/nutrition; crafts/hobbies; ethnic/cultural interests; gay/lesbian issues; health/medicine; juvenile nonfiction; music/dance/theater/film; new age/metaphysics; psychology; true crime/investigative; self-help/personal improvement; sports; women's issues/women's studies. "We also like to see manuscripts aimed at the 50 and above age group, since this is where 90% of the disposable income in the US comes from. We are looking for 50+ how-to sports manuscripts." Will consider these fiction areas: action/adventure; confessional; detective/police/crime; juvenile; literary; mainstream; mystery/suspense; psychic/supernatural; romance (contemporary, gothic); science fiction; sports; thriller/espionage; young adult. Query with synopsis plus first 3 chapters. Will report in 3 weeks on queries; 8 weeks on mss.
Terms: Agent receives 15% on domestic sales; 20% on foreign sales. Offers a written contract. "As long as our relationship is mutually satisfactory, our contract is binding. Either party can cancel the contract at any time."
Fees: "We charge no reading fee in accordance with WGA guidelines." Offers criticism service: $50 per chapter for books; $35 for query letter and outline; $35 for short story; $25 per 16-line poem; $70 for screenplays up to 115 pages, $1 each additional page. "Agents critique works for clients. Critiques include plot analysis and characterization, as well as mechanics such as grammatical or spelling errors.

We charge a $25 file set-up fee that covers initial copies, postage and long-distance telephone expense. Once the $25 is depleted, the client may be billed for additional photocopying, postage or long-distance telephone expense. We may waive the additional expenses if a sale looks promising." 95% of business is derived from commissions on ms sales; 5% is derived from reading fees or criticism services. Payment of a criticism fee does not ensure representation.

Writers' Conferences: Attends Southwest Writer's Workshop Annual Conference, Philadelphia Writer's Conference.

Tips: "We obtain new clients from referrals, registration with WGAWest and through advertising." If you're interested in agency representation, "there are three strikes and then you're out, unless a writer is irresistably good (which we haven't seen happen yet). First, please include a SASE if you want a reply. Second, use sex-fair language. Don't assume a man is going to sign you, so address your query "Dear Sir or Madam," etc. Third, your query letter says a lot about your writing capability, so proofread carefully to avoid spelling and grammatical errors. Show off your talent in your query! Excite us! Make us want to read your manuscript! We would also like to say that books seem to sell more quickly than screenplays because more books are published annually than movies are made. We prefer to represent novels, self-help, how-to and books that appeal to the over-50 crowd and to women. These are the two groups that buy most of the books. We will look at screenplays, TV scripts and stage plays that are strong and that have a studio or actor in mind."

*SEBASTIAN LITERARY AGENCY (III), P.O. Box 1369, #303, 1250 San Carlos Ave., San Carlos CA 94070. (415)598-0310. FAX: (415)637-9615. Contact: Laurie Harper. Estab. 1985. Represents approximately 50 clients. Specializes in psychology, sociology and business. Currently handles: 75% nonfiction books; 25% fiction (novels).

Will Handle: Nonfiction books, novels. "No children's or YA." Will consider these nonfiction areas: anthropology/archaeology; art/architecture/design; biography/autobiography; business; child guidance/parenting; computers/electronics; current affairs; ethnic/cultural interests; government/politics/law; health/medicine; history; military/war; money/finance/economics; nature/environment; psychology; true crime/investigative; science/technology; self-help/personal improvement; sociology; sports; women's issues/women's studies. Will consider these fiction areas: action/adventure; contemporary issues; detective/police/crime; ethnic; family saga; gay; glitz; historical; literary; mainstream; mystery/suspense; thriller/espionage; westerns/frontier. Query with outline plus 3 sample chapters and author bio. Will report in 3 weeks on queries; 4-6 weeks on mss.

Recent Sales: *Beating the Odds*, by Scott A. Clark (Amacom); *Enterprise Information Architecture*, by Bruce Love (Van Nostrand Reinhold).

Terms: Agent receives 15% commission on domestic sales; 20% on foreign sales. Offers a written contract, binding for 2 years.

Fees: Charges a $100, one-time nonrefundable fee when signing with this agency *for previously unpublished authors* and charges for photocopies of manuscript for submission to publisher.

Tips: Obtains new clients through "referrals from authors and editors, some at conferences and some from unsolicited queries from around the country. If interested in agency representation, for *fiction*, "know the category that your novel belongs in, according to market study, and be sure that you have made it conforming to that category. Too many novels fall in-between categories, and are unsalable as a result. For *nonfiction*, it is important to convey more than the facts and statistics about the subject of your book—you need to convey its *relevance* to us, and your fascination or enthusiasm for it."

SINGER MEDIA CORPORATION (III), 3164 Tyler Ave., Anaheim CA 92801. (714)527-5650/51. FAX: (714)527-0268. Contact: Kurt Singer. Estab. 1940. Represents 100+ clients for "books, features, cartoons." 15% of clients are new/previously unpublished writers. Specializes in romance, business, self-help, dictionaries, quiz books, cartoons, interviews. Currently handles: 25% nonfiction books; 35% novels; 40% syndicated material. Member agents: John Kearns (general novels); Dorothy Rosati (romance titles); Kurt Singer (business books); Katherine Han (self-help); Veena Uberoi (Asia department).

Will Handle: Nonfiction books, syndicated material, business titles, cartoons. Will consider these nonfiction areas: biography/autobiography; business; child guidance/parenting; computers/electronics; health/medicine; money/finance/economics; psychology; true crime/investigative; self-help/personal improvement; translations; women's issues/women's studies; cartoons; dictionaries; juvenile activities; interviews with celebrities. Will consider these fiction areas: cartoon/comic; detective/police/crime; erotica; fantasy; glitz; mystery/suspense; picture book; psychic/supernatural; romance (contemporary); science fiction; thriller/espionage; westerns/frontier; teenage romance. Query. "Give writing credits." Will report in 3 weeks on queries; 4-6 weeks on mss.

Recent Sales: *Dark Shadows* series, 32 titles by W.E.D. Ross (Quelle Germany); 20 western titles (Ulverscroft Thorpe, UK/U.S.A.); 2 crossword books and crossword dictionary (PSI).
Terms: Agent receives 15% commission on domestic sales; 20% on foreign sales.
Fees: Charges $300 reading fee "only to unpublished writers, refundable if script is sold. Criticism service is part of our reading fee. Our readers are published authors or ghostwriters." 87% of business is derived from commissions on manuscript and book sales; 3% is derived from reading fees or criticism service. Payment of a criticism fee ensures representation "unless it is not salable to the commercial market."
Writers' Conference: Attends Romance Writers of America Conference.
Tips: "We have been in business for 50 years and are known." If interested in agency representation, "books are not written, but rewritten and rewritten. Syndication is done on a worldwide basis, and must be of global interest. Hollywood's winning formula is God/inspiration, sex and action. Try to get reprints of books overseas and in the USA if out of print."

*SOUTHERN WRITERS (II), Suite 1020, 635 Gravier St., New Orleans LA 70130. (504)525-6390. FAX: (504)524-7349. Contact: Pamela G. Ahearn. Estab. 1979. Member of Romance Writers of America. Represents 30 clients. 40% of clients are new/previously unpublished writers. Specializes in fiction/nonfiction based in the Deep South; romance (both historical and contemporary). Currently handles: 30% nonfiction books; 10% juvenile books; 60% novels.
Will Handle: Nonfiction books, juvenile books, ("young adult and young readers, not children's picture books"), novels. Will consider these nonfiction areas: biography; business; child guidance/parenting; current affairs; gay/lesbian issues; health/medicine; history; juvenile nonfiction; money/finance/economics; music/dance/theater/film; psychology; religious/inspirational; true crime/investigative; self-help/personal improvement; women's issues/women's studies. Will consider these fiction areas: action/adventure; contemporary issues; detective/police/crime; family saga; fantasy; feminist; gay; glitz; historical; humor/satire; juvenile; lesbian; literary; mainstream; mystery/suspense; psychic/supernatural; regional; religious/inspiration; romance; science fiction; thriller/espionage; westerns/frontier; young adult. Query. Will report in 2-3 weeks on queries; 6-8 weeks on mss.
Recent Sales: *Lions and Lace*, by Meagan McKinney (Dell); *Deadly Currents* and *Fatal Ingredients*, by Caroline Burnes (Harlequin Intrigue); *Second Son*, by Kate Moore (Avon).
Terms: Agent receives 15% commission on domestic sales; 20% on foreign sales. Offers a written contract, binding for 1 year.
Fees: Charges a reading fee of up to $450 for 200,000-word ms. "Reading fees are charged to unpublished authors, and to authors writing in areas other than those of previous publication (i.e., nonfiction authors writing fiction). Fee is nonrefundable. We offer criticism at a fee slightly higher than our reading fees. Authors who pay a reading fee or criticism fee receive a 3-5 page, single-spaced letter, explaining what we feel the problems of their books are from both a qualitative and marketing standpoint. Letters are written by Pamela G. Ahearn. We charge for postage on an author's first book only if it is sold. On subsequent books there's no charge." 75% of business is derived from commissions on ms sales. 25% is derived from reading fees or criticism services. Payment of a criticism fee does not ensure representation.
Writers' Conferences: Attends Romance Writers of America Conference; Gulf Coast Writers Association; New Orleans Writer's Conference.
Tips: Obtains new clients through solicitation at conferences and most frequently through recommendations from others. "You should query an agent first, and only send what he/she asks to see. If asked to send 3 chapters, make sure they're the first 3, not the ones you consider to be the strongest. Your manuscript should be in complete form and polished before you contact an agent. It should be double-spaced on 8½×11 white bond paper, unbound. Make your query letter brief and to the point, listing publishing credentials, writer's groups and organizations you may belong to, awards, etc. Do *not* make it cute, outlandish or hostile!"

STATE OF THE ART LTD. (II), Suite 200, 1625 S. Broadway, Denver CO 80210. (303)722-7191. FAX: (303)744-9825. Contact: Carol Ayers. Estab. 1983. Represents 10 clients. Currently handles: 50% nonfiction books, 50% novels.
Will Handle: Nonfiction and novels. Will consider these nonfiction areas: art; new age/metaphysics; self-help/personal improvement; women's studies; also open to other areas. Will consider these fiction areas: contemporary issues; feminist; mystery/suspense; science fiction. Query with SASE first. If they respond, send 3 sample chapters. Reports in 1 week on queries.
Terms: Agent receives 10% and up commission on domestic sales. Offers written contract, binding for 2 years.
Fees: Charges a reading fee. Charges $75 minimum; over 100 pages, $30/hour. Offers criticism service.
Tips: Usually obtains new clients from directory listings. "Do some research. Find out what professional presentation is like."

MICHAEL STEINBERG LITERARY AGENCY (III), P.O. Box 274, Glencoe IL 60027. (708)835-8881. Contact: Michael Steinberg. Estab. 1980. Represents 27 clients. 5% of clients are new/previously unpublished writers. Specializes in business and general nonfiction, mysteries, science fiction. Currently handles: 75% nonfiction books; 25% novels.
Will Handle: Nonfiction books; novels. Will consider these nonfiction areas: biography; business; child guidance; computer; current affairs; ethnic/cultural interests; government/politics/law; history; money/finance/economics; nature/environment; psychology; self-help/personal improvement. Will consider these fiction areas: action/adventure; contemporary issues; detective/police/crime; erotica; mainstream; mystery/suspense; science fiction; thriller/espionage. "Query for guidelines." Will report in 2 weeks on queries; 6 weeks on mss.
Terms: Agent receives 15% on domestic sales; 15-20% on foreign sales. Offers a written contract, which is binding, "but at will."
Fees: Charges $75 reading fee for outline and chapters 1-3; $200 for a full ms to 100,000 words. Offers a criticism service, which is part of the reading fee. Charges actual phone and postage, which is billed back quarterly. 95% of business is derived from commissions on ms sales; 5% is derived from reading fees or criticism services.
Tips: Obtains new clients through unsolicited inquiries and referrals from editors and authors. "We do not solicit new clients. Do not send unsolicited material. Write for guidelines and include SASE. Do not send generically addressed, photocopied query letters.

*MARIANNE STRONG (III), 65 E. 96th St., New York NY 10128. (212)249-1000. FAX: (212)831-3241. Contact: Marianne Strong, Tonia Shoumatoff. Estab. 1978. Represents 10 clients.
Will Handle: Nonfiction books, novels, movie and TV scripts. Will consider these nonfiction areas: current affairs; interior design/decorating; money/finance/economics; true crime/investigative. Will consider these fiction areas: confessional; detective/police/crime; family saga; romance; thriller/espionage. Send outline plus 3 sample chapters. Will report "quickly."
Terms: Agent receives 15% commission on domestic sales; 15% on foreign sales. Offers a written contract, binding for the life of book or play "assuming it is sold."
Fees: Charges a reading fee for new writers only, "fee refundable when manuscript sold." Offers a criticism service.
Tips: Obtains new clients through recommendations from others.

*MARK SULLIVAN ASSOCIATES (II), Suite 1700, 521 Fifth Ave., New York NY 10175. (212)682-5844. FAX: (212)315-3860. Contact: Mark Sullivan. Estab. 1989. 50% of clients are new/previously unpublished writers. Currently handles: 20% nonfiction books; 5% textbooks; 60% novels; 5% poetry books; 10% movie scripts. Specializes in "science fiction, women's romance, detective/mystery/spy, but handles all genres."
Will Handle: Nonfiction books, textbooks, scholarly books, novels, novellas, short story collections, poetry books, movie scripts. Will consider these nonfiction areas: anthropology/archaeology; biography/autobiography; business; cooking/food/nutrition; crafts/hobbies; current affairs; health/medicine; interior design/decorating; language/literature/criticism; military/war; money/finance/economics; music/dance/theater/film; nature/environment; new age/metaphysics; photography; psychology; religious/inspirational; science/technology; sports. Will consider all fiction areas. Query or send query with 3 sample chapters and outline. Will report in 2 weeks on queries; 3-4 weeks on mss.
Terms: Agent receives 10-15% commission on domestic sales; 20% on foreign sales. Offers a written contract.
Fees: Charges $85 reading fee for new writers whose work is chosen from among queries and sample chapters submitted. Critique is provided with reading fee. Charges for photocopying and long-distance telephone calls. 90% of business is derived from commissions on ms sales; 10% of business is derived from reading fees or criticism services. Payment of fees does not ensure agency representation. "However, the firm's offer to read an entire manuscript is a reflection of our strong interest."
Tips: Obtains new clients through "advertising, reputation, recommendations, conferences. Quality of presentation of query letter, sample chapters and manuscript is important. Completed manuscripts are preferred to works in progress."

The publishing field is constantly changing! If you're still using this book and it is 1993 or later, buy the newest edition of Guide to Literary Agents & Art/Photo Reps *at your favorite bookstore or order directly from Writer's Digest Books.*

TIGER MOON ENTERPRISES (I), 1850 Chester Lane, Cambria CA 93428. (805)927-3920. Contact: Terry Kennedy or Mark James Miller. Estab. 1991. Represents 13 clients. 50% of clients are new/previously unpublished writers. "We prefer books written by successful entrepreneurs, teaching their skills to others. Children's books which teach the five human values of love, truth, peace, nonviolence and righteous living also interest us." Currently handles: 40% novels; 20% poetry books; 40% short story collections (10% of these are new age). Member agents: Terry Kennedy (business, how-to, children's); Mark Miller (fiction, history, investigative research).
Will Handle: Nonfiction books, scholarly books, juvenile books, novels, novellas, short story collections, poetry books and work that is "spiritually uplifting, life-guiding." Will consider these nonfiction areas: cooking; crafts; health/medicine; history; juvenile nonfiction; military/war; money; music; nature; new age; religious; self-help. Will consider these fiction areas: contemporary issues; family saga; historical; literary; psychic; regional; religious. Query with a 10-page sample and SASE. Will report "immediately" on queries; in 2 weeks on mss.
Recent Sales: *Frontage Road*, by Frank Sisti (Tiger Moon Press); *Voices of the Boat People*, by Mark James Miller (Golden West College).
Terms: Agent receives 15% commission on domestic sales; 15% on foreign sales. Offers a written contract, duration varies.
Fees: Charges a reading fee. Offers four service options: manuscript reading service for $1.50/page. Provides 750-word critique; copyediting service for $3/page; rewriting package for $4.50/page. Provides publication-ready copy with major mechanical and technical reconstruction; total book packaging. Cost estimates on request. Critiques are written by agents. "We agent a manuscript for a specific fee, custom designed for each client. We offer book packaging services to clients who do not want to wait for mainstream publishing houses to back them." 50% of business derived from ms sales; 50% is derived from reading or criticism (or other) fees. Payment of a criticism fee does not ensure agency representation.
Tips: "We have been in the writing business for 14 years. We have many personal contacts. We have a huge mailing list to draw from, but we are always interested in new contacts. If you are the type of person who really believes in your work, we are interested in doing business with you. We are not equipped to build up your self esteem as a writer. Believe that what you have written is going to be of genuine interest to many readers, send us a professional package and we'll be attentive to your proposal."

*JEANNE TOOMEY ASSOCIATES (II), 95 Belden St., Falls Village CT 06031. (203)824-0831/5469. FAX: (203)824-5460. Contact: Jeanne Toomey. Estab. 1985. Represents 10 clients. 50% of clients are new/previously unpublished writers. Specializes in "nonfiction; biographies of famous men and women; history with a flair—murder and detection. No children's books, no poetry, no Harlequin-type romances." Currently handles: 45% nonfiction books; 20% novels; 35% movie scripts.
Will Handle: Nonfiction books, novels, short story collections, movie scripts. Will consider these nonfiction areas: agriculture/horticulture; animals; anthropology/archaeology; art/architecture/design; biography/autobiography; government/politics/law; history; interior design/decorating; money/finance/economics; nature/environment; true crime/investigative. Will consider these fiction areas: detective/police/crime; psychic/supernatural; thriller/espionage. Send outline plus 3 sample chapters. Will report in 1 month.
Terms: Agent receives 15% commission on domestic sales.
Fees: Charges $100 reading fee for unpublished authors; no fee for published authors. "The $100 covers marketing fee, office expenses, postage, photocopying. We absorb those costs in the case of published authors."

PHYLLIS TORNETTA AGENCY (II), Box 423, Croton-on-Hudson NY 10521. (914)737-3464. President: Phyllis Tornetta. Estab. 1979. Represents 22 clients. 35% of clients are new/unpublished writers. Specializes in romance, contemporary, mystery. Currently handles: 90% novels and 10% juvenile.
Will Handle: Novels and juvenile. Query with outline. Does not read unsolicited mss. Reports in 1 month.
Recent Sales: *Intimate Strangers*, by S. Hoover (Harlequin); *Accused* (Silhouette) and *Ride Eagle* (Worldwide).
Terms: Agent receives 15% commission on domestic sales and 20% on foreign sales.
Fees: Charges a reading fee "for full manuscripts." Charges $75/300 pages.

*SUSAN P. URSTADT INC. WRITERS AND ARTISTS AGENCY (II), P.O. Box 1676, New Canaan CT 06840. (203)966-6111. Contact: Susan Urstadt. Estab. 1975. Member of ILAA. Represents 45 clients. 10% of clients are new/previously unpublished authors. Specializes in illustrated books, popular reference, art, antiques, decorative arts, gardening, travel, horses, armchair cookbooks, business, self-help, crafts, hobbies, collectibles. Currently handles: 95% nonfiction books.

Will Handle: Nonfiction books. Will consider these nonfiction areas: agriculture/horticulture; animals; anthropology/archaeology; art/architecture/design; biography/autobiography; business; child guidance/parenting; cooking/food/nutrition; crafts/hobbies; current affairs; health/medicine; interior design/decorating; military/war; money/finance/economics; music/dance/theater/film; nature/environment; photography; self-help/personal improvement; sports. "No unsolicited fiction please." Send outline plus 2 sample chapters, SASE and short author bio. Will report in 3 weeks on queries.

Recent Sales: *History of American Folk Art*, by Elizabeth Stillinger, (Henry Holt); *History of American Wildflowers*, by Tim Coffey (Facts on File); *Southern Christmas Traditions*, by Emyl Jenkins (Crown).

Terms: Agent receives 15% commission on domestic sales; 20% on foreign sales. Offers written contract.

Fees: Charges $275 "start-up" fee *for new authors* (only for authors who are accepted as clients). 95% of business is derived from commissions on ms sales.

Tips: Obtains new clients through recommendations from others. "We are interested in building a writer's career through the long term and only want dedicated writers with special knowledge, which they share in a professional way."

CARLSON WADE (II), Room K-4, 49 Bokee Ct., Brooklyn NY 11223. (718)743-6983. President: Carlson Wade. Estab. 1949. Represents 40 clients. 50% of clients are new/unpublished writers. Eager to work with new/unpublished writers. Will consider all types of fiction and nonfiction. Currently handles: 10% magazine articles; 10% magazine fiction; 40% nonfiction books; 40% novels.

Will Handle: Magazine articles, magazine fiction, nonfiction books and novels. Query or send entire manuscript.

Recent Sales: *Eat Away Illness* (Prentice Hall) and *Nutritional Therapy* (Prentice Hall).

Terms: Agent receives 10% commission on domestic sales; 10% on dramatic sales; 10% on foreign sales.

Fees: Charges handling fee: $1/1,000 words on short ms; $50/book. 20% of income derived from reading and handling fees. Charges a criticism fee if ms requires extensive work. 10% of income derived from criticism fees. "Short manuscript receives 5 pages of critique, book receives 15 (single space, page-by-page critique)." 20% of income derived from reading and handling fees; 80% of income derived from commission on ms sales. Payment of a criticism fee does not ensure that agency will represent a writer. "If a writer revises a manuscript properly, then we take it on. Further help is available at no cost."

*THE GERRY B. WALLERSTEIN AGENCY (II), Suite 12, 2315 Powell Ave., Erie PA 16506. (814)833-5511. Contact: Ms. Gerry B. Wallerstein. Estab. 1984. Member of The Authors Guild, Inc. and Society of Professional Journalists. Represents 40 clients. 25% of clients are new/previously unpublished writers. Specializes in nonfiction books; "personalized help for new novelists." Currently handles: 50% nonfiction books; 2% scholarly books; 4% juvenile books; 35% novels; 2% short story collections; 2% TV scripts; 5% short material. (Note: Juvenile books, scripts and short material marketed for *clients only!*)

Will Handle: Nonfiction books, scholarly books, novels, short story collections. Will consider all nonfiction areas provided book is for general trade ("no textbooks"). Will consider these fiction areas: action/adventure; contemporary issues; detective/police/crime; family saga; glitz; historical; humor/satire; literary; mainstream; mystery/suspense; regional; romance; thriller/espionage; westerns/frontier; young adult. To query, send entire manuscript for fiction; a proposal (including 3 chapters) for nonfiction books. "No manuscripts are reviewed until writer has received my brochure." Will report in 1 week on queries; 2 months on mss.

Recent Sales: *How to Become Successfully Self-Employed*, by Brian R. Smith (Bob Adams, Inc.); *Derailing the Tokyo Express*, by Jack D. Coombe (Stackpole Books).

Terms: Agent receives 15% on domestic sales; 20% on foreign sales. Offers a written contract, which "can be cancelled by either party, with 60 days' notice of termination."

Fees: "To justify my investment of time, effort and expertise in working with newer or beginning writers, I charge a reading/critique fee based on length of manuscript, for example: $350 for each manuscript of 105,000 to 125,000 words." Critique included as part of reading fee. "Reports are 1-2 pages for proposals and short material; 2-4 pages for full-length mss; done by agent." Charges clients $20/month postage/telephone fee; and if required, manuscript photocopying or typing, copyright fees, cables, attorney fees (if approved by author), travel expense (if approved by author). 50% of business is derived from commissions on ms sales; 50% is derived from reading fees and criticism services. Payment of a criticism fee does not ensure representation.

Writers' Conferences: Attends Westminster College Conference; Midwest Writers' Conference.

Tips: Obtains new clients through recommendations; listings in directories; referrals from clients and publishers/editors. "A query letter that tells me something about the writer and his/her work is more likely to get a personal response."

JAMES WARREN LITERARY AGENCY (II), 13131 Welby Way, North Hollywood CA 91606. (818)982-5423. Agent: James Warren. Editors: Audrey Langer, Bob Carlson. Estab. 1969. Represents 60 clients. 60% of clients are new/unpublished writers. "We are willing to work with select unpublished writers." Specializes in fiction, history, textbooks, professional books, craft books, how-to books, self-improvement books, health books and diet books. Currently handles 40% nonfiction books; 20% novels; 10% textbooks; 5% juvenile books; 10% movie scripts; 15% TV scripts and teleplays.
Will Handle: Juvenile books, historical romance novels, movie scripts (especially drama and humor) and TV scripts (drama, humor, documentary). Query with outline. Does not read unsolicited mss. No reply without SASE. Brochure available with SASE. Reports in 1 week on queries; 1 month on mss.
Recent Sales: *The Woman Inge*, by Audrey R. Langer (New Saga) and *Ashes Under Uricon*, by Audrey R. Langer (New Saga); *Unlife*, by Dale Hoover (Dell/Bantam/Doubleday).
Terms: Agents receives 10% commission on domestic sales; 20% on foreign sales.
Fees: Charges reading fee of $2.50/1,000 words; refunds reading fee if material sells. 20% of total income derived from fees charged to writers; 80% of income derived from commission on ms sales. Payment of fees does not ensure that agency will represent writer.

WATERSIDE PRODUCTIONS, INC. (II), 2191 San Elijo Ave., Cardiff-by-the-Sea CA 92007. (619)632-9190. FAX: (619)632-9295. President: Bill Gladstone. Estab. 1982. Represents 200 clients. 20% of clients are new/previously unpublished writers. Currently handles: 80% nonfiction, 20% novels. Member agents: Bill Gladstone (trade computer titles, business); Julie Castiglia (women's issues, serious nonfiction, fiction); Matthew Wagner (trade computer titles, nonfiction).
Will Handle: Nonfiction books, novels. Will consider these nonfiction areas: anthropology/archaeology; art/architecture/design; biography/autobiography; business; child guidance/parenting; computers/electronics; ethnic/cultural interests; health/medicine; money/finance/economics; music/dance/theater/film; nature/environment; new age/metaphysics; psychology; true crime/investigative; sociology; sports; women's issues/women's studies. Will consider these fiction areas: action/adventure; contemporary issues; detective/police/crime; glitz; literary; mainstream; mystery/suspense; romance; thriller/espionage. Query with outline/proposal. Will report in 2 weeks on queries; 6-8 weeks on mss.
Recent Sales: *Made in America*, by Philippe Kahn (Bantam); *Women in Debt*, by Karen O'Connor (Thomas Nelson); *Sidewinder*, by Mike Dunn (Avon); *Mastering Wordperfect 5.1*, by Alan Simpson (Sybex).
Terms: Agent receives 15% commission on domestic sales; 25% on foreign sales. Offers a written contract.
Fees: Does not charge a reading fee. Offers a criticism service. Charges $50 an hour. Agents write critiques. Charges for photocopying and other unusual expenses. 99.9% of business is derived from commissions on ms sales; .1% derived from reading fees or criticism services.
Tips: Usually obtains new clients through recommendations from others. "Be professional. The more professional a submission, the more seriously it's viewed. Beginning writers should go to a writers workshop and learn how a presentation should be made."

*SANDRA WATT & ASSOCIATES (II), Suite 4053, 8033 Sunset Blvd., Hollywood CA 90046. (213)653-2339. Contact: David South. Estab. 1977. Member of WGA, SAG, AFTRA. Represents 55 clients. 15% of clients are new/previously unpublished writers. Specializes in scripts: film noir, romantic comedies; books: women's fiction, mystery, commercial nonfiction. Currently handles: 40% nonfiction books, 35% novels, 25% movie scripts. Member agents: Sandra Watt (scripts, nonfiction, novels); Larry Bolton (scripts); Robert Drake (gay fiction).
Will Handle: Nonfiction books, novels, movie scripts. Will consider these nonfiction areas: animals; anthropology/archaeology; new age/metaphysics; true crime/investigative; self-help/personal improvement; sports; women's issues/women's studies. Will consider these fiction areas: detective/police/crime; glitz; mainstream; mystery/suspense; thriller/espionage. Query. Will report in 1 week on queries; 2 months on mss.
Recent Sales: *You Can't Grow Tomatoes in Central Park*, by Frank Ruegg (N.A.L.); "Ethel," by Tema Nason (Lorimar); *The Way of Kings*, by Drew Lawrence (Putnam); *The Romantic Imperative*, by Jay Russell (Tarcher).
Terms: Agent receives 15% commission on domestic sales; 25% on foreign sales. Offers written contract, binding for 1 year.
Fees: Does not charge reading fee. Charges a one-time nonrefundable marketing fee of $100 *for unpublished authors.*
Tips: Obtains new clients through recommendations from others, referrals and "from wonderful query letters. Don't forget the SASE!"

WEST COAST LITERARY ASSOCIATES (II), Suite 151, 7960-B Soquel Dr., Aptos CA 95003. FAX: (408)662-0755. Telex: 7101114419. Contact: Acquisitions Editor. Estab. 1986. Member of Authors League of America. Represents 30 clients. 20% of clients are new/previously unpublished clients.

Currently handles: 10% nonfiction books; 60% novels; 30% movie scripts.

Will Handle: Nonfiction books, novels, movie scripts. Will consider these nonfiction areas: biography/autobiography; current affairs; ethnic/cultural interests; government/politics/law; history; language/literature/criticism; music/dance/theater/film; nature/environment; psychology; true crime/investigative; women's issues/women's studies. Will consider these fiction areas: action/adventure; contemporary issues; detective/police/crime; experimental; historical; literary; mainstream; mystery/suspense; regional; contemporary and historical romance; science fiction; thriller/espionage; westerns/frontier. Query first. Will report in 2 weeks on queries; 1 month on mss.

Terms: Agent receives 10% commission on domestic sales; 20% commission on foreign sales. Offers a written contract, binding for 1 year.

Recent Sales: "Available to prospective clients."

Fees: Does not charge a reading fee. Charges an agency marketing and materials fee between $75 and $125, depending on genre and length. Fees are refunded in full upon sale of the property.

Tips: "Query with SASE for submission guidelines before sending material."

THE WILSHIRE LITERARY AGENCY (I), #600, 8601 Wilshire Blvd., Beverly Hills CA 90211. (213)652-3967. Contact: Carol McCleary. Estab. 1990. Specializes in mystery novels. Currently handles: 100% novels.

Will Handle: Novels. Will consider these fiction areas: action/adventure; detective/police/crime; literary; mainstream; mystery/suspense. Send outline plus 3 sample chapters. Will report in 1 month on queries and mss.

Terms: Agent receives 15% commission on domestic sales; 15% on foreign sales. Offers a written contract.

Fees: Does not charge reading fee. Offers criticism service: $2 per page. "We use two freelance editors for line editing and 10-15-page critique." Charges for postage and photocopying; "only fee charged." 98% of business is derived from commission on ms sales; 2% is derived from reading fees and criticism services. Payment of criticism does not ensure representation.

Tips: Obtains new clients through recommendations from others.

*STEPHEN WRIGHT AUTHORS' REPRESENTATIVE (III), P.O. Box 1341, F.D.R. Station, New York NY 10150. (212)213-4382. Authors' Representative: Stephen Wright. Estab. 1984. Prefers to work with published/established authors. Works with a small number of new/unpublished authors. Specializes in fiction, nonfiction and screenplays. Currently handles: 20% nonfiction, 60% novels, 10% movie scripts, 10% TV scripts.

Will Handle: Nonfiction books, novels, young adult and juvenile books, movie scripts, radio scripts, stage plays, TV scripts, syndicated material. Query or send entire ms. SASE required. Reports in 3 weeks on queries.

Terms: Agent receives 10-15% commission on domestic sales; 10-15% on dramatic sales; 15-20% on foreign sales.

Fees: "When the writer is a beginner or has had no prior sales in the medium for which he or she is writing, we charge a reading criticism fee; does not waive fee when representing the writer." Charges $500/300 pages. We simply do not "read" a ms, but give the writer an in-depth criticism. "If we like what we read, we would represent the writer. Or if the writer revises ms to meet our professional standards and we believe there is a market for said ms, we would also represent the writer. We tell the writer whether we believe his/her work is marketable. I normally provide the critiques."

*WRITER'S CONSULTING GROUP (II, III), P.O. Box 492, Burbank CA 91503. (818)841-9294. Director: Jim Barmeier. Estab. 1983. Represents 10 clients. "We prefer to work with established writers unless the author has an unusual true story." Currently handles: 40% nonfiction books; 20% novels; 40% movie scripts.

Will Handle: True stories for which the author has the right; nonfiction books (educational books, how-to, health, true crime, science, business, self-help); novels (women's, mainstream, contemporary thrillers); movie scripts (romantic comedies, character-based dramas). Query or send entire ms. Include SASE. Reports in 1 month on queries; 3 months on mss.

Recent Sales: "We have helped writers sell everything from episodes for children's TV shows ('Smurfs') to movie-of-the-week options (including the Craig Smith espionage story)."

Terms: "We will explain our terms to clients when they wish to sign. We receive a 10% commission on domestic sales."

Fees: Sometimes charges 50¢/page reading fee up to $200. "Additionally, we offer ghostwriting and editorial services, as well as book publicity services for authors. Mr Barmeier is a graduate of Stanford University's Master's Degree in Creative Writing Program."

Tips: "We are looking for good women's stories that could be turned into a movie-of-the-week."

TOM ZELASKY LITERARY AGENCY (II), 3138 Parkridge Crescent, Chamblee (Atlanta) GA 30341. (404)458-0391. Contact: Tom Zelasky. Estab. 1986. Represents 8 clients. 90% of clients are new/ previously unpublished writers. Specializes in detectives and westerns, Vietnam, others (depending on quality and marketability). Currently handles: 10% nonfiction books; 10% juvenile books; 80% novels.

Will Handle: Nonfiction books, juvenile books, novels, novellas, short story collections, movie scripts, stage plays, westerns, detectives. Will consider these nonfiction areas: biography/autobiography; current affairs; government/politics; juvenile nonfiction; military/war; true crime/investigative; self-help/ personal improvement; women's issues/women's studies. Will consider these fiction areas: confessional; contemporary issues; detective/police/crime; family saga; feminist; historical; juvenile; literary; mainstream; mystery/suspense; romance (contemporary); science fiction; thriller/espionage; westerns/ frontier; young adult. Query first, then send entire ms with synopsis. Will report in 1-2 weeks on queries; 2-3 months on mss.

Terms: Agent receives 10-15% commission on domestic sales; 20-25% on foreign sales. Offers a written contract, binding for 1 year and "renewed automatically by 90 days after end of year."

Fees: "A reading fee of $100 is charged. The reading fee is for reviewing and reading a manuscript. A one-page critique is sent if the manuscript is rejected by the agency. My readers and I write the critique, which covers basic writing concerns, the physical format presentation of the manuscript and especially the technique. Postage and photocopying is deducted from the reading fee or after the royalty commission is earned." 50% of business is derived from commissions on ms sales; 50% is derived from reading fees and criticism services. Payment of a criticism fee ensures representation.

Writers' Conferences: Attends the Florida Suncoast Writers' Conference, Tennessee Mountain Writers Conference, Dixie Council Authors' and Journalists' Conference, South Eastern Writers Conference and other conferences. "I don't attend these conferences every year, but use the scatter theory."

Tips: Obtains new clients through query letters, phone queries, conferences, directories, "publishers from everywhere. Know the mechanics and techniques of the art of writing. Practice and produce. Don't rely on past laurels. Use writing knowledge at all facets of writing. Go where the writing is done to acquaint oneself about the writing/publishing profession. And, set a daily pattern of writing as a laboring job, 8 hours or what hours preferable, depending upon a job-for-living necessity. You will be successful in the long run but it may take years, decades. Who knows?"

Additional Fee-charging Agents

The following fee-charging agencies have full listings in other sections of this book. These agencies have indicated they are *primarily* interested in handling the work of scriptwriters, artists or photographers, but are also interested in book manuscripts. After reading the listing (you can find the page number in the Listings Index), send them a query to obtain more information on their needs and manuscript submission policies.

Berzon Agency, The Marian
Lee Literary Agency, L. Harry
Pacific Design Studio

Raintree Agency
Southeastern Entertainment
    Agency Inc.
Talent Bank Agency, The

Script Agents

Finding and Working with Script Agents

by Kerry Cox

As editor and publisher of a newsletter targeted solely at aspiring and professional script-writers, I've talked to dozens of agents and hundreds of writers, all embroiled in a daily search for each other. Each wants what the other has to offer: The agent needs material to sell and the writer needs someone to sell material. Seems like it should be a piece of cake to find the right match and start making money, right?

Of course, the reality is that it's not easy at all. The reason? According to writers, it's, "They don't recognize my talent; they read my stuff and send it back." Talk to an agent, though, and the story you'll hear is, "Ninety-five percent of what I receive is garbage. When I find a truly talented writer, I fall all over myself to sign that writer right away!"

So there's the clue. If you, the writer, want to attract and land an agent, you have to concentrate your efforts not on finding the agent, but on writing top-notch scripts. The simple fact is, if you can write an outstanding script, you can find an outstanding agent.

Now, there are some basic rules to follow in bringing that script to the agent's attention. But before we go into that, let's answer the question that's probably uppermost in your mind as you begin your Agent Quest.

Do I really need an agent?

Nope. If you want, you can approach production companies on your own, and try to convince them to let you submit your script with a release form. The smaller companies will probably let you do that. The larger ones, studios included, might possibly let you do it too, although it's becoming less and less likely. Television producers will almost invariably ignore, if not prohibit, unagented submissions.

So, if you really want to give your script the best shot possible, yes, you should very, very seriously consider getting an agent. For one thing, production companies and studios are plagued by "nuisance" lawsuits, where a writer claims that his or her script has been stolen. To protect themselves from these legal hassles, producers have come to rely on agents to provide a kind of safety screen and keep things on a professional level.

Additionally, producers have no time to wade through the oceans of scripts that get sent to Hollywood every day by prospective writers. They rely on the agent to handle that, and perform a quality control function in weeding out the bad and circulating only the worthwhile scripts.

Kerry Cox *is a scriptwriter with over two dozen television credits with Aaron Spelling Productions, The Disney Channel and others. He has had a play produced in New York, written a feature film on assignment, and co-authored* Successful Scriptwriting, *by Writer's Digest Books. He is the editor and publisher of* The Hollywood Scriptwriter.

All right, so you need an agent to submit your script for you. Is that all an agent does?

What they do

In an interview with *The Hollywood Scriptwriter*, one agent refers to her function as a "yenta" for writers. "My job is to introduce writers to producers, and hope they'll build a business relationship. I find work for my writers, and negotiate the deals for them." An agent will act, on any given day, as a negotiator, mediator, trouble-shooter, critic, advisor and salesperson. And most of them do all of this for the standard ten percent off the top.

Let's talk a minute about commissions and fees, because script agents differ somewhat from their "literary" counterparts in this regard. First, there's the matter of reading fees. The Writers Guild of America specifically prohibits signatory agents from charging reading fees. Period. Now, there is no rule that says that an agent has to be a Guild-signatory, but this goes back to the question of respectability and credibility; producers are more likely to seriously consider material sent by recognized professionals, and *all* the top agencies (and the vast majority of mid-size and small agencies, for that matter) are Guild-signatory agencies.

On the other hand, there is no rule that prohibits an agency from offering a critique service, and there are a number of agencies that do so. Be careful, however, of agencies who will (for a fee) "develop" your work until it is ready for representation—most likely this "development" will go on a mighty long time, and be quite expensive.

Finally, a script agent customarily gets ten percent of the "deal." For example, if you were hired to write a single television episode, your agent would be entitled to ten percent of the writing fee. It is not mandatory to pay an agent's commission on residuals (money you get for reruns of the episode), although some writers choose to do so.

In case where an agent has had to cut another agent in on the deal, such as a foreign sale, the writer might have to pay a 15% commission. In all cases, the commission is well worth the time, trouble, and expense a good agent puts forth in marketing your work.

What they don't do

An agent can't guarantee you will have a successful career. They are not the end—they are the means to an end. Keep in mind that once you have an agent, you are still the one who is responsible for your career, and will be expected to write, and try to make professional contacts, and write some more.

An agent won't necessarily represent everything you write. If you turn in something they honestly feel they can't sell, they will explain to you that the work is not up to your usual standards, and feel it would be harmful to your reputation to send it out. If you insist, they will either send it to a few friends in the business for an objective opinion, or they will refuse to put it on the market. Obviously, at that point you have a decision to make.

An agent won't give you a daily update on how your material is doing. There simply isn't enough time. The best thing to do is check in with your agent about once every two weeks.

Unless your agent is also a lawyer, he or she cannot represent you in court. Generally speaking, an agent provides no legal protection or resources, although most have a working relationship with at least one entertainment attorney and can recommend one when necessary.

An agent's job is to sell your work, and/or find you writing work. That's all.

So how do I get one?

A successful agent once told us, "An agent doesn't like to be 'got' any more than anyone else." Instead, she likened the process to something more akin to a "romance," where there is a courtship period and eventual commitment.

The courtship begins with you, the writer, taking the initiative. If you have a friend or acquaintance who has an agent and might be willing to recommend your work, that's the best way to go. If you have attended a seminar or workshop in which an agent was a guest speaker or panelist, and you are able to make some personal contact, that's another good avenue.

If, however, you're coming in from the cold, like the majority of writers are, your approach needs to begin with a query letter. This letter isn't all that different from the query letters you may have sent to magazines or book publishers in the past, and the goals are the same: a) demonstrate to the agent that you are a relatively sane, competent professional who understands the craft; and b) pique the agent's personal and professional interest enough to request a look at your work.

When you write your query letter, consider the fact that the agent will probably get about a dozen others that day, along with an assortment of scripts, business mail, and the junk mail we all get. Your job is to make your letter practically jump out of that pile, excite the reader and encourage a fast response.

Start by making sure the letter and even the envelope you mail it in are professional in appearance. Get some decent letterhead. It doesn't have to be fancy, but it should look like you take your writing career seriously. Listings for agents in directories such as this usually give contact names. If not, call an agency, and talk to the receptionist, a secretary, or even an agent, and get the name of someone specific to whom you can address the letter. Addressing the letter to, "Dear Sir/Madam," just doesn't cut it.

Third step: plan the letter. You don't want it to take up more than one page if at all possible. Leave out any information that isn't absolutely necessary. Avoid hardsell, glittering claims about the abundance of money your script will make the agent, or the sheer genius you demonstrated in crafting this masterpiece. Instead, you'll want to include two things: a) Your credentials, if any (and not just writing credentials. For instance, if your script is a detective drama, and you're a detective, by all means mention that fact); b) A brief summary of your script—"brief" meaning no more than a paragraph or two.

Some other items that might be important would be related to the type of script you've written. If it's an historical drama, for instance, you might note that you have spent *x* number of years researching the period, especially if your story is based upon true events. You might also want to mention that you have written a number of other spec scripts, too (assuming you have—and you should), which shows the agent that you are not sending out your first effort, but have been earnestly working at this a while.

When summarizing your story in the letter, you may feel reluctant to tell the whole tale, and give away the ending. There are no rules about this. A good generalization would be to craft your query letter in such a way that it leaves the agent wanting more—whether wanting to find out the ending, or find out how you managed to create the ending you've described.

Once you've written the letter, be sure to include a SASE for response, send it off to as many agents as you'd like, and get to work on your next script.

What if they say yes?

Writers are so preconditioned for—and often experienced with—failure, that a positive response tends to induce sudden euphoria and a subsequent lack of judgment.

If an agent expresses an interest in seeing your material, stop and think for a moment. First, is your script already being considered by another agent, one who responded more promptly? If so, it's generally considered poor etiquette to circulate your script to more than one prospective agent at a time (although it's not necessarily an uncommon practice).

Second, are you absolutely sure your script is ready to be seen? This could represent a very important moment in your career, and you don't want to blow it by being overeager. Even though you were positive it was ready when you sent out the query letter, take an hour or so and read the script one more time, keeping as objective a frame of mind as possible. If any part of it feels weak to you, or bothers you in some way—if you even find a typo or two—don't sent it out until it's *perfect*.

Assuming you send the script and the agent likes it, several things might happen. You might be asked, "What else have you got?" This is pretty common, and usually means that your script showed some real writing talent, but the agent doesn't feel quite ready to invest the time and effort necessary to develop a new client without first determining if you are a "One-Script Wonder." An agent is interested not only in selling your first script, but wants to know that you have long-term potential as well. This is a very crucial stage of the "romance," and this next point can't be stressed enough: *Don't send another script if it's not just as good as the first one.* Presumably, you have already sent what you consider to be your best work; but it should have been a tough call, because you weren't sure if your second one was really your best. If you have a second script that's good, send it. If you don't, tell the agent you're working on one, and will be happy to submit it once you're finished. If you panic, and send one of your earlier scripts that isn't quite as good, but it's all you've got—you'll lose your chance with that agent, who will probably send both scripts back to you, most likely with one of those highly personal form rejection letters.

Now, let's say the agent calls, and wants to represent you. In fact, she wants you to sign a one-year, or even (less common) a two-year contract. Do you do it? What if it turns out you don't like this agent after six months—are you stuck with her for two years?

Thanks to the Writers Guild, you aren't stuck. There is a 90-day clause built in to the contract of every Guild-signatory agent, which states, roughly speaking, that either you or the agent can exercise the right to sever the relationship if the agent hasn't found you above-scale work within a 90-day period. (The term "scale" refers to minimum fees set by the WGA.) Of course, it isn't *mandatory* that you call it quits within that period, and in fact it would be a little unrealistic for a new writer to expect his or her agent to make a sale or find work that quickly; however, it does offer an "escape" for those who feel they need it. (If you are not dealing with a signatory agent, you may want to consider asking for such a clause in your contract.)

Are there agents for scriptwriters who don't write for TV or movies?

Yes, although they are usually the same agents who do handle movie and television writers. Playwrights, for instance, can greatly benefit from an agent. Naturally, there is more action on the East Coast than the West for a playwright, but Hollywood agencies tend to either have a New York office or work closely with a New York agent.

The way for a playwright to get an agent is to invite several to a performance, or even a staged reading, of the play. Not all agents want to represent playwrights, for one reason or another, so be sure to call and ascertain if there is any interest before sending out the invitations. Notice too that it's up to you, the playwright, to get yourself produced at the local level before approaching an agent. That's not the case for television and movie writers.

Interested in writing for animation? There are a limited number of agencies that handle that type of work, and a couple of them who specialize almost exclusively in cartoon writers. The fact is, however, it's not necessary for an animation writer to have an agent. The animation houses and producers are much more accessible than their live-action counterparts, and bring new writers on-board all the time.

Ancillary scriptwriting markets, such as industrials, corporate films or video, marketing, radio, etc. are generally not handled by literary agents. There has been some movement within the Writers Guild to bring educational and informational scriptwriting into the fold in terms of fee schedules and so forth, but it's been a half-hearted effort at best. For the time being, educational and informational scriptwriters remain on their own in terms of finding work and negotiating fees.

Some final advice

Stay informed. There are a number of trade publications and specialty newsletters that should be regular reading for aspiring scriptwriters. *Daily Variety* and *The Hollywood Reporter* are the daily business papers of the entertainment industry. *The Hollywood Scriptwriter* is my newsletter targeted specifically for aspiring and professional scriptwriters, and features agency updates throughout the year, along with an Annual Agency Issue every summer that surveys open agencies. Addresses for these publications appear in Resources near the back of this book.

Know your craft. Invest in some scriptwriting books. *Successful Scriptwriting*, Writer's Digest Books, offers an instructional overview of each type of scriptwriting, and includes a chapter on finding an agent, along with a standard release form you can use when submitting material. Some other books: *Making a Good Script Great*, by Dr. Linda Seger; *How to Sell Your Screenplay*, by Carl Sautter; *Writing Screenplays That Sell*, by Michael Hauge; and of course *Adventures in the Screen Trade*, by William Goldman, which isn't exactly an instructional book but is required reading for all screenwriters.

Be professional. Understand and follow the correct format for whatever type of script you're writing (just about any of the books mentioned will provide you with detailed format specifications). Always include a SASE with any correspondence. Keep phone calls brief and to the point. Send only your best work. Continue to perfect your skills as you search for and after you find an agent. Treat your writing not as a hobby or a dream, but as a chosen career.

Keep the faith. Remember, everyone, even the most successful writers, began their career without an agent. As a top agent once said, "(An agent) is always looking for writing that has a spark, that shows imagination, that has vision . . . and style."

If that's you she's talking about, then keep at it. Persevere. As Jim Cash ("Top Gun," "Dick Tracy") put it in one interview, "There's only one way to succeed: accept failure as a temporary state, however long that state may be, and simply outlast it."

Good luck.

Script Agents:
Nonfee and Fee-charging

If you've written a screenplay, teleplay or stage play and would like help approaching television and film producers or theatrical companies, you may find the agents listed in this section very helpful. While many of the agencies listed in the literary agents' sections of this book also handle scripts, agencies who *primarily* sell scripts make up this section.

As with literary agents, approach a screen agent well-informed. For starters, read Finding and Working with Script Agents, by Kerry Cox on page 133 and check our Resources section on the subject. For a good general discussion of the script markets, you may also want to take a look at the introduction to the scriptwriting section in *Writer's Market*.

Many of the signatories to the Writers Guild of America/West are script agents. You can contact this organization for more information on specific agencies. Agents who are affiliated with this group are not permitted to charge for reading scripts, but they can charge for critiques and other services. The guild also offers a registration service and it's a good thing to register your script with the group before sending it out. Write the Guild for more information on this and on membership (see Resources).

Since different types of scripts require different formats, make sure you know how to present your script. The *Writer's Digest Guide to Manuscript Formats* and *Successful Script Writing* (by Kerry Cox and Jurgen Wolff) are good sources for script formats.

Help with your search

To help you with your search for an agent, we've included a number of special indexes in the back of this book. The Subject Index is divided into sections for fee-charging and nonfee-charging literary agents and script agents. Each of these sections in the index is then divided by nonfiction and fiction subject categories. In general these subjects apply to scripts as well as to books, and script type (television episode, movie-of-the-week, documentary, stage play) is mentioned within the script agent's listing. We've included the Agents and Reps Index as well. Often you will read about an agent, but since that agent is an employee of a large agency, you may not be able to find that person's business number. We've asked agencies to give us the names of agents on their staffs. Then we've listed the names in alphabetical order along with the name of their agency. Find the name of the person you would like to contact and then check the listing for that agency.

Many of the nonfee- and fee-charging literary agents are also interested in scripts and vice versa. If the agency's primary function is selling books, but it is interested in seeing some scripts, we've included them in the Additional Script Agents list at the end of this section.

About the listings

The listings in this section are set up very much like the those in the literary agent sections. We've asked for the breakdown of the type of script each agency handles and have included this information within the listing. For specifics on listings, see the sample listings at the beginning of the nonfee- and fee-charging literary agent sections.

Unlike literary agency listings, we have not separated nonfee-charging and fee-charging agencies. As already noted above WGA signatories are not permitted to charge reading fees, but many agencies do charge for a variety of other services—critiques, consultations, promotion, marketing, etc. Those agencies who charge some type of fee have been indicated with an open box (□) symbol at the beginning of the listing.

You will also notice differences within the heading, Recent Sales. Often scripts are not titled at the time of sale, so we asked for the production company's name. We've found the film industry is very secretive about sales, but you may be able to get a list of clients or other references upon request.

We've ranked the agencies listed in this section according to their openness to submissions. Below is our ranking system:

I New agency (less than one year in business) actively seeking clients.

II Agency seeking both new and established writers.

III Agency prefers to work with established writers, mostly through referrals.

IV Agency handling only certain types of work or work by writers under certain circumstances.

V Agency not currently seeking new clients. (If an agency chose this designation, only the address is given). We have included mention of agencies rated V only to let you know they are not open to new clients at this time. In addition to those ranked V, we have included a few well-known agencies' names who have declined listings. *Unless you have a strong recommendation from someone well-known in the field, our advice is to approach only those agents ranked I-IV.*

AGENCY FOR THE PERFORMING ARTS (II), Suite 1200, 9000 Sunset Blvd., Los Angeles CA 90069. (213)273-0744. FAX: (213)275-9401. Contact: Stuart M. Miller. Estab. 1962. Member of WGA. Represents 50+ clients. Specializes in film and TV rights.
Will Handle: Movie scripts and TV scripts. Will consider all nonfiction and fiction areas. Query with SASE. Will report in 2-3 weeks on queries.
Terms: Agent receives 10% commission on domestic sales. Offers written contract.
Tips: Obtains new clients through recommendations from others.

□**AMERICAN PLAY CO., INC. (II)**, Suite 1206, 19 W. 44th St., New York NY 10036. (212)921-0545. FAX: (212)869-4032. President: Sheldon Abenal. Estab. 1889. Subsidiary of Century Play Co. Specializes in novels, plays, screenplays.
Will Handle: Novels, movie scripts, stage plays. Will consider all nonfiction and fiction areas. Send entire ms, "double space each page." Will report as soon as possible on ms.
Terms: Agent receives 15% commission on domestic sales; 15% on foreign sales.
Fees: Charges $100 reading fee, which includes a 2-3 page critique. Criticism service: $100.
Tips: Obtains new clients through referrals, unsolicited submissions by authors. "Writers should write novels first before screenplays. They need to know what's going on behind the camera. Before they write or attempt a play, they need to understand the stage and sets. Novels need strong plots, characters who are fully developed."

THE MARY BEAL AGENCY (III), 144 North Pass Ave., Burbank CA 91505. (818)846-7812. Estab. 1988. Member of DGA. Represents 16 clients. 60% of clients are new/previously unpublished writers. Specializes in movie scripts. Currently handles: 75% movie scripts; 25% TV scripts.
Will Handle: Nonfiction books, movie scripts, TV scripts. Will consider these nonfiction areas: gay/ lesbian issues; government/politics/law; psychology; true crime/investigative. Will consider these fiction areas: detective/police/crime; erotica; feminist; gay/lesbian; literary; mainstream; mystery/suspense; psychic/supernatural; science fiction; thriller/espionage. Query with SASE. Will report in 6 weeks on queries; 3 months on mss.

□ *An open box indicates script agents who charge fees to writers. WGA signatories are not permitted to charge for reading manuscripts, but may charge for critiques or consultations.*

Terms: Agent receives 10% on domestic sales; 10% on foreign sales. Offers a written contract, binding for 2 years. "Authors supply photocopies. They need to have legal counsel when contracts arrive."
Tips: Obtains new clients through referrals. "Be sure that a script is 100% there before seeking representation."

LOIS BERMAN, WRITERS' REPRESENTATIVE (III), 240 W. 44th St., New York NY 10036. (212)575-5114. Contact: Lois Berman or Judy Boals. Estab. 1972. Member of SAR. Represents 25 clients. Specializes in dramatic writing for stage, film and TV.
Will Handle: Movie and TV scripts, plays. Query first.
Terms: Agent receives 10% commission.
Tips: Obtains new clients through recommendations from others.

□**BETHEL AGENCY (II)**, Suite 16, 641 W. 59th St., New York NY 10019. (212)664-0455. Contact: Lewis R. Chambers. Estab. 1967. Represents 25+ clients.
Will Handle: Movie scripts and TV scripts. Will consider these nonfiction areas: agriculture/horticulture; animals; anthropology/archaeology; art/architecure/design; biography/autobiography; business; child guidance/parenting; cooking/food/nutrition; crafts/hobbies; current affairs; ethnic/cultural interests; gay/lesbian issues; government/politics/law; health/medicine; history; interior design/decorating; juvenile nonfiction; language/literature/criticism; military/war; money/finance/economics; music/dance/theater/film; nature/environment; photography; psychology; religious/inspirational; true crime/investigative; science/technology; self-help/personal improvement; sociology; sports; translations; women's issues/women's studies. Will consider these fiction areas: action/adventure; cartoon/comic; confessional; contemporary issues; detective/police/crime; ethnic; family saga; fantasy; feminist; gay; glitz; historical; humor/satire; juvenile; lesbian; literary; mainstream; mystery/suspense; picture book; psychic/supernatural; regional; religious/inspiration; romance (contemporary, gothic, historical, regency); sports; thriller/espionage; westerns/frontier; young adult. Query with SASE and outline plus 1 sample chapter. Will report in 1-2 months on queries.
Terms: Agent receives 15% commission on domestic sales; 20% on foreign sales. Offers written contract, binding for 6 months to 1 year.
Fees: Charges reading fee only to unpublished authors; writer will be contacted on fee amount.
Tips: Obtains new clients through recommendations from others. "Never send original material."

□**THE MARIAN BERZON AGENCY (II)**, 336 E. 17th St., Costa Mesa CA 92627. (818)961-0695. Literary Agent: Mike Ricciardi. Estab. 1979. Member of WGA. "We are also a talent agent and signatory of SAG, AFTRA, Equity and AGVA." 88% of clients are new/previously unpublished writers. Specializes in screenplays of all genres, especially comedy, inspirational and thrillers. Currently handles: 4% juvenile books, 2% novels, 1% novellas, 70% movie scripts, 8% stage plays, 10% TV scripts, 5% songs for movies and musical theater (cassettes only).
Will Handle: Movie scripts, stage plays, TV scripts. Will consider these screenplay areas: action/adventure; contemporary issues; detective/police/crime; family saga; fantasy; juvenile comedy/drama; romantic comedy/drama; juvenile; mainstream; mystery/suspense; religious/inspiration; romance (contemporary); thriller/espionage; young adult; screen stories about real people. Query with bio, small photo, cover letter and one-page summary. SASE with #10 envelope. "Unsolicited scripts will be returned unread C.O.D." Will report in 30 days or sooner on queries. "We will not answer any query without SASE. *Please* inquiry telephone calls only between the hours of 9:30-10:30 a.m. M-F and 9:30-noon Saturday (Pacific Time)."
Recent Sales: "Twinkle," by Mark Troy (Norman Lear); "Father Hustle," by Steve Grieger and Tim Irving (DNS Productions); scripts for "Perfect Strangers."
Terms: Agent receives 10% commission on domestic sales; 15% on foreign sales (short fiction and plays 15%; advances 15% on novels). Offers written contract and WGA rider with agreement.
Fees: "Never charges a reading fee. We give a detailed and complete breakdown for free." Offers criticism service, line by line, $450; screenplay, $695. "In line by line criticism, a qualified, experienced professional writer goes over your screenplay, checking every line of dialogue and every sentence of description. Grammar, spelling, punctuation, format and structure are examined. A cassette tape with comments is also sent to the writer. We charge only for postage, fax, long distance and postal insurance directly related to the client for writers who are not established or members of the guild." 80% of business derived from commissions on ms sales; 20% derived from treatment writing or criticism services. Payment of fees does not ensure representation.
Tips: Obtains new clients through recommendations from others and known producers. "If you really want to be represented, take note of the old saying 'you never get a second chance to make a first impression.' Be sure your queries intrigue us. Include sufficient SASE and #10 envelope. Write us a personal cover letter. No computer draft or mimeographed correspondence. Write to us like you really want to be considered. Include bio, photo, résumé. Read and absorb *The Complete Guide to Standard Script Format* (parts 1 & 2) by Cole and Haag and Margaret Mehring's *The Screenplay: A Blend of Film*

Form & Content before submitting. Screenplays should never be longer than 125 pages. They must be visual and not dialogue heavy. Screenplay description must be visually and actually alive. Make certain the opening of your screenplay is a 'grabber.' We believe in the new writer and will even offer six-month probationary contracts to those who show promise but lack immediate ready-to-market product."

BRODY AGENCY (II, IV), P.O. Box 291423, Davie FL 33329-1423. Contact: Ms. Berk. Estab. 1982. Member of WGA. Represents 4 clients. 100% of clients are new/previously unpublished writers. Specializes in screenplays. Currently handles 50% movie scripts, 50% TV scripts.
Will Handle: Movie scripts, TV scripts, "not for existing shows." Will consider these nonfiction areas: biography/autobiography of well-known figures; gay/lesbian issues; history; nature/environment; women's issues/women's studies; "no pornography." Will consider these fiction areas: contemporary issues; experimental; family saga; fantasy; historical; humor/satire; mainstream; mystery/suspense; psychic/supernatural; science fiction; thriller/espionage; young adult. Send outline or query, "must include SASE. No SASE, no answer." Will report in approximately 6-8 weeks on queries; approximately 3 months on mss.
Terms: Agent receives 15% commission on domestic sales; 20% commission on foreign sales. Offers a written contract. Charges for extra expenses, "depends upon project and contract."
Tips: Obtains new clients through the Writer's Guild. "We don't want ideas; we want stories—finished stories! Concentrate on originality, proper format and good story structure."

DON BUCHWALD AGENCY (III), 10 E. 44th St., New York NY 10017. (212)867-1070. Contact: Don Buchwald. Estab. 1977. Member of WGA. Represents 50 clients. "Talent rep and agent specializing in fiction dealing with theater, broadcasting."
Will Handle: Movie scripts, stage plays, TV scripts. Will consider these nonfiction areas: biography/ autobiography; current affairs; history; science/technology; sports. Will consider these fiction areas: action/adventure; family saga; mainstream; romance (contemporary, gothic, historical, regency); science fiction; thriller/espionage; westerns/frontier. Query with SASE only.
Terms: Agent receives 15% commission on domestic sales. Charges for foreign postage, photocopying and fax.
Tips: Obtains new clients through other authors, agents.

□**THE MARSHALL CAMERON AGENCY (II)**, Rt. 1 Box 125, Lawtey FL 32058. (904)964-7013. FAX: (904)964-6905. Contact: Margo Prescott. Estab. 1986. Specializes in feature films and television scripts (true story presentations for MFTS). Currently handles: 5% nonfiction books; 5% novels; 70% movie scripts; 20% TV scripts. Member agents: Wendy Zhornè (literary department); Margo Prescott (film and TV); Ashton Prescott (film and TV).
Will Handle: Nonfiction books, juvenile books, novels, movie scripts, TV scripts. Will consider these nonfiction areas: business; health/medicine; juvenile nonfiction; money/finance/economics; true crime/ investigative; self-help/personal improvement. Will consider these fiction areas: action/adventure; detective/police/crime; historical; literary; mainstream; mystery/suspense; thriller/espionage. Query. Will report in 1 week on queries; 4-8 weeks on mss.
Terms: Agent receives 15% commission on domestic sales; 20% on foreign sales. Offers a written contract, binding for 1 year.
Fees: Charges $45 for film and TV scripts, $55 for books. Charges $85 to review all true story material for TV or film ("maybe higher for extensive material"). Criticism service available for twice the reading fees. Offers overall criticism, some on line criticism. "We recommend changes, usually 3-10 pages depending on length of the material (on request only)." Charges nominal marketing fee which includes postage, phone, fax, Federal Express. 90% of business is derived from commissions on sales; 10% is derived from reading fees or criticism services. Payment of a criticism fee does not ensure representation.
Tips: "Often professionals in film and TV will recommend us to clients. We also actively solicit material."

MARGARET CANATELLA AGENCY (V), P.O. Box 674, Chalmette LA 70044-0674. Agency not currently seeking new clients.

CINEMA TALENT INTERNATIONAL (II), Suite 808, 8033 Sunset Blvd., W. Hollywood CA 90046. (213)656-1937. Contact: George Kriton and George N. Rumanes. Estab. 1976. Represents approximately 23 clients. 3% of clients are new/previously unpublished writers. Currently handles: 1% nonfiction books; 1% novels; 95% movie scripts; 3% TV scripts. Member agents include: George Kriton and George N. Rumanes.

Will Handle: Nonfiction books, novels, movie scripts, TV scripts. Query with outline/proposal plus 2 sample chapters. Will report in 4-5 weeks on queries; 4-5 weeks on ms.
Terms: Agent receives 10% on domestic sales; 20% on foreign sales. Offers a written contract, binding for 2 years.
Tips: Obtains new clients through recommendations from others.

CIRCLE OF CONFUSION LTD. (II), 131 Country Village Ln., New Hyde Park NY 11040. (212)969-0653. Contact: Rajeev K. Agarwal. Estab. 1990. Member of WGA. Represents 20 clients. 80% of clients are new/previously unpublished writers. Specializes in screenplays for film and TV. Currently handles: 5% nonfiction books; 5% novels; 10% novellas; 75% movie scripts; 5% TV scripts.
Will Handle: Nonfiction books, novels, novellas, short story collections, movie scripts, stage plays, TV scripts. Will consider these nonfiction areas: biography/autobiography; business; current affairs; gay/lesbian issues; government/politics/law; health/medicine; history; juvenile nonfiction; true crime/investigative; women's issues/women's studies. Will consider all fiction areas. Send entire ms. Will report in 1 week on queries; 3 weeks on mss.
Terms: Agent receives 10% commission on domestic sales; 10% on foreign sales. Offers a written contract, binding for 1 year.
Tips: Obtains new clients through queries, recommendations. "I am exclusively working in film/TV industry, pitching books, scripts, short stories and plays for film/TV adaptation."

COCONUT GROVE TALENT AGENCY (II), 3525 Vista Court, Miami FL 33133. Contact: Cathy Tully Pearson. Estab. 1980 as talent agency, 1990 as literary agency. Represents 25 clients. 15% of clients are new/previously unpublished writers. Currently handles: 5% nonfiction books; 60% movie scripts; 10% stage plays; 25% TV scripts.
Will Handle: Movie scripts, TV scripts, stage plays, romantic novels. Will consider these fiction areas: action/adventure; historical; mystery/suspense; romance; thriller/espionage. Query. Will report in 1 month on queries; 3-4 months on mss.
Terms: Agent receives 10% commission on domestic and foreign sales. Offers a written contract.
Tips: Obtains new clients through recommendations from others.

DISKANT & ASSOCIATES (III), Suite 202, 1033 Gayley Ave., Los Angeles CA 90024. (213)824-3773. Contact: George Diskant. Estab. 1983. Represents 12 clients. Currently handles: 40% nonfiction books; 20% movie scripts; 20% TV scripts. Will consider these nonfiction areas: biography/autobiography; current affairs; history. Will consider these fiction areas: contemporary issues; historical; mystery/suspense; young adult. "Won't accept any unsolicited manuscripts at this time."
Terms: Agent receives 15% commission on domestic sales.
Tips: "We deal with teleplays and screen plays mostly."

□**EARTH TRACKS AGENCY (I, II)**, Suite 286, 4712 Ave. N, Brooklyn NY 11234. Contact: David Krinsky. Estab. 1990. Member of WGA. Represents 5 clients. 50% of clients are new/previously unpublished writers. Specializes in "movie and TV script sales of original material." Currently handles: 20% novels; 50% movie scripts; 10% stage plays; 20% TV scripts.
Will Handle: Novels, movie scripts, stage plays, TV scripts ("No Star Trek"), TV movie scripts. Will consider all nonfiction areas. Will consider these fiction areas: action/adventure; cartoon/comic; contemporary issues; detective/police/crime; erotica; humor/satire; romance (contemporary); thriller/espionage; young adult. Query with SASE. Will report in 4-6 weeks on queries; 6-8 weeks on mss ("only if requested").
Terms: Agent receives 10-12% commission on domestic sales; 10-12% on foreign sales. Offers a written contract, binding for 6 months to 2 years.
Fees: "There is no fee if I accept to read a TV/movie script. For plays and books I charge $100 a book or manuscript, nonrefundable. Criticism service: $25 per item (treatment or manuscript) submitted. "I personally write the critiques. Critique not provided on scripts. An author *must* provide a *proper* postage (SASE) if author wants material returned. If no SASE enclosed, material is not returned." 90% of business is derived from commissions on ms sales; 10% is derived from reading fees or criticism service. Payment of a criticism fee does not ensure representation.
Tips: Obtains new clients through recommendations and letters of solicitations by mail. "Send a one-page letter describing the material the writer wishes the agency to represent. Do not send anything other than query letter with SASE. Unsolicited script will not be returned. Do not 'hype' the material — just explain exactly what you are selling. If it is a play, do not state 'screen play.' If it is a movie script, do not state 'manuscript,' as that implies a book. Be specific, give description (summary) of material."

FARBER & FREEMAN (II), 14 E. 75th St., New York NY 10021. (212)861-7075. Contact: Ann Farber or Sandra Freeman. Estab. 1989. Member of WGA. Represents 25 clients. 50% of clients are new/previously unpublished writers. Currently handles: 10% nonfiction books; 30% novels, 30% movie scripts; 30% stage plays.

Will Handle: Juvenile books, novels, novellas, movie scripts, stage plays. Will consider these fiction areas: action/adventure; contemporary issues; detective/police/crime; historical; humor/satire; juvenile; mainstream; mystery/suspense; contemporary romance; thriller/espionage; young adult. Send outline plus 3 sample chapters. Will report at once on queries; 1 month on mss.
Terms: Offers a written contract, binding for 2 years.
Tips: Obtains new clients through recommendations from others and listings.

□**FORTHWRITE LITERARY AGENCY (II)**, P.O. Box 922101, Sylmar CA 91392. (818)365-3400. FAX: (818)362-3443. Contact: Wendy L. Zhorne. Estab. 1989. Represents 40 clients. 50% of clients are new/previously unpublished writers. Specializes in juvenile and nonfiction, "but not limited to those categories. Historical fiction and nonfiction book manuscripts are appealing to us. Action (light) and juvenile scripts welcome. We are noted for our family-type materials." Currently handles: 20% nonfiction books; 10% juvenile books; 10% novels; 25% movie scripts; 35% TV scripts.
Will Handle: Nonfiction, scholarly and juvenile books, novels, movie scripts, TV scripts. Will consider these nonfiction areas: agriculture; animals; anthropology; art; biography; business; child guidance; cooking; crafts; health; history; interior design; juvenile nonfiction; economics; theater/film; environment; photography; psychology; inspirational; technology; personal improvement; sociology; women's studies. Will consider these fiction areas: action; family saga; historical; juvenile; literary; mainstream; mystery/suspense; picture book; romance (historical); young adult. Query. Will report in 3-4 weeks on queries; 4-6 weeks on ms. "No unsolicited manuscripts!"
Terms: Agent receives 10% on domestic sales; 15% on foreign sales. Offers a written contract, which is binding for 6 or 12 months.
Fees: Charges $50 reading fee "for all materials requested, unless writer has previous serious credits related to topic (same field/genre); $25 for juvenile under 5,000 words. In extreme circumstances we will critique an exemplary manuscript to aid in improvement so we can represent the writer. Our reading fee includes a one-page overview of major strengths/weaknesses, etc. and the 'why' of acceptance or rejection by us. In some cases, a new writer is asked to contribute to marketing expenses. All writers provide copies of their material to us."
Writers' Conferences: Attends London Book Fair, Texas Children's Ministries, and occasionally lectures at local colleges and universities.
Tips: Obtains new clients through advertising, referrals, conferences, recommendations by producers, chambers of commerce, etc. "Please check your material, including query, for spelling and typing errors before sending. If you are worried whether your material will arrive, send it certified, don't search area codes for agent's home number; always send a SASE with everything. Think about what time it is in agent's state before you call, and only call during business hours. Never tell an agent, 'All my friends loved it.'"

ROBERT A FREEDMAN DRAMATIC AGENCY, INC. (II, III), Suite 2310, 1501 Broadway, New York NY 10036. (212)840-5760. President: Robert A. Freedman. Vice President: Selma Luttinger. Estab. 1928. Member of SAR. Prefers to work with established authors; works with a small number of new authors. Specializes in plays, motion picture and television scripts.
Will Handle: Movie scripts, stage plays and TV scripts. Query. Does not read unsolicited mss. Usually reports in 2 weeks on queries; 3 months on mss.
Terms: Agent receives 10% on dramatic sales; "and, as is customary, 20% on amateur rights." Charges for photocopying manuscripts.
Recent Sales: "We will speak directly with any prospective client concerning sales that are relevant to his/her specific script."

SAMUEL FRENCH, INC. (II, III), 45 W. 25th St., New York NY 10010. (212)206-8990. Editors: William Talbot and Lawrence Harbison. Estab. 1830. Member of SAR. Represents "hundreds" of clients. Prefers to work with published/established authors; works with a small number of new/unpublished authors. Specializes in plays. Currently handles 100% stage plays.
Will Handle: Stage plays. Query or send entire ms. Replies "immediately" on queries; decision in 2-8 months regarding publication. "Enclose SASE."
Terms: Agent receives usually 10% professional production royalties; 20% amateur production royalties.
Recent Sales: *Mastergate*, by Gelbart.

□**THE GARY-PAUL AGENCY (II)**, 84 Canaan CT, #17, Stratford CT 06497-4538. (203)336-0257. Contact: Gary Maynard. Estab. 1990. Member of WGA. Represents 21 clients. 75% of clients are new/previously unpublished writers. Specializes in the promotion of film and television scripts and writer representation (produced and unproduced). Currently handles: 80% movie scripts; 20% TV scripts.

Will Handle: Movie scripts, TV scripts. Query. Will report in 2 weeks on queries; 6 weeks on mss.
Terms: Agent receives 10% commission on domestic sales; 10% on foreign sales. Offers a written contract. Contract is not binding for a specific length of time, but most clients sign for 6 months.
Fees: "We offer an express service which allows a three-week turnaround on submitted material. The cost for this is $35 and includes a comments sheet. Normally we offer advice at no cost unless the writer is in need of complex advice regarding character, structure and dialogue problems. The fee can cost up to $225 depending on the writer's needs. We can advise on all aspects of screen and television writing. Both Paul Carbonaro and I write the criticisms as do contracted professionals. All writers will provide copies of their scripts including SASE for each submission to producers. There are no other charges." 15% of business is derived from commissions on ms sales; 85% is derived from criticism services. "In most cases, a criticism fee ensures representation."
Writers' Conferences: Attends NBC Writers Workshop.
Tips: Obtains new clients through advertisements in trade magazines and reference books. "If you want help in your writing, ask. This agency will help the writer."

THE GERSH AGENCY (II, III), 232 N. Canyon Dr., Beverly Hills CA 90210. (213)274-6611. Contact: Nancy Nigrosh. Estab. 1962. Less than 10% of clients are new/previously unpublished writers. Special interests: "mainstream—convertible to film and television."
Will Handle: Movie and television scripts. Send entire ms. Responds to ms in 4 weeks.
Recent Sales: *Hot Flashes*, by Barbara Raskin (Weintraub Entertainment); *Donato & Daughter* (Universal); *Libra* by Don Dellio (A&M).
Terms: Agent's commission: 10% on domestic sales. "We strictly deal in *published* manuscripts in terms of potential film or television sales, on a strictly 10% commission—sometimes split with a New York literary agency or various top agencies."

GRAHAM AGENCY (II), 311 W. 43rd St., New York NY 10036. (212)489-7730. Owner: Earl Graham. Estab. 1971. Member of SAR. Represents 35 clients. 35% of clients are new/unpublished writers. Willing to work with new/unpublished writers. Specializes in full-length stage plays and musicals.
Will Handle: Stage plays and musicals. "We consider on the basis of the letters of inquiry." Writers *must* query before sending any material for consideration. Reports "as soon as possible on queries."
Terms: Agent receives 10% commission on domestic sales; 10% on dramatic sales; and 10% on foreign sales.

□ALICE HILTON LITERARY AGENCY (II), 13131 Welby Way, North Hollywood CA 91606. (818)982-2546. Estab. 1986. Eager to work with new/unpublished writers. "Interested in any quality material, although agent's personal taste runs in the genre of 'Cheers.' 'L.A. Law,' 'American Playhouse,' 'Masterpiece Theatre' and Woody Allen vintage humor."
Will Handle: Book length mss (fiction and nonfiction), juvenile, movie and television feature length scripts.
Terms: Agent receives 10% commission. Brochure available with SASE. Preliminary phone call appreciated.
Fees: Charges evaluation fee of $2.50/1,000 words. Charges for phone, postage and photocopy expenses.
Recent Sales: Soap opera comedy, by Kris Meijer to VOO Television (Amsterdam); *Counterparts*, by Kurt Fischel (New Saga) and *The Cradled and the Called*, by Roger Sargeant (New Saga).

MICHAEL IMISON PLAYWRIGHTS LTD. (III,IV), 28 Almeida St., Islington London N1 1TD England. 071-354-3174. FAX: 071-359-6273. Contact: Michael Imison. Estab. 1944. Member of PMA. 10% of clients are new/previously unpublished writers. Specializes in stage plays including plays in translation—especially Russian and Italian. Currently handles: 10% movie scripts; 80% stage plays; 10% TV scripts.
Will Handle: Stage plays. Query first (editor's note: North American writers should send SAE with IRCs for response, available at most post offices). Will report in 1 week on queries; 2 months on mss.
Terms: Agent receives 10-15% commission on sales. Charges for photocopying. 100% of business is derived from commissions on mss sales.
Tips: Obtains new clients through personal recommendation. "Biographical details can be helpful. Generally only playwrights whose work has been performed will be considered."

INTERNATIONAL ARTISTS (II), P.O. Box 29000175, San Antonio TX 78229. (512)733-8855. FAX: (512)734-5511. General Manager: Guy Robin Custer. Estab. 1988. Member of WGA. Represents 10 clients. 50% of clients are new/previously unpublished writers. Specializes in screenplays. "We are presently expanding our scope of representation into print media." Currently handles: 10% nonfiction books; 10% scholarly books; 5% textbooks; 10% novels; 30% movie scripts; 5% stage plays; 30% TV scripts. Member agents: Guy Robin Custer (any well-written screenplay, teleplay, for print—reference,

societal issues, avant-garde, "rational recovery"); B.J. Stafford (screenplays, entertainment industry, sports); Lori Ford (screenplays, modern youth topics); Caspar Jasso (any new ideas, ethnic/cultural). "New/unpublished writers are considered by all our agents on a rotating basis."
Will Handle: Movie scripts, stage plays, TV scripts, nonfiction books, scholarly books, textbooks, juvenile books, novels, short story collections. Will consider these nonfiction areas: anthropology/archaeology; biography/autobiography; child guidance/parenting; computers/electronics; cooking/food/nutrition; current affairs; ethnic/cultural; gay/lesbian issues; government/politics/law; health/medicine; history; juvenile nonfiction; language/literature/criticism; music/dance/theater/film; nature/environment; new age/metaphysics; psychology; true crime/investigative; self-help/personal improvement; sociology; sports; translations, women's issues/women's studies; also interested in "international travel, education, exposés, cinematic topics, human rights and rational recovery." Will consider these fiction areas: action/adventure; contemporary issues; detective/police/crime; erotica; ethnic; experimental; feminist; gay; historical; humor/satire; juvenile; lesbian; mystery/suspense; psychic/supernatural; regional; contemporary and historical romance; science fiction; sports; thriller/espionage; young adult; also interested in "avant-garde, interactive computer dramas and political satire." Query with up to 5 pages of dialogue samples. Will report in 3 weeks on queries; 2 months on mss. "Responses require a SASE!"
Terms: Agent receives 10% commission on domestic sales; 20% on foreign sales. Offers a written contract, binding from 3 months to 2 years. Charges for "expenses beyond a liberal allowance on works we actually sell or any unusual expenses agreed upon in advance." Does not offer criticism service, but "we sometimes refer to a list of reputable critics we feel offer reasonable fees and good advice. We most likely will refer a writer to a critic for technical reasons rather than purpose or content."
Writers' Conferences: Attends Brown Symposium.
Tips: "References and recommendations are always helpful. Well-written queries and small samples of writing style get full consideration. We prefer finished work over proposals even at the query stage. SASE is essential for unsolicited queries. We do not accept phone queries. Some kind of resumé or personal information is very helpful when we're considering a new writer."

INTERNATIONAL LEONARDS CORP. (II), 3612 N. Washington Blvd., Indianapolis IN 46205-3534. (317)926-7566. Contact: David Leonards. Estab. 1972. Member of WGA. Currently handles: 50% movie scripts; 50% TV scripts.
Will Handle: Movie scripts, TV scripts. Will consider these nonfiction areas: anthropology/archaeology; biography/autobiography; business; current/affairs; history; money/finance/economics; music/dance/theater/film; new age/metaphysics; psychology; religious/inspirational; true crime/investigative; science/technology; self-help/personal improvement; sports. Will consider these fiction areas: action/adventure; cartoon/comic; contemporary issues; detective/police/crime; family saga; fantasy; historical; humor/satire; mainstream; mystery/suspense; religious/inspiration; romance (contemporary, gothic, historical, regency); science fiction; sports; thriller/espionage. Query. Will report in 1 month on queries; 6 months on mss.
Terms: Agent receives 10% commission on domestic sales; 10% on foreign sales. Offers a written contract, "WGA standard," which "varies."
Tips: Obtains new clients through recommendations and queries.

JOYCE P. KETAY, 334 W. 89th St., New York NY 10024. Prefers not to be listed.

PAUL KOHNER, INC. (IV), 9169 Sunset Blvd., W. Hollywood CA 90069. (213)550-1060. Contact: Gary Salt. Estab. 1938. Member of ATA. Represents 150 clients. 10% of clients are new/previously unpublished writers. Specializes in film and TV rights sales and representation of film and TV writers.
Will Handle: Nonfiction books, movie scripts, stage plays, TV scripts. Will consider these nonfiction areas: history; military/war; music/dance/theater/film; true crime/investigative. Query with SASE. Will report in 2 weeks on queries.
Recent Sales: Has sold scripts to 20th Century Fox, Warner's, Disney.
Terms: Agent receives 10% commission on domestic sales; 10% on foreign sales. Offers a written contract, binding for 1-3 years. "We charge for copying manuscripts or scripts for submission unless a sufficient quantitiy is supplied by the author. All unsolicited material is automatically returned unread."

LAKE & DOUROUX INC., Suite 310, 445 S. Beverly Dr., Beverly Hills CA 90212. (213)557-0700. FAX: (213)557-0700. Contact: Candace L. Lake. Estab. 1979. Member of WGA. Represents 30 clients. Currently handles: 10% nonfiction books; 90% novels, movie scripts and TV scripts.
Will Handle: Will consider "mainstream nonfiction." Will consider these fiction areas: action/adventure; contemporary issues; detective/police/crime; family saga; fantasy; glitz; historical; literary; mainstream; mystery/suspense; science fiction; thriller/espionage; westerns/frontier. "No unsolicited manuscripts. Only by recommendation."

Terms: Agent receives 10% commission on domestic sales. Offers a written contract, binding for 2 years. Charges for photocopying.
Writers' Conferences: Speaks at The Academy of TV Arts & Sciences, U.S.C., American Film Institute and U.C.L.A.
Tips: Obtains new clients through recommendations from others.

□L. **HARRY LEE LITERARY AGENCY (II)**, Box #203, Rocky Point NY 11778. (516)744-1188. Contact: L. Harry Lee. Estab. 1979. Member of WGA, Dramatists Guild. Represents 285 clients. 65% of clients are new/previously unpublished writers. Specializes in motion picture screenplays. "Comedy is our strength, both features and sitcoms, also movie of the week, science fiction, novels and TV. Currently handles 30% novels; 50% movie scripts; 5% stage plays; 15% TV scripts. Member agents: Ralph Schiano (science fiction, horror, adventure); Mary Lee Gaylor (episodic TV, feature films); Charles Rothery (feature films, sitcoms, movie of the week); Katie Polk (features, mini-series, children's TV); Patti Roenbeck (science fiction, fantasy, romance, historical romance); Frank Killeen (action, war stories, American historical, westerns); Hollister Barr (mainstream, feature films, romantic comedies); Ed Van Bomel (sitcoms, movie of the week, mysteries, adventure stories); Colin James (horror, Viet Nam, war stories); Judith Faria (all romance, fantasy, mainstream); Charis Biggis (plays, historical novels, westerns, action/suspense/thriller films); Stacy Parker (love stories, socially significant stories/films, time travel science fiction); Jane Breoge (sitcoms, after-school specials, mini-series, episodic TV); Cami Callirgos (mainstream/contemporary/humor, mystery/suspense); Vito Brenna (action/adventure, romantic comedy, feature films).
Will Handle: Novels, movie scripts, stage plays, TV scripts, humor, sitcoms. Will consider these nonfiction areas: history; military/war. Will consider these fiction areas: action/adventure; detective/police/crime; erotica; family saga; fantasy; historical; humor/satire; literary; mainstream; mystery/suspense; romance (contemporary, gothic, historical, regency); science fiction; sports; thriller/espionage; westerns/frontier; young adult. Query "with a short writing or background resume of the writer. A SASE is a must. No dot matrix, we don't read them." Will report in "return mail" on queries; 3-4 weeks on mss. "We notify the writer when to expect a reply."
Terms: Agent receives 15% commission on domestic sales; 20% on foreign sales; 10% on screenplays/teleplays and plays. Offers a written contract "by the manuscript which can be broken by mutual consent; the length is as long as the copyright runs."
Fees: Does not charge a reading fee. Criticism service: charges $185 for screenplays; $145 for movie of the week; $90 for TV sitcom; $185 for a mini-series; $1 per page for one-act plays. "All of the agents and readers write the carefully thought out critiques, three page checklist, two to four pages of notes, and a manuscript that is written on, plus tip sheets and notes that may prove helpful. It's a thorough service, for which we have received the highest praise." Charges for postage, handling, photocopying per submission, "not a general fee." 90% of business is derived from commissions on ms sales. 10% is derived from criticism services. Payment of a criticism fee does not ensure representation.
Tips: Obtains new clients through recommendations, "but mostly queries." "If interested in agency representation, write a good story with interesting characters and that's hard to do. Learn your form and format. Take courses, workshops. Read *Writer's Digest*; it's your best source of great information."

HELEN MERRILL LTD. (II), Suite 1 A, 435 W. 23rd St., New York NY 10011. (212)691-5326. Contact: Lourdes Lopez or Helen Merrill. Estab. 1975. Member of SAR. Represents 100 clients. Handles 30% nonfiction books, 70% stage plays.
Will Handle: Stage plays, fiction, nonfiction. Will consider biographies. Will consider these fiction areas: contemporary issues; literary; mainstream. Query with SASE. Will report in 3 weeks on queries.
Terms: Agent receives 15% on domestic sales. Charges for postage, photocopies.
Tips: Usually obtains new clients through recommendations from others.

MONTGOMERY-WEST LITERARY AGENCY (IV), 7450 Butler Hills Dr., Salt Lake City UT 84121. Contact: Carole Western. Estab. 1989. Member of WGA. Represents 30 clients. 80% of clients are new/previously unpublished writers. Specializes in movie and television scripts and romance novels. Currently handles: 15% novels; 60% movie scripts; 25% TV scripts. Member agents: Carole Western (movie and TV scripts, novels); Nancy Gummery (romance novels).
Will Handle: Novels, movie scripts, TV scripts. Will consider these fiction areas: action/adventure; detective/police/crime; fantasy; mystery/suspense; psychic/supernatural; romance (contemporary, historical, regency); science fiction; thriller/espionage. Query with outline, 1 sample chapter and SAE. Will report in 6-8 weeks on queries; 8-10 weeks on mss.

Terms: Agent receives 15% commission on domestic sales for novels, 10% on movie scripts; 15% on foreign sales for books, 10% for movie scripts.
Writers' Conferences: Attends 3 workshops a year; Writers Guild of America West Conference.
Tips: "Send in only the finest product you can and keep synopses and treatments brief and to the point. Have patience and be aware of the enormous competition in the writing field."

□**RAINTREE AGENCY (II)**, 360 W. 21 St., New York NY 10011. (212)242-2387. Contact: Diane Raintree. Estab. 1977. Represents 6-8 clients. Specializes in novels, film, scripts, plays and children's books.
Will Handle: Will consider these nonfiction areas: health; nature/environment; psychology; women's issues/women's studies. Will consider all fiction areas. Phone first.
Terms: Agent receives 10% on domestic sales.
Fees: May charge reading fee. "Amount varies from year to year."

STEPHANIE ROGERS AND ASSOCIATES (III), #218, 3855 Lankershim Blvd., Hollywood CA 91604. (818)509-1010. Owner: Stephanie Rogers. Estab. 1980. Represents 24 clients. 20% of clients are new/unproduced writers. Prefers that the writer has been produced (motion pictures or TV), his/her properties optioned or has references. Prefers to work with published/established authors. Specializes in screenplays—dramas (contemporary), action/adventure, romantic comedies and suspense/thrillers for motion pictures and TV. Currently handles 10% novels; 50% movie scripts and 40% TV scripts.
Will Handle: Novels (only wishes to see those that have been published and can translate to screen) and movie and TV scripts (must be professional in presentation and not over 125 pages). Query. Does not read unsolicited mss. SASE required.
Recent Sales: *Shoot to Kill* for Touchstone Pictures; *Steel Dawn* for Vestron.
Terms: Agent receives 10% commission on domestic sales; 10% on dramatic sales; and 20% on foreign sales. Charges for phone, photocopying and messenger expenses.
Tips: "When writing a query letter, you should give a short bio of your background, a thumbnail sketch (no more than a paragraph) of the material you are looking to market and an explanation of how or where (books, classes or workshops) you studied screenwriting."

JACK SCAGNETTI TALENT & LITERARY AGENCY (III), #210, 5330 Lankershim Blvd., N. Hollywood CA 91601. (818)762-3871. Contact: Jack Scagnetti. Estab. 1974. Member of WGA. Represents 40 clients. 50% of clients are new/previously unpublished writers. Specializes in film books with many photographs. Currently handles: 10% nonfiction books; 80% movie scripts; 10% TV scripts.
Will Handle: Will consider these nonfiction areas: health; military/war; true crime/investigative; self-help/personal improvement; sports. Will consider these fiction areas: mainstream; mystery/suspense; sports; thriller/espionage. Query with outline/proposal. Will report in 1 month on queries; 6-8 weeks on mss.
Terms: Agent receives 10% commission on domestic sales; 15% on foreign sales. Offers a written contract, binding for 6 months-1 year. Charges for postage and photocopies.
Tips: Obtains new clients through "referrals by others and query letters sent to us. Write a good synopsis, short and to the point and include marketing data for the book."

SCRIBE AGENCY (IV), P.O. Box 580393, Houston TX 77258-0393. (713)333-1094. Contact: Marta White or Carl Sinclair. Estab. 1988. Member of WGA. Represents 20 clients. 40% of clients are new/previously unpublished writers. Specializes in book-length literary fiction for adults, motion picture and TV scripts. Currently handles: 40% novels; 40% movie scripts; 20% TV scripts.
Will Handle: Novels, movie scripts, TV scripts. Does not want to see "horrors/thrillers or other material promoting violence and/or sexual abuse." Will consider these fiction areas: contemporary issues; literary; mainstream. Query with SASE. Will report in 3-4 weeks on queries; 1 month on mss.
Terms: Agent receives 15% commission on domestic sales; 20% on foreign sales. Offers a written contract, binding time is negotiable.
Tips: Obtains new clients through recommendations. "Call, and submit query with SASE first."

□ *An open box indicates script agents who charge fees to writers. WGA signatories are not permitted to charge for reading manuscripts, but may charge for critiques or consultations.*

SELECTED ARTISTS AGENCY (III), 2nd Fl. Reception, 3575 Cahuenga Blvd., Los Angeles CA 90068. Contact: Flo Joseph/David Kainer. Estab. 1981. Member of WGA. **Will Handle:** Movie scripts. Will consider "very few if any" nonfiction areas. Will consider these fiction areas: action/adventure; contemporary issues; ethnic; experimental; family saga; fantasy; historical; humor/satire; mainstream; mystery/suspense; romance (contemporary, gothic, historical, regency); science fiction; thriller/espionage; young adult. Query with a SASE "only!" Will report "as soon as we can."
Terms: Agent receives 10% commission on domestic sales. Offers written contract.

KEN SHERMAN & ASSOCIATES, 9507 Santa Monica Blvd. Beverly Hills CA 90210. Agency not currently seeking new clients.

□**SOUTHEASTERN ENTERTAINMENT AGENCY INC. (II)**, 4847 NE 12th Ave, Ft. Lauderdale FL 33334. (305)537-3457, 491-1505. Contact: Louis A. Jassin. Estab. 1989. Member of WGA. Represents 37 clients. 80% of clients are new/previously unpublished writers. Specializes in movie scripts. Currently handles: 50% movie scripts; 50% TV scripts. Member agents: Louis A. Jassin (movie scripts, also does contract work); Tom Banic (TV scripts).
Will Handle: Nonfiction books, movie scripts, TV scripts. Will consider these nonfiction areas: money/finance/economics; music/dance/theater/film; sports. Will consider this fiction area: science fiction. Send outline/proposal. Will report in 1 month on queries; 1 month on mss.
Terms: Agent receives 15% commission on domestic sales; 15% on foreign sales. Offers a written contract, binding for 1 year with option.
Fees: Charges new writers $100, "which goes toward an expense fee if we take scripts to New York or California."
Tips: Obtains new clients through recommendations and the WGA's West Coast office.

ELLEN LIVELY STEELE & ASSOCIATES (III), P.O. Drawer 447, Organ NM 88052. (505)382-5440. FAX: (505)382-9821. Contact: Ellen Lively Steele or Belinda S. Anderson. Estab. 1980. Member of WGA. Represents 20 clients. 60% of clients are new/previously unpublished writers. Specializes in New Age, occult, cookbooks, historical fiction, screenplays, children's. Currently handles: 2% nonfiction books; 1% textbooks; 10% juvenile books; 45% novels; 25% movie scripts; 35% TV scripts; 28% New Age.
Will Handle: Nonfiction and juvenile books, novels, movie scripts, TV scripts, New Age. Will consider these nonfiction areas: cooking/food/nutrition; history; new age/metaphysics; true crime/investigative; self-help/personal improvement; women's issues/women's studies. Will consider these fiction areas: action/adventure; detective/police/crime; family saga; glitz; historical; humor/satire; juvenile; mainstream; mystery/suspense; picture book; psychic/supernatural; romance (historical); science fiction; thriller/espionage. Query with outline plus 3 sample chapters. Will report in 6 weeks on queries; 2-3 months on ms.
Terms: Agent receives 10% commission on domestic sales; splits % on foreign sales. Offers a written contract, which is binding for 2 years. Charges for postage, fax, copies, phone calls. "Charges no extraordinary expense without written agreement from client. No office expenses. Marketing and editing expenses would fall into above list, usually."
Tips: Obtains new clients through recommendations from other clients, producers and editors, "very few from queries."

CHARLES STEWART (I), Suite 260, 953 E. Sahara Ave., Las Vegas NV 89104. (702)731-9100. Contact: Charles Stewart. Estab. 1990. Member of WGA. Specializes in screenplays and TV scripts. Currently handles: 90% movie scripts; 10% TV scripts.
Will Handle: Novels, movie scripts, TV scripts, syndicated material. Query. Will report in 2 weeks on queries; 1 month on mss.
Terms: Agent receives 10% commission on domestic sales; 10% on foreign sales. Offers a written contract.
Tips: Obtains new clients through referrals, recommendations.

H.N. SWANSON INC. (III), 8523 Sunset Blvd., Los Angeles CA 90069. President: H.N. Swanson. Vice-president: N.V. Swanson. Head of Operations: Thomas Shanks. Estab. 1934. Member of WGA. Represents 100 clients. 10% of clients are new/previously unpublished writers. Currently handles 60% novels; 40% movie scripts. Member agents: Michael Siegel and Steven Fisher (literary); Andrew Reich, Steven Sellers and Jim Briggamen (assistant literary agents).
Will Handle: Novels, novellas, movie scripts, TV scripts. Will consider these nonfiction areas: current affairs; sports. Will consider these fiction areas: action/adventure; detective/police/crime; historical; humor/satire; mainstream; mystery/suspense; sports; thriller/espionage. Query. Will report in 5 days on queries; 10 days mss.

Recent Sales: "For the most part, we co-agent with publishing agents, representing the motion picture and television sales of their clients. We do represent the publishing interests of a few clients."
Terms: Agent receives 10% commission on domestic sales; varies on foreign sales. Offers a written contract.
Tips: Obtains new clients through recommendations from others.

□**THE TALENT BANK AGENCY (II)**, 1834 S. Gramercy Place, Los Angeles CA 90019. (213)735-2636. Contact: Douglas J. Nigh. Estab. 1990. Member of WGA. Represents 31 clients. "Seeking established writers: few new authors are being added now." 99% of clients are new/previously unpublished writers. Currently handles: 1% juvenile books; 1% novels; 75% movie scripts; 2% stage plays; 22% TV scripts. **Will Handle:** Juvenile books, novels, movie scripts, stage plays, TV scripts. Will consider these fiction areas: action/adventure; contemporary issues; detective/police/crime; ethnic; family saga; fantasy; feminist; gay; historical; humor/satire; juvenile; lesbian; mainstream; mystery/suspense; picture book; science fiction; thriller/espionage; westerns/frontier. Query. Will report in 2 weeks on queries; 6-8 weeks on mss.
Terms: Agent receives 10% commission on domestic sales. Offers a written contract, binding for 1-2 years.
Fees: Does not charge a reading fee now. Will offer a criticism service.
Tips: Obtains new clients through recommendations and solicitations. "Be sure your letter of inquiry is grammatical and well-spelled. Avoid arrogance and modesty. Be forthright and business-like; get to your point succinctly. Pitch your work in a two-paragraph format. Treatment depends on length of piece. When submitting a screenplay, be sure it is correctly formatted. Have a "hook" in the first 10 pages or figure no one will read beyond that. Give me a reason to want to continue."

THE TANTLEFF OFFICE (II), Suite 700, 375 Greenwich St,. New York NY 10013. (212)941-3939. President: Jack Tantleff. Agent: John B. Sanlaiannio. Estab. 1986. Member WGA. Represents 30 clients. 20% of clients are new/unpublished writers. Specializes in television, theater and film. Currently handles 15% movie scripts; 70% stage plays; 15% TV scripts. Query with outline.
Terms: Agent receives 10% commission on domestic sales; 10% on dramatic sales; and 10% on foreign sales.

THIRD MILLENNIUM PRODUCTIONS (II), 301 Exhibition St., Guelph, Ontario N1H 4R8 Canada. (519)821-3701. Contact: John Gandor. Estab. 1988. Member of ACTRA and WGA. Represents 20 clients. 50% of clients are new/previously unpublished writers. Specializes in screenplays. Currently handles: 90% movie scripts; 10% TV scripts.
Will Handle: Movie scripts, TV scripts. Query. Will report in 2 weeks on queries "if interested"; 4-6 weeks on mss.
Terms: Agent receives 10% commission on domestic sales; 10% on foreign sales. Offers a written contract, binding for 1 year. Charges $6 for script return (postage and handling) "if the material is wanted back."
Tips: Send "good quality, e.g. well-written scripts with good story lines, that can be produced on a realistic production budget."

PEREGRINE WHITTLESEY AGENCY (II), 345 E. 80th St., New York NY 10021. (212)737-0153. FAX: (212)734-5176. Contact: Peregrine Whittlesey. Estab. 1986. Represents 12 clients. 60% of clients are new/previously unpublished writers. Specializes in plays and screenplays. Currently handles: 19% movie scripts; 80% stage plays; 1% TV scripts.
Will Handle: Movie scripts; stage plays; TV scripts. Query with entire ms. Will report in 1 week on queries; 2 weeks on mss.
Recent Sales: *2*, by Romulus Linney (Peter Hall Productions); *Frida*, by Migdalia Cruz (American Music Theater Festival).
Terms: Agent receives 10% commission on domestic sales; 10% on foreign sales. Offers a written contract, binding for 2 years.
Tips: Obtains new clients through recommendations from others and direct inquiries.

ANN WRIGHT REPRESENTATIVES, INC. (II, III), 2C, 136 E. 56th St., New York NY 10022. (212)832-0110. Head of Literary Department: Dan Wright. Estab. 1963. Member of WGA. Represents 42 clients. 25% of clients are new/unpublished writers. "Writers must be skilled or have superior material for screenplays, stories or novels that can eventually become motion pictures or television properties." Prefers to work with published/established authors; works with a small number of new/unpublished authors. "Eager to work with any author with material that we can effectively market in the motion picture business worldwide." Specializes in themes that make good motion pictures. Currently handles 10% novels; 75% movie scripts; and 15% TV scripts.

Will Handle: Query with outline—does not read unsolicited mss. Reports in 3 weeks on queries; 2 months on mss. All work must be sent with a SASE to ensure its return.
Terms: Agent receives 10% commission on domestic sales; 10% on dramatic sales; 10% on foreign sales; 20% on packaging. Will critique only works of signed clients. Charges for photocopying expenses.

WRITERS & ARTISTS (III), Suite 501, 70 W. 36th St., New York NY 10018. (212)391-1112. FAX: (212)398-9877. Contact: Scott Hudson or William Craver. Estab. 1970. Member of SAR. Represents 100 clients. West Coast location: Suite 300, 11726 San Vicente Blvd. Los Angeles CA 90049. (213)820-2240. FAX: (213)207-3781.
Will Handle: Movie and TV scripts, stage plays. Query with SASE and brief description of project and about author. Will report in 1-2 weeks on queries.
Recent Sales: *M Butterfly* (Tony Award play for 1989, David Henry Hwang).
Terms: Agent receives 10% commission on domestic sales; commission varies on foreign sales. Offers written contract (required).

Additional Script Agents

The following agencies have full listings in other sections of this book. These agencies have indicated they are *primarily* interested in handling book manuscripts, but are also interested in scripts. After reading the listing (you can find the page number in the Listings Index), send them a query to obtain more information on their needs and script manuscript submission policies.

Agency Chicago
Alden—Literary Service, Farel T.
Allan Agency, Lee
Amsterdam Agency, Marcia
Anthony Agency, Joseph
Appleseeds Management
Author Aid Associates
Becker, Maximilian
Bloom, Harry
Brown Ltd., Curtis
Browne Ltd., Pema
Casselman Literary Agent, Martha
Cook Literary Agency, Warren
Cooper Assoc., Inc., Bill
Creative Concepts Literary Agency
Deering Literary Agency, Dorothy
Erikson Literary Agency, The
Feiler Literary Agency, Florence
Marje Fields-Rita Scott Inc.
Fishbein Ltd., Frieda
Flannery, White and Stone
Garon-Brooke Assoc. Inc., Jay
Gladden Unlimited
Goldfarb, Kaufman, & O'Toole

Hegler Literary Agency, Gary L.
Iorio, Esq., Gary F.
Jones Agency, Leon
Jordan Literary Agency, Lawrence
Kroll Agency, Lucy
Kuller Associates, Doris Francis
Lampack Agency, Inc., Peter
Law Offices of Robert L. Fenton PC
Lazear Agency Incorporated, The
Lighthouse Literary Agency
Literary and Creative Artists Agency
Markson Literary Agency, Elaine
Marshall Agency, The Evan
Merhige-Merdon Marketing/ Promo Co. Inc., Greg
Morris Agency, William
Morrison, Inc., Henry
Nelson Literary Agency & Lecture Bureau, BK
Norma-Lewis Agency, The
Northeast Literary Agency
Northwest Literary Services

Oscard Associates, Fifi
Pegasus International, Inc., Literary & Film Agents
Popkin/Nancy Cooke, Julie
Radley-Regan & Associates, D.
Rising Sun Literary Group, The
Robb Literary Properties, Sherry
Roffman Associates, Richard H.
SBC Enterprises, Inc.
Scott, Synergy Creative Agency, Stacy Ann
Sterling Lord Literistic, Inc.
Sullivan Associates, Mark
Toomey Associates, Jeanne
Wald Associates, Inc., Mary Jack
Wallerstein Agency, The Gerry B.
Warren Literary Agency, James
Watt & Associates, Sandra
West Coast Literary Associates
Wilshire Literary Agency, The
Wright Authors' Representative, Stephen
Writer's Consulting Group
Zelasky Literary Agency, Tom

Art/Photo Reps

Finding and Working with Art/Photo Reps

by Barbara Gordon

There seems to be a lack of information as well as a lot of misinformation on the function and role of artists' and photographers' representatives. Whether or not to get a rep is a major career decision, so it's important to understand first what a representative is, what they can and cannot do for you and how they work.

A good definition of a representative is one who is the marketing and selling arm of a talent. First of all, if comparisons are to be made, an artists' and photographers' representative is comparable to a literary agent or talent agent in some respects. A rep does not employ artists and photographers, but acts as their agent in obtaining assignments from advertisers, publishers, corporations and others.

The representative is responsible for packaging the product (art and photography) by getting the portfolio in selling condition. This involves editing of the portfolio as well as advising the talent on what needs to be added to fill in the missing gaps. The representative must then take the product to market. This is done through sales calls and advertising, promotion and public relations channels. To do this effectively a good representative must obviously have a thorough working knowledge of what clients are prospects for the talent's work as well as the knowledge of what advertising and promotion mediums will most effectively reach those clients at the most efficient cost.

On the practical side the representative negotiates the best prices and working conditions for the talent while keeping the talent competitive in the marketplace. The rep must have a knowledge of current market trends, prices and job situations and enough experience to talk knowledgeably about the product he/she is selling and pricing.

In addition to payment received for completing the assignment, the representative will negotiate expenses, usages, terms of payment, deadlines, royalties, licensing and other rights where applicable. The representative will check out the credit worthiness of the new client, do the billing, collecting of invoices, and collecting and paying of sales taxes when necessary. A representative will also develop publicity programs for the talent, handle agency shows and presentations, service current business, open new markets and expand existing markets.

On a personal level a rep should have the health, energy and flexibility to flow with the ups and downs of the freelancing business, as well as enough financing to stay in business during the down times. It goes without saying that a good representative should be honest,

Barbara Gordon *operates Barbara Gordon Associates in New York City, representing both illustrators and photographers. She is a past president of the Society of Photographers and Artists Representatives, has written for both art and photography publications, and recently co-authored (with her husband, Elliott)* How to Sell Your Photographs and Illustrations.

trustworthy and in tune with the talent and their aspirations and believe in the work of the talent they represent.

Talents reps handle, talents they don't

Most representatives primarily handle commercial photographers and artists. A few handle designers, but since designers have a different buying audience than artists and photographers it is not as common. Designers usually have to search longer and harder for a representative.

Commercial reps do not handle fine artists (by fine artists I mean those who are looking for gallery affiliation). If a fine artist has a commercial style and is interested in doing commercial assignments however, a commercial representative may be interested in handling him. Yet there are a few fine art representatives, and interested artists will find them in the Fine Art Reps section in this book.

Commercial reps also do not handle craftspeople primarily because most commercial assignments involve the buying of flat art or photography. Occasionally there is a craftsperson who can make models or do something that applies to the commercial marketplace, but this is a rare situation and craftspeople looking for representation may be better served by a fine art rep or a crafts gallery. Reps, however, often handle photo-retouchers and hair and make-up people, simply because these skills are very compatible with a representative who is handling photographers.

Finding a representative

How does one go about finding a representative? One of the best places to start is to get the names and addresses of people in the field. This directory and the directories of professional organizations are probably the best sources with which to start. I also suggest that a prospective talent ask art directors and art buyers to give them recommendations, since these are the people that the client deals with and obviously you want a representative who clients feel has knowledge and integrity.

With your list in hand send either a promotion sheet or slides of your work to the representative in question explaining that you are looking for representation. *Never* send original artwork. If you want something returned, send a self-addressed stamped envelope for that purpose. Always label your slides with your name and address just in case the slides become detached from your letter. Indicate "up" and "front" on your slides as well.Most reps ask for 10-15 slides. Plastic slide sleeves are available at most art and photography supply stores.

Since the representative is primarily interested in the salability of your work and must *see* it, this is the best way to approach a prospective representative. Unless a representative specifically requests them, phone calls and résumés are not recommended for first contacting reps since it's the work they are concerned with.

If a representative expresses an interest in you and your work, your next step is to check out the rep. Ask questions. Find out about the talent they currently handle and what type of clients they work with.

Be sure you have a clear understanding of the rep's policies. You might ask a rep:
- Do you handle competitive talents? If yes, do you have a large enough client base to handle talents with similar work?
- Will you share promotion and advertising costs? What is the split?
- What advertising and promotion would you do for my work?
- How long have you been in business?
- How broad is your client base?

You might also want to speak with art directors and buyers in the field about the representative, especially if they deal with the rep on a regular basis:
- Does the rep seem to have heavy talent turnover?

- Does the rep have consistent follow through or does he have an assistant handle the job after the sale is made?
- Is the rep, fair, honest, thorough?
  One final tip—trust your instincts. If everything checks out and you are getting "bad vibes" from the rep in question anyway, trust those instincts and move on. Conversely, if your instincts are telling you "this is the rep for me," go with those feelings too.

How does a representative work?

The most common arrangement, and the one most sought by talent, is the "exclusive" relationship. In this situation the representative will represent a talent "exclusively." That means the representative will not represent a competing talent. In return for this exclusive arrangement, the representative will get a percentage of the creative fee on all assignments, usually 25% on in-town situations and 30% for out-of town.

Under the exclusive arrangement the talent covers all of his or her own expenses, including portfolio costs (shooting transparencies, prints, laminates, etc.) on the theory that the portfolio is the permanent possession of the talent no matter who represents him/her. The representative covers the cost of running his/her office, making sales calls, etc. On advertising and promotion costs, the talent and representative split them on the same basis as the commission with the representative paying 25-30% of the costs and the talent paying 70-75% of the costs.

Some other representative-talent relationships include representatives who work on a straight salary. This usually occurs with a very large photography or design studio or television production house. Brokering is another situation. A representative represents a large group of competing talents and does not get a percentage on all of the assignments. Because the representative does not get a regular commission on all assignments, the rep will "broker" assignments, taking anywhere from 25-60% per assignment. In this case the representative usually does not pay for any part of the advertising and promotion costs involved.

When we talk about sharing expenses of advertising and promotion, what kinds of advertising and promotion are we referring to? The most common forms of advertising and promotion include: sending direct mail pieces to a specialized list of prospective clients; taking out advertising pages in one of the directories specifically for this purpose; arranging showings of the talent's work; and a variety of public relations efforts such as doing press releases on the talent's accomplishments.

All representatives have a "termination" clause in their contracts allowing them to compensation after the talent and representative split. The reasoning behind this is that often it can take a representative years to establish a talent and the representative gets no compensation for this effort. The feeling is the rep is entitled to some part of the talent's compensation after termination based on earlier efforts. The termination compensation is very involved and can range from commissions on assignments for a period of six months or more after termination or sometimes a percentage of the last year's earnings.

As you can gather, the termination and other financial aspects of an agreement between an artist and representative are very complex and all that can be given here are some of the highlights of some of the arrangements. A talent seeking representation should do his/her own research and confer with several representatives before making a final determination.

Do you really need a representative?

This is a very personal question that needs a very personal, individual answer. However, let me counter with another question. With so many legal and medical books around, does one really need a lawyer or doctor? And the answer is that sometimes all you need is a legal form from a stationery store or a remedy from the health food store, and sometimes you need the real thing.

There are artists and photographers who want to totally control their careers and have the high energy level and determination to promote and sell themselves. They do an excellent job of it without any outside assistance. There are also artists and photographers who are too busy doing assignments to handle the selling and promoting of their works. They want and need representation. Some artists simply like the support and interaction they get from a representative in this isolated world of freelancing.

Practically speaking, there are not enough representatives for the people seeking representation so, initially, many artists and photographers may find they have no choice but to represent themselves. As a working representative myself, I feel it's very good experience for a talent to represent himself sometime in his career. It gives him some insight to his buying audience and some familiarity and appreciation of how a representative functions.

One last word of advice: If you can't get a representative at first, keep trying. Representatives' situations change, and while they may be "booked" up in the beginning of the year, as the months go on they may find they have different needs and will be more receptive to your work at a later time.

For more information on artists' and photographers' reps contact SPAR, the Society of Photographers and Artists Representatives, Suite 914, 1123 Broadway, New York NY 10012. This is a nonprofit organization of photographers' and artists' reps who sponsor educational programs for members and provide members with mailing lists and other educational materials. The group publishes a directory of their members with the types and names of talent they represent.

Commercial Art and Photography Reps

When you make the decision to consider working with a commercial art (illustration and sometimes design) or photography representative, you must be prepared to invest both time and money in your career. In return, however, a representative can help you earn back this investment many times over. In fact, having someone else act as your business manager and sales staff can give you more time to devote to the creation of your work.

Sound like a good deal? It can be. But getting a rep is a serious career move. In addition to spending money and time getting your portfolio and self-promotion pieces in shape, you must also be ready to approach your career as a business. Your professionalism will mean as much to a rep (and your clients) as your talent.

Taking a professional approach

For the most part a representative will require you to have a well-developed portfolio. Some have specific requirements for uniformity, but others just expect you to include your best work in a neat format. Before approaching a rep, take a good look at your portfolio. Is only your best work included? (Remember your portfolio is only as strong as your weakest piece or image.) Is your work mounted neatly on a page or are your slides labeled and secured in sleeves?

Since your rep may be sending out more than one portfolio at a time, you may have to make copies of many of your pieces (or slides). It's easy to see you will need to spend money—depending on the requirements, you could spend several hundred dollars getting your portfolio ready. Once you have invested this money, however, your portfolio will be the key your rep uses to unlock many doors.

Most reps also require you to provide a direct mail piece or to participate in a group package with other talents the rep handles. This, too, can be a big investment. You may be asked to take out your own ad in one of the creative directories, such as *American Showcase* or *Creative Black Book*, but in return your work will be seen by hundreds of art directors. One nice little bonus for taking out one of these ads—most of these books provide you with tearsheets of your page which can be used as direct mail pieces. Advertising costs usually are a shared expense. In general, the expense is split on the same proportion as the commission. In other words, most reps receive 25-30% commission and will agree to absorb an equal percentage of advertising costs.

You may be asked to share expenses also, but most reps will absorb the usual office and marketing expenses. Though some reps are now asking for a monthly fee to cover unusual expenses, this does not seem to be a trend.

Most importantly, you must develop a professional attitude. A representative's job is to find you more and better assignments. Yet more assignments mean more deadlines. In this business you must deliver, and on time. Art directors at magazines and ad agencies trust the rep to present to them only those talents who are willing and able to follow through on assignments.

Approaching art or photo reps

Start by approaching a rep with a brief query letter and a direct mail piece, if you have one. If you do not have a flyer or brochure, you will need to send some representation of your work, such as photocopies or (duplicate) slides along with a self-addressed, stamped envelope. Since this can be a costly endeavor, you may want to check the listing or call to make sure the rep is open to queries at this time.

This should go without saying, but never send original work with a query. We hear too many horror stories about originals which have been lost or damaged on route. At a later date (when showing your portfolio) you may be asked to send originals, but this is after the rep has shown strong interest in your work.

When sending slides, be sure to label them. Your name and phone (and/or address) should appear on each slide in case they are separated from your other material. Also label "up" and "front" and any other information you might find helpful.

In your query letter be as brief as possible, but let the rep know a little bit about your background and your career goals. If you already have some established clients, let the rep know who they are and what you have been doing for them. Although most reps prefer an exclusive arrangement, if you have another rep in another part of the country, be sure to mention this too.

Help with your search

To help you with your search for representation, we've included a Geographic Index in the back of the book. It is divided by state and province. There is also an Agents and Reps Index to help you locate individual reps. Often you will read about a rep, but since that rep is an employee of a large agency, you may not be able to find that person's business number. We've asked agencies to give us the names of representatives on their staffs. Then we've listed the names in alphabetical order along with the name of their agency. Find the name of the person you would like to contact and then check the listing for that agency.

Some of the literary agencies and a few of the fine art reps are also interested in commercial illustrators or photographers. This is especially true of agents who deal with children's book publishers. If an agency's *primary* function is selling manuscripts for writers or the work of fine artists, but it's also interested in handling some illustrators or photographers, we've listed them in Additional Commercial Art/Photo Reps at the end of this section.

In addition to examining and contacting the listings in this section, word-of-mouth and referrals are still an important way to find representation. You may also be able to meet a rep at a show or workshop. Artist and photographer organizations provide information on reps to members through newsletters and meetings. For more on a variety of organizations for artists, as well as a wealth of other information on the business of art, see *Artist's Market*. Then, for photographers' organizations and information on the business, see *Photographer's Market* (both by Writer's Digest Books).

For more information on working with art and photo reps, see Barbara Gordon's article, Finding and Working with Art/Photo Reps. See also Resources for a list of other books on the art and photography business.

The Society of Photographers and Artists Representatives (SPAR) is an organization for professional representatives. The group sponsors educational programs for members and also publishes a directory of their membership (including the talent each represents). While some reputable reps do not belong to any organization, SPAR members are required to maintain certain standards and follow a code of ethics. The group has also developed a standard rep-artist agreement. For more information on the group, write to SPAR, Suite 914, 1123 Broadway, New York NY 10012.

About the listings

Many of the representatives listed in this section handle both illustration and photography. Some also handle graphic designers, story board artists, photographer's models and set people. Although most reps like to handle a variety of work, some specialize in fashion or other specific fields. For specifics on listings, please see the following sample listing.

Many representatives do not charge for additional expenses beyond those incurred in preparing your portfolio and sharing advertising costs. A few, however, require you to pay for special portfolios or other advertising materials. A handful also charge monthly retainers to cover marketing expenses. Where possible, we've indicated these listings with a filled-in box (■) symbol.

We've ranked the agencies listed in this section according to their openness to submissions. Below is our ranking system:

I New representative (less than one year in business) actively seeking clients.

II Representative seeking both new and established artists or photographers.

III Representative prefers to work with established artists or photographers, mostly through referrals.

IV Representative handling only certain types of work or work by artists or photographers under certain circumstances.

V Representative not currently seeking new clients. (If an agency chose this designation, only the address is given.) We have included mention of reps rated V only to let you know they are not open to new clients at this time. *Unless you have a strong recommendation from someone well-known in the field, our advice is to approach only those reps ranked I-IV.*

Sample listing

The following is a sample listing for art and photo representatives. Each element of the listing is numbered and numbers correspond to explanations following the listing. For more information on specific terms see the Glossary and introductions to the listings.

(1)ASCIUTTO ART REPS., INC. (II, IV), 3rd Fl., 19 E. 48th St., New York NY 10017. (212)838-0050. FAX: (212)838-0506. **(2)** Contact: Mary Anne Asciutto. **(3)** Commercial illustration representative. **(4)** Estab. 1980. **(5)** Member of SPAR, Society of Illustrators. **(6)** Represents 20 illustrators. **(7)(8)** Specializes in children's illustration for books, magazines, etc. **(9)** Markets include publishing/books.
(10) Will Handle: Illustration.
(11) Terms: Agent receives 25% commission. **(12)** Advertising costs are split: 75% paid by the talent; 25% paid by the representative. **(13)** For promotional purposes, talent must provide "prints (color) or originals within an 11×14 format." **(14)**
(15) How to Contact: For first contact, send a query letter, direct mail flyer/brochure, tearsheets, photocopies, SASE. **(16)** Will report within 2 weeks. **(17)** After initial contact, drop off or mail appropriate materials. **(18)** Portfolio should include original art, tearsheets, photocopies.
(19) Tips: Obtains new talent through recommendations or "just by observing books or by chance." In obtaining representation "be sure to connect with an agent that handles the kind of account you (the artist) *wants* to do."

(1) Name, address, phone number, ranking. If a rep requires a monthly retainer or additional fees beyond commission and expenses, a filled-in box (■) symbol will appear at the start of the listing. Take special note of the ranking codes (I-V) which appear after the name of the agency. Those ranked I or II and some ranked IV are most open to new talent. Agencies ranked III prefer established illustrators or photographers or those with strong referrals from within the field. Those with rankings of V are not looking for new talent and are included only to inform our readers. For the most part these agencies do not wish to list because they are not looking for new talent and will only accept queries from talents with very strong industry references. For a complete explanation of the different rankings, please see the section introduction.
(2) Contact name/s. Send your query or manuscript to the name or one of the names listed. If you are not sure of the gender, it is best to use the full name, such as "Dear Robin Jones." Occasionally no contact name is given. In such a case, "Dear Agency Director" usually is acceptable. If the agency has listed other reps on staff (see #7) and has indicated a specialty with the name, address your query to the rep who handles the work you do.
(3) Type of business. Many reps handle both photography and illustration. Some also act as consul-

tants or brokers. In the fine art section, you will find reps who are also gallery owners or art publishers, or who operate other art-related businesses.

(4) Establishment date. While an agency that has been in business a number of years is a good sign the rep is stable and has built up a network of helpful contacts in the industry, new agencies are often most open to new talent.

(5) Memberships. Many representatives are members of SPAR, the Society of Photographers and Artists Representatives or a variety of other art industry organizations. We use the blanket term "member of" in the listings, but reps listed as members of some artists' or photographers' organizations are actually signatories or associate members. While there are respectable agencies who are not members of any group, membership in a recognized organization suggests the agency has met certain requirements and has agreed to adhere to a code of ethics. For more information on some of the groups listed see Resources following the Glossary.

(6) Number of talents represented. Number of clients. The number of talents will give you an indication of the size of the agency. This must be weighed by the number of reps working in the agency. To determine the talent to agent ratio, see the reps listed in #2 (contact names) and #7 (staff members) or ask the rep how many representatives they have.

(7) Additional reps on staff. Many smaller agencies are one- or two-person operations. In other cases, however, there may be several reps on staff. We've asked representatives to list staff members. This information is included in the Agents and Representatives Index. You may read about a particular rep, but not know where the rep works. You can find this out by locating their name in the Agents and Representatives Index. We've also asked the agencies to list specialties, if any, next to the staff members listed. This will help you determine which rep on staff will be most interested in your work.

(8) Specialty. If an agency specializes in any type of illustration or photography, it is mentioned here.

(9) Markets. Included here are markets targeted by the representative. This information will help you determine if your style is suitable for most of the reps clients. For example, book publishers look for different styles than do advertising agencies. Yet, on the other hand, be careful not to pigeonhole yourself, if you feel your work would be suited to a variety of clients.

(10) Will handle. This is the type of material the representative is interested in handling. If the rep handles some fine art in addition to commercial work (or vice versa), this will be indicated here. The names of other agencies interested in representing commercial illustrators or photographers, but whose *primary* business is handling fine art or the work of writers, that agency appears in the Additional Commercial Art and Photo Reps (full listings elsewhere in this book).

(11) Terms. Included here is the percentage commission the rep will earn on work sold. If the rep charges for specific expenses or other fees, this information is also included. While most reps would like to handle the work of a talent exclusively, they may not require it or require exclusive representation within certain geographic limits. (this listing did not mention exclusivity, but that information, if given, would appear here).

(12) Advertising costs. Advertising costs are usually split based on the same percentages as the commission structure. In other words, if a rep receives 25% commission, then that rep will cover 25% of the advertising costs. Advertising may include direct mail pieces, ads in industry publications, group or individual ads placed in talent books such as *American Showcase*, special exhibitions or portfolio requirements.

(13) Promotional requirements. In addition to advertising placed by the rep, most also require a the talent to provide certain items for promotional purposes. They will expect the talent to have these materials available. Usually this includes a direct mail piece—a flyer or brochure to give clients, a professional-looking portfolio, copies of the portfolio and sometimes additional ads in talent books. Before approaching a rep, be sure your portfolio is in good shape and have on hand a direct-mail package. Check with the rep for specific portfolio or other promotional requirements, before spending additional money on special materials.

(14) Advertises in. Although this listing mentions no talent books or magazines by name, we asked reps to list those publications in which they advertise. If this information is provided, check their ads to get a feel for the type of talents they rep.

(15) How to contact. This is information on what to send when making your initial contact. Include a brief query letter and usually a direct mail piece and slides. Make sure your slides are properly labeled—include your name and address in case they get separated from your query.

(16) Reporting time. Add an additional 4-6 weeks on the amount of time indicated here, before checking on the status of your query.

(17) After initial contact. When a rep responds to your query, you will probably be asked to submit a portfolio. If you live nearby, you may call or write to set up an interview or you may be able to mail in appropriate materials. *Never* stop by without making arrangements first. Reps are very busy and usually do not have the time to stop to look at a portfolio unless they have set aside a specific time to do so.

(18) Portfolio requirements. This includes information on what to include in your portfolio. If you

are sending material by mail, avoid sending original work, unless the rep has first seen slides and has requested originals and you feel comfortable doing so.
(19) Tips. Included here is information on how reps usually obtain new talent. Any other helpful advice from the rep also appears here.

ARTISTS INTERNATIONAL (II), 7 Dublin Hill Drive, Greenwich CT 06830. (203)869-8010. FAX: (203)869-8274. Contact: Michael Brodie. Commercial illustration representative. Estab. 1971. Represents 25 illustrators. Specializes in children's books. Markets include advertising agencies, corporations/client direct, design firms, editorial/magazines, publishing books.
Will Handle: Illustration.
Terms: Agent receives 30% commission. For promotional purposes, talent must provide 2 portfolios. Advertises in *American Showcase*. "We also have our own full-color brochure, 24 pages."
How to Contact: For first contact, send tearsheets, slides, SASE. Will report within 5 days. After initial contact, drop off or mail in appropriate materials for review. Portfolio should include slides.
Tips: Obtains new talent through recommendations from others, solicitation, at conferences, etc. "Just send in your book. I will review."

ASCIUTTO ART REPS., INC. (II, IV), 3rd Fl., 19 E. 48th St., New York NY 10017. (212)838-0050. FAX: (212)838-0506. Contact: Mary Anne Asciutto. Commercial illustration representative. Estab. 1980. Member of SPAR, Society of Illustrators. Represents 15 illustrators. Specializes in children's illustration for books, magazines, etc. Markets include publishing/books.
Will Handle: Illustration.
Terms: Agent receives 25% commission. Advertising costs are split: 75% paid by talent; 25% paid by representative. For promotional purposes, talent should provide "prints (color) or originals within an 11×14 size format."
How to Contact: Send a query letter, direct mail flyer/brochure, tearsheets, photocopies, SASE. Will report within 2 weeks. After initial contact (if requested), drop off or mail in appropriate materials. Portfolio should include original art, tearsheets, photocopies or color prints. If accepted, materials will remain for assembly.
Tips: Obtains new talent through recommendations or "just by observing books or by chance." In obtaining representation "be sure to connect with an agent that handles the kind of accounts you (the artist) *want*."

BARASA & ASSOCIATES, INC., 2001 E. Fremont Ct., Arlington Heights IL 60004. (312)464-7815 or 280-2289 (in Chicago); (708)253-5795 (in suburbs). Contact: Mary Ann. Commercial photography and art representative. Estab. 1983. Member of SPAR. Represents 1 illustrator; 1 photographer; 2 fine aritsts. Specializes in design imaging. Markets include advertising agencies, corporations/client direct, design firms, sales/promotion firms, galleries.
Will Handle: Photography and film.
Terms: Agent receives 30% commission. Charges other fees. Exclusive area representation is required. "Advertising costs are negotiable, each individual is different." For promotional purposes, talent must provide "annual advertising budgets, samples on a regular basis and at least 1 assistant." Advertises in *Creative Black Book*, *The Workbook*, *The Sourcebook*.
How to Contact: For first contact, send tearsheets. Reporting time varies. After initial contact, drop off or mail in appropriate materials for review. What your portfolio should include "depends on, if it's mailed or hand-delivered."
Tips: Obtains new talent through recommendations from others.

NOEL BECKER ASSOCIATES (III, IV), 150 W. 55th St., New York NY 10019. (212)764-1988. Contact: Noel Becker. Commercial illustration and photography representative. Estab. 1975. Member of Graphic Artists Guild. Represents 2 photographers. Specializes in fashion. Markets include corporations/client direct.
Will Handle: Illustration, photography.
Terms: Agent receives 25-30% commission. Advertising costs are paid by talent. For promotional purposes, talent must provide direct mail piece.
How to Contact: For first contact, send direct mail flyer/brochure, photocopies. After initial contact, call to schedule an appointment to show a portfolio. Portfolio should include tearsheets, photographs.

BARBARA BEIDLER INC. (III), #506, 648 Broadway, New York NY 10012. (212)979-6996. FAX: (212)505-0537. Contact: Barbara Beidler. Commercial illustration and photography representative. Estab. 1986. Represents 1 illustrator, 3 photographers, 3 fashion stylists. Specializes in fashion, home furnishings, life style, portraits. Markets include advertising agencies, corporations/client direct, design firms, editorial/magazines, publishing/books, sales/promotion firms.

Will Handle: Photography.
Terms: Agent receives 25% commission (receives 12.5% for editorial work.) Exclusive area representation is required. Advertising costs are split: 75% paid by the talent; 25% paid by the representative. For promotional purposes, talent must provide portfolio. "Also, promotional materials are important (direct mail piece, etc.)."
How to Contact: For first contact, send direct mail flyer/brochure. After initial contact, write to schedule an appointment. Portfolio should include tearsheets, slides.
Tips: Obtains new talent through recommendations from others.

BERENDSEN & ASSOCIATES, INC. (III), 2233 Kemper Lane, Cincinnati OH 45206. (513)861-1400. FAX: (513)861-6420. Contact: Bob Berendsen or Leslie Hibbard Wood. Commercial illustration, photography, graphic design representative. Estab. 1986. Member of Art Directors Club of Cincinnati AAF, Advertising Club of Cincinnati. Represents 24 illustrators, 4 photographers, 4 designers. Specializes in "high-visibility consumer accounts." Markets include advertising agencies, corporations/client direct, design firms, editorial/magazines, paper products/greeting cards, publishing/books, sales/promotion firms.
Will Handle: Illustration, photography. "We are always looking for illustrators that can draw people, product and action well. Also we look for styles that are unique."
Terms: Agent receives 25% commission. Charges "mostly for postage but figures not available." Advertising costs are split: 75% paid by the talent; 25% paid by the representative. For promotional purposes, "artist must co-op in our direct mail promotions, and source books are recommended. Portfolios are updated regularly." Advertises in *RSVP, Creative Illustration Book, The Ohio Source Book.*
How to Contact: For first contact, send query letter, résumé, tearsheets, slides, photographs, photocopies, SASE. Reports back within weeks. After initial contact, drop off or mail in appropriate materials for review. Portfolios should include tearsheets, slides, photographs, photostats, photocopies.
Tips: Obtains new talent "through recommendations from other professionals. Contact Leslie Hibbard Wood, vice president of Berendsen and Associates, Inc. for first meeting."

IVY BERNHARD (III), Suite 401, 270 Lafayette St., New York NY 10012. Contact: Ive Bernhard. Commercial photography representative. Estab. 1985. Represents 2 photographers. Specializes in fashion stylists. Markets include: advertising agencies, corporations/client direct, design firms, editorial/magazines.
Will Handle: Photography.
Terms: Agent receives 25% commission. Exclusive area representation required in New York. Advertises in *Creative Black Book.*
How to Contact: Reports back with 1 day. After initial contact, drop off or mail in appropriate materials for review. Portfolio should include tearsheets, photographs.
Tips: Obtains new talent through recommendations from others.

BERNSTEIN & ANDRIULLI INC. (III), 60 E. 42nd St., New York NY 10165. (212)682-1490. FAX: (212)286-1890. Contact: Sam Bernstein. Commercial illustration and photography representative. Estab. 1975. Member of SPAR. Represents 50 illustrators, 12 photographers. Staff includes Tony Andriulli; Howard Bernstein; Fran Rosenfeld; Judy Miller; Madeline Martinez. Markets include advertising agencies, corporations/client direct, design firms, editorial/magazines, paper products/greeting cards, publishing/books, sales/promotion firms.
Will Handle: Illustration and photography.
Terms: Agent receives a commission. Exclusive career representation is required. Advertises in *American Showcase, Creative Black Book, The Workbook, New York Gold, Creative Illustration Book.*
How to Contact: For first contact, send query letter, direct mail flyer/brochure, tearsheets, slides, photographs, photocopies. Reports back within 1 week. After initial contact, drop off or mail in appropriate materials for review. Portfolio should include tearsheets, slides, photographs.

CAROLYN BRINDLE & PARTNER INC. (II,IV), 203 E. 89th St., New York NY 10128. (212)534-4177. FAX: (212)996-9003. Contact: Carolyn Brindle. Commercial illustration and fine art representative. Estab. 1974. Represents 5 illustrators, 1 fine artist. Specializes in fashion-oriented work. Markets include advertising agencies, corporations/client direct, design firms, editorial/magazines; paper products/greeting cards, publishing/books, corporate and private collections, interior decorators, museums.
Will Handle: Illustration. Looks for "unusual or new technique."
Terms: Agent receives 25% commission. Exclusive representation is required. Advertising costs are split: 75% paid by talent; 25% paid by representative. For promotional purposes, "we require a well-organized portfolio. We create promotional pieces with the artist that we both feel represents their work." Advertises in *RSVP, Creative Illustration.*

How to Contact: For first contact, send a query letter and direct mail flyer/brochure, tearsheets, photocopies and SASE. Will report within 5 days-1 month, if interested. After initial contact, drop off or mail in appropriate materials for review. Portfolio should include original art, tearsheet, "examples of work that has not been published."
Tips: Usually obtains new talent through "recommendations from others in the fashion field, advertising agency art directors, magazine art directors, illustrators that are friends of artists already represented. If possible, before contacting a representative, look at the advertising annuals, e.g. *Creative Illustration* or *RSVP* and see the kind of work the representative shows. See if your work would fit in with what you see. The promotional pages usually reflect the representative's way of thinking and taste.

SAM BRODY, ARTISTS & PHOTOGRAPHERS REPRESENTATIVE (III), 12 E. 46th St., 4th Fl., New York NY 10017. (212)758-0640. FAX: (212)697-4518. Contact: Sam Brody. Commercial illustration and photography representative and broker. Estab. 1948. Member of SPAR. Represents 4 illustrators, 3 photographers, 2 designers. Markets include advertising agencies, corporations/client direct, design firms, editorial/magazines, publishing/books, sales/promotion firms.
Will Handle: Illustration, photography, design, "great film directors."
Terms: Agent receives 25-30% commission. Exclusive area representation is required. Advertising costs are split: 75% paid by the talent; 25% paid by the representative. For promotional purposes, talent must provide 8×10 transparencies (dupes only) and case; plus back-up advertising material, re: cards (reprints—*Black Book*, etc.) and self-promos. Advertises in *Creative Black Book*.
How to Contact: For first contact, send bio, direct mail flyer/brochure, tearsheets. Will report within 3 days or within 1 day if interested. After initial contact, call to schedule an appointment or drop off or mail in appropriate materials for review. Portfolio should include tearsheets, slides, photographs.
Tips: Obtains new talent through recommendations from others, solicitation. In obtaining representation, artist/photographer should "talk to parties he has worked with in the past year."

BROOKE & COMPANY (II), 4323 Bluffview, Dallas TX 75209. (214)352-9192. FAX: (214)350-2101. Contact: Brooke Davis. Commercial illustration and photography representative. Estab. 1988. Represents 13 illustrators, 4 photographers. "Owner has 18 years experience in sales and marketing in the advertising and design fields."
Terms: No information provided.
How to Contact: For first contact, send bio, direct mail flyer/brochure, "sample we can keep on file if possible" and SASE. Will report within 2 weeks. After initial contact, write to schedule an appointment to show a portfolio or drop off or mail in appropriate materials for review. Portfolio should include tearsheets, slides or photographs.
Tips: Obtains new talent through referral or by an interest in a specific style. "Only show your best work. Develop an individual style. Show the type of work that you enjoy doing and want to do more often. Must have a sample to leave with potential clients."

BRUCK AND MOSS ASSOCIATES (IV), 333 E. 49th St,. New York NY 10017. (212)980-8061 or 982-6533. FAX: (212)832-8778. Contact: Moss or Nancy Bruck. Commercial illustration representative. Estab. 1978. Represents 10 illustrators. Markets include advertising agencies, corporations/client direct, design firms, editorial/magazines, publishing/books, sales/promotion firms.
Will Handle: Illustration.
Terms: Agent receives 30% commission. Exclusive area representation is required. Advertising costs are split: 70% paid by the talent; 30% paid by the representative. For promotional purposes, talent must provide "4×5 transparencies mounted on 7×9 black board. Talent pays for promotional card for the first year and for trade ad." Advertises in *American Showcase*.
How to Contact: For first contact, send tearsheets, "if sending slides, include an SASE." After initial contact, drop off or mail in appropriate materials for review. Portfolios should include tearsheets.
Tips: Obtains new talent through referrals by art directors and art buyers, mailings of promo card, source books, art shows, *American Illustration* and *Print Annual*. "Make sure you have had at least 5 years experience repping yourself. Don't approach a rep on the phone, they are too busy for this. Put them on a mailing list and mail samples. Don't approach a rep who is already repping someone with the same style."

To find a rep located near you or one who handles a region in which you need representation, check the art and photography reps geographic index.

TRICIA BURLINGHAM/ARTIST REPRESENTATION (III), Suite 318, 9538 Brighton Way, Beverly Hills CA 90210. (213)271-3982. Office Manager: Tiffany Bowne. Commercial photography representative. Estab. 1979. Member of APA. Represents 7 photographers, 1 set designer/art director. Markets include advertising agencies, corporations/client direct, design firms, editorial/magazines.
Will Handle: Photography.
Terms: Agent receives 25-30% commission. Charges for Federal Express, messengers. Exclusive area representation is required. Advertising costs are paid by the talent. For promotional purposes, "we require all artists to provide promotional material with a mailing piece (envelope/tube, etc.) We require at least two portfolios and a shipping case." Advertises in *The Workbook*.
How to Contact: For first contact, send direct mail flyer/brochure. Reports within 3 weeks, only if interested. Portfolio should include tearsheets, slides, photographs, "all promotional material/direct mail pieces."
Tips: Obtains new talent through "recommendations from others and our solicitations and research. All promotional material sent in is viewed by Tricia Burlingham. Please only send nonreturnable items."

LYDIA CARRIÈRE-CREATIVE REPRESENTATIVE (III), 16 Lyndon Ave., Los Gatos CA 95030. (408)395-8860. FAX: (408)395-5856. Contact: Lydia Carrière. Commercial illustration, photography and graphic design representative. Estab. 1989. Represents 3 illustrators, 4 photographers, 1 designer. Markets include advertising, corporations/client direct, design firms.
Will Handle: Illustration.
Terms: Agent receives 20-25% commission. Charges for general start up fees. Exclusive area representation is required. Advertising costs are split: 75-80% paid by the talent; 20-25% paid by the representative. For promotional purposes, talent should provide 8½ × 11 tearsheets or promotional leave behinds work best. For a portfolio, 11 × 14 outer dimension, prefers transparencies over prints in most cases. Advertises in *The Workbook, Bay Area Creative Sourcebook/San Francisco*
How to Contact: For first contact, send résumé, tearsheets with cover letter and SASE. Reports within 10 days to 2 weeks. Call to schedule an appointment. Portfolio should include roughs, original art, tearsheets, transparencies.
Tips: "Mostly people contact me via sourcebook listings." You should "have focus/direction; remember presentation is important; professionalism is a must; be client oriented."

STAN CARP, INC. (III, IV), 2166 Broadway, New York NY 10024. (212)362-4000. Contact: Stan Carp. Commercial photography representative and director. Estab. 1959. Member of SPAR. Represents 3 photographers. Markets include advertising agencies, corporations/client direct, design firms, editorial/magazines, paper products/greeting cards, publishing/books, sales/promotion firms.
Will Handle: Photography and "commercial directors."
Terms: Agent receives 25% commission. Exclusive area representation is required. Advertising costs are split: 75% paid by the talent; 25% paid by the representative. Advertises in *Creative Black Book*, *The Workbook*, and other publications.
How to Contact: For first contact, send photographs. Reporting time varies. After initial contact, call to schedule an appointment to show a portfolio, which should include tearsheets, slides and photographs.
Tips: Obtains new talent through recommendations from others.

CAROL CHISLOVSKY INC. (II), 853 Broadway, New York NY 10003. (212)677-9100. FAX: (212)353-0954. Contact: Carol Chislovsky. Commercial illustration representative. Estab. 1975. Member of SPAR. Represents 20 illustrators. Markets include advertising agencies, design firms, editorial/magazines, publishing/books.
Will Handle: Illustration.
Terms: Agent receives 30% commission. Advertising costs are split: 70% paid by the talent; 30% paid by the representative. For promotional purposes, talent must provide direct mail piece. Advertises in *American Showcase, Creative Black Book* and sends out a direct mail piece.
How to Contact: For first contact, send direct mail flyer/brochure. Portfolio should include tearsheets, slides, photostats.
Tips: Obtains new talent through solicitation.

WOODY COLEMAN PRESENTS INC. (II), 490 Rockside Rd., Cleveland OH 44131. (216)661-4222. FAX: (216)661-2879. Contact: Woody or George. Commercial illustration representative. Estab. 1978. Member of Graphic Artists Guild. Represents 26 illustrators. Staff includes George Spuhler (Senior Account Executive, Corporate Marketing Director). Markets include advertising agencies, corporations/client direct, design firms, editorial/magazines, paper products/greeting cards, publishing/books, sales/promotion firms, public relations firms.

Will Handle: Illustration.

Terms: Agent receives 25% commission. Advertising costs are split: 75% paid by the talent; 25% paid by the representative. For promotional purposes, talent must provide "all portfolios in 4×5" transparencies." Advertises in *American Showcase, Creative Black Book, The Workbook*, other publications.

How to Contact: For first contact, send query letter, tearsheets, slides, SASE. Reports within 7 days, only if interested. Portfolio should include tearsheets, 4×5 transparencies.

Tips: "Solicitations are made directly to our agency. Concentrate on developing eight to ten specific examples of a single style exhibiting work aimed at a particular specialty, such as fantasy, realism, Americana or a particular industry such as food, medical, architecture, transportation, film, etc." Specializes in "quality service based on being the 'world's best listeners.' We know the business, ask good questions and simplify an often confusing process. We are truly representative of being called a 'service' industry."

JAN COLLIER REPRESENTS (III), 166 S. Park, San Francisco CA 94107. (415)552-4252. Contact: Jan. Commercial illustration representative. Estab. 1978. Represents 12 illustrators. Markets include advertising agencies, design firms.

Will Handle: Illustration, photography.

Terms: Agent receives 25% commission. Exclusive area representation is required. Advertising costs are split: 75% paid by the talent; 25% paid by the representative. Advertises in *American Showcase, Creative Black Book, The Workbook, The Creative Illustration Book*.

How to Contact: For first contact, send tearsheets, slides, SASE. Reports within 5 days, only if interested. After initial contact, call to schedule an appointment to show a portfolio. Portfolios should include slides.

DANIELE COLLIGNON (II), 200 W. 15th St., New York NY 10011. (212)243-4209. Contact: Daniele Collignon. Commercial illustration representative. Estab. 1981. Member of SPAR, Graphic Artists Guild, Art Director's Club. Represents 12 illustrators. Markets include advertising agencies, corporations/client direct, design firms, editorial/magazines, publishing/books.

Will Handle: Illustration.

Terms: Agent receives 30% commission. Exclusive area representation is required. Advertising costs are split: 75% paid by the talent; 25% paid by the representative. For promotional purposes, talent must provide 8×10 transparencies (for portfolio) to be mounted; printed samples; professional pieces. Advertises in *American Showcase, Creative Black Book, The Workbook*.

How to Contact: For first contact, send direct mail flyer/brochure, tearsheets. Reports within 3-5 days, only if interested. After initial contact, drop off or mail in appropriate materials for review. Portfolio should include tearsheets, transparencies.

JAMES CONRAD & ASSOCIATES (II), 2149 Lyon St., #5, San Francisco CA 94185. (415)921-7140. Contact: James Conrad. Commercial illustration and photography representative. Estab. 1984. Member of SPAR, Society of Illustrators, Graphic Artists Guild. Represents 18 illustrators, 6 photographers. Markets include: advertising agencies, corporate art departments, editorial, graphic designers, paper products/greeting crads, books, poster and calender publishers.

Will Handle: Illustration, photography.

Terms: Agent receives 25% commission. Exclusive regional or national representation is required. For promotional purposes, talent must provide a portfolio "and participate in promotional programs."

How to Contact: For first contact, send samples.

CREATIVE ARTS OF VENTURA (V), P.O. Box 684, Ventura CA 93002. Representative not currently seeking new talent.

CREATIVE PRODUCTIONS, INC. (III), 7216 E. 99 St., Kansas City MO 64134. (816)761-7314. Contact: Linda Pool. Commercial photography representative. Estab. 1982. Represents 1 illustrator, 2 photographers. Markets include advertising agencies, corporations/client direct, design firms.

Will Handle: Photography.

Terms: Agent receives 30% commission. Advertising costs are split: 70% paid by the talent; 30% paid by the representative. For promotional purposes, talent must provide transparencies. "I complete promo pieces, but we share the cost." Advertises in *American Showcase, The Workbook*.

How to Contact: For first contact, send "sample of his/her favorite piece, what he enjoyed completing." Reports within 2 weeks, only if interested. After initial contact, call to schedule an appointment to show a portfolio.

CVB CREATIVE RESOURCE, (II), 1856 Elba Circle, Costa Mesa CA 92626. (714)641-9700. FAX: 714)641-9700. Contact: Cindy Brenneman. Commercial illustration, photography and graphic design representative. Estab. 1984. Member of SPAR, ADDOC. Specializes in "high-quality innovative images." Markets include advertising agencies, corporations/client direct, design firms.
Will Handle: Illustration. Looking for "a particular style or specialized medium."
Terms: Agent receives 30% commission. Exclusive area representation is required. Advertising costs are split: 70% paid by the talent; 30% paid by the representative, "if reps name and number appear on piece." For promotional purposes, talent must provide promotional pieces on a fairly consistent basis. Portfolio should be laminated. Include transparencies or cibachromes. Imges to be shown are mutually agreed upon by talent. Advertises in *The Workbook*.
How to Contact: For first contact, send slides or photographs. Reports within 2 weeks, only if interested. After initial contact, call to schedule an appointment to show a portfolio. Portfolio should include tearsheets, slides, photographs, photostats.
Tips: Obtains new talent through referrals. "You usually know if you have a need as soon as you see the work. Be professional. Treat looking for a rep as you would looking for a freelance job. Get as much exposure as you can. Join peer clubs and network. Always ask for referrals. Interview several before settling on one. Personality and how you interact will have a big impact on the final decision."

LINDA DE MORETA REPRESENTS (II), 1839 Ninth St., Alameda CA 94501. (415)769-1421. FAX: (415)521-1674. Contact: Linda de Moreta. Commercial illustration and photography representative; also portfolio and career consultant. Estab. 1988. Represents 6 illustrators, 2 photographers. Markets include advertising agencies; corporations/client direct; design firms; editorial/magazines; paper products/greeting cards; publishing/books; sales/promotion firms.
Will Handle: Illustration and photography.
Terms: Agent receives 25% commission. Mailing costs are split 75%-25% between talent and representative. Exclusive representation requirements vary. Advertising costs are split: 75% paid by talent; 25% paid by representative. Materials for promotional purposes vary with each artist. Advertises in *The Workbook, Bay Area Creative Sourcebook*.
How to Contact: For first contact, send direct mail flyer/brochure, tearsheets, slides, photocopies, photostats and SASE. "Please do *not* send original art. SASE for any items you wish returned." Will report in 2 weeks. After initial contact, call to schedule an appointment. Portfolios should include tearsheets, photostats, transparencies.
Tips: Obtains new talent through clients and artist referrals, primarily, some solicitation. "I look for a personal vision and style of illustration or photography combined with maturity and a willingness to work hard."

DODGE CREATIVE SERVICES INC. (III), 301 N. Water St., Milwaukee WI 53202. (414)271-3388. FAX: (414)347-0493. Contact: Tim Dodge. Commercial illustration, photography, graphic design, television and film representative. Estab. 1982. Represents 5 illustrators, 4 photographers, 6 designers. Specializes in "representation to the Midwest corporate and advertising agency marketplace." Markets include advertising agencies, corporations/client direct, design firms, sales/promotion firms.
Will Handle: Illustration, photography, design. Looking for "absolutely outstanding and unique work only."
Terms: Agent receives 30% commission. Exclusive area representation is required. Advertising costs are split: 70% paid by the talent; 30% paid by the representative. For promotional purposes, talent must provide "portfolios provided as slides/transparencies (at least 3 complete sets)."
How to Contact: For first contact, send query letter, tearsheets, slides. Reports back within 2 weeks. After initial contact, write to schedule an appointment to show a portfolio. Portfolio should include thumbnails, tearsheets, slides.
Tips: Obtains new talent generally through recommendations and direct inquiries. "Make the presentation meticulous, keep the work focused. Show a desire to build a business and make a commitment."

ELDRIDGE CORPORATION (II), Suite 300, 916 Olive St., St. Louis MO 63101. (314)231-6800. FAX: (314)231-3042. Contact: Rene Armstrong. Commercial illustration representative. Estab. 1984. Represents 24 illustrators, 2 designers, 3 fine artists (includes 2 sculptors). Staff includes Rene Armstrong (manager print division, talent coordinator, produces jobs), Brian Fergusson (sales). Markets include advertising agencies, corporations/client direct, design firms, editorial/magazines, publishing/books, sales/promotion firms.
Will Handle: Illustration.
Terms: Agent receives 30% commission. Advertising costs are split between talent and representative (percentages to be decided). For promotional purposes, talent must provide 8-12 mounted 4x5 transparencies and a promotional leave-behind. "We do our own 105-page, full-color book."

How to Contact: For first contact, send a query letter and tearsheets. Will report within 1 month. After initial contact, drop off or mail appropriate materials for review. Portfolio should include tearsheets, slides, photographs or transparencies.
Tips: Obtains new talent through "seeing the work in a sourcebook or ad (commercial application), receiving a request for representation or referral from another artist or, occasionally, an art director. Make certain that your promotional material has work of consistent quality. Don't put three really strong pieces on a page and use one weak one just to balance out the page. The weak piece always draws my attention. You're better off with fewer pieces—but of the same quality level."

RHONI EPSTEIN (II, III), 3814 Franklin Ave,. Los Angeles CA 90027. (213)663-2388. FAX: (213)662-0035. Contact: Rhoni Epstein. Commercial photography representative. Estab. 1984. Member of SPAR, APA. Represents 5 photographers. Staff includes Frolic Taylor (marketing); Annie Consoletti (design/advertising). Specializes in management of creative photographers. Markets include advertising agencies, corporations, designers, editorial/magazines, entertainment.
Will Handle: Photography.
Terms: Terms are negotiated on an individual basis. Advertises in *The Workbook*.
How to Contact: For first contact, send direct mail flyer/brochure. Reports within weeks, only if interested. After initial contact, drop off or mail in appropriate materials for review. Portfolio should include transparencies, prints, tearsheets.
Tips: Obtains new talent through recommendations from others or researsh. "Do great work!!"

PAT FORBES INC. (V), 11459 Waterview Cluster, Reston VA 22090-4315. Representative not currently seeking new talent.

(PAT) FOSTER ARTIST REP. (II), 6 E 36 St., New York NY 10016. (212)685-4580. FAX: same. Contact: Pat Foster. Commercial illustration representative. Estab. 1981. Member of Graphic Artists Guild. Represents 7 illustrators. Markets include advertising agencies, corporations/client direct, sales/promotion firms.
Will Handle: Illustration.
Terms: Agent receives 25% commission. "No additional charge for my services i.e.—shooting, obtaining pix ref/costumes." Advertising costs are split: 75% paid by the talent; 25% paid by the representative. Advertises in *American Showcase*.
How to Contact: For first contact, send direct mail flyer/brochure, tearsheets, slides. After initial contact, call to schedule an appointment or drop off or mail in appropriate materials. Portfolio should include tearsheets, slides, photographs, proofs.
Tips: Obtains new talent through recommendations mostly from associates in the business. "Work must look fresh; good design sense incorporated into illustration."

FRANCISCO COMMUNICATIONS, INC. (II, III), 419 Cynwyd Rd., Bala Cynwyd PA 19004. (215)667-2378. FAX: (215)667-4308. Contact: Carol Francisco. Commercial illustration representative. Estab. 1983. Represents 7 illustrators. Markets include advertising agencies, corporations/client direct.
Will Handle: Illustration.
Terms: Agent receives 25% commission. Advertising costs are split: 75% paid by the talent; 25% paid by the representative. For promotional purposes, talent must provide "promo samples, originals or same size copies of some samples."
How to Contact: For first contact, send query letter, direct mail flyer/brochure, tearsheets. Reports within 2 weeks only if interested. After initial contact, call to schedule an appointment to show a portfolio. Portfolio should include tearsheets, photographs, photostats, photocopies.

JEAN GARDNER & ASSOCIATES, 348 N. Norton Ave., Los Angeles CA 90004. (213)464-2492. FAX: (213)465-7013. Contact: Jean Gardner. Commercial photography representative. Estab. 1985. Member of APA. Represents 6 photographers. Staff includes Jacquie Barnbrook, associate rep. Specializes in photography. Markets include advertising agencies, design firms.
Will Handle: Photography.
Terms: Agent receives 25% commission. Exclusive area representation is required. Advertising costs are paid by the talent. For promotional purposes, talent must provide promos, *Workbook* advertising, a quality portfolio. Advertises in *The Workbook*.
How to Contact: For first contact, send direct mail flyer/brochure. Reports back within 3 weeks. "No appointments."
Tips: Obtains new talent through recommendations from others.

MICHAEL GINSBURG & ASSOCIATES, INC. (II, III), 407 Park Ave., South, New York NY 10016. (212)679-8881. FAX: (212)679-2053. Contact: Michael Ginsburg. Commercial photography representative. Estab. 1978. Represents 5 photographers. Specializes in advertising and editorial photogra-

phers. Markets include advertising agencies, corporations/client direct, design firms, editorial/magazines, sales/promotion firms.
Will Handle: Photography.
Terms: Agent receives 25% commission. Charges for messenger costs, Federal Express charges. Exclusive representation is required. Advertising costs are split: 75% paid by the talent; 25% paid by the representative. For promotional purposes, talent must provide a minimum of five portfolios—direct mail pieces two times per year—and at least one sourcebook per year. Advertises in *Creative Black Book* and other publications.
How to Contact: For first contact, send query letter, direct mail flyer/brochure. Reports within 2 weeks, only if interested. After initial contact, call to schedule an appointment to show a portfolio. Portfolio should include tearsheets, slides, photographs.
Tips: Obtains new talent through personal referrals and solicitation.

BARBARA GORDON ASSOCIATES LTD. (II), 165 E. 32nd St., New York NY 10016. (212)686-3514. Contact: Barbara Gordon. Commercial illustration and photography representative. Estab. 1969. Member SPAR, Society of Illustrators, Graphic Artists Guild. Represents 9 illustrators, 1 photographer. "I represent only a small select group of people therefore give a great deal of personal time and attention to the people I represent."
Terms: No information provided.
How to Contact: For first contact, send direct mail flyer/brochure. Reports back within 2 weeks. After initial contact, drop off or mail in appropriate materials for review. Portfolio should include tearsheets, slides, photographs, "if the talent wants materials or promotion piece returned, include SASE."
Tips: Obtains new talent through recommendations from others, solicitation, at conferences, etc. "I have obtained talent from all of the above. I do not care if an artist or photographer has been published or is experienced. I am essentially interested in people with a good, commercial style. Don't send résumés and don't call to give me a verbal description of your work. Send promotion pieces. *Never* send original art. If you want something back, include a SASE. Always label your slides in case they get separated from your cover letter. And always include a phone number where you can be reached."

T.J. GORDON/ARTIST REPRESENTATIVE (II), P.O. Box 4112, Montebello CA 90640. (213)887-8958. Contact: Tami Gordon. Commercial illustration, photography and graphic design representative; also illustration or photography broker. Estab. 1990. Member of SPAR. Represents 1 illustrator, 2 photographers, 1 graphic designer. Markets include advertising agencies, corporations/client direct, design firms, editorial/magazines.
Will Handle: Illustration, photography, design.
Terms: Agent receives 30% commission. Advertising costs are split: 70% paid by talent; 30% paid by representative (direct mail costs, billable at end of each month). For promotional purposes, talent must provide "a minimum of three pieces to begin a six-month trial period. These pieces will be used as mailers and leave behinds. Portfolio is to be professional and consistent (pieces of the same size, etc.) At the end of the trial period agreement will be made on production of future promotional pieces."
How to Contact: For first contact, send a bio and direct mail flyer/brochure. Will report in 2 weeks, if interested. After initial contact, call to schedule an appointment. Portfolio should include tearsheets.
Tips: Obtains new talent "primarily through recommendations and as the result of artists' solicitations. Have an understanding of what it is you do, do not be afraid to specialize. If you do everything, then you will always conflict with the interests of the representatives' other artists. Find you strongest selling point, vocalize it and make sure that your promos and portfolio show that point."

ANITA GREEN INC. (III), 6C, 718 Broadway, New York NY 10003. Commercial photography representative. Estab. 1975. Member of SPAR. Represents 3 photographers. Specializes in still life. Markets include advertising agencies, corporations/client direct, design firms, editorial/magazines, publishing/books, sales/promotion firms.
Will Handle: Photography.
Terms: Agent receives 25% commission. Exclusive area representation is required. Advertising costs are split 75% paid by the talent; 25% paid by the representative. Advertises in *The Workbook, New York Gold.*
How to Contact: For first contact, send direct mail flyer/brochure. Does not report back. "Do not call."
Tips: Obtains new talent through recommendations.

CAROL GUENZI AGENTS, INC. (II), Suite 1602, 130 Pearl, Denver CO 80203. (303)733-0128. Contact: Carol Guenzi. Commercial illustration, film and animation representative. Estab. 1984. Member of Denver Advertising Federation and Art Directors Club of Denver. Represents 13 illustrators, 4 pho-

tographers, 1 filmaker, 1 animator. Specializes in a "wide selection of talent in all areas of visual communications." Markets include advertising agencies, corporations/client direct, design firms, editorial/magazine.
Will Handle: Illustration, photography. Looking for "unique style application."
Terms: Agent receives 25% commission. Exclusive area representation is required. Advertising costs are split: 75% paid by talent; 25% paid by the representation. For promotional purposes, talent must provide "promotional material after 6 months, some restrictions on portfolios." Advertises in *American Showcase, Creative Black Book, The Workbook*, "periodically."
How to Contact: For first contact, send direct mail flyer/brochure. Reports within 2 weeks, only if interested. After initial contact, drop off or mail in appropriate materials for review. Portfolio should include slides, photocopies.
Tips: Obtains new talent through solicitation, art directors' referrals, an active pursuit by individual. "Show your strongest style and have at least twelve samples of that style, before introducing all your capabilities."

PAT HACKETT/ARTIST REPRESENTATIVE (III), Suite 502, 101 Yesler Way, Seattle WA 98104-2525. (206)447-1600. FAX: (206)447-0739. Contact: Pat Hackett. Commercial illustration and photography representative. Estab. 1979. Member of Seattle Design Association. Represents 23 illustrators, 2 photographers. Markets include advertising agencies, corporations/client direct, design firms, editorial/magazines.
Will Handle: Illustration.
Terms: Agent receives 25-33% commission. Exclusive area representation is required. Advertising costs are split: 75% paid by the talent; 25% paid by the representative. For promotional purposes, talent must provide "standardized portfolio, i.e. all pieces within the book are the same format. Reprints are nice, but not absolutely required." Advertises in *American Showcase, Creative Black Book, The Workbook, Creative Illustration*.
How to Contact: For first contact, send direct mail flyer/brochure. Reports within 1 week, only if interested. After initial contact, drop off or mail in appropriate materials for review. Portfolio should include tearsheets, slides, photographs, photostats, photocopies.
Tips: Obtains new talent through "recommendations and calls/letters from artists moving to the area. We prefer to handle artists who live in the area unless they do something that is not available locally."

HALL & ASSOCIATES (III), 1010 S. Robertson Blvd, #10, Los Angeles CA 90035. (213)652-7322. FAX: (213)652-3835. Contact: Marni Hall. Commercial illustration and photography representative. Estab. 1983. Member of SPAR, APA. Represents 10 illustrators and 5 photographers. Markets include advertising agencies, design firms.
Will Handle: Illustration and photography.
Terms: Agent receives 25-28% commission. Exclusive area representation is required. Advertising costs are paid 100% by talent. For promotional purposes, talent must advertise in "one or two source books a year (double page), provide two direct mail pieces and one specific, specialized mailing. No specific portfolio requirement except that it be easy and light to carry and send out." Advertises in *Creative Black Book, The Workbook*.
How to Contact: For first contact, send a direct mail flyer/brochure. Will report in 5 days. After initial contact, drop off or mail in appropriate materials for review. Portfolios should include tearsheets, transparencies, prints (8x10 or larger).
Tips: Obtains new talent through recommendations from others or artists' solicitations. "Don't show work you think should sell but what you enjoy shooting. Only put in tearsheets of great ads, not bad ads even if they are a highly visible client."

WENDY HANSEN (II), 126 Madison Ave., New York NY 10016. (212)684-7139. Contact: Wendy Hansen. Commercial photography representative. Estab. 1980. Represents 3 photographers. Markets include advertising agencies, design firms, editorial/magazines, retail outlets.
Will Handle: Photography.
Terms: Agent receives 25% commission. Advertising costs are split: 75% paid by talent; 25% paid by representative. For promotional purposes, talent must provide "a portfolio and promotional pieces." Advertises in *Creative Black Book, New York Gold*.

If you're looking for a particular rep, check the Agents and Reps Index to find at which agency the rep works. Then look up the listing for that agency in this section.

How to Contact: For first contact, send a query letter with promotional pieces and a description of clients. Will report in 2 weeks, if interested. After initial contact, call to schedule an appointment. Portfolio should include tearsheets, photographs.

GRETCHEN HARRIS & ASSOCIATES (III), 5230 13th Ave. S., Minneapolis MN 55417. (612)822-0650. FAX: (612)822-0358. Contact: Gretchen Harris. Commercial illustration and photography representative. Estab. 1981. Member of AIGA. Represents 6 illustrators, 2 photographers. Markets include advertising agencies, corporations/client direct, design firms, editorial/magazines, sales/promotion firms.
Will Handle: Illustration, photography.
Terms: Agent receives 25% commission. Advertising costs are split: 75% paid by the talent; 25% paid by the representative. For promotional purposes, talent must provide "promotional leave behinds. We usually work together on direct mail campaigns. Portfolio is usually made up of mounted transparencies no smaller than 4×5"." Advertises in *American Showcase, Twin Cities Creative Sourcebook*.
How to Contact: For first contact, send query letter, tearsheets. Reports back within 1 week, only if interested. After initial contact, drop off or mail in appropriate materials for review. Portfolio should include tearsheets.
Tips: "I prefer to have talent come recommended through an art director or designer, but that does not offer any guarantees. I might also pursue someone I am interested in. I strongly suggest that artists represent themselves for at least two years before looking for a rep. I will not rep anyone without experience as a freelancer. Working in this field is tough and competitive and I want artists who understand deadlines and budgets. When I stick my neck out I want positive results. Also, I prefer an artist who has a strong style one that would set them apart from others in my group and from other artists in general!"

■**JOANNE HEDGE/ARTIST REPRESENTATIVE (III),** Suite 3, 1838 El Cerrito Place, Hollywood CA 90068. (213)874-1661. FAX: (213)874-0136. Contact: J. Hedge. Commercial illustration representative. Estab. 1975. Member of Graphic Artists Guild, Art Directors Club of LA. Represents 12 illustrators. Specializes in "high-quality, painterly and realistic illustration and lettering." Markets include advertising agencies, design firms.
Will Handle: Illustration. Looking for "painterly impressionist – oils or other with skill in 'California' colors and strong lighting feel – people and scenics."
Terms: Agent receives 30% commission. Charges quarterly portfolio maintenance expenses and freight fees usually when no job netted. Advertising costs are split: 75% paid by talent; 25% paid by representative. For promotional purposes, talent should provide "ad reprint flyer, 4x5 or 8x10 copy transparencies, matted on 11x14 laminate mattes." Advertises in *The Workbook, Creative Black Book* and *Graphic Artists Guild Directory of Illustration.*
How to Contact: For first contact, send a query letter with direct mail flyer or brochure and 35mm slides ok with SASE. Will report in 1 week, if interested. After initial contact, call or write to schedule an appointment to show a portfolio. Portfolios should include tearsheets (laminated), photocopies, 4x5 or 8x10 transparencies.
Tips: Obtains new talent through contact after talent sees directory ad or through referrals from art directors or other talent. "Have an 8½×11 advertising promo already ready and a small roster of client 'fans' – and *no*New York rep!"

HK PORTFOLIO (III), 458 Newtown Turnpike, Weston CT 06883. (203)454-4687. FAX: (203)227-1366. Contact: Harriet Kasak. Commercial illustration representative. Estab. 1986. Member of SPAR. Represents 23 illustrators. Specializes in children's book illustration. Markets include advertising agencies, editorial/magazines, publishing/books.
Will Handle: Illustration.
Terms: Agent receives 25% commission. Advertising costs are split: 75% paid by the talent; 25% paid by the representative. Advertises in *American Showcase, RSVP.*
How to Contact: For first contact, send query letter, direct mail flyer/brochure, tearsheets, slides, photographs, photostats, SASE. Will report within 1 week. After initial contact, drop off or mail in appropriate materials for review. Portfolio should include tearsheets, slides, photographs, photostats, photocopies.
Tips: Obtains new talent through recommendations from others, solicitation, at conferences, etc.

RITA HOLT & ASSOCIATES, INC. (II,III), 920 Main St., Fords NJ 08863. Contact: Rita Holt. Commercial photography representative. Estab. 1976. Member of SPAR. Represents 4 photographers. Specializes in automotive and location photography. Markets include advertising agencies, corporations/client direct, design firms, sales/promotion firms.

Will Handle: Photography, especially automotive.
Terms: Commission taken by agent varies. Charges for all expenses. Advertising costs are paid 100% by talent. For promotional purposes, talent must provide direct mail piece or package and portfolio— "specifics depend on market." Advertises in *Creative Black Book, The Workbook* ("depends on the market").
How to Contact: For first contact, send direct mail flyer/brochure, photographs, portfolio with a return Federal Express air bill. Will report only if interested (time varies). After initial contact, drop off or mail in appropriate materials.
Tips: Obtains new talent through recommendations from others. "Sell a rep the same way you would sell a client."

SCOTT HULL ASSOCIATES (III), 68 E. Franklin S., Dayton OH 45459. (513)433-8383. FAX: (513)433-0434. Contact: Scott Hull or Frank Sturges. Commercial illustration representative. Estab. 1981. Represents 20 illustrators.
Terms: No information provided.
How to Contact: For first contact, send slides. Reports back within 2 weeks. After initial contact, drop off or mail in appropriate materials for review. Portfolio should include tearsheets, slides.
Tips: Obtains new talent through solicitation.

PEGGY KEATING (III, IV), 30 Horatio St., New York NY 10014. (212)691-4654. Contact: Peggy Keating. Commercial illustration representataive. Estab. 1969. Member of Graphic Artists Guild. Represents 7 illustrators. Specializes in fashion illustration (men, women, children and also fashion-related products). Markets include advertising agencies, corporations/client direct, editorial/magazines, sales/promotion firms, "mostly pattern catalog companies and retail."
Will Handle: "Fashion illustration, but only if top-drawer."
Terms: Agent receives 25% commission. Exclusive area representation is required. For promotional purposes, talent must provide "strong sample material that will provide an excellent portfolio presentation." Advertises by direct mail.
How to Contact: For first contact, send tearsheets, photocopies. Reports back within days only if interested. After initial contact, drop off or mail in appropriate materials for review. Portfolio should include thumbnails, roughs, original art, tearsheets, slides, photographs, photostats, photocopies. "It might include all or one or more of these materials. The selection and design of the material are the important factor."
Tips: Obtains new talent through "recommendations from others, or they contact me directly. The talent must be first-rate. The field has diminished and the competition if fierce. There is no longer the tolerance of not yet mature talent, nor is there a market for mediocrity."

RALPH KERR (II), 239 Chestnut St., Philadelphia PA 19106. (215)592-1359. FAX: (215)592-7988. Contact: Ralph Kerr. Commercial illustration and photography representative. Estab. 1987. Represents 1 photographer. Markets include advertising agencies, corporations/client direct, design firms, editorial/magazines, paper products/greeting cards, publishing/books.
Will Handle: Illustration, photography.
Terms: Agent receives 20% commission. Exclusive area representation required. Advertising costs are split: 50% paid by the talent; 50% paid by the representative. For promotional purposes, portfolio required. Advertises in *Creative Black Book*.
How to Contact: For first contact, send query letter. Reports within 1 week. After initial contact, call to schedule an appointment. Portfolio should include tearsheets, slides, photographs.

TANIA KIMCIE (III), 10F, 425 W. 23 St., New York NY 10011. (212)242-6367. FAX: (212)691-6501. Contact: Tania. Commercial illustration representative. Estab. 1981. Member of SPAR. Represents 9 illustrators. "We do everything, a lot of design firm, corporate/conceptial work." Markets include advertising agencies, corporations/client direct, design firms, editorial/magazines, publishing books, sales/promotion firms.
Will Handle: Illustration. Looking for "conceptual/corporate work."
Terms: Agent receives 25% commission if the artist is in town; 30% if the artist is out of town. Splits postage and envelope expense for mailings with artists. Advertising costs are split: 75% paid by the talent; 25% paid by the representative. For promotional purposes, talent "must go into *American Showcase* each year. Advertises in *American Showcase*.
How to Contact: For first contact, send bio, tearsheets, slides. Reports back within months, only if interested. After initial contact, drop off or mail in appropriate materials for review. Portfolio should include tearsheets, slides, photostats.
Tips: Obtains new talent through recommendations from others or "they contact me. Do not call. Send promo material in the mail. Don't waste time with a résumé—let me see the work."

KIRCHOFF/WOHLBERG, INC. ARTIST REPRESENTATION DIVISION (II), #525, 866 United Nations Plaza, New York NY 10017. (212)644-2020. FAX: (212)223-4387. Director of Operations: John R. Whitman. Commercial illustration and photography representative. Estab. 1930s. Member of SPAR, Society of Illustrators, AIGA, Assn. of American Publishers, Book Builders of Boston, New York Bookbinders' Guild. Represents 50 illustrators and photographers. Elizabeth Ford (juvenile and young adult trade book and textbook illustrators). Specializes in juvenile and young adult trade books and textbooks. Markets include publishing/books.
Will Handle: Illustration and photography (juvenile and young adult).
Terms: Agent receives 25% commission. Exclusive representation to book publishers is usually required. Advertising costs paid 100% by the representative ("for all Kirchoff/Wohlberg advertisements only"). "We will make transparencies from portfolio samples; keep some original work on file." Advertises in *American Showcase, Society of Illustrators Annual*, children's book issue of *Publishers Weekly*.
How to Contact: For first contact, send query letter, "any materials artists feel are appropriate." Will report within 4-6 weeks. "We will contact you for additional materials." Portfolios should include: "whatever artists feel best represents their work. We like to see children's illustration in any style."

BILL AND MAURINE KLIMT (II), 7-U, 15 W. 72nd St., New York NY 10023. (212)799-2231. Contact: Bill or Maurine. Commercial illustration representative. Estab. 1978. Member of Society of Illustrators, Graphic Artists Guild. Represents 14 illustrators. Specializes in paperback covers, young adult, romance, science fiction, mystery, etc. Markets include advertising agencies, corporations/client direct, design firms, editorial/magazines, paper products/greeting cards, publishing/books, sales/promotion firms.
Will Handle: Illustration.
Terms: Agent receives 25% commission, 30% commission for "out of town if we do shoots. Supplying reference on jobs. The artist is responsible for only their own portfolio. We supply all promotion and mailings other than the publications." Exclusive area representation is required. Advertising costs are split: 75% paid by the talent; 25% paid by the representative. For promotional purposes, talent must provide 4×5 or 8×10 mounted transparencies. Advertises in *American Showcase, RSVP*.
How to Contact: For first contact, send direct mail flyer/brochure, and "any image that doesn't have to be returned unless supplied with self-addressed stamped envelope." Reports back within 5 days. After initial contact, call to schedule an appointment to show a portfolio. Portfolios should include professional, mounted transparencies.
Tips: Obtains new talent through recommendations from others and solicitation.

CLIFF KNECHT–ARTIST REPRESENTATIVE (II, III), 309 Walnut Rd., Pittsburgh PA 15202. (412)761-5666. FAX: (412)261-3712. Contact: Cliff Knecht. Commercial illustration representative. Estab. 1972. Represents 10 illustrators, 1 designer/film, 2 fine artists. Markets include advertising agencies, corporations/client direct, design firms, editorial/magazines, paper products/greeting cards, publishing/books, sales/promotion firms.
Will Handle: Illustration.
Terms: Agent receives 25% commission. Advertising costs are split: 75% paid by the talent; 25% paid by the representative. For promotional purposes, talent must provide a direct mail piece. Advertises in *American Showcase*.
How to Contact: For first contact, send résumé, direct mail flyer/brochure, tearsheets, slides. Reports back within 1 week. After initial contact, call to schedule an appointment to show a portfolio. Portfolio should include original art, tearsheets, slides, photographs.
Tips: Obtains new talent through directly or recommendations from others.

PETER KUEHNEL & ASSOCIATES (III), #2308, 30 E. Huron Plaza, Chicago IL 60611-2717. (312)642-6499. FAX: (312)642-0377. Contact: Peter Kuehnel. Commercial illustration, photography and film representative. Estab. 1984. Member of SPAR. Represents 5 illustrators and 2 photographers. Staff includes Denise Redding. Markets include advertising agencies, corporations/client direct, design firms, editorial/magazines and sales/promotion firms.
Will Handle: Illustration, photography, film production.
Terms: Agent receives 25% commission. "Any and all expenses billed to artist involved on a 75/25 basis." Exclusive area representation is required. Advertising costs are split 75% paid by talent; 25% paid by representative. Materials talent must provide for promotion vary case by case. Advertises in *Creative Black Book, The Workbook, Chicago Sourcebook*.
How to Contact: For first contact, send query letter, direct mail flyer/brochure, SASE. Will report within 2 weeks. After initial contact, call to schedule an appointment to show portfolio.
Tips: Obtains new talent through "recommendations from buyers, etc." To obtain representation, "work hard, practice, practice, practice."

FRANK & JEFF LAVATY & ASSOCIATES (II), Suite 1014, 509 Madison Ave., New York NY 10022. (212)355-0910. Commercial illustration and fine art representative. Represents 15 illustrators.
Will Handle: Illustration.
Terms: No information provided.
How to Contact: For first contact, send query letter, direct mail flyer/brochure, tearsheets, slides, SASE. Reports back within 1 week. After initial contact, call to schedule an appointment to show a portfolio. Portfolio should include tearsheets and 8×10 or 4×5 transparencies.
Tips: Obtains new talent through solicitation. "Specialize! Your portfolio must be focused."

PETER & GEORGE LOTT (II), 60 E. 42nd St., New York NY 10165. (212)953-7088. Commercial illustration representative. Estab. 1958. Member of Society of Illustrators, Art Directors Club. Represents 15 illustrators. Markets include advertising agencies, corporations/client direct, design firms, editoraial/ magazines, publishing/books, sales/promotion firms, "all types fashion and beauty accounts (men's, women's children's still life and accessories).
Will Handle: Illustration. "We are currently looking for romance novel illustrators. As a general rule, we're interested in any kind of saleable commercial art."
Terms: Agent receives 25% commission. Advertises in *American Showcase, Creative Black Book, The Workbook* and other publications.
How to Contact: For first contact "call to drop off portfolio."
Tips: "Check with us first to make sure it is a convenient time to drop off a portfolio. Then either drop it off or send it with return postage. The format does not matter, as long as it shows what you can do and what you want to do."

THE MCCANN COMPANY (III), 4113 Rawlins, Dallas TX 75219. (214)526-2252. FAX: (214)526-5565. Contact: Liz McCann or Kari Spence. Commercial illustration and photography representative. Estab. 1978. Member of AIGA. Represents 9 illustrators, 2 photographers. Markets include advertising agencies, corporations/client direct, design firms, editorial/magazines, sales/promotion firms.
Will Handle: Illustration, photography.
Terms: Agent receives 25-35% commission. Advertising costs are split: 75% paid by the talent; 25% paid by the representative. For promotional purposes, talent must provide direct mail pieces, source book advertising. Advertises in *Creative Black Book, The Workbook.*
How to Contact: For first contact, send query letter, direct mail flyer/brochure. Reports back within 1 week, only if interested. After initial contact, write to schedule an appointment to show a portfolio. Portfolio should include tearsheets, transparencies.
Tips: Obtains new talent through "recommendations, finding them in source books, seeing what/who art directors are using."

COLLEEN MCKAY PHOTOGRAPHY (III), #2, 229 E. 5th St., New York NY 10003. (212)598-0469. FAX: (212)598-0762. Contact: Colleen McKay. Commercial editorial and fine art photography representative. Estab. 1985. Member of SPAR. Represents 4 photographers. Staff includes Cara Sadownick. "Our photographers cover a wide range of work from location, still life, fine art, fashion and beauty." Markets include advertising agencies, design firms, editorial/magazines, stores.
Will Handle: Commercial and fine art photography.
Terms: Agent receives 25% commission. Exclusive area representation is required. Advertising costs are split: 75% paid by the talent; 25% paid by the representative. "Promotional pieces are very necessary. They must be current. The portfolio should be established already." Advertises in *Creative Black Book, Select, New York Gold.*
How to Contact: For first contact, send query letter, résumé, bio, direct mail flyer/brochure, tearsheets, slides, photographs. Reports within 2-3 weeks. "I like to respond to everyone but if we're really swamped I may only get a chance to respond to those we're most interested in." Portfolio should include tearsheets, slides, photographs, transparencies (usually for still life).
Tips: Obtains talent through recommendations of other people and solicitations. "I recommend that you look in current resource books and call the representatives that are handling the kind of work that you admire or is similar to your own. Ask these reps for an initial consultation and additional references. Do not be intimidated to appraoch anyone. Even if they do not take you on a meeting with a good rep can prove to be very fruitful! Never give up! A clear, positive attitude is very important."

MARTHA PRODUCTIONS, INC. (III, IV), 4445 Overland Ave., Culver City CA 90230. (213)204-1771. FAX: (213)204-4598. Contact: Martha Spelman. Commercial illustration and graphic design representative. Estab. 1978. Member of Graphic Artists Guild. Represents 20 photographers, 1 designer (studio). Staff includes Michelle Secof (assignment illustration). Specializes in black-and-white and four-color illustration. Markets include advertising agencies, corporations/client direct, design firms, editorial/magazines, paper products/greeting cards.

Will Handle: Illustration.
Terms: Agent receives 30% commission. Exclusive area representation is required. Advertising costs are split: 70% paid by the talent; 30% paid by the representative. For promotional purposes, talent must provide "a minimum of 12 images, 3 4×5″ transparencies of each. (We put the transparencies into our own format.) In addition to the transparencies, we require four-color promo/tearsheets and participation in the bi-annual Martha Productions brochure." Advertises in *The Workbook, Single Image.*
How to Contact: For first contact, send query letter, direct mail flyer/brochure, tearsheets, slides, SASE (if materials are to be returned). Reports back only if interested. After initial contact, drop off or mail in appropriate materials for review. Portfolio should include tearsheets, slides, photographs, photostats.
Tips: Obtains new talent through recommendations and solicitation.

MATTELSON ASSOCIATES LTD. (II), 37 Cary Road, Great Neck NY 11021. (212)684-2974. FAX: (516)466-5835. Contact: Judy Mattelson. Commercial illustration representative. Estab. 1980. Member of SPAR, Graphic Artists Guild. Represents 2 illustrators. Markets include advertising agencies, corporations/client direct, design firms, editorial/magazines, paper products/greeting cards, publishing/books, sales/promotion firms.
Will Handle: Illustration.
Terms: Agent receives 25-30% commission. Exclusive area representation is required. Advertising costs are split: 75% paid by talent; 25% paid by representative. For promotional purposes, talent must provide c-prints and tearsheets, custom-made portfolio. Advertises in *American Showcase, Creative Black Book, RSVP, New York Gold.*
How to Contact: For first contact, send direct mail flyer/brochure, tearsheets and SASE. Will report in 2 weeks, if interested. After initial contact, call to schedule an appointment. Portfolio should include tearsheets, c-prints.
Tips: Obtains new talent through "recommendations from others, solicitation. Illustrator should have ability to do consistent, professional-quality work that shows a singular direction and a variety of subject matter. You should have a portfolio that shows the full range of your current abilities. Work should show strong draftsmanship and technical facility. Person should love their work and be willing to put forth great effort in each assignment."

MAUD ART (II), 25 Gray St., Boston MA 02116. (617)236-1920. FAX: (617)482-5940. Contact: Maud Geng. Commercial illustration and photography representative. Estab. 1982. Represents 7 illustrators, 1 photographer. Markets include advertising agencies, corporations/client direct, design firms, editorial/magazines, publishing/books, sales/promotion firms.
Will Handle: Illustration, photography.
Terms: Agent receives 25-30% commission. Advertising costs are split: 75% paid by the talent; 25% paid by the representative. For promotional purposes, talent must provide portfolios plus promo pieces. Advertises in *Creative Black Book* and *Select.*
How to Contact: For first contact, send tearsheets, slides. After initial contact, drop off or mail in appropriate materials for review. Portfolio should include tearsheets, slides, photographs.
Tips: Obtains new talent through recommendations from others.

MENDOLA ARTISTS (II), 420 Lexington Ave. Penthouse, New York NY 10170. (212)986-5680. FAX: (212)818-1246. Contact: Tim Mendola. Commercial illustration representative. Estab. 1961. Member of Society of Illustrators, Graphic Artists Guild. Represents 60 or more illustrators, 3 photographers. Markets include advertising agencies, corporations/client direct, design firms, editorial/magazines, sales/promotion firms.
Will Handle: Illustration. "We work with the top agencies and publishers. The calibre of talent must be in the top 5%."
Terms: Agent receives 25% commission. Artist pays for all shipping not covered by client and 75% of promotion costs. Exclusive area representation is sometimes required. Advertising costs are split: 75% paid by the talent; 25% paid by the representative. For promotional purposes, talent must provide 8×10 transparencies and usually promotion in at least one source book. Advertises in *American Showcase, Creative Black Book, RSVP, The Workbook.*
How to Contact: For first contact, send direct mail flyer/brochure, tearsheets, slides. Reports within 1 week. After initial contact, drop off or mail in appropriate materials for review. Portfolio should include original art, tearsheets, slides, photographs.

FRANK MEO (II, III), 170 Norfolk St., New York NY 10002. (212)353-0907. FAX: (212)673-86979. Contact: Frank Meo. Commercial photography representative. Estab. 1983. Member of SPAR. Represents 2 photographers. Markets include advertising agencies, corporations/client direct, design firms.

Will Handle: Photography.
Terms: Agent receives 30% commission. Advertising costs are paid by the talent. Advertises in *Creative Black Book*.
How to Contact: For first contact, send query letter, photographs. Will report within 2 days. After initial contact, drop off or mail in appropriate materials for review. Portfolio should include tearsheets, photographs.
Tips: Obtains new talent through recommendations and solicitation.

MONTAGANO & ASSOCIATES (II), #1606, 405 N. Wabash, Chicago IL 60611. (312)527-3283. FAX: (312)527-9091. Contact: David Montagano. Commercial illustration photography and television production representative and broker. Estab. 1983. Member of SPAR. Represents 4 illustrators, 2 photographers. Markets include advertising agencies, corporations/client direct, design firms, editorial/magazines, paper products/greeting cards.
Will Handle: Illustration, photography, design.
Terms: Agent receives 25-30% commission. Advertises in *American Showcase, Sourcebook*.
How to Contact: For first contact, send direct mail flyer/brochure, tearsheets, photographs. Portfolios should include original art, tearsheets, photographs.
Tips: Obtains new talent through recommendations from others.

VICKI MORGAN ASSOCIATES, (III), 194 Third Ave., New York NY 10003. (212)475-0440. Contact: Vicki Morgan. Commercial illustration representative. Estab. 1974. Member of SPAR, Graphic Artists Guild. Represents 11 illustrators. Markets include advertising agencies, corporations/client direct, design firms, editorial/magazines, paper products/greeting cards, publishing/books, sales/promotion firms.
Will Handle: Illustration. "Full-time illustrators only."
Terms: Agent receives 25-30% commission. Exclusive area representation is required. Advertising costs are split: 75% paid by the talent; 25% paid by the representative. "We can develop an initial direct mail piece together. We require samples for three duplicate portfolios; the presentation form is flexible." Advertises in *American Showcase*.
How to Contact: For first contact, send any of the following: direct mail flyer/brochure, tearsheets, slides with SASE. Reports back within weeks only if interested. After initial contact, call to schedule an appointment to show a portfolio. Portfolios should include tearsheets or "anything that shows your work at its best."
Tips: Obtains new talent through "recommendations from artists I represent and mail solicitation."

PAMELA NEAIL ASSOCIATES (III), 27 Bleecker St., New York NY 10012. (212)673-1600. FAX: (212)673-7687. Contact: Pamela Neail. Commercial illustration representative. Estab. 1983. Member of SPAR, Society of Illustrators. Represents 15 illustrators. Markets include advertising agencies, corporations/client direct, design firms, editorial/magazines, publishing/books, fashion and beauty.
Will Handle: Illustration.
Terms: Agent receives 25% commission. Exclusive area representation is required. Advertising costs are split: 75% paid by the talent; 25% paid by the representative. Talent must provide established portfolio; "several copies are helpful." Advertises in *American Showcase, Creative Black Book, RSVP, The Workbook*.
How to Contact: For first contact, send query letter, direct mail flyer/brochure, SASE. "We contact only if interested."
Tips: Obtains new talent through recommendations from others.

THE NEIS GROUP (II), 11440 Oak Dr., Shelbyville MI 49344. (616)672-5756. FAX: (616)672-5757. Contact: Judy Neis. Commercial illustration and photography representative. Estab. 1982. Represents 30 illustrators, 7 photographers. Markets include advertising agencies, design firms, editorial/magazines, publishing/books.

Reps ranked I and II are most open to new, as well as established talents. Those ranked III prefer established talent with references from others in the art or photography field.

Will Handle: Illustration, photography.
Terms: Agent receives 25% commission. Advertising costs are split: 75% paid by talent; 25% paid by the representative. Advertises in *The American Showcase*.
How to Contact: For first contact, send direct mail flyer/brochure, tearsheets, photographs. Reports within 5 days. After initial contact, drop off or mail in appropriate materials for review. Portfolio should include tearsheets, photographs.
Tips: "I am mostly sought out by the talent. If I pursue, I call and request a portfolio review."

PACIFIC DESIGN STUDIO (II), P.O. Box 1396, Hilo HI 96721. (808)935-6056. FAX: (808)966-7232. Contact: Francine H. Siedlecki. Commercial illustration and photography representative. Also handles fine art, graphic design and is an illustration or photography broker. Estab. 1980. Represents 4 illustrators, 4 photographers, 2 designers, 12 fine artists (includes 3 sculptors). "This is a small 3-person office." Specializes in "art and design of the Hawaiian Islands; the Big Island in particular." Markets include advertising agencies, editorial/magazines, paper products/greeting cards, t-shirt manufacturers and resorts.
Will Handle: Illustration, photography, fine art. Looking for "underwater artists, ocean and sea life artists, Pacific Rim artists, Hawaiiana design."
Terms: Agent receives 15-20% commission. Charges for "real costs of freight, etc., which come off the top of a sale." Exclusive area representation is "preferred, but not required." For promotional purposes, "transparencies are required, full-color tearsheet or mailer is preferred; artist must have minimum of 12 pieces for sale."
How to Contact: For first contact, send query letter, résumé, bio, direct mail flyer/brochure, tearsheets, slides, SASE. Reports back within 2 weeks, only if interested, "depending on what is sent for first contact." After initial contact, write to schedule an appointment to show a portfolio or drop off or mail in appropriate materials for review. Portfolios should include original art, slides, photographs, transparencies.
Tips: Obtains new talent through studio visits, recommendations, client reference, architect reference, local news and print media. "Send only your best work and be patient. Good representation requires good timing and creativity as well as client contacts."

JACKIE PAGE (III), 219 E. 69th St., New York NY 10021. (212)772-0346. Commercial photography representative. Estab. 1987. Member of SPAR and Ad Club. Represents 10 photographers. Markets include advertising agencies.
Will Handle: Photography.
Terms: "Details given at a personal interview." Advertises in *The Workbook*.
How to Contact: For first contact send direct mail flyer/brochure. After initial contact, call to schedule an appointment to show a portfolio. Portfolios should include tearsheets, slides, photographs.
Tips: Obtains new talent through recommendations from others and mailings.

JOANNE PALULIAN (III), 18 McKinley St., Rowayton CT 06853. (203)866-3734 or (212)581-8338. FAX: (203)857-0842. Commercial illustration representative. Estab. 1976. Member of SPAR. Represents 7 illustrators. Markets include advertising agencies, corporations/client direct, design firms, editorial/magazines, sales/promotion firms.
Will Handle: Illustration.
Terms: Agent receives 30% commission. Exclusive area representation is required. Advertising costs are split: 75% paid by the talent; 25% paid by the representative. For promotional purposes, talent must provide a portfolio and promotional materials. Advertises in *American Showcase, Creative Black Book*.
How to Contact: For first contact send direct mail flyer/brochure. Reports within 2 days, only if interested. After initial contact, drop off or mail in appropriate materials for review. Portfolio should include tearsheets, transparencies (4×5 or 8×10) of original art.
Tips: "Talent usually contacts me, follows up with materials that I can keep. If interest is there, I interview. Do not send materials without my consent. Include return packaging with necessary postage. Be courteous and friendly. You are asking someone to give you his or her time and attention for your benefit."

A IV ranking indicates reps who specialize in a particular type of illustration or photography such as fashion illustration or food photography.

PARALLAX (IV), #5805, 350 Fifth Ave., New York NY 10118. (212)695-0445. FAX: (212)629-5624. Contact: Lylla Demeny. Commercial/editorial photography representative. Estab. 1989. Represents 5 photographers. Specializes in fashion/beauty photography and production; represents hair/make-up also. Markets include advertising agencies, editorial/magazines, catalogs.
Will Handle: Photography.
Terms: Agent receives 25% commission. Splits costs for messengers and promo pieces. Exclusive area representation is required. Advertising costs are split: 50% paid by the talent; 50% paid by the representative. For promotional purposes, talent must provide promo piece "or one can be designed."
How to Contact: For first contact, send direct mail flyer/brochure. Reports back within 2 weeks. After initial contact, drop off or mail in appropriate materials for review. Portfolios should include original art, tearsheets.
Tips: Obtains new talent through recommendations or from published work.

■**PHOTO AGENTS LTD. (III)**, 113 E. 31st St., New York NY 10016. (212)683-5777. FAX: (212)779-3697. Contact: Gary Lerman. Commercial photography representative. Estab. 1973. Member of SPAR. Represents 2-3 photographers. Markets include advertising agencies, corporations/client direct, design firms, editorial/magazines, publishing/books, sales/promotion firms.
Will Handle: Photography. Looking for specialties in "kids or portraits."
Terms: Agent receives 25-30% commission. Charges other fees which are "defined with talent." Exclusive area representation is required. Advertises in *Creative Black Book*.
How to Contact: For first contact, send direct mail flyer/brochure, "follow with call." Reports back within 1 week, only if interested. After initial contact, call to schedule an appointment to show a portfolio. Portfolio should include tearsheets, photographs.
Tips: Obtains new talent through referrals. "Don't rush into representation. Look for a good and lasting relationship!"

MARIA PISCOPO (IV), 2038 Calvert Ave., Costa Mesa CA 92626-3520. (714)556-8133. FAX: (714)556-0899. Contact: Maria Piscopo. Commercial photography representative. Estab. 1978. Member of SPAR, Women in Photography, Society of Illustrative Photographers. Represents 5 photographers. Markets include advertising agencies, design firms.
Will Handle: Photography. Looking for "unique, unusual styles; handle only established photography."
Terms: Agent receives 25-30% commission. Exclusive area representation is required. Advertising costs are split: 75% paid by the talent; 25% paid by the representative. For promotional purposes, talent must provide one show portfolio, three travelling portfolios, leave-behinds and at least six new promo pieces per year. Advertises in *American Showcase, The Workbook, New Media*.
How to Contact: For first contact, send query letter, direct mail flyer/brochure, SASE. Reports within 2 weeks, only if interested. After initial contact, write to schedule an appointment to show a portfolio. Portfolio should include 4×5 or 8×10 transparencies.
Tips: Obtains new talent through personal referral and photo magazine articles. "Be very business-like, organized, professional and follow the above instructions!"

PUBLISHERS' GRAPHICS (II, III, IV), 251 Greenwood Ave., Bethel CT 06801. (203)797-8188. FAX: (203)798-8848. Commercial illustration representative for juvenile markets. Estab. 1970. Member of Graphic Artists Guild, Author's Guild Inc.. Staff includes Paige C. Gillies (President, selects illustrators, develops talent); Susan P. Schwarzchild (sales manager); Diane Carlson (field representative). Specializes in children's book illustration. Markets include design firms, editorial/magazines, paper products/greeting cards, publishing/books, sales/promotion firms.
Will Handle: Illustration.
Terms: Agent receives 25% commission. Exclusive area representation is required. For promotional purposes, talent must provide original art, proofs and photocopies "to start. The assignments generate most sample/promotional material thereafter unless there is a stylistic change in the work." Advertises in *Literary Market Place*.
How to Contact: For first contact send résumé, photocopies, SASE. Reports back within 6 weeks. After initial contact, "We will contact them. We don't respond to phone inquiries." Portfolios should include original art, tearsheets, photocopies.

Reps ranked I-IV are actively seeking new talents. Those ranked V or those who prefer not to be listed have been included to inform you they are not currently looking for new talent.

Tips: Obtains new talent through "clients recommending our agency to artists. We ask for referrals from our illustrators. We receive submissions by mail."

GERALD & CULLEN RAPP, INC. (III), 108 E. 35th St., New York NY 10016. (212)889-3337. FAX: (212)889-3341. Contact: Carla Hansen. Commercial illustration, photography and graphic design representative. Estab. 1945. Member of SPAR, Society of Illustrators, Graphic Artists Guild. Represents 25 illustrators, 2 photographers, 1 designer. Markets include advertising agencies, corporations/client direct, design firms, editorial/magazines, paper products/greeting cards, publishing/books, sales/promotion firms.
Will Handle: Illustration, photography.
Terms: Agent receives 25-30% commission. Exclusive area representation is required. Advertising costs are split: 50% paid by the talent; 50% paid by the representative. Advertises in *American Showcase, Creative Black Book, The Workbook,* and *CA, Print, Art Director* magazines. "Conducts active direct mail program, costs split 50-50."
How to Contact: For first contact, send query letter, direct mail flyer/brochure. Reports back within 1 week. After initial contact, call to schedule an appointment to show a portfolio. Portfolio should include tearsheets, slides.
Tips: Obtains new talent through recommendations from others, solicitations.

REDMOND REPRESENTS (III), 8634 Chelsea Bridge Way, Lutherville MD 21093. (301)823-7422. Contact: Sharon Redmond. Commercial illustration and photography representative. Estab. 1987. Markets include advertising agencies, corporations/client direct, design firms.
Will Handle: Illustration, photography.
Terms: Agent receives 30% commission. Exclusive area representation is required. Advertising costs and expenses are split: 50% paid by the talent; 50% paid by the representative. For promotional purposes, talent must provide a small portfolio (easy to Federal Express) and at least 6 direct mail pieces (with fax number included). Advertises in *American Showcase, Creative Black Book.*
How to Contact: For first contact, send photocopies. Will report within 1 week. After initial contact, representative will call talent to set an appointment.
Tips: Obtains new talent through recommendations from others, advertising a "black book," etc. "Even if I'm not taking in new talent, I do want *photocopies* sent of new work. You never know when an ad agency will require a different style of illustration/photography and it's always nice to refer to my files."

KAY REESE & ASSOCIATES (III), 225 Central Park W., New York NY 10024. (212)799-1133. FAX: (212)533-2509. Illustration or photography broker. Estab. 1971. Member of PAI, ASMP. Represents 20 photographers. Specializes in worldwide corporate photojournalism. Markets include corporations/client direct, design firms, sales/promotion firms.
Terms: Agent receives 30% commission (per SPAR). Exclusive area representation is required. Advertising costs are split: 50% paid by the talent; 50% paid by the representative. For promotional purposes, talent must provide portfolios with original material and tearsheets of published work (color and black and white).
How to Contact: For first contact, send query letter only, "please!" Reports within 2 weeks, only if interested. After initial contact, call or write to schedule an appointment to show a portfolio. Portfolio should include tearsheets, slides, photographs.
Tips: Obtains new talent through referrals.

REPERTOIRE (III), Suite 104-338, 5521 Greenville, Dallas TX 75206. (214)369-6990. FAX: (214)369-6938. Contact: Larry Lynch (photography) or Andrea Lynch (illustration). Commercial illustration and photography representative and broker. Estab. 1974. Member of SPAR. Represents 12 illustrators and 6 photographers. Specializes in "importing specialized talent into the Southwest." Markets include advertising agencies, corporations/client direct, design firms, editorial/magazines.
Will Handle: Illustration, photography.
Terms: Agent receives 25% commission. Exclusive area representation is required. Advertising costs are split: printing costs are paid by the talent; distribution costs are paid by the representative. Talent must provide promotion, both direct mail and a national directory. Advertises in *The Workbook.*
How to Contact: For first contact, send direct mail flyer/brochure, tearsheets. Will report within 1 month. After initial contact, write to schedule an appointment or drop off or mail appropriate materials for review. Portfolio should include tearsheets, slides, photographs.
Tips: Obtains new talent through referrals, solicitations. "Have something worthwhile to show."

RIDGEWAY ARTISTS REPRESENTATIVE (II), 444 Lentz Ct., Lansing MI 48917. (517)371-3086. FAX: (517)371-5160. Contact: Edwin Bonnen. Commercial illustration and photography representative. Estab. 1985. Member of SPAR. Represents 1 illustrator, 2 photographers. Markets include advertising agencies, corporations/client direct, design firms, editorial/magazines.

Will Handle: Illustration, photography. "We are primarily looking for individuals who have developed a distinctive style, whether they be a photographer or illustrator. Photographers must have an area they specialize in. We want artists who are pros in the commercial words; i.e. working with tight deadlines in sometimes less than ideal situations."

Terms: Agent receives 25% commission in the state of Michigan, 35% out of state. Exclusive area representation is required. Advertising costs are split: 75% paid by the talent; 25% paid by the representative. For promotional purposes, talent "should be prepared to invest at least $1,000 on your portfolio. We will develop a yearly marketing plan that focuses on where you want your career to go. Plan on spending approximately 10-15% of yearly gross receipts on advertising."

How to Contact: For first contact, send query letter, résumé, direct mail flyer/brochure, tearsheets, SASE "if they want material returned." Reports within 2 weeks, only if interested. After initial contact, call to schedule an appointment to show a portfolio. Portfolios should include thumbnails, roughs, original art, slides, photographs. "Send it."

Tips: "We obtain talent primarily through their solicitation of our services." If interested in obtaining representation, "approach all representatives as you would a potential client. Don't waste their time. Have an organized portfolio that shows off your talent and the direction you want to go. Show new material often. Put them on your mailing list. Follow-up, follow-up, follow-up."

ARLENE ROSENBERG (II), 377 W. 11th St., New York NY 10014. (212)675-7983. FAX: (212)691-1318. Contact: Arlene Rosenberg. Commercial photography representative. Estab. 1980. Member of SPAR. Represent 2 photographers. Staff includes Erin Wilheim, assistant. Markets include advertising agencies, design firms, editorial/magazines.

Will Handle: Photography.

Terms: Agent receives 25% commission. Exclusive area representation is required. Advertising costs are split: 75% paid by the talent; 25% paid by the representative. "Would review with talent" what to provide a portfolio. Advertises in *Creative Black Book*.

How to Contact: For first contact, send a direct mail flyer/brochure. Will report on queries within 5 day. After initial contact, call to schedule an appointment to show a portfolio. Portfolio should include tearsheets and chromes.

Tips: Obtains new talent through recommendations.

ROSENTHAL REPRESENTS (IV), 3443 Wade St., Los Angeles CA 90066. (213)390-9595. FAX: (213)306-6878. Commercial illustration representative and licensing agent for artists who do advertising, entertainment, action/sports, children's humorous, storyboard, animal, graphic, floral, realistic, impressionistic and game packaging art." Estab. 1979. Member of SPAR, Society of Illustrators, Graphic Artists Guild, Women in Design and Art Directors Club. Represents 100 illustrators, 3 photographers, 2 designers and 5 fine artists. Specializes in game packaging, personalities, licensing, merchandise art and storyboard artists. Markets include advertising agencies, corporations/client direct, paper products/greeting cards, sales/promotion firms, licensees and manufacturers.

Will Handle: Illustration.

Terms: Agent receives 25-30% as a rep; 40% as a licensing agent. Exclusive area representation is required. Advertising costs are 100% paid by the talent. For promotion purposes, talent must provide 1-2 sets of transparencies (mounted and labeled), 10 sets of slides of your best work (labeled with name on each slide) and 1-3 promos. Advertises in *American Showcase*, *Creative Black Book* and *The Workbook*.

How to Contact: For first contact, send direct mail flyer/brochure, tearsheets, slides, photocopies, photostats and SASE. Will report within 1 week. After initial contact, call to schedule an appointment to show a portfolio. Portfolios should include tearsheets, slides, photographs and photocopies.

Tips: Obtains new talent through seeing their work in an advertising book or at an award show.

■**RICHARD SALZMAN (II, III)**, 716 Sanchez St., San Francisco CA 94114. (415)285-8267. FAX: (415)285-8268. Contact: Richard Salzman, Nicola Theilen. Commercial illustration representative. Estab. 1982. Member of SPAR, Graphic Artists Guild, AIGA, SFCA. Represents 14 illustrators. Markets include advertising agencies, corporations/client direct, design firms, editorial/magazines, publishing books.

Will Handle: Illustration. "We're always looking for the next superstar and are also interested in digital art or other 'new' media."

Terms: Agent receives 30% commission. Charges for "portfolios." Talent is required to pay cost of the portfolio (6 copies) created by the representative. Exclusive area representation is required (all of USA). Advertising costs are split: 70% paid by the talent; 30% paid by the representative. "We share promotional costs." Advertises in *American Showcase*, *Creative Black Book*, *The Workbook*.

How to Contact: For first contact, send tearsheets, slides, photocopies. After initial contact, call to schedule an appointment to show a portfolio.
Tips: "We receive 20 to 30 solicitors a week. We sign an average of one new artist a year. Solicit to reps the way you would to a 'client' or art director."

TRUDY SANDS & ASSOCIATES (III), 233 Yorktown, Dallas TX 75208. (214)748-8663. FAX: (214)748-4965. Contact: Trudy. Commercial illustration and photography representative. Estab. 1984. Member of SPAR and AIGA. Represents 10 illustrators, 1 photographer. Markets include advertising agencies, corporations/client direct, design firms, editorial/magazines, publishing/books.
Will Handle: Illustration, photography.
Terms: Agent receives 25% commission. Exclusive area representation is required. Advertising costs are split: 75% paid by the talent; 25% paid by the representative. For promotional purposes, talent must provide portfolio. "Portfolios must be a certain format. Rep chooses samples, two new pieces a month, direct mail pieces and leave-behinds." Advertises in *RSVP, The Workbook, Creative Illustration Book.*
How to Contact: For making first contact, send tearsheets. Reports back within 2 weeks, only if interested. After initial contact, call to schedule an appointment to show a portfolio, or drop off or mail appropriate materials for review. Portfolio should include tearsheets, photocopies.
Tips: Obtains new talent through recommendations. "Follow up your mailer with a phone call. If the rep is interested, be persistent in trying to set up appointment. Do not expect the rep to call you back. Ask art directors which rep they like to work with. Look at source books to see who the rep is handling. Know something about the rep before you call. Don't just call from a list."

THE SCHUNA GROUP, INC. (V), 700 3rd St., #301, Minneapolis MN 55415. Representative not currently seeking new talent.

LAURENS R. SCHWARTZ, ESQUIRE (II, III), Suite 15D, 5 E. 22nd St., New York NY 10010-5315. (212)228-2614. FAX: (212)228-2614. Commercial illustration, design, photography and fine art representative. Estab. 1984. Represents 100 artists and 2 photographers. Specializes in use of computer in photography, art, illustration, video, film, etc. Markets include advertising agencies, editorial/magazines, publishing/books, galleries. Fine art markets include art publishers, corporate collections, museums.
Will Handle: Illustration, photography, fine art.
Terms: Commission is negotiable. Exclusive area representation is required. Advertising costs are negotiated.
How to Contact: For first contact, send query letter, résumé, bio, direct mail flyer/brochure, tearsheets, slides, photographs, photostats, SASE. Will report within 2 weeks, if SASE enclosed. After initial contact, "we contact the talent." Portfolios should include tearsheets, slides, photographs, photostats.
Tips: Obtains new talent through referrals.

FREDA SCOTT, INC. (III), 244 9th St., San Francisco CA 94103. (415)621-2992. FAX: (415)621-5202. Contact: Barry Guillfoil or Freda Scott. Commercial illustration and photography representative. Estab. 1980. Member of SPAR. Represents 7 illustrators, 5 photographers. Markets include advertising agencies, corporations/client direct, design firms, editorial/magazines, paper products/greeting cards, publishing/books, sales/promotion firms.
Will Handle: Illustration, photography.
Terms: Agent receives 25% commission. Advertising costs are split: 75% paid by the talent; 25% paid by the representative. For promotional purposes, talent must provide "promotion piece and ad in a directory. I also need at least 3 portfolios." Advertises in *American Showcase, Creative Black Book, The Workbook.*
How to Contact: For first contact, send direct mail flyer/brochure, tearsheets, SASE. If you send transparencies, reports within 1 week, if interested. "You need to make follow up calls." After initial contact, call to schedule an appointment to show a portfolio or drop off or mail in appropriate materials for review. Portfolio should include tearsheets, photographs, 4×5's or 8×10's.
Tips: Obtains new talent sometimes through recommendations, sometimes solicitation. "If you are seriously interested in getting repped, keep sending promos—once every 6 months or so. Do it yourself a year or two until you know what you need a rep to do."

DAVID SCROGGY AGENCY, (III), 2124 Froude St., San Diego CA 92107-2315. (619)222-2476. FAX: (619)544-0743. Contact: David Scroggy. Commercial illustration representative and comic book packages. Estab. 1981. Member of Society of Illustrators, Communicating Arts Group of San Diego. Represents 7 illustrators. Specializes in illustration only. Markets include advertising agencies, corporations/

client direct, design firms, editorial/magazines, paper products/greeting cards, publishing/books, comic books.
Will Handle: Illustration and comic books.
Terms: Agent receives 25% commission. Advertising costs are split: 75% paid by the talent; 25% paid by the representative. For promotional purposes, talent must provide "samples of professional work done for clients (i.e., advertising agency, magazine/book publisher, corporation, etc.)." Advertises in *American Showcase, RSVP, San Diego Creative Directory.*
How to Contact: For first contact, send query letter, direct mail flyer/brochure, tearsheets. Reports within 3 weeks. After initial contact, mail in appropriate materials for review. Portfolio should include tearsheets, photographs.
Tips: "Develop a truly unique and marketable style."

■**SOLDAT & CARDONI, (II),** Suite 1008, 307 N. Michigan, Chicago IL 60601. (312)201-9662. FAX: (312)236-5752. Contact: Rick Soldat or Pam Cardoni. Commercial illustration and photography representative. Estab. 1990. Member of SPAR. Represents 2 illustrators, 4 photographers. Markets include advertising agencies, corporations/client direct, design firms, publishing/books, sales/promotion firms.
Will Handle: Illustration, photography.
Terms: Agent receives 25-30% commission. Charges for postage, shipping, long-distance travel. Exclusive area representation in the Midwest is required. Advertising costs are split: 75% paid by the talent; 25% paid by the representative. For promotional purposes, talent must provide "a promo for direct mail and other purposes." Advertises in *The Workbook* and *Chicago Talent Sourcebook.*
How to Contact: For first contact, send query letter, tearsheets. Reports within 1 week. After initial contact, call to schedule an appointment to show a portfolio. Portfolio should include original art, tearsheets, slides, photographs.
Tips: Obtains new talent through "recommendations from others, talent search, talent calling us directly."

JANICE STEFANSKI REPRESENTS, (II), 2022 Jones St., San Francisco CA 94133. (415)928-0457. FAX: (415)775-6337. Commercial illustration representative. Estab. 1983. Member of Society of Illustrators. Represents 10 illustrators, 1 photographer, 1 designer. Markets include advertising agencies, corporations/client direct, design firms.
Will Handle: Illustration.
Terms: Agent receives 25% commission. Exclusive area representation is required. Advertising costs are split: 75% paid by the talent; 25% paid by the representative. Advertises in *American Showcase.*
How to Contact: For first contact send, tearsheets, photocopies or photostats. Reports within 2 weeks. Portfolio should include roughs, original art, tearsheets.

■**STORYBOARDS, INC. (IV),** 4052 Del Rey Ave., Venice CA 90292. (213)305-1998. FAX: (213)305-1810. Contact: Roger Shank or Kathy Stewart. Commercial illustration representative. Estab. 1979. Represents 40-50 illustrators. Staff includes Kathy Stewart (general manager); Roger Shank (creative director/coordinator); Mark Stroh (sales representative); Christine Carrillo (coordinator); Chris Hawkins (accountant). Specializes in storyboards and comps for advertising agencies; shooting boards for commercial production companies and feature films; production illustration; set sketches. Markets include advertising agencies, corporations/client direct, design firms, sales/promotion firms, commercial production companies and feature film companies.
Will Handle: Artists "who have a sense for visual continuity and exceptional drawing abilities. Marker rendering abilities a plus."
Terms: Agent receives 10-30% commission. Charges $1,500 "annual ceiling for corporate promotional materials and advertising." Exclusive area representation is required. Advertising costs are split: 70% paid by the talent; 30% paid by the representative. For promotional purposes, talent must provide "a promo card, a portfolio sheet and updated photocopies are all required. Storyboards, Inc. oversees and facilitates the production of all required materials." Advertises *The Workbook, Daily Variety, Backstage, Adweek, LA-411, Creative Handbook, E.T.C.*
How to Contact: For first contact, send fax, color photocopy, originals. Reports back within 5 days. After initial contact, call to schedule an appointment to show a portfolio or drop off or mail appropriate materials for review. Portfolio should include thumbnails, roughs, original art, photocopies.

■ *A solid box indicates reps who charge a fee for expenses or who charge special fees in addition to commission and advertising costs.*

Tips: Obtains new talent through "our ads in the trades or our clients refer them or referrals from other artists." If interested in obtaining representation, "don't give up. If you can't find representation, do it on your own. If you can show a representative that you were able to form a client base, they'll feel better about taking a chance on you. It is not easy, but if you want it badly enough, if you're tenacious, if you're talented, and you refuse to quit, you can realize your goals."

STUDIO ARTISTS/DON PEPPER (II), 638 S. Van Ness Ave., Los Angeles CA 90005. (213)385-4585. FAX: (213)381-6763. Contact: Don Pepper. Illustration or photography broker. Estab. 1984. Represents 5 illustrators, 2 designers. Specializes in "full range of styles plus handlettering, layout and design."
Will Handle: Illustration, design.
Terms: No information provided.
How to Contact: For first contact, send a bio, direct mail flyer/brochure, tearsheets. Will report in "a few" days, if interested. After initial contact, call to schedule an appointment, drop off or mail in appropriate materials for review. Portfolio should include "whatever best represents your capabilities."
Tips: Obtains new talent through solicitation.

JOSEPH TRIBELLI DESIGNS, LTD. (II, IV), 254-33 Iowa Rd., Great Neck NY 11020. (516)482-2699. Contact: Joseph Tribelli. Representative of textile designers only. Estab. 1988. Member of Graphic Artists Guild. Represents 9 designers. Specializes in textile surface design for apparel (women and men). "All designs are on paper."
Will Handle: Textile design for apparel.
Terms: Agent receives 40% commission. Exclusive area representation is required.
How to Contact: "Telephone first." Reports back within 2 weeks. After initial contact, drop off or mail appropriate materials. Portfolio should include original art.
Tips: Obtains new talent through "placing ads, recommendations. I am interested in only textile designers who can paint on paper. Do not apply unless you have a flair for fashion."

TRLICA/REILLY: REPS (II), P.O. Box 13025, Charlotte NC 28270. (704)372-6007. FAX: same. Contact: Jack Trlica or Kerry Reilly. Commercial illustration and photography representative. Estab. 1990. Represents 16 illustrators, 3 photographers. Markets include advertising agencies, corporations/client direct, design firms, editorial/magazines.
Will Handle: Illustration, photography. Looking for computer graphics, freehand, etc.
Terms: Agent receives 25% commission. Exclusive area representation is required. Advertising costs are split: 75% paid by the talent; 25% paid by the representative. For promotional purposes, talent must provide printed leave-behind samples, at least two pages. Preferred format is 9×12 pages, portfolio work on 4×5 transparencies. Advertises in *American Showcase*.
How to Contact: For first contact, send direct mail flyer/brochure or samples of work. Reports within 2 weeks. After initial contact, call to schedule an appointment to show a portfolio or drop off or mail appropriate materials. Portfolio should include original art, tearsheets, slides, 4×5 transparencies.
Tips: Obtains new talent through recommendations from others. "It's essential to have printed samples—a lot of printed samples."

URSULA INC., (V), 63 Adrian Ave., Marble Hill (Bronx) NY 10463. Representative not currently seeking new talent.

PHILIP M. VELORIC, ARTIST REPRESENTATIVE (II), 128 Beechtree Dr., Broomall PA 19008. (215)356-0362. FAX: (215)353-7531. Contact: Philip M. Veloric. Commercial illustration representative. Estab. 1963. Member of Art Directors Club of Philadelphia. Represents 22 illustrators. "Most of my business is from textbook publishing, but not all of it." Markets include advertising agencies, design firms, publishing/books.
Will Handle: Illustration. "Artists should be able to do (and have samples to show) all ethnic children (getting ages right; tell a story; develop a character); earth science, life and physical science; some trade books also."
Terms: Agent receives 25% commission. Exclusive area representation is required. Advertising costs are split: 75% paid by the talent; 25% paid by the representative. Advertises in *American Showcase*, *RSVP*.
How to Contact: For first contact, call. After initial contact, call to schedule an appointment to show a portfolio. Portfolio should include original art, tearsheets, photocopies, laser copies.
Tips: Obtains new talent through recommendations from others.

WARNER & ASSOCIATES (IV), 1425 Belleview Ave., Plainfield NJ 07060. (201)755-7236. Contact: Bob Warner. Commercial illustration and photography representative. Estab. 1986. Represents 4 illustrators, 4 photographers. "My specialized markets are advertising agencies that service pharmaceutical, medical, health-care clients."
Will Handle: Illustration, photography. Looking for medical illustrators; microscope photographers (photomicrography); science illustrators; special effects photographers.
Terms: Agent receives 25% commission. "Promo pieces and portfolios obviously are needed; who makes up what and at what costs and to whom, varies widely in this business."
How to Contact: For first contact send query letter "or phone me." Reports back within days. Portfolio should include "anything that talent considers good sample material."
Tips: Obtains new talent "by hearsay and recommendations. Also, specialists in my line of work often hear about my work from art directors and they call me."

WARSHAW BLUMENTHAL, INC. (III), 400 E. 56th St., New York NY 10022. (212)759-7171. FAX: (212)867-4154. Contact: Andrea Warshaw. Commercial illustration representative. Estab. 1988. Member of SPAR. Represents 20 illustrators. "We service the ad agencies in offering high-tech storyboard, comp art and animatic art for testing."
Terms: No information provided.
How to Contact: For first contact, send resume, direct mail flyer/brochure, photocopies. Will report within 2 days. After initial contact, call to schedule an appointment or drop off or mail appropriate materials for review. Portfolios should include "finished-looking animatic art and/or a reel."
Tips: Obtains new talent through word of mouth and recommendations.

WASHINGTON-ARTIST REPRESENTATIVES (II), Suite 152, 4901 Broadway, San Antonio TX 78209. (512)822-1336. FAX: (512)822-1375. Contact: Dick Washington. Commercial illustration and photography representative. Estab. 1983. Member of CASSA. Represents 10 illustrators, 2 photographers.
Terms: No information provided.
How to Contact: For first contact, send tearsheets. Reports within 2 weeks, only if interested. After initial contact, call to schedule an appointment. Portfolio should include original art, tearsheets, slides.
Tips: Usually obtains, new talent through recommendations and solicitation. "Make sure that you are ready for a real commitment and relationship. It's an important step for an artist, and should be taken seriously. Don't allow an art rep to sign you to an exclusive contract. You will want representation in all the major markets eventually."

ELYSE WEISSBERG (II,III), 299 Pearl St., New York NY 10038. (212)406-2566. FAX: (212)571-7568. Contact: Elyse Weissberg. Commercial photography representative. Estab. 1982. Member of SPAR. Represents 2 photographers. Markets include advertising agencies, corporations/client direct, design firms, editorial/magazines, publishing/books, sales/promotion firms.
Will Handle: Photography. "I'm not looking for talent now, but I'm always interested in seeing what's out there."
Terms: "Each of my contacts are negotiated separately." No specific promotional requirements. "Some younger talents I have represented did not have stationery when we started together—my only requirement is ambition." Advertises in *American Showcase, Creative Black Book, The Workbook*.
How to Contact: For first contact, send direct mail flyer/brochure. Will report in 1 week, if interested. After initial contact, drop off or mail in appropriate materials for review. Portfolio should include tearsheets, photographs.
Tips: Obtains new talent through recommendations, direct mail. "Don't give up! Someone is always looking for new talent."

SUSAN WELLS ASSOCIATES (III), 5134 Timber Trail NE, Atlanta GA 30342. (404)255-1430. FAX: (404)255-3449. Contact: Susan Wells. Commercial illustration representative. Estab. 1981. Represents 17 illustrators. Markets include advertising agencies, corporations/client direct, design firms.

The needs of art and photography reps are constantly changing! If you are using this book and it is 1993 or later, buy the newest edition of Guide to Literary Agents and Art/ Photo Reps *at your favorite book or art supply store or order directly from* Writer's Digest Books.

Will Handle: Illustration.
Terms: Agent receives 25% commission. Exclusive area representation is required. Advertising costs are split: 75% paid by talent; 25% paid by representative. For promotional purposes, talent must provide matted 4x5 or 8x10 transparencies for portfolio presentation, 8½x11 promotional piece for direct mail. Advertises in *Creative Illustration Book*.
How to Contact: For first contact, send a query letter and direct mail flyer/brochure, slides and SASE. Will report in 6 weeks, if interested. After initial contact, write to schedule an appointment. Portfolio should include 4x5 or 8x10 transparencies or laminated tearsheets.
Tips: Obtains new talent through "recommendations or direct contact initiated by artist."

WINSTON WEST, LTD. (III, IV), 195 S. Beverly Dr., Beverly Hills CA 90213. (212)275-2858. FAX: (213)275-0917. Contact: Bonnie Winston. Commercial photography representative (fashion/entertainment). Estab. 1986. Represents 8 photographers. Specializes in "editorial fashion and commercial advertising (with an edge)." Markets include advertising agencies, client direct, editorial/magazines.
Will Handle: Photography.
Terms: Agent receives 25% commission. Charges for courier services. Exclusive area representation is required. Advertising costs are split: 75% paid by the talent; 25% paid by the representative. Advertises by direct mail.
How to Contact: For first contact, send direct mail flyer/brochure, photographs, photocopies, photostats. Reports back within days, only if interested. After initial contact, call to schedule an appointment to show a portfolio. Portfolios should include tearsheets.
Tips: Obtains new talent through "recommendations from the modeling agencies. If you are a new fashion photographer or a photographer that's relocated recently, develop relationships with the modeling agencies in town. They are invaluable sources for client leads and know all the reps."

Additional Commercial Art and Photography Reps

The following representatives have full listings in other sections of this book. These reps and agents have indicated they are *primarily* interested in handling book manuscripts or the work of fine artists, but are also interested in illustrators or photographers. After reading the listing (you can find the page number in the Listings Index), send them a query to obtain more information on their needs and artwork or photography submission policies.

Ajlouny Agency, The Joseph S.
Arts Counsel Inc.
Authors And Artists Resource Center/Tarc Literary Agency, The
Brown Literary Agency, Inc., Andrea
Corporate Art Associates, Ltd.

Curtis Bruce Agency, The
Elek Associates, Peter
Gusay Literary Agency, The Charlotte
Hamersfield Agency, The
Nathan, Ruth
Norma-Lewis Agency, The

Northwest Literary Services
Rubenstein, Literary Agent, Pesha
Spatt, Esq., David M.
Storer, Richard R.
ToLease Lautrec
Wecksler-Incomco

Fine Art Reps

While much of what we've said about dealing with reps in the intro to the Commercial Art/Photo Reps section holds true for fine art reps, there are some differences. First of all there are fewer "official" fine art reps. Yet many gallery owners, art consultants, art publishers and art distributors also act as reps for the artists they handle.

Since there are fewer fine art reps, there are also fewer established norms. And fewer norms mean more room for variety in the way reps work. Some promote their talent by presenting portfolios or slide shows to clients; others hold exhibitions; others maintain extensive slide files. It's important to ask a potential rep for as much information about how they work as possible so that you can make the best informed decision.

What do fine art reps do?

Fine art reps promote the work of fine artists, sculptors, craftspeople and fine art photographers to galleries and museums, but they also sell to corporate art collectors, developers, interior designers, art publishers and even some book publishers. They may operate their own gallery as well or they may be in the art publishing or other art-related business.

In general, fine art reps call on clients with your portfolio or other promotional material. Like commercial reps, they may have certain promotional requirements. Most do not advertise in commercial talent books, but they do advertise in art publications—those seen by decorators, gallery owners and collectors.

Although some fine art reps' terms are identical to those of a commercial rep, most take a higher commission and do not charge talent for advertising costs. Most require an exclusive area of representation. In addition to selling the work you've already created, many arrange commission work for you.

Why get a fine art rep?

Reps can help by taking over the sales, marketing and other business aspects of your work so you can devote more time to the creative process. They can handle the recordkeeping, billing and other paper work—keeping track of the money owed you and the particulars of who is considering your work.

Most galleries do an excellent job of promoting and selling work within their immediate areas. Those situated to attract tourists help to "spread the word" about your work across the country, but a rep can broaden your exposure considerably. Depending on the rep, you may find yourself working with clients on a national or even international level.

Reps cultivate contacts. They watch the market carefully and can advise you on trends and prices. They may be able to get you into shows, help get you your own shows or even put on a show for you.

A few considerations

Before approaching a rep, make sure you are ready. That is, you must be willing to make a commitment to your career as an artist. You should have a sizable body of work ready to show and sell. Consider carefully the idea of doing commissioned work—can you do work "on demand" and deliver it on time?

Prepare your portfolio with care. Include slides and other material for promotion. When sending slides, make sure they are labeled individually with your name and address. Also include directions ("up" and "front") on your slides. For finished work, you will need to include a price list with your slides. Make sure your pricing is consistent and logical. One artist suggests pricing by size only. She feels pricing by other, less tangible, considerations puts out signals that you feel some of your work is not as good as your other work. Your rep should be able to advise you on prices or check out your competition at local galleries.

For more information on working with reps see Finding and Working with Art/Photo Reps by Barbara Gordon and the books listed in the Resources section. *Artist's Market* and *Photographer's Market* include more in depth information on the business of art or photography and are a must for your business bookshelf.

Help with your search

To help you with your search for representation, we've included a Geographic Index in the back of the book. It is divided by state and province. The Agents and Representatives Index is provided to help you locate individual reps. Often you will read about a rep, but since that rep is an employee of a large agency, you may not be able to find that person's business number. We've asked agencies to give us the names of representatives on their staffs. Then we've listed the names in alphabetical order along with the name of their agency. Find the name of the person you would like to contact and then check the listing for that agency.

A few of the commercial illustration and photography representatives are also interested in fine artists. This is especially true of reps who work with book publishers. If a rep's *primary* function is selling illustration, but is also interested in handling some fine artists or fine art photographers, we've listed them in Additional Fine Art Reps at the end of this section.

In addition to examining and contacting the listings in this section, word-of-mouth and referrals are still an important way to find representation. You may also be able to meet a rep at a show or workshop. Artist and photographer organizations provide information on reps to members through newsletters and meetings.

About the listings

Most fine art representatives do not charge for additional expenses beyond those incurred preparing your portfolio. Depending on the arrangement, you may have to help pay for shipping of your work to the rep. A few reps require you to pay for special portfolios or other advertising materials. A handful also charge monthly retainers to cover marketing expenses. Where possible, we've indicated these listings with a filled-in box (■) symbol.

We've ranked the agencies listed in this section according to their openness to submissions. Below is our ranking system:

I   New representative (less than one year in business) actively seeking clients.

II Representative seeking both new and established artists or photographers.

III Representative prefers to work with established artists or photographers, mostly through referrals.

IV Representative handling only certain types of work or work by artists or photographers under certain circumstances.

V   Representative not currently seeking new clients. (If an agency chose this designation, only the address is given.) We have included mention of reps rated V only to let you know they are not open to new clients at this time. *Unless you have a strong recommendation from someone in the field, our advice is to approach only those reps ranked I-IV.*

ADMINISTRATIVE ARTS (II), P.O. Box 547935, Orlando FL 32854-7935. (407)578-1266. Contact: Brenda B. Harris. Fine art advisor. Estab. 1983. Registry includes 900 fine artists (includes fine art crafts). Markets include architects, corporate collections, developers, private collections.

Will Handle: Fine art. "We prefer artists with at least established local and regional credentials as emerging talent."
Terms: "Trade discount requested varies from 15-50% depending on project and medium. Submissions should include: 1) complete résumé; 2) artist's statement or brief profile; 3) slides (with artists name on each and either slide information or numbered with information attached on separate sheet). 4) slide information: title and date of work, image size, medium, availability, etc.; 5) pricing."
How to Contact: For first contact send query letter, résumé, bio, tearsheets, slides, copies of reviews, etc. and SASE. Reports back within 1-2 weeks. After initial contact, call to schedule an appointment. "Artists usually have sent information prior to an appointment. If art is transportable, original work is shown in a meeting. Art professionals who have accepted artists' information may not be able to meet with the artists immediately. We are often busy getting clients and opening doors for the artist!"
Tips: "Artists are generally referred by their business or art advisor, another art professional, from a university or arts journal that has researched our firm, or are referred by other artists. "Make sure that slides are good representations of your work. Always place your name and slide identification on each slide. Understand retail and net pricing structures in the art industry, trends, etc. – and include pricing information. A good impression is made by a well organized, typed résumé. Many artists include concise but very creative cover letters which help introduce the work."

JACK ARNOLD FINE ARTS (II, IV), 5 E. 67 St., New York NY 10021. (212)249-7218. FAX: (212)249-7232. Contact: Jack Arnold. Fine art representative. Estab. 1979. Represents 15 fine artists (includes 1 sculptor). Specializes in contemporary graphics. Markets include galleries, museums, private collections, corporate collections.
Will Handle: Looking for contemporary impressionists and realists.
Terms: Agent receives 50% commission. Exclusive area representation is required. For promotional purposes, talent must provide color prints or slides.
How to Contact: For first contact send bio, photographs, retail prices. Reports back within days. After initial contact, drop off or mail in appropriate materials for review. Portfolios should include slides, photographs.
Tips: Obtains new talent through referrals.

ART SOURCE L.A. (II), 671 N. La Cienega Blvd., Los Angeles CA 90069. (213)652-9285. FAX: (213)652-0336. Contact: Francine Ellman. Fine art representative. Estab. 1980. Member of Architectural Design Council. Represents 6 photographers, 20 fine artists (includes 3 sculptors). Specializes in fine art consulting and curating. Markets include architects, corporate collections, developers, galleries, interior decorators, museums, private collections, publishing/books.
Will Handle: Fine art and fine photography.
Terms: Agent receives commission, amount varies. Exclusive area representation required in some cases. "We request artists or photographers to submit a minimum of five slides/visuals, biography and SASE. Advertises in *Art News, Artscene.*
How to Contact: For first contact, send a résumé, bio, slides or photographs and SASE. Will report in 1-2 months. After initial contact, "we will call to schedule an appointment." Portfolio should include original art, slides, photographs.
Tips: Obtains new talent through recommendations, artists' submission and trade shows.

ARTCO INCORPORATED (II, III), 3148 RFD Cuba Rd., Long Grove IL 60047. (708)438-8420. FAX: (708)438-6464. Contact: Sybil Tillman. Fine art representative. Estab. 1970. Member of International Society of Appraisers. Represents 60 fine artists. Specializes in contemporary artists' originals and limited edition graphics. Markets include architects, art publishers, corporate collections, galleries, private collections.
Will Handle: Fine art.
Terms: "Each commission is determined mutually." "For promotional purposes, I would like to see original work or transparencies." Advertises in newspapers, magazine, etc.
How to Contact: For first contact send query letter, résumé, bio, slides, photographs or transparencies. Reports back within 2 weeks. After initial contact, call to schedule an appointment to show a portfolio. Portfolios should include original art, slides, photographs.
Tips: Obtains new talent through recommendations from others, solicitation, at conferences, advertising.

ARTS COUNSEL INC., 116 E. 27th St., 12th Fl., New York NY 10016, (212)725-3806. FAX: (212)779-9589. Contact: Fran Black. Fine art, commercial illustration, commercial photography representative. Estab. 1985. Represents 2 illustrators, 5 photographers, 12 fine artists (includes 4 sculptors). Specializes in marketing, proposal and guide writing, presentation techniques and public relations. Markets include advertising agencies, corporations/client direct, design firms, art publishers, corporate collections, interior decorators, museums, private collections.

Will Handle: Fine art, illustration, photography. "We are not actively looking, but we will review the work of artists with museum credentials."
Terms: Agent receives 25% commission. Charges 5% for long-distance calls. Advertising costs are split: 75% paid by the talent; 25% paid by the representative. For promotional purposes, talent must provide "promotional materials on hand as well as three to four complete portfolios." Advertises in *Creative Black Book, The Workbook, Graphis.*
How to Contact: For first contact, send query letter, bio, direct mail flyer/brochure. Reports back within 5 days. After initial contact, call to schedule an appointment to show a portfolio. Portfolio should include original art, tearsheets, photographs, laminates.
Tips: Obtains new talent through recommendations from others as well as through select advertising and promotion materials. "Know what you want to achieve in the commercial world. Be open to growth and development while maintaining a distinctive style."

ARTSOURCE, INC. (II), P.O. Box 7697, Richmond VA 23231. (804)222-3600. FAX: (804)222-1744. President: Emily Reynolds. Fine art representative. "Also a designer of crafts and site-specific art installations." Estab. 1982. Represents 8 photographers, 3 designers, 40 fine artists (includes 10 sculptors). Specializes in corporate interiors, comprehensive art services. Markets include architects, corporate collections, developers, interior decorators, medical facilities.
Will Handle: Fine art. Looking for "people working on atrium installations, large hanging sculptures."
Terms: Agent receives 50% commissions. 100% of advertising costs paid by the representative. For promotional purposes, talent must provide color photographs (3×5 or 5×7 sufficient) and color slides. "For kinetic art, send a videotape."
How to Contact: For first contact, send query letter, résumé, tearsheets, slides, photographs, sizes and prices of work and SASE. Reports back with 2 weeks. "Portfolio review appointment will follow if appropriate after seeing slides, photos, etc." Portfolio should include original art.
Tips: Obtains new talent through recommendations from others, or "spotting something of interest at a show, usually."

CATHY BAUM & ASSOCIATES, 384 Stevick Dr., Atherton CA 94027. (415)854-5668. FAX: (415)854-8522. Contact: Cathy Baum or Kris Hartman. Art advisory firm. Estab. 1976. Member of National Association for Corporate Art. Manages 100 fine artists. "Cathy Baum & Associates is a fine arts advisory firm. We do not represent artists, but will work directly with artists, if their work is appropriate for our client's art program. We have slide files on artists in all visual media of the fine arts." Markets include architects, corporate collections, developers, interior designers.
Will Handle: Fine art media – painting, sculpture, prints, photography.
Terms: Agent receives 20-50% commission. For promotional purposes, talent must provide slides of artwork, prices, biography.
How to Contact: For first contact, send bio, slides, price list. Reports back within 2 weeks. After initial contact, firm will request additional material. Portfolio should include slides.
Tips: Obtains new talent through "contacts in the arts, artists sending slides, galleries, etc."

JAMES CORCORAN FINE ARTS (II), 2341 Roxboro Rd., Cleveland OH 44106. (216)397-0777. FAX: (216)397-0222. Contact: James Corcoran. Fine art representative. Estab. 1986. Member of NOADA (Northeast Ohio Dealers Association); ISA (International Society of Appraisers). Represents 5 photographers, 11 fine artists (includes 3 sculptors). Staff includes Meghan Wilson (gallery associate); Brian Keough (office administrator); James Corcoran (owner/manager). Specializes in representing high-quality contemporary work. Markets include architects, corporate collections, developers, galleries, interior decorators, museums, private collections.
Will Handle: Fine art.
Terms: Agent receives 50% commission. Exclusive area representation is required. Advertising costs are "decided case by case."
How to Contact: For first contact send a query letter, résumé, bio, slides, photographs, SASE. Reports back within 1 month. After initial contact, drop off or mail in appropriate materials for review. Portfolio should include slides, photographs.
Tips: Usually obtains new talent by solicitation.

CORPORATE ART ASSOCIATES, LTD. (II), Suite 402, 270 Lafayette St., New York NY 10012. (212)941-9685. Directors: James Cavello, Charles Thurman Rosoff. Fine art representative. Also handles commercial illustration and photography, graphic design. Art consultant. Estab. 1988. Represents 15 illustrators, 50 photographers, 20 designers, 2,000 fine artists (includes 40 sculptors). Markets include advertising agencies, corporations/client direct, design firms, editorial/magazines, paper products/greeting cards, publishing/books, sales/promotion firms, architects, art publishers, corporate collections, developers, galleries, interior decorators, private collections.

Will Handle: Fine art, illustration, photography, design.
Terms: Agent receives 50% commission. Advertising costs are 100% paid by the talent.
How to Contact: For first contact, send query letter, résumé, bio, direct mail flyer/brochure, tearsheets, slides, photographs, photocopies, photostats, SASE. Reports back within days. After initial contact, drop off or mail in appropriate materials for review. Portfolio should include thumbnails, roughs, original art, tearsheets, slides, photographs, photostats, photocopies.
Tips: Obtains new talent through recommendations from others.

FINE ART ASSOCIATES (II), 1114 Barkdull, Houston TX 77006. Contact: Henry Reyna. Fine art representative and illustration or photography broker. Estab. 1972. Represents 4 photographers, 5 fine artists (includes 1 sculptor). Specializes in paintings, works on paper, and ceramic and glass objects. Markets include corporations/client direct, corporate collections, developers, private collections.
Will Handle: Fine art, photography, ceramic objects and glass sculpture. Looking for "realistic landscape subject matter and other representational artworks on canvas and paper. Also colorful ceramics and glassworks."
Terms: Agent receives 50% commission. Charges for "postage and photo/slide reproduction and transparencies (average $100 yearly)." Exclusive area representation is required (100 mile radius of Houston). Advertising costs are split: 50% paid by the talent; 50% paid by the representative. For promotional purposes, talent must provide "promotional materials at the discretion of the individual artist."
How to Contact: For first contact send bio, direct mail flyer/brochure, tearsheets, photographs, SASE; "always send self-addressed stamped return envelope." Reports back within 5 days. After initial contact, mail in appropriate materials for review. Portfolio should include slides, photographs.
Tips: Obtains new talent through "recommendations from other artists, collectors and museum curators. "A well-organized presentation of visual materials gives a quick impression of artworks."

FINE ART REPRESENTATIVE (II), 729 Pine Crest, Prospect Heights IL 60070. (708)459-3990. Contact: Gerard J. Perez. Fine art representative. Estab. 1977. Represents 45 fine artists. Specializes in "selling to art galleries." Markets include corporate collections, galleries, interior decorators.
Will Handle: Fine art.
Terms: "We buy for resale." Exclusive area representation is required. For promotional purposes talent must provide slides, color prints, "any visuals." Advertises in *Art News*, *Decor*, *Art Business News*.
How to Contact: For first contact send tearsheets, slides, photographs, SASE. Reports back within 30 days, only if interested. "Don't call us—if interested, we will call you." Portfolio should include slides, photographs.
Tips: Obtains new talent through recommendations from others and word of mouth."

ROBERT GALITZ FINE ART/ACCENT ART (II), 166 Hilltop Ct., Sleepy Hollow IL 60118. (708)426-8842. FAX: (708)426-8846. Contact: Robert Galitz. Fine art representative. Estab. 1985. Represents 100 fine artists (includes 2 sculptors). Specializes in contemporary/abstract corporate art. Markets include architects, corporate collections, galleries, interior decorators, private collections.
Will Handle: Fine art.
Terms: Agent receives 25-40% commission. For promotional purposes talent must provide "good photos and slides." Advertises in monthly art publications and guides.
How to Contact: For first contact send query letter, slides, photographs. Reports back within 2 weeks. After initial contact, call to schedule an appointment to show a portfolio. Portfolio should include original art.
Tips: Obtains new talent through recommendations from others, solicitation, at conferences. "Be confident, persistent. Never give up or never quit."

GILMARTIN ASSOCIATES (II, IV), 190 Tally Ho Dr., Springfield MA 01118. (413)782-5901. Contact: Jim Gilmartin. Fine art representative. Estab. 1965. Member of POFA. Represents 2 illustrators, 2 fine artists. Specializes in "calling on galleries, frame shops, commercial accounts." Markets include corporations/client direct, galleries, corporate collections.
Will Handle: Fine art.
Terms: Agent receives 20-25% commission. Exclusive area representation is required. For promotional purposes, talent must provide advertising and actual sample of original finished work, catalog sheets.
How to Contact: For first contact, send query letter, bio, direct mail flyer/brochure. Reports back within 2 weeks. After initial contact, drop off or mail in appropriate materials for review.
Tips: Obtains new talent through recommendations from others and solicitation.

ICEBOX, 2401 Central Ave. NE, Minneapolis MN 55418. (612)788-1790. Contact: Howard Christopherson. Fine art representative. Estab. 1988. Represents 4 photographers, 6 fine artists (includes 2 sculptors). Specializes in "thought-provoking art work and photography, predominatly Minnesota artists." Markets include corporate collections, interior decorators, museums, private collections.
Will Handle: Fine art and fine art photographs. Looking for "new photography and thought-provoking works."
Terms: Agent receives 33-50% commission. Exclusive area representation in Minnesota is required. For promotional purposes, talent must provide slides. Advertises in *Art Paper* and local newspapers and magazines.
How to Contact: For first contact, send résumé, bio, slides, SASE. Reports back within 60 days. After initial contact, drop off or mail in appropriate materials for review. Portfolio should include slides.

INTERNATIONAL ART CONNECTION AND ART CONNECTION PLUS (II), #51, 444 Brickell Ave., Miami FL 33131. (305)361-9997. FAX: (305)361-9997. President: Jane Chambeaux. (between June 15 and November 15, contact Ms. Chambeaux at Museum of the Commanderiè of Unet, 47400, Tonneins, Bordeaux France) "Nonprofit organization dedicated to helping artists." Estab. 1966 in Europe, 1987 in USA. Represents photographers, fine artists and sculptors. "We organize exhibits and promote artists." Markets include galleries, museums, private collectors.
Terms: Not-for-profit service. $25 fee.
How to Contact: For first contact, send résumé, slides, photographs, SASE. Reports back within 4 days. After initial contact, drop off or mail in appropriate materials for review. Portfolios should include original art (or framed), photocopies.
Tips: Obtains new talent through "an ad in *Photo* or *Art Review* and contacts in the museums." If interested in obtaining representation, "make international exhibits in museums."

L.A. ART EXCHANGE (II), 2451 Broadway, Santa Monica CA 90404. (213)828-6866. FAX: (213)828-2643. Contact: Jayne Zehngut. Fine art representative. Estab. 1987. Member of Professional Picture Framers Assoc. Represents 20 fine artists. "We deal with retail, wholesale and corporate accounts." Markets include corporations/client direct design firms, architects, corporate collections, developers, galleries, interior decorators.
Will Handle: Fine art, photography, design.
Terms: No information provided. Exclusive area representation is "preferred."
How to Contact: For first contact, send résumé, bio, slides, photographs, SASE. Reports back within 1 week. After initial contact, write to schedule an appointment or drop off or mail in appropriate materials for review.
Tips: Obtains new talent through "advertising in *Decor* magazine and *Art Business News* and local newspapers. Primary businesses are custom picture framing; fine art and poster sales; art consulting (corporate and residential)."

HELDA LEE INC. (III), 2610 21st St., Odessa TX 79761. (915)366-8426. FAX: (915)550-2830. Contact: Helda Lee. Fine art representative. Estab. 1967. Member of American Society of Appraisers, Texas Association of Art Dealers, Appraisers Association of America. Represents 50-60 artists, including 4 sculptors. Markets include corporate collections, developers, galleries, interior decorators, museums, private collections.
Will Handle: Fine art, illustration.
Terms: Agent receives 40-50% commission. Exclusive area representation is required. Advertising costs are 100% paid by representative. Advertises in *Texas Monthly, Southwest Art*, local tv and newspapers.
How to Contact: For first contact, send a query letter and photographs ("include phone number"). Will report within 10 days. After initial contact, call to schedule an appointment. Portfolios should include original art and photographs.
Tips: Obtains new talent through "direct contact from talent. Don't give up. Keep contacting—about every six months to a year. Everybody's needs change."

LESLI ART, INC. (II), Box 6693, Woodland Hills CA 91365. (818)999-9228. Contact: Stan Shevrin. Fine art representative. Estab. 1965. Represents 28 fine artists. Specializes in "artists paintings in oil or acrylic, in the manner of the impressionists. Also represent illustrators whose figurative work can be placed in art galleries."
Terms: Negotiable.
How to Contact: For first contact, send bio, slides, photographs, SASE. Reports back within 2 weeks.
Tips: Obtains new talent through "reviewing portfolios. Artists should show their most current works and state a preference for subject matter and medium."

WOULD YOU USE THE SAME CALENDAR YEAR AFTER YEAR?

Of course not! If you scheduled your appointments using last year's calendar, you'd risk missing important meetings and deadlines, so you keep up-to-date with a new calendar each year. Just like your calendar, *Guide to Literary Agents & Art/Photo Reps* changes every year, too. Many of the agents/reps move, fees change, and even agents/reps' needs change from the previous year. You can't afford to use an out-of-date book to plan your marketing efforts!

So save yourself the frustration of getting your work returned in the mail, stamped MOVED: ADDRESS UNKNOWN. And of NOT submitting your work to new listings because you don't know they exist. **Make sure you have the most current marketing information by ordering *1993 Guide to Literary Agents & Art/Photo Reps* today.** All you have to do is complete the attached post card and return it with your payment or charge card information. Order now, and there's one thing that won't change from your *1992 Guide to Literary Agents & Art/Photo Reps* - the price! That's right, we'll send you the 1993 edition for just $15.95. *1993 Guide to Literary Agents & Art/Photo Reps* will be published and ready for shipment in February 1993.

Let an old acquaintance be forgot, and toast the new edition of *Guide to Literary Agents & Art/Photo Reps*. Order today!

(See other side for more books to help sell your work)

To order, drop this postpaid card in the mail.

☐ **Yes!** I want the most current edition of *Guide to Literary Agents & Art/Photo Reps*. Please send me the 1993 edition at the 1992 price - $15.95.* (NOTE: *1993 Guide to Literary Agents & Art/Photo Reps* will be ready for shipment in February 1993.) #10277

Plus postage & handling: $3.00 for one book, $1.00 for each additional book. Ohio residents add $5^{1}/_{2}\%$ sales tax. Also send me the following books:

___(#10204) 1992 Writer's Market, $25.95* (available NOW)
___(#10205) 1992 Artist's Market, $21.95* (available NOW)
___(#10207) 1992 Photographer's Market, $21.95* (available NOW)

☐ Payment enclosed (Slip this card and your payment into an envelope)
☐ Please charge my: ☐ Visa ☐ MasterCard

Account # _____ Exp. Date _____

Signature _____ Phone ( ) _____

Name _____

Address _____

City _____ State _____ Zip _____

(This offer expires August 1, 1993)

Credit Card Orders Call Toll-Free 1-800-289-0963

Writer's Digest Books
1507 Dana Avenue
Cincinnati, OH 45207

6051

THESE BUYERS WANT TO PURCHASE YOUR WORK!

1992 Writer's Market
edited by Mark Kissling
This new edition contains up-to-date information on 4,000 buyers of freelance materials, as well as listings of workshops, contests and awards. Helpful articles and interviews with top professionals make this the source for your marketing efforts.
1056 pages/$25.95, hardcover

1992 Artist's Market
edited by Lauri Miller
You'll find 2,500 buyers of all types of art in this indispensable directory. Handy geographical indexes are included, in addition to articles and interviews with successful professionals.
608 pages/$21.95, hardcover

1992 Photographer's Market
edited by Sam Marshall
The most comprehensive book of its kind, this directory contains 2,500 up-to-date listings of U.S. and international buyers of freelance photos.
608 pages/$21.95, hardcover

Use coupon on other side to order today!

MADRAZO ARTS (II), 2962 Le Jeune Rd., Coral Gables FL 33134. (305)443-1023. FAX: (305)446-1303. Contact: Mr. Madrazo. Fine art representative. Estab. 1986. Member of Society of Illustrators. Represent 12-13 fine artists (includes 3 sculptors). Specializes in art for hospitality and health care work. Markets include architects, galleries, interior decorators, private collections.
Will Handle: Fine art and sculpture.
Terms: Agent receives 15-30% commission. Exclusive area representation is required. Advertising costs are split: 50% paid by the talent; 50% paid by the representative. For promotional purposes, talent must provide "visuals, whether photo or slides and curriculum vitae."
How to Contact: For first contact, send query letter, résumé, direct mail flyer/brochure, slides, photographs. Reports back within 10 days. After initial contact, call to schedule an appointment to show a portfolio or write to schedule an appointment. Portfolio should include original art, slides, photographs.
Tips: Obtains new talent through recommendations from others.

MEDIA GALLERY/ENTERPRISES (II), 145 W. 4th Ave., Garnett KS 66032-1313. (913)448-5813. Contact: Robert Cugno. Fine art representative. Estab. 1963. Number of artists and sculptors represented varies. Specializes in clay—contemporary and modern. Markets include galleries, museums, private collections.
Will Handle: Fine art and clay.
Terms: Agent receives 40-60% commission. For promotional purposes, talent must provide photos and slides.
How to Contact: For first contact send bio, slides, SASE. Reports back within 1-2 weeks. After initial contact, drop off or mail in appropriate materials for review.
Tips: Obtains new talent through recommendations from other artists, collectors, art consultants and gallery directors.

PALM FINE ART (II), #333, Boston Design Ctr., Boston MA 02210. (617)345-9595. Contact: Eric Palm. Fine art representative. Estab. 1989. Represents 10 fine artists. Markets include design firms, galleries, interior decorators.
Will Handle: Fine art, design.
Terms: Agent receives 40% commission. Exclusive area representation is "sometimes" required.
How to Contact: For first contact send direct mail flyer/brochure. Reports back within weeks. After initial contact, write to schedule an appointment to show a portfolio. Portfolio should include photographs.
Tips: Obtains new talent through recommendations.

■**PENNAMENITIES (IV)**, R.D. #2, Box 1080, Schuylkill Haven PA 17972. (717)754-7744. FAX: (717)754-7744. Contact: Deborah A. Miller. Fine art representative. Estab. 1988. Member of Summit Arts Fellowship. Represents 20 fine artists. Specializes in "arranging New York City art exhibits." Markets include galleries, private collections.
Will Handle: Fine art (originals and prints).
Terms: Agent receives 30-50% commission. Charges $350 annual fee which covers correspondence, copies, phone and fax or services involved in setting up NYC exhibit."
How to Contact: For first contact send résumé, bio, slides, price list, SASE required. After initial contact, drop off or mail in appropriate materials for review. Portfolio should include original art, slides.
Tips: "Initial contact is usually made by artist seeking representative's services."

JOAN SAPIRO ART CONSULTANTS (II, IV), 4750 E. Belleview Ave., Littleton CO 80121. (303)793-0792. FAX: (303)721-1401. Contact: Joan Sapiro or Jennifer Kalin. Fine art representative. Estab. 1980. Specializes in "corporate art with other emphasis on hospitality and health care."
Will Handle: Fine art.
Terms: No information provided.
How to Contact: For first contact, send résumé, bio, direct mail flyer/brochure, tearsheets, slides, photographs, SASE, price list—net (wholesale). Reports back within 2 weeks. After initial contact, drop off or mail in appropriate materials for review. Portfolios should include tearsheets, slides, SASE and price list.
Tips: Obtains new talent through recommendations, publications, travel and research.

SEIFFER & ASSOCIATES, (II), 913 Tanglewood Dr., Plano TX 75075. (214)881-9350. FAX: (214)881-9443. Contact: Wendy Seiffer. Fine art representative. Estab. 1987. Represents 2 photographers, 22 fine artists. "We license artwork to be reproduced as: limited-edition serigraphs and lithographs, poster and prints, collectible plates and sculpture, T-shirts, puzzles, greeting cards, etc. We're a full-scale licensing agency. Collectibles are our strongest area, plates in particular. Posters are our second

area of strength." Markets include paper products/greeting cards, art publishers, collectibles manufacturers (Lenox, The Hamilton Collection, The Danbury Mint, etc.)."
Will Handle: Fine art and exceptional illustration. Looking for "colorful, well-executed and realistic, photorealistic, or impressionistic work. Purely decorative is fine as well."
Terms: Agent receives 40% commission. Exclusive area representation is usually required. Marketing costs are 100% paid by the agent. For promotional purposes, "good visuals are essential. Photographs, tearsheets, etc., (supplied by the talent) are fine. They must be labeled (I provide labels). I prefer having multiple sets (6-12) for marketing."
How to Contact: For first contact, send query letter, résumé, bio, flyer/brochure, tearsheets, photographs, SASE. Reports back within 2 months, "as soon as we can do it!" After initial contact, mail in appropriate materials for review. Portfolio should include tearsheets, photographs, at least 12-24 images.
Tips: Obtains new talent through referrals. "My artists and my clients are continually referring other talented artists to our agency." If interested in obtaining representation, "have great visuals. Even 4×6 photos that are well done are fine. Have at least 12-24 great images to show consistency. Include a bio/artists statement. For successful licensing, artist should have a healthy inventory of original paintings and/or transparencies, ideally several dozen images."

NICKI SHEARER ART SOURCE (II), 6101 Walhonding Rd., Bethesda MD 20816. (301)320-2211. FAX: (301)320-2210. Contact: Nicki Shearer. Fine art representative. Estab. 1979. Represents "many" fine artists (several are sculptors). Specializes in art for hotels, hospitals, other commercial space (law firms, etc.). Markets include architects, corporate collections, developers, interior decorators.
Will Handle: Fine art. Looking for "lobby art — large wallhangings/sculpture."
Terms: Agent receives 40-50% commission. Exclusive area representation is not required, however "I would like to represent artists who are not represented in this area." Advertising costs are paid by representative. For promotional purposes, talent must provide slides, photographs, résumé, "any other promotional materials" and SASE. Advertises in *Washington Art.*
How to Contact: For first contact, send a résumé, bio, direct mail flyer/brochure, 2 or 3 slides, photographs — "call first, if possible." Will report in 1 month, if interested. After initial contact, drop off or mail in appropriate materials for review.
Tips: Obtains new talent through "recommendations from others, museum shows, other exhibits, as well as juried shows."

SIMPATICO ART & STONE (II), 1221 Demaret Ln., Houston TX 77055-6115. (713)467-7123. Contact: Billie Blake Fant. Fine art broker/consultant/exhibitor. Estab. 1973. Specializes in "unique fine art, sculpture and Texas domestic stone furniture, carvings architectural elements." Markets include corporations, designers, institutional and residential clients.
Will Handle: Looking for "unique and exceptionally fine painters and sculptors who are not presently being represented in Houston, Texas."
Terms: Standard commission. Exclusive area representation is required.
How to Contact: For first contact, send query letter, résumé, slides.
Tips: Obtains new talent through "travels, publications, exhibits and referrals."

RICHARD R. STORER (II, III), 710 Sierra Pt., Brisbane CA 94005. Fine art representative. Estab. 1973. Represents 1 illustrator, 3 photographers, 2 designers, 2 fine artists (includes 1 sculptor). Specializes in "fine art erotica in painting, sculpture and jewelry. Also sculptural and fine art commissioned for film properties (cinema)." Markets include advertising agencies, corporations/client direct, design firms, editorial/magazines, publishing/books, sales/promotion firms, corporate collections, interior decorators, private collections, publishing/books, "high-rung clothing and furniture displayers."
Will Handle: Photography, fine art and "fine art erotica."
Terms: Agent receives 30% commission.
How to Contact: For first contact, send query letter, direct mail flyer/brochure, slides, photographs. Reports back within 1 month, only if interested. Portfolio should include thumbnails, slides, photographs.
Tips: Obtains new talent through recommendations from others. Show a "concise, non-philosophical presentation! We do believe an artist's work speaks for itself."

PARK THEDE ASSOCIATES, 13104 Woods Creek Rd., Monroe WA 98272. (206)794-6609. FAX: (206)656-4182. Contact: Park Thede. Fine art representative. Estab. 1984. Represents 3 fine artists. Specializes in limited edition prints and the Northwest. Markets include galleries.
Will Handle: Fine art, posters, prints. Looking for Northwest artists, "preferably."
Terms: Agent receives 20% commission. Exclusive area representation is required. For promotional purposes, talent must provide samples for salesmen and a brochure with résumé.
How to Contact: For first contact send direct mail flyer/brochure. Reports back within days.
Tips: Obtains new talent through art shows such as ABC, etc.

TOLEASE LAUTREC, #C, 4832 Eastwood, Wichita KS 67218. (316)686-2470. Contact: C. Matthew Foley. Fine art, commercial illustration, graphic art representative. Estab. 1984. Member of Societas Artis Illuminatorum/Nepenthe Mundi Society. Represents 3 illustrators, 10 photographers, 5 designers, 36 fine artists (includes 12 sculptors). Specializes in Native American art. Markets includes advertising agencies, corporations/client direct, design firms, editorial/magazines, publishing/books, sales/promotion firms, corporate collections, galleries, interior decorators, museums, private collections, publishing/books. Member agents: Mary McKenzie (painting); John Pearl (marketing director, publicist, art agent); Mattphisto Idol (sculpture).
Will Handle: Fine art, illustration, photography. Agent receives 25-40% commission. Exclusive area representation is required. Advertising costs are split: 50% paid by the talent; 50% paid by the representative.
How to Contact: For first contact, send query letter, résumé, bio, direct mail flyer/brochure, tearsheets, slides, photographs, photocopies, photostats, SASE, "whatever the talent has currently available." Reports back within 2 weeks. Reports back with 1 week, only if interested. After initial contact, write to schedule an appointment to show a portfolio, or drop off or mail in appropriate materials for review. Portfolios should include tearsheets, slides, photographs, photostats, photocopies. "Send no originals."
Tips: Obtains new talent "from many sources. Always on the lookout for exceptional talent. Keep after it!"

WALKINGSTICK PRODUCTIONS (IV), P.O. Box 958, Moss Beach CA 94038. (415)728-9188. FAX: (415)728-7333. Contact: Suzanne Hayes Kane. Fine art representative. Estab. 1987. Represents 2 fine artists. Specializes in "large paintings for public buildings." Markets include architects, developers, interior decorators, publishing/books.
Will Handle: Fine art.
Terms: Agent receives 40% commission. For promotional purposes, talent must provide 4×5 transparencies and a postcard with photo of work.
How to Contact: For first contact send direct mail flyer/brochure, SASE. Reports back within 2 weeks, only if interested. After initial contact, drop off or mail in appropriate materials for review. Portfolio should include 4×5 transparencies or prints.
Tips: Obtains new talent through advertising. "Be persistent."

■ELAINE WECHSLER (III), Suite 5B, 245 W. 104th St., New York NY 10025. (212)222-3780. Contact: Elaine Wechsler. Fine art representative. Estab. 1986. Represents 10 fine artists and sculptors. Specializes in "fine art painting, printmaking and sculpture." Markets include architects, corporate collections, galleries, museums, private collections.
Will Handle: Fine art.
Terms: Agent receives 20-40% commission (depending on circumstance). Charges a retainer of $50-$100/week to cover time, phone, installation, marketing. Exclusive area representation is required (for 1 year). Advertising costs are split: 70% paid by talent; 30% paid by representative. For promotional purposes, talent must provide slide dupes, word-processed bio, direct mail piece and, eventually, original art—at least 2-5 pieces. Advertises in "local newspapers, gallery guides, some professional magazines."
How to Contact: For first contact, send a query letter with résumé, bio, direct mail flyer/brochure, tearsheets, slide (a sheet of slides) and SASE. Will report in 3 months, if interested. After initial contact, call or write to schedule an appointment. Portfolio should include original art (only when requested), slides, photographs.
Tips: Obtains new talent through recommendations from others, solicitation at exhibitions.

Additional Fine Art Reps

The following representatives have full listings in other sections of this book. These reps and agents have indicated they are *primarily* interested in commercial illustration or photography (and in rare cases, book manuscripts), but are also interested in the work of fine artists. After reading the listing (you can find the page number in the Listings Index), send them a query to obtain more information on their needs and artwork submission policies.

Brindle & Partner Inc., Carolyn
Eldridge Corporation
Lavaty & Associates, Frank & Jeff

McKay Photography, Colleen
Pacific Design Studio
Rosenthal Represents
Schwartz, Esquire, Laurens R.

Resources

Recommended Books & Publications

For writers and scriptwriters

ADVENTURES IN THE SCREEN TRADE, by William Goldman, published by Warner Books, 666 Fifth Ave., New York NY 10103. An insider's view of screenwriting and the entertainment business.

AGENT & MANAGER, 7th Fl., 650 First Ave., New York NY 10016. Monthly trade magazine for all types of agents and managers. Information on new agents, news and deals.

BEYOND THE BESTSELLER: A LITERARY AGENT TAKES YOU INSIDE PUBLISHING, by Richard Curtis, published by NAL, 375 Hudson St., New York NY 10014. The "inside story" on publishing by a New York agent.

BUSINESS & LEGAL FORMS FOR AUTHORS AND SELF-PUBLISHERS, by Tad Crawford, published by Allworth Press, c/o Writer's Digest Books, 1507 Dana Ave., Cincinnati OH 45207. Forms for all types of agreements and contracts needed in the publishing business.

CHILDREN'S WRITER'S & ILLUSTRATOR'S MARKET, edited by Lisa Carpenter, published by Writer's Digest Books, 1507 Dana Ave., Cincinnati OH 45207. Annual market directory for children's writers and illustrators. Includes information on writing and art business.

THE COMPLETE BOOK OF SCRIPTWRITING, by J. Michael Straczyniski, published by Writer's Digest Books, 1507 Dana Ave., Cincinnati OH 45207. How to write and sell all types of scripts.

THE COMPLETE GUIDE TO STANDARD SCRIPT FORMAT (Parts 1 and 2), by Hillis Cole and Judith Haag, published by CMC Publishing, 11642 Otsego St., N. Hollywood CA 91601. Standard script formats and other information for scriptwriters.

DAILY VARIETY, 5700 Wilshire Blvd., Los Angeles CA 90036. Publication featuring information on the entertainment business, trade oriented.

DRAMATISTS SOURCEBOOK, edited by Angela E. Mitchell and Gilliam Richards, published by Theatre Communications Group, Inc., 355 Lexington Ave., New York NY 10017. Directory listing opportunities for playwrights. Includes agents.

THE GUIDE TO WRITERS CONFERENCES, published by Shaw Associates, Suite 1406, Biltmore Way, Coral Gables FL 33134. Directory of writers' conferences.

HOLLYWOOD REPORTER, Billboard Publications, Inc., 6715 Sunset Blvd., Hollywood CA 90028. Publication covering news and information on the entertainment industry. Includes information on scriptwriters and sales of scripts.

HOLLYWOOD SCRIPTWRITER, #385, 1626 N. Wilcox, Hollywood CA 90028. Newsletter featuring information for scriptwriters. Includes an annual agents issue.

HOW TO PITCH & SELL YOUR TV SCRIPT, by David Silver, published by Writer's Digest Books, 1507 Dana Ave., Cincinnati OH 45207. Information on marketing your television scripts. Includes information on working with script agents.

HOW TO SELL YOUR SCREENPLAY, by Carl Sautter, published by New Chapter Press, Suite 1122, 381 Park Ave. S., New York NY 10016. Tips on selling screenplays.

HOW TO WRITE A BOOK PROPOSAL, by Michael Larsen, published by Writer's Digest Books, 1507 Dana Ave., Cincinnati OH 45207. How to put together a professional-quality book proposal package.

HOW TO WRITE IRRESISTIBLE QUERY LETTERS, by Lisa Collier Cool, published by Writer's Digest Books, 1507 Dana Ave., Cincinnati OH 45207. How to write professional, effective queries.

THE INSIDER'S GUIDE TO BOOK EDITORS & PUBLISHERS, by Jeff Herman, published by Prima Publishing & Communications, Box 1260, Rocklin CA 95677-1260. An inside look at the publishing industry. Includes information on agents.

LITERARY AGENTS: A WRITER'S GUIDE, by Debby Mayer, published by Poets & Writer's, 72 Spring St., New York NY 10012. Directory of literary agents. Includes articles on working with agents. Published every five years.

LITERARY AGENTS: HOW TO GET AND WORK WITH THE RIGHT ONE FOR YOU, *by Michael Larsen, published by Paragon House, 90 Fifth Ave., New York NY 10011. How to approach and work with an agent.*

LITERARY MARKET PLACE (LMP), *R.R. Bowker Company, 121 Chanlon Road, New Providence NJ 07974. Book publishing industry directory. In addition to publishing companies, includes a list of literary agents and a list of art representatives.*

MAKING A GOOD SCRIPT GREAT, *by Dr. Linda Seger, published by Samuel French Trade, 7623 Sunset Blvd., Hollywood CA 90046. Information on improving your script.*

MANUSCRIPT SUBMISSION, *by Scott Edelstein, published by Writer's Digest Books, 1507 Dana Ave., Cincinnati OH 45207. How to prepare submissions for publishers and agents, especially for the fiction writer.*

NOVEL & SHORT STORY WRITER'S MARKET, *edited by Robin Gee, published by Writer's Digest Books, 1507 Dana Ave., Cincinnati OH 45207. Annual market directory for fiction writers. Includes information on the writing business, organizations and conferences for fiction writers.*

POETS AND WRITERS, *72 Spring St., New York NY 10012. Magazine for writers. Includes interviews and articles of interest to poets and literary writers. Poets and Writers also publishes several books and directories for writers.*

PROFESSIONAL WRITER'S GUIDE, *revised and expanded edition, edited by Donald Bower and James Lee Young, National Writers Press, Suite 620 S., 1450 Havana, Aurora CO 80012. The basics of starting and building a writing career.*

PUBLISHERS WEEKLY, *205 W. 42nd St., New York NY 10017. Weekly magazine covering industry trends and news in the book publishing industry. Contains announcements of new agencies.*

PUBLISHING NEWS, *Hanson Publishing Group, Box 4949, Stamford CT 06907-0949. Bimonthly newsmagazine of the publishing industry.*

SUCCESSFUL SCRIPTWRITING, *by Jurgen Wolff and Kerry Cox, published by Writer's Digest Books, 1507 Dana Ave., Cincinnati OH 45207. Includes information on the movie and television business, as well as tips on marketing and selling scripts.*

THEATRE DIRECTORY, *Theatre Communications Group, Inc., 355 Lexington Ave., New York NY 10017. Directory listing theaters in the U.S.*

THE TV SCRIPTWRITER'S HANDBOOK, *by Alfred Brenner, published by Writer's Digest Books, 1507 Dana Ave., Cincinnati OH 45207. Includes all aspects of writing for television including marketing scripts.*

THE WRITER, *120 Boylston St., Boston MA 02116. Magazine for writers. Includes articles on technique and writing issues.*

WRITER'S DIGEST, *1507 Dana Ave., Cincinnati OH 45207. Monthly magazine for writers. Includes technique, lifestyle, business and market information.*

THE WRITER'S DIGEST GUIDE TO MANUSCRIPT FORMATS, *by Dian Dincin Buchman and Seli Groves, published by Writer's Digest Books, 1507 Dana Ave., Cincinnati OH 45207. Models for all types of manuscript formats including query and cover letters to editors, publishers and agents.*

WRITER'S ESSENTIAL DESK REFERENCE, *edited by Glenda Tennant Neff, published by Writer's Digest Books, 1507 Dana Ave., Cincinnati OH 45207. Reference guide for writers including business, tax and legal information for both U.S. and Canadian writers.*

A WRITER'S GUIDE TO CONTRACT NEGOTIATIONS, *by Richard Balkin, published by Writer's Digest Books, 1507 Dana Ave., Cincinnati OH 45207. Written by an agent, this is an insider's view of book contract negotiations.*

THE WRITER'S LEGAL COMPANION, *by Brad Bunnin and Peter Beren, published by Addison Wesley, Jacob Way, Reading MA 01867. Legal guide for writers. Bunnin is a publishing-industry lawyer.*

WRITER'S MARKET, *edited by Mark Kissling, published by Writer's Digest Books, 1507 Dana Ave., Cincinnati OH 45207. Annual market directory for writers and scriptwriters. Includes information on the writing business.*

WRITING SCRIPTS THAT SELL, *by Michael Hauge, published by McGraw-Hill, 1221 Ave. of the Americas, New York NY 10020. Technique information for scriptwriters.*

For artists and photographers

ADVERTISING AGE, *740 Rush St., Chicago IL 60611-2590. Weekly advertising and marketing tabloid.*

ADWEEK, *A/S/M Communications, Inc., 49 E. 21st St., New York NY 10010. Weekly advertising and marketing magazine.*

AMERICAN ARTIST, *P.O. Box 1944, Marion OH 43306-2044. Magazine featuring instructional articles, profiles and technique information for artists.*

AMERICAN PHOTO, *43rd Fl., 1633 Broadway, New York NY 10019. Monthly magazine emphasizing the craft and philosophy of photography.*

AMERICAN SHOWCASE, *14th Fl., 915 Broadway, New York NY 10010., Annual talent sourcebook featuring illustrators, photographers and designers.*

ART DIRECTION, *6th Fl., 10 E. 39th St., New York NY 10016-0199. Monthly magazine featuring art directors' views on advertising and photography.*

ART IN AMERICA, *575 Broadway, New York NY 10012. Features in-depth articles on art issues, news and reviews. August issue includes an annual guide to artists, galleries and museums.*

THE ARTIST'S FRIENDLY LEGAL GUIDE, *by Floyd Conner, Peter Karlan, Jean Perwin & David M. Spatt, published by North Light Books, 1507 Dana Ave., Cincinnati OH 45207. Tips on taxes and legal matters by tax experts and lawyers familiar with the art business.*

THE ARTIST'S MAGAZINE, *1507 Dana Ave., Cincinnati OH 45207. Monthly art magazine featuring how-to technique and business information for artists.*

ARTIST'S MARKET, *edited by Lauri Miller, published by Writer's Digest Books, 1507 Dana Ave., Cincinnati OH 45207. Annual markets directory for artists. Includes art business information.*

ASMP BULLETIN, *monthly newsletter of American Society of Magazine Photographers, 419 Park Ave. South, New York NY 10016. Subscription comes with membership in ASMP.*

BUSINESS AND LEGAL FORMS FOR FINE ARTISTS, *by Tad Crawford, published by Allworth Press, % North Light Books, 1507 Dana Ave., Cincinnati OH 45207. Forms for agreements and other contracts for fine artists.*

BUSINESS AND LEGAL FORMS FOR ILLUSTRATORS, *by Tad Crawford, published by Allworth Press, c/o North Light Books, 1507 Dana Ave., Cincinnati OH 45207. Forms for agreements and contracts for illustrators.*

CHICAGO CREATIVE DIRECTORY, *Suite 810, 333 N. Michigan Ave., Chicago IL 60610. Annual talent sourcebook featuring illustrators and designers in the Chicago area.*

CHICAGO MIDWEST FLASH, *Alexander Communications, Suite 203, 212 W. Superior, Chicago IL 60610. Quarterly magazine including articles and news on graphic art and advertising in the Midwest.*

COMMUNICATIONS ARTS, *410 Sherman Ave., Box 10300, Palo Alto CA 94303. Magazine covering design, illustration and photography. Published 8 times a year.*

CREATIVE BLACK BOOK, *3rd Fl., 115 Fifth Ave., New York NY 10003. Annual talent sourcebook featuring illustrators, photographers and designers.*

CREATIVE SOURCE, *Wilcord Publications Ltd., Suite 110, 511 King St. West, Toronto, Ontario M5V 2Z4. Annual talent sourcebook featuring illustrators and designers in Canada.*

DECOR, *Commerce Publications, 408 Olive St., St. Louis MO 63102. Monthly magazine covering trends in art publishing, home accessories and framing.*

THE DESIGNER'S COMMONSENSE BUSINESS BOOK, *by Barbara Ganim, published by North Light Books, 1507 Dana Ave., Cincinnati OH 45207. Includes information on business matters for graphic designers.*

DIRECTORY OF FINE ART REPRESENTATIVES, *edited by Constance Franklin, published by Directors Guild Publishers & The Consultant Press. DGP address: 13284 Rices Crossing Road, P.O. Box 369, Renaissance CA 95962. Directory listing fine art reps and corporate art collectors.*

EDITOR & PUBLISHER, *The Editor & Publisher Co., Inc., 11 W. 19th St., New York NY 10011. Weekly magazine covering latest developments in journalism and newspaper production.*

THE FINE ARTIST'S GUIDE TO SHOWING & SELLING YOUR WORK, *by Sally Prince Davis, published by North Light Books, 1507 Dana Ave., Cincinnati OH 45207. Information on developing a marketing plan for fine artists.*

FOLIO, *Box 4949, Stamford CT 06907-0949. Monthly magazine featuring trends in magazine circulation, production and editorial.*

GETTING STARTED AS A FREELANCE ILLUSTRATOR OR DESIGNER, *by Michael Fleishman, published by North Light Books, 1507 Dana Ave., Cincinnati OH 45207. Book presenting information on promotion, portfolios and markets open to freelancers.*

THE GRAPHIC ARTIST'S GUIDE TO MARKETING & SELF-PROMOTION, *by Sally Prince Davis, published by North Light Books, 1507 Dana Ave., Cincinnati OH 45207. Contains information on marketing and promotion for graphic artists and designers.*

GRAPHIS, *Graphis U.S. Inc., 141 Lexington Ave., New York NY 10016. Bimonthly international journal of the graphic design industry.*

GUILFOYLE REPORT, *% AG Editions, 142 Bank St., New York NY 10014. Quarterly market tips newsletter for nature and stock photographers.*

HOW, *1507 Dana Ave., Cincinnati OH 45207. Bimonthly magazine featuring trends in graphic design and illustration.*

HOW TO SELL YOUR PHOTOGRAPHS AND ILLUSTRATIONS, *by Elliott and Barbara Gordon, published by Allworth Press, % North Light Books, 1507 Dana Ave., Cincinnati OH 45207. Business-building tips from commercial reps Elliott and Barbara Gordon. Contains information on working with art/photo reps.*

HUMOR & CARTOON MARKETS, *edited by Bob Staake, published by Writer's Digest Books, 1507 Dana Ave., Cincinnati OH 45207. Annual directory of markets for humor writers and cartoonists. Includes business information for writers and artists (cartoonists).*

INTERIOR DESIGN, *249 W. 17th St., New York NY 10011. Monthly magazine featuring industry news and trends in furnishing and interior design.*

LEGAL GUIDE FOR THE VISUAL ARTIST, *by Tad Crawford, published by Allworth Press, c/o North Light Books, 1507 Dana Ave., Cincinnati OH 45207. Guide to art law covering copyright and contracts.*

MAGAZINE DESIGN AND PRODUCTION, *Suite 106, 8340 Mission Road, Prairie Village KS 66206. Monthly magazine with information on all aspects of magazine design and production.*

NEW YORK GOLD, *10 E. 21st St., New York NY 10010. Annual talent sourcebook featuring photographers.*

THE PERFECT PORTFOLIO, *by Henrietta Brackman, published by Amphoto Books, c/o Watson Guptill*

Publishing, 1515 Broadway, New York NY 10036. Information on how to develop and improve your photography portfolio.

PHOTO DISTRICT NEWS, *49 East 21st St., New York NY 10010. Monthly trade magazine for the photography industry.*

PHOTO/DESIGN, *1515 Broadway, New York NY 10036. Monthly magazine emphasizing photography in the advertising/design fields.*

THE PHOTOGRAPHER'S BUSINESS & LEGAL HANDBOOK, *by Leonard Duboff, published by Images Press, c/o Writer's Digest Books, 1507 Dana Ave., Cincinnati OH 45207. A guide to copyright, trademarks, libel law and other legal concerns for photographers.*

PHOTOGRAPHER'S GUIDE TO MARKETING AND SELF-PROMOTION, *by Maria Piscopo, published by Writer's Digest Books, 1507 Dana Ave., Cincinnati OH 45207. Information on marketing and promotion for photographers. Includes information on photographers' reps.*

PHOTOGRAPHER'S MARKET, *edited by Sam Marshall, published by Writer's Digest Books, 1507 Dana Ave., Cincinnati OH 45207. Annual market directory for photographers. Includes photography business information.*

PHOTOGRAPHING YOUR ART WORK, *by Russell Hart, published by North Light Books, published by Writer's Digest Books, 1507 Dana Ave., Cincinnati OH 45207. How to photograph all types of artwork to create the best slides for your portfolio.*

THE PROFESSIONAL DESIGNER'S GUIDE TO MARKETING YOUR WORK, *by Mary Yeung, published by North Light Books, 1507 Dana Ave., Cincinnati OH 45207. Tips on marketing for graphic designers. Includes information on finding a rep.*

PROMO, *by Rose DeNeve, published by North Light Books, 1507 Dana Ave., Cincinnati OH 45207. A collection of outstanding promo pieces that have worked for illustrators and graphic designers.*

RSVP, *Box 314, Brooklyn NY 11205. Annual talent sourcebook featuring illustrators and designers.*

STEP-BY-STEP GRAPHICS, *Dynamic Graphics, Inc., 6000 N. Forest Park Drive, Peoria IL 61614-3597. Bimonthly magazine featuring instruction for graphic design and illustration projects.*

U&lc, *Upper and Lower Case, 2 Hammarskjold Plaza, New York NY 10017. Newspaper format quarterly featuring news and information for the graphic artist.*

THE ULTIMATE PORTFOLIO, *by Martha Metzdorf, published by North Light Books, 1507 Dana Ave., Cincinnati OH 45207. A showcase of some of the best and most successful portfolios by illustrators and graphic designers.*

WOMEN'S WEAR DAILY, *Fairchild Publications, 7 West 34th St., New York NY 10001. Tabloid (Monday through Friday) focusing on women's and children's apparel.*

THE WORK BOOK, *Scott & Daughters Publishing, Suite A, 940 N. Highland Ave., Los Angeles CA 90038. Annual talent sourcebook listing illustrators, photographers and designers primarily in the Los Angeles area.*

Professional Organizations

Organizations for agents and reps

INDEPENDENT LITERARY AGENTS ASSOCIATION (ILAA), Suite 1801, 915 E. 26th St., New York NY 10010. A list of member agents is available for a SASE with 52 cents for postage. (Note: at press time ILAA and SAR were discussing the possibility of merging in Fall 1992. Check with one of the two groups for information.)

SOCIETY OF AUTHOR'S REPRESENTATIVES (SAR), 3rd Fl., 10 Astor Place, New York NY 10003. A list of member agents is available for a SASE with a 29-cent first class stamp. (Note: at press time ILAA and SAR were discussing the possibility of merging in Fall 1992. Check with one of the two groups for information.)

SOCIETY OF PHOTOGRAPHERS' AND ARTISTS' AGENTS (SPAR), Suite 914, 11123 Broadway, New York NY 10010. A membership directory is available for about $35 (check for current price).

Organizations for writers, artists and photographers

The following professional organizations for writers, artists and photographers publish newsletters and hold conferences and meetings in which they often share information on agents or reps.

ADVERTISING PHOTOGRAPHERS OF AMERICA (APA), Room 601, 27 W. 20th St., New York NY 10011.

AMERICAN INSTITUTE OF GRAPHIC ARTS (AIGA), 1059 Third Ave., New York NY 10021. (212)752-0813.

AMERICAN SOCIETY OF JOURNALISTS & AUTHORS, Suite 302, 1501 Broadway, New York NY 10036. (212)997-0947.

AMERICAN SOCIETY OF MAGAZINE PHOTOGRAPHERS (ASMP), Suite 1407, 419 Park Ave. S., New York NY 10016.

AMERICAN SOCIETY OF PHOTOGRAPHERS (ASP), Box 52900, Tulsa OK 74152.

THE AUTHORS GUILD INC., 330 W. 42nd St., New York NY 10036. (212)563-5904.

GRAPHIC ARTIST GUILD, 8th Fl., 11 W. 20th St., New York NY 10011. (212)463-7730.

INTERNATIONAL ASSOCIATION OF CRIME WRITERS (North American branch), JAF Box 1500, New York NY 10116. (212)757-3915.

THE INTERNATIONAL WOMEN'S WRITING GUILD, P.O. Box 810, Gracie Station, New York NY 10028. (212)737-7536. Provides a literary agents list to members. Also holds "Meet the Agents and Editors" sessions for members twice a year (April and October).

MYSTERY WRITERS OF AMERICA (MWA), 236 W. 27th St., New York NY 10001. (212)255-7005.

NATIONAL WRITERS CLUB, Suite 620, 1450 S. Havana, Aurora CO 80012. (303)751-7844. In addition to agent referrals, also operates an agency for members.

NATIONAL WRITERS UNION, 13 Astor Place, New York NY 10003. (212)254-0279. A trade union, this organization has an agent data base available to members.

PROFESSIONAL PHOTOGRAPHERS OF AMERICA, INC. (PPA), 1090 Executive Way, Des Plaines IL 60018. (708)299-8161.

ROMANCE WRITERS OF AMERICA (RWA), 13700 Veterans Memorial Dr., #315, Houston TX 77014. (713)440-6885. Publishes an annual agent's list, available for $8.50.

SOCIETY OF CHILDREN'S BOOK WRITERS (SCBW), P.O. Box 66296, Mar Vista Station, Los Angeles CA 90066. (818)342-2849. Provides a literary agents list to members.

WRITERS GUILD OF AMERICA (WGA) — EAST, 555 W. 57th St., New York NY 10019. (212)245-6180. Provides a list of WGA signatory agents for $1.33 and SASE. Signatories are required to follow certain standards and a code of ethics.

WRITERS GUILD OF AMERICA (WGA) — WEST, 8955 Beverly Blvd., West Hollywood CA 90048. (213)550-1000. Provides a list of WGA signatory agents for $1 and SASE, addressed to the Agency Department. Signatories are required to follow certain standards and a code of ethics.

Glossary

Advance. A sum of money that a publisher pays a writer prior to publication of a book. It is usually paid in installments, such as one-half upon signing the contract; one-half upon delivery of the complete and satisfactory manuscript. The advance is paid against the royalty money that will be earned by the book. Agents take their percentage off the top of the advance as well as from the royalties earned.

Advertising costs. Costs incurred by placing advertisements in newspapers or magazines, purchasing pages in industry talent books, promoting a show or exhibition, creation and mailing of direct mail or other promo pieces, list rental, slide copying—anything that promotes the work of the talent and may lead to sales.

Auction. Publishers sometimes bid for the acquisition of a book manuscript that has excellent sales prospects. The bids are for the amount of the author's advance, guaranteed dollar amounts, advertising and promotional expenses, royalty percentage, etc.

Backlist. A publisher's list of its books that were not published during the current season, but which are still in print.

Bio. Brief (usually one page) background information about an artist, writer or photographer. Includes work and educational experience.

Boilerplate. A standardized publishing contract. "Our standard contract" usually means the boilerplate without changes. Most authors and agents make many changes on the boilerplate before accepting the contract.

Book. When used in commercial art circles, it refers to a portfolio. See *portfolio*.

Book proposal. See *proposal*.

Broker. A situation in which a rep handles only some of the work of an artist or photographer or in which the rep sells just what the talent has brought to them to sell. A percentage is taken from each sale. The rep is not handling the talent's career, only certain work.

Business-size envelope. Also known as a #10 envelope, it is the standard-size envelope used in most business situations.

Category fiction. A term used to include all various types of fiction. See *genre*.

Cibachrome. Trademark for a full-color positive print made from a transparency.

Client. When referring to a literary or script agent "client" is used to mean the writer whose work the agent is handling, but when referring to art or photography representation, "client" refers to the art/photo buyer. The word "talent" is used to refer to the artist or photographer whose work is handled by the rep.

Client direct. Sales directly to a corporate client instead of to a middle person such as a developer, architect or interior decorator.

Clips. Writing samples, usually from newspapers or magazines, of your published work.

Coffee table book. A heavily illustrated, oversized book, suitable for display on a coffee table.

Collaterals. Accompanying or auxiliary pieces, such as brochures, especially used in advertising. Samples of these may be included in a portfolio.

Commercial novel. A novel designed to appeal to a broad audience. It often falls into a category or genre such as western, romance, mystery and science fiction. See also *genre*.

Concept. A statement that summarizes a screenplay or teleplay—before the outline or treatment is written.

Contemporary. Material dealing with popular current trends, themes or topics.

Contributor's copies. Copies of the author's book sent to the author. Often the number of contributor's copies is negotiated in the publishing contract.

Copyediting. Editing of a manuscript for writing style, grammar, punctuation and factual accuracy. Some agents offer this service.

Cover letter. A brief descriptive letter sent along with a complete manuscript submitted to an agent or publisher.

C-print. Any enlargement printed from a negative. Any enlargement from a transparency is called an R-print.

Creative sourcebook. Also known as creative or talent directory. An annual book sent to art directors and others who buy the work of illustrators or photographers. Each page is an advertisement for the work of a talent or a group of talents and includes a representation of their style and contact information. Pages may be purchased by the rep or talent.

Critiquing service. A service offered by some agents in which writers pay a fee for comments on the salability or other qualities of their manuscript. Sometimes the critique includes suggestions on how to improve the work. Fees vary, as do the quality of the critiques.

Demo. A sample reel of film or sample videocassette which includes excerpts of a filmmaker's or videographer's production of work for clients.

Direct mail package. Sales or promotional material that is distributed by mail. Usually consists of an outer envelope, a cover letter, brochure or flyer, SASE or postpaid reply card.

Direct mail piece. A flyer or brochure used in advertising the work of an artist, designer or photographer. The piece usually includes more than one image or one striking image that best shows the artist's or photographer's style.

Division. An unincorporated branch of a company (e.g., Penguin Books, a division of Viking, Penguin, Inc.)

Docudrama. A fictional film rendition of recent newsmaking events or people.

Editing service. A service offered by some agents in which writers pay a fee—either lump sum or a per-page fee—to have the agent edit their manuscript. The quality and extent of the editing varies from agent to agent.

Electronic submission. A submission made by modem or computer disk. For permission and information on how to make an electronic submission, talk to your agent or publisher.

El-hi. Elementary to high school. A term used in textbook publishing to indicate reading or interest level.

Evaluation fees. Fees an agent may charge to evaluate material. The extent and quality of this evaluation varies, but comments usually concern the salability of the manuscript.

Exclusive. Offering a manuscript, usually for a set period of time, to just one agent and guaranteeing that agent is the only one looking at the manuscript.

Exclusive area representation. Requirement that an artist's or photographer's work be handled by only one rep within a given area.

Floor bid. If a publisher is very interested in a manuscript he may offer to enter a floor bid when the book goes to auction. The publisher sits out of the auction, but agrees to take the book by topping the highest bid by an agreed-upon percentage (usually 10%).

Foreign rights agent. An agent who handles selling the rights to a country other than that of the first book agent. Usually an additional percentage (about 5%) will be added on to the first book agent's commission to cover the foreign rights agent.

Galleys. The first typeset version of a manuscript that has not yet been divided into pages.

Genre. Refers to either a general classification of writing such as a novel, poem or short story or to the categories within those classifications, such as problem novels or sonnets. Genre fiction is a term that covers various types of commercial novels such as mystery, romance, western or science fiction.

Ghosting or ghost writing. When a writer puts into literary form the words, ideas or knowledge of another person under that person's name it is called ghostwriting. Some agents offer this service. Others will pair ghostwriters with celebrities or experts.

Glossy. A black and white photograph with a shiny surface as opposed to one with a non-shiny matte finish.

Imprint. The name applied to a publisher's specific line of books (e.g. Aerie books, an imprint of Tor Books.)

IRC. International Reply Coupons; purchased at a post office to enclose with material sent outside your country to cover the cost of return postage. The recipient can turn in the coupons for stamps in their own country.

Leave-behinds. Promotional or direct mail flyers, brochures or other information about a talent designed to be left with a prospective buyer.

Letter-quality submission. A computer printout that looks like a typewritten manuscript.

Mainstream fiction. Fiction on subjects or trends that transcend popular novel categories such as mystery or romance. Using conventional methods, this kind of fiction tells stories about people and their conflicts.

Marketing fee. Fee charged by some agents to cover marketing expenses. It may be used to cover postage, telephone calls, faxes, photocopying or any other expense incurred in marketing a manuscript.

Mass market paperbacks. Softcover book, usually around 4 × 7, on a popular subject directed at a general audience and sold in groceries and drugstores as well as bookstores.

MFTS. Made for TV series. A series developed for television also known as episodics, usually used when referring to a dramatic series.

Middle reader. The general classification of books written for readers 9-11 years old.

Midlist. Those titles on a publisher's list expected to have limited sales. Midlist books are mainstream, not literary, scholarly or genre, and are usually written by new or unknown writers.

Mini-series. A limited dramatic series written for television, often based on a popular novel.

MOW. Movie of the week. A movie script written especially for television, usually seven acts with time for commercial breaks. Topics are often contemporary, sometimes controversial, fictional accounts. Also known as a made-for-TV-movie.

Multiple submission. The practice of submitting copies of the same manuscript to several agents or publishers at the same time. Also called simultaneous submissions.

Net receipts. One method of royalty payment based on the amount of money a book publisher receives on the sale of the book after the booksellers' discounts, special sales discounts and returned copies.

Novelization. A novel created from the script of a popular movie, usually called a movie "tie-in" and published in paperback.

Novella. A short novel or long short story, usually 7,000 to 15,000 words. Also called a novelette.

Outline. A summary of a book's contents in five to 15 double-spaced pages; often in the form of chapter headings with a descriptive sentence or two under each one to show the scope of the book. A screenplay's or teleplay's outline is a scene-by-scene narrative description of the story (10-15 pages for a ½-hour teleplay; 15-25 pages for 1-hour; 25-40 pages for 90 minutes and 40-60 pages for a 2-hour feature film or teleplay).

Over-the-transom. Slang for the path of an unsolicited manuscript into the slush pile.

Photostats. Black-and-white copies produced by an inexpensive photographic process using paper negatives; only line values are held with accuracy. Also called a stat.

Picture book. A type of book aimed at the preschool to 8-year-old that tells the story primarily or entirely with artwork. Agents and reps interested in selling to publishers of these books often handle both artists and writers.

PMT. Photomechanical transfer, photostat produced without a negative, somewhat like the Polaroid process.

Portfolio. A group of photographs or artwork samples (slides, originals, tearsheets, photocopies) assembled to demonstrate an artist's or photographer's style and abilities, often presented to clients.

Promotional piece. Also called promo piece. Material designed to promote an artist's or photographer's work. Usually more expensively produced and elaborate than a direct-mail or leave-behind piece, a promo piece can be colorful, include special printing techniques or folds.

Proofreading. Close reading and correction of a manuscript's typographical errors. A few agents offer this service for a fee.

Proofs. A typeset version of a manuscript used for correcting errors and making changes, often a photocopy of the galleys.

Proposal. An offer to an editor or publisher to write a specific work, usually a package consisting of an outline and sample chapters.

Prospectus. A preliminary, written description of a book, usually one page in length.

Query. A letter written to an agent, rep, or a potential market, to elicit interest in a writer's, artist's or photographer's work.

Release. A statement that your idea is original, has never been sold to anyone else and that you are selling negotiated rights to the idea upon payment.

Remainders. Leftover copies of an out-of-print or slow-selling book, which can be purchased from the publisher at a reduced rate. Depending on the author's contract, a reduced royalty or no royalty is paid on remaindered books.

Reporting time. The time it takes the agent or rep to get back to you on your query or submission.

Roughs. Preliminary sketches or drawings.

Royalties. A percentage of the retail price paid to the author for each copy of the book that is sold. Agents take their percentage from the royalties earned as well as from the advance.

SASE. Self-addressed, stamped envelope. This or a self-addressed, stamped postcard should be included with all your correspondence with reps or agents.

Scholarly books. Books written for an academic or research audience. These are usually heavily researched, technical and often contain terms used only within a specific field.

Screenplay. Script for a film intended to be shown in movie theaters.

Script. Broad term covering teleplay, screenplay or stage play. Sometimes used as a shortened version of the word "manuscript" when referring to books.

Simultaneous submission. Sending the same manuscript to several agents or publishers at the same time. Simultaneous query letters are common, but simultaneous submissions are unacceptable to many agents or publishers. See also *multiple submission*.

Sitcom. Situation comedy. Episodic comedy script for a television series. Term comes from the characters dealing with various situations with humorous results.

Slides. Usually called transparencies; positive color slides.

Slush pile. A stack of unsolicited submissions in the office of an editor, agent or publisher.

Standard commission. The commission an agent or rep earns on the sales of a manuscript, illustration or photograph. For literary agents, this commission percentage (usually between 10 and 20 percent) is taken from the advance and royalties paid to the writer. For script agents, the commission is taken from script sales; if handling plays, agents take a percentage from the box office proceeds. For art and photo reps the commission (usually 25 to 30 percent) is taken from sales.

Stock photo agency. A business that maintains a large collection of photos which it makes available to clients such as advertising agencies and periodicals. These agencies (not listed in this book) take a percentage from work sold for the photographer. Unlike photo reps, these agencies do not handle the careers of individual photographers, but sell the work of various photographers to clients looking for specific images. Stock agency listings may be found in *Photographer's Market*.

Storyboards. Series of panels which illustrates a progressive sequence or graphics and story copy for a TV commercial, film or filmstrip. Serves as a guide for an eventual finished product. Some artists specialize in doing storyboard work.

Subagent. An agent who handles certain subsidiary rights. This agent usually works in conjunction with the agent who has handled the book rights and the percentage paid the book agent is increased to cover paying the subagent.

Subsidiary. An incorporated branch of a company or conglomerate (e.g. Alfred Knopf, Inc., is a subsidiary of Random House, Inc.)

Subsidiary rights. All rights other than book publishing rights included in a book publishing contract, such as paperback rights, bookclub rights, movie rights. Part of an agent's job is to negotiate those rights and advise you on which to sell and which to keep.

Synopsis. A brief summary of a story, novel or play. As a part of a book proposal, it is a comprehensive summary condensed in a page or page and a half, single-spaced. See also *outline*.

Talent. When used in commercial art circles, talent refers to the artist or photographer. See *client*.

Tearsheet. Published samples of your work, usually pages torn from a magazine.

Textbook. Book to be used in a classroom situation—may be on the elementary, high school or college level.

Thumbnail. A rough layout in miniature, usually used in reference to a book or other large project.

Trade book. Either a hard cover or soft cover book; subject matter frequently concerns a special interest for a general audience; sold mainly in bookstores.

Trade paperback. A softbound volume, usually around 5 × 8, published and designed for the general public, available mainly in bookstores.

Transparencies. Positive color slides; not color prints.

Treatment. Synopsis of a television or film script (40-60 pages for a 2-hour feature film or teleplay).

Unsolicited manuscript. An unrequested manuscript sent to an editor, agent or publisher. A cold submission of an entire manuscript.

Young adult. The general classification of books written for readers age 12-18.

Young reader. Books written for readers 5-8 years old. Unlike picture books, artwork only supports the text.

Indexes

Subject Index

The following subject index is divided into nonfiction and fiction subject categories for each of three sections—Nonfee-charging Literary Agents, Fee-charging Literary Agents and Script Agents. To find an agent who is interested in the type of manuscript you've written, see the appropriate sections under subject headings that best describe your work. Check the Listings Index for the page number of the agent's listing. Agents who said they were open to most nonfiction or fiction subjects appear in the "Open" heading.

Nonfee charging agents

Fiction

Action/adventure
Acton and Dystel, Inc.; Allan Agency, Lee; Amsterdam Agency, Marcia; Appleseeds Management; Barrett Literary Agency, Helen; Brandt & Brandt Literary Agents Inc.; Carvainis Agency, Inc., Maria; Cohen, Inc. Literary Agency, Ruth; Curtis Associates, Inc., Richard; Curtis Bruce Agency, The; Diamant, The Writer's Workshop, Inc., Anita; Diamond Literary Agency, Inc.; Dight Literary Agency, Janet; Dijkstra Literary Agency, Sandra; Ducas, Robert; Dupree/Miller and Associates Inc. Literary; Ellenberg Literary Agency, Ethan; Fields-Rita Scott Inc., Marje; Flaming Star Literary Enterprises; Garon-Brooke Assoc. Inc., Jay; Gotler Inc., Joel; Greenburger Associates, Stanford J.; Hawkins & Associates, Inc., John; Hegler Literary Agency, Gary L.; Hull House Literary Agency; Jarvis & Co., Inc., Sharon; Jones Agency, Leon; Jones Literary Agency, Lloyd; Klinger, Inc., Harvey; Lampack Agency, Inc., Peter; Lantz-Joy Harris Literary Agency, The Robert; Leavitt Agency, The Ned; Leone Agency, Inc., The Adele; Lincoln Literary Agency, Ray; Literary Group, The; Love Literary Agency, Nancy; Merhige-Merdon Marketing/Promo Co. Inc., Greg; Millard Literary Agency, Martha; Naggar Literary Agency, Jean V.; Parks Agency, The Richard; Pelter, Rodney; Perkins Associates, L.; Picard Literary Agent, Alison J.; Schmidt Literary Agency, Harold; Siegel Literary Agency, Bobbe; Wald Associates, Inc., Mary Jack; Weiner Literary Agency, Cherry; Zeckendorf Assoc. Inc., Susan

Cartoon/comic
Axelrod Agency, The; Dupree/Miller and Associates Inc. Literary; Ellenberg Literary Agency, Ethan; Hawkins & Associates, Inc., John; Lampack Agency, Inc., Peter; Lantz-Joy Harris Literary Agency, The Robert; Merhige-Merdon Marketing/Promo Co. Inc., Greg; Pelter, Rodney; Perkins Associates, L.; Rees Literary Agency, Helen; Rubinstein, Literary Agent, Pesha; Van Der Leun & Associates

Confessional
Barrett Literary Agency, Helen; Dight Literary Agency, Janet; Fields-Rita Scott Inc., Marje; Flaming Star Literary Enterprises; Gotler Inc., Joel; Jones Literary Agency, Lloyd; Lantz-Joy Harris Literary Agency, The Robert; Merhige-Merdon Marketing/Promo Co. Inc., Greg; Naggar Literary Agency, Jean V.; Pelter, Rodney; Rees Literary Agency, Helen

Contemporary issues
Acton and Dystel, Inc.; Agents Inc. for Medical and Mental Health Professionals; Barrett Literary Agency, Helen; Blassingame, McCauley & Wood; Boates Literary Agency, Reid; Bova Literary Agency, The Barbara; Brandt Agency, The Joan; Brandt & Brandt Literary Agents Inc.; Cantrell-Colas Inc., Literary Agency; Carvainis Agency, Inc., Maria; Casselman Literary Agent,

Martha; Coopersmith Literary Agency, Julia; de la Haba Agency, The Lois; Diamant, The Writer's Workshop, Inc., Anita; Diamond Literary Agency, Inc.; Dijkstra Literary Agency, Sandra; Ducas, Robert; Dupree/Miller and Associates Inc. Literary; Elder Agency, Joseph; Flaming Star Literary Enterprises; Fogelman Publishing Interests Inc.; Garon-Brooke Assoc. Inc., Jay; Greenburger Associates, Stanford J.; Hawkins & Associates, Inc., John; Jones Agency, Leon; Jones Literary Agency, Lloyd; Kouts, Literary Agent, Barbara S.; Kroll Literary Agency, Edite; Lampack Agency, Inc., Peter; Lantz-Joy Harris Literary Agency, The Robert; Lasbury Literary Agency, M. Sue; Leavitt Agency, The Ned; Lescher & Lescher Ltd.; Levine Communications, James; Lincoln Literary Agency, Ray; Los Angeles Literary Associates; Love Literary Agency, Nancy; McGrath, Helen; Millard Literary Agency, Martha; Neighbors Inc., Charles; Noetzli Literary Agency, Regula; Parks Agency, The Richard; Pelter, Rodney; Picard Literary Agent, Alison J.; Quicksilver Books-Literary Agents; Rees Literary Agency, Helen; Schlessinger-Van Dyck Agency; Schwartz, Esquire, Laurens R.; Schmidt Literary Agency, Harold; Seligman, Literary Agent, Lynn; Shepard Agency, The; Siegel Literary Agency, Bobbe; Singer Literary Agency, Evelyn; Spitzer Literary Agency, Philip; Stauffer Associates, Nancy; Stern Literary Agency, Gloria; Van Der Leun & Associates; Wald Associates, Inc., Mary Jack; Watkins Loomis Agency, Inc.; Weiner Literary Agency, Cherry; Weingel-Fidel Agency, The; Zeckendorf Assoc. Inc., Susan

Detective/police/crime

Acton and Dystel, Inc.; Agency Chicago; Allan Agency, Lee; Allen, Literary Agency, James; Appleseeds Management; Axelrod Agency, The; Bach Literary Agency, Julian; Barrett Literary Agency, Helen; Boates Literary Agency, Reid; Brandt Agency, The Joan; Brandt & Brandt Literary Agents Inc.; Cantrell-Colas Inc., Literary Agency; Carvainis Agency, Inc., Maria; Casselman Literary Agent, Martha; Cohen, Inc. Literary Agency, Ruth; Curtis Associates, Inc., Richard; Diamant, The Writer's Workshop, Inc., Anita; Diamond Literary Agency, Inc.; Dijkstra Literary Agency, Sandra; Ducas, Robert; Dupree/Miller and Associates Inc. Literary; Elder Agency, Joseph; Ellenberg Literary Agency, Ethan; Fields-Rita Scott Inc., Marje; Flaming Star Literary Enterprises; Fogelman Publishing Interests Inc.; Garon-Brooke Assoc. Inc., Jay; Gotler Inc., Joel; Greenburger Associates, Stanford J.; Hawkins & Associates, Inc., John; Hegler Literary Agency, Gary L.; Hull House Literary Agency; Jarvis & Co., Inc., Sharon; J de S Associates Inc.; Jones Agency, Leon; Jones Literary Agency, Lloyd; Kidde, Hoyt & Picard; Klinger, Inc., Harvey; Lampack Agency, Inc., Peter; Lantz-Joy Harris Literary Agency, The Robert; Lasbury Literary Agency, M. Sue; Leavitt Agency, The Ned; Leone Agency, Inc., The Adele; Lincoln Literary Agency, Ray; Literary Group, The; Love Literary Agency, Nancy; McGrath, Helen; Merhige-Merdon Marketing/Promo Co. Inc., Greg; Millard Literary Agency, Martha; Multimedia Product Development, Inc.; Neighbors Inc., Charles; Noetzli Literary Agency, Regula; Nugent Literary Agency, Ray E.; Parks Agency, The Richard; Pelter, Rodney; Perkins Associates, L.; Picard Literary Agent, Alison J.; Rees Literary Agency, Helen; Rubinstein, Literary Agent, Pesha; Schlessinger-Van Dyck Agency; Schmidt Literary Agency, Harold; Seligman, Literary Agent, Lynn; Siegel Literary Agency, Bobbe; Singer Literary Agency, Evelyn; Spitzer Literary Agency, Philip; Steele & Co., Ltd., Lyle; Stern Literary Agency, Gloria; Wald Associates, Inc., Mary Jack; Weiner Literary Agency, Cherry; Weingel-Fidel Agency, The; Zeckendorf Assoc. Inc., Susan

Erotica

Agency Chicago; Authors and Artists Group, Inc.; Brandt & Brandt Literary Agents Inc.; Diamond Literary Agency, Inc.; Gotler Inc., Joel; Jones Literary Agency, Lloyd; Lantz-Joy Harris Literary Agency, The Robert; Leavitt Agency, The Ned; Nugent Literary Agency, Ray E.; Pelter, Rodney; Spatt, Esq., David M.

Ethnic

Acton and Dystel, Inc.; Brandt & Brandt Literary Agents Inc.; Cantrell-Colas Inc., Literary Agency; Cohen, Inc. Literary Agency, Ruth; Crown International Literature and Arts Agency, Bonnie R.; Diamond Literary Agency, Inc.; Dight Literary Agency, Janet; Dijkstra Literary Agency, Sandra; Gotler Inc., Joel; Greenburger Associates, Stanford J.; Hawkins & Associates, Inc., John; Jones Literary Agency, Lloyd; Lantz-Joy Harris Literary Agency, The Robert; Lincoln Literary Agency, Ray; Love Literary Agency, Nancy; Merhige-Merdon Marketing/Promo Co. Inc., Greg; Naggar Literary Agency, Jean V.; Noetzli Literary Agency, Regula; Pelter, Rodney; Perkins Associates, L.; Picard Literary Agent, Alison J.; Schmidt Literary Agency, Harold; Seligman, Literary Agent, Lynn; Stern Literary Agency, Gloria; Van Der Leun & Associates; Wald Associates, Inc., Mary Jack; Zeckendorf Assoc. Inc., Susan

Experimental
Agency Chicago; Brandt & Brandt Literary Agents Inc.; Cantrell-Colas Inc., Literary Agency; de la Haba Agency, The Lois; Diamant, The Writer's Workshop, Inc., Anita; Flaming Star Literary Enterprises; Gotler Inc., Joel; Hawkins & Associates, Inc., John; Lantz-Joy Harris Literary Agency, The Robert; Millard Literary Agency, Martha; Pelter, Rodney; Stern Literary Agency, Gloria; Wald Associates, Inc., Mary Jack

Family saga
Acton and Dystel, Inc.; Axelrod Agency, The; Barrett Literary Agency, Helen; Boates Literary Agency, Reid; Brandt & Brandt Literary Agents Inc.; Buchanan Literary Agency, Jane; Cantrell-Colas Inc., Literary Agency; Carvainis Agency, Inc., Maria; Curtis Associates, Inc., Richard; Curtis Bruce Agency, The; Diamant, The Writer's Workshop, Inc., Anita; Diamond Literary Agency, Inc.; Elder Agency, Joseph; Ellenberg Literary Agency, Ethan; Fields-Rita Scott Inc., Marje; Flaming Star Literary Enterprises; Fogelman Publishing Interests Inc.; Gotler Inc., Joel; Greenburger Associates, Stanford J.; Hawkins & Associates, Inc., John; Jones Agency, Leon; Klinger, Inc., Harvey; Kouts, Literary Agent, Barbara S.; Lampack Agency, Inc., Peter; Lantz-Joy Harris Literary Agency, The Robert; Leavitt Agency, The Ned; McGrath, Helen; Merhige-Merdon Marketing/Promo Co. Inc., Greg; MGA Agency Inc.; Millard Literary Agency, Martha; Naggar Literary Agency, Jean V.; Noetzli Literary Agency, Regula; Parks Agency, The Richard; Pelter, Rodney; Rees Literary Agency, Helen; Schmidt Literary Agency, Harold; Shepard Agency, The; Siegel Literary Agency, Bobbe; Steele & Co., Ltd., Lyle; Wald Associates, Inc., Mary Jack; Weiner Literary Agency, Cherry; Zeckendorf Assoc. Inc., Susan

Fantasy
Allan Agency, Lee; Allen, Literary Agency, James; Appleseeds Management; Butler, Art and Literary Agent, Jane; Carvainis Agency, Inc., Maria; Curtis Associates, Inc., Richard; Curtis Bruce Agency, The; Diamant, The Writer's Workshop, Inc., Anita; Dight Literary Agency, Janet; Dijkstra Literary Agency, Sandra; Elder Agency, Joseph; Ellenberg Literary Agency, Ethan; Garon-Brooke Assoc. Inc., Jay; Gotler Inc., Joel; Greenburger Associates, Stanford J.; Jarvis & Co., Inc., Sharon; Leavitt Agency, The Ned; Leone Agency, Inc., The Adele; Lincoln Literary Agency, Ray; Millard Literary Agency, Martha; Naggar Literary Agency, Jean V.; Schwartz, Esquire, Laurens R.; Seligman, Literary Agent, Lynn; Siegel Literary Agency, Bobbe; Smith, Literary Agent, Valerie; Spatt, Esq., David M.; Stern Literary Agency, Gloria; Wald Associates, Inc., Mary Jack; Weiner Literary Agency, Cherry

Feminist
Bach Literary Agency, Julian; Brandt & Brandt Literary Agents Inc.; Cantrell-Colas Inc., Literary Agency; Curtis Associates, Inc., Richard; Diamant, The Writer's Workshop, Inc., Anita; Diamond Literary Agency, Inc.; Dight Literary Agency, Janet; Dijkstra Literary Agency, Sandra; Ducas, Robert; Dupree/Miller and Associates Inc. Literary; Gotler Inc., Joel; Greenburger Associates, Stanford J.; Hawkins & Associates, Inc., John; Kidde, Hoyt & Picard; Kouts, Literary Agent, Barbara S.; Kroll Literary Agency, Edite; Lantz-Joy Harris Literary Agency, The Robert; Lincoln Literary Agency, Ray; Merhige-Merdon Marketing/Promo Co. Inc., Greg; Millard Literary Agency, Martha; Naggar Literary Agency, Jean V.; Noetzli Literary Agency, Regula; Pelter, Rodney; Picard Literary Agent, Alison J.; Rees Literary Agency, Helen; Schaffner Agency, Inc.; Schmidt Literary Agency, Harold; Seligman, Literary Agent, Lynn; Siegel Literary Agency, Bobbe; Stern Literary Agency, Gloria; Wald Associates, Inc., Mary Jack

Gay
Bach Literary Agency, Julian; Brandt & Brandt Literary Agents Inc.; Diamant, The Writer's Workshop, Inc., Anita; Ducas, Robert; Dupree/Miller and Associates Inc. Literary; Fields-Rita Scott Inc., Marje; Garon-Brooke Assoc. Inc., Jay; Greenburger Associates, Stanford J.; Hawkins & Associates, Inc., John; Kidde, Hoyt & Picard; Lantz-Joy Harris Literary Agency, The Robert; Lincoln Literary Agency, Ray; Naggar Literary Agency, Jean V.; Parks Agency, The Richard; Picard Literary Agent, Alison J.; Schmidt Literary Agency, Harold; Steele & Co., Ltd., Lyle; Wald Associates, Inc., Mary Jack

Glitz

Acton and Dystel, Inc.; Amsterdam Agency, Marcia; Authors and Artists Group, Inc.; Carvainis Agency, Inc., Maria; Diamond Literary Agency, Inc.; Dight Literary Agency, Janet; Dijkstra Literary Agency, Sandra; Dupree/Miller and Associates Inc. Literary; Ellenberg Literary Agency, Ethan; Flaming Star Literary Enterprises; Garon-Brooke Assoc. Inc., Jay; Greenburger Associates, Stanford J.; Hawkins & Associates, Inc., John; Jarvis & Co., Inc., Sharon; Klinger, Inc., Harvey; Lampack Agency, Inc., Peter; Lantz-Joy Harris Literary Agency, The Robert; Leavitt Agency, The Ned; Leone Agency, Inc., The Adele; Multimedia Product Development, Inc.; Naggar Literary Agency, Jean V.; Parks Agency, The Richard; Pelter, Rodney; Picard Literary Agent, Alison J.; Rees Literary Agency, Helen; Rubinstein, Literary Agent, Pesha; Schmidt Literary Agency, Harold; Siegel Literary Agency, Bobbe; Teal Literary Agency, Patricia; Wald Associates, Inc., Mary Jack; Weiner Literary Agency, Cherry; Zeckendorf Assoc. Inc., Susan

Historical

Acton and Dystel, Inc.; Allan Agency, Lee; Allen, Literary Agency, James; Amsterdam Agency, Marcia; Appleseeds Management; Authors and Artists Group, Inc.; Axelrod Agency, The; Barrett Literary Agency, Helen; Blassingame, McCauley & Wood; Brandt & Brandt Literary Agents Inc.; Buchanan Literary Agency, Jane; Butler, Art and Literary Agent, Jane; Cantrell-Colas Inc., Literary Agency; Carvainis Agency, Inc., Maria; Cohen, Inc. Literary Agency, Ruth; Crown International Literature and Arts Agency, Bonnie R.; Curtis Associates, Inc., Richard; Davie Literary Agency, Elaine; de la Haba Agency, The Lois; Diamant, The Writer's Workshop, Inc., Anita; Dijkstra Literary Agency, Sandra; Ducas, Robert; Dupree/Miller and Associates Inc. Literary; Elder Agency, Joseph; Ellenberg Literary Agency, Ethan; Elmo Agency Inc., Ann; Fields-Rita Scott Inc., Marje; Flaming Star Literary Enterprises; Fogelman Publishing Interests Inc.; Garon-Brooke Assoc. Inc., Jay; Gotler Inc., Joel; Greenburger Associates, Stanford J.; Hawkins & Associates, Inc., John; Hull House Literary Agency; Jarvis & Co., Inc., Sharon; J de S Associates Inc.; Jones Agency, Leon; Kouts, Literary Agent, Barbara S.; Lampack Agency, Inc., Peter; Lantz-Joy Harris Literary Agency, The Robert; Lasbury Literary Agency, M. Sue; Leavitt Agency, The Ned; Leone Agency, Inc., The Adele; Lescher & Lescher Ltd.; Lincoln Literary Agency, Ray; Millard Literary Agency, Martha; Multimedia Product Development, Inc.; Naggar Literary Agency, Jean V.; Noetzli Literary Agency, Regula; Parks Agency, The Richard; Pelter, Rodney; Picard Literary Agent, Alison J.; Rees Literary Agency, Helen; Rosenthal Literary Agency, Jean; Rubinstein, Literary Agent, Pesha; Schlessinger-Van Dyck Agency; Schmidt Literary Agency, Harold; Seligman, Literary Agent, Lynn; Shepard Agency, The; Siegel Literary Agency, Bobbe; Singer Literary Agency, Evelyn; Steele & Co., Ltd., Lyle; Van Der Leun & Associates; Wald Associates, Inc., Mary Jack; Wecksler-Incomco; Weiner Literary Agency, Cherry; Zeckendorf Assoc. Inc., Susan

Humor/satire

Agency Chicago; Ajlouny Agency, The Joseph S.; Allan Agency, Lee; Amsterdam Agency, Marcia; Appleseeds Management; Bach Literary Agency, Julian; Brandt & Brandt Literary Agents Inc.; Cantrell-Colas Inc., Literary Agency; Carvainis Agency, Inc., Maria; Curtis Bruce Agency, The; Dijkstra Literary Agency, Sandra; Ducas, Robert; Dupree/Miller and Associates Inc. Literary; Ellenberg Literary Agency, Ethan; Gotler Inc., Joel; Greenburger Associates, Stanford J.; Hawkins & Associates, Inc., John; Jones Agency, Leon; Kidde, Hoyt & Picard; Kroll Literary Agency, Edite; Lantz-Joy Harris Literary Agency, The Robert; Leavitt Agency, The Ned; Lescher & Lescher Ltd.; Lincoln Literary Agency, Ray; Literary Group, The; Merhige-Merdon Marketing/Promo Co. Inc., Greg; Noetzli Literary Agency, Regula; Pelter, Rodney; Picard Literary Agent, Alison J.; Rees Literary Agency, Helen; Seligman, Literary Agent, Lynn; Shepard Agency, The; Wald Associates, Inc., Mary Jack

Juvenile

Allan Agency, Lee; Brown Literary Agency, Inc., Andrea; Carvainis Agency, Inc., Maria; Casselman Literary Agent, Martha; Cohen, Inc. Literary Agency, Ruth; Curtis Bruce Agency, The; de la Haba Agency, The Lois; Diamant, The Writer's Workshop, Inc., Anita; Dight Literary Agency, Janet; Dijkstra Literary Agency, Sandra; Elek Associates, Peter; Ellenberg Literary Agency, Ethan; Gotham Art & Literary Agency Inc.; Gotler Inc., Joel; Greenburger Associates, Stanford J.; Hawkins & Associates, Inc., John; Hegler Literary Agency, Gary L.; J de S Associates Inc.; Jones Agency, Leon; Jones Literary Agency, Lloyd; Kouts, Literary Agent, Barbara S.; Kroll

Lesbian

Literary

Mainstream

Stanford J.; Hawkins & Associates, Inc., John; Hegler Literary Agency, Gary L.; Hull House Literary Agency; International Publisher Associates Inc.; Jarvis & Co., Inc., Sharon; J de S Associates Inc.; Jones Agency, Leon; Jones Literary Agency, Lloyd; Kidde, Hoyt & Picard; Klinger, Inc., Harvey; Kouts, Literary Agent, Barbara S.; Kroll Literary Agency, Edite; Lampack Agency, Inc., Peter; Lantz-Joy Harris Literary Agency, The Robert; Lasbury Literary Agency, M. Sue; Leavitt Agency, The Ned; Leone Agency, Inc., The Adele; Levant & Wales, Literary Agency, Inc.; Lincoln Literary Agency, Ray; Lipkind Agency, Wendy; Lord Literistic, Inc., Sterling; Los Angeles Literary Associates; Love Literary Agency, Nancy; Lowenstein Associates, Inc.; Maccoby Literary Agency, Gina; McGrath, Helen; Merhige-Merdon Marketing/Promo Co. Inc., Greg; Millard Literary Agency, Martha; Multimedia Product Development, Inc.; Naggar Literary Agency, Jean V.; Neighbors Inc., Charles; Noetzli Literary Agency, Regula; Parks Agency, The Richard; Paton Literary Agency, Kathi J.; Pelter, Rodney; Perkins Associates, L.; Picard Literary Agent, Alison J.; Quicksilver Books-Literary Agents; Rees Literary Agency, Helen; Schlessinger-Van Dyck Agency; Schmidt Literary Agency, Harold; Schwartz, Esquire, Laurens R.; Seligman, Literary Agent, Lynn; Siegel Literary Agency, Bobbe; Smith, Literary Agent, Valerie; Spitzer Literary Agency, Philip; Stauffer Associates, Nancy; Sterling Lord Literistic, Inc.; Stern Literary Agency, Gloria; Teal Literary Agency, Patricia; Van Der Leun & Associates; Wald Associates, Inc., Mary Jack; Ware Literary Agency, John A.; Watkins Loomis Agency, Inc.; Weiner Literary Agency, Cherry; Weingel-Fidel Agency, The; Wreschner, Authors' Representative, Ruth; Zeckendorf Assoc. Inc., Susan

Mystery/suspense

Acton and Dystel, Inc.; Allan Agency, Lee; Allen, Literary Agency, James; Amsterdam Agency, Marcia; Appleseeds Management; Axelrod Agency, The; Barrett Literary Agency, Helen; Blassingame, McCauley & Wood; Boates Literary Agency, Reid; Bova Literary Agency, The Barbara; Brandt Agency, The Joan; Brandt & Brandt Literary Agents Inc.; Cantrell-Colas Inc., Literary Agency; Carvainis Agency, Inc., Maria; Cohen, Inc. Literary Agency, Ruth; Columbia Literary Associates, Inc.; Curtis Associates, Inc., Richard; Curtis Bruce Agency, The; Davie Literary Agency, Elaine; de la Haba Agency, The Lois; Diamant, The Writer's Workshop, Inc., Anita; Diamond Literary Agency, Inc.; Dight Literary Agency, Janet; Dijkstra Literary Agency, Sandra; Ducas, Robert; Dupree/Miller and Associates Inc. Literary; Eisenberg Literary Agency, Vicki; Elder Agency, Joseph; Ellenberg Literary Agency, Ethan; Fallon Literary Agency, The; Fields-Rita Scott Inc., Marje; Flaming Star Literary Enterprises; Fox Chase Agency Inc., The; Garon-Brooke Assoc. Inc., Jay; Gartenberg, Literary Agent, Max; Goodman Literary Agency, Irene; Gotler Inc., Joel; Greenburger Associates, Stanford J.; Hawkins & Associates, Inc., John; Hegler Literary Agency, Gary L.; Hull House Literary Agency; Jarvis & Co., Inc., Sharon; J de S Associates Inc.; Jones Agency, Leon; Jones Literary Agency, Lloyd; Kidde, Hoyt & Picard; Klinger, Inc., Harvey; Kouts, Literary Agent, Barbara S.; Kroll Literary Agency, Edite; Lampack Agency, Inc., Peter; Lantz-Joy Harris Literary Agency, The Robert; Lasbury Literary Agency, M. Sue; Leavitt Agency, The Ned; Leone Agency, Inc., The Adele; Lescher & Lescher Ltd.; Lincoln Literary Agency, Ray; Lipkind Agency, Wendy; Literary Group, The; Love Literary Agency, Nancy; Maccoby Literary Agency, Gina; McGrath, Helen; Merhige-Merdon Marketing/Promo Co. Inc., Greg; MGA Agency Inc.; Millard Literary Agency, Martha; Multimedia Product Development, Inc.; Naggar Literary Agency, Jean V.; Noetzli Literary Agency, Regula; Nugent Literary Agency, Ray E.; Parks Agency, The Richard; Pelter, Rodney; Perkins Associates, L.; Picard Literary Agent, Alison J.; Rees Literary Agency, Helen; Rosenthal Literary Agency, Jean; Rubinstein, Literary Agent, Pesha; Schlessinger-Van Dyck Agency; Schmidt Literary Agency, Harold; Seligman, Literary Agent, Lynn; Siegel Literary Agency, Bobbe; Singer Literary Agency, Evelyn; Snell Literary Agency, Michael; Spitzer Literary Agency, Philip; Steele & Co., Ltd., Lyle; Stern Literary Agency, Gloria; Teal Literary Agency, Patricia; Wald Associates, Inc., Mary Jack; Ware Literary Agency, John A.; Watkins Loomis Agency, Inc.; Weiner Literary Agency, Cherry; Weingel-Fidel Agency, The; Wreschner, Authors' Representative, Ruth; Zeckendorf Assoc. Inc., Susan

Open to all fiction areas

Allen Literary Agency, Linda; Barrett Books Inc., Loretta; Brown Ltd., Curtis; Buck Agency, Howard; Cohen Literary Agency Ltd., Hy; Collier Associates; Congdon Associates, Inc., Don; Eisenbach Inc., Robert; Evans and Associates; Goldfarb, Kaufman, & O'Toole; Goodman Associates; Gusay Literary Agency, The Charlotte; Hamilburg Agency, The Mitchell J.; Hoffman Literary Agency, Berenice; Kirchoff/Wohlberg, Inc., Authors' Representation Division; Larsen/Elizabeth Pomada Literary Agents, Michael; Lazear Agency Incorporated, The; Maccampbell

Science fiction

Allan Agency, Lee; Allen, Literary Agency, James; Amsterdam Agency, Marcia; Appleseeds Management; Blassingame, McCauley & Wood; Brandt & Brandt Literary Agents Inc.; Cantrell-Colas Inc., Literary Agency; Curtis Associates, Inc., Richard; Curtis Bruce Agency, The; de la Haba Agency, The Lois; Diamant, The Writer's Workshop, Inc., Anita; Dight Literary Agency, Janet; Dijkstra Literary Agency, Sandra; Dupree/Miller and Associates Inc. Literary; Elder Agency, Joseph; Ellenberg Literary Agency, Ethan; Flaming Star Literary Enterprises; Fox Chase Agency Inc., The; Garon-Brooke Assoc. Inc., Jay; Gotler Inc., Joel; Greenburger Associates, Stanford J.; Hawkins & Associates, Inc., John; Jarvis & Co., Inc., Sharon; Jones Agency, Leon; Leavitt Agency, The Ned; Leone Agency, Inc., The Adele; Lincoln Literary Agency, Ray; McGrath, Helen; MGA Agency Inc.; Millard Literary Agency, Martha; Naggar Literary Agency, Jean V.; Neighbors Inc., Charles; Parks Agency, The Richard; Rees Literary Agency, Helen; Schmidt Literary Agency, Harold; Siegel Literary Agency, Bobbe; Smith, Literary Agent, Valerie; Spatt, Esq., David M.; Stern Literary Agency, Gloria; Wald Associates, Inc., Mary Jack; Watkins Loomis Agency, Inc.

Sports

Acton and Dystel, Inc.; Brandt & Brandt Literary Agents Inc.; Curtis Bruce Agency, The; de la Haba Agency, The Lois; Dight Literary Agency, Janet; Dijkstra Literary Agency, Sandra; Ducas, Robert; Dupree/Miller and Associates Inc. Literary; Elder Agency, Joseph; Ellenberg Literary Agency, Ethan; Fields-Rita Scott Inc., Marje; Flaming Star Literary Enterprises; Fox Chase Agency Inc., The; Greenburger Associates, Stanford J.; Hawkins & Associates, Inc., John; Jones Agency, Leon; Lantz-Joy Harris Literary Agency, The Robert; Leavitt Agency, The Ned; Lincoln Literary Agency, Ray; Literary Group, The; McGrath, Helen; Merhige-Merdon Marketing/Promo Co. Inc., Greg; Noetzli Literary Agency, Regula; Pelter, Rodney; Picard Literary Agent, Alison J.; Rees Literary Agency, Helen; Shepard Agency, The; Spitzer Literary Agency, Philip; Wald Associates, Inc., Mary Jack

Thriller/espionage

Acton and Dystel, Inc.; Allan Agency, Lee; Amsterdam Agency, Marcia; Appleseeds Management; Authors and Artists Group, Inc.; Axelrod Agency, The; Barrett Literary Agency, Helen; Boates Literary Agency, Reid; Brandt Agency, The Joan; Brandt & Brandt Literary Agents Inc.; Cantrell-Colas Inc., Literary Agency; Carvainis Agency, Inc., Maria; Columbia Literary Associates, Inc.; Curtis Associates, Inc., Richard; Curtis Bruce Agency, The; Darhansoff & Verrill Literary Agents; de la Haba Agency, The Lois; Diamant, The Writer's Workshop, Inc., Anita; Diamond Literary Agency, Inc.; Dight Literary Agency, Janet; Dijkstra Literary Agency, Sandra; Ducas, Robert; Dupree/Miller and Associates Inc. Literary; Elder Agency, Joseph; Ellenberg Literary Agency, Ethan; Fields-Rita Scott Inc., Marje; Flaming Star Literary Enterprises; Gotler Inc., Joel; Greenburger Associates, Stanford J.; Hawkins & Associates, Inc., John; Hull House Literary Agency; Jarvis & Co., Inc., Sharon; Jones Agency, Leon; Jones Literary Agency, Lloyd; Kidde, Hoyt & Picard; Klinger, Inc., Harvey; Lampack Agency, Inc., Peter; Lantz-Joy Harris Literary Agency, The Robert; Leavitt Agency, The Ned; Leone Agency, Inc., The Adele; Lescher & Lescher Ltd.; Lincoln Literary Agency, Ray; Literary Group, The; Los Angeles Literary Associates; Love Literary Agency, Nancy; Maccoby Literary Agency, Gina; McGrath, Helen; Merhige-Merdon Marketing/Promo Co. Inc., Greg; Millard Literary Agency, Martha; Multimedia Product Development, Inc.; Naggar Literary Agency, Jean V.; Noetzli Literary Agency, Regula; Parks Agency, The Richard; Pelter, Rodney; Perkins Associates, L.; Picard Literary Agent, Alison J.; Rees Literary Agency, Helen; Schmidt Literary Agency, Harold; Shepard Agency, The; Siegel Literary Agency, Bobbe; Singer Literary Agency, Evelyn; Snell Literary Agency, Michael; Steele & Co., Ltd., Lyle; Stern Literary Agency, Gloria; Wald Associates, Inc., Mary Jack; Ware Literary Agency, John A.; Wecksler-Incomco; Weiner Literary Agency, Cherry; Weingel-Fidel Agency, The; Zeckendorf Assoc. Inc., Susan

Westerns/frontier

Allan Agency, Lee; Amsterdam Agency, Marcia; Brandt & Brandt Literary Agents Inc.; Carvainis Agency, Inc., Maria; Curtis Associates, Inc., Richard; Curtis Bruce Agency, The; Davie Literary Agency, Elaine; de la Haba Agency, The Lois; Diamant, The Writer's Workshop, Inc., Anita; Dight Literary Agency, Janet; Ducas, Robert; Dupree/Miller and Associates Inc. Literary; Elder Agency, Joseph; Ellenberg Literary Agency, Ethan; Fields-Rita Scott Inc., Marje; Flaming Star Literary Enterprises; Greenburger Associates, Stanford J.; Hawkins & Associates, Inc.,

John; Hegler Literary Agency, Gary L.; J de S Associates Inc.; Leavitt Agency, The Ned; Leone Agency, Inc., The Adele; McGrath, Helen; Merhige-Merdon Marketing/Promo Co. Inc., Greg; Multimedia Product Development, Inc.; Neighbors Inc., Charles; Parks Agency, The Richard; Pelter, Rodney; Picard Literary Agent, Alison J.; Schmidt Literary Agency, Harold; Wald Associates, Inc., Mary Jack; Weiner Literary Agency, Cherry

Young adult

Allan Agency, Lee; Amsterdam Agency, Marcia; Brandt & Brandt Literary Agents Inc.; Brown Literary Agency, Inc., Andrea; Cantrell-Colas Inc., Literary Agency; Carvainis Agency, Inc., Maria; Casselman Literary Agent, Martha; Cohen, Inc. Literary Agency, Ruth; Curtis Bruce Agency, The; de la Haba Agency, The Lois; Diamant, The Writer's Workshop, Inc., Anita; Dight Literary Agency, Janet; Dijkstra Literary Agency, Sandra; Elder Agency, Joseph; Elek Associates, Peter; Ellenberg Literary Agency, Ethan; Fields-Rita Scott Inc., Marje; Hegler Literary Agency, Gary L.; J de S Associates Inc.; Jones Agency, Leon; Kouts, Literary Agent, Barbara S.; Lantz-Joy Harris Literary Agency, The Robert; Levine Communications, James; Lincoln Literary Agency, Ray; Maccoby Literary Agency, Gina; Merhige-Merdon Marketing/Promo Co. Inc., Greg; MGA Agency Inc.; Naggar Literary Agency, Jean V.; Parks Agency, The Richard; Picard Literary Agent, Alison J.; Rubinstein, Literary Agent, Pesha; Smith, Literary Agent, Valerie; Spatt, Esq., David M.; Stern Literary Agency, Gloria; Wald Associates, Inc., Mary Jack; Weiner Literary Agency, Cherry

Nonfiction

Agriculture/horticulture

de la Haba Agency, The Lois; Dijkstra Literary Agency, Sandra; Gartenberg, Literary Agent, Max; Hawkins & Associates, Inc., John; Jarvis & Co., Inc., Sharon; Lincoln Literary Agency, Ray; Parks Agency, The Richard; Shepard Agency, The

Animals

Acton and Dystel, Inc.; Agency Chicago; Balkin Agency, Inc.; Boates Literary Agency, Reid; Brandt & Brandt Literary Agents Inc.; Brown Literary Agency, Inc., Andrea; de la Haba Agency, The Lois; Diamant, The Writer's Workshop, Inc., Anita; Diamond Literary Agency, Inc.; Dight Literary Agency, Janet; Ducas, Robert; Flaming Star Literary Enterprises; Fuhrman Literary Agency, Candice; Gartenberg, Literary Agent, Max; Hawkins & Associates, Inc., John; Hegler Literary Agency, Gary L.; Kidde, Hoyt & Picard; Lasbury Literary Agency, M. Sue; Lincoln Literary Agency, Ray; Literary Group, The; Merhige-Merdon Marketing/Promo Co. Inc., Greg; Noetzli Literary Agency, Regula; Parks Agency, The Richard; Rosenthal Literary Agency, Jean; Shepard Agency, The; Writers House

Anthropology

Bach Literary Agency, Julian; Balkin Agency, Inc.; Barrett Literary Agency, Helen; Boates Literary Agency, Reid; Borchardt Inc., George; Brandt & Brandt Literary Agents Inc.; Buchanan Literary Agency, Jane; Cantrell-Colas Inc., Literary Agency; Casselman Literary Agent, Martha; Coover Agency, The Doe; Darhansoff & Verrill Literary Agents; de la Haba Agency, The Lois; Dight Literary Agency, Janet; Dijkstra Literary Agency, Sandra; Fuhrman Literary Agency, Candice; Hawkins & Associates, Inc., John; Hull House Literary Agency; Ketz Agency, Louise B.; Lincoln Literary Agency, Ray; Mann Agency, Carol; Noetzli Literary Agency, Regula; Parks Agency, The Richard; Peter Associates, Inc., James; Quicksilver Books-Literary Agents; Rosenthal Literary Agency, Jean; Schmidt Literary Agency, Harold; Seligman, Literary Agent, Lynn; Siegel Literary Agency, Bobbe; Singer Literary Agency, Evelyn; Steele & Co., Ltd., Lyle; Stern Literary Agency, Gloria; 2M Communications Ltd.; Ware Literary Agency, John A.; Wecksler-Incomco; Weingel-Fidel Agency, The

Art/architecture/design

Agency Chicago; Axelrod Agency, The; Boates Literary Agency, Reid; Brandt & Brandt Literary Agents Inc.; Cantrell-Colas Inc., Literary Agency; de la Haba Agency, The Lois; Diamant, The Writer's Workshop, Inc., Anita; Dijkstra Literary Agency, Sandra; Fuhrman Literary Agency, Candice; Gartenberg, Literary Agent, Max; Gregory Associates, Maia; Hawkins & Associates, Inc., John; Hull House Literary Agency; Lincoln Literary Agency, Ray; Mann Agency, Carol; Merhige-Merdon Marketing/Promo Co. Inc., Greg; Millard Literary Agency, Martha; Nathan,

Ruth; Parks Agency, The Richard; Perkins Associates, L.; Peter Associates, Inc., James; Picard Literary Agent, Alison J.; Rosenthal Literary Agency, Jean; Schmidt Literary Agency, Harold; Seligman, Literary Agent, Lynn; Stern Literary Agency, Gloria; Watkins Loomis Agency, Inc.; Wecksler-Incomco; Weingel-Fidel Agency, The; Writers House; Zeckendorf Assoc. Inc., Susan

Biography/autobiography

Acton and Dystel, Inc.; Allan Agency, Lee; Andrews & Associates Inc., Bart; Appleseeds Management; Authors and Artists Group, Inc.; Bach Literary Agency, Julian; Balkin Agency, Inc.; Barrett Literary Agency, Helen; Blassingame, McCauley & Wood; Boates Literary Agency, Reid; Borchardt Inc., George; Brandt & Brandt Literary Agents Inc.; Buchanan Literary Agency, Jane; Cantrell-Colas Inc., Literary Agency; Carvainis Agency, Inc., Maria; Casselman Literary Agent, Martha; Clausen Associates, Connie; Coover Agency, The Doe; Curtis Associates, Inc., Richard; Curtis Bruce Agency, The; Darhansoff & Verrill Literary Agents; de la Haba Agency, The Lois; Diamant, The Writer's Workshop, Inc., Anita; Diamond Literary Agency, Inc.; Dight Literary Agency, Janet; Dijkstra Literary Agency, Sandra; Ducas, Robert; Ellenberg Literary Agency, Ethan; Fallon Literary Agency, The; Fields-Rita Scott Inc., Marje; Flaming Star Literary Enterprises; Fogelman Publishing Interests Inc.; Fuhrman Literary Agency, Candice; Garon-Brooke Assoc. Inc., Jay; Gartenberg, Literary Agent, Max; Gotler Inc., Joel; Hawkins & Associates, Inc., John; Hegler Literary Agency, Gary L.; Holub & Associates; Hull House Literary Agency; Jarvis & Co., Inc., Sharon; J de S Associates Inc.; Jones Agency, Leon; Jordan Literary Agency, Lawrence; Ketz Agency, Louise B.; Kidde, Hoyt & Picard; Klinger, Inc., Harvey; Kouts, Literary Agent, Barbara S.; Lampack Agency, Inc., Peter; Lasbury Literary Agency, M. Sue; Leavitt Agency, The Ned; Leone Agency, Inc., The Adele; Lescher & Lescher Ltd.; Levant & Wales, Literary Agency, Inc.; Lincoln Literary Agency, Ray; Lipkind Agency, Wendy; Literary and Creative Artists Agency; Literary Group, The; Los Angeles Literary Associates; Love Literary Agency, Nancy; McCauley, Gerard; Maccoby Literary Agency, Gina; McGrath, Helen; Mann Agency, Carol; Merhige-Merdon Marketing/Promo Co. Inc., Greg; Millard Literary Agency, Martha; Multimedia Product Development, Inc.; Naggar Literary Agency, Jean V.; Nathan, Ruth; New England Publishing Associates, Inc.; Noetzli Literary Agency, Regula; Nugent Literary Agency, Ray E.; Parks Agency, The Richard; Peter Associates, Inc., James; Picard Literary Agent, Alison J.; Rees Literary Agency, Helen; Rosenthal Literary Agency, Jean; Schaffner Agency, Inc.; Schmidt Literary Agency, Harold; Seligman, Literary Agent, Lynn; Shepard Agency, The; Siegel Literary Agency, Bobbe; Singer Literary Agency, Evelyn; Spitzer Literary Agency, Philip; Stauffer Associates, Nancy; Steele & Co., Ltd., Lyle; Stern Literary Agency, Gloria; Teal Literary Agency, Patricia; 2M Communications Ltd.; Wald Associates, Inc., Mary Jack; Ware Literary Agency, John A.; Wecksler-Incomco; Weingel-Fidel Agency, The; Writers House; Zeckendorf Assoc. Inc., Susan

Business

Acton and Dystel, Inc.; Allan Agency, Lee; Appleseeds Management; Authors and Artists Group, Inc.; Axelrod Agency, The; Bach Literary Agency, Julian; Blassingame, McCauley & Wood; Boates Literary Agency, Reid; Brandt & Brandt Literary Agents Inc.; Buchanan Literary Agency, Jane; Carvainis Agency, Inc., Maria; Clausen Associates, Connie; Columbia Literary Associates, Inc.; Coover Agency, The Doe; Curtis Associates, Inc., Richard; Diamond Literary Agency, Inc.; Dight Literary Agency, Janet; Dijkstra Literary Agency, Sandra; Ducas, Robert; Ellenberg Literary Agency, Ethan; Flaming Star Literary Enterprises; Fogelman Publishing Interests Inc.; Fuhrman Literary Agency, Candice; Hawkins & Associates, Inc., John; Hull House Literary Agency; Jarvis & Co., Inc., Sharon; J de S Associates Inc.; Jones Literary Agency, Lloyd; Jordan Literary Agency, Lawrence; Ketz Agency, Louise B.; Kouts, Literary Agent, Barbara S.; Lampack Agency, Inc., Peter; Lasbury Literary Agency, M. Sue; Leavitt Agency, The Ned; Leone Agency, Inc., The Adele; Levant & Wales, Literary Agency, Inc.; Levine Communications, James; Lincoln Literary Agency, Ray; Literary and Creative Artists Agency; Literary Group, The; Los Angeles Literary Associates; Love Literary Agency, Nancy; McGrath, Helen; Mann Agency, Carol; Millard Literary Agency, Martha; Multimedia Product Development, Inc.; Naggar Literary Agency, Jean V.; New England Publishing Associates, Inc.; Odenwald Connection, The; Parks Agency, The Richard; Paton Literary Agency, Kathi J.; Peter Associates, Inc., James; Picard Literary Agent, Alison J.; Quicksilver Books-Literary Agents; Rees Literary Agency, Helen; Rock Literary Agency; Rosenthal Literary Agency, Jean; Schmidt Literary Agency, Harold; Seligman, Literary Agent, Lynn; Shepard Agency, The; Singer Literary Agency, Evelyn; Spitzer Literary Agency, Philip; Steele & Co., Ltd., Lyle; Stern Literary Agency, Gloria; Wecksler-Incomco; Writers House; Zeckendorf Assoc. Inc., Susan

Child guidance/parenting

Acton and Dystel, Inc.; Agents Inc. for Medical and Mental Health Professionals; Allan Agency, Lee; Authors and Artists Group, Inc.; Balkin Agency, Inc.; Blassingame, McCauley & Wood; Boates Literary Agency, Reid; Brandt & Brandt Literary Agents Inc.; Buchanan Literary Agency, Jane; Cantrell-Colas Inc., Literary Agency; Casselman Literary Agent, Martha; Columbia Literary Associates, Inc.; Coover Agency, The Doe; Curtis Associates, Inc., Richard; Curtis Bruce Agency, The; Diamant, The Writer's Workshop, Inc., Anita; Diamond Literary Agency, Inc.; Dight Literary Agency, Janet; Dijkstra Literary Agency, Sandra; Ellenberg Literary Agency, Ethan; Flaming Star Literary Enterprises; Fogelman Publishing Interests Inc.; Fuhrman Literary Agency, Candice; Garon-Brooke Assoc. Inc., Jay; Gartenberg, Literary Agent, Max; Hawkins & Associates, Inc., John; Jones Agency, Leon; Kouts, Literary Agent, Barbara S.; Kroll Literary Agency, Edite; Leavitt Agency, The Ned; Leone Agency, Inc., The Adele; Lescher & Lescher Ltd.; Levine Communications, James; Lincoln Literary Agency, Ray; Literary Group, The; Love Literary Agency, Nancy; Mann Agency, Carol; Merhige-Merdon Marketing/Promo Co. Inc., Greg; Millard Literary Agency, Martha; Naggar Literary Agency, Jean V.; New England Publishing Associates, Inc.; Noetzli Literary Agency, Regula; Parks Agency, The Richard; Peter Associates, Inc., James; Picard Literary Agent, Alison J.; Quicksilver Books-Literary Agents; Rosenthal Literary Agency, Jean; Rubinstein, Literary Agent, Pesha; Seligman, Literary Agent, Lynn; Shepard Agency, The; Siegel Literary Agency, Bobbe; Singer Literary Agency, Evelyn; Steele & Co., Ltd., Lyle; Stern Literary Agency, Gloria; Teal Literary Agency, Patricia; 2M Communications Ltd.; Writers House; Zeckendorf Assoc. Inc., Susan

Computers/electronics

Allan Agency, Lee; Axelrod Agency, The; Diamond Literary Agency, Inc.; Jordan Literary Agency, Lawrence; Levine Communications, James; Moore Literary Agency; Shepard Agency, The; Singer Literary Agency, Evelyn

Cooking/food/nutrition

Acton and Dystel, Inc.; Agents Inc. for Medical and Mental Health Professionals; Allan Agency, Lee; Authors and Artists Group, Inc.; Bach Literary Agency, Julian; Brandt & Brandt Literary Agents Inc.; Cantrell-Colas Inc., Literary Agency; Casselman Literary Agent, Martha; Clausen Associates, Connie; Columbia Literary Associates, Inc.; Coover Agency, The Doe; Diamant, The Writer's Workshop, Inc., Anita; Diamond Literary Agency, Inc.; Dight Literary Agency, Janet; Dijkstra Literary Agency, Sandra; Ellenberg Literary Agency, Ethan; Elmo Agency Inc., Ann; Fields-Rita Scott Inc., Marje; Fogelman Publishing Interests Inc.; Fuhrman Literary Agency, Candice; Hawkins & Associates, Inc., John; Klinger, Inc., Harvey; Leone Agency, Inc., The Adele; Lescher & Lescher Ltd.; Levant & Wales, Literary Agency, Inc.; Lincoln Literary Agency, Ray; Literary and Creative Artists Agency; Love Literary Agency, Nancy; Merhige-Merdon Marketing/Promo Co. Inc., Greg; Millard Literary Agency, Martha; Multimedia Product Development, Inc.; Naggar Literary Agency, Jean V.; Neighbors Inc., Charles; Parks Agency, The Richard; Picard Literary Agent, Alison J.; Quicksilver Books-Literary Agents; Seligman, Literary Agent, Lynn; Shepard Agency, The; Siegel Literary Agency, Bobbe; Steele & Co., Ltd., Lyle; Stern Literary Agency, Gloria; 2M Communications Ltd.; Writers House

Crafts/hobbies

Brandt & Brandt Literary Agents Inc.; Diamant, The Writer's Workshop, Inc., Anita; Diamond Literary Agency, Inc.; Dight Literary Agency, Janet; Ellenberg Literary Agency, Ethan; Fuhrman Literary Agency, Candice; Hawkins & Associates, Inc., John; Jarvis & Co., Inc., Sharon; Leone Agency, Inc., The Adele; Lincoln Literary Agency, Ray; Neighbors Inc., Charles; Parks Agency, The Richard; Peter Associates, Inc., James; Rees Literary Agency, Helen; Rubinstein, Literary Agent, Pesha; Shepard Agency, The

Current affairs

Acton and Dystel, Inc.; Allan Agency, Lee; Bach Literary Agency, Julian; Balkin Agency, Inc.; Barrett Literary Agency, Helen; Boates Literary Agency, Reid; Borchardt Inc., George; Brandt Agency, The Joan; Brandt & Brandt Literary Agents Inc.; Cantrell-Colas Inc., Literary Agency; Carvainis Agency, Inc., Maria; Casselman Literary Agent, Martha; Clausen Associates, Connie; Darhansoff & Verrill Literary Agents; Diamant, The Writer's Workshop, Inc., Anita; Diamond Literary Agency, Inc.; Dight Literary Agency, Janet; Dijkstra Literary Agency, Sandra; Ducas, Robert; Ellenberg Literary Agency, Ethan; Flaming Star Literary Enterprises; Fogelman Publishing Interests Inc.; Fox Chase Agency Inc., The; Fuhrman Literary Agency, Candice; Gartenberg, Literary Agent, Max; Hawkins & Associates, Inc., John; Hull House Literary Agency; J de S Associates Inc.; Jones Literary Agency, Lloyd; Ketz Agency, Louise B.; Kouts, Literary Agent, Barbara S.; Kroll Literary Agency, Edite; Lampack Agency, Inc., Peter; Lasbury Literary Agency, M. Sue; Leone Agency, Inc., The Adele; Lescher & Lescher Ltd.; Levine Communications, James; Lincoln Literary Agency, Ray; Lipkind Agency, Wendy; Literary Group, The; Love Literary Agency, Nancy; McCauley, Gerard; Maccoby Literary Agency, Gina; McGrath, Helen; Mann Agency, Carol; Millard Literary Agency, Martha; Multimedia Product Development, Inc.; Naggar Literary Agency, Jean V.; Noetzli Literary Agency, Regula; Odenwald Connection, The; Parks Agency, The Richard; Perkins Associates, L.; Peter Associates, Inc., James; Picard Literary Agent, Alison J.; Rees Literary Agency, Helen; Schmidt Literary Agency, Harold; Seligman, Literary Agent, Lynn; Shepard Agency, The; Singer Literary Agency, Evelyn; Spitzer Literary Agency, Philip; Stauffer Associates, Nancy; Steele & Co., Ltd., Lyle; Stern Literary Agency, Gloria; 2M Communications Ltd.; Wald Associates, Inc., Mary Jack; Ware Literary Agency, John A.; Wecksler-Incomco

Ethnic/cultural interests

Acton and Dystel, Inc.; Agency Chicago; Boates Literary Agency, Reid; Brandt & Brandt Literary Agents Inc.; Cantrell-Colas Inc., Literary Agency; Casselman Literary Agent, Martha; Clausen Associates, Connie; Cohen, Inc. Literary Agency, Ruth; Coover Agency, The Doe; Crown International Literature and Arts Agency, Bonnie R.; Diamond Literary Agency, Inc.; Dight Literary Agency, Janet; Dijkstra Literary Agency, Sandra; Fuhrman Literary Agency, Candice; Hawkins & Associates, Inc., John; Hull House Literary Agency; J de S Associates Inc.; Jones Literary Agency, Lloyd; Kouts, Literary Agent, Barbara S.; Leone Agency, Inc., The Adele; Lincoln Literary Agency, Ray; Love Literary Agency, Nancy; Maccoby Literary Agency, Gina; Mann Agency, Carol; Merhige-Merdon Marketing/Promo Co. Inc., Greg; Millard Literary Agency, Martha; Noetzli Literary Agency, Regula; Parks Agency, The Richard; Perkins Associates, L.; Peter Associates, Inc., James; Picard Literary Agent, Alison J.; Rees Literary Agency, Helen; Schmidt Literary Agency, Harold; Seligman, Literary Agent, Lynn; Siegel Literary Agency, Bobbe; Spitzer Literary Agency, Philip; Stauffer Associates, Nancy; Steele & Co., Ltd., Lyle; Stern Literary Agency, Gloria; Wald Associates, Inc., Mary Jack

Gay/lesbian issues

Acton and Dystel, Inc.; Brandt & Brandt Literary Agents Inc.; Clausen Associates, Connie; Ducas, Robert; Fields-Rita Scott Inc., Marje; Garon-Brooke Assoc. Inc., Jay; Hawkins & Associates, Inc., John; Kidde, Hoyt & Picard; Leone Agency, Inc., The Adele; Lincoln Literary Agency, Ray; Literary Group, The; Naggar Literary Agency, Jean V.; Parks Agency, The Richard; Picard Literary Agent, Alison J.; Schmidt Literary Agency, Harold; Steele & Co., Ltd., Lyle

Government/politics/law

Acton and Dystel, Inc.; Allan Agency, Lee; Axelrod Agency, The; Bach Literary Agency, Julian; Barrett Literary Agency, Helen; Black Literary Agency, David; Boates Literary Agency, Reid; Brandt & Brandt Literary Agents Inc.; Cantrell-Colas Inc., Literary Agency; Carvainis Agency, Inc., Maria; Casselman Literary Agent, Martha; Diamant, The Writer's Workshop, Inc., Anita; Dight Literary Agency, Janet; Dijkstra Literary Agency, Sandra; Ducas, Robert; Ellenberg Literary Agency, Ethan; Flaming Star Literary Enterprises; Fogelman Publishing Interests Inc.; Hawkins & Associates, Inc., John; Hull House Literary Agency; J de S Associates Inc.; Lampack Agency, Inc., Peter; Lasbury Literary Agency, M. Sue; Leone Agency, Inc., The Adele; Lescher & Lescher Ltd.; Levine Communications, James; Lincoln Literary Agency, Ray; Literary and Creative Artists Agency; Love Literary Agency, Nancy; Mann Agency, Carol; Naggar Literary Agency, Jean V.; New England Publishing Associates, Inc.; Parks Agency, The Richard; Peter Associates, Inc., James; Picard Literary Agent, Alison J.; Rees Literary Agency, Helen; Schmidt Literary Agency, Harold; Seligman, Literary Agent, Lynn; Shepard Agency, The; Singer Literary Agency, Evelyn; Spitzer Literary Agency, Philip; Steele & Co., Ltd., Lyle; Stern Literary Agency, Gloria

Health/medicine

Acton and Dystel, Inc.; Agents Inc. for Medical and Mental Health Professionals; Allan Agency, Lee; Appleseeds Management; Axelrod Agency, The; Balkin Agency, Inc.; Blassingame, McCauley & Wood; Boates Literary Agency, Reid; Brandt & Brandt Literary Agents Inc.; Bu-

History

Interior design/decorating

Juvenile nonfiction

Allan Agency, Lee; Brandt & Brandt Literary Agents Inc.; Brown Literary Agency, Inc., Andrea; Cantrell-Colas Inc., Literary Agency; Casselman Literary Agent, Martha; Cohen, Inc. Literary Agency, Ruth; Curtis Bruce Agency, The; de la Haba Agency, The Lois; Diamant, The Writer's Workshop, Inc., Anita; Dight Literary Agency, Janet; Elek Associates, Peter; Ellenberg Literary Agency, Ethan; Elmo Agency Inc., Ann; Feiler Literary Agency, Florence; Hawkins & Associates, Inc., John; Hegler Literary Agency, Gary L.; Jones Agency, Leon; Jones Literary Agency, Lloyd; Kouts, Literary Agent, Barbara S.; Kroll Literary Agency, Edite; Lescher & Lescher Ltd.; Lincoln Literary Agency, Ray; Maccoby Literary Agency, Gina; Merhige-Merdon Marketing/ Promo Co. Inc., Greg; Naggar Literary Agency, Jean V.; Norma-Lewis Agency, The; Picard Literary Agent, Alison J.; Rosenthal Literary Agency, Jean; Rubinstein, Literary Agent, Pesha; Shepard Agency, The; Singer Literary Agency, Evelyn; Stern Literary Agency, Gloria; Wald Associates, Inc., Mary Jack; Writers House

Language/literature/criticism

Authors and Artists Group, Inc.; Bach Literary Agency, Julian; Balkin Agency, Inc.; Boates Literary Agency, Reid; Brandt & Brandt Literary Agents Inc.; Cantrell-Colas Inc., Literary Agency; Casselman Literary Agent, Martha; Coover Agency, The Doe; Darhansoff & Verrill Literary Agents; Dight Literary Agency, Janet; Fallon Literary Agency, The; Fuhrman Literary Agency, Candice; Gregory Associates, Maia; Hawkins & Associates, Inc., John; Leone Agency, Inc., The Adele; Lincoln Literary Agency, Ray; New England Publishing Associates, Inc.; Parks Agency, The Richard; Quicksilver Books-Literary Agents; Rosenthal Literary Agency, Jean; Schmidt Literary Agency, Harold; Seligman, Literary Agent, Lynn; Shepard Agency, The; Siegel Literary Agency, Bobbe; Stauffer Associates, Nancy; Stern Literary Agency, Gloria; Wald Associates, Inc., Mary Jack

Military/war

Acton and Dystel, Inc.; Allan Agency, Lee; Bach Literary Agency, Julian; Brandt & Brandt Literary Agents Inc.; Cantrell-Colas Inc., Literary Agency; Carvainis Agency, Inc., Maria; Curtis Associates, Inc., Richard; Diamond Literary Agency, Inc.; Dijkstra Literary Agency, Sandra; Ducas, Robert; Ellenberg Literary Agency, Ethan; Flaming Star Literary Enterprises; Garon-Brooke Assoc. Inc., Jay; Gartenberg, Literary Agent, Max; Hawkins & Associates, Inc., John; Hegler Literary Agency, Gary L.; Jarvis & Co., Inc., Sharon; J de S Associates Inc.; Jones Agency, Leon; Ketz Agency, Louise B.; Leone Agency, Inc., The Adele; McCauley, Gerard; McGrath, Helen; Merhige-Merdon Marketing/Promo Co. Inc., Greg; Neighbors Inc., Charles; New England Publishing Associates, Inc.; Nugent Literary Agency, Ray E.; Parks Agency, The Richard; Peter Associates, Inc., James; Picard Literary Agent, Alison J.; Schmidt Literary Agency, Harold; Spitzer Literary Agency, Philip; Wald Associates, Inc., Mary Jack; Writers House

Money/finance/economics

Acton and Dystel, Inc.; Allan Agency, Lee; Appleseeds Management; Axelrod Agency, The; Brandt & Brandt Literary Agents Inc.; Buchanan Literary Agency, Jane; Cantrell-Colas Inc., Literary Agency; Carvainis Agency, Inc., Maria; Casselman Literary Agent, Martha; Clausen Associates, Connie; Coover Agency, The Doe; Curtis Associates, Inc., Richard; Diamant, The Writer's Workshop, Inc., Anita; Diamond Literary Agency, Inc.; Dight Literary Agency, Janet; Dijkstra Literary Agency, Sandra; Ducas, Robert; Ellenberg Literary Agency, Ethan; Fogelman Publishing Interests Inc.; Fox Chase Agency Inc., The; Fuhrman Literary Agency, Candice; Gartenberg, Literary Agent, Max; Hawkins & Associates, Inc., John; Hegler Literary Agency, Gary L.; Hull House Literary Agency; Jarvis & Co., Inc., Sharon; Jones Literary Agency, Lloyd; Ketz Agency, Louise B.; Lampack Agency, Inc., Peter; Lasbury Literary Agency, M. Sue; Leone Agency, Inc., The Adele; Levine Communications, James; Lincoln Literary Agency, Ray; Los Angeles Literary Associates; Love Literary Agency, Nancy; Mann Agency, Carol; Millard Literary Agency, Martha; Multimedia Product Development, Inc.; Naggar Literary Agency, Jean V.; Neighbors Inc., Charles; New England Publishing Associates, Inc.; Noetzli Literary Agency, Regula; Parks Agency, The Richard; Peter Associates, Inc., James; Rock Literary Agency; Schmidt Literary Agency, Harold; Seligman, Literary Agent, Lynn; Shepard Agency, The; Singer Literary Agency, Evelyn; Steele & Co., Ltd., Lyle; Stern Literary Agency, Gloria; Wald Associates, Inc., Mary Jack; Writers House

Music/dance/theater/film

Acton and Dystel, Inc.; Agency Chicago; Allan Agency, Lee; Andrews & Associates Inc., Bart; Appleseeds Management; Axelrod Agency, The; Bach Literary Agency, Julian; Balkin Agency, Inc.; Brandt & Brandt Literary Agents Inc.; Casselman Literary Agent, Martha; Clausen Associates, Connie; Curtis Associates, Inc., Richard; Diamond Literary Agency, Inc.; Dight Literary Agency, Janet; Dijkstra Literary Agency, Sandra; Fuhrman Literary Agency, Candice; Garon-Brooke Assoc. Inc., Jay; Gartenberg, Literary Agent, Max; Gotler Inc., Joel; Gregory Associates, Maia; Hawkins & Associates, Inc., John; Hull House Literary Agency; Jones Agency, Leon; Kouts, Literary Agent, Barbara S.; Leone Agency, Inc., The Adele; Lincoln Literary Agency, Ray; Literary Group, The; Merhige-Merdon Marketing/Promo Co. Inc., Greg; Millard Literary Agency, Martha; Naggar Literary Agency, Jean V.; Nathan, Ruth; Nugent Literary Agency, Ray E.; Parks Agency, The Richard; Perkins Associates, L.; Picard Literary Agent, Alison J.; Schmidt Literary Agency, Harold; Seligman, Literary Agent, Lynn; Shepard Agency, The; Siegel Literary Agency, Bobbe; Spitzer Literary Agency, Philip; Stauffer Associates, Nancy; 2M Communications Ltd.; Wald Associates, Inc., Mary Jack; Wecksler-Incomco; Weingel-Fidel Agency, The; Writers House; Zeckendorf Assoc. Inc., Susan

Nature/environment

Acton and Dystel, Inc.; Allan Agency, Lee; Axelrod Agency, The; Bach Literary Agency, Julian; Balkin Agency, Inc.; Boates Literary Agency, Reid; Brandt & Brandt Literary Agents Inc.; Buchanan Literary Agency, Jane; Cantrell-Colas Inc., Literary Agency; Casselman Literary Agent, Martha; Clausen Associates, Connie; Coover Agency, The Doe; Crown International Literature and Arts Agency, Bonnie R.; Darhansoff & Verrill Literary Agents; Diamant, The Writer's Workshop, Inc., Anita; Diamond Literary Agency, Inc.; Dight Literary Agency, Janet; Dijkstra Literary Agency, Sandra; Ducas, Robert; Ellenberg Literary Agency, Ethan; Flaming Star Literary Enterprises; Fox Chase Agency Inc., The; Fuhrman Literary Agency, Candice; Gartenberg, Literary Agent, Max; Hawkins & Associates, Inc., John; Hegler Literary Agency, Gary L.; Jarvis & Co., Inc., Sharon; Kouts, Literary Agent, Barbara S.; Lasbury Literary Agency, M. Sue; Leavitt Agency, The Ned; Leone Agency, Inc., The Adele; Levant & Wales, Literary Agency, Inc.; Lincoln Literary Agency, Ray; Literary Group, The; Love Literary Agency, Nancy; Millard Literary Agency, Martha; Multimedia Product Development, Inc.; New England Publishing Associates, Inc.; Noetzli Literary Agency, Regula; Parks Agency, The Richard; Picard Literary Agent, Alison J.; Quicksilver Books-Literary Agents; Rubinstein, Literary Agent, Pesha; Schaffner Agency, Inc.; Schmidt Literary Agency, Harold; Seligman, Literary Agent, Lynn; Shepard Agency, The; Siegel Literary Agency, Bobbe; Spitzer Literary Agency, Philip; Stauffer Associates, Nancy; Steele & Co., Ltd., Lyle; 2M Communications Ltd.; Wald Associates, Inc., Mary Jack; Wecksler-Incomco; Writers House

New age/metaphysics

Authors and Artists Group, Inc.; Bach Literary Agency, Julian; Cantrell-Colas Inc., Literary Agency; Diamant, The Writer's Workshop, Inc., Anita; Dight Literary Agency, Janet; Dijkstra Literary Agency, Sandra; Ellenberg Literary Agency, Ethan; Fuhrman Literary Agency, Candice; Hawkins & Associates, Inc., John; Jarvis & Co., Inc., Sharon; J de S Associates Inc.; Leavitt Agency, The Ned; Leone Agency, Inc., The Adele; Naggar Literary Agency, Jean V.; Noetzli Literary Agency, Regula; Picard Literary Agent, Alison J.; Quicksilver Books-Literary Agents; Rees Literary Agency, Helen; Schmidt Literary Agency, Harold; Steele & Co., Ltd., Lyle

Open to all nonfiction areas

Allen Literary Agency, Linda; Barrett Books Inc., Loretta; Brown Ltd., Curtis; Buck Agency, Howard; Cohen Literary Agency Ltd., Hy; Collier Associates; Congdon Associates, Inc., Don; Dupree/Miller and Associates Inc. Literary; Eisenbach Inc., Robert; Eisenberg Literary Agency, Vicki; Elder Agency, Joseph; Ellison Inc., Nicholas; Evans and Associates; Goldfarb, Kaufman, & O'Toole; Goodman Associates; Gotham Art & Literary Agency Inc.; Greenburger Associates, Stanford J.; Gusay Literary Agency, The Charlotte; Hamilburg Agency, The Mitchell J.; Herman Agency, Inc., The Jeff; Hoffman Literary Agency, Berenice; International Publisher Associates Inc.; Kirchoff/Wohlberg, Inc., Authors' Representation Division; Larsen/Elizabeth Pomada Literary Agents, Michael; Lazear Agency Incorporated, The; Martell Agency, The; Mendez Inc., Toni; MGA Agency Inc.; Ober Associates, Harold; Pelter, Rodney; Snell Literary Agency, Michael; Writers' Productions

Photography

Bach Literary Agency, Julian; Diamond Literary Agency, Inc.; Hawkins & Associates, Inc., John; Kidde, Hoyt & Picard; Merhige-Merdon Marketing/Promo Co. Inc., Greg; Millard Literary Agency, Martha; Nugent Literary Agency, Ray E.; Wald Associates, Inc., Mary Jack; Wecksler-Incomco

Psychology

Acton and Dystel, Inc.; Agents Inc. for Medical and Mental Health Professionals; Allan Agency, Lee; Appleseeds Management; Authors and Artists Group, Inc.; Bach Literary Agency, Julian; Boates Literary Agency, Reid; Brandt & Brandt Literary Agents Inc.; Cantrell-Colas Inc., Literary Agency; Carvainis Agency, Inc., Maria; Clausen Associates, Connie; Coover Agency, The Doe; Curtis Bruce Agency, The; Diamant, The Writer's Workshop, Inc., Anita; Diamond Literary Agency, Inc.; Dight Literary Agency, Janet; Dijkstra Literary Agency, Sandra; Ellenberg Literary Agency, Ethan; Fallon Literary Agency, The; Flaming Star Literary Enterprises; Fuhrman Literary Agency, Candice; Garon-Brooke Assoc. Inc., Jay; Gartenberg, Literary Agent, Max; Hawkins & Associates, Inc., John; Hegler Literary Agency, Gary L.; Jarvis & Co., Inc., Sharon; Jones Literary Agency, Lloyd; Kidde, Hoyt & Picard; Klinger, Inc., Harvey; Kouts, Literary Agent, Barbara S.; Lasbury Literary Agency, M. Sue; Leavitt Agency, The Ned; Leone Agency, Inc., The Adele; Lescher & Lescher Ltd.; Levant & Wales, Literary Agency, Inc.; Levine Communications, James; Lincoln Literary Agency, Ray; Literary Group, The; Love Literary Agency, Nancy; McGrath, Helen; Mann Agency, Carol; Millard Literary Agency, Martha; Naggar Literary Agency, Jean V.; New England Publishing Associates, Inc.; Noetzli Literary Agency, Regula; Parks Agency, The Richard; Paton Literary Agency, Kathi J.; Peter Associates, Inc., James; Picard Literary Agent, Alison J.; Quicksilver Books-Literary Agents; Rees Literary Agency, Helen; Schmidt Literary Agency, Harold; Seligman, Literary Agent, Lynn; Shepard Agency, The; Siegel Literary Agency, Bobbe; Spitzer Literary Agency, Philip; Steele & Co., Ltd., Lyle; Stern Literary Agency, Gloria; Teal Literary Agency, Patricia; 2M Communications Ltd.; Ware Literary Agency, John A.; Weingel-Fidel Agency, The; Writers House; Zeckendorf Assoc. Inc., Susan

Religious/inspirational

Bach Literary Agency, Julian; Coover Agency, The Doe; Curtis Bruce Agency, The; Diamant, The Writer's Workshop, Inc., Anita; Diamond Literary Agency, Inc.; Dight Literary Agency, Janet; Ellenberg Literary Agency, Ethan; Fuhrman Literary Agency, Candice; Gregory Associates, Maia; Hegler Literary Agency, Gary L.; Holub & Associates; Jones Agency, Leon; Jordan Literary Agency, Lawrence; Kidde, Hoyt & Picard; Leavitt Agency, The Ned; Living Faith Literary Agency; Naggar Literary Agency, Jean V.; Quicksilver Books-Literary Agents; Rees Literary Agency, Helen; Shepard Agency, The; Siegel Literary Agency, Bobbe

Science/technology

Acton and Dystel, Inc.; Agents Inc. for Medical and Mental Health Professionals; Allan Agency, Lee; Axelrod Agency, The; Balkin Agency, Inc.; Boates Literary Agency, Reid; Bova Literary Agency, The Barbara; Brandt & Brandt Literary Agents Inc.; Brown Literary Agency, Inc., Andrea; Cantrell-Colas Inc., Literary Agency; Coover Agency, The Doe; Curtis Associates, Inc., Richard; Darhansoff & Verrill Literary Agents; de la Haba Agency, The Lois; Diamant, The Writer's Workshop, Inc., Anita; Diamond Literary Agency, Inc.; Dight Literary Agency, Janet; Dijkstra Literary Agency, Sandra; Ducas, Robert; Ellenberg Literary Agency, Ethan; Flaming Star Literary Enterprises; Fuhrman Literary Agency, Candice; Gartenberg, Literary Agent, Max; Gotler Inc., Joel; Hawkins & Associates, Inc., John; Hegler Literary Agency, Gary L.; Jarvis & Co., Inc., Sharon; Jordan Literary Agency, Lawrence; Ketz Agency, Louise B.; Klinger, Inc., Harvey; Lasbury Literary Agency, M. Sue; Leavitt Agency, The Ned; Leone Agency, Inc., The Adele; Levant & Wales, Literary Agency, Inc.; Lincoln Literary Agency, Ray; Lipkind Agency, Wendy; Love Literary Agency, Nancy; Lowenstein Associates, Inc.; Millard Literary Agency, Martha; Moore Literary Agency; Multimedia Product Development, Inc.; Neighbors Inc., Charles; New England Publishing Associates, Inc.; Noetzli Literary Agency, Regula; Parks Agency, The Richard; Picard Literary Agent, Alison J.; Rees Literary Agency, Helen; Schmidt Literary Agency, Harold; Seligman, Literary Agent, Lynn; Singer Literary Agency, Evelyn; Steele & Co., Ltd., Lyle; Stern Literary Agency, Gloria; Wald Associates, Inc., Mary Jack; Ware Literary Agency, John A.; Watkins Loomis Agency, Inc.; Weingel-Fidel Agency, The; Writers House; Zeckendorf Assoc. Inc., Susan

Self-help/personal improvement
Acton and Dystel, Inc.; Agents Inc. for Medical and Mental Health Professionals; Allan Agency, Lee; Appleseeds Management; Authors and Artists Group, Inc.; Bach Literary Agency, Julian; Boates Literary Agency, Reid; Brandt & Brandt Literary Agents Inc.; Buchanan Literary Agency, Jane; Cantrell-Colas Inc., Literary Agency; Casselman Literary Agent, Martha; Clausen Associates, Connie; Columbia Literary Associates, Inc.; Coopersmith Literary Agency, Julia; Curtis Associates, Inc., Richard; Curtis Bruce Agency, The; Davie Literary Agency, Elaine; Diamant, The Writer's Workshop, Inc., Anita; Diamond Literary Agency, Inc.; Dight Literary Agency, Janet; Dijkstra Literary Agency, Sandra; Ellenberg Literary Agency, Ethan; Fallon Literary Agency, The; Fields-Rita Scott Inc., Marje; Flaming Star Literary Enterprises; Fogelman Publishing Interests Inc.; Fox Chase Agency Inc., The; Fuhrman Literary Agency, Candice; Garon-Brooke Assoc. Inc., Jay; Gartenberg, Literary Agent, Max; Hawkins & Associates, Inc., John; Hegler Literary Agency, Gary L.; Jarvis & Co., Inc., Sharon; J de S Associates Inc.; Jones Agency, Leon; Jordan Literary Agency, Lawrence; Kidde, Hoyt & Picard; Klinger, Inc., Harvey; Kouts, Literary Agent, Barbara S.; Lasbury Literary Agency, M. Sue; Leavitt Agency, The Ned; Leone Agency, Inc., The Adele; Lincoln Literary Agency, Ray; Literary and Creative Artists Agency; Literary Group, The; Los Angeles Literary Associates; Love Literary Agency, Nancy; McGrath, Helen; Mann Agency, Carol; Merhige-Merdon Marketing/Promo Co. Inc., Greg; Millard Literary Agency, Martha; Naggar Literary Agency, Jean V.; New England Publishing Associates, Inc.; Noetzli Literary Agency, Regula; Odenwald Connection, The; Parks Agency, The Richard; Peter Associates, Inc., James; Picard Literary Agent, Alison J.; Quicksilver Books-Literary Agents; Rees Literary Agency, Helen; Rosenthal Literary Agency, Jean; Rubinstein, Literary Agent, Pesha; Schmidt Literary Agency, Harold; Seligman, Literary Agent, Lynn; Shepard Agency, The; Siegel Literary Agency, Bobbe; Singer Literary Agency, Evelyn; Stauffer Associates, Nancy; Steele & Co., Ltd., Lyle; Stern Literary Agency, Gloria; Teal Literary Agency, Patricia; 2M Communications Ltd.; Weiner Literary Agency, Cherry; Writers House

Sociology
Agents Inc. for Medical and Mental Health Professionals; Authors and Artists Group, Inc.; Balkin Agency, Inc.; Brandt & Brandt Literary Agents Inc.; Cantrell-Colas Inc., Literary Agency; Casselman Literary Agent, Martha; Coopersmith Literary Agency, Julia; Coover Agency, The Doe; Diamond Literary Agency, Inc.; Dight Literary Agency, Janet; Dijkstra Literary Agency, Sandra; Fox Chase Agency Inc., The; Hawkins & Associates, Inc., John; Hull House Literary Agency; J de S Associates Inc.; Lasbury Literary Agency, M. Sue; Lincoln Literary Agency, Ray; Lipkind Agency, Wendy; Literary Group, The; Love Literary Agency, Nancy; Mann Agency, Carol; Merhige-Merdon Marketing/Promo Co. Inc., Greg; Naggar Literary Agency, Jean V.; New England Publishing Associates, Inc.; Noetzli Literary Agency, Regula; Parks Agency, The Richard; Paton Literary Agency, Kathi J.; Rees Literary Agency, Helen; Schmidt Literary Agency, Harold; Seligman, Literary Agent, Lynn; Shepard Agency, The; Spitzer Literary Agency, Philip; Stauffer Associates, Nancy; Steele & Co., Ltd., Lyle; Stern Literary Agency, Gloria; Wald Associates, Inc., Mary Jack; Weiner Literary Agency, Cherry; Weingel-Fidel Agency, The; Zeckendorf Assoc. Inc., Susan

Sports
Acton and Dystel, Inc.; Agency Chicago; Agents Inc. for Medical and Mental Health Professionals; Allan Agency, Lee; Bach Literary Agency, Julian; Black Literary Agency, David; Boates Literary Agency, Reid; Brandt & Brandt Literary Agents Inc.; Curtis Associates, Inc., Richard; Curtis Bruce Agency, The; Diamant, The Writer's Workshop, Inc., Anita; Dight Literary Agency, Janet; Dijkstra Literary Agency, Sandra; Ducas, Robert; Ellenberg Literary Agency, Ethan; Fields-Rita Scott Inc., Marje; Flaming Star Literary Enterprises; Fox Chase Agency Inc., The; Fuhrman Literary Agency, Candice; Gartenberg, Literary Agent, Max; Hawkins & Associates, Inc., John; J de S Associates Inc.; Jones Agency, Leon; Jones Literary Agency, Lloyd; Jordan Literary Agency, Lawrence; Ketz Agency, Louise B.; Klinger, Inc., Harvey; Lasbury Literary Agency, M. Sue; Leavitt Agency, The Ned; Leone Agency, Inc., The Adele; Lincoln Literary Agency, Ray; Literary Group, The; McCauley, Gerard; McGrath, Helen; Merhige-Merdon Marketing/Promo Co. Inc., Greg; Millard Literary Agency, Martha; Noetzli Literary Agency, Regula; Picard Literary Agent, Alison J.; Rees Literary Agency, Helen; Rosenthal Literary Agency, Jean; Shepard Agency, The; Siegel Literary Agency, Bobbe; Spitzer Literary Agency, Philip; Stauffer Associates, Nancy; Steele & Co., Ltd., Lyle; Stern Literary Agency, Gloria; Wald Associates, Inc., Mary Jack; Ware Literary Agency, John A.

Translations

Balkin Agency, Inc.; Crown International Literature and Arts Agency, Bonnie R.; Dijkstra Literary Agency, Sandra; J de S Associates Inc.; Leavitt Agency, The Ned; Rubinstein, Literary Agent, Pesha; Schmidt Literary Agency, Harold; Seligman, Literary Agent, Lynn; Stauffer Associates, Nancy; Wald Associates, Inc., Mary Jack; Watkins Loomis Agency, Inc.

True crime/investigative

Acton and Dystel, Inc.; Allan Agency, Lee; Appleseeds Management; Bach Literary Agency, Julian; Balkin Agency, Inc.; Barrett Literary Agency, Helen; Boates Literary Agency, Reid; Brandt & Brandt Literary Agents Inc.; Cantrell-Colas Inc., Literary Agency; Carvainis Agency, Inc., Maria; Casselman Literary Agent, Martha; Clausen Associates, Connie; Cohen, Inc. Literary Agency, Ruth; Coover Agency, The Doe; Curtis Associates, Inc., Richard; Davie Literary Agency, Elaine; Diamant, The Writer's Workshop, Inc., Anita; Diamond Literary Agency, Inc.; Dight Literary Agency, Janet; Dijkstra Literary Agency, Sandra; Ducas, Robert; Ellenberg Literary Agency, Ethan; Fields-Rita Scott Inc., Marje; Flaming Star Literary Enterprises; Fogelman Publishing Interests Inc.; Fuhrman Literary Agency, Candice; Garon-Brooke Assoc. Inc., Jay; Gartenberg, Literary Agent, Max; Gotler Inc., Joel; Hawkins & Associates, Inc., John; Hegler Literary Agency, Gary L.; Hull House Literary Agency; Jarvis & Co., Inc., Sharon; Jones Agency, Leon; Jones Literary Agency, Lloyd; Ketz Agency, Louise B.; Klinger, Inc., Harvey; Lampack Agency, Inc., Peter; Lasbury Literary Agency, M. Sue; Leavitt Agency, The Ned; Leone Agency, Inc., The Adele; Levine Communications, James; Literary Group, The; Love Literary Agency, Nancy; Mann Agency, Carol; Merhige-Merdon Marketing/Promo Co. Inc., Greg; Millard Literary Agency, Martha; Multimedia Product Development, Inc.; Naggar Literary Agency, Jean V.; New England Publishing Associates, Inc.; Noetzli Literary Agency, Regula; Nugent Literary Agency, Ray E.; Parks Agency, The Richard; Picard Literary Agent, Alison J.; Quicksilver Books-Literary Agents; Rees Literary Agency, Helen; Rubinstein, Literary Agent, Pesha; Schmidt Literary Agency, Harold; Seligman, Literary Agent, Lynn; Siegel Literary Agency, Bobbe; Spitzer Literary Agency, Philip; Steele & Co., Ltd., Lyle; Stern Literary Agency, Gloria; Teal Literary Agency, Patricia; Wald Associates, Inc., Mary Jack; Ware Literary Agency, John A.; Weingel-Fidel Agency, The; Writers House; Zeckendorf Assoc. Inc., Susan

Women's issues/women's studies

Acton and Dystel, Inc.; Authors and Artists Group, Inc.; Bach Literary Agency, Julian; Barrett Literary Agency, Helen; Boates Literary Agency, Reid; Borchardt Inc., George; Brandt & Brandt Literary Agents Inc.; Buchanan Literary Agency, Jane; Cantrell-Colas Inc., Literary Agency; Carvainis Agency, Inc., Maria; Clausen Associates, Connie; Cohen, Inc. Literary Agency, Ruth; Coover Agency, The Doe; Davie Literary Agency, Elaine; Diamant, The Writer's Workshop, Inc., Anita; Diamond Literary Agency, Inc.; Dight Literary Agency, Janet; Dijkstra Literary Agency, Sandra; Elmo Agency Inc., Ann; Fallon Literary Agency, The; Flaming Star Literary Enterprises; Fogelman Publishing Interests Inc.; Fox Chase Agency Inc., The; Fuhrman Literary Agency, Candice; Gartenberg, Literary Agent, Max; Hawkins & Associates, Inc., John; Jones Agency, Leon; Jones Literary Agency, Lloyd; Kidde, Hoyt & Picard; Klinger, Inc., Harvey; Kouts, Literary Agent, Barbara S.; Kroll Literary Agency, Edite; Lasbury Literary Agency, M. Sue; Leavitt Agency, The Ned; Leone Agency, Inc., The Adele; Lescher & Lescher Ltd.; Levine Literary Agency, Inc., Ellen; Lincoln Literary Agency, Ray; Literary Group, The; Love Literary Agency, Nancy; Maccoby Literary Agency, Gina; McGrath, Helen; Mann Agency, Carol; Merhige-Merdon Marketing/Promo Co. Inc., Greg; Millard Literary Agency, Martha; Naggar Literary Agency, Jean V.; New England Publishing Associates, Inc.; Noetzli Literary Agency, Regula; Parks Agency, The Richard; Paton Literary Agency, Kathi J.; Picard Literary Agent, Alison J.; Rees Literary Agency, Helen; Schmidt Literary Agency, Harold; Seligman, Literary Agent, Lynn; Shepard Agency, The; Siegel Literary Agency, Bobbe; Stauffer Associates, Nancy; Stern Literary Agency, Gloria; Teal Literary Agency, Patricia; 2M Communications Ltd.; Weingel-Fidel Agency, The; Writers House; Zeckendorf Assoc. Inc., Susan

Fee-charging agents

Fiction

Action/adventure

Alden—Literary Service, Farel T.; Anthony Agency, Joseph; Authors' Marketing Services Ltd.; Brady Literary Management; Browne Ltd., Pema; Chadd-Stevens Literary Agency; Cook Liter-

Your Guide to Getting Published

Learn to write publishable material and discover the best-paying markets for your work. Subscribe to *Writer's Digest*, the magazine that has instructed, informed and inspired writers since 1920. Every month you'll get:

- Fresh markets for your writing, including the names and addresses of editors, what type of writing they're currently buying, how much they pay, and how to get in touch with them.
- Insights, advice, and how-to information from professional writers and editors.
- In-depth profiles of today's foremost authors and the secrets of their success.
- Monthly expert columns about the writing and selling of fiction, nonfiction, poetry and scripts.

Plus, a $16.00 discount. Subscribe today through this special introductory offer, and receive a full year (12 issues) of Writer's Digest for only $17.00—that's a $16.00 savings off the $33 newsstand rate. Enclose payment with your order, and we will add an extra issue to your subscription, absolutely **free**.

Detach postage-free coupon and mail today!

Subscription Savings Certificate
Save $16.00

Yes, I want professional advice on how to write publishable material and sell it to the best-paying markets. Send me 12 issues of Writer's Digest for just $17...a $16 discount off the newsstand price. Outside U.S. add $7 (includes GST in Canada) and remit in U.S. funds.

☐ Payment enclosed (send me an extra issue *free*— 13 in all).

☐ Please bill me.

Guarantee: If you are not satisfied with your subscription at any time, you may cancel it and receive a full refund for all unmailed issues due you.

Name (please print)

Address   Apt.

City

State   Zip

Basic rate, $24.   VVLA9

Writer's®
DIGEST

How would you like to get:

- up-to-the-minute reports on new markets for your writing
- professional advice from editors and writers about what to write and how to write it to maximize your opportunities for getting published
- in-depth interviews with leading authors who reveal their secrets of success
- expert opinion about writing and selling fiction, nonfiction, poetry and scripts
- ...all at a $16.00 discount?

ary Agency, Warren; Creative Concepts Literary Agency; Dorese Agency Ltd.; Doyen Literary Services, Inc.; Fishbein Ltd., Frieda; Flaherty, Literary Agent, Joyce A.; Flannery, White and Stone; Gladden Unlimited; Independent Publishing Agency; Iorio, Esq., Gary F.; Kaltman Literary Agency, Larry; Kellock & Associates Ltd., J.; Kern Literary Agency, Natasha; Lighthouse Literary Agency; Marshall Agency, The Evan; Nelson Literary Agency & Lecture Bureau, BK; Northeast Literary Agency; Northwest Literary Services; Panettieri Agency, The; Pegasus International, Inc., Literary & Film Agents; Peterson Associates Literary Agency; Pine Associates, Inc, Arthur; Rising Sun Literary Group, The; Scott, Synergy Creative Agency, Stacy Ann; Sebastian Literary Agency; Southern Writers; Steinberg Literary Agency, Michael; Wallerstein Agency, The Gerry B.; Waterside Productions, Inc.; West Coast Literary Associates; Wilshire Literary Agency, The

Cartoon/comic

Colby: Literary Agency; Flannery, White and Stone; Independent Publishing Agency; Lighthouse Literary Agency; Northeast Literary Agency; Singer Media Corporation

Confessional

Independent Publishing Agency; Kaltman Literary Agency, Larry; Northeast Literary Agency; Northwest Literary Services; Pegasus International, Inc., Literary & Film Agents; Scott, Synergy Creative Agency, Stacy Ann; Strong, Marianne; Zelasky Literary Agency, Tom

Contemporary issues

Brady Literary Management; Browne Ltd., Pema; Chester, Literary Agency, Linda; Connor Literary Agency; Creative Concepts Literary Agency; Dorese Agency Ltd.; Doyen Literary Services, Inc.; Fishbein Ltd., Frieda; Flaherty, Literary Agent, Joyce A.; Flannery, White and Stone; Independent Publishing Agency; Iorio, Esq., Gary F.; Kaltman Literary Agency, Larry; Kellock & Associates Ltd., J.; Law Offices of Robert L. Fenton PC; Lighthouse Literary Agency; Marshall Agency, The Evan; Nelson Literary Agency & Lecture Bureau, BK; Northeast Literary Agency; Northwest Literary Services; Pegasus International, Inc., Literary & Film Agents; Rising Sun Literary Group, The; Sebastian Literary Agency; Southern Writers; State of the Art Ltd.; Steinberg Literary Agency, Michael; Tiger Moon Enterprises; Wallerstein Agency, The Gerry B.; Waterside Productions, Inc.; West Coast Literary Associates; Zelasky Literary Agency, Tom

Detective/police/crime

Alden—Literary Service, Farel T.; Anthony Agency, Joseph; Authors' Marketing Services Ltd.; Brady Literary Management; Browne Ltd., Pema; Colby: Literary Agency; Creative Concepts Literary Agency; Dorese Agency Ltd.; Doyen Literary Services, Inc.; Fishbein Ltd., Frieda; Flaherty, Literary Agent, Joyce A.; Flannery, White and Stone; Independent Publishing Agency; Iorio, Esq., Gary F.; Kaltman Literary Agency, Larry; Kellock & Associates Ltd., J.; Law Offices of Robert L. Fenton PC; Lighthouse Literary Agency; Marshall Agency, The Evan; Northeast Literary Agency; Northwest Literary Services; Oceanic Press; Panettieri Agency, The; Pegasus International, Inc., Literary & Film Agents; Pine Associates, Inc, Arthur; Rising Sun Literary Group, The; Scott, Synergy Creative Agency, Stacy Ann; Sebastian Literary Agency; Singer Media Corporation; Southern Writers; Steinberg Literary Agency, Michael; Strong, Marianne; Toomey Associates, Jeanne; Wallerstein Agency, The Gerry B.; Waterside Productions, Inc.; Watt & Associates, Sandra; West Coast Literary Associates; Wilshire Literary Agency, The; Zelasky Literary Agency, Tom

Erotica

Anthony Agency, Joseph; Independent Publishing Agency; Iorio, Esq., Gary F.; Kaltman Literary Agency, Larry; Northwest Literary Services; Oceanic Press; Panettieri Agency, The; Pegasus International, Inc., Literary & Film Agents; Peterson Associates Literary Agency; Rising Sun Literary Group, The; Singer Media Corporation; Steinberg Literary Agency, Michael

Ethnic

Backman, Elizabeth H.; Chester, Literary Agency, Linda; Connor Literary Agency; Dorese Agency Ltd.; Doyen Literary Services, Inc.; Flannery, White and Stone; Independent Publishing Agency; Kaltman Literary Agency, Larry; Kellock & Associates Ltd., J.; Lighthouse Literary Agency; Northeast Literary Agency; Northwest Literary Services; Pegasus International, Inc., Literary & Film Agents; Rising Sun Literary Group, The; Sebastian Literary Agency

Experimental
Alden—Literary Service, Farel T.; Chadd-Stevens Literary Agency; Doyen Literary Services, Inc.; Independent Publishing Agency; Iorio, Esq., Gary F.; Kellock & Associates Ltd., J.; Lighthouse Literary Agency; Northeast Literary Agency; Northwest Literary Services; Oceanic Press; Pegasus International, Inc., Literary & Film Agents; Peterson Associates Literary Agency; Rising Sun Literary Group, The; West Coast Literary Associates

Family saga
Alden—Literary Service, Farel T.; Brady Literary Management; Creative Concepts Literary Agency; Dorese Agency Ltd.; Doyen Literary Services, Inc.; Fishbein Ltd., Frieda; Flaherty, Literary Agent, Joyce A.; Flannery, White and Stone; Kellock & Associates Ltd., J.; Lighthouse Literary Agency; Marcil Literary Agency, The Denise; Marshall Agency, The Evan; Nelson Literary Agency & Lecture Bureau, BK; Northeast Literary Agency; Northwest Literary Services; Panettieri Agency, The; Peterson Associates Literary Agency; Rising Sun Literary Group, The; Sebastian Literary Agency; Southern Writers; Strong, Marianne; Tiger Moon Enterprises; Wallerstein Agency, The Gerry B.; Zelasky Literary Agency, Tom

Fantasy
Alden—Literary Service, Farel T.; Anthony Agency, Joseph; Backman, Elizabeth H.; Chadd-Stevens Literary Agency; Doyen Literary Services, Inc.; Fishbein Ltd., Frieda; Flannery, White and Stone; Gladden Unlimited; Independent Publishing Agency; Iorio, Esq., Gary F.; Kellock & Associates Ltd., J.; Northeast Literary Agency; Northwest Literary Services; Panettieri Agency, The; Pegasus International, Inc., Literary & Film Agents; Rising Sun Literary Group, The; Singer Media Corporation; Southern Writers

Feminist
Browne Ltd., Pema; Chester, Literary Agency, Linda; Dorese Agency Ltd.; Fishbein Ltd., Frieda; Flaherty, Literary Agent, Joyce A.; Flannery, White and Stone; Independent Publishing Agency; Kellock & Associates Ltd., J.; Lighthouse Literary Agency; Northwest Literary Services; Rising Sun Literary Group, The; Southern Writers; State of the Art Ltd.; Writer's Consulting Group; Zelasky Literary Agency, Tom

Gay
Dorese Agency Ltd.; Flannery, White and Stone; Rising Sun Literary Group, The; Sebastian Literary Agency; Southern Writers

Glitz
Brady Literary Management; Browne Ltd., Pema; Connor Literary Agency; Creative Concepts Literary Agency; Dorese Agency Ltd.; Doyen Literary Services, Inc.; JLM Literary Agents; Kellock & Associates Ltd., J.; Law Offices of Robert L. Fenton PC; Marshall Agency, The Evan; Northeast Literary Agency; Panettieri Agency, The; Robb Literary Properties, Sherry; Singer Media Corporation; Southern Writers; Wallerstein Agency, The Gerry B.; Waterside Productions, Inc.; Watt & Associates, Sandra

Historical
Alden—Literary Service, Farel T.; Backman, Elizabeth H.; Brady Literary Management; Browne Ltd., Pema; Creative Concepts Literary Agency; Dorese Agency Ltd.; Doyen Literary Services, Inc.; Fishbein Ltd., Frieda; Flaherty, Literary Agent, Joyce A.; Flannery, White and Stone; Independent Publishing Agency; Iorio, Esq., Gary F.; Kellock & Associates Ltd., J.; Kern Literary Agency, Natasha; Lighthouse Literary Agency; Marcil Literary Agency, The Denise; Marshall Agency, The Evan; Northeast Literary Agency; Northwest Literary Services; Panettieri Agency, The; Pegasus International, Inc., Literary & Film Agents; Rising Sun Literary Group, The; Sebastian Literary Agency; Southern Writers; Tiger Moon Enterprises; Wallerstein Agency, The Gerry B.; West Coast Literary Associates; Zelasky Literary Agency, Tom

Humor/satire
Alden—Literary Service, Farel T.; Browne Ltd., Pema; Colby: Literary Agency; Connor Literary Agency; Cook Literary Agency, Warren; Doyen Literary Services, Inc.; Fishbein Ltd., Frieda; Flannery, White and Stone; Independent Publishing Agency; Kaltman Literary Agency, Larry; Kellock & Associates Ltd., J.; Law Offices of Robert L. Fenton PC; Lighthouse Literary Agency;

Northeast Literary Agency; Northwest Literary Services; Pegasus International, Inc., Literary & Film Agents; Peterson Associates Literary Agency; Rising Sun Literary Group, The; Southern Writers; Wallerstein Agency, The Gerry B.

Juvenile

Alden—Literary Service, Farel T.; Browne Ltd., Pema; Catalog Literary Agency, The; Doyen Literary Services, Inc.; Flannery, White and Stone; Hamersfield Agency, The; Independent Publishing Agency; Kellock & Associates Ltd., J.; Lighthouse Literary Agency; March Media Inc.; Northeast Literary Agency; Northwest Literary Services; Panettieri Agency, The; Pegasus International, Inc., Literary & Film Agents; Popkin/Nancy Cooke, Julie; Porcelain, Sidney E.; Rising Sun Literary Group, The; Scott, Synergy Creative Agency, Stacy Ann; Southern Writers; Zelasky Literary Agency, Tom

Lesbian

Dorese Agency Ltd.; Flannery, White and Stone; Rising Sun Literary Group, The; Southern Writers

Literary

Brady Literary Management; Browne Ltd., Pema; Chester, Literary Agency, Linda; Connor Literary Agency; Cook Literary Agency, Warren; Creative Concepts Literary Agency; Dorese Agency Ltd.; Flaherty, Literary Agent, Joyce A.; Flannery, White and Stone; Independent Publishing Agency; Iorio, Esq., Gary F.; Kaltman Literary Agency, Larry; Kellock & Associates Ltd., J.; Lighthouse Literary Agency; Nelson Literary Agency & Lecture Bureau, BK; Northeast Literary Agency; Northwest Literary Services; Pegasus International, Inc., Literary & Film Agents; Pine Associates, Inc, Arthur; Popkin/Nancy Cooke/Julie; Rising Sun Literary Group, The; Robb Literary Properties, Sherry; Scott, Synergy Creative Agency, Stacy Ann; Sebastian Literary Agency; Tiger Moon Enterprises; Wallerstein Agency, The Gerry B.; Waterside Productions, Inc.; West Coast Literary Associates; Wilshire Literary Agency, The; Zelasky Literary Agency, Tom

Mainstream

Alden—Literary Service, Farel T.; Brady Literary Management; Browne Ltd., Pema; Catalog Literary Agency, The; Chester, Literary Agency, Linda; Creative Concepts Literary Agency; Dorese Agency Ltd.; Doyen Literary Services, Inc.; Fishbein Ltd., Frieda; Flaherty, Literary Agent, Joyce A.; Flannery, White and Stone; Gladden Unlimited; Independent Publishing Agency; Iorio, Esq., Gary F.; Kaltman Literary Agency, Larry; Kellock & Associates Ltd., J.; Kern Literary Agency, Natasha; Lee Shore Agency; Lighthouse Literary Agency; Marshall Agency, The Evan; Nelson Literary Agency & Lecture Bureau, BK; Northeast Literary Agency; Northwest Literary Services; Oceanic Press; Panettieri Agency, The; Pegasus International, Inc., Literary & Film Agents; Peterson Associates Literary Agency; Popkin/Nancy Cooke, Julie; Rising Sun Literary Group, The; Robb Literary Properties, Sherry; Scott, Synergy Creative Agency, Stacy Ann; Sebastian Literary Agency; Southern Writers; Steinberg Literary Agency, Michael; Wallerstein Agency, The Gerry B.; Waterside Productions, Inc.; Watt & Associates, Sandra; West Coast Literary Associates; Wilshire Literary Agency, The; Writer's Consulting Group; Zelasky Literary Agency, Tom

Mystery/suspense

Alden—Literary Service, Farel T.; Anthony Agency, Joseph; Authors' Marketing Services Ltd.; Backman, Elizabeth H.; Brady Literary Management; Browne Ltd., Pema; Chadd-Stevens Literary Agency; Chester, Literary Agency, Linda; Colby: Literary Agency; Connor Literary Agency; Cook Literary Agency, Warren; Creative Concepts Literary Agency; Dorese Agency Ltd.; Doyen Literary Services, Inc.; Fishbein Ltd., Frieda; Flaherty, Literary Agent, Joyce A.; Flannery, White and Stone; Independent Publishing Agency; Iorio, Esq., Gary F.; JLM Literary Agents; Kaltman Literary Agency, Larry; Kellock & Associates Ltd., J.; Kern Literary Agency, Natasha; Law Offices of Robert L. Fenton PC; Lighthouse Literary Agency; Marshall Agency, The Evan; Nelson Literary Agency & Lecture Bureau, BK; Northeast Literary Agency; Northwest Literary Services; Oceanic Press; Panettieri Agency, The; Pegasus International, Inc., Literary & Film Agents; Popkin/Nancy Cooke, Julie; Porcelain, Sidney E.; Rising Sun Literary Group, The; Robb Literary Properties, Sherry; Scott, Synergy Creative Agency, Stacy Ann; Sebastian Literary Agency; Singer Media Corporation; Southern Writers; State of the Art Ltd.; Steinberg Literary

Agency, Michael; Wallerstein Agency, The Gerry B.; Waterside Productions, Inc.; Watt & Associates, Sandra; West Coast Literary Associates; Wilshire Literary Agency, The; Writer's Consulting Group; Zelasky Literary Agency, Tom

Open to all areas of fiction
Author Aid Associates; Bernstein Literary Agency, Meredith; Deering Literary Agency, Dorothy; Erikson Literary Agency, The; Glenmark Literary Agency; Goodkind, Larney; Jenks Agency, Carolyn; Kamaroff Associates, Alex; Kuller Associates, Doris Francis; Morgan Literary Agency, Inc.; Northeast Literary Agency; Sullivan Associates, Mark

Picture book
Alden—Literary Service, Farel T.; Brady Literary Management; Connor Literary Agency; Doyen Literary Services, Inc.; Flannery, White and Stone; Independent Publishing Agency; Kellock & Associates Ltd., J.; Lighthouse Literary Agency; Northeast Literary Agency; Northwest Literary Services; Pegasus International, Inc., Literary & Film Agents; Rising Sun Literary Group, The; Singer Media Corporation

Psychic/supernatural
Alden—Literary Service, Farel T.; Anthony Agency, Joseph; Brady Literary Management; Browne Ltd., Pema; Chadd-Stevens Literary Agency; Dorese Agency Ltd.; Doyen Literary Services, Inc.; Flaherty, Literary Agent, Joyce A.; Flannery, White and Stone; Independent Publishing Agency; JLM Literary Agents; Kellock & Associates Ltd., J.; Marshall Agency, The Evan; Northeast Literary Agency; Northwest Literary Services; Oceanic Press; Panettieri Agency, The; Pegasus International, Inc., Literary & Film Agents; Peterson Associates Literary Agency; Rising Sun Literary Group, The; Scott, Synergy Creative Agency, Stacy Ann; Singer Media Corporation; Southern Writers; Tiger Moon Enterprises

Regional
Backman, Elizabeth H.; Dorese Agency Ltd.; Flannery, White and Stone; Lighthouse Literary Agency; Northeast Literary Agency; Pegasus International, Inc., Literary & Film Agents; Rising Sun Literary Group, The; Southern Writers; Tiger Moon Enterprises; Wallerstein Agency, The Gerry B.; West Coast Literary Associates; Browne Ltd., Pema; Creative Concepts Literary Agency; Northwest Literary Services; Southern Writers; Tiger Moon Enterprises

Romance
Anthony Agency, Joseph; Authors' Marketing Services Ltd.; Browne Ltd., Pema; Creative Concepts Literary Agency; Doyen Literary Services, Inc.; Fishbein Ltd., Frieda; Flaherty, Literary Agent, Joyce A.; Flannery, White and Stone; JLM Literary Agents; Kaltman Literary Agency, Larry; Kellock & Associates Ltd., J.; Kern Literary Agency, Natasha; Law Offices of Robert L. Fenton PC; Marcil Literary Agency, The Denise; Marshall Agency, The Evan; Nelson Literary Agency & Lecture Bureau, BK; Northeast Literary Agency; Northwest Literary Services; Oceanic Press; Panettieri Agency, The; Pegasus International, Inc., Literary & Film Agents; Popkin/ Nancy Cooke, Julie; Rising Sun Literary Group, The; Scott, Synergy Creative Agency, Stacy Ann; Singer Media Corporation; Southern Writers; Strong, Marianne; Wallerstein Agency, The Gerry B.; Waterside Productions, Inc.; West Coast Literary Associates; Zelasky Literary Agency, Tom

Science fiction
Anthony Agency, Joseph; Backman, Elizabeth H.; Browne Ltd., Pema; Doyen Literary Services, Inc.; Fishbein Ltd., Frieda; Flannery, White and Stone; Gladden Unlimited; Iorio, Esq., Gary F.; Law Offices of Robert L. Fenton PC; Lighthouse Literary Agency; Northeast Literary Agency; Northwest Literary Services; Oceanic Press; Panettieri Agency, The; Pegasus International, Inc., Literary & Film Agents; Peterson Associates Literary Agency; Popkin/Nancy Cooke, Julie; Rising Sun Literary Group, The; Scott, Synergy Creative Agency, Stacy Ann; Singer Media Corporation; Southern Writers; State of the Art Ltd.; Steinberg Literary Agency, Michael; West Coast Literary Associates

Sports
Backman, Elizabeth H.; Colby: Literary Agency; Connor Literary Agency; Dorese Agency Ltd.; Flaherty, Literary Agent, Joyce A.; Flannery, White and Stone; Iorio, Esq., Gary F.; Kaltman

Literary Agency, Larry; Kellock & Associates Ltd., J.; Law Offices of Robert L. Fenton PC; Lighthouse Literary Agency; Nelson Literary Agency & Lecture Bureau, BK; Northeast Literary Agency; Northwest Literary Services; Oceanic Press; Pegasus International, Inc., Literary & Film Agents; Scott, Synergy Creative Agency, Stacy Ann

Thriller/espionage
Anthony Agency, Joseph; Authors' Marketing Services Ltd.; Backman, Elizabeth H.; Brady Literary Management; Browne Ltd., Pema; Chester, Literary Agency, Linda; Colby: Literary Agency; Cook Literary Agency, Warren; Creative Concepts Literary Agency; Doyen Literary Services, Inc.; Fishbein Ltd., Frieda; Flaherty, Literary Agent, Joyce A.; Flannery, White and Stone; Gladden Unlimited; Independent Publishing Agency; Iorio, Esq., Gary F.; JLM Literary Agents; Kaltman Literary Agency, Larry; Kellock & Associates Ltd., J.; Kern Literary Agency, Natasha; Law Offices of Robert L. Fenton PC; Lighthouse Literary Agency; Marshall Agency, The Evan; Nelson Literary Agency & Lecture Bureau, BK; Northeast Literary Agency; Northwest Literary Services; Oceanic Press; Panettieri Agency, The; Pegasus International, Inc., Literary & Film Agents; Peterson Associates Literary Agency; Pine Associates, Inc, Arthur; Rising Sun Literary Group, The; Scott, Synergy Creative Agency, Stacy Ann; Sebastian Literary Agency; Singer Media Corporation; Southern Writers; Steinberg Literary Agency, Michael; Strong, Marianne; Toomey Associates, Jeanne; Wallerstein Agency, The Gerry B.; Waterside Productions, Inc.; Watt & Associates, Sandra; West Coast Literary Associates; Zelasky Literary Agency, Tom

Westerns/frontier
Brady Literary Management; Colby: Literary Agency; Doyen Literary Services, Inc.; Iorio, Esq., Gary F.; Kellock & Associates Ltd., J.; Kern Literary Agency, Natasha; Law Offices of Robert L. Fenton PC; Lighthouse Literary Agency; Northeast Literary Agency; Northwest Literary Services; Oceanic Press; Pegasus International, Inc., Literary & Film Agents; Rising Sun Literary Group, The; Sebastian Literary Agency; Singer Media Corporation; Southern Writers; Wallerstein Agency, The Gerry B.; West Coast Literary Associates; Zelasky Literary Agency, Tom

Young adult
Anthony Agency, Joseph; Brady Literary Management; Browne Ltd., Pema; Cook Literary Agency, Warren; Creative Concepts Literary Agency; Dorese Agency Ltd.; Doyen Literary Services, Inc.; Fishbein Ltd., Frieda; Flannery, White and Stone; Follendore Literary Agency, Joan; Independent Publishing Agency; Kaltman Literary Agency, Larry; Kellock & Associates Ltd., J.; Kern Literary Agency, Natasha; Lighthouse Literary Agency; Northeast Literary Agency; Northwest Literary Services; Oceanic Press; Panettieri Agency, The; Pegasus International, Inc., Literary & Film Agents; Rising Sun Literary Group, The; Scott, Synergy Creative Agency, Stacy Ann; Southern Writers; Wallerstein Agency, The Gerry B.; Zelasky Literary Agency, Tom

Nonfiction

Agriculture/horticulture
Catalog Literary Agency, The; Lighthouse Literary Agency; Northwest Literary Services; Toomey Associates, Jeanne; Urstadt Inc. Writers and Artists Agency, Susan P.

Animals
Alden—Literary Service, Farel T.; Author Aid Associates; Brady Literary Management; Creative Concepts Literary Agency; Fishbein Ltd., Frieda; Flaherty, Literary Agent, Joyce A.; Kellock & Associates Ltd., J.; Lighthouse Literary Agency; Nelson Literary Agency & Lecture Bureau, BK; Northwest Literary Services; Pegasus International, Inc., Literary & Film Agents; Rising Sun Literary Group, The; Toomey Associates, Jeanne; Urstadt Inc. Writers and Artists Agency, Susan P.; Watt & Associates, Sandra

Anthropology
Author Aid Associates; Browne Ltd., Pema; Erikson Literary Agency, The; Independent Publishing Agency; Kellock & Associates Ltd., J.; Lighthouse Literary Agency; Nelson Literary Agency & Lecture Bureau, BK; Northwest Literary Services; Pegasus International, Inc., Literary & Film Agents; Peterson Associates Literary Agency; Sebastian Literary Agency; Sullivan

Associates, Mark; Toomey Associates, Jeanne; Urstadt Inc. Writers and Artists Agency, Susan P.; Waterside Productions, Inc.; Watt & Associates, Sandra

Art/architecture/design

Browne Ltd., Pema; Chester, Literary Agency, Linda; Dorese Agency Ltd.; Independent Publishing Agency; Kellock & Associates Ltd., J.; Lighthouse Literary Agency; Marcil Literary Agency, The Denise; Northwest Literary Services; Pegasus International, Inc., Literary & Film Agents; Popkin/Nancy Cooke, Julie; Rising Sun Literary Group, The; Sebastian Literary Agency; State of the Art Ltd.; Toomey Associates, Jeanne; Urstadt Inc. Writers and Artists Agency, Susan P.; Waterside Productions, Inc.

Biography/autobiography

Alden—Literary Service, Farel T.; Author Aid Associates; Authors' Marketing Services Ltd.; Backman, Elizabeth H.; Brady Literary Management; Browne Ltd., Pema; Chester, Literary Agency, Linda; Cook Literary Agency, Warren; Creative Concepts Literary Agency; Dorese Agency Ltd.; Fishbein Ltd., Frieda; Flaherty, Literary Agent, Joyce A.; Independent Publishing Agency; Iorio, Esq., Gary F.; JLM Literary Agents; Kellock & Associates Ltd., J.; Kern Literary Agency, Natasha; Law Offices of Robert L. Fenton PC; Lighthouse Literary Agency; Marshall Agency, The Evan; Miller Agency, The Peter; Nelson Literary Agency & Lecture Bureau, BK; Northwest Literary Services; Oceanic Press; Pegasus International, Inc., Literary & Film Agents; Robb Literary Properties, Sherry; Scott, Synergy Creative Agency, Stacy Ann; Sebastian Literary Agency; Singer Media Corporation; Southern Writers; Steinberg Literary Agency, Michael; Sullivan Associates, Mark; Toomey Associates, Jeanne; Urstadt Inc. Writers and Artists Agency, Susan P.; Waterside Productions, Inc.; West Coast Literary Associates; Zelasky Literary Agency, Tom

Business

About Books Inc.; Authors' Marketing Services Ltd.; Backman, Elizabeth H.; Browne Ltd., Pema; Catalog Literary Agency, The; Chester, Literary Agency, Linda; Creative Concepts Literary Agency; Dorese Agency Ltd.; Flaherty, Literary Agent, Joyce A.; Flannery, White and Stone; Independent Publishing Agency; Iorio, Esq., Gary F.; JLM Literary Agents; Kellock & Associates Ltd., J.; Kern Literary Agency, Natasha; Law Offices of Robert L. Fenton PC; Lighthouse Literary Agency; Marcil Literary Agency, The Denise; Marshall Agency, The Evan; Nelson Literary Agency & Lecture Bureau, BK; Northwest Literary Services; Oceanic Press; Pegasus International, Inc., Literary & Film Agents; Peterson Associates Literary Agency; Pine Associates, Inc, Arthur; Rising Sun Literary Group, The; Scott, Synergy Creative Agency, Stacy Ann; Sebastian Literary Agency; Singer Media Corporation; Southern Writers; Steinberg Literary Agency, Michael; Sullivan Associates, Mark; Urstadt Inc. Writers and Artists Agency, Susan P.; Waterside Productions, Inc.; Writer's Consulting Group

Child guidance/parenting

Author Aid Associates; Authors' Marketing Services Ltd.; Authors and Artists Resource Center/TARC Literary Agency, The; Backman, Elizabeth H.; Brady Literary Management; Browne Ltd., Pema; Catalog Literary Agency, The; Chester, Literary Agency, Linda; Connor Literary Agency; Creative Concepts Literary Agency; Dorese Agency Ltd.; Flaherty, Literary Agent, Joyce A.; Flannery, White and Stone; Independent Publishing Agency; Kellock & Associates Ltd., J.; Kern Literary Agency, Natasha; Law Offices of Robert L. Fenton PC; Lighthouse Literary Agency; Marcil Literary Agency, The Denise; Marshall Agency, The Evan; Nelson Literary Agency & Lecture Bureau, BK; Northwest Literary Services; Oceanic Press; Panettieri Agency, The; Pegasus International, Inc., Literary & Film Agents; Rising Sun Literary Group, The; Scott, Synergy Creative Agency, Stacy Ann; Sebastian Literary Agency; Singer Media Corporation; Southern Writers; Steinberg Literary Agency, Michael; Urstadt Inc. Writers and Artists Agency, Susan P.; Waterside Productions, Inc.

Computers/electronics

Catalog Literary Agency, The; Creative Concepts Literary Agency; Lighthouse Literary Agency; Nelson Literary Agency & Lecture Bureau, BK; Oceanic Press; Pegasus International, Inc., Literary & Film Agents; Rising Sun Literary Group, The; Sebastian Literary Agency; Singer Media Corporation; Steinberg Literary Agency, Michael; Waterside Productions, Inc.

Cooking/food/nutrition

Crafts/hobbies

Current affairs

Ethnic/cultural interests

Gay/lesbian issues

Government/politics/law

Health/medicine

History

Alden—Literary Service, Farel T.; Author Aid Associates; Backman, Elizabeth H.; Brady Literary Management; Chester, Literary Agency, Linda; Cook Literary Agency, Warren; Dorese Agency Ltd.; Flaherty, Literary Agent, Joyce A.; Independent Publishing Agency; Iorio, Esq., Gary F.; Kellock & Associates Ltd., J.; Lighthouse Literary Agency; Marshall Agency, The Evan; Northwest Literary Services; Pegasus International, Inc., Literary & Film Agents; Popkin/Nancy Cooke, Julie; Rising Sun Literary Group, The; Sebastian Literary Agency; Southern Writers; Steinberg Literary Agency, Michael; Tiger Moon Enterprises; Toomey Associates, Jeanne; West Coast Literary Associates

Interior design/decorating

Backman, Elizabeth H.; Creative Concepts Literary Agency; Dorese Agency Ltd.; Lighthouse Literary Agency; Marcil Literary Agency, The Denise; Marshall Agency, The Evan; Strong, Marianne; Sullivan Associates, Mark; Toomey Associates, Jeanne; Urstadt Inc. Writers and Artists Agency, Susan P.

Juvenile nonfiction

Alden—Literary Service, Farel T.; Author Aid Associates; Brady Literary Management; Browne Ltd., Pema; Catalog Literary Agency, The; Creative Concepts Literary Agency; Fishbein Ltd., Frieda; Flannery, White and Stone; Hamersfield Agency, The; Independent Publishing Agency; Kellock & Associates Ltd., J.; Lighthouse Literary Agency; March Media Inc.; Northwest Literary Services; Pegasus International, Inc., Literary & Film Agents; Rising Sun Literary Group, The; Scott, Synergy Creative Agency, Stacy Ann; Southern Writers; Tiger Moon Enterprises; Zelasky Literary Agency, Tom

Language/literature/criticism

Author Aid Associates; Creative Concepts Literary Agency; Dorese Agency Ltd.; Independent Publishing Agency; Kellock & Associates Ltd., J.; Northwest Literary Services; Sullivan Associates, Mark; West Coast Literary Associates

Military/war

Anthony Agency, Joseph; Author Aid Associates; Authors' Marketing Services Ltd.; Brady Literary Management; Browne Ltd., Pema; Creative Concepts Literary Agency; Dorese Agency Ltd.; Fishbein Ltd., Frieda; Flaherty, Literary Agent, Joyce A.; Independent Publishing Agency; Iorio, Esq., Gary F.; JLM Literary Agents; Law Offices of Robert L. Fenton PC; Lighthouse Literary Agency; Nelson Literary Agency & Lecture Bureau, BK; Pegasus International, Inc., Literary & Film Agents; Sebastian Literary Agency; Sullivan Associates, Mark; Tiger Moon Enterprises; Urstadt Inc. Writers and Artists Agency, Susan P.; Zelasky Literary Agency, Tom

Money/finance/economics

About Books Inc.; Catalog Literary Agency, The; Chester, Literary Agency, Linda; Connor Literary Agency; Creative Concepts Literary Agency; Dorese Agency Ltd.; Flaherty, Literary Agent, Joyce A.; Flannery, White and Stone; Independent Publishing Agency; Iorio, Esq., Gary F.; JLM Literary Agents; Kellock & Associates Ltd., J.; Law Offices of Robert L. Fenton PC; Lighthouse Literary Agency; Marcil Literary Agency, The Denise; Marshall Agency, The Evan; Nelson Literary Agency & Lecture Bureau, BK; Oceanic Press; Pegasus International, Inc., Literary & Film Agents; Pine Associates, Inc, Arthur; Rising Sun Literary Group, The; Sebastian Literary Agency; Singer Media Corporation; Southern Writers; Steinberg Literary Agency, Michael; Strong, Marianne; Sullivan Associates, Mark; Tiger Moon Enterprises; Toomey Associates, Jeanne; Urstadt Inc. Writers and Artists Agency, Susan P.; Waterside Productions, Inc.

Music/dance/theater/film

Alden—Literary Service, Farel T.; Author Aid Associates; Backman, Elizabeth H.; Brady Literary Management; Chester, Literary Agency, Linda; Dorese Agency Ltd.; Flannery, White and Stone; Independent Publishing Agency; Kellock & Associates Ltd., J.; Law Offices of Robert L. Fenton PC; Lighthouse Literary Agency; Marshall Agency, The Evan; Nelson Literary Agency & Lecture Bureau, BK; Northwest Literary Services; Oceanic Press; Rising Sun Literary Group, The; Scott, Synergy Creative Agency, Stacy Ann; Southern Writers; Sullivan Associates, Mark; Tiger Moon Enterprises; Urstadt Inc. Writers and Artists Agency, Susan P.; Waterside Productions, Inc.; West Coast Literary Associates

Nature/environment

Author Aid Associates; Brady Literary Management; Browne Ltd., Pema; Catalog Literary Agency, The; Chester, Literary Agency, Linda; Cook Literary Agency, Warren; Creative Concepts Literary Agency; Fishbein Ltd., Frieda; Flaherty, Literary Agent, Joyce A.; Flannery, White and Stone; Independent Publishing Agency; JLM Literary Agents; Kellock & Associates Ltd., J.; Lighthouse Literary Agency; Marcil Literary Agency, The Denise; Nelson Literary Agency & Lecture Bureau, BK; Northwest Literary Services; Pegasus International, Inc., Literary & Film Agents; Rising Sun Literary Group, The; Sebastian Literary Agency; Steinberg Literary Agency, Michael; Sullivan Associates, Mark; Tiger Moon Enterprises; Toomey Associates, Jeanne; Urstadt Inc. Writers and Artists Agency, Susan P.; Waterside Productions, Inc.; West Coast Literary Associates

New age/metaphysics

Alden—Literary Service, Farel T.; Author Aid Associates; Browne Ltd., Pema; Dorese Agency Ltd.; Kellock & Associates Ltd., J.; Marshall Agency, The Evan; New Age World Services; Northwest Literary Services; Oceanic Press; Pegasus International, Inc., Literary & Film Agents; Peterson Associates Literary Agency; Scott, Synergy Creative Agency, Stacy Ann; State of the Art Ltd.; Sullivan Associates, Mark; Tiger Moon Enterprises; Waterside Productions, Inc.; Watt & Associates, Sandra

Open to all areas of nonfiction

Authors and Artists Resource Center/Tarc Literary Agency; Bernstein Literary Agency, Meredith; Deering Literary Agency, Dorothy; Doyen Literary Services, Inc.; Follendore Literary Agency, Joan; Glenmark Literary Agency; Goodkind, Larney; Jenks Agency, Carolyn; Kamaroff Associates, Alex; Morgan Literary Agency, Inc.; Northeast Literary Agency; Wallerstein Agency, The Gerry B.

Photography

Author Aid Associates; Backman, Elizabeth H.; Connor Literary Agency; Dorese Agency Ltd.; Hamersfield Agency, The; Independent Publishing Agency; Lighthouse Literary Agency; Northwest Literary Services; Pegasus International, Inc., Literary & Film Agents; Rising Sun Literary Group, The; Sullivan Associates, Mark; Urstadt Inc. Writers and Artists Agency, Susan P.

Psychology

Anthony Agency, Joseph; Author Aid Associates; Backman, Elizabeth H.; Brady Literary Management; Browne Ltd., Pema; Catalog Literary Agency, The; Chester, Literary Agency, Linda; Creative Concepts Literary Agency; Dorese Agency Ltd.; Flaherty, Literary Agent, Joyce A.; Flannery, White and Stone; Independent Publishing Agency; JLM Literary Agents; Kern Literary Agency, Natasha; Lighthouse Literary Agency; Marcil Literary Agency, The Denise; Marshall Agency, The Evan; Nelson Literary Agency & Lecture Bureau, BK; Northwest Literary Services; Oceanic Press; Panettieri Agency, The; Pegasus International, Inc., Literary & Film Agents; Peterson Associates Literary Agency; Pine Associates, Inc, Arthur; Rising Sun Literary Group, The; Scott, Synergy Creative Agency, Stacy Ann; Sebastian Literary Agency; Singer Media Corporation; Southern Writers; Steinberg Literary Agency, Michael; Sullivan Associates, Mark; Waterside Productions, Inc.; West Coast Literary Associates

Religious/inspirational

Author Aid Associates; Backman, Elizabeth H.; Browne Ltd., Pema; Independent Publishing Agency; JLM Literary Agents; Law Offices of Robert L. Fenton PC; Nelson Literary Agency & Lecture Bureau, BK; Pegasus International, Inc., Literary & Film Agents; Rising Sun Literary Group, The; Rising Sun Literary Group, The; Southern Writers; Sullivan Associates, Mark; Tiger Moon Enterprises

Science/technology

Anthony Agency, Joseph; Author Aid Associates; Backman, Elizabeth H.; Browne Ltd., Pema; Catalog Literary Agency, The; Cook Literary Agency, Warren; Creative Concepts Literary Agency; Flannery, White and Stone; Independent Publishing Agency; JLM Literary Agents; Kaltman Literary Agency, Larry; Kern Literary Agency, Natasha; Nelson Literary Agency & Lecture Bureau, BK; Oceanic Press; Pegasus International, Inc., Literary & Film Agents; Peterson Associates Literary Agency; Sebastian Literary Agency; Sullivan Associates, Mark; Writer's Consulting Group

Self-help/personal improvement
Alden—Literary Service, Farel T.; Anthony Agency, Joseph; Author Aid Associates; Authors and Artists Resource Center/TARC Literary Agency, The; Backman, Elizabeth H.; Brady Literary Management; Browne Ltd., Pema; Catalog Literary Agency, The; Connor Literary Agency; Creative Concepts Literary Agency; Dorese Agency Ltd.; Fishbein Ltd., Frieda; Flaherty, Literary Agent, Joyce A.; Flannery, White and Stone; Independent Publishing Agency; JLM Literary Agents; Kaltman Literary Agency, Larry; Kellock & Associates Ltd., J.; Kern Literary Agency, Natasha; Law Offices of Robert L. Fenton PC; Lee Shore Agency; Lighthouse Literary Agency; Marcil Literary Agency, The Denise; Marshall Agency, The Evan; Nelson Literary Agency & Lecture Bureau, BK; Northwest Literary Services; Oceanic Press; Panettieri Agency, The; Pegasus International, Inc., Literary & Film Agents; Peterson Associates Literary Agency; Popkin/Nancy Cooke, Julie; Rising Sun Literary Group, The; Scott, Synergy Creative Agency, Stacy Ann; Sebastian Literary Agency; Singer Media Corporation; Southern Writers; State of the Art Ltd.; Steinberg Literary Agency, Michael; Tiger Moon Enterprises; Urstadt Inc. Writers and Artists Agency, Susan P.; Watt & Associates, Sandra; Writer's Consulting Group; Zelasky Literary Agency, Tom

Sociology
Cook Literary Agency, Warren; Creative Concepts Literary Agency; Dorese Agency Ltd.; Erikson Literary Agency, The; Flannery, White and Stone; Independent Publishing Agency; Iorio, Esq., Gary F.; JLM Literary Agents; Nelson Literary Agency & Lecture Bureau, BK; Pegasus International, Inc., Literary & Film Agents; Sebastian Literary Agency; Waterside Productions, Inc.

Sports
Author Aid Associates; Backman, Elizabeth H.; Browne Ltd., Pema; Connor Literary Agency; Dorese Agency Ltd.; Flaherty, Literary Agent, Joyce A.; Flannery, White and Stone; Independent Publishing Agency; Iorio, Esq., Gary F.; Kaltman Literary Agency, Larry; Kellock & Associates Ltd., J.; Law Offices of Robert L. Fenton PC; Lighthouse Literary Agency; Nelson Literary Agency & Lecture Bureau, BK; Northwest Literary Services; Oceanic Press; Pegasus International, Inc., Literary & Film Agents; Rising Sun Literary Group, The; Scott, Synergy Creative Agency, Stacy Ann; Sebastian Literary Agency; Sullivan Associates, Mark; Urstadt Inc. Writers and Artists Agency, Susan P.; Waterside Productions, Inc.; Watt & Associates, Sandra

Translations
Author Aid Associates; Hamersfield Agency, The; Northwest Literary Services; Pegasus International, Inc., Literary & Film Agents; Rising Sun Literary Group, The; Singer Media Corporation

True crime/investigative
Alden—Literary Service, Farel T.; Anthony Agency, Joseph; Author Aid Associates; Authors' Marketing Services Ltd.; Brady Literary Management; Browne Ltd., Pema; Chester, Literary Agency, Linda; Connor Literary Agency; Cook Literary Agency, Warren; Dorese Agency Ltd.; Fishbein Ltd., Frieda; Flaherty, Literary Agent, Joyce A.; Flannery, White and Stone; Independent Publishing Agency; Iorio, Esq., Gary F.; JLM Literary Agents; Kellock & Associates Ltd., J.; Kuller Associates, Doris Francis; Law Offices of Robert L. Fenton PC; Lighthouse Literary Agency; Marcil Literary Agency, The Denise; Marshall Agency, The Evan; Miller Agency, The Peter; Nelson Literary Agency & Lecture Bureau, BK; Northwest Literary Services; Oceanic Press; Panettieri Agency, The; Pegasus International, Inc., Literary & Film Agents; Rising Sun Literary Group, The; Robb Literary Properties, Sherry; Scott, Synergy Creative Agency, Stacy Ann; Sebastian Literary Agency; Singer Media Corporation; Southern Writers; Strong, Marianne; Toomey Associates, Jeanne; Waterside Productions, Inc.; Watt & Associates, Sandra; West Coast Literary Associates; Writer's Consulting Group; Zelasky Literary Agency, Tom

Women's issues/women's studies
Author Aid Associates; Backman, Elizabeth H.; Brady Literary Management; Browne Ltd., Pema; Catalog Literary Agency, The; Chester, Literary Agency, Linda; Creative Concepts Liter-

ary Agency; Dorese Agency Ltd.; Fishbein Ltd., Frieda; Flaherty, Literary Agent, Joyce A.; Flannery, White and Stone; Independent Publishing Agency; JLM Literary Agents; Kellock & Associates Ltd., J.; Kern Literary Agency, Natasha; Law Offices of Robert L. Fenton PC; Lighthouse Literary Agency; Marcil Literary Agency, The Denise; Nelson Literary Agency & Lecture Bureau, BK; Northwest Literary Services; Oceanic Press; Panettieri Agency, The; Rising Sun Literary Group, The; Scott, Synergy Creative Agency, Stacy Ann; Sebastian Literary Agency; Southern Writers; State of the Art Ltd.; Waterside Productions, Inc.; Watt & Associates, Sandra; West Coast Literary Associates; Zelasky Literary Agency, Tom

Script agents

Fiction

Action/adventure
Berzon Agency, The Marian; Bethel Agency; Buchwald Agency, Don; Cameron Agency, The Marshall; Coconut Grove Talent Agency; Earth Tracks Agency; Farber & Freeman; ForthWrite Literary Agency; International Artists; International Leonards Corp.; Lake & Douroux Inc.; Lee Literary Agency, L. Harry; Montgomery-West Literary Agency; Rogers and Associates, Stephanie; Selected Artists Agency; Steele & Associates, Ellen Lively; Swanson Inc., H.N.; Talent Bank Agency, The

Cartoon/comic
Bethel Agency; Earth Tracks Agency; International Leonards Corp.

Confessional
Bethel Agency; Lake & Douroux Inc.

Contemporary issues
Berzon Agency, The Marian; Bethel Agency; Brody Agency; Diskant & Associates; Earth Tracks Agency; Farber & Freeman; International Artists; International Leonards Corp.; Merrill Ltd., Helen; Rogers and Associates, Stephanie; Scribe Agency; Selected Artists Agency; Talent Bank Agency, The

Detective/police/crime
Beal Agency, The Mary; Berzon Agency, The Marian; Bethel Agency; Cameron Agency, The Marshall; Earth Tracks Agency; Farber & Freeman; International Artists; International Leonards Corp.; Lake & Douroux Inc.; Lee Literary Agency, L. Harry; Montgomery-West Literary Agency; Steele & Associates, Ellen Lively; Swanson Inc., H.N.; Talent Bank Agency, The

Erotica
Beal Agency, The Mary; Earth Tracks Agency; International Artists; Lee Literary Agency, L. Harry

Ethnic
Bethel Agency; International Artists; Selected Artists Agency; Talent Bank Agency, The

Experimental
Brody Agency; International Artists; Selected Artists Agency

Family saga
Berzon Agency, The Marian; Bethel Agency; Brody Agency; Buchwald Agency, Don; ForthWrite Literary Agency; International Leonards Corp.; Lake & Douroux Inc.; Lee Literary Agency, L. Harry; Selected Artists Agency; Steele & Associates, Ellen Lively; Talent Bank Agency, The

Fantasy
Berzon Agency, The Marian; Bethel Agency; Brody Agency; International Leonards Corp.; Lake & Douroux Inc.; Lee Literary Agency, L. Harry; Montgomery-West Literary Agency; Selected Artists Agency; Talent Bank Agency, The

Feminist
Beal Agency, The Mary; Bethel Agency; International Artists; Talent Bank Agency, The

Gay
Beal Agency, The Mary; Bethel Agency; International Artists; Talent Bank Agency, The

Glitz
Bethel Agency; Lake & Douroux Inc.; Steele & Associates, Ellen Lively

Historical
Bethel Agency; Brody Agency; Cameron Agency, The Marshall; Coconut Grove Talent Agency; Diskant & Associates; Farber & Freeman; ForthWrite Literary Agency; International Artists; International Leonards Corp.; Lake & Douroux Inc.; Lee Literary Agency, L. Harry; Selected Artists Agency; Steele & Associates, Ellen Lively; Swanson Inc., H.N.; Talent Bank Agency, The

Humor/satire
Bethel Agency; Brody Agency; Earth Tracks Agency; Farber & Freeman; International Artists; International Leonards Corp.; Lee Literary Agency, L. Harry; Selected Artists Agency; Steele & Associates, Ellen Lively; Swanson Inc., H.N.; Talent Bank Agency, The

Juvenile
Berzon Agency, The Marian; Farber & Freeman; ForthWrite Literary Agency; International Artists; Steele & Associates, Ellen Lively; Talent Bank Agency, The

Lesbian
Beal Agency, The Mary; Bethel Agency; International Artists

Literary
Beal Agency, The Mary; Bethel Agency; Cameron Agency, The Marshall; ForthWrite Literary Agency; International Artists; Lake & Douroux Inc.; Lee Literary Agency, L. Harry; Merrill Ltd., Helen; Scribe Agency

Mainstream
Beal Agency, The Mary; Berzon Agency, The Marian; Bethel Agency; Brody Agency; Buchwald Agency, Don; Cameron Agency, The Marshall; Farber & Freeman; ForthWrite Literary Agency; International Leonards Corp.; Lake & Douroux Inc.; Lee Literary Agency, L. Harry; Merrill Ltd., Helen; Scagnetti Talent & Literary Agency, Jack; Scribe Agency; Selected Artists Agency; Steele & Associates, Ellen Lively; Swanson Inc., H.N.; Talent Bank Agency, The

Mystery/suspense
Beal Agency, The Mary; Berzon Agency, The Marian; Bethel Agency; Brody Agency; Cameron Agency, The Marshall; Coconut Grove Talent Agency; Diskant & Associates; Farber & Freeman; ForthWrite Literary Agency; International Artists; International Leonards Corp.; Lake & Douroux Inc.; Lee Literary Agency, L. Harry; Montgomery-West Literary Agency; Scagnetti Talent & Literary Agency, Jack; Selected Artists Agency; Steele & Associates, Ellen Lively; Swanson Inc., H.N.; Talent Bank Agency, The

Open to all areas of fiction
Agency for the Performing Arts; American Play Co., Inc.; Circle of Confusion Ltd.; Raintree Agency

Picture book
Bethel Agency; ForthWrite Literary Agency; Steele & Associates, Ellen Lively; Talent Bank Agency, The

Psychic/supernatural
Beal Agency, The Mary; Bethel Agency; Brody Agency; International Artists; Montgomery-West Literary Agency; Steele & Associates, Ellen Lively

Regional
Bethel Agency; International Artists; International Leonards Corp.; Berzon Agency, The Marian; Bethel Agency

Romance
Berzon Agency, The Marian; Bethel Agency; Buchwald Agency, Don; Coconut Grove Talent Agency; Earth Tracks Agency; Farber & Freeman; ForthWrite Literary Agency; International Artists; International Leonards Corp.; Lee Literary Agency, L. Harry; Montgomery-West Literary Agency; Rogers and Associates, Stephanie; Selected Artists Agency; Steele & Associates, Ellen Lively

Science fiction
Beal Agency, The Mary; Brody Agency; Buchwald Agency, Don; International Artists; International Leonards Corp.; Lake & Douroux Inc.; Lee Literary Agency, L. Harry; Montgomery-West Literary Agency; Selected Artists Agency; Steele & Associates, Ellen Lively; Talent Bank Agency, The

Sports
Bethel Agency; International Artists; International Leonards Corp.; Lee Literary Agency, L. Harry; Scagnetti Talent & Literary Agency, Jack; Swanson Inc., H.N.

Thriller/espionage
Beal Agency, The Mary; Berzon Agency, The Marian; Bethel Agency; Brody Agency; Buchwald Agency, Don; Cameron Agency, The Marshall; Coconut Grove Talent Agency; Earth Tracks Agency; Farber & Freeman; International Artists; International Leonards Corp.; Lake & Douroux Inc.; Lee Literary Agency, L. Harry; Montgomery-West Literary Agency; Rogers and Associates, Stephanie; Scagnetti Talent & Literary Agency, Jack; Selected Artists Agency; Steele & Associates, Ellen Lively; Swanson Inc., H.N.; Talent Bank Agency, The; Bethel Agency; Buchwald Agency, Don; Lake & Douroux Inc.; Lee Literary Agency, L. Harry; Talent Bank Agency, The

Young adult
Berzon Agency, The Marian; Bethel Agency; Brody Agency; Diskant & Associates; Earth Tracks Agency; Farber & Freeman; ForthWrite Literary Agency; International Artists; Lee Literary Agency, L. Harry; Selected Artists Agency

Nonfiction

Agriculture/horticulture
Bethel Agency; ForthWrite Literary Agency

Animals
Bethel Agency; ForthWrite Literary Agency

Anthropology
Bethel Agency; ForthWrite Literary Agency; International Artists; International Leonards Corp.

Art/architecture/design
Bethel Agency; ForthWrite Literary Agency

Biography/autobiography
Bethel Agency; Brody Agency; Buchwald Agency, Don; Circle of Confusion Ltd.; Diskant & Associates; ForthWrite Literary Agency; International Artists; International Leonards Corp.; Merrill Ltd., Helen

Business
Bethel Agency; Cameron Agency, The Marshall; Circle of Confusion Ltd.; ForthWrite Literary Agency; International Leonards Corp.

Child guidance/parenting
Bethel Agency; ForthWrite Literary Agency; International Artists

Computers/electronics
International Artists

Cooking/food/nutrition
Bethel Agency; ForthWrite Literary Agency; International Artists; Steele & Associates, Ellen Lively

Crafts/hobbies
Bethel Agency; ForthWrite Literary Agency

Current affairs
Bethel Agency; Buchwald Agency, Don; Circle of Confusion Ltd.; Diskant & Associates; International Artists; International Leonards Corp.; Swanson Inc., H.N.

Ethnic/cultural interests
Bethel Agency; International Artists

Gay/lesbian issues
Beal Agency, The Mary; Bethel Agency; Brody Agency; Circle of Confusion Ltd.; International Artists

Government/politics/law
Beal Agency, The Mary; Bethel Agency; Circle of Confusion Ltd.; International Artists

Health/medicine
Bethel Agency; Cameron Agency, The Marshall; Circle of Confusion Ltd.; ForthWrite Literary Agency; International Artists; Raintree Agency; Scagnetti Talent & Literary Agency, Jack

History
Bethel Agency; Brody Agency; Buchwald Agency, Don; Circle of Confusion Ltd.; Diskant & Associates; ForthWrite Literary Agency; International Artists; International Leonards Corp.; Kohner, Inc., Paul; Lee Literary Agency, L. Harry; Steele & Associates, Ellen Lively

Interior design/decorating
Bethel Agency; ForthWrite Literary Agency

Juvenile nonfiction
Bethel Agency; Cameron Agency, The Marshall; Circle of Confusion Ltd.; ForthWrite Literary Agency; International Artists

Language/literature/criticism
Bethel Agency; International Artists

Military/war
Bethel Agency; Kohner, Inc., Paul; Lee Literary Agency, L. Harry; Scagnetti Talent & Literary Agency, Jack

Money/finance/economics
Bethel Agency; Cameron Agency, The Marshall; ForthWrite Literary Agency; International Leonards Corp.; Southeastern Entertainment Agency Inc.

Music/dance/theater/film
Bethel Agency; ForthWrite Literary Agency; International Artists; International Leonards Corp.; Kohner, Inc., Paul; Southeastern Entertainment Agency Inc.

Nature/environment
Bethel Agency; Brody Agency; ForthWrite Literary Agency; International Artists; Raintree Agency

New age/metaphysics
International Artists; International Leonards Corp.; Steele & Associates, Ellen Lively

Open to all areas of nonfiction
Agency for the Performing Arts; American Play Co., Inc.; Earth Tracks Agency

Photography
Bethel Agency; ForthWrite Literary Agency; Beal Agency, The Mary; Bethel Agency; Forth-Write Literary Agency; International Artists; International Leonards Corp.

Psychology
Raintree Agency

Religious/inspirational
Bethel Agency; ForthWrite Literary Agency; International Leonards Corp.

Science/technology
Bethel Agency; Buchwald Agency, Don; ForthWrite Literary Agency; International Leonards Corp.

Self-help/personal improvement
Bethel Agency; Cameron Agency, The Marshall; ForthWrite Literary Agency; International Artists; International Leonards Corp.; Scagnetti Talent & Literary Agency, Jack; Steele & Associates, Ellen Lively

Sociology
Bethel Agency; ForthWrite Literary Agency; International Artists

Sports
Bethel Agency; Buchwald Agency, Don; International Artists; International Leonards Corp.; Scagnetti Talent & Literary Agency, Jack; Southeastern Entertainment Agency Inc.; Swanson Inc., H.N.

Translations
Bethel Agency; Imison Playwrights Ltd., Michael; International Artists

True crime/investigative
Beal Agency, The Mary; Bethel Agency; Cameron Agency, The Marshall; Circle of Confusion Ltd.; International Artists; International Leonards Corp.; Kohner, Inc., Paul; Scagnetti Talent & Literary Agency, Jack; Steele & Associates, Ellen Lively

Women's issues/women's studies
Bethel Agency; Brody Agency; Circle of Confusion Ltd.; ForthWrite Literary Agency; International Artists; Raintree Agency; Steele & Associates, Ellen Lively

Commercial Art/Photo and Fine Art Reps Geographic Index

All art/photo and fine art reps are listed together in this index by state. Some talents have just one rep to handle all their work, but many talents choose to have more than one rep covering different sections of the country.

California
Art Source L.A.
Baum & Associates, Cathy
Burlingham/Artist Representation, Tricia
Carrière-Creative Representative, Lydia
Collier Represents, Jan
Conrad & Associates, James
CVB Creative Resource
De Moreta Represents, Linda
Epstein, Rhoni
Gardner & Associates, Jean
Gordon/Artist Representative, T.J.
Hall & Associates
Hedge/Artist Representative, Joanne
L.A. Art Exchange
Lesli Art, Inc.
Martha Productions, Inc.
Piscopo, Maria
Rosenthal Represents
Salzman, Richard
Scott, Inc., Freda
Scroggy Agency, David
Stefanski Represents, Janice
Storer, Richard R.
Storyboards, Inc.
Studio Artists/Don Pepper
Walkingstick Productions
Winston West, Ltd.

Colorado
Guenzi Agents, Inc., Carol
Sapiro Art Consultants, Joan

Connecticut
Artists International
HK Portfolio
Palulian, Joanne
Publishers' Graphics

Florida
Administrative Arts
International Art Connection and Art Connection Plus
Madrazo Arts

Georgia
Wells Associates, Susan

Hawaii
Pacific Design Studio

Illinois
Artco Incorporated
Barasa & Associates, Inc.
Fine Art Representative
Galitz Fine Art/Accent Art, Robert
Kuehnel & Associates, Peter
Montagano & Associates
Soldat & Cardoni

Kansas
Media Gallery/Enterprises
ToLease Lautrec

Massachusetts
Gilmartin Associates
Maud Art
Palm Fine Art

Maryland
Redmond Represents
Shearer Art Source, Nicki

Michigan
Neis Group, The
Ridgeway Artists Representative

Minnesota
Harris & Associates, Gretchen
Icebox

Missouri
Creative Productions, Inc.
Eldridge Corporation

North Carolina
Trlica/Reilly: Reps

New Jersey
Holt & Associates, Inc., Rita
Warner & Associates

New York
Arnold Fine Arts, Jack
Arts Counsel Inc.
Asciutto Art Reps., Inc.
Becker Associates, Noel
Beidler Inc., Barbara
Bernhard, Ivy
Bernstein & Andriulli Inc.
Brindle & Partner Inc., Carolyn

Brody, Artists & Photographers Representative, Sam
Bruck and Moss Associates
Carp, Inc., Stan
Chislovsky Inc., Carol
Collignon, Daniele
Corporate Art Associates, Ltd.
Foster Artist Rep., (Pat)
Ginsburg & Associates, Inc., Michael
Gordon Associates Ltd., Barbara
Green, Anita Inc.
Hansen, Wendy
Keating, Peggy
Kimcie, Tania
Kirchoff/Wohlberg Artist Representation Division
Klimt, Bill and Maurine
Lavaty & Associates, Frank & Jeff
Lott, Peter & George
McKay Photography, Colleen
Mattelson Associates Ltd.
Mendola Artists
Meo, Frank
Morgan Associates, Vicki
Neail Associates, Pamela
Page, Jackie
Parallax
Photo Agents Ltd.
Rapp, Inc., Gerald & Cullen
Reese & Associates, Inc., Kay
Rosenberg, Arlene
Schwartz, Esquire, Laurens R.
Tribelli Designs, Ltd., Joseph
Warshaw Blumenthal, Inc.
Wechsler, Elaine
Weissberg, Elyse

Ohio
Berendsen & Associates, Inc.
Coleman Presents Inc., Woody
Corcoran Fine Arts, James
Hull Associates, Scott

Pennsylvania
Francisco Communications, Inc.
Kerr, Ralph
Knecht – Artist Representative, Cliff
Pennamenities
Veloric, Artist Representative, Philip M.

Texas
Brooke & Company
Fine Art Associates
Lee Inc., Helda
McCann Company, The
Repertoire
Sands & Associates, Trudy
Seiffer & Associates
Simpatico Art & Stone
Washington-Artist Representatives

Virginia
Artsource, Inc.

Washington
Hackett/Artist Representative, Pat
Thede Associates, Park

Wisconsin
Dodge Creative Services Inc.

Agents and Reps Index

This index of agent and rep names was created to help you locate agents or reps even when you do not know for which agency they work. You may have read or heard about a particular representative, but do not know how to contact them. Agent and rep names are listed with their agencies' names. Check the Listing Index for the page number of the agency listed.

A

Abel, Dominick (Dominick Abel Literary Agency, Inc.)
Abenal, Sheldon (American Play Co., Inc.)
Acton, Jay (Acton and Dystel, Inc.)
Agarwal, Rajeev K. (Circle of Confusion Ltd.)
Ahearn, Pamela G. (Southern Writers)
Ajlouny, Joe (The Joseph S. Ajlouny Agency)
Alden, Farel T. (Farel T. Alden-Literary Service)
Aley, Elizabeth (Maxwell Aley Associates of Aspen)
Aley, Maxwell (Maxwell Aley Associates of Aspen)
Allen, James (James Allen, Literary Agency)
Allen, Linda (Linda Allen Literary Agency)
Allman, K. (Literary Marketing Consultants)
Amparan, Joann (Wecksler-Incomco)
Amsterdam, Marcia (Marcia Amsterdam Agency)
Anderson, Belinda S. (Ellen Lively Steele & Associates)
Andrews, Bart (Bart Andrews & Associates, Inc.)
Anthony, Joseph (Joseph Anthony Agency)
Appel, Bill (BK Nelson Literary Agency & Lecture Bureau)
Armstrong, Rene (Eldridge Corporation)
Arnold, Jack (Jack Arnold Fine Arts)
Asciutto, Mary Anne (Asciutto Art Reps., Inc.)
Ayers, Carol (State of the Art Ltd.)

B

Bach, Julian (Julian Bach Literary Agency)
Bach, Lisa S. (Connie Clausen Associates)
Backman, Elizabeth (Elizabeth H. Backman)
Baldi, Malaga (Malaga Baldi Literary Agency)
Balkin, R. (Balkin Agency, Inc.)
Banic, Tom (Southeastern Entertainment Agency Inc.)
Barmeier, Jim (Writer's Consulting Group)
Barnbrook, Jacquie (Jean Gardner & Associates)
Barnes, Morgan (Loretta Barrett Books, Inc.)
Barr, Hollister (L. Harry Lee Literary Agency)
Barr, Mary (Sierra Literary Agency)
Barrett, Helen (Helen Barrett Literary Agency)
Barrett, Loretta A. (Loretta Barrett Books, Inc.)
Baum, Cathy (Cathy Baum & Associates)
Becker, Maximilian (Maximilian Becker)
Becker, Noel (Noel Becker Associates)
Beidler, Barbara (Barbara Beidler Inc.)
Beisch, Karin (Elaine Markson Literary Agency)
Benson, John (BK Nelson Literary Agency & Lecture Bureau)
Berendsen, Bob (Berendsen & Associates, Inc.)
Berk, Ms. (Brody Agency)
Berkower, Amy (Writers House)
Berman, Lois (Lois Berman, Writers' Representative)
Bernard, Alec (SBC Enterprises, Inc.)
Bernhard, Ive (Ivy Bernhard)
Bernstein, Meredith (Meredith Bernstein Literary Agency)
Bernstein, Sam (Bernstein & Andrulli Inc.)
Berry, Henry (Independent Publishing Agency)
Biggis, Charis (L. Harry Lee Literary Agency)
Black, Fran (Arts Counsel Inc.)
Blake, Laura (Curtis Brown Ltd.)
Blanton, Sandra (Peter Lampack Agency, Inc.)
Blodgett, Bonnie (The Lazear Agency Incorporated)
Boals, Judy (Lois Berman, Writers' Representative)
Boates, Reid (Reid Boates Literary Agency)
Bollini, Ursula (MGA Agency Inc.)
Bolton, Larry (Sandra Watt & Associates)
Bonnen, Edwin (Ridgeway Artists Representative)
Bonnett, Carol (MGA Agency Inc.)
Boorn, Joyce (Florence Feiler Literary Agency)
Bowne, Tiffany (Tricia Burlingham/Artist Representation)
Brady, Sally Ryder (Brady Literary Management)
Brady, Upton Birnie (Brady Literary Management)
Brandenburgh, Don (Brandenburgh & Associates Literary Agency)
Brandt, Carl (Brandt & Brandt Literary Agents, Inc.)
Brenna, Vito (L. Harry Lee Literary Agency)
Brenneman, Cindy (CVB Creative Resource)
Breoge, Jane (L. Harry Lee Literary Agency)
Briggamen, Jim (H.N. Swanson Inc.)
Brindle, Carolyn (Carolyn Brindle & Partner Inc.)
Brod, A.T. (Ruth Hagy Brod Literary Agency)
Brodie, Michael (Artists International)
Brody, Sam (Sam Brody, Artists & Photographers Representative)
Brophy, Phillipa (Sterling Lord Literistic, Inc.)
Brown, Andrea (Andrea Brown Literary Agency, Inc.)
Brown, Marie (Marie Brown Associates, Inc.)
Browne, Jane Jordan (Multimedia Product Development, Inc.)
Browne, Pema (Pema Browne Ltd.)
Browne, Perry (Pema Browne Ltd.)

Bruck, Moss (Bruck and Moss Associates)
Bruck, Nancy (Bruck and Moss Associates)
Buchanan, Jane (Jane Buchanan Literary Agency)
Buchwald, Don (Don Buchwald Agency)
Buck, Howard (Howard Buck Agency)

C

Callamaro, Lisa (Elaine Markson Literary Agency)
Callirgos, Cami (L. Harry Lee Literary Agency)
Cane, Nikki (Gary L. Hegler Literary Agency)
Caravela, Jack (The Lazear Agency Incorporated)
Carbone, Peter, (Oceanic Press)
Cardoni, Pam (Soldat & Cardoni)
Carlson, Bob (James Warren Literary Agency)
Carlson, Diane (Publishers' Graphics)
Carlson, Heidi (Frieda Fishbein Ltd.)
Carp, Stan (Stan Carp, Inc.)
Carriere, Lydia (Lydia Carriere-Creative Representative)
Carrillo, Christine (Storyboards, Inc.)
Cartaino, Carol (Collier Associates)
Carvainis, Maria (Maria Carvainis Agency, Inc.)
Castiglia, Julie (Waterside Productions, Inc.)
Cavanaugh, Teresa (Jean V. Naggar Literary Agency)
Cavello, James (Corporate Art Associates, Ltd.)
Cerea, Doris (Farel T. Alden-Literary Service)
Chambeaux, Jane (International Art Connection and Art Connection Plus)
Chambers, Lewis R. (Bethel Agency)
Chester, Linda (Linda Chester Literary Agency)
Childs, Faith (Faith Childs Literary Agency)
Chislovsky, Carol (Carol Chislovsky Inc.)
Choron, Sandra (March Tenth, Inc.)
Christopherson, Howard (Icebox)
Chu, Lynn (Writers' Representatives, Inc.)
Clausen, Connie (Connie Clausen Associates)
Cleaver, Diane (Stanford J. Greenburger Associates)
Cochran, John (M. Sue Lasbury Literary Agency)
Cohen, Eugenia (SBC Enterprises, Inc.)
Cohen, Hy (Hy Cohen Literary Agency Ltd.)
Cohen, Roberta (Richard Curtis Associates, Inc.)
Cohen, Ruth (Ruth Cohen Inc. Literary Agency)
Cohen, Susan Lee (Riverside Literary Agency)
Cohen, Susan (Writers House)
Colas, Maryanne C. (Cantrell-Colas Inc., Literary Agency)
Colby, Pat (Colby: Literary Agency)
Colby, Richard (Colby: Literary Agency)
Cole, Joanna (Elaine Markson Literary Agency)
Coleman, George (Woody Coleman Presents Inc.)
Coleman, Woody (Woody Coleman Presents Inc.)
Collier, Jan (Jan Collier Represents)
Collier, Oscar (Collier Associates)
Collignon, Daniele (Daniele Collignon)
Congdon, Don (Don Congdon Associates, Inc.)
Congdon, Michael (Don Congdon Associates, Inc.)
Connor, Marlene K. (Connor Literary Agency)

Conrad, James (James Conrad & Associates)
Consoletti, Annie (Rhoni Epstein)
Cook, Warren (Warren Cook Literary Agency)
Cooke, Nancy (Julie Popkin/Nancy Cooke)
Cooper, Renee (The Joseph S. Ajlouny Agency)
Cooper, William (Bill Cooper Assoc., Inc.)
Coover, Doe (The Doe Coover Agency)
Corcoran, James (James Corcoran Fine Arts)
Craver, William (Writers & Artists)
Crown, Bonnie (Bonnie R. Crown International Literature and Arts Agency)
Cugno, Robert (Media Gallery/Enterprises)
Curtis, Richard (Richard Curtis Associates, Inc.)
Custer, Guy Robin (International Artists)

D

Daley, Aleta (Maximilian Becker)
Dalton, Pat (Diamond Literary Agency, Inc.)
Darhansoff, Liz (Darhansoff & Verrill Literary Agents)
Davie, Elaine (Elaine Davie Literary Agency)
Davis, Brooke (Brooke & Company)
de la Haba, Lois (The Lois de la Haba Agency)
de Moreta, Linda (Linda de Moreta Represents)
de Rogatis, Joseph De (International Publisher Associates Inc.)
de Spoelberch, Jacques (J De S Associates Inc.)
Deering, Dorothy (Dorothy Deering Literary Agency)
Demeny, Lylla (Parallax)
Diamant, Anita (Anita Diamant, The Writer's Workshop, Inc.)
Dight, Janet (Janet Dight Literary Agency)
Dijkstra, Sandra (Sandra Dijkstra Literary Agency)
Dilworth, B.G. (Authors and Artists Group, Inc.)
Diskant, George (Diskant & Associates)
Dodge, Tim (Dodge Account Services Inc.)
Dolger, Jonathan (The Jonathan Dolger Agency)
Donlan, Thomas C. (Thomas C. Donlan)
Donnelly, Dave (BK Nelson Literary Agency & Lecture Bureau)
Dorese, Alyss Barlow (Dorese Agency Ltd.)
Doyen, B.J. (Doyen Literary Services, Inc.)
Drake, Robert (Sandra Watt & Associates)
Dubuisson, Anne (Ellen Levine Literary Agency, Inc.)
Ducas, R. (Robert Ducas)
Dunow, Henry (Curtis Brown Ltd.)
Dystel, Jane (Acton and Dystel, Inc.)

E

Edgar, Wendell (Frieda Fishbein Ltd.)
Edmunds, Jeanine (Curtis Brown Ltd.)
Eisenbach, Robert (Robert Eisenbach Inc.)
Elder, Joseph (Joseph Elder Agency)
Ellenberg, Ethan (Ethan Ellenberg Literary Agency)
Ellinger, Andrew (Los Angeles Literary Associates)
Ellman, Francine (Art Source L.A.)
Elmo, Ann (Ann Elmo Agency Inc.)
Engel, Anne (Jean V. Naggar Literary Agency)
Epstein, Rhoni (Rhoni Epstein)

Harris, Gretchen (Gretchen Harris & Associates)
Harris, Joy (The Robert Lantz-Joy Harris Literary Agency)
Harrison, Lesley (MGA Agency Inc.)
Hart, Al (The Fox Chase Agency Inc.)
Hart, J. (The Fox Chase Agency Inc.)
Hartley, Glen (Writers' Representataives, Inc.)
Hartman, Kris (Cathy Baum & Associates)
Hawkins, Chris (Storyboards, Inc.)
Hawkins, John (John Hawkins & Associates, Inc.)
Hayes, Linda (Columbia Literary Associates, Inc.)
Hazlewood, Katherine (Dupree/Miller and Associates Inc. Literary)
Heacock, Jim (Heacock Literary Agency, Inc.)
Heacock, Rosalie (Heacock Literary Agency, Inc.)
Hedge, J. (Joanne Hedge/Artist Representative)
Hegler, Gary L. (Gary L. Hegler Literary Agency)
Heifetz, Merrillee (Writers House)
Hensen, Carla (Gerald & Cullen Rapp, Inc.)
Henshaw, Richard (Richard Curtis Associates, Inc.)
Herman, Jeffrey H. (The Jeff Herman Agency Inc.)
Herner, Susan (Susan Herner Rights Agency)
Hochman, Gail (Brandt & Brandt Literary Agents, Inc.)
Hochmann, John L. (John L. Hochmann Books)
Hoffman, Berenice (Berenice Hoffman Literary Agency)
Hoffman, Larry (Authors' Marketing Services Ltd.)
Hogenson, Barbara (Lucy Kroll Agency)
Holt, Rita (Rita Holt & Associates)
Holtje, Bert (James Peter Associates, Inc.)
Holub, William (Holub & Associates)
Hotchkiss, Jody (Sterling Lord Literistic, Inc.)
Hudson, Scott (Writers & Artists)
Hull, David Stewart (Hull House Literary Agency)
Hull, Scott (Scott Hull Associates)

I

Idol, Matlphisto (Tolease Lautrec)
Imison, Michael (Michael Imison Playwrights, LTD.)
Iorio, Gary (Gary F. Iorio Esq.)

J

Jacobsen, Emilie (Curtis Brown Ltd.)
James, Colin (L. Harry Lee Literary Agency)
Jarvis, Sharon (Sharon Jarvis & Co.)
Jassin, Louis A. (Southeastern Entertainment Agency Inc.)
Jasso, Caspar (International Artists)
Jenks, Carolyn (Carolyn Jenks Agency)
Jones, Leon (Leon Jones Agency)
Jones, Lloyd (Lloyd Jones Literary Agency)
Jones, M.L. (Living Faith Literary Agency)
Jordan, L.F. (Chadd-Stevens Literary Agency)
Jordan, Lawrence (Lawrence Jordon Literary Agency)
Joseph, Flo (Selected Artists Agency)

K

Kainer, David (Selected Artists Agency)
Kalin, Jennifer (Joan Sapiro Art Consultants)
Kaltman, Larry (Larry Kaltman Literary Agency)
Kamaroff, Alex (Alex Kamaroff Associates)
Kamaroff, Logan (Alex Kamaroff Associates)
Kane, Suzanne Hayes (Walkingstick Productions)
Kangas, Sandra (Lighthouse Literary Agency)
Kaplan, Elizabeth (Sterling Lord Literistic, Inc.)
Kasak, Harriet (HK Portfolio)
Kaufman, Joshua (Goldfarb, Kaufman, & O'Toole)
Kearns, John J. (Oceanic Press Service)
Kearns, John (Singer Media Corporation)
Keating, Peggy (Peggy Keating)
Kellock, Joanne (J. Kellock & Associates)
Kelly, Peggy (The Lazear Agency Incorporated)
Keough, Brian (James Corcoran Fine Arts)
Kepler, Jim (Lyle Steele & Co., Ltd.)
Kern, Natasha (Natasha Kern Literary Agency)
Kerr, Ralph (Ralph Kerr)
Ketz, Louise B. (Louise B. Ketz Agency)
Kidde, Katherine (Kidde, Hoyt & Picard)
Killeen, Frank (L. Harry Lee Literary Agency)
Kimcie, Tania (Tania Kimcie)
Klimt, Bill (Bill and Maurine Klimt)
Klimt, Maurine (Bill and Maurine Klimt)
Klinger, Harvey (Harvey Klinger, Inc.)
Knappman, Edward W. (New England Publishing Associates, Inc.)
Knappman, Elizabeth Frost (New England Publishing Associates, Inc.)
Knecht, Cliff (Cliff Knecht-Artist Representative)
Knickerbocker, Andrea (Lee Allan Agency)
Knowlton, Perry (Curtis Brown Ltd.)
Knowlton, Timothy (Curtis Brown Ltd.)
Knowlton, Virginia (Curtis Brown Ltd.)
Kouts, Barbara (Barbara S. Kouts, Literary Agent)
Kramer, Sidney B. (Mews Books Ltd.)
Krichevsky, Stuart (Sterling Lord Literistic, Inc.)
Krinsky, David (Earth Tracks Agency)
Kriton, George (Cinema Talent International)
Kroll, Edite (Edite Kroll Literary Agency)
Kuehnel, Peter (Peter Kuehnel & Associates)
Kuller, Doris Francis (Doris Francis Kuller Associates)
Kurman, B. (Rights Unlimited)
Kurz, Norman (Lowenstein Associates, Inc.)

L

Lake, Candace L. (Lake & Douroux Inc.)
Lampack, Peter (Peter Lampack Agency, Inc.)
Lange, Heide (Stanford J. Greenburger Associates)
Langer, Audrey (James Warren Literary Agency)
Larsen, Mike (Michael Larsen/Elizabeth Pomada Literary Agents)
Lasbury, Sue (M. Sue Lasbury Literary Agency)
Laughren, Brent (Northwest Literary Services)
Leavitt, Ned (The Ned Leavitt Agency)
Lee, Helda (Helda Lee Inc.)
Lee, L. Harry (L. Harry Lee Literary Agency)

Lee, Lettie (Ann Elmo Agency Inc.)

Lehr, Donald (The Betsy Nolan Literary Agency)

Leonards, David (International Leonards Corp.)

Leone, Adele (The Adele Leone Agency, Inc.)

Leone, Ralph (The Adele Leone Agency, Inc.)

Lerman, Gary (Photo Agents Ltd.)

Lescher, Robert (Lescher & Lescher Ltd.)

Lescher, Susan (Lescher & Lescher Ltd.)

Levant, Dan (Levant & Wales, Literary Agency, Inc.)

Levine, Ellen (Ellen Levine Literary Agency, Inc.)

Levine, James A. (James Levine Communications)

Levine, Victor A., (Northeast Literary Agency)

Liebert, Norma (The Norma-Lewis Agency)

Lincoln, Mrs. Ray (Ray Lincoln Literary Agency)

Lipkind, Wendy (Wendy Lipkind Agency)

Liss, Laurie (Aaron M. Priest Literary Agency)

Lloyd, Lem (Mary Jack Wald Associates, Inc.)

Lockwood, Hal (Penmarin Books)

Lord, Sterling (Sterling Lord Literistic, Inc.)

Lourdes, Lopez (Helen Merrill Ltd.)

Love, Nancy (Nancy Love Literary Agency)

Lovitz, Gene (Pegasus International, Inc. Literary & Film Agents)

Lowenstein, Barbara (Lowenstein Associates, Inc.)

Lowman, Alfred P. (Authors and Artists Group, Inc.)

Lundgren, Curtis H.C. (The Curtis Bruce Agency)

Luttinger, Selma (Robert A. Freedman Dramatic Agency, Inc.)

Lynch, Andrea (Repertoire)

Lynch, Larry (Repertoire)

M

McCann, Liz (The McCann Company)

McCleary, Carol (The Wilshire Literary Agency)

Maccoby, Gina (Gina Maccoby Literary Agency)

McDonald, Lisa (The Joseph S. Ajlouny Agency)

McDonough, Richard P. (Richard P. McDonough, Literary Agent)

McGrath, Helen (Helen McGrath)

McKay, Colleen (Colleen McKay Photography)

McKenzie, Mary (Tolease Lautrec)

Mackey, Elizabeth (The Robbins Office)

Malo, Vik (Sherry Robb Literary Properties)

Mann, Carol (Carol Mann Agency)

Manus, Janet Wilkens (Janet Wilkens Manus Literary Agency)

Marcil, Denise (The Denise Marcil Literary Agency)

Markham, Ann (About Books Inc.)

Markowitz, Barbara (Barbara Markowitz Literary Agency)

Marlowe, Marilyn (Curtis Brown Ltd.)

Marshall, Evan (The Evan Marshall Agency)

Martell, Alice Fried (The Martell Agency)

Mary Ann (Barasa & Associates, Inc.)

Matson, Peter (Sterling Lord Literistic, Inc.)

Mattelson, Judy (Mattelson Associates LTD.)

Matthews, Anne (Wingra Woods Press/Agenting Division)

Matthias, Lee (Lee Allan Agency)

Maynard, Gary (The Gary-Paul Agency)

Mazmamian, Joan (Helen Rees Literary Agency)

Meehan, Mary (The Lazear Agency Incorporated)

Melnick, Jeff (Curtis Brown Ltd.)

Mendez, Toni (Toni Mendez Inc.)

Mendola, Tim (Mendola Artists)

Meo, Frank (Frank Meo)

Merhige, Greg (Greg Merhige-Merdon Marketing/Promo Co. Inc.)

Merrill, Helen (Helen Merrill Ltd.)

Merritt, Susan (Julian Bach Literary Agency)

Meth, David L. (Writers' Productions)

Michael, Douglas (Frieda Fishbein Ltd.)

Michael Ginsburg (Michael Ginsburg & Associates, Inc.)

Millard, Martha (Martha Millard Literary Agency)

Miller, Deborah A. (Pennamenities)

Miller, Jan (Dupree/Miller and Associates Inc. Literary)

Miller, Peter (The Peter Miller Agency, Inc.)

Miller, Stuart M. (Agency for the Performing Arts)

Mr. Madrazo (Madrazo Arts)

Monaco, Richard (The Adele Leone Agency, Inc.)

Montagano, David (Montagano & Associates)

Moore, Claudette (Moore Literary Agency)

Moran, Maureen (Donald MacCampbell Inc.)

Morel, Madeleine (2M Communications Ltd.)

Morgan, David (Mogan Literary Agency)

Morgan, Katherine (Morgan Literary Agency)

Morgan, Vicki (Vicki Morgan Associates)

Morling, Carole (Pegasus International, Inc., Literary & Film Agents)

Morrison, Henry (Henry Morrison, Inc.)

Morrow, Lee (Rising Sun Literary Group)

Mortimer, Lydia (Hull House Literary Agency)

N

Nadell, Bonnie (Frederick Hill Associates)

Naggar, Jean (Jean V. Naggar Literary Agency)

Neail, Pamela (Pamela Neail Associates)

Neighbors, Charles (Charles Neighbors, Inc.)

Neighbors, Margaret (Charles Neighbors, Inc.)

Neis, Judy (The Neis Group)

Nellis, Muriel (Literary and Creative Artists Agency)

Nelson, Bonita (BK Nelson Literary Agency & Lecture Bureau)

Nichols, Mary (Kidde, Hoyt & Picard)

Nigh, Douglas J. (The Talent Bank Agency)

Nigrosh, Nancy (The Gersh Agency)

Noetzli, Regula (Regula Noetzli Literary Agency)

Nolan, Betsy (The Betsy Nolan Literary Agency)

Nugent, Ray E. (Ray E. Nugent Agency)

Null, Julia (The Robbins Office)

O

Odenwald, Sylvia (The Odenwald Connection)

Olm, Sandrine (Lucianne S. Goldberg Literary

Sellers, Steven (H.N. Swanson Inc.)
Semler, Judy (JLM Literary Agents)
Sewach, Michele Glance (Creative Concepts Literary Agency)
Shank, Roger (Storyboards, Inc.)
Shanks, Thomas (H.N. Swanson Inc.)
Shearer, Nicki (Nicki Shearer Art Source)
Sheedy, Charlotte (Charlotte Sheedy Literary Agency, Inc.)
Shelton, Ken (Executive Excellence)
Shepard, Jean (The Shepard Agency)
Shepard, Lance (The Shepard Agency)
Shepherd, Peter (Harold Ober Associates)
Sher, Danis (Mary Jack Wald Associates, Inc.)
Shevrin, Stan (Lesli Art, Inc.)
Shoumatoff, Tonia (Marianne Strong)
Siedlecki, Francine H. (Pacific Design Studio)
Siegel, Bobbe (Bobbe Siegel Literary Agency)
Siegel, Michael (H.N. Swanson Inc.)
Silverstein, Bob (Quicksilver Books-Literary Agents)
Sinclair, Carl (Scribe Agency)
Singer, Evelyn (Evelyn Singer Literary Agency)
Singer, Katherine (Oceanic Press)
Singer, Kurt (Singer Media Corporation)
Skolnick, Irene (Curtis Brown Ltd.)
Smith, Claire (Harold Ober Associates)
Smith, Patricia (Michael Snell Literary Agency)
Smith, Valerie (Valerie Smith, Literary Agent)
Snell, Michael (Michael Snell Literary Agency)
Soldat, Rick (Soldat & Cardoni)
Solowiej, Constance (Flannery, White and Stone)
Sommer, Elyse (Elyse Sommer, Inc.)
South, David (Sandra Watt & Associates)
Spatt, David M. (David M. Spatt, Esq.)
Spelman, Martha (Martha Productions, Inc.)
Spence, Kari (The McCann Company)
Spitzer, Philip (Philip E. Spitzer Literary Agency)
Stafford, B.J. (International Artists)
Stauffer, Nancy (Nancy Stauffer Associates)
Steel, Ellen Lively (Ellen Lively Steele & Associates)
Steele, Lyle (Lyle Steele & Co., Ltd.)
Steinberg, Michael (Michael Steinberg Literary Agency)
Sterling, Cynthia (Lee Shore Agency)
Stern, Gloria (Gloria Stern Literary Agency)
Stewart, Charles (Charles Stewart)
Stewart, Kathy (Storyboards, Inc.)
Stone, Ivey Fischer (Fifi Oscard Associates)
Storey, Douglas (The Catalog Literary Agency)
Stroh, Mark (Storyboards, Inc.)
Strong, Marianne (Marianne Strong)
Sturges, Frank (Scott Hull Associates)
Sturgess, Chris (Stacy Ann Scott, Synergy Creative Agency)
Sullivan, Mark (Mark Sullivan Associates)
Suter, Anne Elisabeth (Gotham Art & Literary Agency, Inc.)
Sutton, Sheree (Lloyd Jones Literary Agency)
Swanson, H.N. (H.N. Swanson Inc.)
Swanson, N.V. (H.N. Swanson Inc.)
Sweeney, Emma (Julian Bach Literary Agency)

T
Talbot, William (Samuel French, Inc.)

Tantleff, Jack (The Tantleff Office)
Taylor, Clyde (Curtis Brown Ltd.)
Taylor, Frolic (Rhoni Epstein)
Taylor, Jess (Curtis Brown Ltd.)
Taylor, Kendra (Watkins Loomis Agency, Inc.)
Teal, Patricia (Patricia Teal Literary Agency)
Tenney, Craig (Harold Ober Associates)
Thede, Park (Park Thede Associates)
Theilen, Nicola (Richard Salzman)
Thomas, Abigail (Darhansoff & Verrill Literary Agents)
Thomas, Geri (Elaine Markson Literary Agency)
Tillman, Sybil (Artco Incorporated)
Toomey, Jeanne (Jeanne Toomey Associates)
Tornetta, Phyllis (Phyllis Tornetta Agency)
Tribelli, Joseph (Joseph Tribelli Designs, Ltd.)
Trlica, Jack (Trlica/Reilly: Reps)
Trupin, James (Jet Literary Associates, Inc.)

U
Uberoi, Veena (Singer Media Corporation)
Urstadt, Susan (Susan P. Urstadt Inc. Writers and Artists Agency)

V
Vallely, Joseph B. (Flaming Star Literary Enterprises)
Van Bomel, Ed (L. Harry Lee Literary Agency)
Van der Leun, Patricia (Van der Leun & Associates)
Van Dyck, Barrie (Schlessinger-Van Dyck Agency)
Vandertuin, Victoria (New Age World Services New)
Veloric, Philip M. (Philip M. Veloric, Artist Representative)
Verrill, Charles (Darhansoff & Verrill Literary Agents)
Vesel, Beth (Stanford J. Greenburger Associates)
Vitale, Joe (Lyle Steele & Co., Ltd.)

W
Wade, Carlson, (Carlson Wade)
Wagner, Matthew (Waterside Productions, Inc.)
Wales, Elizabeth (Levant & Wales, Literary Agency, Inc.)
Wallerstein, Gerry B. Ms. (The Gerry B. Wallerstein Agency)
Walters, Maureen (Curtis Brown Ltd.)
Ware, John (John A. Ware Literary Agency)
Warner, Bob (Warner & Associates)
Warren, James (James Warren Literary Agency)
Warshaw, Andrea (Warshaw Blumenthal, Inc.)
Washington, Dick (Washington-Artist Representative)
Wasserman, Harriet (Harriet Wasserman Literary Agency)
Watson, Lynn (Rising Sun Literary Group)
Watt, Sandra (Sandra Watt & Associates)
Wecksler, Sally (Wecksler-Incomco)
Weimann, Frank (The Literary Group)
Weiner, Cherry (Cherry Weiner Literary Agency)
Weissberg, Elyse (Elyse Weissberg)
Wells, Susan (Susan Wells Associates)

Listing Index

Other Books of Interest

Annual Market Books

    Artist's Market, edited by Lauri Miller $21.95

    Children's Writer's & Illustrator's Market, edited by Lisa Carpenter (paper) $16.95

    Humor & Cartoon Markets, edited by Bob Staake (paper) $16.95

    Novel & Short Story Writer's Market, edited by Robin Gee (paper) $18.95

    Photographer's Market, edited by Sam Marshall $21.95

    Writer's Market, edited by Mark Kissling $25.95

General Writing Books

    Beginning Writer's Answer Book, edited by Kirk Polking (paper) $13.95

    Discovering the Writer Within, by Bruce Ballenger & Barry Lane $16.95

    Getting the Words Right: How to Rewrite, Edit and Revise, by Theodore A. Rees Cheney (paper) $12.95

    How to Write a Book Proposal, by Michael Larsen (paper) $10.95

    Make Your Words Work, by Gary Provost $17.95

    On Being a Writer, edited by Bill Strickland $19.95

    12 Keys to Writing Books That Sell, by Kathleen Krull (paper) $12.95

    The 29 Most Common Writing Mistakes & How to Avoid Them, by Judy Delton (paper) $9.95

    The Wordwatcher's Guide to Good Writing & Grammar, by Morton S. Freeman (paper) $15.95 (paper) $14.95

    The Writer's Digest Guide to Manuscript Formats, by Buchman & Groves $18.95

    The Writer's Essential Desk Reference, edited by Glenda Neff $19.95

Fiction Writing Books

    The Art & Craft of Novel Writing, by Oakley Hall $17.95

    Best Stories from New Writers, edited by Linda Sanders $16.95

    Characters & Viewpoint, by Orson Scott Card $13.95

    The Complete Guide to Writing Fiction, by Barnaby Conrad $17.95

    Cosmic Critiques: How & Why 10 Science Fiction Stories Work, edited by Asimov & Greenberg (paper) $12.95

    Creating Characters: How to Build Story People, by Dwight V. Swain $16.95

    Creating Short Fiction, by Damon Knight (paper) $10.95

    Dare to Be a Great Writer: 329 Keys to Powerful Fiction, by Leonard Bishop $16.95

    Dialogue, by Lewis Turco $13.95

    The Fiction Writer's Silent Partner, by Martin Roth $19.95

    Handbook of Short Story Writing: Vol. I, by Dickson and Smythe (paper) $10.95

    Handbook of Short Story Writing: Vol. II, edited by Jean Fredette (paper) $12.95

    How to Write & Sell Your First Novel, by Collier & Leighton (paper) $12.95

    Manuscript Submission, by Scott Edelstein $13.95

    Mastering Fiction Writing, by Kit Reed $18.95

    Plot, by Ansen Dibell $13.95

    Revision, by Kit Reed $13.95

    Spider Spin Me a Web: Lawrence Block on Writing Fiction, by Lawrence Block $16.95

    Theme & Strategy, by Ronald B. Tobias $13.95

    Writing the Novel: From Plot to Print, by Lawrence Block (paper) $10.95

Special Interest Writing Books

    Armed & Dangerous: A Writer's Guide to Weapons, by Michael Newton (paper) $14.95

    The Children's Picture Book: How to Write It, How to Sell It, by Ellen E.M. Roberts (paper) $18.95

    The Complete Book of Feature Writing, by Leonard Witt $18.95

    The Complete Book of Scriptwriting, by J. Michael Straczynski (paper) $11.95

    The Complete Guide to Writing Biographies, by Ted Schwarz $19.95

    Deadly Doses: A Writer's Guide to Poisons, by Serita Deborah Stevens with Anne Klarner (paper) $16.95

    Hillary Waugh's Guide to Mysteries & Mystery Writing, by Hillary Waugh $19.95

    How to Pitch & Sell Your TV Script, by David Silver $17.95

    How to Write a Play, by Raymond Hull (paper) $12.95

    How to Write & Sell True Crime, by Gary Provost $17.95

    How to Write Horror Fiction, by William F. Nolan $15.95

    How to Write Mysteries, by Shannon OCork $13.95

    How to Write Romances, by Phyllis Taylor Pianka $13.95

    How to Write Science Fiction & Fantasy, by Orson Scott Card $13.95

Write Tales of Horror, Fantasy & Science Fiction, edited by J.N. Williamson (paper) $12.95

.y Writer's Handbook, by The Mystery Writers of America (paper) $11.95

.ssful Scriptwriting, by Jurgen Wolff & Kerry Cox (paper) $14.95

criptwriter's Handbook, by Alfred Brenner (paper) $10.95

: Writer's Complete Crime Reference Book, by Martin Roth $19.95

riting for Children & Teenagers, 3rd Edition, by Lee Wyndham & Arnold Madison (paper)
.2.95

Writing the Modern Mystery, by Barbara Norville $15.95

Writing A to Z, edited by Kirk Polking $22.95

usiness Art Books

Artist's Friendly Legal Guide, by Floyd Conner, Peter Karlan, Jean Perwin & David M. Spatt $18.95 (paper)

Business & Legal Forms for Illustrators, by Tad Crawford $15.95

The Complete Book of Caricature, by Bob Staake $18.95

The Complete Guide to Greeting Card Design & Illustration, by Eva Szela $27.95 (cloth)

Getting Started as a Freelance Illustrator or Designer, by Michael Fleishman $16.95 (paper)

Handbook of Pricing & Ethical Guidelines, 7th edition, by The Graphic Artist's Guild $22.95 (paper)

Legal Guide for the Visual Artist, Revised Edition by Tad Crawford $18.95 (paper)

Licensing Art & Design, by Caryn Leland $12.95 (paper)

Make It Legal, by Lee Wilson $18.95 (paper)

Photography Books

Sell & Re-Sell Your Photos, by Rohn Engh $14.95 (paper)

A Guide to Travel Writing & Photography, by Ann & Carl Purcell $22.95 (paper)

The Professional Photographer's Guide to Shooting & Selling Nature & Wildlife Photos, by Jim Zuckerman $22.95 (paper)

Photo Gallery & Workshop Handbook, by Jeff Carson $19.95 (paper)

Nikon System Handbook, by Moose Peterson $19.95 (paper)

Photographer's Publishing Handbook, by Harold Davis $19.95 (paper)

Winning Photo Contests, by Jeanne Stallman $14.95 (paper)

The Photographer's Business & Legal Handbook, by Leonard Duboff $18.95 (paper)

Photo Marketing Handbook, by Jeff Carson & Peter Lawrence $19.95 (paper)

Lighting Secrets for the Professional Photographer, by Alan Brown, Tim Grondin, & Joe Braun $22.95 (paper)

How to Shoot Stock Photos That Sell, by Michal Heron $16.95 (paper)

How to Sell Your Photographs & Illustrations, by Elliott & Barbara Gordon $16.95 (paper)

How You Can Make $25,000 a Year with Your Camera (No Matter Where You Live), by Larry Cribb $12.95 (paper)

The Photographer's Guide to Marketing & Self-Promotion, by Maria Piscopo $16.95 (paper)

To order directly from the publisher, include $3.00 postage and handling for 1 book and $1.00 for each additional book. Allow 30 days for delivery.

Writer's Digest Books/North Light Books
1507 Dana Avenue, Cincinnati, Ohio 45207
Credit card orders call TOLL-FREE
1-800-289-0963
Prices subject to change without notice.

Write to this same address for information on *Writer's Digest* magazine, *The Artist's Magazine*, *Story* magazine, Writer's Digest Book Club, Graphic Artist's Book Club, North Light Book Club, Writer's Digest School, North Light Art School and Writer's Digest Criticism Service.